The political nature of Absolutism has long been a subject of controversy within historical materialism. Developing considerations advanced in *Passages from Antiquity to Feudalism*, this book situates the Absolutist states of the early modern epoch against the prior background of European feudalism. It is divided into two parts. The first discusses the overall structures of Absolutism as a state-system in Western Europe, from the Renaissance onwards; and the difficult question of the relations between monarchy and nobility institutionalised by it, for which it suggests a general periodization. It then looks in turn at the trajectory of each of the specific Absolutist states in the dominant countries of the West – Spain, France, England and Sweden, set off against the case of Italy, where no major indigenous Absolutism developed.

The second part of the work sketches a comparative prospect of Absolutism in Eastern Europe. It begins with an enquiry into the reasons why the divergent social conditions in the more backward half of the continent should have produced political forms apparently similar to those of the more advanced West. The peculiarities, as well as affinities, of Eastern Absolutism as a distinct type of royal state, are examined. The variegated monarchies of Prussia, Austria and Russia are surveyed, and the lessons asked of the counter-example of Poland. Finally, the structure of the Ottoman Empire in the Balkans is taken as an external gauge by which the singularity of Absolutism as a European phenomenon is assessed. The work ends with some observations on the special position occupied by European development within universal history, which draws themes from both *Passages from Antiquity to Feudalism* and *Lineages of the Absolutist State* together into a single argument – within their common limits – as materials for debate.

Two postscript notes treat, respectively, the notion of the 'Asiatic mode of production,' with particular reference to Islamic and Chinese history, and the experience of Japanese feudalism, as relevant controls for a study of the evolution of Europe up to the advent of industrial capitalism.

Lineages of the
Absolutist State

PERRY ANDERSON

VERSO

London · New York

First published by NLB 1974

© Perry Anderson 1974

Verso Edition 1979
Second impression 1984
Third impression 1986
Fourth impression 1987
Fifth impression 1989
Sixth impression 1993

Verso
UK: 6 Meard Street, London W1V 3HR
USA: 29 West 35th Street, New York, NY 10001-2291

Printed in Great Britain by
Redwood Books, Trowbridge, Wiltshire

ISBN 86091 710 X

Foreword

The object of this work is to attempt a comparative survey of the nature and development of the Absolutist State in Europe. Its general character and limits as a reflection on the past are explained in the foreword to the study that precedes it.[1] Some specific remarks about the relationship of the enquiry undertaken in this volume to historical materialism may be added. Conceived as a Marxist study of Absolutism, the work below is deliberately situated between two different planes of Marxist discourse, which normally lie at a considerable distance from each other. It has been a general phenomenon of the last decades that Marxist historians, the authors of a now impressive corpus of research, have not always been directly concerned with the theoretical questions of implications raised by their work. At the same time, Marxist philosophers, who have sought to clarify or solve the basic theoretical problems of historical materialism, have often done so at a considerable remove from the specific empirical issues posed by historians. An attempt has been made here to explore a mediate ground between the two. It is possible that it may serve only by negative example. At all events, the aim of this study is to examine European Absolutism simultaneously 'in general' and 'in particular': that is to say, both the 'pure' structures of the Absolutist State, which constitute it as a fundamental historical category, and the 'impure' variants presented by the specific and diverse monarchies of post-mediaeval Europe. These two orders of reality are customarily separated by a major gap in much Marxist writing today. On the one hand, 'abstract' general models are constructed, or presupposed – not only of the absolutist state, but equally of the bourgeois revolution or the capitalist state, without concern for their effective variations; on the other hand, 'concrete' local cases are explored, without reference to their reciprocal implications and

1. *Passages from Antiquity to Feudalism*, London 1974, pp. 7–9.

interconnections. The conventional dichotomy between these procedures derives, doubtless, from the widespread belief that an intelligible
necessity only inhabits the broadest and most general trends in history,
which operate so to speak 'above' the multiple empirical circumstances of specific events and institutions, whose actual course or shape
becomes by comparison largely the outcome of chance. Scientific laws
– if the notion of them is accepted at all – are held to obtain only for
universal categories: singular objects are deemed the domain of the
fortuitous. The practical consequences of this division are often to
render general concepts – such as the absolutist state, the bourgeois
revolution or the capitalist state – so remote from historical reality that
they cease to have any explicative power at all; while particular studies
– confined to delimited areas or periods – fail vice-versa to develop or
refine any global theory. The premise of this work is that there is no
plumb-line between necessity and contingency in historical explanation, dividing separate types of enquiry – 'long-run' versus 'short-run',
or 'abstract' versus 'concrete' – from each other. There is merely that
which is known – established by historical research – and that which is
not known: the latter may be either the mechanisms of single events or
the laws of motion of whole structures. Both are equally amenable, in
principle, to adequate knowledge of their causality. (In practice, the
surviving historical evidence can often be so insufficient or contradictory that definite judgements are not feasible: but this is another
question – of documentation, not intelligibility.) One of the main
purposes of the study undertaken here is thus to try to hold together
in tension two orders of reflection which have often been unwarrantably divorced in Marxist writing, weakening its capacity for rational
and controllable theory in the domain of history.

The actual scope of the study below is marked by three anomalies
or discrepancies from orthodox treatments of the subject. The first of
these is the much longer ancestry accorded to Absolutism, implicit in
the nature of the study that is the prologue to it. Secondly, within the
bounds of the continent explored in these pages – Europe – a relatively
systematic effort has been made to give equivalent and complementary
treatment to its Western and Eastern zones, as was done in the preceding discussion of feudalism. This is not something that can be taken for
granted. Although the division between Western and Eastern Europe

is an intellectual commonplace, it has very rarely been the object of a direct and sustained historical reflection. The most recent vintage of serious works on European history has to some extent redressed the traditional geo-political imbalance of Western historiography, with its characteristic neglect of the Eastern half of the continent. But a reasonable balance of interest has still largely to be struck. Moreover, it is not so much a mere parity of coverage within the two regions that is needed, as a comparative explanation of their division, analysis of their differences, and account of the dynamic of their interconnections. The history of Eastern Europe is not merely a poorer copy of that of Western Europe, which can simply be added side by side to it, without affecting study of the latter; the development of the more 'backward' regions of the continent casts an unwonted light on that of the more 'advanced' regions, and often throws into relief novel problems within it, concealed by the limits of a purely Western introspection. Thus, contrary to normal practice, the vertical division of the continent between West and East is here taken throughout as a central organizing principle of the materials discussed. Within each zone, of course, major social and political variations have always existed, and these are contrasted and explored in their own right. The aim of this procedure is to suggest a regional *typology* that can help to clarify the divergent trajectories of the major Absolutist States of both Eastern and Western Europe. Such a typology may serve to indicate, if only in outline, precisely the sort of intermediate conceptual plane that is so often missing between generic theoretical constructs and particular case-histories, in studies of Absolutism as of much else.

Thirdly, and finally, the selection of the *object* of this study – the Absolutist State – has determined a temporal articulation unlike that of the orthodox genres of historiography. The traditional frameworks of historical writing are either single countries or closed periods. The great majority of qualified research is conducted strictly within national bounds; and where a work exceeds these for an international perspective, it usually takes a delimited epoch as its frontiers. In either case, historical time normally seems to present no problem: whether in 'old-fashioned' narrative studies or 'modern' sociological studies, events or institutions appear to bathe in a more or less continuous and homogeneous temporality. Although all historians are naturally aware that rates of change vary between different layers or sectors of society, convenience and custom usually dictate that the form of a work implies or conveys a chronological monism. That is to say, its materials are treated as if they share a common departure and common conclusion, spanned by a single stretch of time. In this study, there is no such uniform temporal medium: for the *times* of the major Absolutisms of Europe – Eastern and Western – were, precisely, enormously diverse, and this diversity was itself constitutive of their respective nature as State systems. Spanish Absolutism suffered its first great defeat in the late 16th century in the Netherlands; English Absolutism was cut down in the mid-17th century; French Absolutism lasted until the end of the 18th century; Prussian Absolutism survived until the later 19th century; Russian Absolutism was only overthrown in the 20th century. The wide disjunctures in the dating of these great structures inevitably corresponded to deep distinctions in their composition and evolution. Since the specific object of this study is the whole spectrum of European Absolutism, no single temporality covers it. The story of Absolutism has many, overlapping beginnings and disparate, staggered endings. Its underlying unity is real and profound, but it is not that of a linear continuum. The complex duration of European Absolutism, with its multiple breaks and displacements from region to region, commands the presentation of the historical material in this study. Thus, the whole cycle of processes and events which assured the triumph of the capitalist mode of production in Europe after the early modern epoch, is omitted here. The first bourgeois revolutions occurred long before the last metamorphoses of absolutism, chronologically. For the purposes of this work, however, they remain categorically posterior to the latter, and will be considered in a subsequent study. Thus such fundamental phenomena as the primitive accumulation of capital, the onset of religious reformation, the formation of nations, the expansion of overseas imperialism, the advent of industrialization – all of which fall well within the formal compass of the 'periods' treated here, as contemporaneous with various phases of Absolutism in Europe – are not discussed or explored. Their dates are the same: their times are separate. The unfamiliar and disconcerting history of the successive bourgeois revolutions is not our concern here:

the present essay is confined to the nature and development of the Absolutist States, their political antecedent and adversary. Two subsequent studies will deal specifically, in turn, with the chain of the great bourgeois revolutions, from the Revolt of the Netherlands to the Unification of Germany; and with the structure of the contemporary capitalist states that eventually, after a long process of ulterior evolution, emerged from them. Certain of the theoretical and political implications of arguments in the present volume will only become fully apparent in these sequels.

A last word is perhaps needed on the choice of the *State* itself as a central theme for reflection. Today, when 'history from below' has become a watchword in both Marxist and non-Marxist circles, and has produced major gains in our understanding of the past, it is nevertheless necessary to recall one of the basic axioms of historical materialism: that secular struggle between classes is ultimately resolved at the *political* – not at the economic or cultural – level of society. In other words, it is the construction and destruction of States which seal the basic shifts in the relations of production, so long as classes subsist. A 'history from above' – of the intricate machinery of class domination – is thus no less essential than a 'history from below': indeed, without it the latter in the end becomes one-sided (if the better side). Marx in his maturity wrote: 'Freedom consists in the conversion of the State from an organ superimposed on society into one completely subordinated to it, and today too, the forms of the State are more free or less free to the extent that they restrict the "freedom" of the State.' The abolition of the State altogether remains, a century later, one of the goals of revolutionary socialism. But the supreme significance accorded to its final disappearance, testifies to all the weight of its prior presence in history. Absolutism, the first international State system in the modern world, has by no means yet exhausted its secrets or lessons for us. The aim of this work is to contribute towards a discussion of some of them. Its errors, misconceptions, oversights, solecisms, illusions can safely be left to the criticism of a collective debate.

I. Western Europe

The Absolutist State in the West

The long crisis of European economy and society during the 14th and 15th centuries marked the difficulties and limits of the feudal mode of production in the late mediaeval period.[1] What was the final *political* outcome of the continental convulsions of this epoch? In the course of the 16th century, the Absolutist State emerged in the West. The centralized monarchies of France, England and Spain represented a decisive rupture with the pyramidal, parcellized sovereignty of the mediaeval social formations, with their estates and liege-systems. Controversy over the historical nature of these monarchies has persisted ever since Engels, in a famous dictum, pronounced them to be the product of a class equilibrium between the old feudal nobility and the new urban bourgeoisie: 'By way of exception, however, periods occur where the warring classes balance each other (*Gleichgewicht halten*) so nearly that the State power, as ostensible mediator, acquires, for the moment, a certain degree of independence of both. Such was the absolute monarchy of the 17th and 18th centuries, which held the balance (*gegeneinander balanciert*) between the nobility and the class of burghers.'[2] The multiple qualifications of this passage indicate a certain conceptual unease on the part of Engels. But a careful examination of successive formulations by both Marx and Engels reveals that a similar conception of Absolutism was, in fact, a comparatively consistent theme in their work. Engels repeated the same basic thesis elsewhere in more categorical form, remarking that 'the basic condition of

1. See the discussion in *Passages from Antiquity to Feudalism*, London 1974, which precedes this study.
2. *The Origin of the Family, Private Property and the State*, in Marx-Engels, *Selected Works*, London 1968, p 588; Marx-Engels, *Werke* Bd 21, p. 167

the old absolute monarchy' was 'an equilibrium (*Gleichgewicht*) between the landowning aristocracy and the bourgeoisie'.[3] Indeed, the classification of Absolutism as a political balancing-mechanism between nobility and bourgeoisie frequently glides towards an implicit or explicit designation of it as fundamentally a type of bourgeois State as such. This slippage is most evident within the *Communist Manifesto* itself, where the political role of the bourgeoisie 'in the period of manufactures proper' is characterized in a single breath as 'serving either the semi-feudal or the absolute monarchy as a counterpoise (*Gegengewicht*) against the nobility, and, in fact, corner-stone (*Hauptgrundlage*) of the great monarchies in general'.[4] The suggestive transition from 'counter-poise' to 'corner-stone' is echoed in other texts. Engels could refer to the epoch of Absolutism as the age in which 'the feudal nobility were made to understand that the period of their social and political domination had come to an end'.[5] Marx, for his part, repeatedly asserted that the administrative structures of the new Absolutist States were a peculiarly bourgeois instrument. 'Under the absolute monarchy,' he wrote, 'bureaucracy was only the means of preparing the class rule of the bourgeoisie.' Elsewhere Marx declared that: 'The centralised State power, with its ubiquitous organs of standing army, police, bureaucracy, clergy and judicature – organs wrought after the plan of a systematic and hierarchic division of labour – originates from the days of absolute monarchy, serving nascent middle-class society as a mighty weapon in its struggles against feudalism.'[6]

These reflections on Absolutism were all more or less casual and allusive: no direct theorization of the new centralized monarchies which emerged in Renaissance Europe was ever made by either of the founders of historical materialism. Their exact weight was left to the judgement of later generations. Marxist historians, in fact, have debated the problem of the social nature of Absolutism down to this day. A

3. *Zur Wohnungsfrage*, in *Werke*, Bd 18, p. 258.
4. Marx-Engels, *Selected Works*, p. 37; *Werke*, Bd 4, p. 464.
5. *Über den Verfall des Feudalismus und das Aufkommen der Bourgeoisie*, in *Werke*, Bd 21, p. 398. 'Political' domination is expressly *staatliche* in the sentence cited here.
6. The first formulation is from *The Eighteenth Brumaire of Louis Bonaparte*, in *Selected Works*, p. 171; the second is from *The Civil War in France*, in *Selected Works*, p. 289.

correct solution of it is, indeed, vital for any understanding of the passage from feudalism to capitalism in Europe, and of the political systems which distinguished it. The Absolute monarchies introduced standing armies, a permanent bureaucracy, national taxation, a codified law, and the beginnings of a unified market. All these characteristics appear to be preeminently capitalist. Since they coincide with the disappearance of serfdom, a core institution of the original feudal mode of production in Europe, the descriptions of Absolutism by Marx and Engels as a State system representing either an equilibrium between bourgeoisie and nobility, or even an outright dominance of capital itself, have often seemed plausible. A more careful study of the structures of the Absolutist State in the West, however, inevitably infirms such judgements. For the end of serfdom did not thereby mean the disappearance of feudal relations from the countryside. Identification of the two is a common error. Yet it is evident that private extra-economic coercion, personal dependence, and combination of the immediate producer with the instruments of production, did not necessarily vanish when the rural surplus ceased to be extracted in the form of labour or deliveries in kind, and became rent in money: so long as aristocratic agrarian property blocked a free market in land and factual mobility of manpower – in other words, as long as labour was not separated from the social conditions of its existence to become 'labour-power' – rural relations of production remained feudal. In his properly theoretical analysis of ground-rent, Marx himself made this clear in *Capital*: 'The transformation of labour rent into rent in kind changes nothing fundamental in the nature of ground-rent. . . . By money-rent we here mean the ground-rent which arises from a mere change in the form of rent in kind, just as the latter in turn is but a modification of labour rent. . . . The basis of this type of rent, although approaching its dissolution, remains the same as that of rent in kind, which constitutes its point of departure. The direct producer as before is still possessor of the land, either through inheritance or some other traditional right, and must perform for his lord, as owner of his most essential condition of production, excess corvée-labour, that is, unpaid labour for which no equivalent is returned, in the form of a surplus-product transformed into money.'[7] The lords who remained the proprietors of the fundamental

7. *Capital*, III, pp. 774, 777. Dobb's exposition of this fundamental question in

means of production in any pre-industrial society were, of course, the noble landowners. Throughout the early modern epoch, the dominant class – economically and politically – was thus the *same* as in the mediaeval epoch itself: the feudal aristocracy. This nobility underwent profound metamorphoses in the centuries after the close of the Middle Ages: but from the beginning to the end of the history of Absolutism, it was never dislodged from its command of political power.

The changes in the *forms* of feudal exploitation which supervened at the end of the mediaeval epoch were, of course, far from insignificant. Indeed, it was precisely these changes which changed the forms of the State. Absolutism was essentially just this: *a redeployed and recharged apparatus of feudal domination*, designed to clamp the peasant masses back into their traditional social position – despite and against the gains they had won by the widespread commutation of dues. In other words, the Absolutist State was never an arbiter between the aristocracy and the bourgeoisie, still less an instrument of the nascent bourgeoisie against the aristocracy: it was the new political carapace of a threatened nobility. The consensus of a generation of Marxist historians, from England and Russia, was summed up by Hill twenty years ago: 'The absolute monarchy was a different form of feudal monarchy from the feudal-estates monarchy which preceded it; but the ruling class remained the same, just as a republic, a constitutional monarchy and a fascist dictatorship can all be forms of the rule of the bourgeoisie.'[8] The new form of noble power was in its turn determined by the spread of commodity production and exchange, in the transitional social formations of the early modern epoch. Althusser has in this sense correctly specified its character: 'The political regime of the absolute monarchy

---

his 'Reply' to Sweezy in the famous debate of the fifties on the Transition from Feudalism to Capitalism is trenchant and lucid: *Science and Society*, XIV, No. 2, Spring 1950, pp. 157–67, esp. 163–4. The theoretical importance of the problem is evident. In the case of a country like Sweden, for example, standard historical accounts still claim that 'it had no feudalism' because there was an absence of serfdom proper. In fact, of course, feudal relations predominated in the Swedish countryside throughout the late mediaeval era.

8. Christopher Hill, 'Comment' (on the Transition from Feudalism to Capitalism), *Science and Society*, XVII, No. 4, Fall 1953, p. 351. The terms of this judgement should be treated with care. The general and epochal character of Absolutism renders any formal comparison of it with the local, exceptionalist régimes of fascism inappropriate, of course.

is only the new political form needed for the maintenance of feudal domination and exploitation in the period of development of a commodity economy.'[9] But the dimensions of the historical transformation involved in the advent of Absolutism must in no way be minimized. It is essential, on the contrary, to grasp the full logic and import of the momentous change in the structure of the aristocratic State, and of feudal property, that produced the new phenomenon of Absolutism.

Feudalism as a mode of production was originally defined by an organic *unity* of economy and polity, paradoxically distributed in a chain of parcellized sovereignties throughout the social formation. The institution of serfdom as a mechanism of surplus extraction fused economic exploitation and politico-legal coercion at the molecular level of the village. The lord in his turn typically owed liege-loyalty and knight-service to a seigneurial overlord, who claimed the land as his ultimate domain. With the generalized commutation of dues into money rents, the cellular unity of political and economic oppression of the peasantry was gravely weakened, and threatened to become dissociated (the end of this road was 'free labour' and the 'wage contract'). The class power of the feudal lords was thus directly at stake with the gradual disappearance of serfdom. The result was a *displacement* of politico-legal coercion upwards towards a centralized, militarized summit – the Absolutist State. Diluted at village level, it became concentrated at 'national' level. The result was a reinforced apparatus of royal power, whose permanent political function was the repression of the peasant and plebeian masses at the foot of the social hierarchy. This new State machine, however, was also by its nature vested with a

9. Louis Althusser, *Montesquieu, Le Politique et l'Histoire*, Paris 1969, p. 117. This formulation is selected as recent and representative. Belief in the capitalist or quasi-capitalist character of Absolutism can still, however, occasionally be found. Poulantzas commits the imprudence of so classifying Absolutist States in his otherwise important work *Pouvoir Politique et Classes Sociales*, pp. 169–80, although his phrasing is vague and ambiguous. The recent debate on Russian Absolutism in Soviet historical journals revealed isolated similar instances, although chronologically more nuanced; see for example, A. Ya. Avrekh, 'Russkii Absoliutizm i evo Rol' v Utverzhdenie Kapitalizma v Rossii', *Istoriya SSSR*, February 1968, pp. 83–104, who deems Absolutism the 'prototype of the bourgeois State' (p. 92). Avrekh's views were heavily criticized in the debate which followed, and were not typical of the general tenor of the discussion.

coercive force capable of breaking or disciplining individuals and groups *within* the nobility itself. The arrival of Absolutism was thus, as we shall see, never a smooth evolutionary process for the dominant class itself: it was marked by extremely sharp ruptures and conflicts within the feudal aristocracy to whose collective interests it ultimately ministered. At the same time, the objective complement of the political concentration of power at the height of the social order, in a centralized monarchy, was the economic consolidation of the units of feudal property beneath it. With the growth of commodity relations, the dissolution of the primary nexus of economic exploitation and politico-legal coercion led not only to an increasing projection of the latter onto the royal apex of the social system, but also to a compensatory strengthening of the titles of property guaranteeing the former. In other words, with the reorganization of the feudal polity as a whole, and the dilution of the original fief system, landownership tended to become progressively less 'conditional' as sovereignty became correspondingly more 'absolute'. The weakening of the mediaeval conceptions of vassalage worked in both directions: while it conferred new and extraordinary powers on the monarchy, it at the same time emancipated from traditional restraints the estates of the nobility. Agrarian property in the new epoch was silently allodialized (to use a term which was itself to become anachronistic in an altered juridical climate). Individual members of the aristocratic class, who steadily lost political rights of representation in the new epoch, registered economic gains in ownership as the obverse of the same historical process. The final effect of this general redisposition of the social power of the nobility was the State machine and juridical order of Absolutism, whose coordination was to increase the efficacy of aristocratic rule in pinning down a non-servile peasantry into new forms of dependence and exploitation. The royal States of the Renaissance were first and foremost modernized instruments for the maintenance of noble domination over the rural masses.

Simultaneously, however, the aristocracy had to adjust to a second antagonist: the mercantile bourgeoisie which had developed in the mediaeval towns. It has been seen that it was precisely the intercalation of this third presence that prevented the Western nobility from settling its accounts with the peasantry in Eastern fashion, by smashing its resistance and fettering it to the manor. The mediaeval town had been able to develop because the hierarchical dispersal of sovereignties in the feudal mode of production for the first time freed urban economies from direct domination by a rural ruling class.[10] The towns in this sense were never exogenous to feudalism in the West, as we have seen: in fact, the very condition of their existence was the unique 'detotalization' of sovereignty within the politico-economic order of feudalism. Hence the resilience of the towns in the West throughout the worst crisis of the 14th century, which temporarily bankrupted so many of the patrician families of the Mediterranean cities. The Bardi and Peruzzi collapsed in Florence, Siena and Barcelona declined; but Augsburg, Geneva or Valencia were just starting their ascent. Important urban industries such as iron, paper and textiles grew throughout the feudal depression. From a distance, this economic and social vitality acted as a constant, objective interference in the class struggle on the land, and blocked any regressive solution to it by the nobles. Indeed, it is significant that the years from 1450 to 1500, which saw the emergence of the first prodromes of unified Absolute Monarchies in the West, were

10. The celebrated debate between Sweezy and Dobb, with contributions by Takahashi, Hilton and Hill, in *Science and Society* 1950–3, remains to this day the only systematic Marxist treatment of the central problems of the transition from feudalism to capitalism. In one important respect, however, it revolved on a false issue. Sweezy argued (following Pirenne) that the 'prime mover' in the transition was an 'external' agent of dissolution – the urban enclaves which destroyed the feudal agrarian economy by their expansion of commodity exchange in the towns. Dobb replied that the impetus to the transition must be located within the contradictions of the agrarian economy itself, which generated social differentiation of the peasantry and the rise of the small producer. In a subsequent essay on the subject, Vilar explicitly formulated the problem of the transition as that of defining the correct combination of 'endogenous' agrarian and 'exogenous' urban-commercial changes, while himself emphasizing the importance of the new Atlantic trading economy in the 16th century: 'Problems in the Formation of Capitalism', *Past and Present*, No. 10, November 1956, pp. 33–4. In an important recent study, 'The Relation between Town and Country in the Transition from Feudalism to Capitalism' (unpublished), John Merrington has effectively resolved this antinomy, by demonstrating the basic truth that European feudalism – far from constituting an exclusively agrarian economy – was the *first* mode of production in history to accord an autonomous structural place to urban production and exchange. The growth of towns was in this sense as 'internal' a development as the dissolution of the manor, in Western European feudalism.

also those in which the long crisis of the feudal economy was sur-
mounted, by a recombination of production factors in which for the
first time specifically *urban* technological advances played the leading
role. The cluster of inventions which coincides with the hinge between
the 'mediaeval' and the 'modern' epochs is too well-known to need
discussion here. The discovery of the *seiger* process for separating
silver from copper ore restarted the mines of Central Europe, and the
flow of metals into the international economy; monetary production
from Central Europe quintupled between 1460 and 1530. The development of bronze-cast cannon made gunpowder for the first time the
decisive arm of warfare, rendering baronial castellar defences anachronistic. The invention of movable type brought the advent of printing.
The construction of the three-masted, stern-ruddered galleon made the
oceans navigable for conquests overseas.[11] All these technical breakthroughs, which laid the foundations of the European Renaissance,
were concentrated in the latter half of the 15th century; and it was then
that the secular agrarian depression finally lifted, towards 1470 in
England and France.

This was precisely the epoch in which a sudden, concurrent revival
of political authority and unity occurred in country after country. From
the pit of extreme feudal chaos and turmoil of the Wars of the Roses,
the Hundred Years War and the second Castilian Civil War, the first
'new' monarchies straightened up virtually together, during the reigns
of Louis XI in France, Ferdinand and Isabella in Spain, Henry VII in
England and Maximilian in Austria. Thus when the Absolutist States
were constituted in the West, their structure was fundamentally determined by the feudal regroupment against the peasantry, after the
dissolution of serfdom; but it was secondarily *over-determined* by the

11. For cannons and galleons, see Carlo Cipolla, *Guns and Sails in the Early
Phase of European Expansion 1400–1700*, London 1965. For printing, the most
audacious recent reflections, although marred by a monomania familiar to his-
torians of technology, are Elizabeth L. Eisenstein, 'Some Conjectures about the
Impact of Printing on Western Society and Thought: a Preliminary Report',
Journal of Modern History, March–December 1968, pp. 1–56, and 'The Advent
of Printing and the Problem of the Renaissance', *Past and Present*, No. 45,
November 1969, pp. 19–89. The critical technical inventions of this epoch can be
seen, in one respect, as variations in a common field, that of communications.
They concern respectively, money, language, travel and war: in a later age, all
among the great philosophical themes of the Enlightenment.

rise of an urban bourgeoisie which after a series of technical and commercial advances was now developing into pre-industrial manufactures on a considerable scale. It was this secondary impact of the urban bourgeoisie on the forms of the Absolutist State which Marx and Engels sought to capture with the misleading notions of 'counter-poise' or 'cornerstone'. Engels, in fact, expressed the real relationship of forces accurately enough on more than one occasion: discussing the new maritime discoveries and manufacturing industries of the Renaissance, he wrote that 'this mighty revolution in the conditions of the economic life of society was, however, not followed by any immediate corresponding change in its political structure. The political order remained feudal, while society became more and more bourgeois.'[12] The threat of peasant unrest, unspokenly constitutive of the Absolutist State, was thus always conjoined with the pressure of mercantile or manufacturing

12. *Anti-Dühring*, Moscow 1947, p. 126: see also pp. 196–7, where correct and incorrect formulae are mixed. These pages are cited by Hill in his 'Comment' to exculpate Engels from the errors of the notion of 'equilibrium'. In general, it is possible to find passages in both Marx and Engels where Absolutism is more adequately grasped than in the texts discussed earlier. (For example, in the *Communist Manifesto* itself, there is a straightforward reference to 'feudal Absolutism': *Selected Works*, p. 56; see also Marx's article *Die moralisierende Kritik und die kritisierende Moral* of 1847, in *Werke*, Bd 4, pp. 347, 352–3.) It would be surprising if it were otherwise, given that the logical consequence of baptizing the Absolutist States as bourgeois or semi-bourgeois would be to deny the nature and reality of the bourgeois revolutions of Western Europe themselves. But there is no doubt that, amidst a recurrent confusion, the *main* drift of their comments was in the direction of the 'counter-poise' conception, with its concomitant slide towards that of the 'corner-stone'. There is no need to hide this fact. The immense intellectual and political respect we owe to Marx and Engels is incompatible with any piety towards them. Their mistakes – often more revealing than the truths of others – should not be eluded, but located and surpassed. A further warning is necessary here. It has long been fashionable to depreciate the relative contribution of Engels to the creation of historical materialism. For those who are still inclined to accept this received notion, it is necessary to say calmly and scandalously: Engels's *historical* judgements are nearly always superior to those of Marx. He possessed a deeper knowledge of European history, and had a surer grasp of its successive and salient structures. There is nothing in the whole of Engels's oeuvre to compare with the illusions and prejudices of which Marx was on occasion capable in this field, such as the fantasmagoric *Secret Diplomatic History of the Eighteenth Century*. (The supremacy of Marx's overall contribution to the *general theory* of historical materialism scarcely needs to be reiterated.) Engels's stature in his historical writings is precisely what makes it worth drawing attention to the specific errors in them.

capital within the Western economies as a whole, in moulding the contours of aristocratic class power in the new age. The peculiar form of the Absolutist State in the West derives from this double determination.

The dual forces which produced the new monarchies of Renaissance Europe found a single juridical condensation. The revival of Roman law, one of the great cultural movements of the age, ambiguously corresponded to the needs of both social classes whose unequal power and rank shaped the structures of the Absolutist State in the West. Renewed knowledge of Roman jurisprudence dated back, in itself, to the High Middle Ages. The dense overgrowth of customary law had never completely suppressed the memory and practice of Roman civil law in the peninsula where its tradition was longest, Italy. It was in Bologna that Irnerius, the 'lamp of the law', had started the systematic study of Justinian's codifications once again, in the early 12th century. The school of Glossators founded by him methodically reconstituted and classified the legacy of the Roman jurists over the next hundred years. They were followed, in the 14th and 15th centuries, by 'Commentators' more concerned with contemporary application of Roman legal norms, than with scholarly analysis of their theoretical principles; and in the process of adapting Roman law to the drastically altered conditions of the time, they both corrupted its pristine form and cleansed it of its particularist contents.[13] The very infidelity of their transpositions of Latin jurisprudence paradoxically 'universalized' it, by removing the large portions of Roman civil law that were strictly related to the historical conditions of Antiquity (for example, of course, its comprehensive treatment of slavery).[14] Beyond Italy, Roman legal concepts gradually began to spread outwards from the original re-

13. See H. D. Hazeltine, 'Roman and Canon Law in the Middle Ages', *The Cambridge Mediaeval History*, V, Cambridge 1968, pp. 737–41. Renaissance classicism proper was consequently to be very critical of the work of the Commentators.

14. 'Now when this law was transposed into entirely strange fact situations, unknown in Antiquity, the task of "construing" the situation in a logically impeccable way became almost the exclusive task. In this way that conception of law which still prevails today and which sees in law a logically consistent and gapless complex of "norms" waiting to be "applied" became the decisive conception for legal thought.' Weber, *Economy and Society*, II, p. 855.

discovery of the 12th century onwards. By the end of the Middle Ages, no major country in Western Europe was unaffected by this process. But the decisive 'reception' of Roman law – its general juridical triumph – occurred in the age of the Renaissance, concurrently with that of Absolutism. The historical reasons for its deep impact were two-fold, and reflected the contradictory nature of the original Roman legacy itself.

Economically, the recovery and introduction of classical civil law was fundamentally propitious to the growth of free capital in town and country. For the great distinguishing mark of Roman civil law had been its conception of absolute and unconditional private property. The classical conception of Quiritary ownership had sunk virtually out of sight in the obscured depths of early feudalism. For the feudal mode of production, as we have seen, was precisely defined by juridical principles of 'scalar' or conditional property, the complement of its parcellized sovereignty. This property statute was well adapted to the overwhelmingly natural economy which emerged in the Dark Ages; although it was never wholly adequate for the urban sector which developed in the mediaeval economy. The reemergence of Roman law during the Middle Ages thus had already led to juristic efforts to 'harden' and delimit notions of ownership, inspired by the classical precepts now available. One such attempt was the invention in the late 12th century of the distinction between *dominium directum* and *dominium utile*, to account for the existence of a vassal hierarchy and hence multiplicity of rights over the same land.[15] Another was the characteristic mediaeval notion of 'seisin', an intermediate conception between Latin 'property' and 'possession', which guaranteed a protected ownership against casual appropriations and conflicting claims, while retaining the feudal principle of multiple titles to the same object: the right of 'seisin' was neither exclusive nor perpetual.[16] The full reappearance of the idea of absolute private property in land was a

15. See the discussion in J-P. Lévy, *Histoire de la Propriété*, Paris 1972, pp. 44–6. Another ironic side-effect of the efforts towards a new juridical clarity inspired by mediaeval researches into Roman codes was, of course, the emergence of the definition of serfs as *glebae adscripti*.

16. For the import of the concept of seisin, see P. Vinogradoff, *Roman Law in Mediaeval Europe*, London 1909, pp. 74–7, 86, 95–6; Levy, *Histoire de la Propriété*, pp. 50–2.

product of the early modern epoch. For it was not until commodity production and exchange had reached overall levels – in both agriculture and manufactures – equal to or above those of Antiquity, that the juridical concepts created to codify them could come into their own once again. The maxim of *superficies solo cedit* – single and unconditional ownership of land – now for the second time became an operative principle in agrarian property (if by no means yet a dominant one), precisely because of the spread of commodity relations in the countryside that was to define the long transition from feudalism to capitalism in the West. In the towns themselves, a relatively developed commercial law had, of course, spontaneously developed during the Middle Ages. Within the urban economy, commodity exchange had already achieved considerable dynamism in the mediaeval epoch, as we have seen, and in certain important respects its forms of legal expression were more advanced than Roman precedents themselves: for example, proto-company law and marine law. But there was no uniform framework of legal theory or procedure here either. The superiority of Roman law for mercantile practice in the cities thus lay not only in its clear-cut notions of absolute property, but also in its traditions of equity, its rational canons of evidence, and its emphasis of a professional judiciary – advantages which customary courts normally failed to provide.[17] The reception of Roman law in Renaissance Europe was thus a sign of the spread of capitalist relations in towns and country: *economically*, it answered to vital interests of the commercial and manufacturing bourgeoisie. In Germany, the country where the impact of Roman law was most dramatic, abruptly superseding local courts in the homeland

17. The relation of prior mediaeval law to Roman law in the cities still needs considerable investigation. The comparative advance of legal rules governing commenda-type operations and maritime trade in the Middle Ages is not surprising: the Roman world, as we have seen lacked entrepreneurial companies and comprised a unitary Mediterranean. Hence there was no reason for it to develop either. On the other hand, the early study of Roman law in the Italian cities suggests that what appeared by the time of the Renaissance as 'mediaeval' contract practice may well have often been originally informed by legal precepts derived from Antiquity. Vinogradoff had no doubt that Roman contract law exercised a direct influence on the business codes of urban burghers in the Middle Ages: *Roman Law in Mediaeval Europe*, pp. 79–80, 131. Urban real estate, with its 'burgage tenures', was always, of course, closer to Roman norms than rural property in the Middle Ages.

of Teutonic customary law in the late 15th and 16th centuries, the initial impetus for its adoption occurred in the Southern and Western cities, and came from below through the pressure of urban litigants for a clear and professional justiciary law.[18] It was soon, however, taken up by the German princes and applied on an even more imposing scale in their territories, to serve very different ends.

For *politically*, the revival of Roman law corresponded to the constitutional exigencies of the reorganized feudal States of the epoch. In fact, there is no doubt that on a European scale, the *primary* determinant of the adoption of Roman jurisprudence lay in the drive of royal governments for increased central powers. For the Roman legal system, it will be remembered, comprised two distinct – and apparently contrary – sectors: civil law regulating economic transactions between citizens, and public law governing political relations between the State and its subjects. The former was *jus*, the latter *lex*. The juridically unconditional character of private property consecrated by the one found its contradictory counterpart in the formally absolute nature of the imperial sovereignty exercised by the other, at least from the Dominate onwards. It was the theoretical principles of this political *imperium* which exercised a profound influence and attraction on the new monarchies of the Renaissance. If the rebirth of notions of Quiritary ownership both translated and promoted the general growth of commodity exchange in the transitional economies of the epoch, the revival of authoritarian prerogatives of the Dominate expressed and consolidated the concentration of aristocratic class power in a centralized State apparatus that was the noble reaction to it. The double social movement engraved in the structures of Western Absolutism thus found its juridical concordance in the reintroduction of Roman law. Ulpian's famous maxim – *quod principi placuit legis habet vicem*, 'the ruler's will has force of law' – became a constitutional ideal of Renaissance monarchies all over the West.[19] The complementary idea that

18. Wolfgang Kunkell, 'The Reception of Roman Law in Germany: An Interpretation', and Georg Dahm, 'On the Reception of Roman and Italian Law in Germany', in G. Strauss (ed.), *Pre-Reformation Germany*, London 1972, pp. 271, 274–6, 278, 284–92.

19. *An* ideal, but by no means the only one: we shall see that the complex practice of Absolutism was always very far from corresponding to Ulpian's maxim.

kings and princes were themselves *legibus solutus*, or freed from anterior legal constraints, provided the juristic protocols for overriding mediaeval privileges, ignoring traditional rights, and subordinating private franchises.

In other words, the enhancement of private property from below was matched by the increase of public authority from above, embodied in the discretionary power of the royal ruler. The Absolutist States in the West based their novel aims on classical precedents: Roman law was the most powerful intellectual weapon available for their typical programme of territorial integration and administrative centralism. It was no accident, in fact, that the one mediaeval monarchy which had achieved complete emancipation from any representative or corporate restraints was the Papacy, which had been the first political system of feudal Europe to utilize Roman jurisprudence wholesale, with the codification of canon law in the 12th and 13th centuries. The Pope's assertion of a *plenitudo potestatis* within the Church set the precedent for the later pretensions of secular princes, often realized precisely against its religious exorbitance. Moreover, just as it was the canon lawyers within the Papacy who had essentially built and operated its far-reaching administrative controls over the Church, so it was semi-professional bureaucrats trained in Roman law who were to provide the key executive servants of the new royal States. The Absolutist monarchies of the West characteristically relied on a skilled stratum of legists to staff their administrative machines: the *letrados* in Spain, the *maîtres de requêtes* in France, the *doctores* in Germany. Imbued with Roman doctrines of princely decretal authority and Roman conceptions of unitary legal norms, these lawyer-bureaucrats were the zealous enforcers of royal centralism in the first critical century of Absolutist State-construction. It was the imprint of this international corps of legists, more than any force, that Romanized the juridical systems of Western Europe in the Renaissance. For the transformation of law inevitably reflected the distribution of power between the propertied classes of the epoch: Absolutism, as the reorganized State apparatus of noble domination, was the central architect of the reception of Roman law in Europe. Even where, as in Germany, autonomous towns initiated the movement, it was princes who captured and drove it home; and where, as in England, royal power failed to impose civil law, it did not take root in the urban milieu.[20] In the overdetermined process of the Roman revival, it was the political pressure of the dynastic State which had primacy: the demands of monarchical 'clarity' dominated those of mercantile 'certainty'.[21] The growth in formal rationality, still extremely imperfect and incomplete, of the legal systems of early modern Europe was preponderantly the work of aristocratic Absolutism.

The superior effect of juridical modernization was thus to reinforce the rule of the traditional feudal class. The apparent paradox of this phenomenon was reflected in the whole structure of the Absolutist monarchies themselves – exotic, hybrid compositions whose surface 'modernity' again and again betrays a subterranean archaism. This can be seen very clearly from a survey of the institutional innovations which heralded and typified its arrival: army, bureaucracy, taxation, trade, diplomacy. These can be briefly considered in order. It has often been remarked that the Absolutist State pioneered the professional army, which with the military revolution introduced in the late 16th and 17th centuries by Maurice of Orange, Gustavus Adolphus and Wallenstein (infantry drill and line by the Dutchman; cavalry salvo and platoon system by the Swede; unitary vertical command by the Czech) grew immensely in size.[22] Philip II's armies numbered some

20. Roman law was never naturalized in England, largely because of the early centralization of the Anglo-Norman State, whose administrative unity rendered the English monarchy comparatively indifferent to the advantages of civil law during its mediaeval diffusion: see the pertinent comments of N. Cantor, *Mediaeval History*, London 1963, pp. 345–9. In the early modern epoch, the Tudor and Stuart dynasties did introduce new juridical institutions of a civil-law type (Star Chamber, Admiralty, or Chancery), but were ultimately unable to prevail over common law: after sharp conflicts between the two in the early 17th century, the English Revolution of 1640 sealed the victory of the latter. For some reflections on this process, see W. Holdsworth, *A History of English Law*, IV, London 1924, pp. 284–5.

21. These were the two terms used by Weber to denote the respective interests of the two forces working for Romanization: 'While thus the bourgeois classes seek after "certainty" in the administration of justice, officialdom is generally interested in "clarity" and "orderliness" of the law.' See his excellent discussion, *Economy and Society*, II, pp. 847–8.

22. Michael Roberts, 'The Military Revolution 1560–1660', in *Essays in Swedish History*, London 1967, pp. 195–225 – a basic text; *Gustavus Adolphus. A History of Sweden 1611–1632*, London 1958, Vol. II, pp. 169–89. Roberts perhaps slightly overestimates the quantitative growth of armies in this epoch.

60,000 or so, while a hundred years later Louis XIV's ran to 300,000. Yet both the form and the function of these troops diverged immensely from that which later became characteristic of the modern bourgeois State. They were not normally a national conscript force, but a mixed mass in which foreign mercenaries played a constant and central role. These mercenaries were typically recruited from areas outside the perimeter of the new centralized monarchies, often mountain regions which specialized in providing them: the Swiss were the Gurkhas of early modern Europe. French, Dutch, Spanish, Austrian or English armies included Swabians, Albanians, Swiss, Irish, Wallachians, Turks, Hungarians or Italians.[23] The most obvious social reason for the mercenary phenomenon was, of course, the natural refusal of the noble class to arm its own peasants wholesale. 'It is virtually impossible to train all the subjects of a commonwealth in the arts of war, and at the same time keep them obedient to the laws and magistrates', confided Jean Bodin. 'This was perhaps the principal reason why Francis I disbanded in 1534 the seven regiments, each of 6,000 infantry, which he had created in this kingdom.'[24] Conversely, mercenary troops ignorant of the very language of the local population, could be relied on to stamp out social rebellion. German *Landsknechten* dealt with the East Anglian peasant risings of 1549 in England, while Italian arquebusiers ensured the liquidation of the rural revolt in the West country; Swiss Guards helped to repress the Boulonnais and Camisard guerrillas of 1662 and 1702 in France. The key importance of mercenaries, already increasingly visible in the later Middle Ages, from Wales to Poland, was not merely an interim expedient of Absolutism at the dawn of its existence: it marked it down to its very demise in the West. In the late 18th century, even after the introduction of conscription into the main European countries, up to two-thirds of a given 'national' army could be composed of hired foreign soldateska.[25] The example of Prussian Absolutism, both bidding and kidnapping manpower beyond its

---

23. Victor Kiernan, 'Foreign Mercenaries and Absolute Monarchy', *Past and Present*, No. 11, April 1957, pp. 66–86, reprinted in T. Aston (ed.), *Crisis in Europe 1560–1660*, London 1965, pp. 117–40, is a peerless survey of the mercenary phenomenon, to which little has since been added.
24. Jean Bodin, *Les Six Livres de la République*, Paris 1578, p. 669.
25. Walter Dorn, *Competition for Empire*, New York 1940, p. 83.

border, using auction and empressment, is a reminder that there was not necessarily a clear distinction between the two.

At the same time, however, the function of these vast new agglomerations of soldiers was also visibly distinct from that of later capitalist armies. There has hitherto been no Marxist theory of the variant social functions of war in different modes of production. This is not the place to explore the subject. Yet it can be argued that war was possibly the most *rational* and *rapid* single mode of expansion of surplus extraction available for any given ruling class under feudalism. Agricultural productivity was, as we have seen, by no means stagnant during the Middle Ages: nor was the volume of trade. But both grew very slowly for the lords, compared with the sudden and massive 'yields' afforded by territorial conquest, of which the Norman invasions of England or Sicily, the Angevin seizure of Naples or the Castilian conquest of Andalusia were only the most spectacular examples. It was thus logical that the social definition of the feudal ruling class was military. The economic rationality of war in such a social formation is a specific one: it is a maximization of wealth whose role cannot be compared to that which it plays in the developed forms of the successor mode of production, dominated by the basic rhythm of the accumulation of capital, and the 'restless and universal change' (Marx) of the economic foundations of every social formation. The nobility was a landowning class whose profession was war: its social vocation was not an external accretion but an intrinsic function of its economic position. The normal medium of inter-capitalist competition is economic, and its structure is typically additive: rival parties may both expand and prosper – although unequally – throughout a single confrontation, because the production of manufactured commodities is inherently unlimited. The typical medium of inter-feudal rivalry, by contrast, was military and its structure was always potentially the zero-sum conflict of the battle-field, by which fixed quantities of ground were won or lost. For land is a natural monopoly: it cannot be indefinitely extended, only re-divided. The categorial object of noble rule was territory, regardless of the community inhabiting it. Land as such, not language, defined the natural perimeters of its power. The feudal ruling class was thus essentially motile, in a way that a capitalist ruling class later could never be. For capital itself is *par excellence* internationally mobile, thereby permitting its holders to be nationally fixed: land is nationally immobile, and nobles had to travel to take possession of it. A given barony or dynasty could thus typically transfer its residence from one end of the continent to the other without dislocation. Angevin lineages could rule indifferently in Hungary, England or Naples; Norman in Antioch, Sicily or England; Burgundian in Portugal or Zeeland; Luxemburger in the Rhineland or Bohemia; Flemish in Artois or Byzantium; Habsburg in Austria, the Netherlands or Spain. No common tongue had to be shared between lords and peasants in these varied lands. For public territories formed a continuum with private estates, and their classical means of acquisition was force, invariably decked out in claims of religious or genealogical legitimacy. Warfare was not the 'sport' of princes, it was their fate; beyond the finite diversity of individual inclinations and characters, it beckoned them inexorably as a social necessity of their estate. For Machiavelli, as he surveyed the Europe of the early 16th century, the final rule of their being was a verity as obvious and unimpeachable as the sky above them: 'A prince should thus have no other thought or aim than war, nor acquire mastery in anything except war, its organization and discipline; for war is the only art expected of a ruler.'[26]

The Absolutist States reflect this archaic rationality in their inmost structure. They were machines built overwhelmingly for the battle-field. It is significant that the first regular national tax to be imposed in France, the *taille royale*, was levied to finance the first regular military units in Europe – the *compagnies d'ordonnance* of the mid-15th century, of which the premier unit was composed of Scots soldiers of fortune. By the mid-16th century, 80 per cent of Spanish State revenues went on military expenditure: Vicens Vives could write that 'the impulse towards the modern type of administrative monarchy began in Western Europe with the great naval operations of Charles V against the Turks in the Western Mediterranean from 1535 onwards.'[27] By the mid-17th century, the annual outlays of continental principalities from Sweden

26. Niccolò Machiavelli, *Il Principe e Discorsi*, Milan 1960, p. 62.

27. J. Vicens Vives, 'Estructura Administrativa Estatal en los Siglos XVI y XVII', *XIe·Congrès International des Sciences Historiques*, Rapports IV, Göteborg 1960; now reprinted in Vicens Vives, *Cojuntura Económica y Reformismo Burgués*, Barcelona 1968, p. 116.

to Piedmont were everywhere predominantly and monotonously devoted to the preparation or conduct of war, now immensely more costly than in the Renaissance. Another century later, on the peaceful eve of 1789, according to Necker two-thirds of French state expenditure were still allocated to the military establishment. It is manifest that this morphology of the State does not correspond to a capitalist rationality: it represents a swollen memory of the mediaeval functions of war. Nor were the grandiose military apparatuses of the late feudal state left idle. The virtual permanence of international armed conflict is one of the hallmarks of the whole climate of Absolutism. Peace was a meteorological exception in the centuries of its dominance in the West. It has been calculated that in the entire 16th century, there were only 25 years without large-scale military operations in Europe;[28] while in the 17th century, only 7 years passed without major wars between states.[29] Such calendars are foreign to capital, although as we shall see, it eventually contributed to them.

The characteristic civilian bureaucracy and tax system of the Absolutist State was no less paradoxical. It appears to represent a transition to Weber's rational legal administration, in contrast to the jungle of particularist dependencies of the high Middle Ages. Yet at the same time, the Renaissance bureaucracy was treated as saleable property to private individuals: a central confusion of two orders that the bourgeois State has everywhere kept distinct. Thus the prevalent mode of integration of the feudal nobility into the Absolutist State in the West took the form of acquisition of 'offices'.[30] He who privately purchased a position in the public apparatus of the State could then recoup himself by licensed privileges and corruption (fee-system), in a kind of monetarized caricature of investiture in a fief. Indeed, the Marqués del Vasto, Spanish governor of Milan in 1544, could request the Italian office-holders of that city to pledge their fortunes to Charles V in his hour of need after the defeat of Ceresole, on an exact

28. R. Ehrenberg, *Das Zeitalter der Fugger*, Jena 1922, I, p. 13.

29. G. N. Clark, *The Seventeenth Century*, London 1947, p. 98. Ehrenberg, with a slightly different definition, gives a somewhat lower estimate, 21 years.

30. The best overview of this international phenomenon is K. W. Swart, *Sale of Offices in the Seventeenth Century*, The Hague 1949; the most comprehensive national study is Roland Mousnier, *La Vénalité des Offices sous Henri IV et Louis XIII*, Rouen (n.d.).

model of feudal traditions.[31] Such office-holders, who proliferated in France, Italy, Spain, Britain or Holland, could hope to make up to 300–400 per cent profit, and perhaps very much more, on their purchase. The system was born in the 16th century and became a central financial support of the Absolutist States during the 17th century. Its grossly parasitic character is evident: in extreme situations (France during the 1630's is an example), it could even cost a royal budget something like as much in disbursements (via tax-farms and exemptions) as it supplied in remunerations. The growth of the sale of offices was, of course, one of the most striking by-products of the increased monetarization of the early modern economies and of the relative ascent of the mercantile and manufacturing bourgeoisie within them. Yet by the same token, the very integration of the latter into the State apparatus by the private purchase and inheritance of public positions and honours, marked its subordinate assimilation into a feudal polity in which the nobility always necessarily constituted the summit of the social hierarchy. The *officiers* of the French parlements who played with municipal republicanism and sponsored the Mazarinades in the 1650's became the most die-hard rampart of noble reaction in the 1780's. Absolutist bureaucracy both registered the rise of mercantile capital, and arrested it.

If the sale of offices was an indirect means of raising revenue from the nobility and the mercantile bourgeoisie on terms profitable to them, the Absolutist State also, and above all, of course, taxed the poor. The economic transition from labour dues to money rents in the West was accompanied by the emergence of royal taxes levied for war, which in the long feudal crisis at the end of the Middle Ages had already been one of the main provocations for the desperate peasant upheavals of the time. 'A chain of peasant uprisings clearly directed against taxation exploded all over Europe. . . . There was little to choose between foragers and friendly or enemy armies: one took as much as the other. Then the tax-collectors appeared and swept up all they could find. Lastly the lords recovered from their men the amount of the "aid" they themselves were obliged to pay their sovereign. There is no doubt that

31. Federico Chabod, *Scritti sul Rinascimento*, Turin 1967, p. 617. The Milanese functionaries refused the demand of their governor: but their homologues elsewhere might not have been so resolute.

of all the ills which afflicted them, the peasants suffered more painfully and less patiently from the burdens of war and remote taxation.'[32] Virtually everywhere, the overwhelming weight of taxation – *taille* and *gabelle* in France, or *servicios* in Spain – fell on the poor. There was no conception of the juridical 'citizen' subject to fiscality, by the very fact of belonging to the nation. The seigneurial class was in practice everywhere effectively exempt from direct taxation. Porshnev has thus aptly dubbed the new taxes imposed by the Absolutist States 'centralized feudal rent' as opposed to the seigneurial dues which formed a 'local feudal rent':[33] this doubled system of exactions led to a tormented epidemic of rebellions by the poor in 17th century France, in which provincial nobles often led their own peasants against the tax-collectors so as the better to be able to extort their local dues from them. Fiscal officials had to be guarded by units of fusiliers to be able to perform their duties in the countryside: re-embodiments in a modernized guise of the immediate unity of politico-legal coercion with economic exploitation constitutive of the feudal mode of production as such.

The economic functions of Absolutism were not exhausted, however, by its tax and office system. Mercantilism was the ruling doctrine of the epoch, and it presents the same ambiguity as the bureaucracy which was intended to enforce it, with the same underlying reversion to an earlier prototype. For mercantilism undoubtedly demanded the suppression of particularistic barriers to trade within the national realm, and strove to create a unified domestic market for commodity production. Aiming to increase the power of the State relative to that of all other States, it encouraged exports of goods, while banning exports of bullion or coins, in the belief that there was a fixed quantity of commerce and wealth in the world. In Hecksher's famous phrase: 'The State was both the subject and the object of mercantilist economic policy.'[34]

32. Duby, *Rural Economy and Country Life in the Mediaeval West*, p. 333.
33. B. F. Porshnev, *Les Soulèvements Populaires en France de 1623 à 1648*, Paris 1965, pp. 395–6.
34. Hecksher argued that the object of mercantilism was to increase the 'power of the State' rather than the 'wealth of nations', and that this meant a subordination, in Bacon's words, of 'considerations of plenty' to 'considerations of power' (Bacon praised Henry VII for having restricted wine imports to English ships on these grounds). Viner, in an effective reply, had no difficulty in showing that

Its characteristic creations were the royal manufactures and state-regulated guilds in France, and the chartered companies in England. The mediaeval and corporatist lineage of the former scarcely needs comment; the tell-tale fusion of political and economic orders in the latter scandalized Adam Smith. For mercantilism exactly represented the conceptions of a feudal ruling class that had adapted to an integrated market, yet had preserved its essential outlook on the unity of what Francis Bacon called 'considerations of plenty' and 'considerations of power'. The classical bourgeois doctrines of laissez-faire, with their rigorous formal separation of the political and economic systems, were to be its antipode. Mercantilism was precisely a theory of the coherent intervention of the political State into the workings of the economy, in the joint interests of the prosperity of the one and the power of the other. Logically, whereas laissez-faire was consistently 'pacifist', urging the benefits of peace among nations to increase mutually profitable international trade, mercantilist theory (Montchrétien, Bodin) was heavily 'bellicist', emphasizing the necessity and profitability of warfare.[35] Vice-versa, the aim of a strong economy was successful prosecution of a conquering foreign policy. Colbert told Louis XIV that the royal manufactures were his economic regiments, and the corporations his reserves. This greatest practitioner of mercantilism, who restored the finances of the French State in ten miraculous years of intendancy, then launched his sovereign on the fateful invasion of Holland in 1672, with this expressive piece of advice: 'If the king were to subjugate all the United Provinces to his authority, their commerce would become the commerce of the subjects of his majesty, and there would be

most mercantilist writers on the contrary gave equal emphasis to both, and believed the two to be compatible. 'Power versus Plenty as Objectives of Foreign Policy in the 17th and 18th Centuries', *World Politics*, I, No. I, 1948, now reprinted in D. C. Coleman (ed.), *Revisions in Mercantilism*, London 1969, pp. 61–91. At the same time, Viner plainly underestimated the difference between mercantilist theory and practice, and those of the *laissez-faire* which followed it. In fact, both Hecksher and Viner in different ways miss the essential point, which is the *indistinction* of economy and polity in the transitional epoch which produced mercantilist theories. Dispute as to whether either of the two had 'primacy' over the other is an anachronism, because there was no such rigid separation of them in practice until the advent of *laissez-faire*.

35. E. Silberner, *La Guerre dans La Pensée Economique du XVIᵉ au XVIIIᵉ Siècle*, Paris 1939, pp. 7–122.

nothing more to ask.'[36] Four decades of European conflict were to follow this sample of economic reasoning, which perfectly captures the social logic of Absolutist aggression and predatory mercantilism: the trade of the Dutch treated as the land of the Anglo-Saxons or the estates of the Moors, a physical object to be taken and enjoyed by military force as the natural mode of appropriation, and possessed permanently thereafter. The optical error in this particular judgement does not make it unrepresentative: it was with such eyes that Absolutist States gazed at one another. The mercantilist theories of wealth and of war were, indeed, conceptually interlocked: the zero-sum model of world trade which inspired its economic protectionism was derived from the zero-sum model of international politics which was inherent in its bellicism.

Trade and war were not the only external activities of the Absolutist State in the West, of course. Its other great effort was invested in *diplomacy*. This was one of the great institutional inventions of the epoch – inaugurated in the miniature area of Italy in the 15th century, institutionalized there with the Peace of Lodi, and adopted in Spain, France, England, Germany and throughout Europe in the 16th century. Diplomacy was, in fact, the indelible birth-mark of the Renaissance State: with its emergence an international State system was born in Europe, in which there was a perpetual 'probing of the weak points in the environment of a State or the dangers to it emanating from other States'.[37] Mediaeval Europe had never been composed of a clearly demarcated set of homogeneous political units – an international State system. Its political map was an inextricably superimposed and tangled one, in which different juridical instances were geographically interwoven and stratified, and plural allegiances, asymmetrical suzerainties

36. Pierre Goubert, *Louis XIV et Vingt Millions de Français*, Paris 1966, p. 95.
37. B. F. Porshnev, 'Les Rapports Politiques de l'Europe Occidentale et de l'Europe Orientale à l'Epoque de la Guerre de Trente Ans', *XIe Congrès International des Sciences Historiques*, Uppsala 1960, p. 161: an extremely speculative foray into the Thirty Years War, that is a good example of Porshnev's strengths and weaknesses. Contrary to the intimations of his Western colleagues, it is not a rigid 'dogmatism' that is his major failing, but an over-fertile 'ingenuity' not always adequately restrained by the discipline of evidence; yet the same trait is in another respect what makes him an original and imaginative historian. The brief suggestions at the end of his essay on the concept of 'an international state system' are well-taken.

and anomalous enclaves abounded.[38] Within this intricate maze, there was no possibility of a formal diplomatic system emerging, because there was no uniformity or parity of partners. The concept of Latin Christendom of which all men were members provided a universalist ideological matrix for conflicts and decisions, which was the necessary obverse of the extreme particularist heterogeneity of the political units themselves. Thus 'embassies' were sporadic and unpaid voyages of address, which could equally well be sent by a vassal or a rear-vassal within a given territory, or between the princes of two territories, or a prince and his suzerain. The contraction of the feudal pyramid into the new centralized monarchies of Renaissance Europe produced for the first time a formalized system of inter-State pressure and exchange, with the establishment of the novel institutions of reciprocal fixed embassies abroad, permanent chancelleries for foreign relations, and secret diplomatic communications and reports, shielded by the new concept of 'extra-territoriality'.[39] The resolutely secular spirit of political egoism which henceforward inspired the practice of diplomacy was limpidly expressed by Ermolao Barbaro, the Venetian Ambassador who was its inaugural theorist: 'The first duty of an ambassador is exactly the same as that of any other servant of a government, that is, to do, say, advise and think whatever may best serve the preservation and aggrandizement of his own state.'

Yet these instruments of diplomacy, ambassadors or state secretaries, were not the weapons of a modern national State. The ideological conceptions of 'nationalism' as such were foreign to the inmost nature of Absolutism. The royal States of the new epoch did not disdain to mobilize patriotic sentiments in their subjects, in the political and military conflicts which constantly opposed the various monarchies of Western Europe to one another. But the diffuse existence of a popular

38. Engels liked to cite the example of Burgundy: 'Charles the Bold, for example, was the feoffee of the Emperor for a part of his lands, and the feoffee of the French king for another part of them; on the other hand, the King of France, his feoffor, was at the same time the feoffee of Charles the Bold, his own vassal, for certain regions.' See his important manuscript, posthumously entitled *Uber den Verfall des Feudalismus und das Aufkommen der Bourgeoisie*, in *Werke*, Bd 21, p. 396.

39. For this whole development of the new diplomacy in early modern Europe, see Garrett Mattingly's great work, *Renaissance Diplomacy*, London 1955, *passim*. The quotation from Barbaro is cited on p. 109.

proto-nationalism in Tudor England, Bourbon France or Habsburg Spain was basically a token of bourgeois presence within the polity,[40] and it was always manipulated by grandees or sovereigns more than it governed them. The national aureole of Absolutism in the West, often apparently very pronounced (Elizabeth I, Louis XIV), was in reality contingent and borrowed. The ruling norms of the age lay elsewhere. For the ultimate instance of legitimacy was the *dynasty*, not the territory. The State was conceived as the patrimony of the monarch, and therefore the title-deeds to it could be gained by a union of persons: *felix Austria*. The supreme device of diplomacy was therefore marriage – peaceful mirror of war, which so often provoked it. For, less costly as an avenue of territorial expansion than armed aggression, matrimonial manoeuvring afforded less immediate results (often only at one generation's remove) and was thereby subject to unpredictable hazards of mortality in the interval before the consummation of a nuptial pact and its political fruition. Hence the long detour of marriage so often led back directly to the short route of war. The history of Absolutism is littered with such conflicts, whose names bear them witness: Wars of the Spanish, Austrian, or Bavarian Successions. Their outcome might, indeed, accentuate the 'flotation' of dynasty over territory that had occasioned them. Paris could be defeated in the ruinous military struggle over the Spanish Succession; the Bourbon house inherited Madrid. In diplomacy, too, the index of feudal dominance in the Absolutist State is evident.

Immensely magnified and reorganized, the feudal State of Absolutism was nevertheless constantly and profoundly over-determined by the growth of capitalism within the composite social formations of the early modern period. These formations were, of course, a combination of different modes of production under the – waning – dominance of one of them: feudalism. All the structures of the Absolutist State thus reveal the action from a distance of the new economy at work within

40. The rural and urban masses themselves, of course, evinced spontaneous forms of xenophobia: but this traditional negative reaction to alien communities was quite distinct from the positive national identification that started to emerge within literate bourgeois milieux in the early modern epoch. The fusion of the two could, in crisis situations, produce patriotic outbursts from below of an uncontrolled and seditious character: the Comuneros in Spain or the League in France.

the framework of an older system: hybrid 'capitalizations' of feudal forms abounded, whose very perversion of future institutions (army, bureaucracy, diplomacy, trade) was a conversion of past social objects to repeat them.

Yet the premonitions of a new political order contained within them was not a false promise. The bourgeoisie in the West was already strong enough to leave its blurred impress on the State, under Absolutism. For the apparent paradox of Absolutism in Western Europe was that it fundamentally represented an apparatus for the protection of aristocratic property and privileges, yet at the same time the means whereby this protection was promoted could *simultaneously* ensure the basic interests of the nascent mercantile and manufacturing classes. The Absolutist State increasingly centralized political power and worked towards more uniform legal systems: Richelieu's campaigns against the Huguenot redoubts in France were typical. It did away with a large number of internal barriers to trade, and sponsored external tariffs against foreign competitors: Pombal's measures in Enlightenment Portugal were a drastic example. It provided lucrative if risky investments in public finance for usury capital: 16th century Augsburg bankers and 17th century Genoese oligarchs could make fortunes from their loans to the Spanish State. It mobilized rural property by seizure of ecclesiastical lands: dissolution of the monasteries in England. It offered rentier sinecures in the bureaucracy: the Paulette in France ordained stable tenure of them. It sponsored colonial enterprises and trading companies: to the White Sea, to the Antilles, to Hudson Bay, to Louisiana. In other words, it accomplished certain partial functions in the *primitive accumulation* necessary for the eventual triumph of the capitalist mode of production itself. The reasons why it could perform this 'dual' role lie in the specific nature of merchant or manufacturing capital: since neither rested on the mass production characteristic of machine industry proper, neither in themselves demanded a radical rupture with the feudal agrarian order which still enclosed the vast majority of the population (the future wage-labour and consumer market of industrial capitalism). In other words, they could develop within the limits set by the reorganized feudal framework. This is not to say that they everywhere did so: political, religious or economic conflicts could well fuse into revolutionary explosions against Absolutism after a certain period of maturation, in specific conjunctures. There was, however, always a potential *field of compatibility* at this stage between the nature and programme of the Absolutist State and the operations of mercantile and manufacturing capital. For in the international competition between noble classes that produced the endemic warfare of the age, the size of the commodity sector within each 'national' patrimony was always of critical importance to its relative military and political strength. Every monarchy thus had a stake in gathering treasure and promoting trade under its own banners, in the struggle against its rivals. Hence the 'progressive' character that subsequent historians have so often conferred on the official policies of Absolutism. Economic centralization, protectionism and overseas expansion aggrandized the late feudal State while they profited the early bourgeoisie. They increased the taxable revenues of the one by providing business opportunities for the other. The circular maxims of mercantilism, proclaimed by the Absolutist State, gave eloquent expression to this provisional coincidence of interests. It was appropriately enough the Duc de Choiseul, in the last decades of the aristocratic *ancien régime* in the West, who declared: 'Upon the navy depend the colonies, upon the colonies commerce, upon commerce the capacity of a State to maintain numerous armies, to increase its population and to make possible the most glorious and useful enterprises.'[41]

Yet, as the final cadence of 'glorious and useful' implies, the irreducibly feudal character of Absolutism remained. It was a State founded on the social supremacy of the aristocracy and confined by the imperatives of landed property. The nobility could deposit power with the monarchy, and permit the enrichment of the bourgeoisie: the masses were still at its mercy. No 'political' derogation of the noble class ever occurred in the Absolutist State. Its feudal character constantly ended by frustrating and falsifying its promises for capital. The Fuggers were eventually ruined by Habsburg bankruptcies; English nobles appropriated most of the monastic lands; Louis XIV destroyed the benefits of Richelieu's work by revoking the Edict of Nantes; London merchants were plundered by the Cockayne project; Portugal reverted to the

41. Cited by Gerald Graham, *The Politics of Naval Supremacy*, Cambridge 1965, p. 17.

Methuen system after Pombal's death; Parisian speculators were defrauded by Law. Army, bureaucracy, diplomacy and dynasty remained a hardened feudal complex which governed the whole State machine and guided its destinies. The rule of the Absolutist State was that of the feudal nobility in the epoch of transition to capitalism. Its end would signal the crisis of the power of its class: the advent of the bourgeois revolutions, and the emergence of the capitalist State.

2

Class and State:
Problems of Periodization

The typical institutional complex of the Absolutist State in the West has now been outlined. It remains to sketch very briefly some aspects of the trajectory of this historical form, which naturally underwent significant modifications in the three or more centuries of its existence. At the same time, it is necessary to give some account of the relationship between the noble class and Absolutism, because nothing could be less justified than to assume that this was an unproblematic one of natural harmony from the start. On the contrary, it may be argued that the real *periodization* of Absolutism in the West is at bottom to be found precisely in the changing rapport between the nobility and the monarchy, and the multiple attendant political shifts which were correlated with it. At any rate, a provisional periodization of the State and an attempt to trace the relationship of the dominant class to it, will be proposed below.

The mediaeval monarchies, as we have seen, were an unstable amalgam of feudal suzerains and anointed kings. The extraordinary regalian rights of the latter function were, of course, a necessary counterweight against the structural weakness and limitations of the former: the contradiction between these two alternate principles of royalty was the central tension of the feudal State in the Middle Ages. The role of the feudal suzerain at the summit of a vassal hierarchy was ultimately the dominant component of this monarchical model, as the retrospective light shed on it by the contrasting structure of Absolutism was to show. This role dictated very narrow limits to the economic base of monarchy in the early mediaeval period. In effect, the feudal ruler of this epoch had to raise his revenues primarily from his own estates, in his capacity as a particular landlord. The dues from his demesne would initially be delivered in kind, and then increasingly in cash.[1] In addition to this income, he would normally enjoy certain financial privileges from his territorial lordship: above all, feudal 'incidences' and special 'aids' from his vassals, tied to investiture in their fiefs, plus seigneurial tolls exacted on markets or trade-routes, plus emergency levies from the Church, plus the profits of royal justice in the forms of fines and confiscations. Naturally, these fragmented and restricted forms of revenue were soon inadequate even for the exiguous governmental duties characteristic of the mediaeval polity. Recourse could be had, of course, to credit from merchants and bankers in the towns, who controlled relatively large reserves of liquid capital: this was the earliest and most widespread expedient of feudal monarchs when confronted with shortage of income for the conduct of affairs of State. But borrowing only postponed the problem, since bankers normally demanded secure pledges from future royal income against their loans.

The pressing and permanent need to acquire substantial sums outside the range of their traditional revenues thus led virtually all mediaeval monarchies to summon the 'Estates' of their realm from time to time, in order to raise taxes. These Estates became increasingly frequent and prominent from the 13th century onwards in Western Europe, when the tasks of feudal government had become more complex and the scale of finance involved in them correspondingly demanding.[2] They nowhere acquired a regular basis of recall, independent of the will of the ruler, and hence their periodicity varied enormously from country to country, and within countries. However, these institutions should

1. The Swedish monarchy was actually to receive much of its income in kind, both in dues and taxes, well into the early modern epoch.

2. A full-scale study of mediaeval Estates in Europe is badly needed. At present, the only work with some international sidelights appears to be Antonio Marongiu, *Il Parlamento in Italia, nel Medio Evo e nell'Età Moderna: Contributo alla Storia delle Istituzioni Parlamentari dell'Europa Occidentale*, Milan 1962, recently and somewhat misleadingly translated into English as *Mediaeval Parliaments: A Comparative Study*, London 1968. In fact, Marongiu's book – as its original title indicates – is essentially concerned with Italy, the one region in Europe where Estates were absent or relatively unimportant. Its brief sections on other countries (France, England or Spain) scarcely constitute a satisfactory introduction to them, and it ignores Northern and Eastern Europe altogether. Moreover, the book is a juristic survey, innocent of any sociological enquiry.

not be regarded as contingent or extrinsic growths on the mediaeval body politic. On the contrary, they constituted an intermittent mechanism that was an inevitable consequence of the structure of the early feudal State as such. For precisely because the political and economic orders were *fused* in a chain of *personal* obligations and dues, there was never any legal basis for *general* economic levies by the monarch outside the hierarchy of mediate sovereignties. In fact, it is striking that the very idea of universal taxation – so central to the whole edifice of the Roman Empire – lapsed altogether during the Dark Ages.[3] Thus no feudal king could decree imposts at will. Every ruler had to obtain the 'consent' of specially assembled bodies – Estates – for major taxation, under the rubric of the legal principle *quod omnes tangit*.[4] It is significant that most of the direct general taxes which were slowly introduced into Western Europe, subject to the assent of mediaeval parliaments, had been initially pioneered in Italy, where the initial feudal synthesis was most tilted towards the Roman and urban heritage. Not only did the Church levy general taxation on the faithful for the Crusades; municipal governments – compact councils of patricians without investiture or rank stratification – had no great difficulties in imposing taxes on their own town populations, still less on a subjugated *contado*. The Commune of Pisa actually had property taxes. The peninsula also initiated many indirect taxes: the salt monopoly or *gabelle* originated in Sicily. Soon a variegated fiscal pattern developed in the main West European countries. English princes relied mainly on custom duties because of their insular situation, French on excises and the *taille*, and German on intensification of tolls. These taxes, however, were not regular grants. They normally remained occasional levies down to the end of the Middle Ages, during which few Estates ever yielded to royal rulers the right to raise permanent or general taxation without the consent of their subjects.

Naturally, the social definition of 'subjects' was a predictable one. The 'estates of the realm' customarily represented the nobility, the clergy and the urban burgesses, and were organized either in a straight-forward three-curia or a somewhat distinct two-chamber (magnate/

---

3. Carl Stephenson, *Mediaeval Institutions*, pp. 99–100.
4. *Ab omnibus debet comprobari*: what touches all must be approved by all.

non-magnate) system.[5] Such assemblies were virtually universal throughout Western Europe, with the exception of Northern Italy where the urban density and absence of feudal suzerainty naturally inhibited their emergence: the Parliament in England, États-Généraux in France, Landtage in Germany, Cortes in Castile or Portugal, Riksdag in Sweden, and so on. Besides their essential role as the fiscal faucets of the mediaeval State, these Estates fulfilled another critical function in the feudal polity. They were collective representations of one of the deepest principles of feudal hierarchy within the nobility, the duty of the vassal to provide not only *auxilium*, but *consilium* to his liege-lord: in other words, the right to give his solemn advice in matters of gravity affecting both parties. Such consultation did not necessarily weaken the mediaeval ruler: in foreign or domestic crises, it might well strengthen him by providing welcome political support. Outside the particular nexus of individual homage relationships, the public application of this conception was initially confined to the small number of baronial magnates who were the tenants-in-chief of the monarch, formed his entourage, and expected to be consulted by him in important affairs of State. With the growth of Estates proper in the 13th century because of fiscal exigencies, the baronial prerogative of consultation in the *ardua negotia regni* was gradually extended to these new assemblies, and came to form an important part of the political tradition of the noble class as a whole, which naturally everywhere dominated the Estates. The 'ramification' of the feudal polity in the High Middle Ages by the growth of Estates institutions from the main trunk, thus did not alter the relationship between the monarchy and nobility in any unilateral direction. These institutions were essentially summoned into existence to expand the fiscal base of the monarchy, but while fulfilling this aim, they also increased the potential collective control of the nobility over the latter. They should not therefore be regarded either as mere checks or tools of royal power: rather they reduplicated a

5. These alternative patterns are discussed by Hintze, in 'Typologie der Ständischen Verfassungen des Abendlandes', *Gesammelte Abhandlungen*, Vol. I, pp. 110–29, which remains the best single text on the phenomenon of feudal estates in Europe, although curiously inconclusive by comparison with most of Hintze's other essays: as if the full implications of his findings had yet to be elucidated by him.

pristine balance between the feudal suzerain and his vassals in a more complex and effective framework.

In practice, the Estates remained sporadic occasions, and the taxes levied by the monarchy relatively modest affairs. One important reason for this was that the problem of an extensive paid bureaucracy had not as yet interposed itself between the monarchy and the nobility. Royal government throughout the Middle Ages relied to a considerable extent on the services of the very large clerical bureaucracy of the Church, whose top personnel could devote themselves full-time to civil administration without a financial charge on the State, since they already received ample salaries from a separate ecclesiastical apparatus. The higher clergy who century after century provided so many of the supreme administrators of the feudal polity – from England to France to Spain – were themselves, of course, mostly recruited from the nobility, for whom access to episcopal and abbatial positions was an important social and economic privilege. The stepped feudal hierarchy of personal homage and fealty, the corporate Estates assemblies exercising their rights of voting taxes and deliberating on affairs of the realm, the informal character of an administration partly maintained by the Church, a Church often staffed at its summit by magnates – all these formed a legible and intimate political system binding the noble class to a State with which, despite and through constant conflicts with specific monarchs, it was at one.

The contrast between this pattern of the mediaeval Estates-Monarchy and that of early modern Absolutism is marked enough for historians today. It was naturally no less – far more – so for the nobles who actually lived through it. For the great, silent structural force impelling a complete reorganization of feudal class power was inevitably concealed from them. The type of historical causality that was at work in dissolving the original unity of extra-economic exploitation at the base of the whole social system, by the spread of commodity production and exchange, and recentralizing it at the summit, was not visible within their categorial universe. For many individual nobles, it meant new opportunities for fortune and fame, which were avidly grasped; for many others, it signified indignity or ruin, against which they rebelled; for most it involved a protracted and difficult process of adaptation and conversion, across succeeding generations, before harmony between class and State was precariously restored. In the course of this process, the late feudal aristocracy was obliged to abandon old traditions and acquire many new skills.[6] It had to shed military exercise of private violence, social patterns of vassal loyalty, economic habits of hereditary insouciance, political rights of representative autonomy, and cultural attributes of unlettered ignorance. It had to learn the new avocations of a disciplined officer, a literate functionary, a polished courtier, and a more or less prudent estate-owner. The history of Western Absolutism is largely the story of the slow reconversion of the landed ruling class to the necessary form of its own political power, despite and against most of its previous experience and instincts.

The Renaissance epoch thus witnessed the first phase in the consolidation of Absolutism, when it was still comparatively close to an antecedent monarchical pattern. Estates persisted in France, Castile or the Netherlands up to mid-century and flourished in England. Armies were relatively small, mainly mercenary forces with only seasonal campaigning capacity. They were led in person by aristocrats who were magnates of the first water in their respective realms (Essex, Alba, Condé or Nassau). The great secular boom of the 16th century, provoked both by rapid demographic growth and the advent of American bullion and trade, eased credit for European princes, and allowed great increases in outlay without a correspondingly sound expansion of the fiscal system, although there was a general intensification of taxation: this was the golden age of the South German financiers. There was a steady growth of bureaucratic administration, but it was typically everywhere prey to colonization by grandee houses competing for the

6. Lawrence Stone, *The Crisis of the Aristocracy 1558–1641*, Oxford 1965, is the deepest existent case-study of the metamorphoses of a European nobility in this epoch. Criticism has focused on its thesis that the economic position of the English peerage deteriorated significantly in the century examined. However, this is essentially a secondary issue, for the 'crisis' was a much wider one than a simple question of the quantity of manors held by lords: it was a pervasive travail of adaptation. Stone's discussion of the problem of aristocratic military power in this context is particularly valuable (pp. 199–270). The limitation of the book is rather its confinement to the English peerage, a very small élite within the landed ruling class; moreover, as will be seen below, the English aristocracy was extremely atypical of Western Europe as a whole. Studies of continental nobilities, with a comparable wealth of material, are much needed.

political privileges and economic profits of office, and commanding parasitic clientages of lesser nobles who were infiltrated into the State apparatus and formed rival patronage networks within it: a modernized version of the late mediaeval retainer system and its conflicts. Factional feuds between great families, each with a segment of the State machine at their behest, and often a solid regional base within a tenuously unified country, constantly occupied the front of the political stage.[7] In England, the virulent Dudley/Seymour and Leicester/Cecil rivalries, in France the murderous three-cornered war between the Guise, Montmorency and Bourbon lineages, in Spain the brutal backstairs struggle for power between the Alva and Eboli groups, were a keynote of the time. The Western aristocracies had begun to acquire university education and the cultural fluency hitherto reserved for clerics:[8] they were by no means yet demilitarized in their private life, even in England, let alone France, Italy or Spain. The reigning monarchs generally had to reckon with their magnates as an independent force, to be accorded the positions appropriate to their rank: the traces of a symmetrical mediaeval pyramid were still visible in the approaches to the sovereign. It was only in the second half of the century that the first theorists of Absolutism started to propagate divine right conceptions that elevated royal power totally above the limited and reciprocal fealty of mediaeval kingly suzerainty. Bodin was the first and most rigorous of them. But the 16th century closed in the major countries without the accomplished form of Absolutism in existence anywhere: even in Spain, Philip II was impotent to send troops across the border into Aragon without the permission of its lords.

Indeed, the very term 'Absolutism' was a misnomer. No Western monarchy ever enjoyed an absolute power over its subjects, in the sense of an untrammelled despotism.[9] All were limited, even at the

7. For a recent discussion, see J. H. Elliott, *Europe Divided 1559–1598*, London 1968, pp. 73–7.

8. J. H. Hexter, 'The Education of the Aristocracy in the Renaissance', in *Reappraisals in History*, London 1961, pp. 45–70.

9. Roland Mousnier and Fritz Hartung, 'Quelques Problèmes Concernant la Monarchie Absolue', *X Congresso Internazionale di Scienze Storici, Relazioni IV*, Florence 1955, esp. pp. 4–15, is the first and most fundamental contribution to the debate on this topic over recent years. Earlier writers had perceived the same truth, if in a less systematic fashion, among them Engels: 'The decadence of feudalism and the development of towns were both decentralizing forces, which

height of their prerogatives, by the complex of conceptions designated 'divine' or 'natural' law. Bodin's theory of sovereignty, which dominated European political thought for a century, eloquently embodies these contradictions of Absolutism. For Bodin was the first thinker systematically and resolutely to break with the mediaeval conception of authority as the exercise of traditional justice, and to formulate the modern idea of political power as the sovereign capacity to create new laws, and impose unquestioning obedience to them. 'The principal mark of sovereign majesty and absolute power is essentially the right to impose laws on subjects generally without their consent. . . . There is indeed a distinction between justice and law, for the one merely implies equity, while the other implies command. Law is nothing other than the command of the sovereign in the exercise of his power.'[10] Yet while enunciating these revolutionary axioms, Bodin simultaneously upheld the most conservative feudal maxims limiting the basic fiscal and economic rights of rulers over their subjects. 'It is not within the competence of any prince in the world to levy taxes at will on his people, or seize the goods of another arbitrarily'; for 'since the sovereign prince has no power to transgress the laws of nature, which God – whose image he is on earth – has ordained, he cannot take the property of another without a just and reasonable cause.'[11] Bodin's passionate exegesis of the novel idea of sovereignty was thus combined with a call for the reinvigoration of the fief system for military service, and a reaffirmation of the value of Estates: 'The sovereignty of a monarch is no way altered or diminished by the existence of Estates; on the contrary, his majesty is the greater and more illustrious when his people acknowledge him as sovereign, even if in such assemblies princes, not wanting to antagonize their subjects, grant and permit many things to

---

precisely determined the necessity of absolute monarchy as a power capable of welding together nationalities. Monarchy *had* to be absolute, just because of the centrifugal pressure of all these elements. Its *absolutism*, however, must not be understood in a vulgar sense. It was in permanent conflict with Estates, and with rebellious feudatories and cities: it nowhere abolished Estates altogether.' Marx-Engels, *Werke*, Bd 21, p. 402. The last clause is, of course, an overstatement.

10. Jean Bodin, *Les Six Livres de la République*, Paris 1578, pp. 103, 114. I have translated *droit* as 'justice' in this passage, to bring out the distinction alluded to above.

11. *Les Six Livres de la République*, pp. 102, 114.

which they would not have consented without the requests, prayers and just complaints of their people. . . .'[12] Nothing reveals more clearly the real nature of Absolute Monarchy in the later Renaissance than this authoritative theorization of it. For the practice of Absolutism corresponded to Bodin's theory of it. No Absolutist State could ever dispose at will of the liberty or landed property of the nobility itself, or the bourgeoisie, in the fashion of the Asian tyrannies coeval with them. Nor did they ever achieve any complete administrative centralization or juridical unification; corporative particularisms and regional heterogeneities inherited from the mediaeval epoch marked the Ancien Régimes down to their ultimate overthrow. Absolute monarchy in the West was thus, in fact, always doubly limited: by the persistence of traditional political bodies below it and the presence of an overarching moral law above it. In other words, the sway of Absolutism ultimately operated within the necessary bounds of the class whose interests it secured. Sharp conflicts between the two were to break out as the dismantling of many familiar noble landmarks by the monarchy proceeded in the next century. But throughout them, it should be remembered that just as no absolute power was ever exercised by the Absolutist State of the West, no struggle between these States and their aristocracies could ever be absolute either. The social unity of the two determined the terrain and temporality of the political contradictions between them. These, however, were to have their own historical importance.

The next hundred years witnessed the full emplacement of the Absolutist State, in a century of agrarian and demographic depression and downward-drifting prices. It was now that the effects of the 'military revolution' made themselves decisively felt. Armies rapidly multiplied in size, becoming astronomically expensive, in a series of ceaselessly expanding wars. Tilly's operations were not so much larger than those of Alva; they were dwarfed by those of Turenne. The cost of these massive military machines created acute revenue crises for the Absolutist States. Tax pressures on the masses generally intensified. Simultaneously, the sale of public offices and honours now became a central financial expedient for all monarchies, and was systematized in a way that it had not been in the previous century. The result was to integrate a growing number of *arriviste* bourgeois into the columns of

12. *Les Six Livres de la République*, p. 103.

State functionaries, which became increasingly professionalized, and to reorganize the links between the nobility and the State apparatus itself.

For the sale of offices was not merely an economic device to raise revenue from the propertied classes. It also served a political function: by making the acquisition of bureaucratic position a market transaction, and vesting ownership of it with rights of inheritance, sale of offices blocked the formation of grandee clientage systems within the State dependent not on impersonal cash equivalents, but on the personal connections and prestige of a great lord and his house. Richelieu stressed in his Testament the critical 'sterilizing' role of the *paulette* in putting the whole administrative system beyond the reach of tentacular aristocratic lineages like that of the House of Guise. Of course, one parasitism was only exchanged for another: instead of patronage, venality. But the mediation of the market was a safer one for the monarchy than that of the magnates: the Parisian financial syndicates who advanced loans to the State, farmed taxes and bought up offices in the 17th century were much less dangerous to French Absolutism than the provincial dynasties of the 16th, who not only had sections of the royal administration beholden to them, but could field their own armed troops as well. The augmented bureaucratization of office in its turn produced new types of ruling administrators, normally recruited from the nobility and expecting the conventional benefits of office, but imbued with a rigorous respect for the State as such and a fierce determination to uphold its long-term interests against short-sighted cabals of ambitious or disaffected grandees. These were the austere reforming Ministers of the 17th century monarchies, essentially civilian functionaries, with no autonomous regional or military base, directing the affairs of State from their cabinets: Oxenstierna, Laud, Richelieu, Colbert or Olivares. (The complementary type in the new era was the feckless personal intimate of the reigning sovereign, the *válido* of whom Spain was to be so prodigal, from Lerma to Godoy; Mazarin was a strange mixture of the two.) It was these generations which extended and codified the practices of bilateral 16th century diplomacy into a multilateral international system, of which the Treaty of Westphalia was the founding charter, and the magnified scope of the wars of the 17th century the material crucible.

Escalation of war, bureaucratization of office, intensification of taxation, erosion of clientage, all led in the same direction: towards a decisive elimination of what Montesquieu in the next century was to theorize nostalgically as the 'intermediary powers' between the monarchy and the people. In other words, the Estates systems progressively went under as the class power of the nobility assumed the form of a centripetal dictatorship exercised under the royal ensign. The actual power of the monarchy as an institution, of course, in no way necessarily corresponded to that of the monarch: the sovereign who actually directed administration and conducted policy was as much the exception as the rule, although for obvious reasons the creative unity and efficacy of Absolutism was always at its height when the two coincided (Louis XIV or Frederick II). The maximum florescence and vigour of the Absolutist State of the *grand siècle* was necessarily also a stifling compression of the traditional rights and autonomies of the noble class, which dated back to the original mediaeval decentralization of the feudal polity and were sanctioned by venerable custom and interest. The last Estates-General before the Revolution was held in France in 1614; the last Castilian Cortés before Napoleon in 1665; the last Landtag in Bavaria in 1669; while in England, the longest surcease of Parliament in a century occurred, from 1629 to the Civil War. This epoch is thus not only that of a political and cultural apogee of Absolutism, but also of widespread aristocratic disaffection and alienation from it. Particularist privileges and customary rights were not abandoned without a struggle, especially in a time of pervasive economic recession and tautened credit.

The 17th century was thus repeatedly the scene of local noble revolts against the Absolutist State in the West, which often blended with incipient sedition by lawyers or merchants, and sometimes even utilized the suffering rage of the rural and urban masses themselves, as a temporary weapon against the monarchy.[13] The Fronde in France,

13. Trevor-Roper's justly celebrated essay, 'The General Crisis of the Seventeenth Century', *Past and Present*, No. 16, November 1959, pp. 31–64, now modified and reprinted in *Religion, The Reformation and Social Change*, London 1967, pp. 46–89, for all its merits, restricts the scope of these revolts too narrowly, by presenting them essentially as protests against the expense and waste of the post-Renaissance courts. In fact, as numerous historians have pointed out, war was a very much larger item in the State budgets of the 17th century than the court. Louis XIV's palace establishment was far more lavish than that of Anne of

the Catalonian Republic in Spain, the Neapolitan Revolution in Italy, the Estates Revolt in Bohemia and the Great Rebellion in England itself all had, in very different proportions, something of this aspect of a nobiliary revolt against the consolidation of Absolutism.[14] Naturally, this reaction could never become a full-scale, united aristocratic onslaught on the monarchy, for the two were tied together by an umbilical class cord: nor was there any case of a *purely* noble revolt in the century. The characteristic pattern was rather an overdetermined explosion in which a *regionally* delimited part of the nobility raised the banner of aristocratic separatism, and was joined by a discontented urban bourgeoisie and plebeian mobs in a general upheaval. Only in England, where the capitalist component of the revolt was preponderant in both the rural and urban propertied classes, did the Great Rebellion succeed. Everywhere else, in France, Spain, Italy and Austria, insurrections dominated or infected by noble separatism were crushed and Absolutist power reinforced. Necessarily so. No feudal ruling class could afford to jettison the advances achieved by Absolutism, which were the expression of profound historical necessities working themselves out right across the continent, without jeopardizing its own existence; none, in fact, ever was wholly or mainly won to the cause of revolt. But the regional or partial character of these struggles does not minimize their significance: factors of local autonomism merely *condensed* a diffuse dissatisfaction that often existed throughout the nobility, and gave it a violent politico-military form.

Austria, but it was not thereby more unpopular. Apart from this, the fundamental rift between the aristocracy and the monarchy in this epoch was not really an economic one, although war-taxes could and did set off wider revolts. It was *political*, concerned with the total position of the nobility in an incipient polity whose outlines were often still opaque to all the actors involved in the drama.

14. The Neapolitan upheaval, socially much the most radical of these movements, naturally least so. But even there, the first storm signal of anti-Spanish explosion were the aristocratic conspiracies of Sanza, Conversano and other nobles, who were hostile to vice-regal fiscalism and the speculative cliques which battened on it, and were intriguing with France against Spain from 1634 onwards. Baronial plots were multiplying in Naples in early 1647, when the popular tumult headed by Masaniello suddenly burst out, and drove the bulk of the Neapolitan aristocracy back to loyalism. For this process, see the excellent analysis in Rosario Villari, *La Rivolta Anti-Spagnuola a Napoli. Le Origini (1585–1647)*, Bari 1967, pp. 201–16.

The protests of Bordeaux, Prague, Naples, Edinburgh, Barcelona or Palermo had a wider resonance. Their ultimate defeat was a central episode in the difficult travail of the whole class in this century, as it slowly transformed itself to fit the new, unwonted exigencies of its own State power. No class in history immediately comprehends the logic of its own historical situation, in epochs of transition: a long period of disorientation and confusion may be necessary for it to learn the necessary rules of its own sovereignty. The Western nobility in the tense age of 17th century Absolutism was no exception: it had to be broken in to the harsh and unawaited discipline of its own conditions of government.

This is essentially the explanation of the apparent paradox of the later trajectory of Absolutism in the West. For if the 17th century is the noon of turmoil and disarray in the relationship between class and State within the total system of aristocratic political rule, the 18th century is by comparison the golden evening of their tranquillity and reconciliation. A new stability and harmony prevailed, as the international economic conjuncture changed and a hundred years of relative prosperity set in for most of Europe, while the nobility regained confidence in its capacity to direct the fortunes of the State. A polished rearistocratization of the higher bureaucracy occurred in one country after another, making the previous epoch seem by illusory contrast assorted with *parvenus*. The French Regency and the Swedish Hat oligarchy are the most striking examples of this phenomenon. But it can be seen in Caroline Spain and even in Georgian England or Periwig Holland, where bourgeois revolutions had actually converted state and dominant mode of production to capitalism. The Ministers of State who symbolize the period lack the creative energy and austere force of their predecessors: but they were serenely at peace with their class. Fleury or Choiseul, Enseñada or Aranda, Walpole or Newcastle are the representative figures of this epoch.

The civilian performance of the Absolutist State in the West in the age of the Enlightenment reflects this pattern: there was a trimming of excesses and a refinement of techniques, a certain further imprint of bourgeois influences, coupled with a general loss of dynamism and creativity. The extreme distortions generated by sale of offices were pared away, and the bureaucracy rendered correspondingly less venal:

but often at the price of a public loan system for raising equivalent revenues which, imitated from the more advanced capitalist countries, soon tended to waterlog the State with accumulated debts. Mercantilism was still preached and practised, although the new 'liberal' economic doctrines of the physiocrats, advocating free trade and agrarian investment, made some limited headway in France, Tuscany and elsewhere. Perhaps the most important and interesting development within the landed ruling class in the last hundred years before the French Revolution, however, was a phenomenon outside the ambit of the State itself. This was the European spread of *vincolismo* – the rash of aristocratic devices for the protection and consolidation of large landed property against the disintegrating pressures and vagaries of the capitalist market.[15] The English nobility after 1689 was one of the first to pioneer this trend, with the invention of the 'strict settlement', preventing owners of estates from alienating family property and vesting rights in the eldest son only: two measures designed to freeze the whole land market in the interests of aristocratic supremacy. Soon, one after another, the main Western countries developed or perfected their own variants of this 'vinculism' or tying of the land to its traditional owners. The *mayorazgo* in Spain, the *morgado* in Portugal, *fideicommissum* in Italy and Austria, and the *maiorat* in Germany, all fulfilled the same function: to preserve intact great blocks of magnate estates and large latifundia against the dangers of fragmentation or sale on an open commercial market.[16] Much of the recovered stability of the European nobility in the 18th century was doubtless due to the economic underpinning provided by these legal devices. There was, in fact, probably less social turnover within the ruling class in this age

---

15. There is no comprehensive study of this phenomenon. It is discussed in passing by, *inter alia*, S. J. Woolf, *Studi sulla Nobiltà Piemontese nell' Epoca dell' Assolutismo*, Turin 1963, who dates its spread from the preceding century. Most of the contributors to A. Goodwin (ed.), *The European Nobility in the 18th Century*, London 1953, also touch on it.

16. The Spanish *mayorazgo* was much the oldest of these devices, dating back over two hundred years; but it steadily increased in both numbers and scope, eventually coming to include even movable goods. The English 'strict settlement' was in fact somewhat less rigid than the general continental pattern of the *fideicommissum*, since it was formally operative only for a single generation: but in practice successive heirs were expected to reaccept it.

than in the preceding epochs, when families and fortunes had fluctuated far more rapidly amidst greater political and social upheavals.[17]

It was against this background that a cosmopolitan élite culture of court and salon spread across Europe, typified by the new preeminence of French as an international idiom of diplomatic and intellectual discourse. In fact, of course, beneath its veneer this culture was more deeply penetrated than ever before by the ideas of the ascendant bourgeoisie, now triumphantly finding expression in the Enlightenment. The specific weight of mercantile and manufacturing capital within most of the Western social formations was rising throughout this century, which saw the second great wave of commercial and colonial expansion overseas. But it only determined State policy where a bourgeois revolution had already occurred and Absolutism had been overthrown, in England and Holland. Elsewhere, there is no more striking sign of the structural continuity of the late feudal State into its final phase than the persistence of its traditional military traditions. Actual troop strengths generally levelled off or dropped somewhat in Western Europe after the Treaty of Utrecht: the physical apparatus of war had ceased to expand, at least on land (at sea, it was another matter). But the frequency of war and its centrality to the international state system

17. The whole question of mobility within the noble class, from the dawn of feudalism to the end of absolutism, needs a great deal of further exploration. At present, only approximate guesses are possible for successive phases of this long history. Duby records his surprise at finding that Bloch's conviction of a radical discontinuity between the Carolingian and mediaeval aristocracies in France was mistaken: in fact, a high proportion of the lineages who supplied the *vassi dominici* of the 9th century survived to become the barons of the 12th century. See G. Duby, '*Une Enquête à Poursuivre: La Noblesse dans la France Médiévale*', *Revue Historique*, CCXXVI, 1961, pp. 1–22. On the other hand, Perroy found an extremely high level of mobility within the gentry of the County of Forez from the 13th century onwards: there the average duration of any noble line was 3–4, or more conservatively, 3–6 generations, largely because of the hazards of mortality. Edouard Perroy, 'Social Mobility among the French Noblesse in the Later Middle Ages', *Past and Present*, No. 21, April 1962, pp. 25–38. In general, the later Middle Ages and early Renaissance seem to have been periods of rapid turnover in many countries, in which most of the greatest mediaeval houses disappeared. This is certainly true in England and France, although probably less so in Spain. The restabilization of the ranks of the aristocracy seems equally plain by the late 17th century, after the last and most violent reshuffle of all, in Habsburg Bohemia during the Thirty Years War, had come to an end. But the subject may well reserve further surprises for us.

did not seriously alter. In fact, perhaps more geographical territory – classical object of every aristocratic military struggle – changed hands in Europe during this century than either of its two predecessors: Silesia, Naples, Lombardy, Belgium, Sardinia and Poland were among the prizes. War 'functioned' in this sense down to the end of the Ancien Regime. Typologically, of course, the campaigns of European Absolutism present a certain evolution in and through a basic repetition. The common determinant of all of them was the feudal-territorial drive discussed above, whose characteristic form was the dynastic conflict pure and simple of the early 16th century (Habsburg/Valois struggle for Italy). Superimposed on this for a hundred years, from 1550 to 1650, was the religious conflict between Reformation and Counter-Reformation powers, which never initiated but frequently intensified and exacerbated geopolitical rivalries and provided their contemporary ideological idiom. The Thirty Years War was the greatest, and last, of these 'mixed' struggles.[18] It was promptly succeeded by the first of a wholly new type of military conflict in Europe, fought for different objectives in a different element – the Anglo-Dutch commercial wars of the 1650's and 1660's, in which virtually all engagements were maritime. These confrontations, however, were confined to the two States in Europe which had experienced bourgeois revolutions, and were strictly inter-capitalist contests. The attempt to 'adopt' their objectives by Colbert in France proved a fiasco in the 1670's. However, from the War of the League of Augsburg onwards, trade was nearly always an auxiliary co-presence in the major European military struggles for land – if only because of the participation in them of England, whose geographical expansion overseas was now wholly commercial in character, and whose goal was effectively a world colonial monopoly. Hence the hybrid character of the last 18th century wars, juxtaposing two different times and types of conflict in a strange, single mêlée, of which the Seven Years War furnishes the clearest example:[19] the first in history to be fought right across the globe, yet as a sideshow for most of the participants, for whom Manila or Montreal

18. H. G. Koenigsberger's chapter, 'The European Civil War', in *The Habsburgs in Europe*, Ithaca 1971, pp. 219–85, is a succinct and exemplary account.
19. The best general analysis of the Seven Years War is still Dorn, *Competition for Empire*, pp. 318–84.

were remote skirmishes compared with Leuthen or Kunersdorf. Nothing reveals the failing feudal vision of the Ancien Régime in France more than its inability to perceive the real stakes involved in these dual wars: together with its rivals, it remained basically fixated on the traditional contest for land to the end.

3

Spain

Such was the general character of Absolutism in the West. The specific territorial States which came into existence in the different countries of Renaissance Europe, however, cannot simply be assimilated to a single pure type. They exhibited wide variations, in fact, which were to have crucial consequences for the subsequent histories of the countries concerned, and can still be felt to this day. Some survey of these variants is therefore a necessary complement to any consideration of the general structure of Western Absolutism. Spain, the earliest great power of modern Europe, provides a logical starting-point.

For the rise of Habsburg Spain was not merely one episode within a set of concurrent and equivalent experiences of State-construction in Western Europe: it was also an auxiliary determinant of the whole set as such. It thus occupies a qualitatively distinct position in the general process of Absolutization. For the reach and impact of Spanish Absolutism was in a strict sense 'inordinate', among the other Western monarchies of the age. Its international pressure acted as a special over-determination of the national patterns elsewhere in the continent, because of the disproportionate wealth and power at its command: the historical *concentration* of these assets in the Spanish State could not but affect the overall shape and direction of the emergent State-system of the West. The Spanish monarchy owed its preeminence to a combination of two complexes of resources – themselves sudden projections of common constituents of ascendant Absolutism to an exceptional magnitude. On the one hand, its ruling house benefited more than any other line in Europe from the compacts of dynastic marriage-policy. The Habsburg family connection yielded the Spanish State a scale of territory and influence in Europe, which no rival monarchy could match: a supreme artefact of feudal mechanisms of political expansion.

On the other hand, the colonial conquest of the New World supplied it with a superabundance of precious metals, which gave it a treasury beyond the range of any of its counterparts. Conducted and organized within still notably seigneurial structures, the plunder of the Americas was nevertheless at the same time the most spectacular single act in the primitive accumulation of European capital during the Renaissance. Spanish Absolutism thus drew strength both from the inheritances of feudal aggrandizement at home and the booty of extractive capital overseas. There was never, of course, any question as to the social and economic interests to which the political apparatus of the Spanish monarchy principally and permanently answered. No other major Absolutist State in Western Europe was to be so finally noble in character, or so inimical to bourgeois development. The very fortune of its early control of the mines of America, with their primitive but lucrative economy of extraction, disinclined it to promote the growth of manufactures or foster the spread of mercantile enterprise within its European empire. Instead, it bore down with a massive weight on the most active commercial communities of the continent, even while threatening every other landed aristocracy in a cycle of inter-aristocratic wars that lasted for a hundred and fifty years. Spanish power stifled the urban vitality of North Italy, and crushed the flourishing towns of half the Low Countries – the two most advanced zones of the European economy at the turn of the 16th century. Holland eventually escaped its control, in a long struggle for bourgeois independence. In the same period, the royal states of Southern Italy and Portugal were absorbed by Spain. The monarchies of France and England were battered by Hispanic attacks. The principalities of Germany were repeatedly invaded by *tercios* from Castile. While Spanish fleets rode the Atlantic or patrolled the Mediterranean, Spanish armies ranged across most of Western Europe: from Antwerp to Palermo, and Regensburg to Kinsale. The menace of Habsburg dominance, however, in the end quickened the reactions and fortified the defenses of the dynasties arrayed against it. Spanish priority gave the Habsburg monarchy a system-setting role for Western Absolutism as a whole. Yet it also, as we shall see, critically limited the nature of Spanish Absolutism itself within the system it helped to originate.

*   *   *

Spanish Absolutism was born from the Union of Castile and Aragon, effected by the marriage of Isabella I and Ferdinand II in 1469. It started with an apparently firm economic basis. During the labour shortages produced by the general crisis of Western feudalism, increasing areas of Castile were converted to a lucrative wool economy, which had made it the 'Australia of the Middle Ages',[1] and a major partner of Flemish trade; while Aragon had long been a territorial and commercial power in the Mediterranean, controlling Sicily and Sardinia. The political and military dynamism of the new dual state was soon dramatically revealed in a series of sweeping external conquests. The last Moorish stronghold of Granada was destroyed and the Reconquista completed; Naples was annexed; Navarre was absorbed; and above all, the Americas were discovered and subjugated. The Habsburg connection soon added Milan, the Franche-Comté and the Netherlands. This sudden avalanche of successes made Spain the premier power in Europe for the whole of the 16th century, enjoying an international position which no other continental Absolutism was ever later able to emulate. Yet the State which presided over this vast Empire was itself a ramshackle assemblage, ultimately united only by the person of the monarch. Spanish Absolutism, so awesome to Northern Protestantism abroad, was in fact notably modest and limited in its domestic development. Its internal articulations were perhaps uniquely loose and heteroclite. The reasons for this paradox are doubtless to be sought essentially in the curious triangular relationship between the American Empire, the European Empire and the Iberian homelands.

The composite realms of Castile and Aragon united by Ferdinand and Isabella presented an extremely diverse basis for the construction of the new Spanish monarchy in the late 15th century. Castile was a land with an aristocracy of enormous estates and powerful military orders; it also had a considerable number of towns, although, significantly, not yet a fixed capital. The Castilian nobility had seized vast quantities of agrarian property from the monarchy during the civil wars of the later Middle Ages; 2–3 per cent of the population now controlled some 97 per cent of the soil. More than half of this, in turn,

1. The phrase is Vicens's. See J. Vicens Vives, *Manual de Historia Económica de España*, pp. 11–12, 231.

was owned by a few magnate families who towered over the numerous *hidalgo* gentry.[2] Cereal agriculture was steadily yielding to sheep-farming on these great estates. The wool boom which provided the basis for the fortunes of so many aristocratic houses had, at the same time, stimulated urban growth and foreign trade. Castilian towns and Cantabrian shipping benefited from the prosperity of the pastoral economy of late mediaeval Spain, which was linked by a complex commercial system to the textile industry of Flanders. The economic and demographic profile of Castile within the Union was thus from the outset an advantageous one: with a population calculated at between 5 and 7 million, and a buoyant overseas trade with Northern Europe, it was easily the dominant state in the peninsula. Politically, its constitution was curiously unsettled. Castile-Leon had been one of the first mediaeval kingdoms in Europe to develop an Estates system in the 13th century; while by the mid 15th century, the factual ascendancy of the nobility over the monarchy had for a time become far-reaching. But the grasping power of the late mediaeval aristocracy had not set in any juridical mould. The Cortes, in fact, remained an occasional and indefinite assembly: perhaps because of the migrant character of the Castilian kingdom as it shifted southwards and shuffled its social pattern in doing so, there had never developed a firm and fixed institutionalization of the Estates system. Thus both the convocation and composition of the Cortes was subject to the arbitrary decision of the monarchy, with the result that sessions were spasmodic, and no regular three-curia system emerged from them. On the one hand, the Cortes had no initiatory legislative powers; on the other, the nobility and clergy enjoyed fiscal immunity. The result was an Estates system in which only the towns had to pay the taxes voted by the Cortes, which otherwise fell virtually exclusively on the masses beneath it. The aristocracy thus had no direct economic stake in its representation within the Castilian Estates, which formed a comparatively weak and isolated institution. Aristocratic corporatism found separate expression in the rich and formidable military orders – Calatrava, Alcantara and Santiago – which had been created by the Crusades: but these by nature lacked the collective authority of a noble Estate proper.

2. J. H. Elliott, *Imperial Spain 1469–1716*, London 1970, pp. 111–13.

The economic and political character of the Realm of Aragon[3] was in sharp contrast to this. The high interior of Aragon itself harboured the most repressive seigneurial system in the Iberian peninsula; the local aristocracy was vested with a full range of feudal powers in the barren countryside, where serfdom still survived and a captive *morisco* peasantry toiled for its Christian landlords. Catalonia, on the other hand, had traditionally been the centre of a mercantile empire in the Mediterranean: Barcelona was the largest city in mediaeval Spain, and its urban patriciate the richest commercial class of the region. Catalan prosperity, however, had suffered grievously during the long feudal depression. The epidemics of the 14th century had struck the principality with especial violence, returning again and again after the Black Death itself to ravage the population, which fell by over a third between 1365 and 1497.[4] Commercial bankruptcies had been compounded by aggressive Genoese competition in the Mediterranean, while smaller merchants and artisan guilds revolted against the patriciates in the towns. In the countryside the peasantry had risen to throw off the 'evil customs' and seize deserted lands in the *remença* rebellions of the 15th century. Finally, a civil war between the monarchy and nobility, pulling other social groups into its maelstrom, had further weakened the Catalan economy. Its overseas bases in Italy, however, remained intact. Valencia, the third province of the realm, was socially intermediate between Aragon and Catalonia. The nobility exploited *morisco* labour; a merchant community expanded during the 15th century, as financial dominance passed down the coast from Barcelona. The growth of Valencia, however, did not adequately compensate for the decline of Catalonia. The economic disparity between the two Realms of the Union created by the marriage of Ferdinand and Isabella can be seen from the fact that the population of the three provinces of Aragon together perhaps totalled only some 1 million inhabitants – compared with Castile's 5–7 million. The political contrast between the two Kingdoms, on the other hand, was no less striking. For in the Realm of Aragon, there was to be found perhaps the most sophisticated and entrenched Estates structure anywhere in Europe. All three

---

3. The Aragonese Kingdom was itself a union of three principalities: Aragon, Catalonia and Valencia.

4. Elliott, *Imperial Spain*, p. 37.

provinces of Catalonia, Valencia and Aragon had their own separate Cortes. Each had, in addition, special watchdog institutions of permanent judicial control and economic administration derived from the Cortes. The Catalan *Diputació* – a standing committee of the Cortes – was the most effective exemplar of these. Each Cortes, moreover, had statutorily to be summoned at regular intervals, and was technically subject to a rule of unanimity – a device unique in Western Europe. The Aragonese Cortes itself had the further refinement of a four-curia system of magnates, gentry, clergy and burghers.[5] *In toto*, this complex of mediaeval 'liberties' presented a singularly intractable prospect for the construction of a centralized Absolutism. The asymmetry of institutional orders in Castile and Aragon was, in fact, to shape the whole career of the Spanish monarchy henceforward.

For Ferdinand and Isabella, understandably, took the obvious course of concentrating on the establishment of an unshakeable royal power in Castile, where the conditions for it were most immediately propitious. Aragon presented far more formidable political obstacles to the construction of a centralized State, and much less profitable prospects for economic fiscalization. Castile had five or six times the population, and its greater wealth was not protected by any comparable constitutional barriers. A methodical programme for its administrative reorganization was thus set in train by the two monarchs. The military orders were decapitated and their vast lands and incomes annexed. Baronial castles were demolished, marcher lords ousted, and private wars banned. The municipal autonomy of the towns was broken by the planting of official *corregidores* to administer them; royal justice was reinforced and extended. Control of ecclesiastical benefices was captured for the State, detaching the local Church apparatus from the reach of the Papacy. The Cortes was progressively domesticated by the effective omission of the nobility and clergy from its assemblies after 1480; since the main purpose of summoning it was to raise taxes for military expenditure (on the Granadan and Italian wars, above all),

5. The spirit of Aragonese constitutionalism was expressed in the arresting oath of allegiance attributed to its nobility: 'We who are as good as you swear to you who are no better than we to accept you as our king and sovereign lord, provided you observe all our liberties and laws; but if not, not.' The formula itself was perhaps legendary, but its sense was engraved in the institutions of Aragon.

from which the First and Second Estate were exempted, the latter had little reason to resist this restriction. Fiscal yields rose impressively: Castilian revenues increased from some 900,000 *reales* in 1474 to 26,000,000 in 1504.[6] The Royal Council was reformed and grandee influence excluded from it; the new body was staffed by lawyer-bureaucrats or *letrados*, recruited from the smaller gentry. Professional secretaries worked directly under the sovereigns, dispatching ongoing business. The Castilian State machine, in other words, was rationalized and modernized. But the new monarchy never counterposed it to the aristocratic class as a whole. Top military and diplomatic positions were always reserved for magnates, who kept their great viceroyalties and governorships, while lesser nobles filled the ranks of the *corregidores*. Royal domains usurped since 1454 were recovered by the monarchy, but those appropriated earlier – the majority – were left in the hands of the nobility; new estates in Granada were added to its possessions, and the immobilization of rural property by the device of the *mayorazgo* was confirmed. Moreover, wide privileges were deliberately granted to the pastoral interests of the *Mesta* wool cartel in the countryside, dominated by Southern latifundists; while discriminatory measures against cereal farming eventually fixed retail prices for grain crops. In the towns, a constricting guild system was foisted on nascent urban industry, and religious persecution of the *conversos* led to an exodus of Jewish capital. All these policies were pursued with great energy and resolution in Castile.

In Aragon, on the other hand, no political programme of comparable scope was ever attempted. There, on the contrary, the most that Ferdinand could achieve was a social pacification, and restoration of the late mediaeval constitution. The *remença* peasants were finally granted remission of their dues with the Sentence of Guadelupe in 1486, and rural unrest subsided. Access to the Catalan *Diputació* was broadened by the introduction of a sortition system. Otherwise, Ferdinand's rule unambiguously confirmed the separate identity of the Eastern realm: Catalan liberties were expressly acknowledged in their entirety by the *Observança* of 1481, and new safeguards against royal infractions of them actually added to the existing arsenal of local

6. For the work of Ferdinand and Isabella in Castile, see Elliott, *Imperial Spain*, pp. 86–99.

weapons against any form of monarchical centralization. Rarely resident within his native country, Ferdinand installed viceroys in all three provinces to exercise a delegated authority for him, and created a Council of Aragon, mostly based in Castile, to liaise with them. Aragon, in effect, was thus virtually left to its own devices; even the great wool interests – all-powerful beyond the Ebro – were unable to secure sanction for their sheep-runs across its agricultural land. Once Ferdinand had been obliged solemnly to reconfirm all its thorny contractual privileges, there was no question whatever of an administrative merger at any level between Aragon and Castile. Far from creating a unified kingdom, their Catholic Majesties failed even to establish a single currency,[7] let alone a common tax or legal system within their realms. The Inquisition – a unique creation in Europe at the time – should be seen in this context: it was the one unitary 'Spanish' institution in the peninsula, an overwrought ideological apparatus compensating for the actual administrative division and dispersal of the State.

The accession of Charles V was to complicate, but not substantially alter, this pattern; if anything, it ultimately accentuated it. The most immediate result of the advent of a Habsburg sovereign was a new and heavily expatriate court, dominated by Flemings, Burgundians and Italians. The financial extortions of the new regime soon provoked a wave of intense popular xenophobia in Castile. The departure of the monarch himself for Northern Europe was thus the signal for a widespread urban rebellion against what was felt to be foreign fleecing of Castilian resources and positions. The *comunero* revolt of 1520–1 won the initial support of many city nobles, and appealed to a traditional set of constitutional demands. But its driving force was the popular artisan masses in the towns, and its dominating leadership was the urban bourgeoisie of northern and central Castile, whose trading and manufacturing centres had enjoyed an economic boom in the preceding period.[8] It found little or no echo in the countryside, either among the peasantry or rural aristocracy; the movement never seriously affected those regions where towns were few or weak – Galicia, Andalusia,

7. The only step towards monetary unification was the minting of three high-denomination gold coins of equivalent value in Castile, Aragon and Catalonia.

8. See J. A. Maravall, *Las Comunidades de Castilla. Una Primera Revolución Moderna*, Madrid 1963, pp. 216–22.

Estremadura or Guadalajara. The 'federative' and 'proto-national' programme of the revolutionary Junta which the Castilian communes created during their insurrection clearly marked it as basically a revolt of the Third Estate.[9] Its defeat by royal armies, behind which the bulk of the aristocracy had rallied once the potential radicalism of the upheaval became evident, was thus a critical step in the consolidation of Spanish Absolutism. The crushing of the *comunero* rebellion effectively eliminated the last vestiges of a contractual constitution in Castile, and doomed the Cortes – for which the *comuneros* had demanded regular tri-annual sessions – to nullity henceforward. More significant, however, was the fact that the Spanish monarchy's most fundamental victory over corporate resistance to royal absolutism in Castile – indeed its only actual armed contest with any opposition in that realm – was the military defeat of the towns, rather than nobles. Nowhere else in Western Europe was this true of nascent absolutism: the primary pattern was the suppression of aristocratic rather than burgher revolts, even where the two were closely mingled. Its triumph over the Castilian communes, at the outset of its career, was to separate the course of the Spanish monarchy from its Western counterparts thereafter.

The most spectacular development of Charles V's reign was, of course, its vast enlargement of the Habsburg international orbit. In Europe, the Netherlands, the Franche-Comté and Milan were now added to the personal patrimony of the rulers of Spain, while Mexico and Peru were conquered in the Americas. During the life-time of the Emperor himself, the whole of Germany was a major theatre of operations over and above these hereditary possessions. This sudden territorial expansion inevitably reinforced the prior tendency of the emergent Absolutist State in Spain towards devolution via separate Councils and Viceroys for the different dynastic possessions. Charles V's Piedmontese Chancellor, Mercurio Gattinara, inspired by universalist Erasmian ideals, strove to confer a more compact and effective executive on the unwieldy bulk of the Habsburg Empire, by creating certain unitary institutions for it of a departmental type – notably a Council of Finances, a Council of War and a Council of State (the latter theoretically becoming the summit of the whole imperial edifice), with overall

9. Maravall, *Las Comunidades de Castilla*, pp. 44–5, 50–7, 156–7.

responsibilities of a trans-regional character. These were backed by a growing permanent secretariat of civil servants at the disposal of the monarch. But at the same time, a new series of territorial Councils was progressively formed, Gattinara himself establishing the first of these for the government of the Indies. By the end of the century, there were eventually to be no less than six such regional Councils, for Aragon, Castile, the Indies, Italy, Portugal and Flanders. Outside Castile itself, none of these had any adequate body of local officials on the ground, where actual administration was entrusted to viceroys, who were subject to often fumbling control and direction from a distance by the Councils.[10] The powers of the viceroys themselves were usually very limited in their turn. Only in the Americas did they command the services of their own bureaucracy, but there they were flanked by *audiencias* which deprived them of the judicial authority they enjoyed elsewhere; while in Europe, they had to come to terms with resident aristocracies – Sicilian, Valencian or Neapolitan – who normally claimed by right a virtual monopoly of public offices. The result was to block any real unification either of the international imperium as a whole, or of the Iberian homelands themselves. The Americas were juridically attached to the kingdom of Castile, Southern Italy to the realm of Aragon. The Atlantic and Mediterranean economies represented by each never met within a single commercial system. The division between the two original realms of the Union within Spain was, in practice, if anything, reinforced by the overseas possessions now subjoined to them. For juridical purposes, Catalonia could simply be assimilated in statute to Sicily or the Netherlands. Indeed, by the 17th century, Madrid's power in Naples or Milan was actually greater than in Barcelona or Zaragoza. The very sprawl of the Habsburg Empire thus overextended its capacity for integration, and helped to arrest the process of administrative centralization within Spain itself.[11]

10. J. Lynch, *Spain under the Habsburgs*, II, Oxford 1969, pp. 19–20.
11. Marx was aware of the paradox of Habsburg Absolutism in Spain. After declaring that, 'Spanish liberty disappeared under the clash of arms, showers of gold, and the terrible illuminations of thé auto-da-fé', he asked: 'But how are we to account for the singular phenomenon that, after nearly three centuries of a Habsburg dynasty, followed by a Bourbon dynasty – either of them quite sufficient to crush a people – the municipal liberties of Spain more or less survive? that in the very country where of all feudal states absolute monarchy first arose in

At the same time, Charles V's reign also inaugurated the fateful sequence of European wars which was to be the price of Spanish power in the continent. In the Southern theatre of his innumerable campaigns, Charles achieved overwhelming success: it was during this period that Italy fell definitively under Hispanic ascendancy, as France was driven from the peninsula, the Papacy intimidated, and the Turkish threat held off. The most advanced urban society in Europe henceforward became an elongated military platform for Spanish Absolutism. In the Northern theatre of his wars, by contrast, the Emperor was forced into a costly stalemate: the Reformation remained unvanquished in Germany, despite his repeated attempts to crush or conciliate it, and hereditary Valois enmity survived every defeat in France. The financial burden of constant war in the North, moreover, had gravely strained the traditional loyalty of the Netherlands by the end of the reign, preparing for the disasters which were to overtake Philip II in the Low Countries. For the size and expense of Habsburg armies had escalated steeply and regularly throughout Charles V's rule. Before 1529, Spanish troops in Italy had never numbered more than 30,000; in 1536–7, 60,000 soldiers were mobilized for war with France; by 1552, there were perhaps 150,000 men under the Emperor's command in Europe.[12] Financial borrowing and fiscal pressures increased commensurately: Charles V's revenues had tripled by the time of his abdication in 1556,[13] yet royal debts were so great that a State bankruptcy had to be formally declared a year later by his heir. The Spanish Empire in the Old World inherited by Philip II, always administratively divided, was becoming economically untenable at mid-century: it was the New World which was to refurbish its treasury and prolong its disunity.

For from the 1560's onwards, the multiple effects of its American Empire on Spanish Absolutism became increasingly determinant for its future, although it is necessary not to confuse the different levels at

its most unmitigated form, centralization has never succeeded in taking root?', K. Marx and F. Engels, *Revolutionary Spain*, London 1939, pp. 24–5. An adequate answer to the question, however, escaped him.

12. G. Parker, *The Army of Flanders and the Spanish Road 1567–1659*, Cambridge 1972, p. 6.

13. Lynch, *Spain under the Habsburgs*, I, Oxford 1965, p. 128: prices had also risen greatly in the interval, of course.

which these worked themselves out. The discovery of the Potosí mines now enormously increased the flow of colonial bullion to Seville. The supply of huge quantities of silver from the Americas henceforward became a decisive 'facility' of the Spanish State, in both senses of the word. For it provided Hispanic Absolutism with a plentiful and permanent extraordinary income that was wholly outside the conventional ambit of State revenues in Europe. This meant that Absolutism in Spain could for a long time continue to dispense with the slow fiscal and administrative unification which was a precondition of Absolutism elsewhere: the stubborn recalcitrance of Aragon was compensated by the limitless compliance of Peru. The colonies, in other words, could act as a structural substitute for provinces, in a total polity where orthodox provinces were substituted by autarchic patrimonies. Nothing is more striking in this respect than the utter lack of any proportionate contribution to the Spanish war effort in Europe during the later 16th and 17th centuries from Aragon or even Italy. Castile was to bear the tax burden of interminable military campaigns abroad virtually alone: behind it, precisely, lay the mines of the Indies. The total incidence of American tribute in the Spanish imperial budgets was, of course, much less than was often popularly supposed at the time: at the height of the treasure-fleets, colonial bullion directly accounted for only 20–25 per cent of its revenues.[14] The bulk of the rest of Philip II's income was furnished by domestic Castilian charges: the traditional sales tax or *alcabala*, the special *servicios* levied on the poor, the *cruzada* collected with the sanction of the church from clergy and laity, and the public bonds or *juros* sold to the propertied. American metals, however, played their part in sustaining the metropolitan tax-base of the Habsburg State: the extremely high fiscal levels of successive reigns were indirectly supported by the private transfers of bullion to Castile, whose volume averaged well over twice that of public inflows;[15] the notable success of the *juros* as a funding device – the first widespread use of such bonds by an Absolute monarchy in Europe – is, no doubt, partly explicable by its capacity to tap this new monetary

14. J. H. Elliott, 'The Decline of Spain', *Past and Present*, No. 20, November 1961, now in T. Aston (ed.), *Crisis in Europe 1560–1660*, p. 189; *Imperial Spain*, pp. 285–6.

15. Lynch makes this point very well: *Spain under the Habsburgs*, I, p. 129.

wealth. Furthermore, the colonial increment to royal revenues was in its own right quite decisive for the conduct of Spanish foreign policy, and for the nature of the Spanish State. For it arrived in the form of liquid specie which could be used to finance troop movements or diplomatic manoeuvres directly, all across Europe; and it afforded exceptional credit opportunities to the Habsburg monarchs, who could raise sums in the international money market to which no other princes could aspire.[16] The huge military and naval operations of Philip II, from the Channel to the Aegean, and Tunis to Antwerp, were possible only because of the extraordinary financial flexibility provided by the American surplus.

At the same time, however, the impact of American metals on the Spanish *economy*, as distinct from the Castilian *State*, was no less critical, if in another way. For the first half of the 16th century, the moderate level of shipments (with a higher gold component) provided a stimulus to Castilian exports, which quickly responded to the price inflation that followed the advent of colonial treasure. Since the 60–70 per cent of this bullion which did not go straight into the royal coffers had to be bought as a commodity like any other from the local entrepreneurs in the Americas, a thriving trade with the colonies developed, mainly in textiles, oil and wine. Monopoly control of this captive market initially benefited Castilian producers, who could sell at inflationary prices in it, although domestic consumers were soon complaining bitterly of the cost of living at home.[17] However, there were two fatal twists in this process for the Castilian economy as a whole. Firstly, increased colonial demand led to further conversion of land away from cereal production, to wine and olives. This reinforced the already disastrous trend encouraged by the monarchy towards a contraction of wheat output at the expense of wool: for the Spanish wool industry, unlike the English, was not sedentary but transhumant. and therefore extremely destructive of arable farming. The combined result of these pressures was to make Spain a major grain-importing country for the first time by the 1570's. The structure of Castilian rural society was now already unlike anything else in Western Europe.

16. Pierre Vilar, *Oro y Moneda en la Historia, 1450–1920*, Barcelona 1969, pp. 78, 165–8.
17. Vilar, *Oro y Moneda*, pp. 180–1.

Dependent tenants and peasant small-holders were a minority in the countryside. In the 16th century, more than half the rural population of New Castile – perhaps as much as 60–70 per cent – were agricultural labourers or *jornaleros*;[18] and the proportion was probably even higher in Andalusia. There was widespread unemployment in the villages, and heavy feudal rents on seigneurial lands. Most striking of all, the Spanish censuses of 1571 and 1586 revealed a society in which a mere one-third of the male population was engaged in agriculture at all; while no less than two-fifths were outside any direct economic production – a premature and bloated 'tertiary sector' of Absolutist Spain, which prefigured secular stagnation to come.[19] But the ultimate damage caused by the colonial nexus was not limited to agriculture, the dominant branch of domestic production at the time. For the influx of bullion from the New World also produced a parasitism that increasingly sapped and halted domestic manufactures. Accelerating inflation drove up the costs of production of the textile industry, which operated within very rigid technical limits, to a point where Castilian cloths were eventually being priced out of both colonial and metropolitan markets. Dutch and English interlopers started to cream off the American demand, while cheaper foreign wares invaded Castile itself. Castilian textiles were thus by the end of the century the victim of Bolivian silver. The cry now went up – *España son las Indias del extranjero*: Spain has become the Americas of Europe, a colonial dumping-ground for foreign goods. Thus both the agrarian and urban economies were ultimately stricken by the blaze from the American treasure, as numerous contemporaries lamented.[20] The productive potential of Castile was being undermined by the same Empire which was pumping resources into the military apparatus of the State for unprecedented adventures abroad.

18. Noel Salomon, *La Campagne de Nouvelle Castille à la Fin du XVIe Siècle*, Paris 1964, pp. 257–8, 266. For tithes, dues and rents, see pp. 227, 243–4, 250.

19. It is a Portuguese historian who has underlined the implications of this extraordinary occupational pattern, which he believes to hold for Portugal as well: Vitorino Magalhães Godinho, *A Estrutura na Antiga Sociedade Portuguesa*, Lisbon 1971, pp. 85–9. As Magalhães Godinho remarks, since agriculture was the main branch of economic production in any pre-industrial society, a diversion of manpower away from it on this scale inevitably resulted in long-term stagnation.

20. For the reactions of contemporaries by the turn of the 17th century, see Vilar's superb essay, 'Le Temps du Quichotte', *Europe*, XXXIV, 1956, pp. 3–16.

Yet there was a close link between the two effects. For, if the American Empire was the undoing of the Spanish economy, it was its *European* Empire which was the ruin of the Habsburg State, and the one rendered the extended struggle for the other financially possible. Without the bullion shipments to Seville, the colossal war effort of Philip II would have been unthinkable. However, it was just this effort which was to bring the original structure of Spanish Absolutism down. The long reign of the Prudent King, covering nearly the whole of the latter half of the 16th century, was not itself a uniform record of foreign failures, despite the immense expense and punishing setbacks which it incurred in the international arena. Its basic pattern was, in fact, not dissimilar to that of Charles V: success in the South, defeat in the North. In the Mediterranean, Turkish naval expansion was definitively checked at Lepanto in 1571, a victory which effectively confined Ottoman fleets henceforward to home waters. Portugal was incorporated smoothly into the Habsburg bloc by dynastic diplomacy and timely invasion: its absorption added the numerous Lusitanian possessions in Asia, Africa and America to the Hispanic colonies in the Indies. The Spanish overseas empire itself was augmented by the conquest of the Philippines in the Pacific – logistically and culturally the most daring colonization of the century. The military apparatus of the Spanish State was honed to a steadily greater degree of skill and efficacy, its organization and supply system becoming the most advanced in Europe. The traditional willingness of Castilian *hidalgos* to serve in the *tercios* stiffened its infantry regiments,[21] while the Italian and Walloon provinces proved a reliable reservoir of soldiers, if not of taxes, for Habsburg international policies; significantly, the multi-national contingents of Habsburg armies all fought better on foreign than on native soil, their very diversity permitting a relatively lesser degree of reliance on external mercenaries. For the first time in modern Europe, a large standing army was successfully maintained at a great distance from the imperial homeland, for decades on end. From Alva's arrival onwards, the Army of Flanders averaged some 65,000 troops over the rest of the

---

21. Alva characteristically commented: 'In our nation nothing is more important than to introduce gentlemen and men of substance into the infantry, so that all is not left in the hands of labourers and lackeys.' Parker, *The Army of Flanders and the Spanish Road*, p. 41.

entire Eighty Years' War with the Dutch – a feat without precedent.[22] On the other hand, the permanent disposition of these troops in the Low Countries told its own story. The Netherlands, already rumbling with discontent at Charles V's fiscal exactions and religious persecution, had exploded into what was to become the first bourgeois revolution in history, under the pressure of Philip II's Tridentine centralism. The Revolt of the Netherlands posed a direct threat to vital Spanish interests, for the two economies – closely linked since the Middle Ages – were largely complementary: Spain exported wool and bullion to the Low Countries, and imported textiles, hardware, grain and naval stores. Flanders, moreover, ensured the strategic encirclement of France and was thus a lynchpin of Habsburg international ascendancy. Yet despite immense exertions, Spanish military power was unable to break the resistance of the United Provinces. Moreover, Philip II's armed intervention in the Religious Wars in France and his naval attack on England – two fatal extensions of the original theatre of war in Flanders – were both repulsed: the scattering of the Armada and the accession of Henri IV marked the double defeat of his forward policy in the North. Yet the international balance-sheet at the end of his reign was still an apparently formidable one – dangerously so for his successors, to whom he bequeathed an undiminished sense of continental stature. The Southern Netherlands had been regained and fortified. The Luso-Hispanic fleets were rapidly reconstituted after 1588 and successfully checked English assaults on the Atlantic bullion routes. The French monarchy was, in the last resort, denied to Protestantism.

At home, on the other hand, the legacy of Philip II at the turn of the 17th century was more visibly sombre. Castile now had for the first time a stable capital in Madrid, facilitating central government. The Council of State, dominated by grandees, and deliberating on major issues of policy, was more than counterbalanced by the enhanced importance of the royal secretariat, whose diligent jurist-functionaries provided the desk-bound monarch with the bureaucratic tools of rule most congenial to him. Administrative unification of the dynastic patrimonies, however, was not pursued with any consistency. Absolutist reforms were pressed in the Netherlands, where they led to a

22. Parker, *The Army of Flanders and the Spanish Road*, pp. 27–31.

debacle, and in Italy, where they secured a modest measure of success. In the Iberian peninsula itself, by contrast, no progress in the same direction was even seriously attempted. Portuguese constitutional and legal autonomy was scrupulously respected; no Castilian interference ruffled the traditional order of this Western acquisition. In the Eastern provinces, Aragonese particularism gave truculent provocation to the King by shielding his fugitive secretary Antonio Perez from royal justice with armed riots: an invasion force in 1591 subdued this blatant sedition, but Philip abstained from any permanent occupation of Aragon, or major modification of its constitution.[23] The chance of a centralist solution was deliberately foregone. Meanwhile, the economic situation of both monarchy and country was deteriorating ominously by the end of the century. Silver shipments ran at record levels from 1590 to 1600: but war-costs had by now grown so much that a new consumption tax levied essentially on food – the *millones* – was imposed in Castile, which henceforward became a further heavy burden on the labouring poor in the countryside and the towns. Philip II's total revenues had more than quadrupled by the end of his reign:[24] even so, official bankruptcy overtook him in 1596. Three years later, the worst plague of the epoch descended on Spain, decimating the population of the peninsula.

The accession of Philip III was followed by peace with England (1604), a further bankruptcy (1607), and then by the reluctant signature of a truce with Holland (1609). The new regime was dominated by the Valencian aristocrat Lerma, a frivolous and venal *privado* who had established his personal ascendancy over the King. Peace brought with it lavish court display, and multiplication of honours; political influence deserted the old secretariat, while the Castilian nobility congregated again towards the now softened centre of the State. Lerma's only two governmental decisions of note were the systematic use of devaluations to extricate royal finances, by flooding the country with the debased copper *vellón*, and the mass expulsion of the *moriscos* from Spain, which merely weakened the Aragonese and Valencian rural economy: price

23. Philip II limited himself to reducing the powers of the local *Diputació* (where the unanimity rule was abolished) and of the office of *Justicia*, and introducing non-native Viceroys in Aragon.

24. Lynch, *Spain under the Habsburgs*, II, pp. 12–13.

inflation and labour shortages were the inevitable result. Much graver in the long-run, however, was the silent shift that was now occurring in the whole commercial relationship between Spain and America. From about 1600 onwards, the American colonies were becoming increasingly self-sufficient in the primary commodities they had traditionally imported from Spain – grain, oil and wine; coarse cloth was also now starting to be locally produced; ship-building developed rapidly, and inter-colonial trade boomed. These changes coincided with the growth of a creole aristocracy in the colonies, whose wealth was derived from agriculture rather than mining.[25] The mines themselves were subject to a deepening crisis from the second decade of the 17th century onwards. Partly because of a demographic collapse in the Indian labour-force, due to devastating epidemics and super-exploitation in underground gangs, and partly because of lode exhaustion, silver output began to contract. The decline from the peak of the previous century was initially a gradual one. But the composition and direction of trade between the Old and the New World was irreversibly altering, to the detriment of Castile. The colonial import pattern was switching to more sophisticated manufactured goods, which Spain could not supply, brought as contraband by English or Dutch merchants; local capital was being reinvested on the spot rather than transferred to Seville; and native American shipping was increasing its share of Atlantic freightage. The net result was a calamitous decrease in Spanish trade with its American possessions, whose total tonnage fell 60 per cent from 1606–10 to 1646–50.

In the days of Lerma, the ultimate consequences of this process still lay hidden in the future. But the relative decline of Spain on the seas, and the rise of the Protestant powers of England and Holland at its expense, were already visible. The reconquest of the Dutch Republic and the invasion of England had both failed in the 16th century. But since that date Spain's two maritime enemies had grown more prosperous and powerful, while the Reformed religion continued to advance in Central Europe. The cessation of hostilities for a decade under Lerma thus merely convinced the new generation of imperialist generals and diplomats – Zuñiga, Gondomar, Osuña, Bedmar, Fuentes

25. Lynch, *Spain under the Habsburgs*, II, p. 11.

– that, if war was expensive, Spain could not afford peace. The accession of Philip IV, bringing the masterful Conde-Duque de Olivares to chief power in Madrid, coincided with the upheaval in the Bohemian lands of the Austrian branch of the Habsburg family: the chance to crush Protestantism in Germany and settle accounts with Holland – an inter-related goal, because of the strategic need to command the corridor through the Rhineland for troop movements between Italy and Flanders – now appeared before them. European war was thus unleashed once again, by proxy through Vienna, but at the initiative of Madrid, in the 1620's. The course of the Thirty Years' War curiously reversed the pattern of the two great bouts of Habsburg arms in the previous century. Whereas Charles V and Philip II had scored initial victories in the South of Europe and suffered eventual defeat in the North, Philip IV's forces achieved early successes in the North only to experience ultimate disasters in the South. The size of the Spanish mobilization for this third and last general engagement was formidable: in 1625 Philip IV claimed 300,000 under his orders.[26] The Bohemian Estates were crushed at the Battle of the White Mountain, with the aid of Hispanic subsidies and veterans, and the cause of Protestantism permanently beaten in the Czech lands. The Dutch were forced backwards by Spinola, with the capture of Breda. The Swedish counter-attack in Germany, after defeating Austrian or Leaguer armies, was undone by Spanish *tercios* under the Cardinal-Infante at Nordlingen. But it was precisely these victories which finally forced France into hostilities, tipping the military balance decisively against Spain: the reaction of Paris to Nordlingen in 1634 was Richelieu's declaration of war in 1635. The results were soon evident. Breda was retaken by the Dutch in 1637. A year later, Breisach – the key to the roads into Flanders – had fallen. Within another year, the bulk of the Spanish fleet was sent to the bottom at the Downs – a far worse blow to the Habsburg navy than the fate of the Armada. Finally, in 1643, the French army ended the supremacy of the *tercios* at Rocroi. Military intervention by Bourbon France had proved a very different matter from the Valois contests of the previous century; it was the new nature and weight of French Absolutism which was now to encompass the downfall of Spanish imperial power in Europe. For whereas in the 16th

26. Parker, *The Army of Flanders and Spanish Road*, p. 6.

century, Charles V and Philip II had both profited from the internal weakness of the French State, by utilizing provincial disaffections to invade France itself, the boot was now on the other foot: a maturing French Absolutism was able to exploit aristocratic sedition and regional separatism in the Iberian peninsula to invade Spain. In the 1520's Spanish troops had marched into Provence, in the 1590's into Languedoc, Brittany and the Ile de France, with the alliance or welcome of local dissidents. In the 1640's, French soldiers and ships were fighting together with anti-Habsburg rebels in Catalonia, Portugal and Naples: Spanish Absolutism was at bay on its own soil.

For the long strain of the international conflict in the North eventually told in the Iberian peninsula itself. State bankruptcy had to be declared again in 1627; the *vellón* was devalued by 50 per cent in 1628; a sharp drop in transatlantic trade followed in 1629–31; the silver fleet failed to arrive in 1640.[27] The huge war costs led to new taxes on consumption, contributions from the clergy, confiscations of interest on public bonds, seizure of private bullion shipments, swelling sales of honours and – especially – seigneurial jurisdictions to the nobility. All these devices, however, remained inadequate to raise the sums needed for the pursuit of the struggle; for its costs were still borne virtually alone by Castile. Portugal yielded no revenues whatever to Madrid, since local subsidies were confined to defense purposes in the Portuguese colonies. Flanders was chronically deficitary. Naples and Sicily had contributed a modest but respectable surplus to the central treasury, in the previous century. Now, however, the cost of covering Milan and maintaining the *presidios* in Tuscany absorbed all their revenues, despite increased taxes, sale of offices and alienations of land: Italy continued to provide invaluable manpower, but no longer money, for the war.[28] Navarre, Aragon and Valencia at best consented to a few small grants to the dynasty in its emergency. Catalonia – the richest region of the Eastern kingdom and the most parsimonious province of all – paid nothing, permitting no taxes to be spent, and no troops to be

27. Elliott, *Imperial Spain*, p. 343.
28. For the financial record of the Italian possessions, see A. Domínguez Ortiz, *Política y Hacienda de Felipe IV*, Madrid 1960, pp. 161–4. In general, the role of the Italian components of the Spanish Empire in Europe has been least studied, although it is evident that no satisfactory account of the imperial system as a whole will be possible until this lacuna has been remedied.

deployed, outside its borders. The historical price of the failure of the Habsburg State to harmonize its realms was already patent by the outset of the Thirty Years' War. Olivares, aware of the acute dangers in the lack of any central integration to the State system, and the isolated and perilous eminence of Castile within it, had proposed a far-reaching reform of the whole structure to Philip IV in a secret memo-randum of 1624 – effectively a simultaneous equalization of fiscal charges and political responsibilities between the different dynastic patrimonies, which would have given Aragonese, Catalan or Italian nobles regular access to the highest positions in royal service, in exchange for a more even distribution of the tax-burden and the acceptance of uniform laws modelled on those of Castile.[29] This blue-print for a unitary Absolutism was too bold to be released publicly, for fear of both Castilian and non-Castilian reaction. But Olivares also drew up a second and more limited project, the 'Union of Arms', for the creation of a common reserve army of 140,000 to be maintained and recruited from all the Spanish possessions, for their common defense. This scheme, officially proclaimed in 1626, was thwarted on all sides by traditional particularism. Catalonia, above all, refused to have any-thing to do with it, and in practice it remained a dead letter.

But as the military conflict wore on, and the Spanish position worsened, pressure to extract some Catalan assistance for it became increasingly desperate in Madrid. Olivares therefore determined to force Catalonia into the war by attacking France across its south-eastern frontiers in 1639, thereby putting the uncooperative province *de facto* into the front-line of Spanish operations. This reckless gamble back-fired disastrously.[30] The morose and parochial Catalan nobility,

29. The best discussion of this scheme is provided by Elliott, *The Revolt of the Catalans*, Cambridge 1963, pp. 199–204. Domínguez has argued that Olivares had no internal policy, being exclusively preoccupied with foreign affairs: *La Sociedad Española en el Siglo XVI*, I, Madrid 1963, p. 15. This view is belied both by his early domestic reforms and the breadth of his recommendations in the memorandum of 1624.

30. Olivares was aware of the magnitude of the risk he was taking: 'My head cannot bear the light of a candle or of the window. . . . To my mind this will lose everything irremediably or be the salvation of the ship. Here go religion, king-dom, nation, everything, and, if our strength is insufficient, let us die in the attempt. Better to die, and more just, than to fall under the dominion of others, and most of all of heretics, as I consider the French to be. Either all is lost, or else

starved of remunerative offices and dabbling in mountain banditry, were enraged by commanders from Castile and casualties suffered against the French. The lower clergy whipped up regionalist fervour. The peasantry, harried by billeting and requisitioning, rose against the troops in a spreading insurrection. Rural labourers and unemployed streaming into the towns set off violent riots in Barcelona and other cities.[31] The Catalan Revolution of 1640 fused the grievances of all social classes except a handful of magnates into an unstoppable explosion. Habsburg power in the province disintegrated. To head off the dangers of popular radicalism, and block a Castilian reconquest, the nobility and patriciate invited in a French occupation. For a decade, Catalonia became a protectorate of France. Meanwhile, on the other side of the peninsula, Portugal had staged its own revolt within a few months of the Catalan rebellion. The local aristocracy, resentful of the loss of Brazil to the Dutch and assured of the anti-Castilian sentiments of the masses, had no difficulty in reasserting its independence, once Olivares had made the blunder of concentrating royal armies against the heavily defended East, where Franco-Catalan forces were victorious, rather than the comparatively demilitarized West.[32] In 1643, Olivares fell; four years later, Naples and Sicily in their turn threw off Spanish rule. The European conflict had exhausted the exchequer and economy of the Habsburg Empire in the South, and disrupted its composite polity. In the cataclysm of the 1640's, as Spain went down to defeat in the Thirty Years' War, and bankruptcy, pestilence, depopulation and invasion followed, it was inevitable that the patchwork union of dynastic patrimonies should come apart: the secessionist revolts of Portugal, Catalonia and Naples were a judgment on the infirmity of Spanish Absolutism. It had expanded too fast too early, because of its overseas fortune, without ever having completed its metropolitan foundations.

Ultimately, the outbreak of the Fronde saved Catalonia and Italy

---

Castile will be head of the world, as it is already head of Your Majesty's Monarchy.' Cit: Elliott, *The Revolt of the Catalans*, p. 310.

31. Elliott, *The Revolt of the Catalans*, pp. 460–8, 473–6, 486–7.

32. A. Domínguez Ortiz, *The Golden Century of Spain 1556–1659*, London 1971, p. 103.

for Spain. Mazarin, himself distracted by domestic turmoil, relinquished the one, after the Neapolitan baronage had rediscovered loyalty to its sovereign in the other, where the rural and urban poor had erupted in a menacing social revolt, and French intervention was abbreviated. War, however, dragged on for another fifteen years even after the recovery of the last Mediterranean province – against the Dutch, the French, the English, the Portuguese. Further losses in Flanders occurred in the 1650's. The slow-motion attempt to reconquer Portugal lasted longest of all. By now the Castilian *hidalgo* class had lost all appetite for the field; military disillusion was universal among Spaniards. The final border campaigns were mostly fought with Italian conscripts, eked out with Irish or German mercenaries.[33] Their only result was to ruin much of Estremadura, and reduce government finances to a nadir of futile manipulation and deficit. Peace and Portuguese independence were not accepted until 1668. Six years later, the Franche-Comté was lost to France. The paralytic reign of Charles II witnessed the re-capture of central political power by the grandee class, which secured direct domination of the State with the aristocratic putsch of 1677, when Don Juan José of Austria – its candidate for the regency – successfully led an Aragonese army on Madrid. It also experienced the darkest economic depression of the century, with a shut-down of industries, collapse of currency, reversion to barter exchange, food shortages and bread riots. Between 1600 and 1700 the total population of Spain fell from 8,500,000 to 7,000,000 – the worst demographic setback in the West. The Habsburg State was moribund by the end of the century: its demise in the person of its spectral ruler Charles II, *El Hechizado*, was awaited in every chancellery abroad as the signal at which Spain would become the spoils of Europe.

In fact, the outcome of the War of the Spanish Succession renovated Absolutism in Madrid, by destroying its unmanageable outworks. The Netherlands and Italy were lost. Aragon and Catalonia, which had rallied to the Austrian candidate, were defeated and subdued in the civil war within the international war. A new French dynasty was installed. The Bourbon monarchy achieved what the Habsburgs had failed to do. The grandees, many of whom had defected to the Anglo-

33. Lynch, *Spain under the Habsburgs*, II, pp. 122–3; Domínguez Ortiz, *The Golden Century of Spain*, pp. 39–40.

Austrian camp in the War of Succession, were subordinated and excluded from central power. Importing the much more advanced experience and techniques of French Absolutism, expatriate civil servants created a unitary, centralized State in the 18th century.[34] The Estates systems of Aragon, Valencia and Catalonia were eliminated, and their particularism suppressed. The French device of royal *intendants* for the uniform government of provinces was introduced. The Army was drastically recast and professionalized, with a semi-conscript base and a rigidly aristocratic command. Colonial administration was tightened and reformed: freed from its European possessions, the Bourbons showed that Spain could run its American Empire competently and profitably. In fact, this was the century in which a cohesive *España* – as opposed to the semi-universal *monarquía española* of the Habsburgs – finally and gradually emerged.[35]

Yet the work of the Caroline bureaucracy which rationalized the Spanish State could not revitalize Spanish society. It was now too late for a development comparable to that of France or England. The once dynamic Castilian economy had received its quietus under Philip IV. Although there was a real demographic recovery (population rose from 7 to 11 million) and a considerable extension of cereal cultivation in Spain, only 60 per cent of the population was still employed in agriculture, while urban manufactures had been virtually excised from the metropolitan social formation. After the collapse of the American mines in the 17th century, there was a new boom of Mexican silver in the 18th century, but in the absence of any sizeable domestic industry, it probably benefited French expansion more than Spanish.[36] Local capital was diverted, as before, into public rents or land. The State administration was numerically not very large, but it remained rife with

34. See Henry Kamen, *The War of Succession in Spain 1700–1715*, London 1969, pp. 84–117. The main architect of the new administration was Bergeyck, a Fleming from Brussels; pp. 237–40.

35. It was in this epoch that a national flag and anthem were adopted. Domínguez's dictum is characteristic: 'Smaller than the Empire, larger than Castile, Spain, precellent creation of our eighteenth century, emerged from its nebula and acquired solid and tangible shape. . . . By the time of the War of Independence, the ideal plastic and symbolic image of the Nation as we know it today, was essentially complete.' Antonio Domínguez Ortiz, *La Sociedad Española en el Siglo XVIII*, Madrid 1955, pp. 41, 43: the best work on the period.

36. Vilar, *Oro y Moneda*, pp. 348–61, 315–17.

empleomania, the job-hunting pursuit of office by the impoverished gentry. Vast latifundia worked by gang labour in the South provided the fortunes of a stagnant grandee nobility, parked in provincial capitals.[37] From the mid-century onwards, there was a reflux of the higher nobility into Ministerial office, as 'civilian' and 'military' factions struggled for power in Madrid: the tenure of the Aragonese aristocrat Aranda corresponded to the high point of direct magnate influence in the capital.[38] The political impetus of the new order, however, was now running out. By the end of the century, the Bourbon court was itself in a full decadence reminiscent of its predecessor, under the slack and corrupt control of Godoy, the last *privado*. The limits of the 18th century revival, whose epilogue was to be the ignominious collapse of the dynasty in 1808, were always evident in the administrative structure of Bourbon Spain. For even after the Caroline reforms, the authority of the Absolutist State stopped at municipal level over vast areas of the country. Down to the invasion of Napoleon, more than half the towns in Spain were not under monarchical, but under seigneurial or clerical jurisdiction. The regime of the *señorios*, a mediaeval relic dating from the 12th and 13th centuries, was of more directly economic than political importance to the nobles who controlled these jurisdictions: yet it assured them not only of profits, but also of local judicial and administrative power.[39] These 'combinations of sovereignty and property' were a telling survival of the principles of territorial lordship into the epoch of Absolutism. The *ancien régime* preserved its feudal roots in Spain to its dying day.

37. There is a memorable portrait of this class in Raymond Carr, 'Spain', in Goodwin (ed.), *The European Nobility in the Eighteenth Century*, pp. 43–59.

38. Domínguez Ortiz, *La Sociedad Española en el Siglo XVIII*, pp. 93, 178.

39. Domínguez provides an ample survey of the whole pattern of the *señorios* in his chapter, 'El Ocaso del Régimen Señorial', *La Sociedad Española en el Siglo XVIII*, pp. 300–42, in which he describes them in the phrase cited above.

4

France

France presents an evolution very distinct from the Hispanic pattern. Absolutism there enjoyed no such early advantages as in Spain, in the form of a lucrative overseas empire. Nor, on the other hand, was it confronted with the permanent structural problems of fusing disparate kingdoms at home, with radically contrasted political and cultural legacies. The Capetian monarchy, as we have seen, had slowly extended its suzerain rights outwards from its original base in the Ile de France, in a gradual movement of concentric unification during the Middle Ages, until they reached from Flanders to the Mediterranean. It never had to contend with another territorial realm within France of comparable feudal rank: there was only one kingship in the Gallic lands, apart from the small and semi-Iberian State of Navarre in the remote folds of the Pyrenees. The outlying duchies and counties of France had always owed nominal allegiance to the central dynasty, even if as vassals initially more powerful than their royal overlord – permitting a juridical hierarchy that facilitated later political integration. The social and linguistic differences that divided the South from the North, although persistent and pronounced, were never quite as great as those set the East off from the West in Spain. The separate legal system and language of the Midi did not coincide, fortunately for the monarchy, with the main military and diplomatic rift which split France in the later Middle Ages: the house of Burgundy, the major rival power ranged against the Capetian dynasty, was a Northern duchy. Southern particularism nevertheless remained a constant, latent force in the early modern epoch, assuming masked forms and novel guises in successive crises. The real political control of the French monarchy was never territorially uniform: it always ebbed at the extremities of the country, progressively decreasing in the more recently acquired provinces farthest from Paris. At the same time, the sheer demographic size of France in itself posed formidable obstacles for administrative unification: some 20 million inhabitants made it at least twice as populous as Spain in the 16th century. The rigidity and clarity of the domestic barriers to a unitary Absolutism in Spain were consequently balanced by the thicker profusion and variety of regional life contained within the French polity. No linear constitutional advance thus occurred after the Capetian consolidation in mediaeval France. On the contrary, the history of the construction of French Absolutism was to be that of a 'convulsive' progression towards a centralized monarchical State, repeatedly interrupted by relapses into provincial disintegration and anarchy, followed by an intensified reaction towards concentration of royal power, until finally an extremely hard and stable structure was achieved. The three great breakdowns of political order were, of course, the Hundred Years' War in the 15th century, the Religious Wars in the 16th century, and the Fronde in the 17th century. The transition from the mediaeval to the Absolute monarchy was each time first arrested, and then accelerated by these crises, whose ultimate outcome was to create a cult of royal authority in the epoch of Louis XIV with no equal anywhere else in Western Europe.

The slow concentric centralization of the Capetian kings, discussed earlier, had come to an abrupt end with the extinction of the line in the mid 14th century, which proved the signal for the onset of the Hundred Years' War. The outbreak of violent magnate feuds within France itself, under weak Valois rulers, eventually led to the combined Anglo-Burgundian attack on the French monarchy of the early 15th century, which shattered the unity of the realm. At the height of the English and Burgundian successes in the 1420's, virtually the entire traditional demesne of the royal house in Northern France lay under alien control, while Charles VII was driven into flight and exile in the South. The general story of the eventual recovery of the French monarchy and the expulsion of the English armies is well known. For our purposes here, the critical legacy of the long ordeal of the Hundred Years' War was its ultimate contribution to the fiscal and military emancipation of the monarchy from the limits of the prior mediaeval polity. For the war was only won by abandoning the seigneurial *ban* system of knightly service, which had proved disastrously ineffective against the English archers, and creating a regular paid army whose artillery proved the decisive weapon for victory. To raise this army, the first important country-wide tax to be collected by the monarchy was granted by the French aristocracy – the *taille royale* of 1439, which became the regular *taille des gens d'armes* in the 1440's.[1] The nobility, clergy and certain towns were exempt from it, and in the course of the next century the legal definition of nobility in France became hereditary exemption from the *taille*. The monarchy thus emerged strengthened in the later 15th century to the extent that it now possessed an embryonic regular army in the *compagnies d'ordonnance*, captained by the aristocracy, and a direct fiscal levy not subject to any representative control.

On the other hand, Charles VII made no attempt to tighten central dynastic authority in the Northern provinces of France, when they were successively reconquered: in fact, he promoted assemblies of regional Estates and transferred financial and judicial powers to local institutions. Just as the Capetian rulers had accompanied their extension of monarchical control with cession of princely appanages, so the early Valois kings combined reassertion of royal unity with provincial devolution to an entrenched aristocracy. The reason in both cases was the same: the sheer administrative difficulty of managing a country the size of France with the instruments of rule available to the dynasty. The coercive and fiscal apparatus of the central State was still very small: Charles VII's *compagnies d'ordonnance* never numbered more than 12,000 troops – a force entirely insufficient for control and repression of a population of 15 million.[2] The nobility thus retained autonomous local power by virtue of its own swords, on which the stability of the whole social structure ultimately depended. The advent of a modest royal army had even increased its economic privileges, the institutionalization of the *taille* securing nobles a complete fiscal immunity they had not hitherto enjoyed. Charles VII's convocation of Estates-Generals, an institution which had lapsed for centuries in

1. P. S. Lewis, *Later Mediaeval France: the Polity*, London 1968, pp. 102–4.
2. For this point, see J. Russell Major, *Representative Institutions in Renaissance France, 1421–1559*, Madison 1960, p. 9.

France, was thus inspired precisely by his need to create a minimal national forum in which he could induce the various provincial estates and towns to accept taxation, ratify treaties and provide advice on foreign affairs: its sessions, however, rarely granted proper satisfaction to his demands. The Hundred Years' War thus bequeathed to the French monarchy permanent troops and taxes, but little new civilian administration on a national scale. English intervention had been cleared from French soil: Burgundian ambitions remained. Louis XI, who succeeded in 1461, tackled both internal and external opposition to Valois power with grim resolution. His steady resumption of provincial appanages such as Anjou, systematic packing of municipal govern-ments in the major towns, arbitrary exaction of heavier taxes and quelling of aristocratic intrigues, greatly increased the royal authority and treasury in France. Above all, Louis XI secured the whole eastern flank of the French monarchy by encompassing the downfall of its most dangerous rival and enemy, the Burgundian dynasty. Fomenting the Swiss cantons against the neighbouring Duchy, he financed the first great European defeat of feudal cavalry by an infantry army: with the rout of Charles the Bold by the Swiss pikemen at Nancy in 1477, the Burgundian State collapsed and Louis XI annexed the bulk of the Duchy. In the next two decades, Charles VIII and Louis XII absorbed Brittany, the last major independent principality, by successive marriages to its heiress. The French realm now for the first time bounded all the vassal provinces of the mediaeval epoch, beneath a single sovereign. The extinction of most of the great houses of the Middle Ages and the reintegration of their domains into the lands of the monarchy, threw into prominent relief the apparent dominance of the Valois dynasty itself.

In fact, however, the 'new monarchy' inaugurated by Louis XI was by no means a centralized or integrated State. France was redivided into some 12 governorships, administration over which was entrusted to royal princes or leading nobles, who legally exercised a wide range of regalian rights down to the end of the century and factually could act as autonomous potentates well into the next.[3] Moreover, there now also developed a cluster of local *parlements*, provincial courts created by the monarchy with supreme judicial authority in their areas, whose

3. Major, *Representative Institutions in Renaissance France*, p. 6.

importance and numbers steadily grew in this epoch: between the accession of Charles VII and the death of Louis XII, new *parlements* were founded in Toulouse, Grenoble, Bordeaux, Dijon, Rouen and Aix. Nor were urban liberties yet gravely curtailed, although the position of the patrician oligarchy within them was reinforced at the expense of the guilds and small masters. The essential reason for these far-reaching limitations of the central State remained the insurmountable organizational problems of imposing an effective apparatus of royal rule over the whole country, amidst an economy without a unified market or modernized transport system, in which the dissociation of primary feudal relations in the village was by no means complete. The social ground for vertical political centralization was not yet ready, despite the notable gains registered by the monarchy. It was in this context that the Estates-General found a new lease of life after the Hundred Years' War, not against but with the revival of the monarchy. For in France, as elsewhere, the initial impulse for the convocation of the Estates was the dynastic need for fiscal or foreign policy support from the subjects of the realm.[4] In France, however, the consolidation of the Estates-General as a permanent national institution was blocked by the same diversity which had obliged the monarchy to accept wide political devolution even in the hour of its unitary victory. It was not that the three estates were especially divided socially when they met: the *moyenne noblesse* dominated their proceedings without much effort. But the regional assemblies which had elected their deputies to the Estates-General always refused to mandate them to vote national taxes; and since the nobility was exempt from the existing fisc, it had little incentive to press for the convocation of the Estates-General.[5]

4. There is a particularly trenchant statement of the general thesis that Estates-Generals in France and elsewhere nearly always served, not hindered, the promotion of royal power in the Renaissance, in Major's excellent study: *Representative Institutions in Renaissance France*, pp. 16–20. In fact, Major perhaps presses the argument somewhat too unilaterally; certainly, in the course of the 16th century, it became steadily less true, if it had once been so, that monarchs 'had no fear of the assemblies of estates' (p. 16). But this is nevertheless one of the most illuminating single discussions of the topic in any language.

5. See the convergent opinions expressed by Lewis and Major: P. S. Lewis, 'The Failure of the French Mediaeval Estates', *Past and Present*, No. 23, November 1962, pp. 3–24, and J. Russell Major, *The Estates-General of 1560*, Princeton 1951, pp. 75, 119–20.

The result was that since the French kings were unable to get the financial contributions they wanted from the national Estates, they gradually ceased to summon them at all. It was thus the regional entrenchment of local seigneurial power, rather than the centralist drive of the monarchy, which frustrated the emergence of a national Parliament in Renaissance France. In the short-run, this was to contribute to a complete break-down of royal authority; in the long-run, of course, it was to facilitate the task of Absolutism.

In the first half of the 16th century, Francis I and Henry II presided over a prosperous and multiplying realm. There was a steady decrease of representative activity: the Estates-General had lapsed again; the towns were no longer summoned after 1517 and foreign policy tended to become a more exclusively royal preserve. Legal officials – *maîtres de requêtes* – gradually extended the juridical rights of the monarchy, and *parlements* were overawed by special sessions or *lits de justice* in the presence of the king. Control of appointments in the ecclesiastical hierarchy was gained by the Concordat of Bologna with the Papacy. But neither Francis I nor Henry II were yet anything like autocratic rulers: they both consulted frequently with regional assemblies and carefully respected traditional noble privileges. The economic immunities of the Church were not infringed by the change of patronage over it (unlike the situation in Spain, where the clergy were heavily taxed by the monarchy). Royal edicts still in principle needed formal registration by the *parlements* to become law. Fiscal revenues doubled between 1517 and the 1540's, but the tax-level at the end of Francis I's reign was not appreciably above that of Louis XI sixty years earlier, although prices and incomes had risen greatly in the interval:[6] the direct fiscal yield as a proportion of national wealth thus actually fell. On the other hand, the issue of public bonds to *rentiers* from 1522 onwards helped to maintain the royal treasury comfortably. Dynastic prestige at home was meanwhile assisted by the constant external wars in Italy into which the Valois rulers led their nobility: for these became a well-established outlet for the perennial pugnacity of the gentry. The long French effort to win ascendancy in Italy, launched by Charles VIII in 1494 and concluded by the Treaty of Cateau-Cambrésis in 1559, was unsuccessful. The Spanish monarchy – politically and militarily more

6. Major, *Representative Institutions in Renaissance France*, pp. 126–7.

advanced, strategically commanding the Habsburg bases in Northern Europe, and navally superior through its Genoese alliance – cleanly routed its French rival for control of the transalpine peninsula. Victory in this contest went to the State whose process of Absolutization was earlier and more developed. Ultimately, however, defeat in its first foreign adventure probably helped to ensure a sounder and more compact foundation for French Absolutism, forced back in on its own domestic territory. Immediately, on the other hand, it was the termination of the Italian wars, combined with the uncertainty of a succession crisis, which was to reveal how insecurely the Valois monarchy was still anchored in the country. The death of Henry II precipitated France into forty years of internecine strife.

The Civil Wars which raged after Cateau-Cambrésis were, of course, set off by the religious conflicts attendant on the Reformation. But they provided a kind of radiography of the body politic in the late 16th century, in the way in which they exposed the multiple tensions and contradictions of the French social formation in the epoch of the Renaissance. For the struggle between the Huguenots and the Holy League for control of the monarchy, in practice politically vacant after the death of Henry II and the regency of Catherine of Medici, served as an arena for the coalescence of virtually every type of internal political conflict characteristic of the transition towards Absolutism. The Religious Wars were led, from first to last, by the three rival magnate lineages of Guise, Montmorency and Bourbon, each controlling a domanial territory, extensive clientele, leverage inside the State apparatus, loyal troops and international connections. The Guise family was master of the North-East from Lorraine to Burgundy; the Montmorency-Châtillon line was based on hereditary lands stretching through the whole Centre of the country; the Bourbon bastions lay essentially in the South-West. The inter-feudal struggle between these noble houses was intensified by the plight of needy rural squires all over France, previously habituated to plundering forays into Italy and now caught by the price inflation; this stratum provided military cadres ready for prolonged civil warfare, quite apart from the religious affiliations which divided it. Moreover, as the struggle wore on, the towns themselves split into two camps: many of the Southern cities rallying to the Huguenots, while the Northern inland towns became

virtually without exception bulwarks of the League. It has been argued
that differing commercial orientations (to the overseas or domestic
market) influenced this division.[7] It seems more probable, however,
that the general geographical pattern of Huguenotism reflected a traditional regional separatism of the South, which had always lain
farthest from the Capetian homelands in the Ile de France, and where
the local territorial potentates had kept their independence longest. At
the start, Protestantism had generally spread from Switzerland into
France via the main river-systems of the Rhône, Loire and Rhine,[8]
providing a fairly even regional distribution of the Reformed faith. But
once official toleration ceased, it rapidly reconcentrated in the Dau-
phiné, Languedoc, Guyenne, Poitou, Saintonge, Béarn and Gascgony –
mountainous or coastal zones beyond the Loire, many of them harsh
and poor, whose common characteristics were not so much commercial
vitality as manorial particularism. Huguenotism always mustered
artisans and burghers in its towns, but the appropriation of tithes by
Calvinist notables ensured that the appeal of the new creed to the
peasantry was very limited. Huguenot social leadership, in fact, was
drawn overwhelmingly from the landowning class, where it could
claim perhaps half the nobility in France in the 1560's – while it never
surpassed more than 10–20 per cent of the population as a whole.[9]
Religion retreated in the South into the embrace of aristocratic
dissidence. The general strain of the confessional conflict can be seen
as thus simply having split the tenuous fabric of French unity along its
inherently weakest seam.

Once under way, however, the struggle unleashed deeper social
conflicts than those of feudal secessionism. When the South was lost

7. This thesis is advanced in the stimulating essay by Brian Pearce, 'The
Huguenots and the Holy League: Class, Politics and Religion in France in the
Second Half of the Sixteenth Century' (unpublished), who suggests that the
Northern towns were consequently more concerned with the consolidation of
French national unity. However, many of the main ports in the South and West
also remained Catholic: Bordeaux, Nantes and Marseille all rallied to the League.
Marseille suffered in consequence, pro-Spanish policies depriving it of its traditional Levantine trade: G. Livet, *Les Guerres de Religion*, Paris 1966, pp. 105–6.
8. Livet, *Les Guerres de Religion*, pp. 7–8.
9. J. H. Elliott, *Europe Divided 1559–1598*, London 1968, p. 96, which includes *inter alia* a skilful narrative of this period in French history, in the setting
of the international political struggles of the age.

to Condé and the Protestant armies, a redoubled weight of royal taxation for the war fell on the beleaguered Catholic cities of the North. The urban misery that resulted from this development in the 1580's provoked a radicalization of the Holy League in the towns, compounded by Henry III's assassination of Guise. While the ducal lords of the Guise clan – Mayenne, Aumale, Elbeuf, Mercoeur – detached Lorraine, Brittany, Normandy and Burgundy in the name of Catholicism, and Spanish armies invaded from Flanders and Catalonia to aid the League, municipal revolutions exploded in the Northern cities. Power was seized in Paris by a dictatorial committee of discontented lawyers and clerics, backed by the famished plebeian masses and a fanatical phalanx of friars and preachers.[10] Orléans, Bourges, Dijon, Lyon followed suit. Once the Protestant Henry of Navarre became the legal successor to the monarchy, the ideology of these urban revolts started to veer towards republicanism. At the same time, the tremendous devastation of the countryside by the constant military campaigns of these decades pushed the South-Central peasantry of Limousin, Périgord, Quercy, Poitou and Saintonge into menacingly non-religious risings in the 1590's. It was this dual radicalization in town and country that finally reunited the ruling class: the nobility started to close ranks as soon as there was a real danger of an upheaval from below. Henry IV tactically accepted Catholicism, rallied the aristocratic patrons of the League, isolated the Committees, and suppressed the peasant revolts. The Religious Wars ended in a reaffirmed royal state.

French Absolutism now came relatively rapidly of age, although there was still to be one radical setback before it was definitively

10. For a political sociology of the municipal leadership of the League in Paris at the height of the Religious Wars, see J. H. Salmon, 'The Paris Sixteen, 1584–1594: The Social Analysis of a Revolutionary Movement', *Journal of Modern History*, 44, No. 4, December 1972, pp. 540–76. Salmon shows the importance in the Council of Sixteen of the middle and lower ranks of the legal profession, and stresses its manipulation of the plebeian masses, together with a provision of some economic relief, under its dictatorship. A brief comparative analysis is sketched in H. G. Koenigsberger, 'The Organization of Revolutionary Parties in France and the Netherlands during the Sixteenth Century', *Journal of Modern History*, 27, December 1955, pp. 335–51. But much work remains to be done on the League, one of the most complex and enigmatic phenomena of the century; the movement which invented urban barricades has yet to find its Marxist historian.

established. Its great administrative architects in the 17th century were, of course, Sully, Richelieu and Colbert. The size and diversity of the country were still largely unconquered when they began their work. Royal princes remained jealous rivals of the monarch, often in possession of hereditary governorships. Provincial *parlements* composed of a combination of rural gentry and lawyers represented bastions of traditional particularism. A commercial bourgeoisie was growing in Paris and other cities, and controlled municipal power. The French masses had been aroused by the civil wars of the previous century, when both sides had at different times appealed to them for support, and retained memories of popular insurgency.[11] The specific character of the French Absolutist state which emerged in the *grand siècle* was designed to fit, and master, this complex of forces. Henry IV fixed royal presence and power centrally in Paris for the first time, rebuilding the city and making it into the permanent capital of the kingdom. Civic pacification was accompanied by official care for agricultural recovery and promotion of export trades. The popular prestige of the monarchy was restored by the personal magnetism of the founder of the new Bourbon dynasty himself. The Edict of Nantes and its supplementary articles contained the problem of Protestantism, by conceding it limited regional autonomy. No Estates-General was summoned, despite promises to do so made during the civil war. External peace was maintained, and with it administrative economy. Sully, the Huguenot Chancellor, doubled the net revenues of the State, mainly by shifting to indirect taxes, rationalizing tax-farms and cutting expenses. The most important institutional development of the reign was the introduction of the *paulette* in 1604: sale of offices in the state apparatus, which had existed for over a century, was stabilized by Paulet's device of rendering them inheritable, in exchange for payment of a small annual percentage on their purchase value – a measure designed not only to increase the income of the monarchy, but also to insulate the bureaucracy from magnate influence. Under the frugal regime of Sully, sale of offices still represented only some 8 per cent of budget receipts.[12]

11. This point is emphasized by J. H. Salmon, 'Venality of Office and Popular Sedition in 17th Century France', *Past and Present*, July 1967, pp. 41–3.

12. Menna Prestwich, 'From Henri III to Louis XIV', in H. Trevor-Roper (ed.), *The Age of Expansion*, London 1968, p. 199.

But from the minority of Louis XIII onwards, this proportion rapidly altered. A recrudescence of noble factionalism and religious unrest, marked by the last and ineffectual session of the Estates-General (1614–15) before the French Revolution, and the first aggressive intervention of the *Parlement* of Paris against a royal government, led to the brief dominance of the Duc de Luynes. Pensions to buy off captious grandees and resumption of war against the Huguenots in the South increased state expenditures greatly. Henceforward, the bureaucracy and judiciary was to pullulate with the largest single volume of venal transactions in Europe. France became the classical land of sale of offices, as an ever-growing number of sinecures and prebends were created by the monarchy for revenue purposes. By 1620–4, the traffic in these provided some 38 per cent of royal revenues.[13] Tax-farms, furthermore, were now regularly auctioned to large financiers, whose collecting systems might tap up to two-thirds of fiscal receipts on their way to the State. The steeply rising costs of foreign and domestic policy in the new international conjuncture of the Thirty Years' War, moreover, were such that the monarchy had constantly to resort to forced loans at high interest rates from the syndicates of its own tax-farmers, who were themselves at the same time *officiers* who had bought positions in the treasury section of the State apparatus.[14] This vicious circle of financial improvisation inevitably maximized confusion and corruption. The multiplication of venal offices, in which a new *noblesse de robe* now became lodged, impeded any firm dynastic hold over major agencies of public justice and finance, and dispersed bureaucratic power both centrally and locally.

Yet it was in the same epoch that, curiously interlaced with this system, Richelieu and his successors started to build a rationalized administrative machine capable for the first time of direct royal control and intervention throughout France. *De facto* ruler of the country from 1624 onwards, the Cardinal proceeded promptly to liquidate the remaining Huguenot fortresses in the South-West, with the siege and capture of La Rochelle; crushed successive aristocratic conspiracies

13. Prestwich, 'From Henri III to Louis XIV', p. 199.

14. There is a good discussion of this phenomenon in A. D. Lublinskaya, *French Absolutism: The Crucial Phase 1620–1629*, Cambridge 1968, pp. 234–43; for the size of the take from the *taille* appropriated by tax-farmers, see p. 308 (13 million out of 19 million *livres* in the mid 1620's).

with summary executions; abolished the highest mediaeval military dignities; levelled noble castles and banned duelling; and suppressed Estates where local resistance permitted (Normandy). Above all, Richelieu effectively created the *intendant* system. The *Intendants de Justice, de Police et de Finances* were functionaries dispatched with omnibus powers into the provinces, at first on temporary and ad hoc missions, who later became permanent commissioners of the central government throughout France. Appointed directly by the monarchy, their offices were revocable and non-purchasable: normally recruited from the earlier *maîtres de requêtes* and themselves small or medium nobles in the 17th century, they represented the new power of the Absolutist State in the farthest reaches of the realm. Extremely unpopular with the *officier* stratum, on whose local prerogatives they infringed, they were used with caution at first, and coexisted with the traditional governorships of the provinces. But Richelieu broke the quasi-hereditary character of these regional lordships, long the peculiar prey of the highest aristocratic magnates, so that by the end of his rule, only a quarter were still held by men who predated his accession to power. There was thus a simultaneous and contradictory development of both *officier* and *commissaire* groups within the overall structure of the State during this period. While the role of the *intendants* grew progressively more prominent and authoritarian, the magistrature of the various *parlements* of the land, champions of legalism and particularism, became the most vocal spokesmen of *officier* resistance to them, intermittently hemming the initiatives of the royal government.

The compositional form of the French monarchy thus came, both in theory and practice, to acquire an extreme, ornate complexity. Kossmann has described its contours for the consciousness of the possessing classes of the time, in a striking passage: 'Contemporaries felt that Absolutism in no way excluded that tension which seemed to them inherent in the State and altered none of their ideas of government. For them, the State was like a baroque church in which a great number of different conceptions mingle, clash and are finally absorbed into a single magnificent system. Architects had recently discovered the oval, and space came alive in their ingenious arrangements of it: everywhere the splendour of oval forms, gleaming from their corners, projected onto the construction as a whole the supple energy and swaying, uncertain rhythms cherished by the new style.'[15] These 'aesthetic' principles of French Absolutism, nevertheless, corresponded to functional purposes. The relationship between taxes and dues in the traditional epoch, as has been seen, has been termed a tension between 'centralized' and 'local' feudal rent. This 'economic' duplication was in a sense reproduced in the 'political' structures of French Absolutism. For it was the very complexity of the architecture of the State which permitted a slow yet relentless unification of the noble class itself, which was gradually adapted into a new centralized mould, subject to the public control of the *intendants*, while still occupying privately owned positions within the *officier* system and local authority in the provincial *parlements*. Simultaneously, moreover, it achieved the feat of integrating the nascent French bourgeoisie into the circuit of the feudal state. For the purchase of offices represented such a profitable investment that capital was perpetually diverted away from manufacturing or mercantile ventures into a usurious collusion with the Absolutist State. Sinecures and fees, tax-farms and loans, honours and bonds all drew bourgeois wealth away from production. The acquisition of noble titles and fiscal immunity became normal entrepreneurial goals for *roturiers*. The social consequence was to create a bourgeoisie which tended to become increasingly assimilated to the aristocracy itself, via the exemptions and privileges of offices. The State, in its turn, sponsored royal manufactures and public trading companies which, from Sully to Colbert, provided business outlets for this class.[16] The result was to 'side-track' the political evolution of the French bourgeoisie for a hundred and fifty years.

The weight of this whole apparatus fell on the poor. The reorganized feudal State proceeded to batten mercilessly on the rural and urban masses. The extent to which local commutation of dues and growth of a monetarized agriculture were compensated by centralized pumping of the surplus from the peasantry can be seen with stark clarity in the

15. 'Or to change the metaphor: if royal authority was a brilliant sun, there was another power which reflected, concentrated and tempered its light, a shade enclosing that source of energy on which no human eye could rest without being blinded. We refer to the Parlements, above all the Parlement of Paris.' Ernst Kossmann, *La Fronde*, Leyden 1954, p. 23.

16. B. F. Porshnev, *Les Soulèvements Populaires en France de 1623 à 1648*, pp. 547–60.

French case. In 1610, the fiscal agents of the State collected 17 million livres from the *taille*. By 1644, the exactions of this tax had trebled to 44 million livres. Total taxation actually quadrupled in the decade after 1630.[17] The reason for this sudden and enormous increase in the fiscal burden was, of course, Richelieu's diplomatic and military intervention in the Thirty Years' War. Mediated at first by subventions to Sweden and then by hire of German mercenaries, it ended with large French armies in the field. The international effect was decisive. France settled the fate of Germany and destroyed the ascendancy of Spain. The Treaty of Westphalia, four years after the historic French victory at Rocroi, extended the frontiers of the French monarchy from the Meuse to the Rhine. The new structures of French Absolutism were thus baptised in the fire of European war. French success in the anti-Spanish struggle, in effect, coincided with domestic consolidation of the dual bureaucratic complex that made up the early Bourbon State. The military emergencies of the conflict facilitated the imposition of intendency in invaded or threatened zones: its huge financial expense at the same time necessitated unprecedented sale of offices and yielded spectacular fortunes for banking syndicates. The real costs of the war were borne by the poor, among whom it wrought social havoc. The fiscal pressures of war-time Absolutism provoked a constant ground-swell of desperate revolts by the urban and rural masses throughout these decades. There were town riots in Dijon, Aix and Poitiers in 1630; jacqueries in the countryside of Angoumois, Saintonge, Poitou, Périgord and Guyenne in 1636–7; a major plebeian and peasant rebellion in Normandy in 1639. The more important regional upsurges were interspersed with constant minor outbreaks of unrest against tax-collectors over large areas of France, frequently patronized by local gentry. Royal troops were regularly deployed for repression at home, while the international conflict was being fought abroad.

The Fronde can in certain respects be regarded as a high 'crest' of this long wave of popular revolts,[18] in which for a brief period sections of the top nobility, the office-holding magistrature and the municipal bourgeoisie used mass discontents for their own ends against the

17. Prestwich, 'From Henri III to Louis XIV', p. 203; Mousnier, *Peasant Uprisings*, London 1971, p. 307.

18. This is Porshnev's view in *Les Soulèvements Populaires en France*.

Absolutist State. Mazarin, who succeeded Richelieu in 1642, had skil-
fully steered French foreign policy through to the end of the Thirty
Years' War, and with it the acquisition of Alsace. After the Peace of
Westphalia, however, Mazarin provoked the crisis of the Fronde by
prolonging the anti-Spanish war into the Mediterranean theatre, where
as an Italian he aimed at the sequestration of Naples and Catalonia.
Fiscal extortion and financial manipulation to support the military
effort abroad coincided with successive bad harvests in 1647, 1649 and
1651. Popular hunger and fury combined with a war-weary revolt of
officiers led by the *Parlement* of Paris against the *intendant* system; the
disgruntlement of *rentiers* at an emergency devaluation of government
bonds; and the jealousy of powerful peers of the realm at an Italian
adventurer manipulating a royal minority. The upshot was a confused
and bitter mêlée in which, once again, the country seemed to fall apart
as provinces detached themselves from Paris, marauding private
armies wandered across the land, towns set up rebel municipal dictatorships, and complex manoeuvres and intrigues divided and reunited the
rival princes competing for control of the court. Provincial governors
sought to settle scores with local *parlements*, while municipal authorities
seized the opportunity to attack the regional magistratures.[19] The
Fronde thus reproduced many elements of the pattern that marked the
Religious Wars. This time, the most radical urban insurrection
coincided with one of the traditionally most disaffected rural zones:
the *Ormée* of Bordeaux and the extreme South-West were the last
centres to hold out against Mazarin's armies. But the popular seizures
of power in Bordeaux and Paris occurred too late to affect the outcome
of the criss-crossed conflicts of the Fronde; local Huguenotism in
general remained studiously neutral in the South; and no coherent
political programme emerged from the *Ormée*, beyond its instinctual
hostility to the local Bordelais bourgeoisie.[20] By 1653, Mazarin and
Turenne had stamped out the last refuges of revolt. The progress of
administrative centralization and class reorganization achieved within
the mixed structures of the French monarchy in the 17th century had
revealed its efficacy. Although the social pressure from below was
probably more urgent, the Fronde was actually less dangerous to the

19. For this aspect, see Kossmann, *La Fronde*, pp. 117–38.
20. Kossmann, *La Fronde*, pp. 20 , 24 250–2.

monarchical State than the Religious Wars, because the propertied classes were by now more united. For all the contradictions between the *officier* and *intendant* systems, both groups were predominantly recruited from the *noblesse de robe*, while the bankers and tax-farmers against whom the *Parlements* protested were in fact closely connected in personnel to them. The annealing process permitted by the coexistence of the two systems within a single State thus ended by ensuring much prompter solidarity against the masses. The very depth of the plebeian unrest revealed by the Fronde shortened the last emotional breakaway of the dissident aristocracy from the monarchy: although there were to be further peasant risings in the 17th century, no conflux of rebellion from above and below ever occurred again. The Fronde cost Mazarin his projected gains in the Mediterranean. But when the Spanish War ended with the Treaty of the Pyrenees, Roussillon and Artois had been added to France; and a picked bureaucratic elite was practised and ready for the imposing administrative order of the next reign. The aristocracy was henceforward to settle down under the consummated, solar Absolutism of Louis XIV.

The new sovereign assumed personal command of the whole state apparatus in 1661. Once royal authority and executive capacity were reunited in a single ruler, the full political potential of French Absolutism was rapidly realized. The *Parlements* were silenced, their claim to present remonstrances before registering royal edicts annulled (1673). The other sovereign courts were reduced to obedience. The provincial Estates could no longer dispute and bargain over taxes: precise fiscal demands were dictated by the monarchy, which they were compelled to accept. The municipal autonomy of the *bonnes villes* was bridled, as mayoralties were domesticated and military garrisons were installed in them. Governorships were granted for three years only, and their holders frequently obliged to reside with the court, rendering them merely honorific. Command of fortified towns in frontier regions was carefully rotated. The higher nobility was forced to reside at Versailles once the new palace complex was completed (1682), and divorced from effective lordship over its territorial domains. These measures against the refractory particularism of traditional institutions and groups provoked, of course, resentment both among the princes and peers, and the provincial gentry. But they did not alter the objective bond between the aristocracy and the State, henceforward more efficacious than ever in protecting the basic interests of the noble class. The degree of economic exploitation guaranteed by French Absolutism can be judged by the recent calculation that throughout the 17th century, the nobility – 2 per cent of the population – appropriated 20–30 per cent of the total national income.[21] The central machinery of royal power was thus now concentrated, rationalized and enlarged without serious aristocratic resistance.

Louis XIV inherited his key ministers from Mazarin: Le Tellier, in charge of military affairs, Colbert who came to combine management of the royal finances, household and navy, Lionne who directed foreign policy, and Séguier who as Chancellor handled internal security. These disciplined and competent administrators formed the apex of the bureaucratic order now at the disposal of the monarchy. The king presided in person over the deliberations of the small *Conseil d'en Haut*, comprising his most trusted political servants and excluding all princes and grandees. This became the supreme executive body of the State, while the *Conseil des Dépêches* dealt with provincial and domestic matters, and the newly created *Conseil des Finances* supervised the economic organization of the monarchy. The departmental efficacy of this relatively taut system, linked by the tireless activity of Louis XIV himself, was much greater than that of the cumbersome conciliar paraphernalia of Habsburg Absolutism in Spain, with its semi-territorial lay-out and interminable collective ruminations. Below it, the *intendant* network now covered the whole of France – Brittany was the last province to receive a commissioner in 1689.[22] The country was divided into 32 *généralités*, in each of which the royal *intendant* now ruled supreme, assisted by *sub-délégués*, and vested with new powers over the assessment and supervision of the *taille* – vital duties that were transferred from the old *officier* 'treasurers' formerly in control of them. The total personnel of the civilian sector of the central state apparatus of French Absolutism in the reign of Louis XIV was still very modest: perhaps 1,000 responsible functionaries in all, both at court and in the

21. Pierre Goubert, 'Les Problèmes de la Noblesse au XVIIe Siècle', *XIIIth International Congress of Historical Sciences*, Moscow 1970, p. 5.
22. Pierre Goubert, *Louis XIV et Vingt Millions de Français*, pp. 164, 166.

provinces.[23] But these were backed by a massively augmented coercive machinery. A permanent police force was created to keep order and repress riots in Paris (1667), which was ultimately extended throughout France (1698–9). The Army was enormously increased in size during the reign, rising from some 30–50,000 to 300,000 by its end.[24] Regular pay, drill and uniforms were introduced by Le Tellier and Louvois; military weaponry and fortifications were modernized by Vauban. The growth of this military apparatus meant the final disarming of the provincial nobility, and the capacity to strike down popular rebellions with dispatch and efficacy.[25] The Swiss mercenaries who provided Bourbon Absolutism with its household troops helped to make short work of the Boulonnais and Camisard peasantry; the new dragoons operated the mass ejection of Huguenots from France. The ideological incense surrounding the monarchy, lavishly dispensed by the salaried writers and clerics of the regime, swathed the armed repression on which it relied, but could not conceal it.

French Absolutism achieved its institutional apotheosis in the last decades of the 17th century. The State structure and concordant ruling culture perfected in the reign of Louis XIV was to become the model for much of the rest of the nobility in Europe: Spain, Portugal, Piedmont and Prussia were only the most direct later examples of its influence. But the political *rayonnement* of Versailles was not an end in itself: the organizational accomplishments of Bourbon Absolutism were designed in the conception of Louis XIV to serve a specific purpose – the superior goal of military expansion. The first decade of the reign, from 1661 to 1672, was essentially one of internal preparation for external adventures ahead. Administratively, economically and culturally these were the most effulgent years of Louis XIV's rule; nearly all its most lasting work dated from them. Under the able superintendancy of the early Colbert, fiscal pressure was stabilized and trade promoted. State expenses were cut by the wholesale suppression of new offices created since 1630; the depredations of tax-farmers were

23. Goubert, *Louis XIV et Vingt Millions de Français*, p. 72.

24. J. Stoye, *Europe Unfolding 1648–1688*, London 1969, p. 223; Goubert, *Louis XIV et Vingt Millions de Français*, p. 186.

25. Roland Mousnier, *Peasant Uprisings*, London 1971, p. 115, justly stresses this point, commenting that the rebellions of 1675 in Brittany and Bordeaux were the last serious social upheavals of the century.

drastically reduced, although collection was not itself resumed by the State; royal demesne lands were systematically recovered. The *taille personnelle* was lowered from 42 to 34 million livres; while the *taille réelle* in the more lightly burdened *pays d'états* was raised by some 50 per cent; the yield of indirect taxes was increased some 60 per cent by vigilant control of the farming system. The net revenues of the monarchy doubled from 1661 to 1671, and a budgetary surplus was regularly achieved.[26] Meanwhile, an ambitious mercantilist programme to accelerate manufacturing and commercial growth in France, and colonial expansion overseas, was launched: royal subventions founded new industries (cloth, glass, tapestry, iron-ware), chartered companies were created to exploit the trade of the East and West Indies, shipyards were heavily subsidised, and finally an extremely protectionist tariff system imposed. It was this very mercantilism, however, which led directly to the decision to invade Holland in 1672, with the intention of suppressing the competition of its trade – which had proved easily superior to French commerce – by incorporating the United Provinces into the French domains. The Dutch war was initially successful: French troops crossed the Rhine, lay within striking distance of Amsterdam, and took Utrecht. An international coalition, however, rapidly rallied to the defense of the *status quo* – above all, Spain and Austria; while the Orange dynasty regained power within Holland, forging a marital alliance with England. Seven years of fighting ended with France in possession of the Franche-Comté and an improved frontier in Artois and Flanders, but with the United Provinces intact and the anti-Dutch tariff of 1667 retracted: a modest balance-sheet abroad. At home, Colbert's fiscal retrenchment had been permanently wrecked: sale of offices was multiplied once again, old taxes were increased, new taxes were invented, loans were floated, commercial subsidies were jettisoned. War was henceforward to dominate virtually every aspect of the reign.[27] The misery and famine caused by the

26. Goubert, *Louis XIV et Vingt Millions de Français*, pp. 90–2.

27. Even in a certain sense its cultural ideals: 'The newly acquired symmetry and order of the parade-ground provided, for Louis XIV and his contemporaries, the model to which life and art must alike conform; and the *pas cadencé* of Martinet – whose name is in itself a programme – echoed again in the majestic monotony of interminable alexandrines.' Michael Roberts, 'The Military Revolution 1560–1660', *Essays in Swedish History*, London 1967, p. 206.

State's exactions and a series of bad harvests led to renewed risings of the peasantry in the Guyenne and Brittany in 1674–5, and summary armed suppression of them: this time no lord or squire attempted to use them for his ends. The nobility, relieved of monetary charges that Richelieu and Mazarin had tried to impose on it, remained loyal throughout.[28]

The restoration of peace for a decade in the 1680s, however, merely accentuated the surquedry of Bourbon Absolutism. The king now became immured in Versailles; ministerial calibre declined, as the generation chosen by Mazarin gave way to more or less mediocre successors by hereditary cooption from the same group of inter-related families in the *noblesse de robe*; clumsy anti-Papal gestures were mixed with heedless expulsion of Protestants from the realm; creaking legal chicanery was used for a series of small annexations in the North-East. Agrarian depression continued at home, if maritime commerce recovered and boomed, to the apprehension of English and Dutch merchants. The defeat of the French candidate for the Electorate of Cologne, and the accession of William III to the English monarchy, were the signals for the resumption of international conflict. The War of the League of Augsburg (1689–97) ranged virtually the whole of Western and Central Europe against France – Holland, England, Austria, Spain, Savoy, and most of Germany. French armies had been more than doubled in strength, to some 220,000 in the intervening decade. The most they proved able to do was hold the coalition to a costly draw: Louis XIV's war aims were everywhere frustrated. The sole gain registered by France at the Treaty of Ryswick was European acceptance of the absorption of Strasbourg, secured before the fighting had broken out: all other occupied territories had to be evacuated, while the French navy was driven from the seas. To finance the war effort, a cascade of new offices was invented for sale, titles were auctioned, forced loans and public rents were multiplied, monetary values manipulated, and for the first time a 'capitation' tax was imposed

28. The Cardinals had sought to subject the aristocracy to disguised imposts, in the form of 'commutations' of the military *ban* owed on fiefs. These were much disliked by the gentry and were abandoned by Louis XIV. See Pierre Deyon, 'A Propos des Rapports entre la Noblesse Française et la Monarchie Absolue pendant la Première Moitié du XVIIe Siècle', *Revue Historique*, CCXXXI, 1964, pp. 355–6.

that the nobility itself did not escape.[29] Inflation, hunger and depopulation ravaged the countryside. But within five years, France was plunged back into the European conflict for the Spanish Succession. Louis XIV's diplomatic ineptitude and brusque provocations once again maximized the coalition against France in the decisive military contest that was now joined: the advantageous testament of Charles II was flouted for the French heir, Flanders occupied by French troops, Spain directed by French emissaries, the slave-contracts with its American colonies annexed by French merchants, the exiled Stuart claimant ostentatiously hailed as legitimate monarch of England. Bourbon determination to monopolize the totality of the Hispanic Empire, refusing any partition or diminution of the vast Spanish haul, inevitably united Austria, England, Holland, and most of Germany against it. By reaching for everything, French Absolutism eventually secured virtually nothing from its supreme effort of political expansion. The Bourbon armies – now 300,000 strong, equipped with rifles and bayonets – were decimated at Blenheim, Ramillies, Turin, Oudenarde, Malplaquet. France itself was battered by invasion, as tax-farms collapsed at home, the currency was debased, bread riots raged in the capital, frost and famine numbed the countryside. Yet apart from the local Huguenot rising in the Cévennes, the peasantry remained still. Above it, the ruling class was compactly serried about the monarchy, even amidst its autocratic discipline and foreign disasters, which were shaking the whole society.

Tranquillity only came with final defeat in the war. The peace was mitigated by divisions in the victorious coalition against Louis XIV, which allowed the junior branch of the Bourbon dynasty to retain the monarchy in Spain, at the price of political separation from France. Otherwise, the ruinous ordeal had yielded Gallic Absolutism no benefit. It had merely established Austria in the Netherlands and Italy, and made England master of colonial commerce in Spanish America. The paradox of French Absolutism, in fact, was that its greatest domestic florescence did not coincide with its greatest international ascendancy: on the contrary, it was the still defective and incomplete State structure of Richelieu and Mazarin, marked by institutional anomalies and torn by internal upheavals, which achieved spectacular foreign successes, while the consolidated and stabilized monarchy of

29. Goubert, *Louis XIV et Vingt Millions de Français*, pp. 158–62.

Louis XIV – with its enormously augmented authority and army – momentously failed to impose itself on Europe, or make notable territorial gains. Institutional construction and international expansion were dephased and inverted in the French case. The reason, of course, lay in the acceleration of a time distinct from that of Absolutism altogether, in the Maritime countries – Holland and England. Spanish Absolutism held European dominance for a hundred years; first checked by the Dutch Revolution, its ascendancy was finally broken by French Absolutism in the mid 17th century, with the aid of Holland. French Absolutism, however, enjoyed no comparable spell of hegemony in Western Europe. Within twenty years of the Treaty of the Pyrenees, its expansion had already been effectively halted. Louis XIV's ultimate defeat was not due to his numerous strategic mistakes, but to the alteration in the relative position of France within the European political system attendant on the advent of the English Revolutions of 1640 and 1688.[30] It was the economic rise of English capitalism and the political consolidation of its State in the later 17th century which 'overtook' French Absolutism, even in the epoch of the latter's own ascent. The real victors of the War of the Spanish Succession were the merchants and bankers of London: a world-wide British imperialism was ushered in by it. The late feudal Spanish State had been brought down by its French counterpart and rival, aided by the early bourgeois State in Holland. The late feudal French State was stopped in its path by two capitalist States of unequal power – England, Holland – assisted by its Austrian counterpart. Bourbon Absolutism was intrinsically much stronger and more unified than Spanish Absolutism had been: but the forces arrayed against it were proportionately more powerful too. The strenuous inner preparations of Louis XIV's reign for outer dominion proved vain. The hour of supremacy for Versailles, which seemed so near in the Europe of the 1660's, never struck.

The advent of the Regency in 1715 announced the social reaction to

30. Louis XIV, of course, proved unable to appreciate this change – hence his constant diplomatic blunders. The temporary weakness of England in the 1660's, when Charles II was a French pensioner, led him to underestimate the island ever afterwards, even when its central political importance in Western Europe was already obvious. Louis XIV's failure to extend any preemptive aid to James II in 1688, before the landing of William III, was thus to be one of the most fatal errors of a career well supplied with them.

this failure. The higher nobility, its pent-up grievances against royal autocracy suddenly released, staged an immediate come-back. The Regent secured the agreement of the *Parlement* of Paris to set aside Louis XIV's will in exchange for restoring its traditional right of remonstrance: government passed into the hands of peers who promptly terminated the Ministerial system of the late king, assuming direct power themselves in the so-called *polysynodie*. Both the *noblesse d'épée* and the *noblesse de robe* were thus institutionally reinstated by the Regency. The new epoch was in fact to accentuate the overt class character of Absolutism: the 18th century witnessed a regression of non-noble influence in the State apparatus, and the collective dominance of an increasingly unified upper aristocracy. The magnate take-over of the Regency itself did not last: under Fleury and then two weak kings who succeeded him, the decision-making system at the summit of the State reverted to the old Ministerial pattern, now no longer controlled by a commanding monarch. But the nobility henceforward maintained a limpet grip on the highest offices of government: from 1714 to 1789, there were only three Ministers who were not titled aristocrats.[31] The judicial magistrature of the *parlements* now likewise formed a closed stratum of nobles, both in Paris and the provinces, from which commoners were effectively barred. The royal *intendants*, once the scourge of provincial landowners, became a virtually hereditary caste in their turn: 14 of them in the reign of Louis XVI were sons of former *intendants*.[32] In the Church, all archbishops and bishops were of noble origin by the second half of the century, and most abbacies, priories and canonries were controlled by the same class. In the Army, the top military commands were solidly occupied by grandees; purchase of companies by *roturiers* was banned in the 1760's, when it became necessary to have unambiguous noble descent in order to qualify for the rank of officer. The aristocratic class as a whole retained a rigorous late feudal statute: it was a legally defined order of some 250,000 persons, which was exempt from the bulk of taxation and enjoyed a monopoly

31. Albert Goodwin, 'The Social Structure and Economic and Political Attitudes of the French Nobility in the 18th Century', *XIIth International Congress of Historical Sciences*, Rapports, I, p. 361.

32. J. McManners, 'France', in Goodwin (ed.), *The European Nobility in the 18th Century*, pp. 33–5.

of the highest echelons of the bureaucracy, judiciary, clergy and army. Its subdivisions were now punctiliously defined in theory, and between the highest peerage and the lowest rural *hobereaux* there existed a great gulf. But in practice the lubricants of money and marriage made its upper reaches in many ways a more flexibly articulated group than ever before. The French nobility in the age of the Enlightenment possessed complete security of tenure within the structures of the Absolutist State. Yet an irreducible sentiment of discomfort and friction subsisted between the two, even in this last period of optimal union between aristocracy and monarchy. For Absolutism, no matter how congenial its personnel and how attractive its service, remained an inaccessible and irresponsible power wielded over the heads of the nobility as a whole. The condition of its efficacy as a State was its structural distance from the class from which it was recruited and whose interests it defended. Absolutism in France never became unquestioningly trusted and accepted by the aristocracy on which it rested: its decisions were not accountable to the titled order which gave it life – necessarily so, as we shall see, because of the inherent nature of the class itself; yet also perilously so, because of the danger of unconsidered or arbitrary actions taken by the executive rebounding on it. Plenitude of royal power, even when mildly exercised, bred seigneurial reserve towards it. Montesquieu – President of the *Parlement* of Bordeaux under the easygoing regime of Fleury – gave unanswerable expression to the new type of aristocratic oppositionism characteristic of the century.

In fact, the Bourbon monarchy of the 18th century made very few moves of a 'levelling' type against the 'intermediary powers' which Montesquieu and his consorts cherished so intensely. The Ancien Régime in France preserved its bewildering jungle of heteroclite jurisdictions, divisions and institutions – *pays d'états, pays d'élections, parlements, sénéschaussées, généralités* – down to the Revolution. After Louis XIV, little further rationalization of the polity occurred: no uniform customs tariff, tax-system, legal code or local administration was ever created. The monarchy's one attempt to impose a new conformity on a corporate body was its persistent effort to secure theological obedience in the clergy by persecution of Jansenism – which was invariably and vigorously combated by the *Parlement* of Paris in the name of traditional Gallicanism. The anachronistic quarrel over this ideological issue became the chief flash-point of relations between Absolutism and the *noblesse de robe* from the Regency to the epoch of Choiseul, when the Jesuits were formally expelled from France by the *parlements*, in a symbolic victory for Gallicanism. Much more serious, however, was to be the financial deadlock which eventually developed between the monarchy and the magistrature. Louis XIV had left a State massively encumbered with debts; the Regency had halved these by the Law system; but the costs of foreign policy from the War of the Austrian Succession onwards, combined with the extravagance of the court, kept the exchequer in steady and deepening deficit. Successive attempts to levy new taxes, puncturing the fiscal immunity of the aristocracy, were resisted or sabotaged in the *Parlements* and provincial Estates, by refusal to register edicts or presentation of indignant remonstrances. The objective contradictions of Absolutism here unfolded in their plainest form. The monarchy sought to tax the wealth of the nobility, while the nobility demanded controls on the policies of the monarchy: the aristocracy, in effect, refused to alienate its economic privileges without gaining political rights over the conduct of the royal State. In their struggle against the Absolutist governments over this issue, the judicial oligarchy of the *Parlements* came increasingly to use the radical language of the *philosophes*: migrant bourgeois notions of liberty and representation started to haunt the rhetoric of one of the most inveterately conservative and caste-like branches of the French aristocracy.[33] By the 1770's and 1780's, a curious cultural contamination of sections of the nobility by the estate below it was pronounced in France.

For the 18th century had meanwhile seen a rapid growth in the ranks and fortunes of the local bourgeoisie. The epoch from the Regency onwards was in general one of economic expansion, with a secular increase of prices, relative agrarian prosperity (at least in the period 1730–74), and demographic recovery: the population of France rose from some 18/19 to 25/26 million between 1700 and 1789. While agriculture remained the overwhelmingly dominant branch of production, manufactures and commerce registered notable advances. French

---

33. For the attitudes of the *Parlements* of the last years of the Ancien Régime, see J. Egret, *La Pré-Révolution Française, 1787–1788*, Paris 1962, pp. 149–60.

industry increased some 60 per cent in output in the course of the century;[34] true factories started to appear in the textile sector; the foundations of iron and coal industries were laid. Far more rapid, however, was the progress of trade, above all in the international and colonial arenas. Foreign commerce proper quadrupled from 1716–20 to 1784–8, with a regular export surplus. Colonial trade achieved faster growth with the rise of the sugar, coffee and cotton plantations in the Antilles: in the last years before the Revolution, it came to two-thirds as much as French foreign trade.[35] The commercial boom naturally stimulated urbanization; there was a wave of new building in the towns, and by the end of the century the provincial cities of France still outdistanced those of England in size and numbers, despite the much higher level of industrialization across the Channel. Meanwhile, sale of offices had dwindled away, with the aristocratic closure of the State apparatus. Absolutism in the 18th century switched increasingly to public loans, which did not create the same degree of intimacy with the State: *rentiers* did not receive ennoblement or tax-immunity as *officiers* had done. The wealthiest single group within the French capitalist class remained the *financiers*, whose speculative investments reaped the huge profits of army contracts, tax farms or royal borrowing. But by and large, the simultaneous diminution of commoner access to the feudal State and development of a commercial economy outside it, emancipated the bourgeoisie from its subaltern dependence on Absolutism. The merchants, manufacturers and ship-owners of the Enlightenment, and the lawyers and journalists who grew up together with them, now increasingly prospered outside the ambit of the State, with inevitable results for the political autonomy of the bourgeois class as a whole.

The monarchy, for its part, now proved incapable of protecting bourgeois interests, even when they nominally coincided with those of Absolutism itself. Nowhere was this clearer than in the external policies of the late Bourbon State. The wars of the century followed an unerringly traditional pattern. Small annexations of land in Europe always in practice achieved priority over defense or acquisition of overseas colonies; maritime and commercial power was sacrificed to

34. A. Soboul, *La Révolution Française*, I, Paris 1964, p. 45.
35. J. Lough, *An Introduction to 18th Century France*, London 1960, pp. 71–3.

territorial militarism.[36] Fleury, bent on peace, successfully ensured the absorption of Lorraine in the brief campaigns over the Polish Succession in the 1730's, from which England stayed aloof. The War of the Austrian Succession in the 1740's, however, saw the British fleet punish French shipping all the way from the Caribbean to the Indian Ocean, inflicting huge trading losses on France, while Saxe conquered the Southern Netherlands in an accomplished but futile land campaign: peace restored the *status quo ante* on both sides, but the strategic lessons were already clear to Pitt in England. The Seven Years' War (1756–63), in which France committed itself to join an Austrian attack on Prussia against every rational dynastic interest, brought disaster for the Bourbon colonial empire. The continental war was this time fought listlessly by French armies in Westphalia, while the naval war launched by Britain swept away Canada, India, West Africa and the West Indies. Choiseul's diplomacy recuperated the Bourbon possessions in the Antilles at the Peace of Paris, but the chance of France presiding over a mercantile imperialism on a world scale was over. The American War of Independence allowed Paris to achieve a political revenge on London, by proxy: but the French role in North America, although vital to the success of the American Revolution, was essentially a spoiling operation, which brought no positive gains to France. Indeed, it was the costs of Bourbon intervention in the War of American Independence which forced on the ultimate fiscal crisis of French Absolutism at home. By 1788, the State debt was so large – payment of interest on it accounting for nearly 50 per cent of current expenditure – and the budgetary deficit so acute, that Louis XVI's last ministers, Calonne and Loménie de Brienne, resolved to impose a land tax on the nobility and clergy. The *Parlements* furiously resisted these schemes; the monarchy in desperation decreed their dissolution; then, retreating before the uproar from the propertied classes, reestablished them; and finally, capitulating to the *Parlements'* demands for an Estates-General before any tax-reform was granted, convoked the three Estates amidst the disastrous grain shortage, widespread unemployment and popular misery of 1789. The aristocratic reaction against Absolutism

36. The naval budget never totalled more than half that of England: Dorn, *Competition for Empire*, p. 116. Dorn presents a telling account of the general deficiencies of the French fleets in this epoch.

therewith passed into the bourgeois revolution which overthrew it. Fittingly, the historical collapse of the French Absolutist State was tied directly to the inflexibility of its feudal formation. The fiscal crisis which detonated the revolution of 1789 was provoked by its juridical inability to tax the class which it represented. The very rigidity of the nexus between State and nobility ultimately precipitated their common downfall.

5

England

In the Middle Ages, the feudal monarchy of England was generally far more powerful than that of France. The Norman and Angevin dynasties created a royal State unrivalled in its authority and efficacy throughout Western Europe. It was precisely the strength of the English mediaeval monarchy that permitted its ambitious territorial adventures on the continent, at the expense of France. The Hundred Years' War, during which successive English kings and their aristocracy attempted to conquer and hold down huge areas of France, across a hazardous maritime barrier, represented a unique military undertaking in the Middle Ages: aggressive sign of the organizational superiority of the insular State. Yet the strongest mediaeval monarchy in the West eventually produced the weakest and shortest Absolutism. While France became the home ground of the most formidable Absolutist State in Western Europe, England experienced a peculiarly contracted variant of Absolutist rule, in every sense. The transition from the mediaeval to the early modern epochs thus corresponded in English history – despite all local legends of unbroken 'continuity' – to a deep and radical reversal of many of the most characteristic traits of prior feudal development. Naturally, certain mediaeval patterns of great importance were also preserved and inherited: it was precisely the contradictory fusion of traditional and novel forces that defined the particular political rupture that occurred in the island during the Renaissance.

The early administrative centralization of Norman feudalism, dictated both by the original military conquest and the modest size of the country, had generated – as we have seen – an unusually small and regionally unified noble class, without semi-independent territorial potentates comparable to those of the Continent. Towns, following Anglo-Saxon traditions, were part of the royal demesne from the outset, and hence enjoyed commercial privileges without the political autonomy of continental communes: they were never numerous or strong enough in the mediaeval epoch to challenge this subordinate status.[1] Nor did ecclesiastical lords ever gain large, consolidated seigneurial enclaves. The mediaeval monarchy in England was thus spared the respective dangers to unitary government that confronted feudal rulers in France, Italy or Germany. The result was a *concurrent* centralization, both of royal power, and of noble representation, within the total mediaeval polity. These two processes were, in fact, not opposites but complements. Within the parcellized system of feudal sovereignty, extra-suzerain monarchical power could in general only be sustained by the assent of exceptional vassal assemblies, capable of voting extraordinary economic and political support, outside the mediatized hierarchy of personal dependences. Mediaeval Estates can therefore virtually never, as pointed out earlier, be directly counterposed to monarchical authority: they were often the precise precondition of it. In England, Angevin royal authority and administration had no exact equivalent anywhere in 12th century Europe. But the personal power of the monarch was soon by the same token followed by precocious collective institutions of the feudal ruling class, of a uniquely unitary character – Parliaments. The existence of such mediaeval parliaments in England from the 13th century onwards was, of course, in no way a national peculiarity. What was distinctive about them was rather that they were both 'singleton' and 'conglomerate' institutions.[2] In other words, there was only one such assembly, which

1. Weber, in his analysis of English mediaeval towns, notes among other things that it is significant that they never experienced guild or municipal revolutions comparable to those of the continent: *Economy and Society*, III, pp. 1276–81. There was briefly an insurgent *conjuratio* in London in 1263–5, for which see Gwyn Williams, *Mediaeval London. From Commune to Capital*, London 1963, pp. 219–35. But this was an exceptional episode, which occurred in the wider context of the Barons' Revolt.

2. The initial judicial functions of the English Parliament were also unusual; it acted as a supreme court for petitions, with which the bulk of its work was concerned in the 13th century, when it was mainly dominated by royal servants. For the origins and evolution of the mediaeval Parliaments, see G. O. Sayles, *The*

coincided with the boundaries of the country itself, not a number for different provinces; and within the assembly, there was no three-fold division of nobles, clergy and burghers such as generally prevailed on the Continent. From the time of Edward III onwards, knights and towns were regularly represented alongside barons and bishops in the English Parliament. The two-chamber system of Lords and Commons was a subsequent development, which did not divide Parliament itself along Estate lines, but basically marked an intra-class distinction within the nobility. A centralized monarchy had produced a unified assembly.

Two further consequences followed from the early centralization of the English feudal polity. The unitary Parliaments which met in London did not achieve the degree of meticulous fiscal control nor the rights of regular convocation which later characterized some of the continental Estates systems. But they did secure a traditional negative limitation of royal *legislative* power, which was to become of great importance in the epoch of Absolutism: it became accepted, after Edward I, that no monarch could decree new statutes without the consent of Parliament.[3] Viewed structurally, this veto corresponded closely to the objective exigencies of noble class power. In effect, since centralized royal administration was from the start geographically and technically easier in England than elsewhere, there was proportionately less need for it to be equipped with any innovatory decretal authority, which could not be justified by inherent dangers of regional separatism or ducal anarchy. Thus while the real executive powers of English mediaeval kings were usually much greater than those of French monarchs, for that very reason, they never won the relative legislative autonomy eventually enjoyed by the latter. A second comparable feature of English feudalism was the unusual fusion between monarchy

Mediaeval Foundations of England, pp. 448–57; G. A. Holmes, *The Later Middle Ages*, London 1962, pp. 83–8.

3. The ultimate significance of this limitation has been underlined by J. P. Cooper, 'Differences between English and Continental Governments in the Early Seventeenth Century', in J. J. Bromley and E. H. Kossmann (ed.), *Britain and the Netherlands*, London 1960, pp. 62–90, esp. 65–71. As he points out, it meant that when the 'new monarchy' emerged in the early modern epoch, it was limited by 'positive' law in England, not merely the divine or natural law of Bodin's theory of sovereignty.

and nobility at the local judicial and administrative level. Whereas on the continent, the court system was typically divided between segregated royal and seigneurial jurisdictions, in England the survival of pre-feudal folk courts had provided a kind of common terrain on which a blend of the two could be achieved. For the sheriffs who presided over the shire-courts were non-hereditary royal appointees; yet they were selected from the local gentry, not from a central bureaucracy; while the courts themselves retained vestiges of their original character as popular juridical assemblies in which the free men of the rural community appeared before their equals. The result was to block the development either of a comprehensive *bailli* system of professionalized royal justice or of an extensive baronial *haute justice*; instead, an unpaid aristocratic self-administration emerged in the counties, which was later to evolve into the Justices of the Peace of the early modern epoch. In the mediaeval period itself, of course, the equipoise of the shire courts still coexisted with manorial courts and some seigneurial franchises of an orthodox feudal type, such as were to be found all over the Continent.

At the same time, the English nobility of the Middle Ages was fully as militarized and predatory a class as any in Europe: indeed it distinguished itself among its counterparts by the scope and constancy of its external aggression. No other feudal aristocracy of the later mediaeval epoch ranged so far and freely, as a whole order, from its territorial base. The repeated ravages of France during the Hundred Years War were the most spectacular feats of this militarism: but Scotland and Flanders, the Rhineland and Navarre, Portugal and Castile, were also traversed by armed expeditions from England in the 14th century. English knights fought abroad from the Forth to the Ebro in this age. The military organization of these expeditions reflected the local development of a monetarized 'bastard' feudalism. The last feudal array proper, summoned on the basis of land tenure, was called out in 1385, for Richard II's attack on Scotland. The Hundred Years' War was essentially fought by indentured companies, raised on the basis of cash contracts by major lords for the monarchy, and owing obedience to their own captains; shire levies and foreign mercenaries provided supplementary forces. No permanent or professional army was involved, and the scale of the expeditions was numerically modest:

troops dispatched to France never numbered much more than 10,000. The nobles who led the successive forays into Valois territory remained basically freebooting in outlook. Private plunder, ransom and land were the objects of their ambition; and the most successful captains enriched themselves massively from the wars, in which English forces again and again outfought much larger French armies mustered to expel them. The strategic superiority of the English aggressors throughout most of the long conflict did not lie, as a retrospective illusion might suggest, in control of sea-power. For mediaeval fleets in Northern seas were little more than improvised troop-transports; mostly composed of temporarily empressed merchant bottoms, they were incapable of patrolling the ocean regularly. Fighting ships proper were still largely confined to the Mediterranean, where the oar-driven galley was the weapon of real maritime warfare. Running battles at sea were consequently unknown in Atlantic waters in this epoch: naval engagements typically occurred in shallow bays or estuaries (Sluys or La Rochelle), where contending ships could lock together for hand-to-hand combat between the soldiers aboard them. No strategic 'command of the sea' was possible in this epoch. The coasts on either side of the Channel thus lay equally undefended against seaborne landings. In 1386, France assembled the largest army and fleet of the entire war for a full-scale invasion of England: defence plans for the island did not even contemplate arresting this force at sea, but relied on keeping the English fleet out of harm's way in the Thames and luring the enemy to conclusions inland.[4] In the event this invasion was cancelled; but the vulnerability of England to maritime attack was amply demonstrated during the war, in which destructive naval raids played a role equivalent to military *chevauchées* on land. French and Castilian fleets, using Southern-type galleys with their much greater mobility, captured, sacked or burnt a redoubtable list of English ports, all the way from Devon to Essex: among other towns, Plymouth, Southampton, Portsmouth, Lewes, Hastings, Winchelsea, Rye, Gravesend and Harwich were all seized or pillaged in the course of the conflict.

English dominance throughout most of the Hundred Years' War, which dictated that the permanent battle-field – with all its train of

4. For this revealing episode, see J. J. Palmer, *England, France and Christendom, 1377–1399*, London 1972, pp. 74–6.

damage and desolation – should be France, was thus not a result of seapower.[5] It was a product of the far greater political integration and solidity of the English feudal monarchy, whose administrative capacity to exploit its patrimony and rally its nobility was until the very end of the war much greater than that of the French monarchy, harried by disloyal vassals in Brittany or Burgundy, and weakened by its earlier inability to dislodge the English fief in Guyenne. The loyalty of the English aristocracy, in its turn, was cemented by the successful external campaigns into which it was led by a series of martial princes. It was not until the French feudal polity was itself reorganized under Charles VII, on a new fiscal and military basis, that the tide turned. Their Burgundian allies gone, English forces were thereafter relatively soon evicted by larger and better equipped French armies. The acrid aftermath of the final collapse of English power in France was the outbreak of the Wars of the Roses at home. Once a victorious royal authority no longer held the higher nobility together, the late-mediaeval machinery of war turned inwards, as brutalized retainers and indentured gangs were unleashed across the countryside by magnate feuds, and rival usurpers clawed for the succession. A generation of civil war eventually ended with the foundation of the new Tudor dynasty in 1485, on the field of Bosworth.

The reign of Henry VII now gradually prepared the emergence of a 'new monarchy' in England. During the later Lancastrian regime, aristocratic factions had prominently developed and manipulated Parliaments for their own ends, whereas Yorkist rulers had striven amidst the prevailing anarchy to concentrate and strengthen the central institutions of royal power again. Himself a Lancastrian by connection, Henry VII essentially developed Yorkist administrative practice. Before the Wars of the Roses, Parliaments were virtually annual, and during the first decade of reconstruction after Bosworth they became so again. But once internal security improved and Tudor power was consolidated, Henry VII discarded the institution: from 1497 to 1509 – the last twelve years of his reign – it only assembled once again.

5. See the pertinent comments by C. F. Richmond, 'The War at Sea', in K. Fowler (ed.), *The Hundred Years' War*, London 1971, p. 117, and 'English Naval Power in the Fifteenth Century', *History*, LII, No. 174, February 1967, pp. 4–5. The subject is only starting to be studied.

Centralized royal government was exercised through a small coterie of personal advisers and henchmen of the monarch. Its primary objective was the subjugation of the rampant magnate power of the preceding period, with its liveried gangs of armed retainers, systematic embracery of juries, and constant private warfare. This programme was applied, however, with much greater persistence and success than in the Yorkist phase. Supreme prerogative justice was enforced over the nobility by the use of the Star Chamber, a conciliar court which now became the main political weapon of the monarchy against riot or sedition. Regional turbulence in the North and West (where marcher lords claimed rights of conquest, not enfeoffment by the monarch) was quelled by the special Councils delegated to control these areas *in situ*. Extended sanctuary rights and semi-regalian private franchises were whittled down; liveries were banned. Local administration was tightened up under royal control by vigilant selection and supervision of JPs; recidivist usurper rebellions were crushed. A small bodyguard was created in lieu of armed police.[6] The royal demesne was greatly enlarged by resumption of lands, whose yield to the monarchy quadrupled during the reign; feudal incidents and customs duties were likewise maximally exploited. By the end of Henry VII's rule, total royal revenues had nearly trebled, and there was a reserve of between one and two million pounds in treasure.[7] The Tudor dynasty had thus made a promising start towards the construction of an English Absolutism by the turn of the 16th century. Henry VIII inherited a powerful executive and a prosperous exchequer.

The first twenty years of Henry VIII's rule brought little change to the secure domestic position of the Tudor monarchy. Wolsey's administration of the State was marked by no major institutional innovation; at most, the Cardinal concentrated unprecedented powers over the Church in his own person, as Papal legate in England. Both king and minister were mainly preoccupied with foreign affairs. The limited campaigns fought against France, in 1512–14 and 1522–5, were the main events of this period; to cope with the costs of these military operations on the continent, two brief bouts of parliamentary

6. S. T. Bindoff, *Tudor England*, London 1966, pp. 56–66, gives a good brief summary of this whole process.

7. G. R. Elton, *England under the Tudors*, London 1956, pp. 49, 53.

convocation were necessary.[8] An attempt at arbitrary taxation by Wolsey thereafter aroused sufficient propertied opposition for Henry VIII to disavow it. There was no sign yet of any dramatic development in the drift of royal policies within England. It was the marriage crisis of 1527–8, caused by the king's decision to divorce his Spanish wife, and the ensuing deadlock with the Papacy over an issue that affected the domestic succession, that suddenly altered the whole political situation. For to deal with Papal obstruction – inspired by the dynastic hostility of the Emperor to the projected remarriage – new and radical legislation was needed, and national political support had to be rallied against Clement VII and Charles V.

Thus in 1529, Henry summoned what became the longest Parliament yet to be held, to mobilize the landed class behind him in his dispute with the Papacy and the Empire, and to secure its endorsement of the political seizure of the Church by the State in England. This revival of a neglected institution was, however, far from a constitutional capitulation by Henry VIII or Thomas Cromwell, who became his political planner in 1531: it did not signify a weakening of royal power, but rather a new drive to enhance it. For the Reformation Parliaments not only greatly increased the patronage and authority of the monarchy by transferring control of the whole ecclesiastical apparatus of the Church to it. Under Cromwell's guidance, they also suppressed the autonomy of seigneurial franchises by depriving them of the power to designate JPs, integrated the marcher lordships into the shires, and incorporated Wales legally and administratively into the Kingdom of England. More significantly still, monasteries were dissolved and their vast landed wealth expropriated by the State. In 1536, the government's combination of political centralization and religious reformation provoked a potentially dangerous rising in the North, the Pilgrimage of Grace, a particularist regional reaction against a reinforced royal State, of a type that was characteristic of Western

8. C. Russell, *The Crisis of Parliaments*, Oxford 1971, pp. 41–2, states flatly that the English Parliament of this period, with its brevity of assembly and infrequency of summons, was a declining force; he correctly emphasizes, on the other hand, that the constitutional compact between monarchy and parliament rested on the class unity of the rulers of the country. For the social basis of English Parliamentarism, see the perceptive remarks by Penry Williams, 'The Tudor State', *Past and Present*, No. 24, July 1963, pp. 39–58.

Europe in this epoch.[9] It was rapidly broken, and a new and permanent Council of the North established to hold down the lands beyond the Trent. Meanwhile, the central bureaucracy was enlarged and reorganized by Cromwell, who converted the office of royal secretary into the highest ministerial post and created the beginnings of a regular privy council.[10] Soon after his fall, the Privy Council was formally institutionalized as the inner executive agency of the monarchy, and henceforward became the hub of the Tudor State machine. A Statute of Proclamations, apparently designed to confer extraordinary legislative powers on the monarchy, emancipating it from reliance on Parliament in the future, was eventually neutralized by the Commons.[11] This rebuff did not, of course, prevent Henry VIII from conducting sanguinary purges of ministers and magnates or creating a secret police system of delation and summary arrest. The State apparatus of repression was steadily increased throughout the reign: nine separate treason laws had been passed by the end of it.[12] Henry VIII's use of Parliament,

9. There is a sensitive discussion of the implications of the Pilgrimage of Grace, habitually underplayed, in J. J. Scarisbricke, *Henry VIII*, London 1971, pp. 444–5, 452.

10. The exaggerated claims made for Cromwell's administrative 'revolution' by Elton, in *The Tudor Revolution in Government*, Cambridge 1953, pp. 160–427, and *England under the Tudors*, pp. 127–37, 160–75, 180–4, have been reduced to more modest proportions by, among others, G. L. Harriss, 'Mediaeval Government and State-Craft', *Past and Present*, No. 24, July 1963, pp. 24–35; for a representative recent comment, see Russell, *The Crisis of Parliaments*, p. 111.

11. Plans were also mooted at this time for a standing army and a juridically privileged peerage – two measures which, if implemented, would have altered the whole course of 16th and 17th century English history. In fact, neither was acceptable to a Parliament which welcomed State control of the Church and a royal peace in the countryside, but was aware of the logic of professional troops and averse to a juridical hierarchy within the nobility which would have militated socially against many of its members. The draft scheme for a standing army, prepared in 1536–7 and found in the files of Cromwell's office, is discussed in L. Stone, 'The Political Programme of Thomas Cromwell', *Bulletin of the Institute of Historical Research*, XXIV, 1951, pp. 1–18. For the proposal of a privileged legal statute in landed property for the titled nobility, see Holdsworth, *A History of English Law*, IV, pp. 450–543.

12. Joel Hurstfield, 'Was there a Tudor Despotism after all?', *Transactions of the Royal Historical Society*, 1967, pp. 83–108, effectively criticizes the apologetic anachronisms in which much writing on the period is still couched. Hurstfield stresses the real thrust behind the Statute of Proclamations, the Treason Acts, and the official censorship and propaganda of the reign. The once received notion that the Tudor monarchy was not a form of Absolutism is given short shrift by

from which he expected and received few inconveniences, was confidently legalistic in approach: it was a necessary means to his own royal ends. Within the inherited framework of the English feudal polity, which had conferred singular powers on Parliament, a national Absolutism was in the making that in practice seemed to bear comparison with that of any of its continental counterparts. Throughout his life, Henry VIII's actual personal power within his realm was fully the equal of that of his contemporary Francis I in France.

Nevertheless, the new Tudor monarchy operated within one fundamental limitation, which set it apart from its equivalents abroad: it lacked a substantial military apparatus. To understand why English Absolutism took the peculiar form that it assumed in the 16th and early 17th centuries, it is necessary to look beyond the indigenous heritage of a law-making Parliament to the whole international context of Renaissance Europe. For while the Tudor State was being successfully constructed at home, the geopolitical position of England abroad had swiftly and silently undergone a drastic change. In the Lancastrian epoch, English external power could match or overtop that of any other country in the continent, because of the advanced nature of the feudal monarchy in England. But by the early 16th century, the balance of forces between the major Western States had totally altered. Spain and France – each victims of English invasion in the previous epoch – were now dynamic and aggressive monarchies, disputing the conquest of Italy between them. England had been suddenly outdistanced by both. All three monarchies had achieved an approximately comparable internal consolidation: but it was just this evening-up which permitted the natural advantages of the two great continental powers of the epoch to become for the first time decisive. The population of France was four to five times that of England. Spain had twice the population of England, not to speak of its American Empire and European possessions. This demographic and economic superiority was heightened by the geographical necessity for both countries to develop modernized land armies on a permanent basis, for the perpetual warfare of the

Mousnier, 'Quelques Problèmes Concernant La Monarchie Absolue', pp. 21–6. Henry's attitude to Parliament is well conveyed bv Scarisbricke, *Henry VIII*, pp. 653–4.

time. The creation of the *compagnies d'ordonnance* and the *tercios*, the utilization of mercenary infantry and field artillery, all led to a new type of royal military apparatus – far larger and more costly than anything known in the mediaeval period. The build-up of their troop-strengths was an indispensable condition of survival for the Renaissance monarchies on the mainland. The Tudor State was subtracted from this imperative, because of its insular situation. On the one hand, the steady growth in the size and expense of armies in the early modern epoch, and the transport problems of ferrying and supplying large numbers of soldiers across the water, rendered the mediaeval type of overseas expedition in which England had once excelled, increasingly anachronistic. The military preponderance of the new land powers, based on their much greater financial and manpower resources, precluded any successful repetition of the campaigns of Edward III or Henry V. On the other hand, this continental ascendancy was not translated into any equivalent strike-capacity at sea: no major transformation of naval warfare had yet occurred, so that England conversely remained relatively immune from the risk of a maritime invasion. The result was that at the critical juncture of the transition towards a 'new monarchy' in England, it was neither necessary nor possible for the Tudor State to build up a military machine comparable to that of French or Spanish Absolutism.

Subjectively, however, Henry VIII and his generation within the English nobility were still incapable of grasping the new international situation. The martial pride and continental ambitions of their late-mediaeval predecessors remained a living memory within the English ruling class of the time. The ultra-cautious Henry VII himself had revived Lancastrian claims to the French monarchy, fought to block the Valois absorption of Brittany, and actively schemed to gain the succession in Castile. Wolsey, who directed English foreign policy for the next twenty years, posed as arbiter of European concord with the Treaty of London, and aimed for nothing less than the Italian Papacy itself. Henry VIII, in turn, entertained hopes of becoming Emperor in Germany. These grandiose aspirations have been dismissed as irrational fantasms by subsequent historians: in fact, they reflected the perceptual difficulty of English rulers to adapt themselves to the new diplomatic configuration, in which the stature of England had in real terms so much diminished, just at a time when their own domestic power was sensibly increasing. Indeed, it was precisely this loss of international standing – unseen by native protagonists – which lay behind the whole miscalculation of the royal divorce. Neither Cardinal nor King realized that the Papacy was virtually bound to submit to the superior pressure of Charles V, because of the dominance of Habsburg power in Europe. England had been marginalized by the Franco-Spanish struggle for Italy: an impotent onlooker, its interests had little weight in the Curia. The surprise of the discovery was to propel the Defender of the Faith into the Reformation. The misadventures of Henry VIII's foreign policy, however, were not confined to this calamitous diplomatic setback. On three occasions, the Tudor monarchy did attempt to intervene in the Valois-Habsburg wars in Northern France, by an expedition across the Channel. The armies dispatched in these campaigns of 1512–14, 1522–5, and 1543–6, were necessarily of considerable size, composed of English levies bulked up with foreign mercenaries: 30,000 in 1512, 40,000 in 1544. Their deployment lacked any serious strategic objective, and yielded no significant gains: English departure from the sidelines of the struggle between Spain and France proved both expensive and futile. Yet these 'aimless' wars of Henry VIII, whose absence of any coherent purpose has so often been remarked, were not a mere product of personal caprice: they corresponded precisely to a curious historical intermission, when the English monarchy had lost its old military importance in Europe but had not yet found the future maritime role awaiting it.

Nor were they without fundamental results in England itself. Henry VIII's last major act, his alliance with the Empire and attack on France in 1543, was to have fateful consequences for the whole ulterior destiny of the English monarchy. Military intervention on the continent was misconducted; its costs escalated greatly, eventually totalling some ten times those of the first French war of his reign; to cover them, the State not only resorted to forced loans and debasement of the coinage, but also started to unload on the market the huge fund of agrarian property it had just acquired from the monasteries – amounting to perhaps a quarter of the land of the realm. The sale of Church estates by the monarchy multiplied as war dragged on towards Henry's death. By the time peace was finally restored, the great bulk of this vast windfall was lost;[13] and with it, the one great chance of English Absolutism to build up a firm economic base independent of parliamentary taxation. This transfer of assets not only weakened the State in the long-run: it also greatly strengthened the gentry who formed the main purchasers of these lands, and whose numbers and wealth henceforward steadily grew. One of the drabbest and most inconsequential foreign wars in English history thus had momentous, if still hidden consequences on the domestic balance of forces within English society.

The dual facets of this final episode of Henrician rule, indeed, presaged much of the evolution of the English landowning class as a whole. For the military conflict of the 1540's was in practice the last aggressive war fought by England on the continent for the rest of the century. The illusions of Crécy and Agincourt died away. But the gradual disappearance of its traditional vocation profoundly altered the cast of the English nobility. The absence of the constraining pressure of constant potential invasion allowed the English aristocracy to dispense with a modernized apparatus of war in the epoch of the Renaissance; it was not directly endangered by rival feudal classes abroad, and it was reluctant – like any nobility at a comparable stage of its evolution – to submit to the massive build-up of royal power at home that was the logical consequence of a large standing army. In the isolationist context of the island kingdom, therefore, there was an exceptionally early demilitarization of the noble class itself. In 1500, every English peer bore arms; by Elizabeth's time, it has been calculated, only half the aristocracy had any fighting experience.[14] On the eve of the Civil War in the 17th century, very few nobles had any military background at all. There was a progressive *dissociation* of the nobility from the basic military function which defined it in the mediaeval social order, much earlier than anywhere else on the continent; and this necessarily had important repercussions on the landowning class itself. In the peculiar maritime context, derogation proper – always linked to an intense feeling for the virtues of the sword, and

13. By the end of the reign, two-thirds of the monastic domains had been alienated; income from sales of church lands averaged 30 per cent above rents from those retained. See F. Dietz, *English Government Finance 1485–1558*, London 1964, pp. 147, 149, 158, 214.

14. Stone, *The Crisis of the Aristocracy*, pp. 265–6.

codified against the temptations of the purse – never appeared. This in turn allowed a gradual conversion of the aristocracy to commercial activities long before any comparable rural class in Europe. The prevalence of wool-farming, which had been the growth sector in agriculture in the 15th century, naturally accelerated this drift greatly, while the rural cloth industry which was contiguous with it provided natural outlets for gentry investment. The economic path which led from the metamorphoses of feudal rent in the 14th and 15th centuries to the emergence of an expanding rural capitalist sector in the 17th century was thus laid open. Once it was taken, the legally separate character of the English nobility became virtually impossible to sustain.

During the later Middle Ages, England had experienced – in common with most other countries – a marked trend towards a formalized stratification of ranks within the aristocracy, with the introduction of new titles, after the original feudal hierarchy of vassals and liege-lords had been eroded by the onset of monetarized social relations and the dissolution of the classical fief system. Everywhere, new and more abundant tables of rank were felt necessary by the nobility, once personal dependences had generally declined. In England, the 14th and 15th centuries had seen the adoption of a series of novel grades – dukes, marquesses, barons and viscounts – within the nobility, which, with devices to ensure primogeniture of inheritance, for the first time separated out a distinct 'peerage' from the rest of the class.[15] This stratum henceforward always comprised the most powerful and opulent group within the aristocracy. At the same time, a College of Heralds was formed which gave legal definition to the gentry by confining it to armigerous families, and setting up procedures for investigating claims to this status. A tighter, two-tiered aristocratic order, legally demarcated from *roturiers* below it, thus might well have developed in

15. The transition from the early mediaeval baronage to the late mediaeval peerage, and the attendant evolution of knightage into a gentry, are traced by N. Denholm-Young, 'En Remontant le Passé de l'Aristocratie Anglaise: le Moyen Age', *Annales*, May 1937, pp. 257–69. (The title 'baron' itself acquired a new meaning as a patented rank in the late 14th century, distinct from its earlier use.) The consolidation of the peerage system is analyzed by K. B. Macfarlane, 'The English Nobility in the Later Middle Ages', *XIIth International Congress of Historical Sciences*, Vienna 1965, Rapports I, pp. 337–45, who stresses its novelty and discontinuity.

England, as it did elsewhere. But the increasingly non-military and proto-commercial bent of the whole nobility – stimulated by the land sales and agrarian boom of the Tudor epoch – rendered the concomitant of a derogation bar impossible.[16] The result was to render the strict armigerous criterion itself largely inoperative. Hence the peculiarity emerged whereby the social aristocracy in England did not coincide with the patented peerage, which was the only section of it with legal privileges, and untitled gentry and younger sons of peers could dominate a so-called House of Commons. The idiosyncrasies of the English landowning class in the epoch of Absolutism were thus to be historically interlocked: it was unusually civilian in background, commercial in occupation and commoner in rank. The correlate of this class was a State that had a small bureaucracy, a limited fiscality, and no permanent army. The inherent tendency of the Tudor monarchy was, as we have seen, strikingly homologous to that of its continental opposites (down to the personality parallels, often noted between Henry VII–Louis XI–Ferdinand II and Henry VIII–Francis I–Maximilian I): but the limits of its development were set by the character of the nobility that surrounded it.

The immediate legacy of Henry VIII's last incursion into France, meanwhile, was sharp popular distress in the countryside as monetary depreciation and fiscal pressures led to rural insecurity and a temporary commercial depression. The minority of Edward VI thus witnessed a swift regression in the political stability and authority of the Tudor State, with a predictable jockeying between the largest territorial lords for control of the court, in a decade punctuated by peasant unrest and religious crises. Rural risings in East Anglia and the South-West were crushed with hired Italian and German mercenaries.[17] But soon afterwards, in 1551, these professional troops were disbanded to relieve the exchequer: the last serious agrarian explosion for nearly three hundred years had been suppressed by the last major force of alien soldiery to be at the domestic disposal of the monarchy. Meanwhile, the rivalry

16. It should be borne in mind that the *loi de dérogeance* was itself a late Renaissance creation in France, which only dates from 1560. Such a legal measure was unnecessary as long as the function of the nobility was unambiguously military; like the graded titles themselves, it was a reaction to a new social mobility.

17. The government could not rely on the loyalty of the shire levies in this crisis: W. K. Jordan, *Edward VI: The Young King*, London 1968, p. 467.

between the Dukes of Somerset and Northumberland, with their respective patronage of lesser nobles, functionaries and men at arms, led to muffled coups and counter-coups in the Privy Council, amidst religious tension and dynastic uncertainty. The whole unity of the Tudor State apparatus seemed temporarily threatened. However, the danger of a real disintegration was not only cut short by the death of the young sovereign; it was unlikely ever to have developed into a full-blown facsimile of the aristocratic conflicts in France, because of the lack of client troops at the disposal of the contending magnates. The upshot of the interlude of rule by Somerset and Northumberland was merely to radicalize the local Reformation and fortify monarchical dignity against the greater nobles. The brief passage of Mary, with its dynastic subordination to Spain and ephemeral Catholic restoration, left little political trace. The last English toe-hold on the continent was lost with the French reconquest of Calais.

The long reign of Elizabeth in the latter half of the century thereafter largely restored and developed the domestic *status quo ante*, without any radical innovations. The religious pendulum swung back to a moderate Protestantism, with the establishment of a domesticated Anglican Church. Ideologically, royal authority was greatly enhanced, as the personal popularity of the queen rose to new heights. Institutionally, however, there was comparatively little development. The Privy Council was concentrated and stabilized under the long and steady secretaryship of Burghley in the first part of the reign. The espionage and police networks – mainly concerned with suppression of Catholic activity – were extended by Walsingham. Legislative activity was very reduced by comparison with Henry VIII's reign.[18] Factional rivalries within the higher nobility now mainly took the form of corridor intrigues for honours and offices at court. The final, guttering attempt at an armed magnate putsch – the rebellion at the end of the reign by Essex, the English Guise – was easily put down. On the other hand, the political influence and prosperity of the gentry – whom the Tudors had initially sponsored as a counter-weight to the peerage – was now an increasingly evident stumbling-block to the

18. See the comparative estimates of statutes made by Elton, in 'The Political Creed of Thomas Cromwell', *Transactions of the Royal Historical Society*, 1956, p. 81.

royal prerogative. Summoned thirteen times in forty-five years, largely because of external emergencies, Parliament now started to evince independent criticism of government policies. Over the century, the House of Commons grew greatly in size, from some 300 to 460 members, of whom the proportion of country gentlemen steadily increased, as borough seats were captured by rural squires or their patrons.[19] The moral dilapidation of the Church, after the secular dominance and doctrinal zigzags of the previous fifty years, permitted the gradual spread of an oppositional Puritanism among considerable sections of this class. The last years of Tudor rule were thus marked by a new recalcitrance and restiveness in Parliament, whose religious importunity and fiscal obstruction led Elizabeth to further sales of royal lands to minimize reliance on it. The coercive and bureaucratic machinery of the monarchy remained very slim, compared with its political prestige and executive authority. Above all, it had lacked the forcing-house of warfare on land which had speeded the development of Absolutism on the Continent.

The impact of Renaissance war, of course, by no means passed Elizabethan England by. Henry VIII's armies had remained hybrid and improvised in character, archaic aristocratic levies raised at home mingled with Flemish, Burgundian, Italian and 'Allmayne' mercenaries hired abroad.[20] The Elizabethan State, now confronted with real and constant foreign dangers in the epoch of Alva and Farnese, resorted to illegal stretching of the traditional militia system in England to assemble adequate forces for its overseas expeditions. Technically supposed to serve only as a home guard, some 12,000 or so were given special training and mostly kept for defense within the country. The remainder – often rounded up from the vagabond population – were empressed for use abroad. The development of this system did not produce a permanent or professional army, but it did provide regular troop-flows, on a modest scale, for the numerous foreign commitments of the Elizabethan government. The lords-lieutenant of the shires acquired greater importance as recruiting authorities; regimental organization

19. J. E. Neale, *The Elizabethan House of Commons*, London 1949, pp. 140, 147–8, 302.

20. C. Oman, *A History of the Art of War in the Sixteenth Century*, London 1937, pp. 288–90.

was slowly introduced, and fire-arms overcame native attachment to the long-bow.[21] The militia contingents themselves were typically combined with mercenary soldiers, Scots or Germans. No army sent to the continent ever numbered more than 20,000 – half the size of the last Henrician expedition; and most were considerably smaller. The performance of these corps, in the Netherlands or Normandy, was a generally bedraggled one. Their cost was disproportionately high in relation to their utility, discouraging any further evolution in the same direction.[22] The military inferiority of English Absolutism continued to preclude any expansionist goals on the mainland. Elizabethan foreign policy was thus largely confined to negative aims: prevention of Spanish reconquest of the United Provinces, prevention of French installation in the Low Countries, prevention of the victory of the League in France. In the event, these limited objectives were attained, although the role of English armies in the outcome of the tangled European conflicts of the period was very secondary. The decisive victory of England in the war with Spain lay elsewhere, in the defeat of the Armada: but it could not be capitalized on land. The lack of any positive continental strategy inevitably resulted in the wasteful and pointless diversions of the last decade of the century. The long Spanish war after 1588, which cost the English monarchy dearly in domestic wealth, ended without acquisitions of territory or treasure.

English Absolutism nevertheless achieved one major military conquest in this period. Elizabethan expansionism, incapable of frontal advance against the leading monarchies of the mainland, threw its largest armies against the poor and primitive clan society of Ireland. This Celtic island had remained the most archaic social formation in the West down to the end of the 16th century, perhaps in the whole continent. 'The last of the children of Europe',[23] in Bacon's phrase,

21. C. G. Cruickshank, *Elizabeth's Army*, Oxford 1966, pp. 12–13, 19–20, 24–30, 51–3, 285.

22. Cruickshank has suggested that the absence of an adult male sovereign, to command field troops in person, for nearly 60 years after Henry VIII, may have contributed to the failure of a regular army to emerge in this epoch: *Army Royal*, Oxford 1969, p. 189.

23. 'Ireland is the last *ex filiis Europae*, which hath been reclaimed from desolation and a desert (in many parts), to population and plantation; and from savage and barbarous customs, to humanity and civility.' *The Works of Francis Bacon*,

had lain outside the Roman world; had not been touched by the Germanic conquests; had been visited but not subdued by the Viking invasions. Christianized in the 6th century, its rudimentary clan system uniquely survived religious conversion without political centralization: the Church rather adapted to the local social order in this distant outpost of the faith, abandoning episcopal authority for communal monastic organization. Hereditary chiefs and optimates ruled over free peasants, grouped in extended kin units, and bound to them by ties of commendation. Pastoralism dominated the countryside. There was no central monarchy, and towns were non-existent, although a literary culture flourished during the 7th to 9th centuries – the nadir of the Dark Ages elsewhere – in the monastic communities. Repeated Scandinavian attacks during the 9th and 10th centuries disrupted both cultural life and clan localism in the island. Norse enclaves created the first towns in Ireland; under foreign pressure, a central royal authority eventually emerged in the interior to expel the Viking danger in the early 11th century. This precarious Irish high-kingship soon collapsed again into warring federations, incapable of resisting a more advanced invasion. In the later 12th century, the Angevin monarchy in England acquired the 'lordship' of Ireland from the Papacy, and Anglo-Norman baronial forces crossed over to subjugate and colonize the island. English feudalism, with its heavy cavalry and strong castles, gradually established formal control of most of the country, with the exception of the far North, over the next hundred years. But the density of Anglo-Norman settlement was never enough to stabilize its military success. In the later mediaeval period, while the energies of the English monarchy and nobility were overwhelmingly engaged in France, Irish clan society steadily recovered ground. The perimeter of English authority

London 1711, Vol. IV, p. 280. For further examples of the same colonial sentiments, see pp. 442–8. Bacon, like all his contemporaries, was keenly aware of the material profits to be derived from England's civilizing mission in Ireland: 'This I will say confidently, that if God bless this kingdom with peace and justice, no usurer is so sure in seventeen years space to double his principal, and interest upon interest, as that kingdom is within the same time to double the stock both of wealth and people. . . . It is not easy, no not upon the continent, to find such confluence of commodities, if the hand of man did join with the hand of nature.' pp. 280, 444. Note the clarity of the conception of Ireland as an alternative outlet for expansion to the continent.

shrank to the small Pale round Dublin, beyond which lay the scattered 'liberties' of territorial magnates of Anglo-Norman origin, now increasingly Gaelicized, surrounded in turn by the renascent Celtic chieftainries, whose zones of control covered most of the island again.[24]

The advent of the renovated Tudor State, at the turn of the early modern epoch, brought the first serious efforts to reassert and enforce English suzerainty over Ireland for a century. Henry VII dispatched his aid Poynings to break the autonomy of the local baronial Parliament in 1494–6. The potentate Kildare dynasty, closely intermarried with leading Gaelic families, nevertheless continued to wield predominant feudal power, accoutred with the dignity of Lord Deputy. Under Henry VIII, Cromwell's administration started to introduce more regular bureaucratic instruments of rule into the Pale: in 1534 Kildare was deposed, and a rebellion by his son crushed. In 1540, Henry VIII – having repudiated the Papacy, which had originally vested the English monarchy with the lordship of Ireland as a fief of Rome – assumed the new title of King of Ireland. In practice, however, most of the island remained outside any Tudor control – dominated either by 'Old Irish' chiefs or 'Old English' lords related to them, both faithful to Catholicism while England underwent the Reformation. Only two counties had been formed outside the Pale down to the time of Elizabeth. Fierce rebellions thereafter exploded – in 1559–66 (Ulster), in 1569–72 (Munster), and 1579–83 (Leinster and Munster), as the monarchy tried to impose its authority and install 'New English' plantations of Protestant colonists to re-settle the country. Finally, during the long war between England and Spain, an island-wide insurrection against Tudor oppression was launched in 1595 by the Ulster clan leader O'Neill, appealing to the Papacy and Spain for aid. Determined to achieve a conclusive settlement of the Irish problem, the Elizabethan regime mobilized the largest armies of the reign to reoccupy the island, and Anglicize the country once and for all. The guerrilla tactics adopted by the Irish were met by policies of ruthless extermination.[25] The war lasted nine years before all resistance was

24. For the situation by the early 16th century, see M. MacCurtain, *Tudor and Stuart Ireland*, Dublin 1972, pp. 1–5, 18, 39–41.

25. For some glimpses of the tactics used to reduce the Irish to submission, see C. Falls, *Elizabeth's Irish Wars*, London 1950, pp. 326–9, 341, 343, 345. The

pulverized by the English commander Mountjoy. By Elizabeth's death, Ireland was militarily annexed.

This signal operation, however, remained a solitary triumph of Tudor arms on land: won with the greatest exertions against a pre-feudal enemy, it was not repeatable in any other arena. The decisive strategic development of the time for the whole character of the English landed class and its State lay elsewhere – in the slow switch towards naval equipment and expansion in the 16th century. Towards 1500, the traditional Mediterranean division between the 'long' oar-powered galley built for war and the 'round' sail-driven cog used for trade, started to be superseded in Northern waters by the construction of large war-ships equipped with fire-arms.[26] In the new type of fighting vessels, sails were substituted for oars, and soldiers started to give way to guns. Henry VII, creating the first English dry-dock at Portsmouth in 1496, built two of these ships. It was Henry VIII, however, who was responsible for 'a sustained and unprecedented' expansion of English naval power;[27] he added 24 warships to the navy by purchase or con-struction in the first five years after his accession, quadrupling it in size. By the end of his reign, the English monarchy possessed 53 ships and a permanent Navy Board, created in 1546. The huge carracks of this phase, with their top-heavy castles and newly installed artillery, were still clumsy instruments. Sea battles continued to be essentially grappling-matches between troops on water; and in Henry VIII's final war, French galleys still held the initiative, attacking up the Solent. A new dock was built at Chatham during the reign of Edward VI, but there was otherwise a sharp decrease in Tudor maritime strength in the succeeding decades, when Spanish and Portuguese naval design moved ahead of English with the invention of the faster galleon. But from

---

English Fury in Ireland was probably just as lethal as the Spanish Fury in the Netherlands: in fact, there is little sign that it was ever restrained by the con-siderations which, for example, prevented Spain from destroying the Dutch dikes – a measure rejected as genocidal by Philip II's government: compare Parker, *The Army of Flanders and the Spanish Road*, pp. 134–5.

26. For this development, see Cipolla, *Guns and Sails in the Early Phase of European Expansion*, pp. 78–81; M. Lewis, *The Spanish Armada*, London 1960, pp. 61–80, who claims a perhaps doubtful English priority in it.

27. G. J. Marcus, *A Naval History of England*, I, *The Formative Centuries* London 1961, p. 30.

1579 onwards, Hawkins's tenure at the Navy Board saw a rapid expansion and modernization of the royal fleet: low-slung galleons were equipped with long-range cannon, making them into highly manoeuvrable gun-platforms, designed to sink enemy craft from maximum distance in a running battle. The onset of a seaborne war with Spain, long rehearsed by English piracy on the Main, demonstrated the technical superiority of these new ships. 'By 1588 Elizabeth I was mistress of the most powerful navy Europe had ever seen.'[28] The Armada was outshot by English demi-culverines, and scattered into the storm and mist. Insular security was assured, and the foundations of an imperial future laid.

The ultimate results of the new marine mastery won by England were to be two-fold. The substitution of naval for terrestrial warfare tended to specialize and segregate the practice of military violence, safely extruding it overseas. (The ships which carried it were, of course, floating prisons in which press-ganged labour was exploited with notorious cruelty.) At the same time, the naval focus of the ruling class was preeminently conducive to a commercial orientation. For while the Army always remained a single-purpose institution, the Navy was by its nature a dual instrument, bracketed not only on war, but on trade.[29] In fact, the bulk of the English fleets throughout the 16th century still remained merchant ships temporarily converted for battle by the addition of cannon, and capable of reverting to commerce afterwards. The State naturally promoted this adaptability by premia for merchant design that conformed to it. The Navy was thus to become not only the 'senior' instrument of the coercive apparatus of the English State, but an 'ambidextrous' one, with profound consequences for the nature of the governing class.[30] For although higher

28. Garrett Mattingly, *The Defeat of the Spanish Armada*, London 1959, p. 175.

29. Indeed, by the 18th century, when the Admiralty was the largest single spending department of the government, the Navy not only relied on the City to lobby for its budget; it had to bargain with it over whether mercantile or strategic interests should have precedence in determining the cruising routes of its squadrons. See Daniel Baugh, *British Naval Administration in the Age of Walpole*, Princeton 1965, p. 19.

30. Hintze commented laconically, and somewhat too simply: 'England in its insular safety needed no standing army, at least not of a continental size, but only a navy, which could serve the interests of trade and the aims of war; it therefore

per unit,[31] the total costs of naval construction and maintenance were far below those of a standing army: in the last decades of Elizabeth's reign, the ratio of expenditure was 1:3 on them. Yet the yields throughout the next centuries were to be far higher: the British colonial empire was to be the sum of them. The full harvest of this navalism was yet to be seen. But it was in large measure because of it that already by the 16th century, the landowning class could develop not in antagonism, but in unison, with mercantile capital in the ports and shires.

The extinction of the Tudor line in 1603, and the advent of the Stuart dynasty, created a fundamentally new political situation for the monarchy. For with the accession of James I, Scotland was for the first time joined in a personal union with England. Two radically distinct polities were now combined under the same ruling house. The Scottish impact on the pattern of English development appeared initially very slight, precisely because of the historical distance between the social formations; but in the long-run it was to prove critical for the fortunes of English Absolutism. Scotland, like Ireland, had remained a Celtic fastness beyond the bounds of Roman control. Receiving an admixture of Irish, Germanic and Scandinavian immigration in the Dark Ages, its variegated clannic map was subjected to a central royal authority, with jurisdiction over the whole country except for the North-West, in the 11th century. In the High Middle Ages the impingement of Anglo-Norman feudalism here too recast the shape of the indigenous political and social system: but whereas in Ireland, it took the form of a precarious military conquest that was soon awash with a Celtic reflux, in Scotland the native Canmore dynasty itself imported English settlers and institutions, promoting intermarriage with the nobility to the South and emulating the structures of the more

---

developed no absolutism.' He added in a characteristic phrase: 'Land power produces an organization that dominates the very body of the state itself and lends it a military form. Sea power is merely an armoured fist thrust out into the world beyond; it is not suitable for use against an "internal army".' *Gesammelte Abhandlungen*, I, pp. 59, 72. Hintze himself, a keen advocate of Wilhelmine naval imperialism before the First World War, had good reasons for his sharp attention to English maritime history.

31. Costs per man in the next century were twice as high on sea as on land; a navy also, of course, needed a much more advanced supply and maintenance industry. See Clark, *The Seventeenth Century*, p. 119.

advanced kingdom on the other side of the Border, with its castles, sheriffs, chamberlains and justiciars. The result was a much deeper and more thorough feudalization of Scottish society. Self-imposed 'Normanization' eliminated the old ethnic divisions of the country, and created a new line of linguistic and social demarcation between the Lowlands, where English speech came to stay, together with manors and fiefs, and the Highlands, where Gaelic remained the language of a backward clan pastoralism. Unlike the situation in Ireland, the purely Celtic sector was permanently reduced to a minority, confined to the North-West. During the later mediaeval period, the Scottish monarchy in general failed to consolidate royal discipline over its dominions. Mutual contamination between Lowland and Highland political patterns led to a semi-seigneurialization of Celtic clan leadership in the mountains, and clan infection of Scottish feudal organization on the plains.[32] Above all, constant frontier warfare with England repeatedly battered the royal State. In the anarchic conditions of the 14th and 15th centuries, amidst ceaseless border turmoil, barons seized hereditary control of sheriffdoms and set up private jurisdictions, magnates wrested provincial 'regalities' from the monarchy, and vassal kin-networks proliferated under both.

The successor Stuart dynasty, dogged by unstable minority and regency governments, was unable to make much headway against the endemic disorder of the country in the next hundred and fifty years, while Scotland became increasingly tied to diplomatic alliance with France, as a shield against English pressure. In the mid 16th century, outright French domination through a Guise regency provoked an aristocratic and popular xenophobia that provided much of the driving-power for the local Reformation: towns, lairds and nobles revolted against the French administration, whose lines of communication to the continent were cut by the English navy in 1560, ensuring the success of Scottish Protestantism. But the religious change, which henceforward set Scotland off from Ireland, did little to alter the political complexion of the country. The Gaelic Highlands, which alone remained loyal to Catholicism, became even wilder and more turbulent

32. For this process, see T. C. Smout, *A History of the Scottish People 1560–1830*, London 1969, pp. 44–7, which includes a socially acute survey of Scotland prior to the Reformation.

in the course of the century. While glass-paned country mansions were the new feature of Tudor landscape to the South, massively fortified castles continued to be constructed in the Border country and the Lowlands. Private armed feuds remained rife throughout the kingdom. It was not until the assumption of power by James VI himself, from 1587 onwards, that the Scottish monarchy seriously improved its position. James VI, employing a mixture of conciliation and coercion, developed a strong Privy Council, patronized and played off the great magnates against each other, created new peerages, gradually introduced bishops into the Church, increased the representation of smaller barons and burghs in the local Parliament, subordinated the latter by the creation of a closed steering committee (the 'Lords of Articles'), and pacified the border.[33] By the turn of the 17th century, Scotland was apparently a recomposed land. Its socio-political structure nevertheless remained in notable contrast to that of contemporary England. Population was thin – some 750,000; towns very few and small, ridden by pastors. The largest noble houses comprised territorial potentates of a type unknown in England – Hamilton, Huntly, Argyll, Angus – controlling huge areas of the country, with full regalian powers, military retinues, and dependent tenantries. Seigneurial lordships were widespread among the lesser baronage; justices of the peace cautiously sent out by the king had been nullified. The numerous class of small lairds was habituated to petty armed disputes. The depressed peasantry, released from serfdom in the 14th century, had never staged a major rebellion. Economically poor and culturally isolated, Scottish society was still heavily mediaeval in character; the Scottish State was little more secure than the English monarchy after Bosworth.

The Stuart dynasty, transplanted to England, nevertheless pursued the ideals of Absolutist royalty that were now the standard norms of courts all over Western Europe. James I, inured to a country where territorial magnates were a law to themselves and parliament was of little account, now found a realm where grandee militarism had been broken and failed to see that parliament, on the other hand, represented the central locus of noble power. The much more developed character of English society thus for a time made it appear delusively easier for him

33. G. Donaldson, *Scot and: James V to James VII*, Edinburgh 1971, pp. 215–28, 284–90.

to rule. The Jacobean regime, contemptuous and uncomprehending of Parliament, made no attempt to assuage the growing oppositional temper of the English gentry. An extravagant court was combined with an immobilist foreign policy, based on rapprochement with Spain: both equally unpopular with the bulk of the landowning class. Divine Right doctrines of monarchy were matched by High Church ritualism in religion. Prerogative justice was used against common law, sale of monopolies and offices against parliamentary refusal of taxation. The unwelcome trend of royal government in England, however, did not encounter similar resistance in Scotland or Ireland, where the local aristocracies were coaxed with calculating patronage by the King, and Ulster was colonized by a mass plantation from the Lowlands to ensure Protestant ascendancy. But by the end of the reign, the political position of the Stuart monarchy was dangerously isolated in its central kingdom. For the underlying social structure of England was sliding away from beneath it, as it sought to pursue institutional goals that were nearly everywhere being successfully accomplished on the Continent.

In the century after the dissolution of the monasteries, while the population of England doubled, the size of the nobility and gentry had trebled, and their share of national wealth increased more than proportionately, with a particularly notable climb in the early 17th century, when rent-rises overtook price increases, benefiting the whole landowning class: the net income of the gentry perhaps quadrupled in the century after 1530.[34] The triadic system of landlord, farmer and agricultural labourer – future archetype of the English countryside – was already emergent in the richer parts of rural England. At the same time, an unprecedented concentration of trade and manufactures had occurred in London, some seven to eight times larger in the reign of Charles I than that of Henry VIII, making it the most dominant capital city of any country in Europe by the 1630's. By the end of the century, England would already form something like a single internal market.[35] Agrarian and mercantile capitalism had thus registered more rapid advances than in any other nation except the Netherlands, and major

34. L. Stone, *The Causes of The English Revolution 1529–1642*, London 1972, pp. 72–5, 131. This work, admirable in its economy and synthesis, is far the best conspectus of the epoch.

35. E. J. Hobsbawm, 'The Crisis of the Seventeenth Century', in Aston (ed.), *Crisis in Europe 1560–1660*, London 1965, pp. 47–9.

swathes of the English aristocracy itself – peerage and gentry – had successfully adapted to it. The political refortification of a feudal State thus no longer corresponded to the social character of much of the class on which it would inevitably have to rest. Nor was there a compelling social danger from below to tighten the links between the monarchy and the gentry. Because there was no need for a large permanent army, the tax-level in England had remained remarkably low: perhaps a third to a quarter of that in France in the early 17th century.[36] Little of this fell on the rural masses, while the parish poor received a prudential charity from public funds. The result was a relative social peace in the countryside, after the agrarian unrest in the mid 16th century. The peasantry, moreover, was not only subject to a much lighter tax burden than elsewhere, but was more internally differentiated. With the gathering commercial impetus in the countryside, this stratification in turn made possible and profitable a virtual abandonment of demesne cultivation for leasing of land by the aristocracy and gentry. The result was the consolidation of a relatively well-off kulak stratum (yeomanry) and a large number of rural wage-labourers, side by side with the general peasant mass. The situation in the villages was thus a reasonably secure one for the nobility, which did not have to fear rural insurrections any longer, and therefore had no stake in a strong central coercive machine at the disposal of the State. At the same time, the low tax-level which contributed to this agrarian calm checked the emergence of any large bureaucracy erected to man the fiscal system. Since the aristocracy had assumed local administrative functions since the Middle Ages, the monarchy was always deprived of any professional regional apparatus. The Stuart drive for a developed Absolutism was thus very handicapped from the start.

In 1625, Charles I conscientiously, if in general ineptly, took up the work of constructing a more advanced Absolutism with the unpromising materials available. The variant auras of successive court administrations did not help the monarchy: the peculiar combination of Jacobean corruption and Caroline censoriousness – from Buckingham

---

36. Christopher Hill, *The Century of Revolution*, London 1961, p. 51. In 1628, Louis XIII derived revenues from Normandy equal to Charles I's total fiscal income from all England: L. Stone, in 'Discussion of Trevor-Roper's General Crisis', *Past and Present*, No. 18, November 1960, p. 32.

to Laud – proved especially jarring to many of the gentry.[37] The vagaries of its foreign policy also weakened it at the outset of the reign: English failure to intervene in the Thirty Years' War was compounded by an unnecessary and unsuccessful war with France, the confused inspiration of Buckingham. Once this episode was terminated, however, the general direction of dynastic policy became relatively coherent. Parliament, which had vigorously denounced the conduct of the war and the minister responsible for it, was dissolved indefinitely. In the succeeding decade of 'personal rule', the monarchy tended to draw closer to the higher nobility once again, reinvigorating the formal hierarchy of birth and rank within the aristocracy by conferring privileges on the peerage, now that the risk of magnate militarism in England was past. In the cities, monopolies and benefits were reserved for the topmost stratum of urban merchants, who formed the traditional municipal patriciates. The bulk of the gentry and the newer mercantile interests were excluded from the royal concert. The same preoccupations were evident in the episcopal reorganization of the Church effected under Charles I, which restored the discipline and morale of the clergy, at the cost of widening the religious distance between local ministers and squires. The successes of Stuart Absolutism, however, were largely confined to the ideological/clerical apparatus of the State, which under both James I and Charles I began to inculcate divine right and hieratic ritual. But the economic/bureaucratic apparatus remained subject to acute fiscal cramp. Parliament controlled the right to taxation proper, and from the earliest years of James I resisted every effort to bypass it. In Scotland, the dynasty could increase taxes virtually at will, especially on the towns, since there was no strong tradition of bargaining over grants in the Estates. In Ireland, Strafford's draconian administration reclaimed lands and

37. These aspects of Stuart rule provided much of the colour, but not the lines, of the growing political conflict of the early 17th century. They are evoked with great bravura by Trevor-Roper, in his powerful discussion of these years: *Historical Essays*, London 1952, pp. 130–45. It is a mistake, however, to think that the problems of the Stuart monarchy were ever soluble merely by greater political adroitness and competence, as he suggests. In practice, probably no Stuart error was as fateful as the improvident sale of lands by their Tudor predecessors. It was not the lack of signal personal abilities, but of institutional foundations, that prevented the consolidation of English Absolutism.

revenues from the carpetbagger gentry who had moved in after the Elizabethan conquest, and made the island for the first time a profitable source of income for the State.[38] But in England itself, where the central problem lay, no such remedies were feasible. Hampered by earlier Tudor profligacy with royal estates, Charles I resorted to every possible feudal and neo-feudal device in the quest for tax-revenues capable of sustaining an enlarged State machine beyond Parliamentary control: revival of wardship, fines for knighthood, use of purveyance, multiplication of monopolies, inflation of honours. It was in these years, especially, that sale of offices for the first time became a major source of royal income – 30–40 per cent – and simultaneously remuneration of office-holders a major share of State expenditure.[39] All these devices proved inadequate: their profusion only antagonized the landowning class, much of it gripped by Puritan aversion to the new court and church alike. Significantly, Charles I's final bid to create a serious fiscal base was an attempt to extend the one traditional defense tax which existed in England: the payment of ship money by ports for the maintenance of the Navy. Within a few years, it was sabotaged by the refusal of unpaid local JPs to operate it.

The selection of this scheme, and its fate, revealed *en creux* the elements which were missing for an English version of Versailles. Continental Absolutism was built on its armies. By a strange irony, insular Absolutism could only exist on its meagre revenues so long as it did not have to raise any army. For Parliament alone could provide the resources for one, and once summoned was soon certain to start dismantling Stuart authority. Yet for the same historical reasons, the rising political revolt against the monarchy in England possessed no ready instruments for an armed insurrection against it; gentry opposition even lacked any focus for a constitutional assault on the personal rule of the king, so long as there was no convocation of Parliament. The deadlock between the two antagonists was broken in Scotland. In 1638, Caroline clericalism, which had already threatened the Scots nobility with resumption of secularized church lands and tithes, finally

38. The significance of Strafford's regime in Dublin, and the reaction it provoked in the New English landlord class, are discussed in T. Ranger, 'Strafford in Ireland: a Revaluation', in Aston (ed.), *Crisis in Europe 1560–1660*, pp. 271–93.

39. G. Aylmer, *The King's Servants. The Civil Service of Charles I*, London 1961, p. 248.

provoked a religious upheaval by the imposition of an Anglicanized liturgy. The Scottish Estates united to reject this: and their Covenant against it acquired immediate material force. For in Scotland, the aristocracy and gentry were not demilitarized: the more archaic social structure of the original Stuart realm preserved the warlike bonds of a late mediaeval polity. The Covenant was able to field a formidable army to confront Charles I within a few months. Magnates and lairds rallied their tenantry in arms, burghs provided funds for the cause, mercenary veterans of the Thirty Years' War supplied professional officers. The command of an army backed by the peerage was entrusted to a general returned from Swedish service.[40] No comparable force could be raised by the monarchy in England. There was thus an underlying logic in the fact that it was the Scottish invasion of 1640 which finally put an end to Charles I's personal rule. English Absolutism paid the penalty for its lack of armour. Its deviation from the rules of the late feudal State only provided a negative confirmation of their necessity. Parliament, convoked *in extremis* by the king to deal with military defeat by the Scots, proceeded to erase every gain registered by the Stuart monarchy, proclaiming a return to a more pristine constitutional framework. A year later, Catholic rebellion erupted in Ireland.[41] The second weak link in the Stuart peace had snapped. The struggle to seize control over the English army that now had to be raised to suppress the Irish insurrection, drove Parliament and King into the Civil War. English Absolutism was brought to crisis by aristocratic particularism and clannic desperation on its periphery: forces that lay historically behind it. But it was felled at the centre by a commercialized gentry, a capitalist city, a commoner artisanate and yeomanry: forces pushing beyond it. Before it could reach the age of maturity, English Absolutism was cut off by a bourgeois revolution.

40. The colonels of the army were nobles, the captains were lairds, the rank-and-file were 'stout young ploughmen' serving as their tenants: Donaldson, *Scotland: James V to James VII*, pp. 100–2. Alexander Leslie, Commander of the Army of the Covenant, was a former Vasa governor of Stralsund and Frankfurt-on-Oder: with him and his colleagues, the European experience of the Thirty Years' War came home to Britain.

41. It is possible, although not certain, that Charles I may have unwittingly triggered the Old Irish rising in Ulster by his clandestine negotiations with Old English notables in Ireland in 1641: see A. Clarke, *The Old English in Ireland*, London 1966, pp. 227–9.

6

Italy

The Absolutist State arose in the era of the Renaissance. A great many of its essential techniques – both administrative and diplomatic – were pioneered in Italy. It is therefore necessary to ask: why did Italy itself never achieve a national Absolutism? It is clear, of course, that the universalist mediaeval institutions of the Papacy and the Empire acted to check the development of an orthodox territorial monarchy in both Italy and Germany. In Italy, the Papacy resisted any attempt at a territorial unification of the peninsula. However, this in itself would not necessarily have sufficed to block such an outcome. For the Papacy was notoriously weak for long periods. A strong French king such as Philippe Le Bel had no difficulty in dealing with it *manu militari*, by simple and obvious means – kidnapping at Anagni, captivity at Avignon. It was the absence of any such ascendant power in Italy which allowed the Papacy's political manoeuvres. The critical determinant of the failure to produce a national Absolutism should be sought elsewhere. It lies precisely in the premature development of *mercantile capital* in the North Italian cities, which prevented the emergence of a powerful reorganized *feudal* State at the national level. It was the wealth and vitality of the Lombard and Tuscan Communes which defeated the most serious effort to establish a unified feudal monarchy which could have provided the basis for a later Absolutism – Frederick II's attempt in the 13th century to extend his relatively advanced baronial State from its base in the South.

The Emperor had many assets for his projects. Southern Italy was the one part of Western Europe where a pyramidal feudal hierarchy, implanted by the Normans, had been combined with a strong Byzantine legacy of imperial autocracy. The Kingdom of Sicily had fallen into disrepair and confusion in the last years of Norman rule, when local barons had seized provincial powers and regal estates for themselves. Frederick II signalled his arrival in Southern Italy with the promulgation of the laws of Capua of 1220, which reasserted formidable centralized control of the *Regno*. Royal bailiffs replaced city mayors in the towns, key castles were repossessed from nobles, inheritance of fiefs was subjected to monarchical supervision, donations of demesne lands were cancelled, and feudal dues for the upkeep of a fleet were restored.[1] The Capuan laws were enforced at the point of the sword; they were completed a decade later by the Constitutions of Melfi (1231), which codified the legal and administrative system of the Kingdom, suppressing the last vestiges of urban autonomy and tightly constricting clerical lordships. Nobles, prelates and towns were subordinated to the monarchy by a sophisticated bureaucratic system, comprising a corps of royal justiciars who acted as both commissioners and judges in the provinces, working with written documents – officials who were revolved to prevent them becoming enmeshed in local seigneurial interests.[2] Castles were multiplied to intimidate rebellious cities or lords. The Muslim population of Western Sicily, which had held out in the mountains to become a constant thorn in the side of the Norman State, was conquered and resettled in Apulia: the Arab colony at Lucera henceforward provided Frederick with a unique force of professional Islamic troops for his campaigns in Italy. Economically, the *Regno* was no less rationally organized. Internal tolls were abolished, and a strict external customs service installed. State control of foreign trade in grain permitted large profits for the royal demesne, the greatest Sicilian wheat producer. Important commodity monopolies and increasingly regular land taxes yielded substantial fiscal revenues; a nominal gold coinage was even minted.[3] The solidity and prosperity of this Hohenstaufen fortress in the South allowed Frederick II to make a redoubtable bid to create a unitary Imperial State throughout the peninsula.

Claiming all Italy as his heritage, and rallying most of the feudal

1. G. Masson, *Frederick II of Hohenstaufen*, London 1957, pp. 77–82.
2. For the justiciars, see E. Kantorowicz, *Frederick the Second*, London 1931, pp. 272–9.
3. Masson, *Frederick II of Hohenstaufen*, pp. 165–70.

lords scattered through the North to his cause, the Emperor seized the Marche and invaded Lombardy. For a brief period, his ambitions seemed to be on the brink of realization: in 1239–40, Frederick fashioned a blue-print for the future administration of Italy as a single royal state, divided into provinces governed by vicars-general and captains-generals modelled on the Sicilian justiciars, appointed by the Emperor and selected from his Apulian entourage.[4] The shifting tides of war prevented any stabilization of this structure: but its logic and coherence were unmistakable. Even the final setbacks and death of the Emperor did not undo the Ghibelline cause. His son Manfred, without even legitimate birth or the imperial title, was soon able to restore the strategic dominance of Hohenstaufen power in the peninsula, routing the Florentine Guelfs at Montaperti; a few years later, his armies threatened to capture the Supreme Pontiff himself at Orvieto, in a move foreshadowing the future French *coup de main* at Anagni. Yet the temporary successes of the dynasty were to prove finally illusory: in the protracted Guelf-Ghibelline wars, the Hohenstaufen line was eventually defeated and destroyed.

The Papacy was the formal victor of this contest, clamorously orchestrating the struggle against the Imperial 'Anti-Christ' and his progeny. But the ideological and diplomatic role of successive popes – Alexander III, Innocent IV and Urban IV – in the attack on Hohen-staufen power in Italy, never corresponded to the real political or military strength of the Papacy. For a long time, the Holy See had lacked even the modest administrative resources of a mediaeval prince-dom: it was not until the 12th century, after the Investiture Conflict with the Empire in Germany, that the Papacy acquired a normal court machinery comparable to that of the secular states of the epoch, with the constitution of the *Curia Romana*.[5] Thereafter, Papal power followed curiously divergent paths, along its dual ecclesiastical and secular tracks. Within the universal Church itself, the Papacy gradually built up an autocratic, centralist authority whose prerogatives far surpassed those of any temporal monarchy of the epoch. The 'plenitude of power' accorded to the Pope was wholly unlimited by normal feudal constraints – estates or councils. Clerical benefices throughout

4. Kantorowicz, *Frederick the Second*, pp. 487–91.
5. G. Barraclough, *The Mediaeval Papacy*, London 1958, pp. 93–100.

Christendom came to be controlled by it; legal transactions were concentrated in its courts; a general income tax on the clergy was successfully imposed.[6] At the same time, however, the position of the Papacy
as an Italian State remained extremely weak and ineffectual. Enormous
efforts were invested by successive Popes in the attempt to consolidate
and expand the 'Patrimony of Peter' in Central Italy. But the mediaeval
Papacy failed to establish any secure or reliable control even of the
modest region under its nominal suzerainty. The small hill-towns of
Umbria and the Marche vigorously resisted Papal intervention in their
government, while the city of Rome itself was often troublesome or
disloyal.[7] No viable bureaucracy was created to administer the Papal
State, whose internal condition was consequently for long periods very
ragged and anarchic. The fiscal receipts of the Patrimony amounted to
a mere 10 per cent of the total income of the Papacy; the cost of
maintaining and protecting it was probably for most of the time much
greater than the revenues it yielded. The military service owed by
Papal subjects – towns and feudatories of the Pontifical territory – was
equally inadequate to cover the defense needs it involved.[8] Financially
and militarily, the Papal State as an Italian principality was a deficitary
unit. Arrayed alone against the *Regno* in the South, it had no chance.

The basic reason for the failure of the Hohenstaufen drive to unify
the peninsula lay elsewhere – in the decisive economic and social
superiority of Northern Italy, which had twice the population of the
South and the overwhelming majority of the productive urban centres
of trade and manufacture. The Kingdom of Sicily had only 3 towns
of over 20,000 inhabitants: the North had more than 20.[9] The cereal
exports which furnished the main wealth of the South were, in fact,
an indirect symptom of the commercial predominance of the North.
For it was the thriving Communes of Lombardy, Liguria and Tuscany
which imported grain because of their advanced division of labour and
demographic concentration, while the surpluses of the Mezzogiorno
were conversely the sign of a thinly settled countryside. The resources
of the Communes were thus always much greater than those the

6. Barraclough, *The Mediaeval Papacy*, pp. 120–6.
7. D. Waley, *The Papal State in the Thirteenth Century*, London 1961, pp. 68–
90, describes the nature and success of this urban recalcitrance.
8. Waley, *The Papal State in the Thirteenth Century*, pp. 273, 275, 295–6.
9. G. Procacci, *Storia degli Italiani*, I, Bari 1969, p. 34.

Emperor was able to mobilize in Italy, although they were often divided, while their very existence as autonomous city republics was menaced by the prospect of a unitary peninsular monarchy. The initial Hohenstaufen attempt to enforce Imperial sovereignty in Italy, Frederick I's descent across the Alps from Germany in the 12th century, had been resoundingly rebuffed by the Lombard League, with the great victory of its urban militias over Barbarossa's army at Legnano in 1160. With the transfer of the dynastic base of Hohenstaufen power from Germany to Sicily, and the implantation of Frederick II's centralized monarchy on South Italian soil, the danger to the Communes of royal and seigneurial absorption increased proportionately. Once again, it was essentially the Lombard cities, led by Milan, which frustrated the advance into the North of the Emperor, flanked by his feudal allies in Savoy and the Veneto. After his death, Manfred's recovery of the Ghibelline position was challenged most effectively in Tuscany. The Guelf bankers of Florence, exiled after Montaperti, were the financial architects of the final ruin of the Hohenstaufen cause. It was their massive loans – some 200,000 *livres tournois* were made available in all – which alone made possible the Angevin conquest of the *Regno*;[10] while at the battles of Benevento and Tagliacozzo, it was the Florentine cavalry which helped to give the French armies their winning margin. In the long struggle against the spectre of a unified Italian monarchy, the Papacy regularly supplied the anathemas; it was the Communes which provided the funds and – until the very end – most of the troops. The Lombard and Tuscan towns proved strong enough to stifle any territorial regroupment on a rural-feudal basis. On the other hand, they were inherently incapable of achieving any peninsular unification themselves: merchant capital had no possibility whatever of dominating a social formation of national dimensions at this date. Thus while the Lombard League could victoriously defend the North against Imperial invasions, it was not itself capable of conquering the feudal South: French knights had to launch the attack on the Kingdom of Sicily. Logically enough, it was not the Tuscan or

10. E. Jordan, *Les Origines de la Domination Angévine en Italie*, Paris 1909, II, pp. 547, 556. The Church had to pledge much of its fixed property in Rome as a collateral, to raise the necessary sums from Tuscan and Roman bankers for its French ally.

Lombard cities which inherited the South, but Angevin nobles – the necessary instrument of urban victory, who appropriated its fruits. Soon afterwards, the revolt of the Sicilian Vespers against French rule ended the integrity of the old *Regno* itself. The baronial territories of the South split apart between warring Angevin and Aragonese claimants in a confused mêlée, whose ultimate result was to finish off any further prospect of a Southern mastery of Italy. The Papacy, now a mere hostage to France, was deported to Avignon, evacuating the peninsula altogether for half a century.

The towns of the North and Centre were thus freed for their own, bewitching political and cultural development. The simultaneous eclipse of the Empire and the Papacy made Italy the weak link of Western feudalism: from the mid 14th century to the mid 16th century, the cities between the Alps and the Tiber lived out the revolutionary historical experience that men themselves termed a 'Renaissance' – the rebirth of the civilization of classical Antiquity, after the intervening darkness of the 'Middle Ages'. The radical reversal of time implied in these definitions, in contradiction of all evolutionary or religious chronology, has provided the foundation of the categoric structures of European historiography ever since: the age which posterity was to regard as a basic dividing-line of the past, itself drew the boundaries that separated it from its predecessors, and demarcated its remote from its immediate antecedence – a unique cultural achievement. No real sense of distance had separated the Middle Ages from Antiquity; it had always regarded the classical era simply as its own natural extension backwards into a still unredeemed, pre-Christian world. The Renaissance discovered itself with a new, intense consciousness of rupture and loss.[11] Antiquity was far in the past, cut off from it by all the obscurity

11. 'The Middle Ages had left antiquity unburied and alternately galvanized and exorcised its corpse. The Renaissance stood weeping at its grave and tried to resurrect its soul. And in one fatally auspicious moment it succeeded.' E. Panofsky, *Renaissance and Renascences in Western Art*, London 1970, p. 113 – the one great historical work on the rebirth of Antiquity, worthy of its subject. In general, the modern literature on the Italian Renaissance is curiously limited and flat: as if the very scale of its creations has tended to unnerve the historians who have approached it. The disproportion between the object and the studies of it is, of course, nowhere more evident than in the legacy of Marx and Engels themselves: always relatively indifferent to the visual arts (or music), neither of them were ever imaginatively engaged by the problems posed for historical material-

of the *medium aevum* between them, and yet far in advance of the crude barbarism which had prevailed throughout the supervening centuries. Petrarch's passionate call, at the threshold of the new age, proclaimed the vocation of the future: 'This slumber of forgetfulness will not last forever: after the darkness has been dispelled, our grandsons will be able to walk back into the pure radiance of the past.' The poignant awareness of a long break and relapse after the fall of Rome was combined with a fierce determination to achieve once more the paragon standard of the ancients. The recreation of the classical world was to be the superb innovation and ideal of the modern. The Italian Renaissance thus witnessed a deliberate revival and imitation of one civilization by another, across its entire range of civic and cultural life, without example or sequel in history. Roman law and Roman magistracies had already resurfaced in the later mediaeval communes: Quiritary property had everywhere left its stamp on the economic relations of the Italian towns, while Latinate consuls replaced episcopal authorities as their rulers. Plebeian tribunes soon provided the model for Captains of the People in the Italian cities. The advent of the Renaissance proper, bringing with it the new sciences of archaeology, epigraphy and textual criticism to illuminate the classical past, suddenly extended the remembrance and emulation of Antiquity on an enormous, explosive scale. Architecture, painting, sculpture, poetry, history, philosophy, political and military theory all vied to recover the liberty or beauty of works once consigned to oblivion. Alberti's churches were derived from his study of Vitruvius; Mantegna drew in emulation of Apelles; Piero di Cosimo painted panels inspired by Ovid; Petrarch's odes were based on Horace; Guicciardini learnt his irony from Tacitus; Ficino's spiritualism descended from Plotinus;

---

ism by the Renaissance as a total phenomenon. Panofsky's book is purely aesthetic in focus: the entire economic, social and political history of the period remains outside it. Its quality and method nevertheless set the appropriate protocols for the work that has still to be accomplished across this whole field. Above all, Panofsky took more seriously than any other scholar has done, the retrospective relationship of the Renaissance to Antiquity, through which the age conceived itself: the classical world is an active pole of real comparison, not merely a vaguely aromatic nomenclature, in his writing. In the absence of this dimension, the political and economic history of the Italian Renaissance has yet to be written with similar depth.

Machiavelli's discourses were a commentary on Livy, his dialogues on war an appeal to Vegetius.

The Renaissance civilization that resulted in Italy was of such iridescent vitality that it still seems a true repeal of that of Antiquity, the only one. Their common historical setting in city-state systems naturally provided the objective basis of the suggestive illusion of correspondent incarnations. The parallels between the urban flowering of classical Antiquity and the Italian Renaissance were striking enough. Both were originally the product of autonomous city-republics, composed of municipally-conscious citizens. Both were dominated at the outset by nobles, and in both the majority of the early citizenry owned landed property in the rural territory surrounding the city.[12] Both were, of course, intense centres of commodity exchange. The same sea provided the main commercial routes of each.[13] Both exacted military service from their citizens, cavalry or infantry according to property qualifications. Even some of the political singularites of the Greek *poleis* had their close counterpart in the Italian communes: the very high proportion of citizens who held temporary office in the State, or the use of sortition for selecting magistrates.[14] All these shared characteristics appeared to form a kind of partial super-imposition of one historical form on the other. In reality, of course, the whole socio-

12. D. Waley, *The Italian City-Republics*, London 1969, p. 24, reckons that in most towns of the later 13th century some ⅔ of the urban households owned land. It should be noted that this pattern was specifically Italian: neither the German nor Flemish towns of the same epoch contained comparable numbers of rural proprietors. Likewise, there was no real equivalent of the *contado* controlled by the cities of Lombardy and Tuscany, in Flanders or the Rhineland. The North European cities were always more exclusively urban in character. For a good discussion of the failure of the Flemish towns to annex their rural environment, see D. Nicholas, 'Towns and Countryside: Social and Economic Tensions in Fourteenth-Century Flanders', *Comparative Studies in Society and History*, X, No. 4, 1968, pp. 458–85.

13. Comparative costs were still massively weighted towards maritime transport. In the 15th century, cargoes could be shipped all the way from Genoa to Southampton for little more than a fifth of the price of lifting them by land the short distance from Geneva to Asti: J. Bernard, *Trade and Finance in the Middle Ages 900–1500*, London 1971, p. 46.

14. Waley, *The Italian City-Republics*, pp. 83–6, 63–4, 107–9, who estimates that perhaps a third of the citizens in a typical Italian commune held office in any given year.

economic natures of the Ancient and Renaissance city-states were profoundly different. Mediaeval towns were, as we have seen, urban enclaves within the feudal mode of production, structurally permitted by its parcellization of sovereignty; they essentially existed in dynamic *tension* with the countryside, where ancient cities were largely an emblematic *resumption* of it. The Italian towns started as market centres, dominated by petty nobles and populated with semi-peasants, often combining rural and urban occupations, cultivation with crafts. But they had rapidly assumed a pattern utterly distinct from their classical forebears. Merchants, bankers, manufacturers or lawyers came to form the patrician elite of the city-republics, while the basic mass of the citizenry were soon artisans – in polar contrast to ancient towns where the dominant class was always a landowning aristocracy, and the bulk of the citizenry were yeomen farmers or dispossessed plebeians, and where slaves constituted the great under-class of immediate producers excluded from citizenship altogether.[15] Mediaeval cities not merely and naturally made no use of slave-labour in domestic industry or agriculture:[16] they typically banned even serfdom within their precincts, too. The entire economic orientation of the two urban civilizations was thus in key respects antipodal. While both represented advanced focal points of commodity exchange, Italian towns were fundamentally centres of urban production, whose internal organization was based on craft guilds, while Ancient cities had always been primarily centres of consumption, articulated in clan or territorial

15. These social antitheses were first systematically discussed by Weber, *Economy and Society*, III, pp. 1340–3. Despite Weber's fluctuating grasp of the relationship between town and country in the Italian republics, the whole section entitled 'Ancient and Mediaeval Democracy', which concludes the work, remains the best and most original discussion of the question to this day. Subsequent advances in research have not on the whole been matched by comparable gains in synthesis.

16. The overseas colonies of Genoa and Venice in the Eastern Mediterranean did employ slave labour, on the sugar plantations of Crete or in the alum mines of Phocaea; and household servants were often slaves in these cities – mostly women, however, in contrast with those of Antiquity. In this sense, there was even a certain recrudescence of slavery; but it never acquired economic importance at home, within Italy. For the nature and limits of the phenomenon, see C. Verlinden, *The Beginnings of Modern Colonization*, Ithaca 1970, pp. 26–32.

associations.[17] The division of labour and technical level of manufacturing industries in the Renaissance cities – textile or metallurgical –
was consequently far more developed than that of Antiquity, as was
maritime transport. Mercantile and banking capital, always lamed in the
classical world by the absence of the necessary financial institutions to
ensure its secure accumulation, now expanded vigorously and freely
with the advent of the joint-stock company, bill of exchange and
double-account book-keeping: the device of the public debt, unknown
to ancient cities, increased both State revenues and investment outlets
for urban rentiers.

Above all, the completely distinct bases of slave and feudal modes of
production were evident in the diametrically opposite relations between
town and country in each. The cities of the classical world formed an
integral civic and economic unity with their rural milieu. The *municipia*
included indistinctly both the urban centre and its agrarian periphery,
and juridical citizenship was common to both. Slave labour linked the
productive system of each, and there was no specifically urban economic policy as such: the town essentially functioned simply as a consumer agglomeration for agrarian produce and landed rents. The
Italian cities, by contrast, were sharply separated from their countryside: the rural *contado* was typically a subject territory, whose inhabitants had no rights of citizenship in the polity. Its name, indeed,
came to furnish the familiar, contemptuous term for 'peasants' –
contadini. The communes customarily combated certain basic institutions of agrarian feudalism: vassalage was often expressly banned
within the towns, and serfdom was abolished in the countryside
controlled by them. At the same time, the Italian cities systematically
exploited their *contado* for urban profit and production, levying grain
and recruits from it, fixing prices and imposing meticulous crop
regulations and directives on the subjugated agricultural population.[18]
These anti-rural policies were part and parcel of the city-republics of
the Renaissance, whose economic *dirigisme* was quite foreign to their
predecessors of Antiquity. The fundamental means of expansion of the
classical town was warfare. Booty in treasure, land and labour were the
economic goals pursuable within the slave mode of production, and the

17. Weber, *Economy and Society*, III, pp. 1343–7.
18. Waley, *The Italian City-Republics*, pp. 93–5.

internal structure of the Greek and Roman cities largely followed from this: the military vocation of hoplites or *assidui* was central to their whole municipal constitution. Armed aggression was constant among the Italian communes, but it never acquired equivalent primacy. The State eluded a comparable military definition, because competition in trade and manufactures – escorted and enforced by extra-economic coercion, the 'protection costs' of the age[19] – had become an economic purpose of the community in its own right: markets and loans were more important than prisoners, plunder was secondary to engrossment. The cities of the Italian Renaissance, as their ultimate fate was to show, were complex commercial and industrial organisms, whose capacity as landed or even naval belligerents was to prove relatively limited.

These great socio-economic contrasts inevitably found their reflection within the cultural and political florescence in which the city-states of Antiquity and the Renaissance seemed to converge most closely. The free craft substructure of the Renaissance cities, where manual labour in the guilds was never tainted with servile social degradation, produced a civilization in which the plastic and visual arts of painting, sculpture and architecture occupied an absolutely predominant position. Sculptors and painters were themselves organized in artisan guilds, and initially enjoyed the median social position accorded to analogous trades: eventually, they were to attain an honour and prestige immeasurably greater than that of their Greek or Roman predecessors. The nine muses of the classical world had significantly omitted the visual arts altogether.[20] Sensuous imagination was the supreme domain of the Renaissance, yielding an artistic wealth and profusion that trumped Antiquity itself, as contemporaries themselves proudly became aware. On the other hand, the intellectual and theoretical achievements of Renaissance culture in Italy were much

19. The notion of 'protection rent' was developed by F. C. Lane, *Venice and History*, Baltimore 1966, pp. 373–428, to bring into relief the economic consequences of the characteristic fusion of warfare and business in the early trading and colonial ventures of the Italian city-states – both the aggressive raiding and piracy, and defensive guarding and convoying, which were inseparable from the commercial practice of the epoch.

20. Only music and poetry were admitted to their company, which otherwise decorated mainly what are today 'sciences' or 'humanities'. See the notable discussion of the changing order and definition of the arts in P. O. Kristeller, *Renaissance Thought*, II, New York 1965, pp. 168–89.

more restricted. Literature, philosophy and science – ranged in descending order of contribution – produced no body of works comparable to that of Ancient civilization. The slave basis of the classical world, divorcing manual from cerebral labour far more radically than mediaeval civilization had ever done, produced a leisured landed class remote from the *affairé* patriciate of the city-states of Italy. Words and numbers, in their abstraction, were more native to the classical universe: images took precedence at its rebirth. Literary and philosophical 'humanism', with its secular and scholarly enquiries, was always confined to a fragile and narrow intellectual elite during the Italian Renaissance;[21] science made its brief and isolated debut only in the aftermath. The aesthetic vitality of the towns had much deeper civic roots, and would survive them both: Galileo was to expire in solitude and silence, while Bernini emblazoned the capital and court that had disbarred him.

The political evolution of the Renaissance towns, however, diverged still more than their cultural configuration from that of their Ancient prototypes. Up to a certain point, there were marked formal analogies between the two. After the eviction of episcopal rule – a pre-history that might be compared with the overthrow of royal rule in Antiquity – the Italian towns were dominated by landed aristocrats. The resultant consular regimes soon gave way to oligarchic government with an external *podestà* system, which was then assailed by the more prosperous plebeian guilds, who created their own civic counter-institutions; while eventually the top stratum of guild-masters, notaries and merchants who led the struggle of the *popolo* coalesced with the urban nobility above them, to form a single municipal bloc of privilege and power, repressing or manipulating the artisan mass beneath them. The exact shape and composition of these struggles varied from city to city, and the political evolution of different towns might abridge or extend their sequence. In Venice, the mercantile patriciate confiscated

21. 'The two Germans who brought printing to Italy in 1465 and to Rome two years later, went bankrupt in 1471 simply because there was no market for their editions of the Latin classics. . . . Even when the Renaissance was its highest, its ideals were only intelligible to and cherished by a very small minority.' R. Weiss, *The Renaissance Discovery of Antiquity*, Oxford 1969, pp. 205–6. Gramsci, of course, was intensely seized with this defect of his country's cultural past: but like Marx and Engels before him, he had little plastic sensibility, and tended to see the Renaissance mainly or merely as a rarefied spiritual enlightenment.

the fruits of a craftsmen's rebellion against the old aristocracy very early on, and blocked any further political development by a rigid closure of its ranks: the *serrata* of 1297 checked any emergence of a *popolo*. In Florence, on the other hand, famished wage-earners, a miserable proletariat below the artisan class, revolted in their turn against a neo-conservative guild government in 1378, before being crushed. But in most of the cities, urban republics with extensive formal suffrages emerged, which were in fact ruled by restricted groups of bankers, manufacturers, merchants and landlords, whose common denominator was no longer birth but wealth, the possession of mobile or fixed capital. The Italian sequence of bishopric to consulate and *podesteria* to *popolo*, and the 'mixed' constitutional systems that were its outcome, is obviously reminiscent in some ways of the trajectory from monarchy to aristocracy and oligarchy to democracy or tribunate, and its complex results, in the classical world. But there was one clear and critical difference between the two orders of succession. In Antiquity, tyrannies had typically supervened between aristocratic and popular constitutions, as transitional systems for enlarging the social bases of the polity: they were a prelude to a wider franchise and freer agora. In the Renaissance, by contrast, tyrannies closed the whole parade of civic forms: the *signorie* were the last episode in the evolution of the city-republics, and signified their final fall to an aristocratic authoritarianism.

The ultimate upshot of the Ancient and Renaissance city-states, in fact, reveals perhaps more than anything else in their history the deep gulf between them. The municipal republics of the classical epoch could give birth to universal empires, without any basic break in their social continuity, because territorial expansionism was a natural prolongation of their agrarian and military bent. The countryside was always the incontestable axis of their existence: they were therefore in principle perfectly adapted to ever greater annexations of it, their economic growth resting on the successful conduct of war, which had always been a central civic purpose. Military conquest thus proved a comparatively straightforward gangway from republican to imperial states, and the latter could come to seem something like a predestined terminus. The Renaissance cities, on the other hand, were always fundamentally towns at variance with the countryside: their laws of motion were centred in the urban economy itself, whose relation to its rural environment was one of structural antagonism. The advent of the *signorie* – princely dictatorships with a pervasive agrarian background – thus ushered in no further cycle of major political or economic growth. Rather they concluded the fortunes of the Italian cities altogether. For the Renaissance republics had no chance of a career of imperial conquest and unification: precisely because they were so quintessentially urban, they could never reassemble and command whole feudal social formations, still massively dominated by the country. There was no economic passage for them to political aggrandisement on a peninsular scale. Moreover, their military forces were radically inadequate for such a task. The emergence of the *signoria* as an institutional form was a presage of their future impasse.

North and Central Italy formed an exceptional zone within the European economy of the later Middle Ages – the most advanced and thriving region in the West, as we have seen. The apogee of the Communes, in the 13th century, was an age of vigorous urban boom and demographic growth. This early lead gave Italy a peculiar position in the subsequent economic development of the continent. Like every other West European country, it was ravaged by the depopulation and depression of the 14th century: commercial regression and banking failures both cut back manufacturing output and probably stimulated building investment, diverting capital into sumptuary expenditure and real estate. The trajectory of the Italian economy in the 15th century is more obscure.[22] The drastic fall in output of woollen

22. Scholarly opinion is sharply divided on the problem of the overall economic balance-sheet of 15th century Italy. Lopez, supported by Miskimin, has argued that the Renaissance was essentially an epoch of depression: among other indices, the capital of the Medici Bank in mid 15th century Florence was only half that of the Peruzzi a hundred years earlier, while Genoese port dues in the early 16th century were still below those of the last decade of the 13th century. Cipolla has questioned the validity of general deductions from such evidence, and suggested that *per capita* production in Italy perhaps increased, together with the international division of labour. For the debate, see R. Lopez, 'Hard Times and Investment in Culture', reprinted in A. Molho (ed.), *Social and Economic Foundations of the Renaissance*, New York 1969, pp. 95–116; R. Lopez and H. Miskimin, 'The Economic Depression of the Renaissance', *Economic History Review*, XIV, No. 3, April 1962, pp. 408–26; C. Cipolla, 'Economic Depression of the Renaissance?', *Economic History Review*, XVI, No. 3, April 1964, pp. 519–24, with replies by Lopez and Miskimin, pp. 525–9. A more recent survey, covering the

textiles was now offset by a switch into production of silks, although the extent of the compensatory effects remains difficult to assess. A renewed growth in population and production may still have left overall levels of economic activity below the peak of the 13th century. Nevertheless, it seems probable that the city-states weathered the general crisis of European feudalism better than any other area in the West. The general resilience of the urban sector and the relative modernity of the agrarian sector, at least in Lombardy, perhaps allowed Northern Italy to recover economic impetus some half a century ahead of the rest of Western Europe, towards 1400. Now, however, the fastest demographic gains seem to have been located in the countryside rather than the towns, and capital investment tended to become increasingly oriented towards the land.[23] The quality of manufactures became increasingly sophisticated, with a shift into elite goods; the silk and glass industries were among the most dynamic sectors of urban production in this epoch. Moreover, for another hundred years thereafter, revived European demand sustained Italian luxury exports at high levels. Yet there were to be fatal limits to the commercial and industrial prosperity of the towns.

For the guild organization which set the Renaissance towns off from classical cities posed in its turn inherent restrictions to the development of capitalist industry in Italy. The craft corporations blocked the full separation of direct producers from the means of production that was the precondition of the capitalist mode of production as such, within the urban economy: they were defined by the persistent unity of the artisan and his tools, which could not be broken within this framework. The woollen textile industry, in certain advanced centres such as Florence, achieved to some extent a proto-factory organization based on wage-labour proper; but the norm in cloth manufactures always remained the putting-out system under the control of merchant capital. In sector after sector, craftsmen tightly grouped in guilds regulated their methods and tempo of work according to corporate traditions and

latter part of the 15th century and the early 16th century, presents a generally optimistic account of Italian trade, finance and manufactures: P. Laven, *Renaissance Italy 1464–1534*, London 1966, pp. 35–108.

23. C. M. Cipolla, 'The Trends in Italian Economic History in the Later Middle Ages', *Economic History Review*, II, No. 2, 1949, pp. 181–4.

customs, which presented formidable obstacles to progress in technique and exploitation. Venice developed the latest and most competitive woollen-cloth industry in Italy in the 16th century, when it captured markets from Florence and Milan – perhaps the most notable commercial success of the time. Yet even in Venice, craft corporations also eventually proved an insuperable barrier to technical progress: there too, 'it may be said that the entire body of guild legislation was aimed at preventing any sort of innovation.'[24] Manufacturing capital proper was thus held within a constricted space, with little possibility of enlarged reproduction: competition from freer, rurally-located industries abroad, with lower costs of production, would eventually ruin it. Mercantile capital flourished longer, because trade was subject to no such fetters; but it too eventually paid the penalty of relative technical inertia, when maritime dominance passed from Mediterranean to Atlantic shipping with the advent of faster and cheaper forms of sea-transport developed by the Dutch and English.[25] Banking capital maintained its profit levels longest of all, because it was most dissociated from the material processes of production. Yet its parasitic dependence on international courts and armies made it peculiarly vulnerable to their vicissitudes. The careers of Florence, Venice and Genoa – victims of English or French cloths, Portuguese or Anglo-Dutch shipping, and Spanish bankruptcies – were to illustrate these successive contingencies. The economic lead of the Renaissance towns of Italy proved a precarious one. At the same time, the political stabilization of the republican oligarchies which generally emerged from the struggles between the patriciates and guilds often proved difficult: the social resentments of the mass of artisans and city poor always remained just below the surface of municipal life, ready to explode again in new crises, whenever the established circle of the powerful became factionally divided.[26] Finally, the great growth in the

24. C. M. Cipolla, 'The Decline of Italy', *Economic History Review*, V, No. 2, 1952, p. 183. The guilds in the cloth export industries maintained high levels of quality and resisted wage-reductions: their fabrics were never modified to adapt to changing fashions. The result was that Italian draperies, expensive and old-fashioned, were ultimately outpriced and driven from the market.

25. F. Lane, 'Discussion', *Journal of Economic History*, XXIV, December 1964, No. 4, pp. 466–7.

26. The multiplication of inter-urban political contacts and rivalries also played

scale and intensity of war with the advent of field artillery and professional pike infantry rendered the modest defense capabilities of small city-states increasingly outmoded. The Italian republics became ever more militarily vulnerable as the size and fire-power of European armies in the early modern epoch developed. These conjoint strains, visible in different degrees at different times in the Northern and Central cities, set the stage for the rise of the *signorie*.

The social backdrop of these parvenu lordships over the towns lay in the feudal hinterlands of the countryside. The network of communes had never covered the North and Centre of the peninsula entirely; large rural interstices, dominated by seigneurial nobles, had always persisted between them. They had provided much of the aristocratic support for the Hohenstaufen campaigns against the Guelf towns, and the origin of the *signorie* can be traced back to the noble allies or lieutenants of Frederick II in the less urbanized regions of Saluzzo or the Veneto.[27] In the Romagna, the very expansion of communes into the countryside, by the creation of a subject *contado*, led to the conquest of the cities by rural lords whose territories were incorporated in them.[28] Most of the early tyrants throughout the North were feudatories or condottieri, who seized power through their tenure of the *podesteria* or *capitaneria* of the cities; in many cases, they enjoyed temporary popular sympathy because of their suppression of hated municipal oligarchies, or their restoration of civic order after endemic outbreaks of factional violence between the previous ruling families. Nearly always, they brought or created an enlarged military apparatus, better adapted to the modern necessities of war. Their provincial conquests then tended by themselves to increase the weight of the rural component of the city-states which they now governed.[29]

---

a major role in the emergence of the *signorie* in this epoch: 'All the *signorie* of North Italy, all without exception, are born with the direct or indirect aid of forces extraneous to the city which is the theatre of the new lordship.' E. Sestan, 'Le Origini delle Signorie Cittadine: Un Problema Storico Esaurito?', *Bollettino dell'Istituto Storico Italiano per il Medio Evo*, No. 73, 1961, p. 57. For the example of Florence, see below.

27. Jordan, *Les Origines de la Domination Angévine*, I, pp. 68–72, 274.
28. J. Larner, *The Lords of the Romagna*, London 1965, pp. 14–17, 76.
29. The contrast between the Italian and German cities is in this respect particularly striking in the 15th century. The Rhenish and Swabian towns never possessed, as we shall see, the rural periphery which distinguished their counter-

For the link of the *signorie* with the land from which they drew troops and revenues remained a close one, as the pattern of their spread testified. Originating in the more backward 'wings' of Northern Italy, along the Alpine passes in the West and the Po delta in the East, princely power moved to the sophisticated centre of the political scene with the Visconti capture of Milan – once the communal soul of the Lombard League – in the late 13th century. Milan thereafter always represented the most stable and powerful princedom of the major Italian cities, because of the specific internal composition of the State. It was neither a maritime port, nor a major manufacturing centre, its industries being numerous and prosperous but also small and fragmented; on the other hand, it possessed the most advanced agricultural zone in Italy, with the irrigated meadows of the Lombard plain, and one which was to resist the agrarian depression of the 14th century probably better than any other region in Europe. Milan, the most rural in wealth of the large Italian cities, was the natural spring-board for the first internationally significant *signoria* in the North. By the end of the 13th century, most of Italy above the Apennines had fallen to petty lords or military adventurers. Tuscany resisted for another hundred years, but in the course of the 15th century it too succumbed to gilded tyrannies. Florence, the greatest manufacturing and banking centre of the peninsula, eventually slid into the smooth hereditary fist of the Medici, although not without recidivist republican episodes: the diplomatic and military protection of the Sforza rulers of Milan,[30] and

---

parts in Lombardy or Tuscany. Their economic hinterland, on the other hand, contained a *mining* complex – silver, copper, tin, zinc and iron – of a type that was quite absent in Italy, and produced a metallurgical industry much more dynamic than anything south of the Alps. Thus while the Italian cities were rife with artistic creations, the German towns of this epoch were the scene of the greatest cluster of technical inventions in Europe: printing, ore-refining, smelting, ordnance, clock-making – virtually all the key technological advances of the age were pioneered or perfected in the milieu of the German cities.

30. The suave discretion of Cosimo de Medici's dominance of Florence, indirectly operated through electoral manipulation, corresponded to the comparative weakness of the social bases of the family's rule. Lorenzo only acceded to power peacefully because of the threat of Milanese intervention if he did not. For the original character of Medici primacy in Florence, and its support from Milan, see N. Rubinstein, *The Government of Florence under the Medici (1434–1494),* Oxford 1966, pp. 128–35, 161, 175.

later the pressure of Medici popes in Rome, was necessary to ensure the final victory of a princely regime in Florence. In Rome itself, the rule of the Della Rovere pope Julius II in the early 16th century for the first time pressed the political and military structure of the Papal State into a form close to that of the rival powers beyond the Tiber. Predictably, the two marine republics, Venice and Genoa, alone withstood the onset of the new type of court and prince – safeguarded by the relative lack of rural belts surrounding them. The Venetian *serrata*, however, produced a tiny hereditary clique of rulers that froze the political development of the city thereafter, and proved incapable of integrating the mainland possessions which the Republic came to acquire into any modern or unitary State.[31] The Genoese patriciate, mercenary and asocial, survived in the car of Hispanic imperialism. Everywhere else, most of the city-republics disappeared.

Culturally, of course, the Renaissance reached its apogee in this final act of Italian urban civilization, before what came to be seen as the new 'barbarian' invasions from the other side of the Alps and the Mediterranean. The princely and clerical patronage of the new and gorgeous courts of the peninsula invested lavishly in arts and letters: architecture, sculpture, painting, philology and history were all beneficiaries, in the conservatory warmth of an overtly aristocratic climate of erudition and etiquette. Economically, the creeping stagnation of technique and enterprise was concealed by the boom in the rest of Western Europe, which continued to expand demand for Italian luxury goods after domestic manufactures had ceased to innovate, and assured the ostentatious wealth of the *signorie*. But politically, the potential of these sub-regal states proved very limited. The mosaic of communes in the North and Centre had given way to a smaller number of consolidated urban tyrannies, which then engaged in constant wars and intrigues against each other to gain predominance in Italy. But none of the five major states in the peninsula – Milan, Florence, Venice, Rome and Naples – had the strength to overcome the others, or even to absorb the numerous lesser principalities and towns. The penning back of Gian Galeazzo Visconti into Lombardy, by the combined pressure of his foes at the turn of the 15th century, marked the end of the most successful bid for paramountcy. The ceaseless political and

31. See the perceptive comments in Procacci, *Storia degli Italiani*, I, pp. 144–7.

military rivalry between middle-strength states eventually reached a precarious equilibrium with the Treaty of Lodi in 1451. By that date, the Renaissance cities had already developed the basic instruments of secular state-craft and aggression which they were to bequeath to European Absolutism – a heritage whose enormous importance has already been seen. Fiscal impositions, funded debts, sale of offices, foreign embassies, espionage agencies – all these were pioneered in the Italian city-states, in a kind of reduced-scale rehearsal of the great international state-system and its conflicts to come.[32]

Nevertheless, the regime of the *signorie* could not alter the basic parameters of the deadlock in Italian political development that had set in after the defeat of the project of a unitary imperial monarchy in the Hohenstaufen epoch. The communes had been structurally incapable of achieving the unification of the peninsula, because of the very precocity of their urban-commercial development. The *signorie* represented a political reassertion of the rural and seigneurial circumambience within which they had always been inserted. But no real social victory of the countryside over the towns was ever possible in Northern and Central Italy: the attractive strength of the cities was much too great, while the local landowning class never formed a cohesive feudal nobility with an ancestral tradition or *esprit de corps*. The lords who usurped power in the republics were frequently mercenaries, upstarts or adventurers, while others were elevated bankers or merchants. The sovereignty of the *signoria* was consequently always in a deep sense illegitimate:[33] it rested on recent force and personal fraud, without any collective social sanction in aristocratic hierarchy or duty behind it. The new princedoms had extinguished the civic vitality of the republican towns; but they could not rely on the loyalty or discipline of a seigneuralized countryside. Thus despite their often apparently *outré* modernism of means and techniques, their famous inauguration of pure 'power politics' as such, the *signorie* were in fact inherently unable to generate the characteristic State form of the early modern epoch, a unitary royal Absolutism.

32. See Mattingly, *Renaissance Diplomacy*, pp. 58–60.
33. The degree and type of this illegitimacy varied, of course; in the Romagna, local tyrants had gradually acquired a certain dynastic normalcy by the 15th century: Larner, *The Lords of the Romagna*, pp. 78, 154.

It was the turbid historical experience of these lordships that produced the political theory of Machiavelli. Conventionally presented as the acme of modern *Realpolitik*, forecasting the practice of the secular monarchies of Absolutist Europe, it was in fact an idealized programme for an all-Italian, or perhaps merely Central Italian, *signoria*, on the eve of the historical supersession of this form.[34] Machiavelli's alert intelligence was aware of the distance between the dynastic States of Spain or France and the provincial tyrannies of Italy. He noted that the French monarchy was surrounded by a powerful aristocracy and based on a venerated legitimacy: its distinctive traits were the prominence of autonomous 'nobles' and traditional 'laws'. 'The king of France is surrounded by a time-honoured company of nobles, who are acknowledged and loved by their own subjects; they have their prerogatives, and the king cannot deprive them of these except at his own peril. . . . The kingdom of France is more regulated by laws than any other of which we have knowledge today.'[35] But he failed to comprehend that the strength of the new territorial monarchies lay in precisely this combination of a feudal nobility and constitutional legality; he believed the French *parlements* were merely a royal facade for the intimidation of the aristocracy and the placation of the masses.[36] For Machiavelli's aversion to aristocracy was so intense and general that he could declare a landed gentry incompatible with any stable or viable political order whatever: 'Those states whose political life remains uncorrupted do not permit any of their citizens to be gentry, or to live after the fashion of gentry. . . . To clarify the term, I will say that by "gentry" are meant those who live idly on the abundant incomes yielded by their estates, without playing any role in cultivation or performing any other tasks

34. Chabod, the most lucid authority, judges that Machiavelli envisaged merely the latter, a strong princedom in Central Italy rather than a peninsular State: *Scritti su Machiavelli*, Turin 1965, pp. 64–7.

35. Niccolò Machiavelli, *Il Principe e Discorsi sopra la Prima Deca de Tito Livio* (Introduction by Giuliano Procacci), Milan 1960, pp. 26, 262: the best recent edition.

36. *Il Principe e Discorsi*, pp. 77–8. Machiavelli's comprehension of the nature and role of the French nobility was, in fact, ultimately insecure and confused. In his *Ritratto di Cose di Francia*, he describes the French aristocracy as 'utterly compliant' (*ossequentissimi*) with the monarchy, in complete contradiction to his later remarks cited above. See *Arte della Guerra e Scritti Politici Minori*, Milan 1961, p. 164.

necessary to life. Such men are pernicious in any republic and in any province; but still more maleficent are those who, in addition to the rents from their estates, control castles and command subjects who obey them. . . . Men of this stamp are wholly inimical to any form of civic government.'[37] Wistfully glancing at the German cities that had no seigneurial periphery at all,[38] he kept a certain nostalgic republicanism, compounded of fading memories of the Republic of Soderini that he had served, and of antiquarian reverence for the heroic age of Rome recorded by Livy.

But Machiavelli's republicanism in the *Discourses* was at bottom sentimental and occasional. For all political regimes were dominated by a small inner circle of power: 'In all states, whatever their type of government, the real rulers are never more than forty or fifty citizens.'[39] The great mass of the population below this elite cared only for its own safety: 'the overwhelming majority of those who demand freedom, merely desire to live in security.' Successful government could always suppress traditional liberties, so long as it left the property and family of its subjects intact; it should, if anything, seek to promote their economic enterprises, since these would contribute to its own resources. 'A prince can always inspire fear yet avoid hatred if he abstains from the property of his subjects and citizens and from their women.'[40] These maxims were indifferently true of any political system – principality or republic. Republican constitutions, however, were adapted only for endurance: they could preserve an existent polity, but not inaugurate a new one.[41] To found an Italian State capable of resisting the barbarian invaders from France, Switzerland and Spain, the concentrated will and ruthless energy of a single prince was necessary. Machiavelli's real passion lay here. His prescriptions were essentially addressed to the future architect of a – necessarily *parvenu* – peninsular lordship. The *Prince* declares at the outset that it will examine the two types of principality, 'hereditary' and 'new', and it never quite loses sight of the distinction between them. But the burning preoccupation of the treatise, which dominates its actual content throughout, is essentially the creation of a new princedom, a task which Machiavelli ends by expressly pronouncing to be the greatest

---

37. *Il Principe e Discorsi*, p. 256.   38. *Ibid.*, pp. 255–6.
39. *Ibid.*, p. 176.   40. *Ibid.*, p. 70.   41. *Ibid.*, p. 265.

achievement of any ruler: 'A new prince, if he carefully observes the lessons set out above, will take on the appearance of a traditional ruler and his government will soon become safer and firmer than if he had been long entrenched in it. For the deeds of a new prince attract much more notice than those of a hereditary ruler; and when his actions are of valour, they captivate and bind men far more than royal blood. . . . The new Prince will have a two-fold glory.'[42]

This covert imbalance of focus is evident throughout the book. Thus Machiavelli states that the two main foundations of government are 'good laws' and 'good arms'; but he promptly adds that since coercion creates legality, and not vice-versa, he will consider only coercion. 'The main foundations of every state – new or ancient or composite – are good laws and good arms; and since there cannot be good laws without good arms, and where there are good arms there must be good laws, I will not consider laws but speak of arms.'[43] In perhaps the most famous passage of the *Prince*, he repeats the same revealing conceptual slide. Law and force are the respective modes of conduct natural to men and beasts, he asserts, and a prince should be a 'centaur', combining both. But in practice the princely 'combination' he discusses is not that of the centaur, half-man and half-beast, but – by immediate slippage – that of two beasts, the 'lion' and the 'fox' – force and fraud. 'There are two ways of fighting: by law or by force. The first is proper to men, and the second to beasts; but as the first way is often inadequate, recourse is necessary to the second. Thus a prince must know how to make good use of the beast and the man. The ancient writers instructed princes in this lesson by an allegory: they told how Achilles and many other rulers of antiquity were given in infancy to the centaur, Chiron, to be reared and trained by him. The meaning of this story of a teacher who is half beast and half man, is that a prince must acquire the nature of both; if he possesses the qualities of one without the other, he will be lost. Therefore, as a prince is obliged to know how to act like a beast, he should learn from the fox and the

42. *Il Principe e Discorsi*, p. 97. Compare the tone here with Bodin: 'He who on his own authority makes himself a sovereign prince, without election, hereditary right, sortition, just war or special divine calling, is a tyrant.' Such a ruler 'tramples on the laws of nature'. *Les Six Livres de la République*, pp. 218, 211.

43. *Il Principe e Discorsi*, p. 53.

lion. . . .'[44] For fear is always preferable to affection in subjects; violence and deception are superior to legality in controlling them. 'One can say this in general of men: they are ungrateful, disloyal, insincere and deceitful, timid of danger and avid of profit. . . . Love is a bond of obligation which these miserable creatures break whenever it suits them to do so; but fear holds them fast by a dread of punishment that never passes.'[45]

These summary precepts were, in effect, the house rules of the petty tyrannies of Italy: they were remote from the realities of the much more complex ideological and political structure of class power in the new monarchies of Western Europe. Machiavelli had little understanding of the immense historical strength of dynastic *legitimacy*, in which emergent Absolutism was rooted. His world was that of the transient adventurers and upstart tyrants of the Italian *signorie*; his cynosure Cesare Borgia. The result of the studied 'illegitimism' of Machiavelli's outlook was his famous 'technicism', the advocacy of morally unsanctioned means for the attainment of conventional political ends, dissociated from ethical restraints and imperatives. The conduct of a Prince could only be a catalogue of perfidy and crime, once all stable juridical and social bases of dominion were dissolved, aristocratic solidarity and fealty annulled. To later epochs, this stripping away of feudal or religious ideology from the practical exercise of power, seemed to be the secret, and greatness, of Machiavelli's modernity.[46] But in fact his political theory, apparently so modern in its intention of clinical rationality, significantly lacked any secure, objective concept of the *State* at all. There is a constant wavering of vocabulary in his writings, in which the terms *città*, *governo*, *republica* or *stato* alternate uncertainly, but all tend to become subordinate to the notion which gave its name to his central work – *principe*, the 'prince' who could be master either of a 'republic' or a 'principality'.[47]

44. *Il Principe e Discorsi*, p. 72.   45. *Il Principe e Discorsi*, pp. 69–70.
46. Nor, of course, were they wrong. It was in a sense precisely Machiavelli's lack of mooring in the mainswell of his own historical epoch which produced a political work of more general and perennial moment, after it had passed.
47. For examples, see *Il Principe e Discorsi*, pp. 129–31; 309–11; 355–7. See Chabod's comments in 'Alcuni Questioni di Terminologia: Stato, Nazione, Patria nel Linguaggio del Cinquecento', *L'Idea di Nazione*, Bari 1967, pp. 145–53.

Machiavelli never fully separated the personal ruler who could in principle parachute anywhere at will (Cesare Borgia or his counter-parts) and the impersonal structure of a political order with territorial fixity.[48] The functional inter-connection between the two in the age of Absolutism was real enough: but Machiavelli, by failing to grasp the necessary social bond between monarchy and nobility which mediated it, tended to reduce his notion of the State simply to that of the passive property of the individual prince, accessory ornament of his will. The consequence of this voluntarism was the curious, central paradox of Machiavelli's work – his constant denunciation of mercenaries and strenuous advocacy of an urban militia as the only military organization capable of executing the projects of a strong Prince, who could be the author of a new Italy. This is the theme of the vibrant closing call of his most celebrated work, addressed to the Medici. 'Mercenaries and auxiliaries are useless and dangerous . . . they have led Italy into slavery and ignominy' – 'therefore if your illustrious House wants to emulate those celebrated men who saved their countries, it must before all else raise its own army.'[49] Machiavelli was later to devote the *Art of War* to arguing out his military case for a citizen army again at full length, buttressed with all the examples of Antiquity.

Machiavelli believed mercenaries to be the bane of Italian political weakness; and as Secretary of the Republic, he had himself tried to arm local peasants to defend Florence. In fact, of course, mercenaries were the precondition of the new royal armies beyond the Alps, while his neo-communal militia were routed by regular troops with the greatest of ease.[50] The reason for his military error, however, went to the core of his political tenets. For Machiavelli confused the European *mercenary*

48. There are a few, fleeting passages in Machiavelli which indicate an aware-ness of the limits of his dominant conception of the state: 'Governments erected in haste, like everything else in nature that is born and grows too quickly, lack firm roots and ramifications, and can be overturned by the first squall.' *Il Principe e Discorsi*, p. 34. Procacci, in his able introduction, makes considerable play of the terms *barbe e correspondenzie* (roots and ramifications), as evidence that Machiavelli did possess an objective notion of the princely state (*Intro-duzione*, pp. L ff). But what is actually most striking about this germane phrase is its general absence of consequences or echoes in *The Prince* as a whole.

49. *Il Principe e Discorsi*, pp. 53, 58, 104.

50. For this episode, see Oman, *A History of War in the Sixteenth Century*, pp. 96–7.

with the Italian *condottieri* system: the difference was precisely that the *condottieri* in Italy owned their troops, auctioning them and switching them from side to side in local wars, while royal rulers beyond the Alps formed or contracted mercenary corps directly under their own control, to constitute the forerunner of permanent, professional armies. It was the combination of Machiavelli's concept of the State as the adventitious property of the Prince, with his acceptance of adventurers as princes, that misled him into thinking the volatile *condottieri* were typical of mercenary warfare in Europe. What he failed to see was the power of dynastic authority, rooted in a feudal nobility, which rendered the use of household mercenary troops not only safe, but superior to any other military system then available. The logical incongruity of a citizen militia under a usurper tyranny, as a formula for the liberation of Italy, was merely a desperate sign of the historical impossibility of a peninsular *signoria*. Beyond it, there remained only the banal recipes of deceit and ferocity that came to bear the name of Machiavellianism.[51] These counsels of the Florentine Secretary were merely a theory of political weakness: their technicism was an unseeing empiricism, incapable of identifying the deeper social causes of the events which it recorded, and confined to a vain surface manipulation of them, mephistophelean and utopian.

Machiavelli's work thus fundamentally reflected, in its inner structure, the final impasse of the Italian city-states, on the eve of their absorption. It remains the best guide to their eventual end. In Prussia and Russia, as will be seen, a super-Absolutism emerged above a void of towns. In Italy, and in Germany west of the Elbe, the density of towns produced a kind of 'micro-absolutism' only – a proliferation of petty princedoms that crystallized the divisions of the country. These miniature States were in no position to resist neighbouring feudal monarchies, and the peninsula was soon forcibly aligned with European norms by foreign conquerors. France and Spain joined issue

---

51. This aspect of Machiavelli's work, which gave rise to his sensational 'legend' for subsequent centuries, is generally glided over by his more serious commentators today, as of little intellectual interest. In fact, it is conceptually inseparable from the theoretical structure of his work, and cannot be urbanely ignored: it is the necessary and logical residue of his thought. Much the best and most forceful discussion of the real meaning of 'machiavellianism' is by Georges Mounin, *Machiavel*, Paris 1966, pp. 202–12.

for its control within the first decades of their respective political integration, in the last years of the 15th century. Unable to produce a national Absolutism from within, Italy was condemned to suffer an alien one from without. In the half century between Charles VIII's march to Naples in 1494 and the defeat of Henri II at Saint Quentin in 1557, the Valois were checked by the Habsburgs and the prize fell to Spain. Henceforward, Spanish rule, anchored in Sicily, Naples and Milan, coordinated the Peninsula and domesticated the Papacy under the banner of the Counter-Reformation. Paradoxically, it was the economic advance of Northern Italy that condemned it to a long cycle of political backwardness thereafterwards. The eventual result, once Habsburg power had been consolidated, was economic retrogression too: a ruralization of the urban patriciates, which in their decadence abandoned finance or manufactures for investment in land. Hence the 'hundred cities of silence', to which Gramsci was to advert again and again.[52] By a curious compression of historical epochs, it was ultimately to be the Piedmontese monarchy which achieved national unification, in the era of bourgeois revolutions in the West. In fact,

---

52. *Passato e Presente*, p. 98; *Note sul Machiavelli*, p. 7; *Il Risorgimento*, p. 95. The phrase was borrowed from D'Annunzio's poem-cycle. Gramsci's analyses of the problem of Italian unity in the Renaissance, with which he was profoundly concerned, suffer from an implicit assumption that the new European monarchies which were unifying France, England and Spain, were bourgeois in character (or at least balanced between bourgeoisie and aristocracy). He thus tends illegitimately to telescope the two distinct historical problems of the absence of a unitary Absolutism in the Renaissance and the subsequent lack of a radical democratic revolution in the Risorgimento. Both become the evidence of a failure of the Italian bourgeoisie, the first because of the corporatism and involution of the Communes in the later mediaeval and early modern epoch, the second because of the collusion of the Moderates with the Southern latifundists in the 19th century. In fact, as we have seen, the truth is the opposite. It was the absence of a dominant *feudal nobility* that prevented a peninsular Absolutism and hence a unitary state coeval with that of France or Spain; and it was the regional presence of such a nobility in Piedmont that permitted the creation of a State that would provide the trampolin for a belated unification in the era of industrial capitalism. Gramsci's misapprehension largely reflects his reliance on Machiavelli as the central prism through which he viewed the Renaissance, and his belief that Machiavelli represented a 'precocious Jacobinism' (see especially *Note sul Machiavelli*, pp. 6–7, 14–16). For Machiavelli, in his own epoch, confused two distinct historical times – imagining that an Italian Prince could form a powerful autocratic state by recreating the citizen militias typical of the 12th century Communes, long since dead in his day.

Piedmont provided the logical base for this unification: for there alone a rigorous and indigenous Absolutism emerged, squarely founded on a feudal nobility in a social formation dominated by serfdom. The State constructed by Emanuele Filiberto and Carlo Emanuele in Savoy was economically rudimentary by comparison with Venice or Milan; precisely for that reason it proved to be the only territorial nucleus capable of later political advance.

Its geographical position astride the Alps was critical for this exceptional destiny. For it meant that for three centuries, Savoy could maintain its autonomy and enlarge its borders, by playing off the two major powers of the continent against each other – first France against Spain, then Austria against France. In 1460, on the eve of the foreign invasions which were to close the Renaissance, Piedmont was the only independent state in Italy with an influential Estates system[53] – precisely, of course, because it was perhaps the most feudal social formation in the peninsula. The Estates were organized in a conventional three-curia system dominated by the nobility. The revenues of the ruling dukes were small and their authority limited, although the clergy, who owned a third of the land, were generally their allies. The Estates refused to grant subsidies for a permanent army. Then, in the 1530's, French and Spanish troops occupied the Western and Eastern parts of Piedmont respectively. In the French zone, the Estates were maintained as provincial *états* of the Valois realm, while in the Spanish they were suppressed from 1555 onwards. The French administration reorganized and modernized the archaic local polity; the beneficiary of their work was Duke Emanuele Filiberto. Educated in Spain and combatant in Flanders, this Habsburg ally and victor of Saint-Quentin regained the whole of his patrimony in 1559 with the Treaty of Cateau-Cambrésis. The vigorous and authoritarian Duke, *Testa di Ferro* to his contemporaries, summoned the Estates for the last time in 1560, raised a large grant for a standing army of 24,000, and then dismissed them for ever. Thereafter, the institutional innovations of thirty years of Valois rule were preserved and developed: executive Council of State,

53. Together with Sicily – which predictably was the other region with a powerful estates system, but was now part of the realm of Aragon: H. G. Koenigsberger, 'The Parliament of Piedmont during the Renaissance, 1640–1560', *Studies Presented to the International Commission for the History of Representative and Parliamentary Institutions*, IX, Louvain 1952, p. 70.

judicial parlements, royal *lettere di giussione* (i.e. *lits de justice*), unitary legal code, single coinage and a reorganized exchequer, sumptuary legislation. Quintupling his revenues, Emanuele Filiberto created a new and loyal court nobility by astute distribution of titles and offices. Under the rule of a Duke who was one of the first rulers in Europe to proclaim himself freed from all legislative restraints – *Noi, come principi, siamo da ogni legge sciolti e liberi*[54] – Piedmont travelled rapidly towards an early princely centralization.

Henceforward the Piedmontese dynasty always tended to borrow the political forms and mechanics of French Absolutism, while resisting its territorial absorption into it. The 17th century, however, witnessed prolonged relapses into anarchic civil wars and noble feuds under weak rulers, graver and longer echoes of the Fronde. The multiple enclaves and uncertain frontiers of the State in a buffer region of Europe hampered firm ducal control of the Alpine uplands. Advance towards a centralized Absolutism was decisively resumed by Vittorio Emanuele II in the early 18th century. A skilful switch of sides in the War of the Spanish Succession, from France to Austria, secured Piedmont the county of Montferrat and the island of Sardinia, and European acknowledgment of its elevation from duchy to monarchy. Sinuous in war, Vittorio Emanuele used the succeeding peace to install a rigid administration modelled on that of Colbert, complete with Council and *intendant* system. He then de-enfiefed large tracts of noble land by a new cadastral register – the *perequazione* of 1731 – thereby increasing fiscal revenues, since allodial estates were liable for tax;[55] built up a

54. 'We, as a prince, are of all laws unbound and freed': the ducal claim was, of course, a direct rendition of the famous Roman maxim. For an account of Emanuele Filiberto's reforms in Piedmont, see Vittorio de Caprariis, 'L'Italia nell'Età della Controriforma', in Nino Valeri (ed.), *Storia d'Italia*, II, Turin 1965, pp. 526–30.

55. The *perequazione* is discussed in S. J. Woolf, *Studi sulla Nobiltà Piemontese nell'Epoca dell'Assolutismo*, Turin 1963, pp. 69–75. The significance of this move for the general history of Absolutism is clear. In a mediaeval polity, where there was no central tax system, a ruler's economic interest was to multiply the number of fiefs – which owed military service and feudal incidents – and reduce the number of allods, with their unconditional tenures and hence absence of obligations to any feudal superior. With the advent of a centralized fiscal system, the situation was reversed: fiefs fell outside the tax assessments, because they owed a military service that was now merely token, while allodial estates could be put under levy like urban or peasant properties. In Prussia at virtually the same time

large military and diplomatic establishment into which the aristocracy was integrated; eliminated clerical immunities and subordinated the Church; and prosecuted a vigorous protectionist mercantilism, including the development of roads and canals, promotion of export manufactures, and construction of an aggrandized capital at Turin. His successor, Carlo Emanuele III, deftly allied with France against Austria in the War of the Polish Succession, to gain part of the Lombard plain, and then with Austria against France in the War of the Austrian Succession, to keep it. Piedmontese Absolutism was thus one of the most coherent and successful of the epoch. Like the two other Southern experiments of a strong, modernized Absolutism in small states – Tanucci's regime in Naples and Pombal's in Portugal – it was chronologically lagged: its creative peak was in the 18th, not the 17th century. But its pattern was otherwise closely similar to that of its larger mentors. Indeed, by the time of its apogee, Piedmontese Absolutism was spending proportionately more on its army, a skilled professional corps, than perhaps any other state in Western Europe.[56] This aristocratic military apparatus was to be a gage for the future.

Frederick William I introduced in 1717 a similar reform to 'commute' knight service for a tax, by converting feudal into allodial property, thus in effect ending the fiscal immunity of the nobility. The measure aroused a storm of junker indignation.

56. G. Quazza, *Le Riforme in Piemonte nella Prima Metà del Settecento*, Modena 1957, pp. 103–6. Quazza thinks it probable that only Prussia equalled or surpassed Piedmont in military expenditures in this century.

7

Sweden

The sudden ascent of a Swedish Absolutism in the first years of the 16th century, passing virtually without transition from an 'early mediaeval' to an 'early modern' type of feudal State, had no real equivalent in Western Europe. The emergence of the new State was precipitated from outside. In 1520 the new Danish king, Christian II, marched with an army into Sweden to enforce his authority there, defeating and executing the oligarchic Sture faction which had *de facto* ruled the country as a local Regency in the last years of the Union of Kalmar. The prospect of a strong foreign monarchy imposing itself on Sweden rallied the local aristocracy and sections of the independent peasantry behind a usurper noble, Gustavus Vasa, who rose against Danish dominion and established his own rule over the country three years later, with the aid of Lübeck – Hanseatic enemy and rival of Denmark. Gustavus, once installed in power, promptly and ruthlessly proceeded to lay the bases of a stable monarchical State in Sweden.

His first, and decisive, move was to set in train the expropriation of the Church, under the timely banner of the Reformation. Initiated in 1527, the process was effectively completed in 1544, when Sweden officially became a Lutheran country. The Vasa Reformation was undoubtedly the most successful economic operation of its kind accomplished by any dynasty in Europe. For, by contrast with the dissipated results of the Tudor seizure of the monasteries, or the German princes' secularization of church lands, virtually the entire windfall of ecclesiastical estates accrued *en bloc* to the Swedish monarchy. By his confiscations, Gustavus quintupled the royal farms, besides annexing two-thirds of the tithes previously levied by the bishops on the population, and seizing massive hoards of plate from churches and monasteries.[1]

1. Michael Roberts, *The Early Vasas*, Cambridge 1968, pp. 178–9. The

Exploiting silver mines, promoting bar-iron exports, and minutely supervising the revenues and receipts in his realm, Gustavus accumulated a vast surplus by the time of his death, without any commensurate increase in taxes. He simultaneously expanded the royal administrative apparatus for the management of the country by trebling the number of bailiffs, and experimenting with a central bureaucracy designed for him by German advisers. Regional autonomies in the turbulent Dalarna mining districts were suppressed and Stockholm was permanently garrisoned. The nobility, whose economic rivalry with the clergy had been used to associate it with the expropriation of church lands, was decreasingly invested with the straightforward knight's fief, the old *län på tjänst*, and was more and more granted the new *förläning*, a type of semi-ministerial benefice that was much more limited in scope, amounting to an allocation of specific royal revenues for specific administrative assignments. This measure of centralization did not antagonize the aristocracy, which evinced a basic solidarity with the regime throughout Gustavus's rule, enhanced by his defeat of peasant rebellions in Dalarna (1527) and Småland (1543-4), and military humbling of Lübeck. The traditional magnate *råd* was preserved for advice in matters of political importance, but excluded from day-to-day administration. The critical innovation of the Vasa political machinery was rather the constant use in the early part of Gustavus's reign of the Estates Assembly, the Riksdag, which was repeatedly summoned to legitimate the acts of the new dynasty by giving the stamp of popular approval to royal policies. Gustavus's most important achievement in this respect was to secure in 1544 the acceptance by the Estates at Västerås of the principle that the monarchy should no longer be elective, but henceforward hereditary in the house of Vasa.[2]

Gustavus I's sons, Erik XIV and John, thus inherited a vigorous, if still somewhat primitive State that had maintained cordial relations

---

English-speaking reader is fortunate in having available the distinguished and ample *oeuvre* of this historian of early modern Sweden.

2. The flinty personality of Gustavus Vasa inevitably recalls that of the state-building succession of West European rulers just before him: Henry VII, Louis XI and Ferdinand II – just as his extravagant eldest son Erik XIV bears certain resemblances to the flamboyant instability of Henry VIII and Francis I. A sober study of such generational shifts and clusters might sometimes prove of wider interest than conventional biographies.

with the aristocratic class by imposing few burdens and injuring no privileges. Erik XIV, who succeeded in 1560, reformed and expanded the Army, intensifying the military service obligations of the nobility. He also created a new title-system, conferring on magnates the ranks of count and baron, and investing them with classical, hereditary fiefs. Externally, his reign inaugurated Swedish expansionism in the Northern Baltic. With the imminent collapse of the Order of Livonian Knights before Russian attack, and the intervention of Poland to secure their inheritance, Sweden occupied Reval on the other side of the Gulf of Finland. A confused and intricate struggle ensued among the Baltic powers for control of Livonia. In 1568, Erik XIV – prey to violent suspicions of leading magnates – was deposed as unbalanced. His brother John III, who succeeded, prosecuted the Livonian Wars with greater success by switching to alliance with Poland against Russia. In the late 1570's, Polish forces swept Ivan IV's armies back to Pskov, while Swedish troops conquered Estonia: the foundation of Sweden's overseas empire was laid. At home, meanwhile, there was an accelerated drift towards the *förläning* benefices, which were increasingly confided by the monarchy to parvenu functionaries and bailiffs, until by the 1590's only one-third were in the hands of the nobility.[3] Friction between the monarchy and aristocracy was thus visibly developing by the end of the century, despite Vasa success in the Livonian Wars. The accession of John III's Catholic son Sigismund, in 1592, soon precipitated a period of acute religious and political conflicts which threatened the whole stability of the royal State. Sigismund, a devout adherent of the Counter-Reformation, had been elected king of Poland five years earlier, partly because of Vasa dynastic ties by marriage with the now defunct Jagellonian line. Obliged by the Swedish nobility, as a condition of acceptance, to respect Lutheranism in Sweden and to refrain from any administrative unification of his two kingdoms, he resided as an absentee monarch in Poland for ten years. In Sweden itself, his uncle Charles, Duke of Södermanland, and the magnate *råd* governed the country: Sigismund was effectively kept out of his northern realm by an entente between the Duke and the nobility. The increasingly arbitrary personal power concentrated by Charles

3. Roberts, *The Early Vasas*, p. 306.

eventually antagonized the higher aristocracy, who rallied to Sigismund when he returned in 1604 to reclaim his patrimony from the usurpation of his uncle. The armed confrontation which followed ended in ducal victory, much assisted by anti-papal propaganda against Sigismund, who was presented as menacing Sweden with re-catholicization.

The seizure of power by the Duke, who now became Charles IX, was sealed by a judicial massacre of the constitutionalist magnates of the *råd* who had sided with the losing contender in the dynastic conflict. Charles IX's repression and neutralization of the *råd* was characteristically accompanied by a flurry of convocations of the Riksdag, which once again proved a docile and manipulable instrument of Swedish Absolutism. The nobility was kept at arm's length from the central administration, and its military obligations were augmented. To mollify aristocratic dislike and contempt for his usurpation, the king distributed lands confiscated from oppositional magnates who had fled into emigation with Sigismund, and accorded a larger share of *förläningar* to the nobility.[4] But on his death in 1611, the degree of tension and suspicion between the dynasty and aristocracy that had built up over the years was sharply revealed. For the nobility immediately seized the opportunity of a royal minority to impose a Charter in 1612 which formally condemned the illegalities of the past reign; restored the power of the *råd* over taxation and affairs of State; guaranteed noble primacy in appointments to the bureaucracy; and gave security of tenure and fixed salaries to state functionaries. The reign of Gustavus Adolphus was thus ushered in by a constitutional compact carefully designed to prevent any repetition of the tyrannies of his father. In fact, Gustavus Adolphus showed no inclination to revert to a crude royal autocracy. His rule, on the contrary, witnessed reconciliation and integration of the monarchy and nobility: the State apparatus ceased to be a rudimentary dynastic patrimony, as the aristocracy collectively enlisted in the modern and powerful administration and army now constructed in Sweden. Gustavus Adolphus's grandee Chancellor Oxenstierna reorganized the whole executive system into five central colleges, staffed by noble bureaucrats. The *råd* became a regular Privy Council for deliberation of public policies. The legislative procedures and com-

4. Roberts, *The Early Vasas*, p. 440.

posiiton of the Riksdag were codified in 1617; an Ordinance legally divided the aristocracy into three grades and accorded it a special Chamber or *Riddarhus* in 1626, which henceforward became the dominant focus of the Estate assemblies. The country was divided into 24 provincial units (formally designated *län*), over each of which a *landhövding* or lord-lieutenant picked from the nobility was installed.[5] A modernized educational system was promoted, while official ideology exalted the ethnic descent of the Swedish ruling class, whose 'Gothic' ancestors had once dominated Europe. Meanwhile, expenditure on the fleet increased six-fold during Gustavus Adolphus's reign, while native troop-strengths quadrupled.[6] This sweeping rationalization and re-invigoration of Swedish Absolutism at home provided the platform for Gustavus Adolphus's military expansion abroad.

Extricating himself from the unsuccessful war with Denmark which Charles IX had bequeathed to him, by signing a costly peace at the start of his reign, the king concentrated his initial objectives in the Northern Baltic theatre, where Russia was still convulsed by the Time of Troubles and his brother Charles Philip was nearly installed as Tsar with boyar and Cossack backing. Territorial gains were soon clinched at Russian expense. By the Treaty of Stolbova in 1617, Sweden acquired Ingria and Karelia, giving it total command of the Gulf of Finland. Four years later, Gustavus Adolphus seized Riga from Poland. Then in 1625–6, Swedish armies rolled up Polish forces throughout Livonia, conquering the whole region. The next operation was an amphibious attack on Poland itself, where Sigismund still ruled. The strategic approaches to East Prussia were seized, with the annexation of Memel, Pillau and Elbing, and heavy tolls henceforward levied on the South Baltic corn trade. The conclusion of the Polish campaign in 1629 was promptly followed by the Swedish landing in Pomerania in 1630, inaugurating Gustavus Adolphus's momentous intervention in the struggle for Germany during the Thirty Years' War. By now, the total strength of the Swedish military apparatus comprised some 72,000 troops, of whom just over half were native soldiers: the war plans for 1630

5. Michael Roberts, *Gustavus Adolphus, A History of Sweden 1611–1632*, I, London 1953, pp. 265–78, 293–7, 319–24.

6. Pierre Jeannin, *L'Europe du Nord-Ouest et du Nord aux XVIIe et XVIIIe Siècles*, Paris 1969, p. 130.

envisaged the deployment of 46,000 men for the expedition to Germany, but in practice this target was not fulfilled.[7] Nevertheless, in two brief years, Gustavus Adolphus led his armies victoriously in a great arc from Brandenburg through the Rhineland and into Bavaria, shattering the Habsburg position in the Empire. At the death of the king in 1632, on the triumphal field of Lützen, Sweden was the arbiter of Germany and the dominant power throughout Northern Europe.

What had rendered possible this meteoric ascent of Swedish Absolutism? To understand its nature and dynamic, it is necessary to look back at the distinctive traits of mediaeval Scandinavia outlined earlier. The central peculiarity of the Swedish social formation on the eve of the Vasa epoch was the markedly incomplete feudalization of the relations of production in the rural economy. A small-holder peasantry of a pre-feudal type still occupied half the cultivated land in the early 16th century. This did not mean, however, that Sweden 'never knew feudalism', as is often asserted.[8] For the other half of Swedish agriculture was in the royal-clerical-noble complex, where conventional surplus-extraction of a feudal character from a dependent peasantry obtained: although the tenants in this sector were never juridically reduced to serfdom, extra-economic coercion pressed dues and services out of them in the fashion familiar all over Western Europe at this time. The *predominant* sector in the Swedish economy throughout the period was thus doubtless always feudal agriculture proper, since while there was an approximate equality of cultivated surface between the two sectors, it may safely be assumed that productivity and output was generally higher on the larger noble and royal estates – the normal rule in Western Europe. Nevertheless, the extreme backwardness of the whole economy was at first glance its most striking characteristic in any comparative perspective. Less than half the soil was suitable for arable cultivation. Barley was overwhelmingly the main grain crop. Demesne consolidation was very limited – as late as the mid 17th century, only

7. Roberts, *Gustavus Adolphus, A History of Sweden 1611–1632*, II, London 1958, pp. 414–15, 444. In effect, the king started his German campaigns with some 26,000 troops.

8. See, for example, E. Hecksher, *An Economic History of Sweden*, Cambridge USA, 1954, pp. 36–8; M. Roberts, 'Introduction' to Ingvar Andersson, *A History of Sweden*, London 1956, p. 5 (contradicted by the book introduced: compare pp. 43–4).

some 8 per cent of farms were manorial units.[9] Moreover, the unique extent of petty production in the villages meant that the index of commercialization in agriculture was probably the lowest anywhere in the continent. A natural economy prevailed over vast areas of the country, to such an extent that as late as the 1570's, a mere 6 per cent of royal revenues – taxes and rents – were paid in cash, while most state officials were equally remunerated in kind.[10] In these conditions, where the temperature of monetary exchange was still sub-arctic, there was no possibility of a blossoming urban economy. Swedish towns were few and feeble, most of them German-founded and settled; foreign trade was virtually a monopoly of Hanseatic merchants. *Prima facie*, this configuration appears notably unpropitious for the sudden and successful emergence of a modern Absolutism. What is the explanation for the historical success of the Vasa State?

The answer to this question takes us to the centre of the specific character of Swedish Absolutism. The centralization of royal power in the 16th and 17th centuries was not a response to the crisis of serfdom and the disintegration of a manorial system by commodity exchange and social differentiation in the villages. Nor did it obliquely reflect the growth of local mercantile capital and an urban economy. Its initial impulse was transmitted from without; it was the threat of a rigorous Danish overlordship that mobilized the Swedish nobility behind Gustavus I, and it was Lübeck capital that financed his war effort against Christian II. But the conjuncture of the 1520's did not form the fundamental matrix of Swedish Absolutism thereafter: this must be sought in the triangular relationship of class forces within the country. The basic, and determinant, social pattern behind it can for our purposes be summarized into a brief formula. The typical Western constellation in the early modern epoch was an aristocratic Absolutism raised above the social foundations of a non-servile peasantry and ascendant towns; the typical Eastern constellation was an aristocratic Absolutism erected over the foundations of a servile peasantry and subjugated towns. Swedish Absolutism, by contrast, was built on a base that was unique, because – for historical reasons outlined earlier – it combined free peasants and nugatory towns: in other words, a set of

9. Roberts, *Gustavus Adolphus*, II, p. 152.
10. Roberts, *Gustavus Adolphus*, II, p. 44.

two 'contradictory' variables running across the master-division of the continent. In the overwhelmingly rural societies of the time, the first term of the peculiar Swedish constellation, a personally free peasantry, was 'dominant', and ensured the fundamental convergence of Swedish history, from its very different point of departure, with that of Western and not Eastern Europe. But its second term – the insignificance of the towns, itself the corollary of a large subsistence peasant sector never pumped by orthodox feudal mechanisms of surplus extraction – sufficed to give the nascent State structure of the Swedish monarchy its distinctive cast. For the nobility, while in one sense much less absolutely paramount in the countryside than its counterparts elsewhere in Western Europe, was also much less objectively constricted by the presence of an urban bourgeoisie. There was little chance of any wholesale reversal of the position of the peasantry, for the balance of social forces in the rural economy was too heavily weighted against the possibility of a violent enserfment. The deep roots and broad expanse of independent peasant property made this unfeasible, particularly since the very extent of this sector conversely reduced the numbers of the nobility outside it to an exceptionally low level. It must always be remembered that the Swedish aristocracy throughout the first century of Vasa rule was a very small class, by any European standards. Thus in 1611, it numbered some 400–500 families, out of a population of 1,300,000. However, at least a half to two-thirds of these were modest bucolic backwoodsmen, or *knapar*, with incomes little different from those of prosperous peasants. When Gustavus Adolphus established a *Riddarhusordning* to fix the limits of the whole estate legally, only 126 families passed the tests for admittance to it, in 1626.[11] Of these, some 25 to 30 families constituted the inner circle of magnates who traditionally provided the counsellors of the *råd*. The 'critical mass' of the Swedish aristocracy in this epoch was thus always structurally inadequate to any frontal assault on the peasantry. At the same time, there was no burgher challenge whatever to its monopoly of political power. The Swedish social order was thus an unusually stable one, so long as no exogenous pressures were brought to bear on it.

It has been seen that it was precisely such pressures which pre-

11. Roberts, *Gustavus Adolphus*, Vol. II, p. 57. The figure for total population above includes Finland: Sweden itself had some 900,000 inhabitants in this period.

cipitated the initial advent of Vasa rule. At this point, a further peculiarity of the Swedish situation became important. There had never been an articulated feudal hierarchy within the aristocracy during the Middle Ages, with full-scale parcellization of sovereignty, or chains of sub-infeudation. The fief system itself was late and imperfect. Thus no territorial potentates or feudal separatism of the continental type ever developed. Just because the vassal system was recent and relatively shallow, it never produced entrenched regional divisions among the small Swedish nobility. The first real emergence of fissiparous provincial power was actually a subsequent creation of the unitary monarchy itself, not a prior obstruction to it: the ducal appanages of Finland, Östergötland and Södermanland left by Gustavus Vasa in his testament to his younger sons, which disappeared in the next century.[12] The result was that while the internal urgency of a centralized Absolutism was not great in Sweden, since depression of the peasantry was not practicable and control of the towns was not arduous, the obstacles to it within the landed ruling class were not very great either. A small and compact nobility could adapt relatively easily to a centralized monarchy. The low-pressure character of the basic class situation which underlay Swedish Absolutism, and determined its form and evolution, was visible in the odd role of the Estates system in it. For, on the one hand, the Riksdag was politically unique in its inclusion of a separate peasant estate within its four-curia system: there was no parallel to this in any other major country in Europe. On the other hand, the Riksdag in general, and the peasant delegates to it above all, formed a curiously passive body throughout this epoch, devoid of legislative initiative and virtually unswerving in complaisance to royal requests. Thus Vasa rule, indeed, had such frequent recourse to the Riksdag that it had been described without paradox as the epitome of 'parliamentary absolutism'; for virtually every important increment of royal power from Gustavus I's seizure of Church lands in 1527 to

12. Gustavus Vasa's death-bed division of his country by the creation of these dangerous appanages, after a life-time of royal centralization, captures a typically feudal trait of many of the pioneers of European Absolutism. It can be compared to the even more drastic testamentary instructions for the dismemberment of the Hohenzollern domains left by the Great Elector himself, supreme architect of the unitary Prussian State. A dynastic patrimony always remained potentially divisible for these rulers.

Charles XI's proclamation of divine right in 1680 was solemnized by a loyal assembly. Aristocratic resistance to the monarchy was thus nearly always focussed in the *råd* – lineal descendant of a mediaeval *curia regis* – and not in the Riksdag, where the reigning sovereign could usually manipulate the non-noble orders against it, if a conflict should arise between the two.[13] The Riksdag, on the surface an audacious institution for its time, was in fact a remarkably innocuous one. The monarchy never had any difficulty in using it for its political purposes in this period. Another, complementary reflection of the same basic social situation underlying the docility of the Estates was to be found in the Army. For precisely because of the existence of an independent peasantry, the Swedish State could afford a conscript army – alone in Renaissance Europe. Gustavus Vasa's decree creating the *utskrivning* system of rural conscription in 1544 never ran the risk of arming a *jacquerie*, because the soldiers thus recruited had never been serfs: their legal and material condition was compatible with loyalty in the field.

The question remains, how Swedish Absolutism acquired not merely the political-ideological accoutrements, but the economic and military resources necessary for its European showing, with a domestic population of no more than 900,000 in the early 17th century. Here the general law that a viable Absolutism presupposed a substantive level of monetarization could not be evaded. A natural rural economy appeared to preclude this. In Sweden, however, there was one crucial enclave of commodity production, whose disproportionate profits compensated for the subnormal commercialization of agriculture, and provided the fortunes of the Vasa state in its phase of outward expansion. This was the mineral wealth of the iron and copper deposits of the Bergslagen. Mining everywhere occupies a special position in the transitional economies of early modern Europe: not only did it represent for a long time the largest concentration of workers in a single form of enterprise, but it was always the direct fulcrum of the monetary economy by its supply of precious metals, yet without itself necessarily involving any advanced level of manufacturing process or

13. The whole tradition and role of the *råd* is examined in Roberts's essay, 'On Aristocratic Constitutionalism in Swedish History, 1520–1720', *Essays in Swedish History*, pp. 14–55.

market demand. Moreover, the tradition of regalian rights over the subsoil in feudal Europe meant that it was often in one way or another an appurtenance of princes. Swedish copper and iron ore can thus be compared with Spanish silver and gold in their impact on the local Absolutism. Both allowed the combination of a powerful and aggressive State with a social formation without either great agrarian wealth or mercantile dynamism: Sweden was, of course, far more bereft of these than Spain. The zenith of the copper boom in Sweden was actually linked directly to the collapse of silver currency in Castile. For it was the issue of the new copper *vellón* by Lerma in the devaluation of 1599 that created a soaring international demand for the output of the Kopparberg at Falun. Gustavus Adolphus levied heavy regalian tolls on the copper mines, organized a royal export company to corner supply and fix price levels, and raised large Dutch credits for his wars against his mineral assets. Although the *vellón* was suspended in 1626, Sweden continued to possess virtually a copper monopoly throughout Europe. Meanwhile, the iron industry steadily progressed, increasing its production five-fold by the end of the 17th century, when it amounted to half of all exports.[14] Moreover, both copper and iron were not merely direct sources of cash revenue for the Absolutist State: they were also the indispensable materials for its arms industry. Bronze-cast cannon were the decisive artillery arm in this epoch, while all other types of weaponry demanded high-grade iron. With the arrival of the legendary Walloon entrepreneur Louis De Geer in the 1620's, Sweden soon possessed one of the largest armaments complexes in Europe. The mines thus felicitously supplied Swedish Absolutism with both the financial and military substructure necessary for its surge across the Baltic. Prussian tolls, German booty and French subsidies completed its war budget for the duration of the Thirty Years' War, and rendered possible the hiring of vast numbers of mercenaries who eventually came to swamp the Swedish expeditionary troops themselves.[15]

14. Stewart Oakley, *The Story of Sweden*, London 1966, p. 125.
15. Gustavus Adolphus started his campaigns in Germany with an army of which half was recruited in Sweden. By the time of Breitenfeld, this had sunk to a quarter. By the time of Lützen, it was less than a tenth (13,000 out of 140,000). Roberts, *Gustavus Adolphus*, Vol. II, pp. 206–7. Domestic conscription thus in no way sufficed to exempt Swedish Absolutism from the general laws of European militarism in this epoch.

The Empire thus won proved, unlike the Spanish possessions in Europe, reasonably profitable. The Baltic provinces, in particular, with their corn shipments to Sweden, always yielded substantial tax revenues, with a large net surplus after local expenditures had been deducted. Their share of total royal receipts was well over a third in the budget of 1699.[16] Moreover, the Swedish nobility gained particularly extensive estates in conquered Livonia, where agriculture approximated much more closely to a manorial pattern than in the homeland. The overseas branches of the aristocracy in their turn played an important role in staffing the expensive military machine of Swedish imperial expansion: in the early 18th century, one out of every three of Charles XII's officers in his Polish and Russian campaigns was from the Baltic provinces. Swedish Absolutism, indeed, always functioned most smoothly during phases of aggressive expansion outwards: it was during the reigns of royal generalissimos – Gustavus Adolphus, Charles X and the early years of Charles XII – that harmony between monarchy and nobility was customarily greatest. But the external success of Swedish Absolutism never wholly cancelled its internal limitations. It suffered from a fundamental *under-determination*, because of the comparatively dormant class configuration within Sweden itself. Thus it always remained a 'facultative' form of rule for the noble class itself. In socially atonic conditions, Absolutism tended to lack the pressure of vital class necessity. Hence the curious pendular trajectory of Swedish Absolutism, unlike that of any other in Europe. Instead of a progression through initial grave contradictions, to an ultimate stabilization and tranquil integration of the nobility, which as we have seen was the normal evolution elsewhere, in Sweden the absolute monarchy suffered recurrent reverses whenever there was a royal minority, and yet later regained lost ground no less recurrently: the aristocratic charters of 1611, 1632 and 1720, limiting royal power, were succeeded by the recrudescence of absolutist power in the 1620's, 1680's and 1772–89.[17] What is striking about these oscillations is the relative ease with which the aristocracy adjusted to either form of state

16. Jeannin, *L'Europe du Nord-Ouest et du Nord*, p. 330.
17. Roberts points out that aristocratic constitutionalism never won a victory over a king of full age: it was the relative frequency of minorities which gave it periodic chances of reassertion: *Essays in Swedish History*, p. 33.

– 'royal' or 'representative'. Throughout the entire three centuries of its existence, Swedish Absolutism suffered frequent institutional relapses, but never a real political upheaval of the nobility against it, comparable to those in Spain, France and England. Just because it was domestically to a certain extent a facultative State for the ruling class, the aristocracy could convert backwards and forwards to it without undue emotion or discomfort. The history of Sweden from the death of Gustavus Adolphus in 1632 to the putsch of Gustavus III in 1789 is largely that of its successive adjustments.

Naturally, divisions and conflicts within the nobility itself were one of the central regulators of these serial changes. Thus the Form of Government imposed by Oxenstierna after Lützen codified magnate rule in the *råd* (now packed with his own relatives) during the regency from 1632–44. The Chancellor was soon confronted with a strategic downturn in Germany: the Imperial victory at Nordlingen in 1634 was followed by the defection of most of the Protestant princes in 1635, while the lucrative Prussian tolls – critical for the Swedish war efforts – now lapsed by treaty. Swedish tax revenues paid only for the maintenance of the Baltic navy – trebled to some 90 ships by Gustavus Adolphus – and home defense. French subsidies henceforward became indispensable for the pursuit of the struggle by Stockholm: in 1641, they amounted to a third of the domestic income of the State.[18] The campaigns in Germany during the last half of the Thirty Years' War, fought with much smaller armies than the huge hosts assembled at Breitenfeld or Lützen, were financed by foreign subventions or loans and ruthless local extortions by the commanders abroad. In 1643, Oxenstierna unleashed Torstensson – the best Swedish general – against Denmark, in a side-campaign. The yield of this stroke was satisfactory: provincial gains along the Norwegian frontier, and island bases in the Baltic which ended Danish control of both sides of the Sound. In the wider conflict, Swedish troops had reached Prague when peace was restored in 1648. The Treaty of Westphalia consecrated the international stature of Sweden as co-victor with France of the long contest in Germany. The Vasa State acquired Western Pomerania and

18. Roberts, 'Sweden and the Baltic 1611–1654', *The New Cambridge Modern History*, IV, p. 401.

Bremen on the German mainland itself, and control of the mouths of the Elbe, Oder and Weser – the three great rivers of Northern Germany.

Meanwhile, however, the accession of Christina in 1644 had formally led to the political reassertion of royal power: but it was used by the light-headed queen to shower titles and lands on the upper stratum of the aristocracy and the swarm of military-bureaucratic adventurers drawn to Swedish service in the Thirty Years' War. Christina sextupled the number of counts and barons in the top rank of the *Riddarhus*, and doubled the size of the two lower ranks. For the first time the Swedish nobility acquired an appreciable numerical strength, mainly drawn from abroad: more than half the aristocracy was to be of foreign descent by 1700.[19] Moreover, encouraged by Oxenstierna who advocated commutation of traditional state revenues in kind into reliable cash flows, the monarchy alienated royal lands and taxes on an enormous scale to its elite of functionaries and retainers: the total area of noble land in Sweden doubled between 1611 and 1652, while state incomes cascaded proportionately downwards under Christina.[20] The alienations to private landowners of fiscal receipts from free peasants threatened to reduce the latter to full dependence on them, and provoked vigorous reactions from the peasantry. But it was the hostility of the lower nobility, which had not benefited from the gratuitous profligacy of the queen, that was to ensure that this upheaval in the property pattern of Sweden would be a brief one.

In 1654 Christina abdicated to embrace Catholicism, after prearranging the succession of her cousin. The new ruler, Charles X, immediately relaunched Swedish expansionism with a savage thrust into Poland in 1655. Cutting off Russian advances from the East, and scattering Polish armies, Swedish expeditionary forces took Poznan, Warsaw and Cracow in quick succession: East Prussia was officially declared a Swedish fief, and Lithuania joined to Sweden. Dutch harrassment by sea and Polish revival weakened the grip of this spectacular occupation: but it was a direct Danish attack on Sweden in the rear of the king that undid the conquest of Poland. Pulling the bulk

19. R. M. Hatton, *Charles XII of Sweden*, London 1968, p. 38.
20. Total receipts dropped 40 per cent in the decade from 1644 to 1653. For the whole episode, see Roberts's essay, 'Queen Christina and the General Crisis of the Seventeenth Century', *Essays in Swedish History*, pp. 111–37.

of his corps rapidly back through Pomerania, Charles X marched to Copenhagen and knocked Denmark out of the war. Victory in the Sound brought annexation of Scania. Renewed hostilities to clinch Swedish control of the gateway to the Baltic were thwarted by Dutch intervention. The death of Charles X in 1660 terminated both the adventure in Poland and the conflict in Denmark. Another magnate regency followed during the minority of 1660–72, dominated by the Chancellor De La Gardie. Royal schemes for resumption of alienated revenues, briefly envisaged by Charles X before his headlong overseas campaigns, were shelved: a drifting government of the high nobility continued to sell off the property of the monarchy, while steering an unambitious foreign policy. It was in this decade, significantly, that manorial codes of *gårdsrätt* were enforced for the first time in Swedish history, giving landowners private jurisdiction over their own peasantry.[21] The outbreak of a major European war, with Louis XIV's attack on Holland, eventually forced this regime, as a French ally and client, into a lethargic diversionary conflict with Brandenburg in 1674. Military failure in Germany discredited the De La Gardie camarilla, and paved the way for the dramatic reascendancy of the monarchy under the new sovereign, who had achieved his majority during the wars.

In 1680, Charles XI used the Riksdag to abolish the traditional privileges of the *råd*, and to reappropriate the alienated lands and revenues of the dynasty, with the support of the lower gentry. The royal 'reductions' were on a very large scale: 80 per cent of all alienated estates were recovered for the monarchy without compensations, and the proportion of cultivated land owned by nobles in Sweden was halved.[22] The creation of new tax-exempt properties was forbidden. Territorial counties and baronies were liquidated. The 'reductions'

21. They were abolished again in the 1670's: Jeannin, *L'Europe du Nord-Ouest et du Nord*, p. 135.

22. For the reductions, see J. Rosen, 'Scandinavia and the Baltic', *The New Cambridge Modern History of Europe*, V, p. 534. In 1655, nobles had owned $\frac{2}{3}$ of all farms in the country. By 1700, the proportions were 33 per cent noble, 36 per cent royal and 31 per cent tax-paying peasant. The reductions had increased the revenues of the monarchy by some 2,000,000 daler a year at the end of the reign; of this increment, $\frac{2}{3}$ was derived from repossessions in the overseas provinces.

were implemented with special thoroughness in the overseas possessions. They did not affect manorial consolidation within the holdings of the aristocracy; their final upshot was to restore the *status quo ante* in the distribution of agrarian property which had prevailed at the beginning of the century.[23] State revenues, refurbished by this programme at the expense of the magnate stratum, were further augmented by higher taxation on the peasantry. The Riksdag submissively assented to the unprecedented increase in the personal power of Charles XI which accompanied the *reduktion*, abdicating virtually all rights to control or check his government. Charles XI used his position to reform the army by planting a soldier-peasantry on specially distributed lands in the so-called *indelningsverket* or allotment system, which relieved the treasury of cash payments for troops at home. The permanent military establishment was enlarged to a force of some 63,000 in the 1680's, of which over a third were professional units stationed overseas. The fleet was assiduously built up, for both strategic and commercial reasons. The bureaucracy, to which the lower nobility now had equal access, was drilled and streamlined. Scania and Livonia were subjected to tightening centralization and Swedification.[24] The royal sway appeared complete by the last decade of the reign: in 1693 the Riksdag ended by passing a fulsome resolution declaring the divine right of the king to absolute sovereignty over his realm, as the anointed delegate of his maker. Charles XI, like Frederick William I of Prussia a thrifty and cautious ruler abroad, brooked no opposition to his will at home.

The best testament to his work was the astonishing reign of his son

23. The dramatic peripeteia of the alienations and reversions of the Swedish royal patrimony in the mid 17th century, which in a brief space reshuffled the whole property pattern of the country, are generally interpreted as the sign of a deep social struggle for the land, in which the Swedish peasantry was only just rescued from a 'Livonian serfdom' by the reductions. However widespread, it is difficult to accept this view. For the origins of this interlude were too manifestly linked to the subjective whims of Christina. Her reckless donations were made in peace-time and corresponded to no objective need of the monarchy; nor were they the result of any irrecusable collective drive or demand of the nobility. Won without effort by the higher aristocracy, they were abandoned without resistance. There was never any class confrontation on the land of a gravity commensurate with the stakes formally involved. It may be assumed that it would have taken more than feckless royal largesse to break the liberties of the Swedish peasantry.

24. Rosen, 'Scandinavia and the Baltic', pp. 535–7.

Charles XII, who surpassed his father in an autocratic power that was ideologically trumpeted from the day of his accession in 1697. The last of the Vasa warrior-kings, he was able to spend eighteen years abroad, nine of them in Turkish captivity, without the civil administration of his country ever being seriously challenged or disrupted in his absence. It is doubtful if any other contemporary ruler could have been so confident of his patrimony. In effect, virtually the entire reign of Charles XII was occupied with his long odyssey in Eastern Europe, during the Great Northern War. For by 1700, the Swedish imperial system in the Baltic was approaching its day of reckoning. Despite the rigorous administrative overhaul it had recently undergone under Charles XI, its demographic and economic base was too small to sustain its spread, against the combined enmity of its neighbours and rivals. A domestic population of perhaps 1,500,000 was doubled by the overseas possessions to some 3,000,000: its manpower and financial reserves permitted a maximum mobilization of some 110,000 troops (including foreign mercenaries) under Charles XII, of whom less than half were available for his major offensive campaigns.[25] Moreover, Vasa centralization had provoked a particularist backlash among the semi-Germanic nobility of the Baltic provinces, who had suffered especially from the royal reclamations of the preceding reign. The experience of Catalonia and Scotland was now to be re-edited in Livonia. By 1699, Denmark, Saxony, Poland and Russia were arrayed against Sweden: the signal for war was given by a secessionist revolt in Latvia, led by local nobles declaring for incorporation into Poland. Charles XII struck first at Denmark, which he rapidly defeated with Anglo-Dutch naval aid; then at Russia, where a small Swedish force annihilated Peter I's army at Narva; then at Poland, where Augustus II was driven from the country after heavy fighting and a Swedish nominee prince installed; and finally at Saxony, which was mercilessly occupied and pillaged. After this circular military progress round the Baltic, the Swedish army was thrown deep into the Ukraine for a juncture with the Zaporozhe Cossacks and march on Moscow.[26]

25. The attack on Russia in 1709 was launched with about 44,000 men: Hatton, *Charles XII of Sweden*, p. 233.

26. The blunder involved in this venture is notorious. It may be remarked that the military flair of Swedish Absolutism was nearly always typically combined

Russian Absolutism under Peter I was now, however, more than a match for the columns of Charles XII: at Poltava and Perevolotchna in 1709, the Swedish Empire was destroyed at the furthest historical point of its military penetration to the east. A decade later, the Great Northern War ended with Sweden bankrupt and stripped of Ingria, Karelia, Livonia, Western Pomerania and Bremen.

The imperious autocracy of Charles XII disappeared with him. When the disasters of the Great Northern War debouched onto the king's death, amid a disputed succession, the nobility deftly engineered a constitutional system which left the Estates politically supreme and the monarchy temporarily a cipher. The 'Age of Liberty' from 1720–72 established a regime of corrupt aristocratic parliamentarism, divided by factional conflicts between Hat and Cap parties, which were manipulated in turn by the nobiliary bureaucracy, and ballasted by English, French and Russian gratifications and subventions. The new order was no longer a magnate one: the mass of the medium and lower aristocracy, which dominated the civil service and army, had increasingly come into its own. The three-rank division within the noble Estate was abolished. The social and economic privileges of the aristocracy as a whole were jealously preserved: commoner access to noble lands or marriages was banned. The Riksdag – from whose key Secret Committee peasant representatives were excluded – became the formal centre of constitutional politics, while its real arena lay in the *Riddarhus*.[27] Eventually, increasing social agitation against noble privileges among the lower clergy, smaller towns and peasantry threatened to break the charmed circle of manoeuvres within this system. The programme of the Younger Cap party in the 1760's, although combined with an unpopular

---

with political myopia. Its rulers consistently applied force with consummate skill to misconceived targets. Gustavus Adolphus careered vainly across Germany, when Swedish long-term interests indicated seizure of Denmark and mastery of the Sound. Charles XII lunged uselessly into the Ukraine, at British prompting, when a French alliance and attack on Austria would have altered the whole course of the War of the Spanish Succession, and saved Sweden from its complete isolation at the conclusion of the struggle in the East. The dynasty never overcame a certain provincialism in its strategic outlook.

27. See Roberts, *Essays in Swedish History*, pp. 272–8; the ban on commoner purchase of noble land was later confined to peasants only, while the marriage restrictions were also mitigated.

deflation of the economy, expressed the rising tide of plebeian discontent. Aristocratic alarm at the prospect of a challenge from below thus produced a final, abrupt abandonment of parliamentarism. The accession of Gustavus III proved the signal for the aristocracy to rally once again back to an Absolutist formula: a royal putsch was smoothly conducted with the help of the Guards and the connivance of the bureaucracy. The Riksdag duly rubber-stamped a new constitution, reconsecrating the authority of the monarchy, initially without a full reversion to the absolutism of Charles XI or XII. The new monarch, however, energetically proceeded towards an enlightened despotism of the 18th century type, renovating the administration, and reserving more and more arbitrary power to his person. When the nobility resisted this trend, Gustavus III forced an emergency Act of Union and Security through the Riksdag, which restored a thorough-going Absolutism in 1789. To gain his ends, the king had to promise the lower Estates access to the civil service and judiciary, the right to purchase noble lands, and other socially egalitarian demands. The last hours of Swedish Absolutism were thus lived in the anomalous atmosphere of a 'career open to the talents' and curbs on the privileges of the nobility. The political rationale of absolute monarchy thereby lost its basic moorings, a sure sign of its approaching end. In a final, bizarre permutation of roles, the 'radical' autocrat became the most fervent European champion of counter-revolutionary intervention against the French Revolution, while disgruntled nobles adopted the republican ideals of the Rights of Man. In 1792, Gustavus was assassinated by a dissident aristocratic officer. The historical 'underdetermination' of Swedish Absolutism was never more visible than in this strange climax. A facultative State finished in apparently full contingency.

II. Eastern Europe

Absolutism in the East

It is now necessary to revert to the Eastern half of Europe, or more accurately that part of it which was spared the Ottoman invasion that over-ran the Balkans in successive waves of advance, subjecting it to a local history separate from that of the rest of the continent. It has been seen how the great crisis which struck the European economies in the 14th and 15th centuries produced a violent manorial reaction east of the Elbe. The seigneurial repression unleashed against the peasants increased in intensity throughout the 16th century. The political result, in Prussia and Russia, was an Absolutism of the East, coeval with that of the West yet basically different in lineage. The Absolutist State in the West was the redeployed political apparatus of a feudal class which had accepted the commutation of dues. It was a *compensation for the disappearance of serfdom*, in the context of an increasingly urban economy which it did not completely control and to which it had to adapt. The Absolutist State in the East, by contrast, was the repressive machine of a feudal class that had just erased the traditional communal freedoms of the poor. It was a *device for the consolidation of serfdom*, in a landscape scoured of autonomous urban life or resistance. The manorial reaction in the East meant that a new world had to be implanted from above, by main force. The dose of violence pumped into social relations was correspondingly far greater. The Absolutist State in the East never lost the signs of this original experience.

Yet at the same time, the internal class struggle within the Eastern social formations and its outcome, the enserfment of the peasantry, do not in themselves provide an exhaustive explanation for the emergence of the distinctive type of Absolutism of the region. The distance between the two can be measured chronologically in Prussia, where the manorial reaction of the nobility had already rolled over much of the peasantry with the spread of the *Gutsherrschaft* in the 16th century, a hundred years before the establishment of an Absolutist State in the 17th century. In Poland, classical land of the 'second serfdom', no Absolutist State ever emerged, although this was a failure for which the noble class was eventually to pay with its national existence. Here, too, however, the 16th century witnessed decentralized feudal rule, dominated by a representative system totally under aristocratic control, and very weak princely authority. In Hungary, the definitive enserfment of the peasantry was accomplished after the Austro-Turkish War at the turn of the 17th century, while the Magyar nobility was successfully resisting the imposition of a Habsburg Absolutism.[1] In Russia, the installation of serfdom and the erection of Absolutism were more closely coordinated, but even there the onset of the first preceded the consolidation of the second, and did not always develop *pari passu* with it thereafter. Since servile relations of production involve an immediate fusion of property and sovereignty, lordship and landlordship, there is nothing in itself surprising in a polycentric nobiliary State, such as initially existed in Ostelbian Germany, Poland or Hungary after the manorial reaction in the East. To explain the subsequent ascent of Absolutism it is necessary first of all to reinsert the whole process of the second serfdom into the *international* state system of late feudal Europe.

We have seen that the pull of the more advanced Western economy on the East has often been exaggerated in this epoch, as the sole or main force responsible for the manorial reaction there. In fact, while the corn trade undoubtedly intensified servile exploitation in Eastern Germany or Poland, it did not inaugurate it in either country, and played no role at all in the parallel development of Bohemia or Russia. In other words, if it is incorrect to ascribe central importance to the economic bonds of the export-import trade from East to West, this is because the feudal mode of production as such – by no means finally surpassed in Western Europe during the 16th and 17th centuries – could not create a unified international economic system; it was only

1. See Zs. Pach, *Die ungarische Agrarentwicklung im 16–17 Jahrhundert*, pp. 38–41, 53–6, for the phases of this process and the impact of the Thirteen Years' War itself on the condition of the peasantry.

the world market of industrial capitalism that accomplished this, radiating out from the advanced countries to mould and dominate the development of backward ones. The composite Western economies of the transitional epoch – typically combining a semi-monetarized and post-servile feudal agriculture[2] with enclaves of mercantile and manufacturing capital – had no such compulsive pull. Foreign investment was minimal, except in the Colonial Empires and to some extent Scandinavia. Foreign trade still represented a small percentage of the national product of all countries except Holland or Venice. Any wholesale integration of Eastern Europe into a Western European economic circuit – often implied by historians' use of such phrases as a 'colonial economy' or 'plantation business concerns' to refer to the *Gutsherrschaft* system beyond the Elbe – is thus inherently implausible.

This is not to say, however, that the impact of Western on Eastern Europe was not determinant for the *state structures* which emerged there. For transnational interaction within feudalism was typically always first at the *political*, not the economic level, precisely because it was a mode of production founded on extra-economic coercion: conquest, not commerce, was its primary form of expansion. The uneven development of feudalism within Europe thus found its most characteristic and direct expression, not in balances of trade, but in balances of arms, between the respective regions of the continent. In other words, the main mediation between East and West in these centuries was military. It was the international pressure of Western

2. The real index of monetarization of the different West European agricultures in the 16th and 17th centuries was probably much lower than is often thought. Jean Meuvret remarks that in 16th century France, 'the peasantry lived virtually everywhere in a regime of domestic quasi-autarchy', while 'the daily life of artisans, including petty-bourgeois, was effectively regulated by the same principle, namely to live above all from foods cultivated on the soil in their possession and otherwise to buy and sell a minimum'; for 'to satisfy ordinary needs, the use of gold or even silver coins was in no way necessary. For the small number of exchange transactions that were indispensable it was often possible to dispense with money.' Jean Meuvret, 'Circulation Monétaire et Utilisation Economique de la Monnaie dans la France du XVIe et du XVIIe Siècle', *Etudes d'Histoire Moderne et Contemporaine*, 1947, Vol. I, p. 20. Porshnev aptly characterizes the general situation as one defined by the 'contradiction between the monetary form and the natural basis of the feudal economy' in this epoch, and comments that the fiscal difficulties of Absolutism were everywhere rooted in this contradiction: *Les Soulèvements Populaires en France*, p. 558.

Absolutism, the political apparatus of a more powerful feudal aristocracy, ruling more advanced societies, which obliged the Eastern nobility to adopt an equivalently centralized state machine, to survive. For otherwise the superior military force of the reorganized and magnified Absolutist armies would inevitably take its toll in the normal medium of inter-feudal competition: war. The very modernization of troops and tactics brought about by the 'military revolution' in the West after 1560 rendered aggression into the vast spaces of the East more feasible than ever before, and the dangers of invasion correspondingly greater for the local aristocracies there. Thus, at a time when infrastructural relations of production were diverging, there was a paradoxical convergence of superstructures in the two zones (itself, of course, an index of an ultimate common mode of production). The concrete form which the military threat from Western Absolutism initially took was, fortunately for the Eastern nobility, historically circuitous and transient. It is nevertheless all the more striking how immediately catalytic its effects were for the whole political pattern in the East. To the South, the front between the two zones was occupied by the long Austro-Turkish duel, which for two hundred and fifty years focussed the Habsburgs on their Ottoman enemies and Hungarian vassals. In the Centre, Germany was a maze of small, weak states divided and neutralized by religious conflicts. It was thus from the relatively primitive North that the attack came. Sweden – most recent and surprising of all the Western Absolutisms, a new country with a very limited population and rudimentary economy – proved to be the Hammer of the East. Its impact on Prussia, Poland and Russia in the ninety years from 1630 to 1720 bears comparison with that of Spain in Western Europe in an earlier age, although it has never received the same study. Yet it was one of the greatest cycles of military expansion in the history of European Absolutism. At its height, Swedish cavalry rode victoriously into the five capitals of Moscow, Warsaw, Berlin, Dresden and Prague – operating across a huge arc of territory in Eastern Europe that exceeded even the campaigns of the Spanish *tercios* in Western Europe. The Austrian, Prussian, Polish and Russian state-systems all experienced its formative shock.

Sweden's first overseas conquest was the seizure of Estonia, in the long Livonian Wars with Russia in the last decades of the 16th century.

It was the Thirty Years' War, however, which produced the first fully formalized international state system in Europe, that appropriately marked the decisive onset of the Swedish irruption into the East. The spectacular march of Gustavus Adolphus's armies into Germany, rolling back Habsburg power to the astonishment of Europe, proved the turning-point of the war; while the later successes of Baner and Torstensson scotched any long-term recovery of the Imperial cause. From 1641 onwards, Swedish troops permanently occupied large parts of Moravia,[3] and when the war ended in 1648, were camped on the left bank of the Vltava in Prague. The intervention of Sweden had definitively broken the prospect of a Habsburg imperial state in Germany: the whole course and character of Austrian Absolutism were henceforward to be determined by this defeat, which deprived it of any chance of a consolidated territorial centre in the traditional lands of the *Reich*, and – to its cost – shifted its whole centre of gravity eastwards. At the same time, the impact of Swedish power on the evolution of Prussia, less visible internationally, was domestically even deeper. Brandenburg was occupied by Swedish armies from 1631 onwards, and although technically an ally in the Protestant cause, was immediately subjected to ruthless military requisitioning and fiscal exactions, such as it had never known before: the traditional privileges of the junker Estates were dismissed out of hand by Swedish commandants.[4] The trauma of this experience was compounded by the Swedish acquisition of Western Pomerania with the Treaty of Westphalia in 1648, which ensured Sweden a large and permanent beachhead on the southern shores of the Baltic. Swedish garrisons now controlled the Oder, posing a direct threat to the hitherto demilitarized and decentralized ruling class of Brandenburg, a country with virtually no army at all. The construction of Prussian Absolutism by the Great Elector from the 1650's onwards was in large measure a direct response to the impending Swedish menace: the standing army which was to be the cornerstone of Hohenzollern autocracy, and its tax system, was accepted by the junkers in 1653 to deal with an imminent war situation in the Baltic

3. See J. V. Polišensky, *The Thirty Years' War*, London 1971, pp. 224–31.

4. Carsten, *The Origins of Prussia*, p. 179. Gustavus Adolphus had a few years earlier seized the strategic fortresses of Memel and Pillau in East Prussia, which commanded access to Königsberg, and levied Swedish tolls there: op. cit., pp. 205–6.

theatre and resist external dangers. In fact, the Swedo-Polish War of 1655–60 proved to be the turning-point in the political evolution of Berlin, which itself avoided the brunt of Swedish aggression by participating as an apprehensive junior partner on the side of Stockholm. The next great step in the construction of Prussian Absolutism was once again taken in response to military conflict with Sweden. It was during the 1670's, in the throes of the Swedish campaigns against Brandenburg that formed a Northern theatre of the war unleashed by France in the West, that the notorious *Generalkriegskommissariat* came to occupy the functions of the earlier privy council and to mould henceforward the whole structure of the Hohenzollern State machine. Prussian Absolutism, and its ultimate shape, came into being during the epoch and under the pressure of Swedish expansionism.

Meanwhile, it was in these same decades after Westphalia that the heaviest Nordic blow of all was unleashed in the East. The Swedish invasion of Poland in 1655 quickly shattered the loose aristocratic confederation of the *szlachta*. Warsaw and Cracow fell, and the whole Vistula valley was torn up by the march and counter-march of Charles X's troops. The main strategic result of the war was to deprive Poland of any suzerainty over Ducal Prussia. But the social results of the devastating Swedish attack were far more serious: Polish economic and demographic patterns were so badly damaged that the Swedish invasion came to be known as the 'Deluge' which for ever after separated the previous prosperity of the *Rzeczpospolita* from the irretrievable crisis and decline into which it sank thereafter. The last brief revival of Polish arms in the 1680's, when Sobieski led the relief of Vienna against the Turks, was soon followed by the second Swedish ravage of the Commonwealth, during the Great Northern War of 1701–21, in which the main theatre of destruction was once again Poland. When the last Scandinavian troops withdrew from Warsaw, Poland had ceased to be a major European power. The Polish nobility, for reasons which will be discussed later, did not succeed in generating an Absolutism during these ordeals. It thereby demonstrated in practice what the consequences of not doing so were, for a feudal class in the East; unable to recover from the lethal blows delivered by Sweden, Poland ultimately ceased to exist as an independent state.

Russia, as always, presents a somewhat different case, within a common historical field. There, the impulse within the aristocracy towards a military monarchy was evident much earlier than anywhere else in Eastern Europe. In part, this was due to the pre-history of the Kievan State, and the Byzantine imperial tradition it transmitted across the chaotic Russian Middle Ages, through the ideology of the 'Third Rome': Ivan III had married the niece of the last Paleologus Emperor of Constantinople and arrogated the title of 'Tsar' or Emperor in 1480. The ideology of the *translatio imperii* was doubtless, however, less important than the constant material pressure on Russia of the Tartar and Turcoman pastoralists of Central Asia. The political suzerainty of the Golden Horde lasted until the late 15th century. The successor Khanates of Kazan and Astrakhan launched constant slaving incursions from the East until their defeat and absorption in the mid 16th century. For another hundred years, the Crimean Tartars – now under Ottoman overlordship – raided Russian territory from the South; their looting and enslaving expeditions kept most of the Ukraine a depopulated wilderness.[5] Tartar horsemen lacked the capacity to conquer or occupy permanently, in the early modern epoch. But Russia, 'sentinel of Europe', had to bear the brunt of their attacks, and the result was an earlier and greater impetus towards a centralized State in the Duchy of Muscovy than in the more sheltered Electorate of Brandenburg or the Polish Commonwealth. But from the 16th century onwards, the military threat in the West was always much greater than that in the East, field artillery and modern infantry now easily outclassing mounted archery as weapons of warfare. Thus in Russia too, the really decisive phases of the transition towards Absolutism occurred during successive phases of Swedish expansion. The pivotal reign of Ivan IV in the late 16th century was dominated by the long Livonian Wars, of which Sweden was the strategic victor, annexing Estonia by the Treaty of Yam Zapolsky in 1582: a springboard for mastery of the Northern Baltic littoral. The Time of Troubles in the early 17th century, which ended with the critical accession of the

5. On the eve of Ivan IV's attack on the Tartar Khanate of Kazan in 1552, there are supposed to have been 100,000 Russian slaves there. The total number of slaves captured by Tartar raids from the Crimea in the first half of the 17th century was upwards of 200,000: G. Vernadsky, *The Tsardom of Moscow 1547–1682*, I, Yale 1969, pp. 51–4, 12.

Romanov dynasty, saw Swedish power unfurled into the depths of Russia. Amidst mounting chaos, a corps commanded by De La Gardie fought its way to Moscow to shore up the usurper Shuisky; three years later a Swedish candidate – Gustavus Adolphus's brother – came within an ace of election to the Russian monarchy itself, only just being blocked by that of Mikhail Romanov in 1613. The new regime was promptly obliged to cede Karelia and Ingria to Sweden, which within another decade had seized the whole of Livonia from Poland, giving it virtually complete control of the Baltic. Swedish influence was also extensive within the Russian political system itself, in the early years of Romanov rule.[6] Finally, of course, the massive statal edifice of Peter I in the early 18th century was erected during and against the supreme Swedish military offensive into Russia, led by Charles XII, which had started by shattering Russian armies at Narva and was eventually to thrust deep into the Ukraine. Tsarist power within Russia was thus tested and forged in the international struggle for ascendancy with the Swedish Empire in the Baltic. The Austrian State had been turned back from Germany by Swedish expansion; the Polish State disjointed altogether; the Prussian and Russian States, by contrast, withstood and repelled it, acquiring their developed form in the course of the contest. Eastern Absolutism was thus centrally determined by the constraints of the international political system into which the nobilities of the whole region were objectively integrated.[7] It was the price of their survival in a civilization of unremitting territorial warfare; the uneven development of feudalism obliged them to match the State structures of the West before they had reached any comparable stage of economic transition towards capitalism.

Yet this Absolutism was, inevitably, also overdetermined by the course of class struggle within the Eastern social formations. It is now necessary to consider the endogenous pressures which contributed to its emergence. An initial concordance is striking. The decisive juridical

6. J. H. Billington, *The Icon and the Axe*, London 1966, p. 110; this is a subject which invites further research.

7. For an acknowledgement of this by a Russian historian, see A. N. Chistozvonov, 'Nekotorye Aspekty Problemy Genezisa Absoliutizma', *Voprosy Istorii*, No. 5, May 1968, pp. 60–1. Although it contains some wild judgments (on Spain, for example), this comparative essay is probably the best recent Soviet discussion of the origins of Absolutism, in Eastern and Western Europe.

and economic consolidation of serfdom in Prussia, Russia and Bohemia occurred during precisely the same decades in which the political foundations of the Absolutist State were firmly laid. This double development – institutionalization of serfdom and inauguration of Absolutism – was in all three cases closely and clearly linked in the history of the social formation concerned. In Brandenburg, the Great Elector and the Estates sealed the famous bargain of 1653, consigned in a formal Charter, whereby the nobility voted taxes for a permanent army, and the prince decreed ordinances binding the rural labour force irretrievably to the land. The taxes were to be levied on the towns and peasants, not on the junkers themselves, while the army was to be the core of the whole Prussian State. It was a pact which both increased the political power of the dynasty over the nobility, and that of the nobility over the peasantry. East German serfdom was now normalized and standardized everywhere in the Hohenzollern lands beyond the Elbe; while the Estates system was relentlessly suppressed by the monarchy, in province after province. By 1683, the Landtage of Brandenburg and East Prussia had lost all power, permanently.[8] Meanwhile, in Russia a very similar conjuncture had occurred. In 1648, the Zemsky Sobor – Assembly of the Land – gathered in Moscow, to pass the historic *Sobornoe Ulozhenie* which for the first time codified and universalized serfdom for the rural population; instituted strict state control over the towns and their inhabitants; while at the same time confirming and clinching the formal liability of all noble lands for military service. The *Sobornoe Ulozhenie* was the first comprehensive legal code to be promulgated in Russia, and its advent was a momentous event: it provided, in effect, Tsarism with the regulative juridical framework for its solidification as a state system. The solemn proclamation of the enserfment of the Russian peasantry was followed, here too, by the swift desuetude of the Estates system. Within a decade the Zemsky Sobor had effectively faded away, while the monarchy built up a large semi-permanent army that eventually superseded the old gentry levies altogether. The last, token Zemsky Sobor passed into

8. When the foregathered nobles recorded their melancholy conviction in Brandenburg that the ancient privileges of the Estates were virtually 'annulled and emaciated so that no *umbra libertatis* seemed to be left'. Cit. Carsten, *The Origins of Prussia*, p. 200.

oblivion in 1683, by now a shadowy court claque. The social pact between the Russian monarchy and aristocracy was sealed, establishing absolutism in exchange for finalizing serfdom.

There was a comparable synchronism of developments in Bohemia, within much the same period, if in the differing context of the Thirty Years' War. The Treaty of Westphalia which ended the long military struggle in 1648, consecrated the dual victory of the Habsburg monarchy over the Bohemian Estates, and the landed magnates over the Czech peasantry. The bulk of the old Czech aristocracy had been eliminated after the Battle of the White Mountain, and with it the political constitution which embodied their local power. The *Verneuerte Landesordnung* which now came into unchallenged effect concentrated all executive power in Vienna: the Estates – their traditional social leadership wiped out – were reduced to a perfunctory ceremonial role. The autonomy of the towns was crushed. In the countryside, ruthless measures of enserfment followed, on the great estates. The wholesale prescriptions and confiscations of the former Czech nobility and gentry created a new, cosmopolitan aristocracy of military adventurers and court functionaries, which together with the Church henceforward controlled nearly three-quarters of all lands in Bohemia. Demographic losses were enormous after the Thirty Years' War, creating acute labour shortages. The labour services of the *robot* soon reached half the working week, while feudal dues, tithes and taxes could take up to two-thirds of the peasants' produce.[9] Austrian Absolutism, checked in Germany, triumphed in Bohemia; and with it, the remaining liberties of the Czech peasantry were extinguished. Thus in all three regions, the consolidation of landlord control over the peasantry, and discrimination against the towns, was tied to a sharp increase in the prerogatives of the monarchy and was succeeded by a disappearance of the estates system.

The cities of Eastern Europe, as we have seen, had been generally curtailed and repressed in the late mediaeval depression. The economic upswing throughout the continent in the 16th century, however, fostered a new if uneven urban growth in certain zones of the East. From 1550 onwards, the Bohemian towns regained much of their prosperity, although under the aegis of urban patriciates closely linked

9. Polišensky, *The Thirty Years' War*, p. 245.

to the nobility by municipal landownership, and without the popular vitality which had once distinguished them in the Hussite epoch. In East Prussia, Königsberg still remained a robust outpost of burgher autonomy. In Russia, Moscow had burgeoned after the formal emergence of the Tsardom with Ivan III, benefiting notably from the long-distance trade between Europe and Asia that crossed Russia, in which the older mercantile centres of Novgorod and Pskov also participated. The maturation of the Absolutist States in the 17th century now effectively dealt a death-blow to the possibility of a revival of urban independence in the East. The new monarchies – Hohenzollern, Habsburg and Romanov – unshakeably assured the political supremacy of the nobility over the towns. The only corporate body seriously to resist the *Gleichschaltung* of the Great Elector after the Recess of 1653 was the city of Königsberg in East Prussia: it was crushed in 1662–3 and 1674, while the local junkers looked on.[10] In Russia, Moscow itself lacked any substantial burgher class, trade being cornered by boyars, officials and a small ring of *gosti* merchants dependent on the government for their status and privileges: but it did contain numerous artisans, an anarchic semi-rural labour force, and the truculent and demoralized musketeers of the *strel'tsy* militia. The immediate cause of the convocation of the fateful Zemsky Sobor which promulgated the *Sobornoe Ulozhenie* had been a sudden explosion by these heterogeneous groups. Rioting mobs enraged by rising prices of basic commodities, following tax-increases by the Morozov administration, seized Moscow and forced the Tsar to flee the city, while disaffection rumbled in the rural provinces towards Siberia. Once royal control of the capital was regained, the Zemsky Sobor was summoned, and the *Ulozhenie* decreed. Novgorod and Pskov revolted against fiscal exactions, and were definitively suppressed, ceasing to have any economic importance thereafter. The last urban tumults in Moscow occurred in 1662, when protesting craftsmen were easily subdued, and in 1683, when Peter I finally liquidated the *strel'tsy*. Thereafter, Russian towns gave no trouble to monarchy or aristocracy. In the Czech lands, the Thirty Years' War finished off the pride and growth of the Bohemian and Moravian cities: the ceaseless devastations and sieges during the campaigns of the war, coupled with the

10. Carsten, *The Origins of Prussia*, pp. 212–14, 220–1.

cancellations of municipal autonomy after it, henceforward reduced them to passive counters within the Habsburg Empire.

The most fundamental domestic rationale of Eastern Absolutism, however, lay in the countryside. Its complex machinery of repression was essentially and primarily directed against the peasantry. The 17th century was an epoch of declining prices and population throughout most of Europe. In the East, wars and civil disasters had created particularly acute labour crises. The Thirty Years' War had inflicted a brutal setback to the whole German economy east of the Elbe. There were demographic losses of up to 50 per cent in many districts of Brandenburg.[11] In Bohemia, the total population declined from 1,700,000 to less than 1,000,000 by the signature of the Peace of Westphalia.[12] In the Russian lands, the intolerable strain of the Livonian Wars and the Oprichnina had led to a calamitous depopulation and evacuation of Central Russia in the last years of the 16th century; from 76 to 96 per cent of the settlements in the province of Moscow itself were abandoned.[13] The Time of Troubles, with its civil wars, foreign invasions and rural rebellions, then compounded the instability and scarcity of the work-force at the disposal of the land-owning class. The demographic down-turn of this epoch thus created, or aggravated, a constant shortage of rural labour for demesne cultivation There was, moreover, a permanent regional background to this phenomenon: the endemic problem for Eastern feudalism of the land/labour ratio – the existence of too few peasants scattered over too vast spaces. A comparison may give some idea of the contrast of conditions with those of Western Europe: the population density of Russia in the 17th century was 3 to 4 persons per square kilometre, at a time when that of France was 40, or some 10 times greater.[14] In the fertile lands of South-Eastern Poland and Western Ukraine, the richest agricultural zone of the *Rzeczspospolita*, demographic density was little more – some 3 to 7 persons per square kilometre.[15] Most of the Central Hungarian Plain – now the borderlands between the Austrian and Turkish

11. Stoye, *Europe Unfolding 1648–1688*, p. 31.
12. Polišensky, *The Thirty Years' War*, p. 245.
13. R. H. Hellie, *Enserfment and Military Change in Muscovy*, p. 95.
14. R. Mousnier, *Peasant Uprisings*, pp. 157, 159.
15. P. Skwarczyński, 'Poland and Lithuania', *The New Cambridge Modern History of Europe*, III, Cambridge 1968, p. 377.

Empires – was equally depopulated. The first objective of the landlord class was thus everywhere, not so much as in the West to fix the level of dues to be paid by the peasant, as to arrest the mobility of the villager and bind him to the estates. Conversely, over huge areas of Eastern Europe, the most typical and effective form of class struggle waged by the peasantry was simply *flight* – collective desertion of the land for uninhabited and uncharted spaces beyond.

The measures taken by the Prussian, Austrian and Czech nobility to prevent this traditional mobility in the late mediaeval epoch have already been described; they were naturally intensified in the inaugural era of Absolutism. Farther east, in Russia and Poland, the problem was even more serious. No stable frontiers or boundaries of settlement existed in the wide Pontic hinterlands lying between the two countries; the deeply forested North of Russia was traditionally a zone of 'black-earth' peasantry beyond seigneurial control; while Western Siberia and the Volga-Don region in the South-East constituted remote, trackless expanses still in the process of gradual colonization. Uncovenanted rural emigration in all these directions offered the possibility of escaping manorial exploitation for independent peasant farming in frontier conditions, however harsh. Throughout the 17th century, the whole, long drawn-out process of the enserfment of Russian peasantry must be set against this inchoate natural context: a huge, friable margin existed all round the pattern of noble land-holdings. Thus it is a historical paradox that Siberia was being opened up largely by peasant smallholders from the 'black-earth' communities of the North, seeking greater personal freedom and economic opportunities, during the very period when the great mass of the central peasantry was sinking into abject bondage.[16] It was this absence of normal territorial fixitude in Russia that accounts for the striking survival of slavery on a very considerable scale; in the later 16th century, slaves still cultivated some 9–15 per cent of Russian estates.[17] For, as has repeatedly been seen, the presence of rural slavery in a feudal social formation always signifies that the system of serfdom itself is not yet closed, and that considerable

---

16. A. N. Sakharov, 'O Dialektike Istoricheskovo Razvitiya Russkovo Krest'yanstva', *Voprosy Istorii*, No. 1, January 1970, pp. 26–7, emphasizes this contrast.

17. Mousnier, *Peasant Uprisings*, pp. 174–5.

numbers of direct producers in the countryside are still obversely free. The possession of slaves was one of the great assets of the boyar class, giving them a critical economic advantage on their estates over the smaller service gentry:[18] it ceased to be necessary only when the net of enserfment had drawn tight over virtually the whole Russian peasantry in the 18th century. Meanwhile, there was unremitting inter-feudal competition for control of 'souls' to cultivate noble or clerical lands: boyars and monasteries with more profitable and rational manors often took in fugitive serfs from smaller estates, obstructing their recovery by their former masters, to the fury of the squire-class. It was not until a stable and powerful central autocracy was established, with a coercive state apparatus capable of enforcing adscription throughout Russian territory, that these conflicts were suspended. It was thus the constant seigneurial preoccupation with the problem of labour mobility in the East which undoubtedly lay behind much of the internal drift towards Absolutism.[19] Seigneurial laws tying the peasantry to the soil had already been widely passed in the preceding epoch. But as we have seen, their implementation usually remained very imperfect: actual labour patterns by no means always corresponded to the provisions of statute-books. The mission of Absolutism was everywhere to convert juridical theory into economic practice. A ruthlessly centralized and unitary repressive apparatus was an objective necessity for the surveillance and suppression of widespread rural mobility in times of economic depression; no mere network of individual landlord jurisdictions, no matter how despotic, could be wholly adequate to cope with the problem. The domestic policing functions necessary for the second serfdom in the East were in this respect more exigent than those needed for the first serfdom in the West: the result was to render possible an Absolutist State in advance of the relations of production

18. See Vernadsky's notable paper, 'Serfdom in Russia', *X Congresso Internazionale di Scienze Storiche, Relazioni III*, Florence 1955, pp. 247–72, which rightly points out the importance of rural slavery in Russia as a peculiarity of the agrarian system.

19. Some idea of the scale of the problem for the ruling class in Russia can be gained from the fact that as late as 1718–19, long after the legal consolidation of general serfdom, the census conducted by Peter I unearthed no less than 200,000 fugitive serfs, amounting to some 3·4 per cent of the total subject population, who were repatriated to their former masters. See M. Ya. Volkov, 'O Stanovlenii Absoliutizma v Rossii', *Istoriya SSSR*, January 1970, p. 104.

on which it was founded, contemporary with that of the West in the transition beyond serfdom.

Poland, again, was the apparent exception to the logic of this process. But just as externally it paid the penalty of the Swedish Deluge for not producing an Absolutism, so internally the price of its failure was the greatest peasant insurrection of the epoch – the ordeal of the Ukrainian Revolution of 1648, which cost it a third of its territory and dealt *szlachta* morale and prowess a blow from which it never fully recovered: which was, indeed, the immediate prelude to the Swedish War, with which it interlocked. The peculiar character of the Ukrainian Revolution was the direct result of the basic problem of peasant mobility and flight in the East.[20] For it was a rebellion set off by relatively privileged 'cossacks' in the Dnieper region, who were in origin fugitive Russian or Ruthenian peasants, or Circassian highlanders, who had settled in the vast borderlands between Poland, Russia and the Tartar Khanate of the Crimea. In these no man's lands, they had come to adopt a semi-nomadic, equestrian mode of life similar to that of the Tartars against whom they customarily fought. Over time, a complex social structure had developed in the Cossack communities. Their political and military centre came to be the fortified island or *sech* below the Dnieper rapids, created in 1557 – which formed a warrior encampment, organized into regiments which elected delegates to a council of officers or *starshina*, that in turn selected a supreme commander or *Hetman*. Outside the Zaporozhe *sech*, roving bands of brigands and foresters mingled with settled villages of farmers under their own elders. The Polish nobility, when it encountered these communities in its expansion into the Ukraine, had found it necessary to tolerate the armed force of the Zaporozhian Cossacks in a limited number of 'registered' regiments technically under Polish command. Cossack troops were used as mounted auxiliaries in Polish campaigns into Moldavia, Livonia and Russia, and successful officers came to constitute a propertied elite, dominating the rank-and-file Cossacks, sometimes eventually becoming Polish nobles themselves.

This social convergence with the local *szlachta*, who had steadily extended their lands eastwards, did not alter the military anomaly of

20. For a full account of Ukrainian social structure and the revolution of 1648–54, see Vernadsky, *The Tsardom of Moscow*, I, pp. 439–81.

the regimental independence of the *sech*, with its semi-popular free-booting basis; nor did it affect the clusters of agricultural cossacks living among the serf population tilling the latifundia of the Polish aristocracy in the region. Peasant mobility had thus given birth in the Pontic grasslands to a sociological phenomenon virtually unknown in the West at the time – commoner rural masses capable of fielding organized armies against a feudal aristocracy. The sudden mutiny of the registered companies under their *Hetman* Khmelnitsky in 1648 was thus professionally able to take on Polish armies sent against them, and their rebellion in its turn set off a vast general rising of the serfs of the Ukraine, who fought side by side with the poor Cossack peasantry to throw off their Polish landlords. Three years later, the Polish peasants themselves revolted in the Cracow region of Podhale, in an agrarian movement inspired by that of the Ukrainian cossacks and serfs. A savage social war was waged in Galicia and the Ukraine, in which the *szlachta* armies were repeatedly worsted by Zaporozhian forces. It ended with the fateful transfer of allegiance by Khmelnitsky from Poland to Russia at the Treaty of Pereyaslavl in 1654, which brought the whole of the Ukraine beyond the Dnieper under the rule of the Tsars, and secured the interests of the Cossack *starshina*.[21] The Ukrainian peasantry – Cossack and non-Cossack – were the victims of the operation: the 'pacification' of the Ukraine with the integration of the officer corps into the Russian State restored their bonds. Eventually, indeed, after a long evolution, Cossack squadrons were to form an elite corps of the Tsarist Autocracy. The Treaty of Pereyaslavl symbolized, in effect, the respective parabola of the two great rivals of the region in the 17th century. The parcellized Polish State proved unable to defeat and subordinate the Cossacks, just as it failed to resist the Swedes. The centralized Tsarist autocracy was able to do both – repel the Swedish threat and not only subjugate, but in the end utilize the Cossacks as repressive dragoons against its own masses.

The Ukrainian rising was the most formidable peasant war of the epoch in the East. But it was not the only one. All the major East European nobilities were at one time or another in the 17th century

---

21. For the negotiations and provisions of the Treaty of Pereyaslavl, see the succinct account in C. B. O'Brien, *Muscovy and the Ukraine*, Berkeley-Los Angeles 1963, pp. 21–7.

confronted with serf rebellions. In Brandenburg, there were repeated outbreaks of rural violence in the central district of Prignitz, during the closing phase of the Thirty Years' War and the decade which succeeded it: in 1645, 1646, 1648, 1650 and again in 1656.[22] The concentration of princely power by the Great Elector must be seen against this background of unrest and despair in the villages. The Bohemian peasantry, subjected to a steady degradation of its economic and legal position after the Treaty of Westphalia, rose against its lords across the country in 1680, when Austrian troops had to be dispatched to suppress them. Above all, in Russia itself, there was an unequalled record of rural insurrections, which stretched from the Time of Troubles at the turn of the 17th century to the era of the Enlightenment in the 18th century. In 1606–7, peasants, plebeians and cossacks in the Dnieper region seized provincial power under the ex-slave Bolotnikov; their armies nearly installed the False Dimitri as Tsar in Moscow. In 1633–4, serfs and deserters in the war zone of Smolensk revolted under the peasant Balash. In 1670–1, virtually the whole of the South-East, from Astrakhan to Simbirsk, threw off landlord control as teeming armies of peasants and cossacks marched up the Volga valley led by the bandit Razin. In 1707–8, the rural masses of the Lower Don followed the cossack Bulavin in a fierce rebellion against the increased tax-loads and forced labour in the ship-yards imposed by Peter I. Finally, in 1773–4, there occurred the last and most formidable insurrection of all: the awesome rising of multiple exploited populations from the foothills of the Urals and the deserts of Bashkiria to the shores of the Caspian, commanded by Pugachev, which mingled mountain and steppe cossacks, empressed factory workers, peasants of the plains, and pastoral tribes in a series of risings that necessitated the full-scale deployment of the Russian imperial armies to be defeated.

All these popular revolts originated in the indeterminate borderlands of Russian territory: Galicia, Belorussia, Ukraine, Astrakhan, Siberia. For there the power of the central state dwindled and shifting masses of free-booters, adventurers and fugitives mixed with settled serfs and noble estates: the four largest rebellions were all led by armed Cossack elements, who provided the military experience and organization which made them so dangerous to the feudal class. Significantly, it was with

22. Stoye, *Europe Unfolding 1648–1688*, p. 30.

the final closure of the Ukrainian and Siberian frontiers in the late 18th century, after Potemkin's colonization schemes were completed, that the Russian peasantry was finally beaten into sullen quiescence. Thus throughout Eastern Europe, the intensity of class struggle in the countryside – always latent in the form of rural flights – also detonated peasant explosions against serfdom in which the collective power and property of the nobility was frontally threatened. The planar social geography of most of the region, which distinguished it from the more segmented space of Western Europe,[23] could lend this menace particularly serious forms. The widespread danger from their own serfs consequently acted as a general centripetal force on the Eastern aristocracies. The ascent of the Absolutist State in the 17th century ultimately answered to social fear: its politico-military apparatus of coercion was the guarantee of the stability of serfdom. There was thus an internal order to Absolutism in the East that complemented its external determination: the function of the centralized State was to defend the class position of the feudal nobility against both its rivals abroad and its peasants at home. The organization and discipline of the one and the fluidity and contumacy of the other dictated a quickened political unity. The Absolutist State was thus reduplicated beyond the Elbe, to become a general European phenomenon.

What were the specific traits of the Eastern variant of this fortified feudal machine? Two basic and inter-related peculiarities may be singled out. Firstly, the influence of war in its structure was even more preponderant than in the West, and took unprecedented forms. Prussia represents perhaps the extreme limit reached by the militarization of the genesis of this State. Functional focus on war here effectively reduced the nascent State apparatus to a by-product of the military machine of the ruling class. The Absolutism of the Great Elector of Brandenburg was, as we have seen, born amidst the turmoil of the Swedish expeditions across the Baltic in the 1650's. Its internal evolution and articulation was to represent an expressive fulfilment of Treitschke's dictum: 'War is the father of culture and the mother of creation.' For

23. The contrast between the endless, flat topography of the East, which facilitated flights, and the more accidented and confined relief of the West, which assisted labour control, is emphasized by Lattimore, 'Feudalism in History', pp. 55–6, and Mousnier, *Peasant Uprisings*, pp. 157, 159.

the entire tax-structure, civil service and local administration of the Great Elector came into being as technical sub-departments of the *Generalkriegskommissariat*. From 1679 onwards, during the war with Sweden, this unique institution became, under the command of Von Grumbkow, the supreme organ of Hohenzollern Absolutism. The Prussian bureaucracy, in other words, was born as an offshoot of the Army. The *Generalkriegskommissariat* formed an omnicompetent war and finance ministry which not only maintained the standing army, but collected taxes, regulated industry and provided the provincial official-dom of the Brandenburger State. The great Prussian historian Otto Hintze described the development of this structure into the next century: 'The whole organization of officialdom was interlocked with military objectives and designed to serve them. The very provincial police officials were derived from the war commissariats. Every Minister of State was simultaneously entitled a War Minister, every councillor in the administrative and fiscal chambers was simultaneously entitled a war councillor. One-time officers became provincial coun-cillors, or indeed presidents and ministers; the administrative officials were mostly recruited from former regimental quarter-masters and auditors; the lower positions were filled as much as possible with retired NCOs and war invalids. The entire State thus acquired a military trim. The whole social system was placed in the service of militarism. Nobles, burghers and peasants were merely there, each in their own sphere, to serve the State and *travailler pour le roi de Prusse*.'[24] By the end of the 18th century, the percentage of the population enrolled in the Army was perhaps 4 times higher than that of contemporary France,[25] and was typically replenished by ruthless pressganging of foreign peasants and deserters. Junker control of its command was virtually absolute. This formidable military machine regularly absorbed some 70–80 per cent of the fiscal revenues of the State by the time of Frederick II.[26]

Austrian Absolutism, as will be seen, was always much more heteroclite in structure, exhibiting an imperfect compound of Western and Eastern traits, befitting its mixed territorial basis in Central

24. Hintze, *Gesammelte Abhandlungen*, I, p. 61.
25. Dorn, *Competition for Empire*, p. 94.
26. A. J. P. Taylor, *The Course of German History*, London 1961, p. 19.

Europe. No concentration comparable to that of Berlin ever prevailed in Vienna. But it is nevertheless noticeable that within the eclectic administrative system of the Habsburg State, much of the hard centre and innovating impetus from the mid 16th to the late 18th centuries derived from the Imperial military complex. Indeed, for a long time, it was this alone which gave practical reality to the dynastic unity of the disparate lands ruled by the Habsburgs. Thus the Supreme War Council or *Hofkriegsrat* was the only governing body with jurisdiction throughout the Habsburg territories in the 16th century, the sole executive agency uniting them under the ruling line. In addition to its defense duties against the Turks, the *Hofkriegsrat* was responsible for direct civil administration of the whole band of territory along the south-eastern frontier of Austria and Hungary, which was garrisoned with *Grenzer* militias subject to it. Its subsequent role in the slow growth of Habsburg centralization, and the construction of a developed Absolutism, was always a determinant one. 'Probably of all the central organs of government, it was ultimately the most influential in assisting the unification of the various hereditary territories, and all, including Bohemia and particularly Hungary, for the protection of which it had been primarily designed, accepted its supreme control over military affairs.'[27] The professional army which emerged after the Thirty Years War sealed the victory of the dynasty over the Bohemian Estates: maintained by the taxes of the Bohemian and Austrian lands, it became the first permanent apparatus of government in both realms, remaining without a real civilian equivalent for over a century. In the Magyar lands, too, it was the extension of the Habsburg army into Hungary in the early 18th century which finally drew it into a closer political union with the other dynastic possessions. Absolutist power here dwelt exclusively within the military branch of the State: Hungary henceforward provided cantonments and troops for the Habsburg armies, which occupied geographical terrain that otherwise remained constitutionally beyond bounds for the rest of the Imperial administration. At the same time, the newly conquered territories further to the East, wrested from the Turks, were put under army control: Transylvania and the Banat were managed directly by the Supreme War Council in

27. H. F. Schwarz, *The Imperial Privy Council in the Seventeenth Century*, Harvard 1943, p. 26.

Vienna, which organized and supervised the systematic colonization of these lands by German immigrants. The machinery of war was thus always the most constant escort of the development of Austrian Absolutism. But the Austrian armies nonetheless never achieved the position of their Prussian counterparts: the militarization of the State was checked by the limits to its centralization. The ultimate lack of a rigorous political unity in the Habsburg domains was to prevent any comparable elevation of the military establishment within Austrian Absolutism.

The role of the military apparatus in Russia, on the other hand, was scarcely less great than in Prussia. In his discussion of the historical specificity of the Muscovite Empire, Kliuchevsky commented: 'The first of these peculiarities was the war-like organization of the State. The Muscovite Empire was Great Rus in arms.'[28] The most celebrated masons of this edifice, Ivan IV and Peter I, both designed their basic administrative system to augment Russian war capacity. Ivan IV tried to reshuffle the whole land-holding pattern of Muscovy to convert it to service tenure, increasingly committing the nobility to permanent military duties in the Muscovite State. 'Land became an economic means of securing to the State a sufficiency of military service, while landownership by the official class became the basis of a system of national defense.'[29] Warfare was perennial throughout most of the 16th century, with Swedes, Poles, Lithuanians, Tartars and other antagonists. Ivan IV finally plunged into the long Livonian Wars which ended in a generalized catastrophe in the 1580's. The Time of Troubles and the subsequent consolidation of the Romanov dynasty, however, developed the basic trend of linking ownership of land to a build-up of the army. Peter I then gave this system its most implacable and universal form. All land became liable for military duty, and all nobles had to start indefinite State service at the age of 15. Two-thirds of the members of every noble family had to enter the Army: only every third son was allowed to do his service in the civilian bureaucracy.[30] Peter's military and naval expenses in 1724 totalled 75 per cent

28. V. O. Kliuchevsky, *A History of Russia*, II, London 1912, p. 319.
29. Kliuchevsky, op. cit., p. 120.
30. M. Beloff, 'Russia', in Goodwin (ed.), *The European Nobility in the 18th Century*, pp. 174–5.

of State revenues[31] – for one of the few years of peace of his reign.

The overwhelming focus of the Absolutist State on war was not supererogatory. It corresponded to much greater upheavals of conquest and expansion than occurred in the West. The cartography of Eastern Absolutism closely corresponded to its dynamic structure. Muscovy multiplied some twelve times over in size during the 15th and 16th centuries, absorbing Novgorod, Kazan and Astrakhan; the Russian State then expanded steadily in the 17th century by annexing the Western Ukraine and part of Belorussia; while in the 18th century it seized the Baltic lands, the rest of the Ukraine and Crimea. Brandenburg acquired Pomerania in the 17th century; the Prussian State then doubled its size by the conquest of Silesia in the 18th century. The Habsburg State, based in Austria, reconquered Bohemia in the 17th century, had subdued Hungary by the 18th century, and annexed Croatia, Transylvania and Oltenia in the Balkans. Finally, Russia, Prussia and Austria divided the whole of Poland between them – once the largest state in Europe. The rationality and necessity of a 'super-absolutism' for the feudal class in the East received in this final dénouement a symmetrical demonstration, from the example of its absence. The manorial reaction of the Prussian and Russian nobles was completed by a perfected Absolutism. Their Polish homologues, after no less ferocious a subjection of the peasantry, failed to generate one. By thus jealously preserving the individual rights of every squireen against every other, and all against any dynasty, the Polish gentry committed collective suicide. Their pathological fear of a central state power institutionalized a nobiliary anarchy. The result was predictable: Poland was wiped off the map by its neighbours, who demonstrated on the battle-field the higher necessity of the Absolutist State.

The extreme militarization of the State was structurally linked to the second major peculiarity of Absolutism in both Prussia and Russia. This lay in the nature of the functional relationship between the feudal landowners and the Absolutist monarchies. The critical difference between the Eastern and Western variants can be seen in the respective modes of integration of the nobility into the new bureaucracy created by them. In neither Prussia nor Russia did sale of offices exist on any considerable scale. The Ostelbian junkers had been charac-

31. V. O. Kliuchevsky, *A History of Russia*, Vol. IV, pp. 144–5.

terized by grasping public greed in the 16th century, when there was generalized corruption and malversation of state funds, farming of sinecures, and manipulations of royal credit.[32] This was to be the epoch of unchallenged domination by the *Herrenstand* and *Ritterscha,t*, and enfeeblement of any central public authority. The advent of Hohenzollern Absolutism in the 17th century radically altered the situation. The new Prussian State henceforward enforced an increasing financial probity in its administration. Purchase of profitable positions in the bureaucracy by nobles was not permitted. Significantly, only in the much more socially advanced Hohenzollern enclaves of Cleves and Mark in the Rhineland, where there was a flourishing urban bourgeoisie, was purchase of office formally sanctioned by Frederick William I and his successors.[33] In Prussia itself, the civil service was on the whole remarkable for its conscientious professionalism. In Russia, on the other hand, frauds and embezzlement were endemic in the Muscovite and Romanov State machines, which regularly lost a large proportion of their revenues in this way. But this phenomenon was merely a straightforward and primitive variety of peculation and theft, if on a huge and chaotic scale. Sale of offices proper – as a regulated and legal system of recruitment to the bureaucracy – never became seriously established in Russia. Nor was it ever a significant practice in the relatively more advanced Austrian State either, which – unlike some of its princely neighbours in South Germany – never harboured an 'officer' class that had purchased its administrative positions. The reasons for the general Eastern disjuncture from the Western pattern are evident. Swart's comprehensive study of the distribution of the phenomenon of sale of offices justly emphasizes its connection with the existence of a local commercial class.[34] In other words, in the West, sale of offices corresponded to the over-determination of the late feudal state by the swift growth of mercantile and manufacturing capital. The contradictory nexus which it established between public office and private persons reflected mediaeval conceptions of sovereignty and contract, in which an impersonal civic order did not exist; yet this was

32. Hans Rosenberg, 'The Rise of the Junkers in Brandenberg-Prussia 1410–1563', *American Historical Review*, October 1943, p. 20.

33. Hans Rosenberg, *Bureaucracy, Aristocracy and Autocracy – The Prussian Experience 1680–1815*, Cambridge 1958, p. 78.

34. K. W. Swart, *Sale of Offices in the Seventeenth Century*, p. 96.

simultaneously a cash nexus, reflecting the presence and interference of a monetary economy and its future masters, the urban bourgeoisie. Merchants, lawyers and bankers had access to the State machine if they could unbelt the sums necessary to buy positions in it. The exchange nature of the transaction was also, of course, an index of the intra-class relationship between the ruling aristocracy and its State: unification by corruption rather than coercion produced a milder and more advanced Absolutism.

In the East, on the other hand, there was no urban bourgeoisie to inflect the character of the Absolutist State; it was not tempered by a mercantile sector. The stiflingly anti-urban policies of the Prussian and Polish nobility have already been seen. In Russia, the Tsars controlled trade – frequently through their own monopoly enterprises – and administered the towns. Uniquely, urban residents were often serfs. The result was to make the hybrid phenomenon of sale of offices impracticable. Undiluted feudal principles were to govern the construction of the State machine. The device of a *service nobility* was in many respects the Eastern correlate of sale of offices in the West. The Prussian junker class was incorporated directly into the War Commissariat and its financial and tax services, by recruitment to the State. In the civilian bureaucracy, there was always an important leavening of non-aristocratic elements, although these were normally ennobled once they reached the top positions in it.[35] In the countryside, the junkers maintained rigorous control of the local *Gutsbezirke* and were thus vested with a complete panoply of fiscal, juridical, police and conscription powers over their peasants. The provincial bureaucratic organs of the 18th century civil service, the suggestively entitled *Kriegs-und-Domänen-Kammern* (War-and-Manorial Chambers) were likewise increasingly dominated by them. In the Army itself, officer command was the professional reserve of the landowning class. 'Only young noblemen were admitted into the cadet companies and schools which he (Frederick William I) founded, and noble non-commissioned officers were listed by name in the quarterly returns made to his son: indicating that noblemen were *eo ipso* considered to be officer aspirants. Although many commoners were commissioned under the stress of the war of the Spanish Succession, they were purged soon after its end.

35. Rosenberg, *Bureaucracy, Aristocracy and Autocracy*, pp. 139–43.

Thus the nobility became a service nobility; it identified its interests with those of the State which gave them positions of honour and profit.'[36]

In Austria, there was no such compact fit between the Absolutist State apparatus and the aristocracy; the insurmountable heterogeneity of the landed classes of the Habsburg realms effectively precluded it. Yet a drastic if incomplete sketch for a service nobility occurred there too: for the Habsburg reconquest of Bohemia in the Thirty Years' War was followed by the systematic destruction of the old Czech and German aristocracy of the Bohemian lands, which were planted with a new and foreign nobility, of Catholic faith and cosmopolitan origins, which owed its estates and fortunes entirely to the fiat of the dynasty that had created it. The new 'Bohemian' aristocracy henceforward provided the dominant contingent of cadres to the Habsburg State, becoming the major social basis of Austrian Absolutism. But the abrupt radicalism of its construction from above was not reproduced in the subsequent forms of its integration into the State machine: the composite dynastic polity ruled by the Habsburgs rendered a uniform or 'regulated' bureaucratic cooption of the nobility into the service of Absolutism impossible.[37] Military positions above certain ranks and after certain periods of duty were to confer titles automatically: but no general or institutionalized linkage between State service and the aristocratic order emerged, to the ultimate detriment of the international strength of Austrian Absolutism.

In the more primitive environment of Russia, on the other hand, the principles of a service nobility were to go much further even than in Prussia. There, Ivan IV promulgated a decree in 1556 which made military service obligatory for every lord, and laid down precise allocations of warriors to be supplied from given units of land, thereby consolidating the *pomeshchik* class of gentry which had started to emerge under his predecessor. Conversely, only persons performing State service could henceforward technically own land in Russia, apart from religious institutions. This system never achieved the universality

36. Carsten, *The Origins of Prussia*, p. 272.

37. Schwarz comments, however, that the old high nobility of the Habsburg State essentially owed its ascent to service in the Imperial Privy Council during the 17th century: *The Imperial Privy Council in the Seventeenth Century*, p. 410.

or efficacy in practice which was conferred on it by law, and by no means ended the autonomous power of the anterior magnate class of boyars whose estates remained in allodial tenure. But despite many zigzags and reverses, Ivan's successors inherited and developed his work. Blum comments on the first Romanov ruler: 'The State over which Michael was called to rule was a unique kind of political organization. It was a Service State and the tsar was its absolute ruler. The activities and obligations of all subjects, from the greatest lord to the meanest peasant, were determined by the State in the pursuit of its own interests and policies. Every subject was bound to certain specific functions that were designed to preserve and aggrandise the power and authority of the State. The seigniors were bound to do service in the army and bureaucracy, and the peasants were bound to the seigniors to provide them with the means to perform their state service. Whatever freedoms or privileges a subject might enjoy were his only because the State allowed them to him as a perquisite of the function he performed in its service.'[38] This is a rhetorical evocation of the claims of Tsarist autocracy or *samoderzhavie*, not a description of the actual state structure itself: the practical realities of the Russian social formation were far from corresponding to the omnipotent political system suggested by it. The ideological theory of Russian Absolutism never coincided with its material powers, which were always much more limited than contemporary Western observers – often prone to travellers' exaggeration – tended to believe. Yet in any comparative European perspective, the peculiarity of the Muscovite service complex was nevertheless unmistakeable. In the late 17th and early 18th centuries, Peter I generalized and radicalized its normative principles yet further. By merging conditional and hereditary estates, he assimilated the *pomeshchik* and *boyar* classes. Every noble henceforward had to become a permanent servitor of the Tsar. The State bureaucracy was divided into fourteen ranks, the top eight of which involved hereditary noble status, and the bottom six non-hereditary aristocratic status. In this way, feudal rank and bureaucratic hierarchy were organically fused: the device of the service nobility in principle made the State a virtual simulacrum of the structure of the landowning class, under the centralized power of its 'absolute' delegate.

38. Jerome Blum, *Lord and Peasant in Russia*, p. 150.

2

Nobility and Monarchy: the Eastern Variant

It remains to establish the historical significance of the service nobility. This can best be done by looking at the evolution of the relationship between the feudal class and its State, this time in the East. It has been seen that prior to the expansion of Western feudalism eastwards in the Middle Ages, the mainly Slav social formations of Eastern Europe had nowhere produced a fully articulated feudal polity of the type which emerged from the Romano-Germanic synthesis in the West. All of them were at different stages in the transition from the inchoate tribal federations of the original settlements to stratified social hierarchies with stabilized State structures. The typical pattern, it will be remembered, combined a ruling warrior aristocracy with a heteroclite population of free peasants, debt peons and captured slaves; while the structure of the State was still often close to the retinue-system of the traditional military leader. Even Kievan Russia, the most advanced sector in the whole region, had not yet produced a unitary hereditary monarchy. The impact of Western feudalism on the social formations of the East has already been discussed at the level of its effects on the prevalent mode of production in the estates and villages, and on the organization of the towns. There has been less study of its influence on the nobility itself, but as we have seen, it is clear that there was an increasing adaptation to Western hierarchical norms within the ruling class. The higher aristocracy in Bohemia and Poland, for example, took shape precisely from the mid-12th to the early 14th centuries, the peak period of German expansion; it was also then that the Czech *rytiri* and *vladky* or knight class emerged, together with the magnate *barones*; while the use of crests and titles was adopted in both countries from

Germany by the second half of the 13th century.[1] Indeed, in most of the Eastern countries, the title system was borrowed from German (or later Danish) usages: Count, Margrave, Duke and so on were successively naturalized in the Slavonic languages.

Nevertheless, throughout both the era of economic expansion in the 11th to 13th centuries, and contraction in the 14th to 15th centuries, two critical features of the Eastern ruling classes can be noted, which date back to the absence of the Western feudal synthesis. Firstly, the institution of *conditional tenure* – the fief system proper – never really became entrenched beyond the Elbe.[2] It is true that it did initially follow the path of German colonization, and always had more grip in the Ostelbian lands permanently occupied by German junkers than elsewhere. But the German estates which owed knight-service in the East were technically allodial in the 14th century, even though they bore military obligations.[3] By the 15th century juridical fictions in Brandenburg were increasingly ignored, and the *Rittergut* was tending to become a patrimonial estate – in this respect, a process not unlike that which was occurring in West Germany. Elsewhere, too, conditional tenure generally failed to become firmly established. In Poland allodial estates outnumbered fiefs during the Middle Ages; but as in Eastern Germany, both types of property owed military service, although it was lighter on the former. From the second half of the 15th century onwards, the gentry successfully turned many feudal into allodial estates, against the efforts of the monarchy to reverse this process. From 1561 to 1588 the Sejm then passed enactments finally commuting feudal to allodial tenures everywhere.[4] In Russia, as we have seen, the typical boyar property was always the allodial *votchina*;

1. F. Dvornik, *The Slavs: Their Early History and Civilization*, p. 324; ibidem, *The Slavs in European History and Civilization*, pp. 121–8.

2. Bloch perceived this, if mistakenly offering a culturalist explanation of it, by asserting that 'the Slavs never knew' the distinction between concession for service and outright gift. See his note, 'Féodalité et Noblesse Polonaises', *Annales*, January 1939, pp. 53–4. In fact, concession of land for service was known in Western Russia from the 14th to the 16th centuries, and later emerged in the *pomest'e* system.

3. Hermann Aubin, 'The Lands East of the Elbe and German Colonization eastwards', in *The Agrarian Life of the Middle Ages*, p. 476.

4. P. Skwarczyński, 'The Problem of Feudalism in Poland up to the Beginning of the 16th century', *Slavonic and East European Review*, 34, 1955–6, pp. 296–9.

the imposition from above of the conditional *pomest'e* system was the later work of the Tsarist autocracy. In all these lands, moreover, there were few or no intermediary lordships between knights and monarchs, tenants-in-chief of the type which played such an important role in the compact feudal hierarchies of the West. Complex chains of rear-vassalage or sub-infeudation were effectively unknown. On the other hand, public authority never became so juridically limited or divided as in the mediaeval West either. Local administrative offices in all these lands were appointive rather than hereditary, and rulers retained the formal right to tax the whole peasant population, which was not subtracted from the public realm by integral private immunities or jurisdictions, although in practice the fiscal and legal powers of princes or dukes were often very limited. The result was a much less cohesive network of intra-feudal relationships than in the West.

There is little doubt that this pattern was linked to the spatial setting of Eastern feudalism. Just as the vast, sparsely populated tracts of land in the East created specific problems of labour exploitation for the nobility, because of the possibility of flights, so they also created special problems for a hierarchical integration of the nobility by princes and overlords. The frontier character of the Eastern social formations rendered it extremely difficult for dynastic rulers to enforce liege obedience from military settlers and landowners, in an unbounded milieu where armed adventurers and anarchic velleities were often at a premium. The result was that vertical feudal solidarity was much weaker than in the West. There were few organic ties binding the various aristocracies internally together. This situation was not substantially altered by the introduction of the manorial system during the great crisis of European feudalism. Demesne farming and servile labour now aligned Eastern agriculture more closely with the production norms of the early mediaeval West. But the seigneurial reaction which created them did not simultaneously reproduce the distinctive fief system that had accompanied it. One consequence of this, of course, was to concentrate seigneurial power over the peasantry to a degree unknown in the West, where parcellized sovereignty and scalar property created plural jurisdictions over villeins, with confusions and overlaps that were objectively propitious to peasant resistance. In Eastern Europe, by contrast, territorial, personal and economic lordship were generally fused in a single manorial authority, which exercised cumulative rights over its subject serfs.[5] This concentration of powers could go so far that in Russia and Prussia serfs might actually be sold, apart from the estates on which they worked, to other landowners – a condition of personal dependence close to that of outright slavery. The manorial system thus did not initially affect the predominant type of aristocratic tenure of land, although it greatly enlarged it at the expense of village commons and peasant small-holdings. On the contrary, if anything it increased despotic local power within the seigneurial class.

The double pressures which eventually created an Absolutist State in the East have been outlined above. What is important to stress here is that the transition towards Absolutism could not take the same path as in the West, not only because of the nullification of the towns and the enserfment of the peasantry, but also because of the peculiar character of the nobility which accomplished these. It had experienced no long, secular adaptation into a relatively disciplined feudal hierarchy to prepare for its integration into an aristocratic Absolutism. Yet once confronted with the historical dangers of foreign conquest or peasant desertions, the nobility needed an instrument capable of endowing itself *ex novo* with an iron unity. The type of political integration realized by Absolutism in Russia and Prussia always bore the marks of this original class situation. Hitherto, we have emphasized the extent to which the clock of Absolutism in Eastern Europe ran fast: to which it was a State structure in advance of the social formations which supported it, because level with the Western States which were in front of them. It is now necessary to underline the converse of the same dialectical contraction. Precisely the construction of the 'modern' Absolutist edifice in the East necessitated the creation of the 'archaic' service relationship once characteristic of the fief system in the West. This relationship had never previously taken serious hold in the East; yet just as it was disappearing in the West with the advent of Absolutism, it was appearing in the East at the behest of Absolutism. Much the clearest case of this was, of course, Russia. The mediaeval centuries

5. Skazkin rightly dwells on this point. 'Osnovnye Problemy tak Nazyvaemovo "Vtorovo Izdaniya Krepostnichestva" v Srednei i Vostochnoi Evrope', pp. 99–100.

after the fall of the Kievan State had known mediatized political authority and mutual suzerain-vassal relationships between princes and nobles: but these were dissociated from manorial lordship and land tenure, which remained dominated by the allodial *votchina* of the boyar class.[6] From the early modern epoch onwards, however, the whole progress of Tsarism was built on the conversion of allodial into conditional tenures, with the implantation of the *pomest'e* system in the 16th century, its domination over the *votchina* in the 17th century, and the eventual merging of the two in the 18th century. For the first time, land was now held in exchange for knight service to the feudal over-lord – the Tsar, in a formal replica of the fief in the mediaeval West. In Prussia, there was no such radical juridical alteration of land tenure, apart from a large-scale resumption of the royal demesne after the alienations of the 16th century, because there the traces of a fief system still survived. But here too, the horizontal dispersal of the junker class was broken by a rigorous vertical integration into the Absolutist State under the ideological imperative of the universal duty of the noble class to serve its feudal suzerain. In fact, the ethos of military service to the State was to go much deeper in Prussia than in Russia, and eventually to produce perhaps the most devoted and disciplined aristocracy in Europe. There was thus correspondingly less need for the legal reformation and material constraint which Tsarism had to apply so ruthlessly in its efforts to force the Russian landowning class into military service for the State.[7] In both cases, however, the 'revival' of the service relationship in Europe in fact inflicted a drastic modification of it. For the military service demanded was no longer simply to a liege lord in the mediatized chain of personal dependence that was the feudal

6. There is an excellent delimitation and discussion of the relevant historical pattern in the Russian lands in Vernadsky's extremely lucid text, 'Feudalism in Russia', *Speculum*, Vol. 14, 1939, pp. 300–23. In the light of the later *pomest'e* system, it is important to stress that the vassal relationships of the mediaeval period were genuinely contractual and reciprocal, as can be seen from the homages of the time. For an account and examples of this, see Alexandre Eck, *Le Moyen Age Russe*, pp. 195–212.

7. It should be noted, however, that Prussian Absolutism did not disdain coercion where it deemed it necessary. The Sergeant King banned all foreign travel by junkers except with his express permission, in order to oblige them to take up officer duties in the Army. A. Goodwin, 'Prussia', in Goodwin (ed.), *The European Nobility in the 18th Century*, p. 88.

hierarchy of the mediaeval epoch: it was to a hyper-centralized, Absolutist State.

There were two inevitable consequences to this displacement of the relationship. Firstly, the service involved was not the occasional and autonomous bearing of arms by a knight at the summons of his feudal superior – the conventional equestrian outing of forty days in the field stipulated in the Norman fief system, for example. It was an induction into a bureaucratic apparatus, and tended to become vocational and permanent in character. The extreme here was reached by the Petrine decrees which made the Russian *dvoriantsvo* legally liable for life-long service to the State. Once again, the very ferocity and irrealism of this system reflected the greater practical difficulty of integrating the Russian nobility into the Tsarist apparatus, rather than any greater degree of actual success in doing so. There was no need for such extreme measures in Prussia, where the junker class was smaller and more pliable from the start. In either case, it is evident that bureaucratic service proper – whether military or civilian – contradicts one central principle of the original feudal contract in the mediaeval epoch in the West: namely, its *reciprocal* nature. The fief system proper always contained an explicit component of mutuality: the vassal had not only duties to his lord, but also rights which the lord was bound to respect. Mediaeval law expressly included the notion of seigneurial felony – the illegal breaking of the compact by the feudal superior, not his inferior. Now it is plain that such a personal reciprocity, with its comparatively strict legal safeguards, was incompatible with a full-scale Absolutism, which presupposed a new and unilateral power of the central State apparatus. So, in fact, the second distinctive trait of the service relationship in the East was necessarily its heteronomy. The *pomeshchik* was not a vassal, with his own rights claimable against the tsar. He was a servitor, who received estates from the autocracy and was bound to unconditional obedience to it. His submission was legally direct and unequivocal, it was not mediatized through intervening instances of a feudal hierarchy. This extreme Tsarist conception never became assimilated in Prussia. But there too the critical element of mutuality was arrestingly lacking in the bond between the junker and the Hohenzollern State. The ideal of the Sergeant King was notoriously expressed in his demand: 'I must be served with life and limb, with house and wealth, with honour and conscience, everything must be committed except eternal salvation – that belongs to God, but all else is mine.'[8] Nowhere did the cult of mechanical military obedience – the *Kadavergehorsamkeit* of the Prussian bureaucracy and army – so come to permeate the landowning class. There was thus never a complete replication of the Western feudal synthesis in the East, either before or after the divide of the late mediaeval crisis. Rather, the component elements of this feudalism were strangely re-shuffled into listing and asynchronous combinations, none of which ever quite possessed the completion or unity of the original synthesis. Thus the manorial system functioned both under nobiliary anarchy and centralized absolutism; dispersed sovereignty existed but in epochs of non-conditional tenure; conditional tenures appeared, but with non-reciprocal service bonds; feudal hierarchy was eventually codified in the framework of state bureaucracy. Absolutism itself represented the most paradoxical reconjugation of all – in Western terms, a bizarre mixture of modern and mediaeval structures, consequence of the peculiar 'squashed' temporality of the East.

The adaptation of the landowners of Eastern Europe to the advent of Absolutism was itself not a smooth process, without vicissitudes, any more than it had been in the West. In fact, the Polish *szlachta* – alone of any such social class in Europe – defeated all efforts to create a strong dynastic state, for reasons which will be discussed later. In general, however, the relationship between monarchy and nobility in the East followed a trajectory not unlike that of the West, if with certain significant regional characteristics of its own. Thus comparative aristocratic insouciance prevailed during the 16th century, succeeded by widespread conflicts and turbulence in the 17th century, which then yielded to a new and confident concord in the 18th century. This political pattern was nevertheless distinct from that in the West in a number of important respects. To start with, the process of Absolutist State construction began much later in the East. There was no real equivalent to the Renaissance monarchies of Western Europe in the Eastern Europe of the same century. Brandenburg was still a provincial backwater without any notable princely power; Austria was

8. R. A. Dorwart, *The Administrative Reforms of Frederick William I of Prussia*, Cambridge USA, 1953, p. 226.

entangled with the mediaeval Imperial system of the Reich; Hungary had lost its traditional dynasty and had been largely overrun by the Turks; Poland remained an aristocratic commonwealth; Russia experienced a premature and forced autocracy that soon collapsed. The only country which produced a genuine Renaissance culture was Poland, whose state system was virtually a nobiliary republic. The only country which witnessed a powerful proto-Absolutist monarchy was Russia, whose culture remained far more primitive than that of any other State in the region. Disjointed, both phenomena were short-lived. It was in the next century that durable Absolutist States were erected in the East, after the full military and diplomatic integration of the continent into a single international system, and the resultant pressure from the West that accompanied it.

The fate of the Estates of the region was everywhere the clearest index of the progress of Absolutization. The three strongest Estates systems of the East were those of Poland, Hungary and Bohemia – all of which claimed the constitutional right to elect their respective monarchs. The Polish Sejm, a bi-cameral assembly in which only nobles were represented, not only thwarted the ascent of any central royal authority in the Commonwealth after its momentous victories in the 16th century; it actually increased the anarchic prerogatives of the gentry with the introduction of the *liberum veto* in the 17th century, whereby any member of the Sejm could dissolve it by a single negative vote. The Polish case was unique in Europe: so unshakeable was the position of the aristocracy that there was not even a serious conflict between monarchy and nobility in this epoch, for no elective king ever accumulated sufficient power to challenge the *szlachta* constitution. In Hungary, on the other hand, the traditional Estates shocked frontally against the Habsburg dynasty when it moved towards administrative centralization from the late 16th century onwards. The Magyar gentry, bolstered by national particularism and sheltered by Turkish power, resisted Absolutism might and main: no other nobility in Europe was to have a record of such ferocious and persistent struggle against the encroachments of monarchy. No less than four times in the space of a hundred years – in 1604–8, 1620–1, 1678–82 and 1701–11, under Bocskay, Bethlen, Tökölli and Rákóczi – major sections of the Hungarian landowning class rose in armed rebellion against the Hofburg. At the end of this prolonged and virulent contest, Magyar separatism was effectively broken and Hungary henceforward occupied by unitary Absolutist armies, while the local serfs were subjected to central taxation. But in virtually every other respect, the privileges of the Estates were preserved, and Habsburg sovereignty in Hungary remained a dim shadow of its counterpart in Austria. In Bohemia, by contrast, the revolt of the Snem which precipitated the Thirty Years' War was crushed at the Battle of the White Mountain in 1620: the victory of Austrian Absolutism in the Czech lands was complete and final, erasing the old Bohemian nobility altogether. The Estates systems formally survived in both Austria and Bohemia, but henceforward were normally obedient sounding-boxes of the dynasty.

In the two zones which gave birth to the most developed and dominant Absolutist States of Eastern Europe, however, the historical pattern was different. In Prussia and Russia, there were no great aristocratic rebellions against the oncoming of a centralized State. Indeed, it is noticeable that in the difficult phase of transition towards Absolutism, the nobility of these countries played a less prominent role in the political upheavals of the time than their counterparts in the West. The Hohenzollern and Romanov States never encountered any real equivalents of the Religious Wars, the Fronde, the Catalan Revolt or even the Pilgrimage of Grace. The Estates system in both countries petered out towards the end of the 17th century, without clamour or complaint. The Landtag of Brandenburg passively acquiesced in the increasing Absolutism of the Great Elector after the Recess of 1653. The only serious resistance to it came from the burghers of Königsberg: the East Prussian landowners, by contrast, accepted the Elector's summary suppression of the ancient rights of the Duchy with relatively few qualms. The relentlessly anti-urban policies pursued by the Eastern nobilities here had their effect, once the process of Absolutization got under way.[9] Relations between the dynasty and the nobility in Prussia were by no means free from tension and suspicion in the late 17th and early 18th centuries: neither the Great Elector nor the Sergeant King were popular rulers among their own class, which was

9. The Prussian Landtag existed formally down to Jena, but was in practice deprived of any but decorative functions by the 1680's. In the 18th century, it merely assembled to pay homage to new monarchs at their accession.

often treated roughly by both of them. But no serious split between the monarchy and aristocracy, even of a transient character, ever developed in Prussia during this epoch. In Russia, the Estates Assembly – the Zemsky Sobor – was a particularly weak and factitious institution,[10] originally created for tactical reasons by Ivan IV in the 16th century. Its composition and convocation were on the whole easily manipulated by the court cliques in the capital; the Estates principle as such never acquired an independent life in Muscovy. It was further weakened by the social divisions within the landowning class between the magnate boyar stratum and the petty *pomeshchik* gentry whose rise had been promoted by the Tsars of the 16th century.

Thus, although gigantic social struggles were unleashed in the course of the transition to Absolutism, on a scale far beyond anything in Western Europe, they were dominated by the exploited rural and urban classes, not by the privileged and propertied, who on the whole revealed considerable prudence in their relationship to Tsarism. 'Throughout our history', Count Stroganov was to write to Alexander I in a confidential memorandum, 'it has been the peasantry that was the source of all disturbances, while nobility never stirred: if the government has any force to fear and any group to watch, it is the serfs and not any other class.'[11] The great events of the 17th century which punctuated the fading away of the Zemsky Sobor and Boyar Duma were not separatist noble rebellions, but the peasant wars of Bolotnikov and Razin, urban riots by artisans in Moscow, upsurges of Cossack turmoil along the Dnieper and the Don. These conflicts provided the historical context within which the intra-feudal contradictions between boyars and *pomeshchiki* – themselves certainly acuter than anything in Prussia – were resolved. For much of the 17th century, boyar groups controlled the central machinery of the State in the absence of strong Tsars, while the gentry lost political ground; but the essential interests of both were protected by the new structures of Russian Absolutism, as it became gradually consolidated. Autocratic repression of individual aristocrats in Russia was, of course, often much fiercer than in the West, because of the lack of any equivalent to the latter's mediaeval

10. See the sharp analysis of its record in J. L. H. Keep, 'The Decline of the Zemsky Sobor', *The Slavonic and East European Review*, 36, 1957–8, pp. 100–22.
11. See H. Seton-Watson, *The Russian Empire 1801–1917*, Oxford 1967, p. 77.

legal traditions. But it is nonetheless striking how stable the Russian monarchy could become, even while small court and military groups within the nobility waged feverish struggles for control of it: the strength of the Absolutist function so far surpassed that of its nominal royal occupants that after Peter I, political life could for a time become a hectic series of intrigues and putsches by palace guards without in any way altering the powers of Tsarism as such, or impairing political stability in the country as a whole.

The 18th century, in fact, witnessed the zenith of harmony between the aristocracy and monarchy in Prussia and Russia, as in Western Europe. This was the epoch in which the nobility of both countries adopted French as the cultural language of the ruling class, the idiom in which Catherine II was candidly to declare: *Je suis une aristocrate, c'est mon métier* – epigraph for the age.[12] The consonance between the landowning class and the Absolutist State was, in fact, even greater in the two great monarchies of the East than in the West. The historical weakness of the mutual and contractual elements of feudal vassalage in Eastern Europe during an earlier epoch has already been noted. The service hierarchy of Prussian and Russian Absolutism never reproduced the reciprocal commitment of mediaeval homage: a bureaucratic pyramid necessarily excluded the inter-personal pledges of a seigneurial hierarchy, replacing allegiances by commands. But the supersession of individual guarantees between lord and vassal, which in principle ensured a chivalrous relationship between them, did not mean that nobles in the East were thereby delivered over to arbitrary or implacable tyranny by their monarchs. For the aristocracy as a class was collectively ratified in its social power by the objective nature of the State which had arisen 'above' it. The service of the nobility in the machinery of Absolutism ensured that the Absolutist State served the political interests of the nobility. The link between the two involved more constraint than in the West, but also more intimacy. The general

12. The spread of French among the Prussian, Austrian and Russian ruling classes in the 18th century is, of course, evidence of the absence in the Eastern European States of the 'proto-nationalist' nimbus acquired by West European Absolutism in an earlier epoch – determined in its turn by the lack of any ascendant bourgeoisie in the Eastern Europe of this era. The Prussian monarchy itself, of course, continued to be avowedly hostile to national ideals down to the eve of German unification: the Austrian to the end of its existence.

rules of European Absolutism were thus – despite ideological appearances – never seriously infringed in the East. The private property and security of the landowning class remained the domestic talisman of royal regimes, no matter how autocratic their pretensions.[13] The composition of the nobility might be forcibly altered and reshuffled in extreme crises, as it had been in the mediaeval West: its structural location within the social formation was always upheld. Eastern Absolutism, no less than Western, stopped at the gates of the manor itself: conversely, the aristocracy drew its fundamental wealth and power from stable possession of the land, not from temporary sojourn in the State. The great bulk of agrarian property remained juridically hereditary and individual within the noble class, right across Europe. Grades of the nobility could be coordinated with ranks in army and administration, but they were never reduced to them; titles always subsisted outside the service of the State, bespeaking honour rather than office.

It is thus not surprising that the parabola of the relationship between monarchy and aristocracy in the East was, despite the great differences in the whole historical formation of the two halves of Europe, so similar to that in the West. The imperious advent of Absolutism met with initial incomprehension and refusal; then, after confusion and resistance, it was finally accepted and embraced by the landed class. The 18th century was an epoch of reconciliation between monarchy and nobility throughout Europe. In Prussia, Frederick II pursued avowedly aristocratic policies of recruitment and promotion in the Absolutist State apparatus, excluding foreigners and *roturiers* from positions in the army and civil service which they had once held. In Russia, too, the professional expatriate officers who had been a mainstay of the reformed Tsarist regiments of the late 17th century were

13. The most striking demonstration of the strict objective limits to Absolutist power was to be the long-successful resistance of the Russian nobility to Tsarist contemplation of emancipation of the serfs in the 19th century. By then, both Alexander I and Nicholas I – two of the most powerful monarchs Russia had known – personally considered serfdom to be in principle a social fetter, yet in practice ended by actually transferring more peasants into private bondage. Even when emancipation was finally decreed by Alexander II, in the second half of the 19th century, the form of its implementation was largely determined by combative aristocratic counter-moves. For these episodes, see Seton-Watson, *The Russian Empire*, pp. 77–8, 227–9, 393–7.

phased out, and the *dvorianstvo* came into its own again in the Imperial armed forces, while its provincial administrative privileges were generously enlarged and confirmed by Catherine II's formal Charter of the Nobility. In the Austrian Empire, Maria Theresa even succeeded to an unprecedented extent in melting Hungarian hostility to the Habsburg dynasty, tying Magyar magnates to court life in Vienna and creating a special Hungarian Guard for her person in the capital. At mid century, the central power of the monarchies was greater than ever before, and yet the rapport between the respective rulers and landowners of the East was closer and more relaxed than at any time in the past. Moreover, unlike that of the West, the later Absolutism of the East was now in its political apogee. The 'Enlightened Despotism' of the 18th century was essentially a Central and East European affair[14] – symbolized by the three monarchs who finally partitioned Poland: Frederick II, Catherine II and Joseph II. The chorus of praises for their work from the bourgeois *philosophes* of the Western Enlightenment, for all their often ironic misconceptions, was not simply a historical accident: dynamic energy and capability seemed to have passed to Berlin, Vienna and St Petersburg. This period was the high point of the development of the Absolutist army, bureaucracy, diplomacy and mercantilist economic policy in the East. The Partition of Poland, calmly and collectively executed in defiance of the impotent Western powers on the eve of the French Revolution, seemed to symbolize its international ascent.

Anxious to shine in the mirror of Western civilization, the Absolutist rulers in Prussia and Russia assiduously emulated the past record of their compeers in France or Spain, and flattered the occidental writers who arrived to report on their splendour.[15] In certain limited respects,

14. This emerges clearly from the best recent study of the subject, François Bluche's *Le Despotisme Eclairé*, Paris 1968. Bluche's book provides a fine comparative survey of the enlightened despotisms of the 18th century. Its explicative framework, however, is defective, relying essentially on a theory of generative examples, whereby Louis XIV is said to have provided an original model of government, which inspired Frederick II, who himself then inspired his fellow-sovereigns of the time (pp. 344–5). Without denying the importance of the – relatively novel – phenomenon of conscious international imitation between states in the 18th century, the limitations of such a genealogy are obvious enough.

15. Bluche's commentary on the breathless and gullible admiration of the

the Eastern Absolutisms of this century were curiously more advanced than their Western prototypes of the previous century, because of the general evolution of the time. Where Philip III and Louis XIV had heedlessly expelled Moriscos and Huguenots, Frederick II not only welcomed religious refugees but set up immigration bureaux abroad to promote the demographic growth of his kingdom – a new twist to mercantilism. Populationist policies were likewise promoted in Austria and Russia, which launched ambitious colonization programmes in the Banat and the Ukraine. Official toleration and anti-clericalism were enforced in Austria and Prussia, by contrast with Spain or France.[16] Public education was inaugurated or expanded, marked progress being achieved in the two Germanic monarchies, particularly in the Habsburg realms. Conscription was introduced everywhere, most successfully in Russia. Economically, Absolutist mercantilism and protectionism were prosecuted with vigour. Catherine presided over a great expansion of the metal industry of the Urals, and accomplished a major reform of the Russian currency. Frederick II and Joseph II both doubled the industrial establishments of their domains; in Austria, traditional mercantilism was even mingled with the more modern influences of physiocracy, with its greater emphasis on agrarian production and the virtues of domestic laissez-faire.

Yet none of these apparent advances actually altered the relative character and position of the Eastern exemplars of European Absolutism in the epoch of the Enlightenment. For the underlying structures

---

philosophes for the royal rulers of the East is particularly sardonic and vigorous: *Le Despotisme Eclairé*, pp. 317–40. Voltaire was the *coryphée* of Prussian Absolutism in the person of Frederick II, Diderot of Russian Absolutism in that of Catherine II; while Rousseau characteristically reserved his commendation for the Polish squirearchy, whom he advised not to rush intemperately into the abolition of serfdom. The Physiocrats Mercier de la Rivière and De Quesnay vaunted the merits of 'patrimonial and legal despotism' generally.

16. Joseph II could declare, in the accents of the age: 'Toleration is an effect of that beneficent increase of knowledge which now enlightens Europe, and which is owing to philosophy and the efforts of great men; it is a convincing proof of the improvement of the human mind, which has boldly reopened a road through the dominions of superstition, which was trodden centuries ago by Zoroaster and Confucius, and which, fortunately for mankind, has now become the highway of monarchs.' S. K. Padover, *The Revolutionary Emperor, Joseph II 1741–1790*, London 1934, p. 206.

of these monarchies remained archaic and retrograde, even in the hour of their greatest prestige. Austria, shaken by defeat in war with Prussia, was the scene of a royal attempt to restore the strength of the State by emancipating the peasantry:[17] Joseph II's agrarian reforms, however, ended in failure, inevitable once the monarchy became isolated from its circumambient nobility. Austrian Absolutism remained permanently weakened and inferior. The future lay with Prussian and Russian Absolutism. Serfdom was preserved by Frederick II and extended by Catherine II: the manorial foundations of Eastern Absolutism survived intact in the two dominant powers of the region into the next century. Then, once again, it was the shock of military attack from the West, which had once contributed to bring Eastern Absolutism into existence, that finally brought the serfdom on which it had rested to an end. For now the assault came from capitalist States, and could not long be resisted. Napoleon's victory at Jena led directly to the legal emancipation of the Prussian peasantry in 1811. Alexander II's defeat in the Crimea precipitated the formal emancipation of the Russian serfs in 1861. Yet in neither case did these reforms mean the end of Absolutism itself, in Eastern Europe. The life-span of the two, contrary to linear expectations, but in conformity with the oblique march of history, did not coincide: the Absolutist State in the East, as we shall see, was to survive the abolition of serfdom.

17. The first official scheme for the abolition of *robot* labour services and the distribution of land to the peasantry was drafted in 1764 by the *Hofkriegsrat*, with the aim of improving recruitment to the army: W. E. Wright, *Serf, Seigneur and Sovereign – Agrarian Reform in Eighteenth Century Bohemia*, Minneapolis 1966, p. 56. The whole Josephine programme must always be seen against the background of Habsburg military humiliations in the War of the Austrian Succession and the Seven Years' War.

3

Prussia

Having surveyed their common determinants, we may now briefly consider the divergent evolution of the particular social formations of the East. Prussia presents the classical case in Europe of an *uneven and combined development*, which eventually produced the largest industrialized capitalist State in the continent from one of the smallest and most backward feudal territories of the Baltic. The theoretical problems posed by this trajectory were specifically raised by Engels, in his famous letter to Bloch in 1890, on the irreducible importance of political, legal and cultural systems in the structure of all historical determination: 'According to the materialist conception of history, the *ultimately* determining element in history is the production and reproduction of real life. More than this neither Marx nor I have ever asserted. . . . The Prussian State also arose and developed from historical, ultimately economic causes. But it could scarcely be maintained without pedantry that among the many small states of North Germany, Brandenburg was specifically determined by economic necessity to become the great power embodying the economic, linguistic and, after the Reformation, also the religious difference between North and South, and not by other elements as well (above all by its entanglement with Poland, owing to the possession of Prussia, and hence with international political relations – which were indeed also decisive in the formation of the Austrian dynastic power).'[1] At the same time, it

1. Marx-Engels, *Selected Correspondence*, p. 417. Althusser has selected this passage as a touchstone in his famous essay, 'Contradiction and Overdetermination', *For Marx*, London 1969, pp. 111–12: but he limits himself to demonstrating the general theoretical importance of Engels's formulations here, without proposing any solution to the actual historical problems raised by it. Engels's express emphasis on the complex and overdetermined character of Prussia's ascent is all the

is evident that the complex causes of Brandenburg's ascent also contain the answer to the central rebus of modern German history as a whole – why the national unification of Germany in the epoch of the industrial revolution was ultimately achieved under the political aegis of the agrarian junkerdom of Prussia. The rise of the Hohenzollern State, in other words, concentrates in a particularly clear form some of the key general issues of the nature and function of Absolutism in European political development.

Its beginnings were not especially auspicious. The Hohenzollern house was originally transplanted by the Emperor Sigismund, during his struggle with the Hussite Revolution in Bohemia, from South Germany – where it had traditionally been an aristocratic line at loggerheads with the trading city of Nuremburg – to Brandenburg in the early 15th century. Frederick, the first Hohenzollern Margrave of Brandenburg, was made an Elector of the Empire for his services to Sigismund in 1415.[2] The next Margrave suppressed the municipal autonomy of Berlin, while his successors prised the other towns of the Mark from the Hanseatic League and subordinated them in turn. By the early 16th century, as we have already seen, Brandenburg was a region voided of free cities. The defeat of the towns, however, ensured the supremacy of the nobility rather than the dynasty in this remote frontier zone. The local aristocracy steadily enlarged its demesnes, enclosing village commons, and deprived small peasants of their land,

––––––––––––––

more remarkable when compared with Marx's comments on the same subject. For Marx precisely *did* reduce the emergence of the Hohenzollern State in Brandenburg to a virtual caricature of merely economic necessity. In his 1856 article, 'Das göttliche Recht der Hohenzollern' (*Werke*, Bd 12, pp. 95–101), he attributed the rise of the dynasty simply to – a squalid series of bribes: 'The Hohenzollerns acquired Brandenburg, Prussia and the royal title merely through bribery'. His private correspondence with Engels at the same date uses the same phraseology: 'Petty thieving, bribery, direct purchase, underhand dealings to capture inheritances, and so on – all this shabby business is what the history of Prussia amounts to.' (*Selected Correspondence*, p. 96). This vulgar materialism with a vengeance is a reminder of the dangers of assuming any general superiority of Marx over Engels in the historical field proper: the balance of insight between the two was perhaps if anything usually the opposite.

2. For the context of this move, see Barraclough, *The Origins of Germany*, p. 358.

as export farming became more lucrative. The landowning class simultaneously seized control of higher justice, bought out Electoral domains, and monopolized administrative offices, while a series of ineffectual rulers slipped into increasing debt and impotence. An entrenched Estates system, dominated by the nobility, vetoed the development of a standing army and virtually any foreign policy, making the Electorate one of the most pronounced examples of a decentralized *Ständestaat* in Reformation Germany. Thus, after the economic crisis of the later Middle Ages, Brandenburg settled down to a modest manorial prosperity, with very weak princely power, during the epoch of the price revolution in the West. Benefiting from the profits of the corn trade, but showing little aggressive political drive, junker society formed a sleepy and provincial backwater throughout the 16th century.[3] Meanwhile, East Prussia had become the hereditary fief of another branch of the Hohenzollern family, when Albert Hohenzollern opportunely wound up the Teutonic Order as its last Grand Master by declaring for the Reformation in 1525, and acquiring the secular title of Duke from his Polish overlord. The dissolution of the ruling military-clerical order, long decadent since its defeat and subjugation by Poland in the 15th century, led to the fusion of its knights with lay landowners and hence to the creation of a unified seigneurial class in East Prussia for the first time. A peasant revolt against the new regime was promptly crushed, and a society very similar to that in Brandenburg consolidated. Eviction and enserfment proceeded in the countryside, where free tenants were soon degraded to the ranks of villeins. A small stratum of *Cölmer*, once petty servitors of the Teutonic Knights, on the other hand survived. Virtually all towns of any importance had been annexed by Poland in the previous century anyway, with the exception of Königsberg – the one relatively large and undaunted city of the region. Constitutionally, princely power in the new Duchy was very limited and fragile, although the ducal lands themselves were extensive. The Prussian Estates, in fact, secured perhaps wider privileges than any other such institutions in Germany, including administrative appointments, judicial powers, and

3. Hans Rosenberg, 'The Rise of the Junkers in Brandenburg-Prussia 1410–1653', *American Historical Review*, October 1943, pp. 1–22, and January 1944, pp. 228–42.

permanent rights of appeal to the Polish monarchy against the Dukes.[4]
The international significance of East Prussia was now even less than
that of Brandenburg.

In 1618, the two principalities – hitherto politically unrelated – were
united when the Elector of Brandenburg acceded to the succession in
East Prussia by an inter-familial marriage; although the Duchy continued to be a Polish fief. Four years earlier, another geographical gain
had been made in the lower Rhineland, when the two small territories
of Cleves and Mark, densely populated and highly urbanized enclaves
in the West, were gathered by inheritance to the Hohenzollern patrimony. The new dynastic acquisitions of the early 17th century, however, remained without any land-bridge to Brandenburg; the three
possessions of the Elector were strategically scattered and vulnerable.
The Electorate itself was still by all-German standards an indigent and
isolated state – contemptuously termed 'the sand-box of the Holy
Roman Empire' by its contemporaries. 'There was nothing to indicate
that Brandenburg or Prussia would ever play a major part in German
or European affairs.'[5] It was the gales of the Thirty Years' War and of
Swedish expansion which were to buffet the Hohenzollern State out of
its inertia. Brandenburg was for the first time put on the map of international politics when Wallenstein's Imperial armies victoriously
marched across Germany to the Baltic. The Elector George William,
a Lutheran hostile to the prospect of a Calvinist ruler in Prague, had
rallied politically to the Habsburg Emperor Ferdinand II over the
original conflict in Bohemia; a military role was beyond him since he
effectively had no army. His defenseless territory was nevertheless
occupied and pillaged by Austrian troops in 1627, while Wallenstein
installed himself in Mecklenburg. In East Prussia, meanwhile, Gustavus
Adolphus had seized Memel and Pillau – the two forts commanding
Königsberg – in pursuit of his war with Poland, and thereafter levied
tolls on all maritime traffic into the Duchy. Then, in 1631, the Swedish
expeditionary army landed in Pomerania and invaded Brandenburg in
its turn. George William, who had helplessly fled to East Prussia, was
obliged by Gustavus Adolphus to change sides and declare against the
Imperial cause. Four years later, he defected to make a separate peace

4. Carsten, *The Origins of Prussia*, pp. 168–9.
5. *Ibid.*, p. 174.

with the Emperor. But for the duration of the rest of the Thirty Years' War, Swedish armies were always garrisoned in the Electorate, which was at the mercy of their financial exactions. The Estates were naturally brushed aside by the occupying power. Brandenburg ended the long conflict as passively as it had begun it. Paradoxically, however, it gained at the Treaty of Westphalia. For in the course of the war, Pomerania had legally reverted to the Hohenzollern line on the death of its last Duke. The Swedish conquest of Pomerania – the main Baltic base for Nordic operations in the Lower Saxon Circle – had prevented this inheritance from taking any effect during the war, but at French insistence the poorer Eastern half of the province was now grudgingly relinquished to Brandenburg, which was also compensated with smaller gains to the south and west of the Electorate. The Hohenzollern State emerged externally from the Thirty Years' War with little political or military credit, yet territorially enlarged by the peace. Internally, its traditional institutions had been deeply shaken, but no new ones had arisen to succeed them.

The new and young Elector, Frederick William I, who had been educated in Holland, came into his patrimony under normal conditions for the first time with the conclusion of the peace. Two indelible lessons had been learnt by the experience of the decades of foreign occupation: the urgent need to build an army capable of withstanding Swedish imperial expansion in the Baltic and – complementarily – the administrative example of coercive Swedish tax-collection in Brandenburg and East Prussia, in defiance of the protests of the local Estates. The immediate preoccupation of the Elector was thus to secure a stable financial basis with which to create a permanent military apparatus for the defense and integration of his realms. Vasa forces, in fact, did not evacuate Eastern Pomerania until 1654. Hence in 1652, the Elector summoned a general Landtag in Brandenburg, convoking the whole nobility and all the towns of the Mark to it, for the purpose of instituting a new financial system to provide for a princely army. Protracted wrangling with the Estates ensued, finally ending the following year with the famous Recess of 1653, which consecrated the beginnings of the social pact between the Elector and the aristocracy which was to provide the lasting foundation of Prussian Absolutism. The Estates refused to grant a general excise tax, but voted a subsidy of half a million thalers over six years for the establishment of an army, which was to become the nucleus of the future bureaucratic State. In exchange, the Elector decreed that henceforward all peasants in Brandenburg were assumed to be *Leibeigene* serfs unless proved otherwise; seigneurial jurisdictions were confirmed; noble estates were closed against commoner purchase; and aristocratic fiscal immunity was preserved.[6] Within two years of this deal being reached, war had broken out again in the Baltic, with the lightning Swedish attack on Poland in 1655. Frederick William opted for the Swedish side in this conflict, and in 1656 his fledgling army entered Warsaw side by side with Charles X's troops. Polish military recovery, backed by Russian and Austrian intervention, soon weakened the Swedish position, which was also attacked in the rear by Denmark. Brandenburg thereupon deftly switched sides, in exchange for formal Polish renunciation of its overlordship of East Prussia. The Treaty of Labiau in 1657 for the first time established unconditional Hohenzollern sovereignty over the Duchy. The Elector then rapidly occupied Western Pomerania with a mixed Polish, Austrian and Brandenburger force. The Treaty of Oliva in 1660, however, returned this province to Sweden with the restoration of peace, at French insistence.

The Baltic War of 1656–60, meanwhile, had abruptly and drastically altered the domestic balance of forces within the Hohenzollern possessions. In Brandenburg, East Prussia and Cleves-Mark, the Elector had overriden all constitutional niceties in the name of military emergency, collecting taxes without the consent of the local assemblies, and building up a troop force of some 22,000, which was halved but not disbanded with the cessation of hostilities. A more drastic reckoning with Estates particularism was now possible. East Prussia, where the nobility had hitherto been accustomed to lean back against Polish suzerainty to resist Hohenzollern pretensions, and the towns had been openly malcontent during the war, was the first domain to experience the new power of the Electorate. In 1661–3, a long Landtag was summoned. The refusal of the burghers of Königsberg to accept full dynastic sovereignty in the Duchy was broken by the summary arrest of the ringleader of urban resistance, and an excise tax was wrested for

6. Carsten, *The Origins of Prussia*, pp. 185–9.

the maintenance of the army. The Elector had to promise to hold tri-
annual sessions of the Estates and not to levy taxes henceforward without its consent: but these concessions were to prove largely formal.
In Cleves-Mark, meanwhile, the Estates had been pressured into
acceptance of the ruler's right to introduce troops and appoint officials
at will.

In 1672, the Franco-Dutch War drew the Hohenzollern State – a
diplomatic ally and financial client of the United Provinces – into
renewed military conflict, this time on a European scale. By 1674, the
Elector was titular commander of the combined German forces
operating against France in the Palatinate and Alsace. In the next year,
Sweden invaded Brandenburg as a French ally, in his absence. Hasten-
ing home, Frederick William struck back at the battle of Fehrbellin in
1675, when for the first time Brandenburg troops overcame Scandinavian veterans, in the marsh-lands north-west of Berlin. By 1678, the
whole of Swedish Pomerania had been overrun by the Elector. But
once again French intervention robbed him of his conquests: Bourbon
armies marched into Cleves-Mark and menaced Minden, the Hohenzollern outposts in the West, and France was able to dictate the
restoration of Western Pomerania to Sweden in 1679. Geographically
fruitless, the war was nevertheless institutionally profitable for the
construction of a princely Absolutism. East Prussia was forcibly subjected to a land-tax and excise collection without representative consent,
to the mutterings of noble dissidence and the louder menaces of burgher
revolt. Königsberg was the centre of resistance: in 1674, a swift
military coup seized the city, and smashed its municipal autonomy
permanently. Thereafter, the Prussian Estates docilely voted the large
contribution demanded of them for the duration of the war.[7]

The conclusion of peace brought no respite in the growing concentration of power in the hands of the Elector. In 1680, an urban
excise tax was made obligatory in Brandenburg, which was deliberately
not extended to the countryside in order to divide the nobility from the
towns. A year later, the same fiscal separatism was introduced in East
Prussia, and by the end of the Elector's reign, it had been extended to
Pomerania, Magdeburg and Minden. Rural charges were paid by the
peasantry alone in Brandenburg and Cleves-Mark; in East Prussia the

7. Carsten, *The Origins of Prussia*, pp. 219–21.

nobility made a slight contribution, but the bulk of the burden was born by their tenants. The administrative division of town and country-side created by this dualism split the potential social opposition to nascent Absolutism irremediably. Taxes were effectively confined to towns and peasants, in a proportion of 3:2. The new fiscal load was particularly damaging to the cities, because the freedom from excise enjoyed by breweries and other enterprises on their estates allowed landowners to compete with impunity against urban manufactures. The economic strength of the towns of Brandenburg and East Prussia, already hard hit by the general depression of the 17th century, was thus further reduced by State policy: and once the excise became a permanent consumption tax, the cities were effectively deleted from further Landtag representation. The nobility, by contrast, received velvet treatment financially and legally. Not only were its traditional privileges confirmed in the major Eastern provinces: in the Western enclaves of Cleves and Mark, the Elector even conferred *de novo* seigneurial jurisdictions and fiscal immunity on the local aristocracy, where it had never possessed these before.[8] The wintry economic climate of the later 17th century provided another incentive for the landowning class to rally to the political edifice of princely power that was now going up in the Hohenzollern realms: the prospects of employment within it were a further inducement to abandon the crabbed ways of earlier tradition.

For while the Estates system had been steadily ground down, the military-bureaucratic apparatus of centralist Absolutism was being rapidly and relentlessly elevated. A Privy Council for the Mark of Brandenburg had existed since 1604, but it had soon been colonized by local noblemen, becoming an unimportant and parochial body whose activity virtually lapsed altogether during the Thirty Years' War. Frederick William revived it after Westphalia, when it started intermittently to assume central direction of the Hohenzollern domains as a whole, while remaining localist in underlying outlook and primitive in administrative function. During the war of 1665–70, however, a specialist department for the conduct of military affairs throughout the dynastic lands was created, the *Generalkriegskommissariat*. With the resumption of peace, this Commissariat was reduced in role and

8. Carsten, *The Origins of Prussia*, pp. 236–9, 246–9.

personnel, but not abolished: it remained under the formal supervision of the Privy Council. Thus far, the evolution of Brandenburger Absolutism followed an administrative path very similar to that of earlier Western monarchies. The onset of the war of 1672–8 marked an abrupt and decisive departure from it. For the *Generalkriegskommissariat* now started to commandeer virtually the whole machinery of the State itself. In 1674 a *Generalkriegskasse* was formed, which within a decade had become the central Hohenzollern treasury, as tax-collection was increasingly entrusted to the officials of the Commissariat. In 1679, the *Generalkriegskommissariat* acquired a professional soldier at its head, the Pomeranian aristocrat Von Grumbkow; its ranks were expanded; a regular bureaucratic hierarchy was created within it; and its responsibilities diversified outwards. In the course of the next decade, it organized the settlement of Huguenot refugees and handled immigration policy, controlled the guild system in the towns, supervised trade and manufactures, and launched the naval and colonial enterprises of the State. The *Generalkriegskommissar* himself was now in practice at once Chief of the General Staff, Minister for War and Minister for Finance. The Privy Council was dwarfed by this huge growth. The officialdom of the Commissariat was recruited on a unitary, inter-provincial basis, and was used as the major bludgeon of the dynasty against local particularism or resistant assemblies.[9] The *Generalkriegskommissariat* was not, however, in any sense a weapon against the aristocracy itself. On the contrary, its top echelons were staffed with leading nobles, both at central and provincial levels: commoners were concentrated in the comparatively lowly department for urban tax-collection.

The prime function of the whole tentacular apparatus of the Commissariat, of course, was to ensure the maintenance and expansion of the armed forces of the Hohenzollern State. To this end, total revenues were tripled from 1640 to 1688, a *per capita* fiscal yield nearly twice as high as that of Louis XIV's France, a vastly richer country. At Frederick William's accession, Brandenburg possessed a mere 4,000 troops; by the end of the reign of the ruler whom contemporaries now called the 'Great Elector', a permanent army of 30,000 well-trained soldiers existed, led by an officer corps recruited from the junker class

9. Carsten, *The Origins of Prussia*, pp. 259–65.

and imbued with martial loyalty towards the dynasty.[10] The death of the Great Elector revealed how well his work was jointed. His vain and inconsequential successor Frederick committed the Hohenzollern house to the European coalition against France from 1688 onwards. Brandenburger contingents acquitted themselves competently in the Wars of the League of Augsburg and the Spanish Succession, while the reigning prince ran through foreign subsidies by his extravagance at home and failed to secure any territorial gains for his international policy. The only prominent achievement of the reign was the acquisition for the dynasty of the royal title of King of Prussia – diplomatically conceded in 1701 by the Emperor Charles VI in exchange for a formal Habsburg-Hohenzollern alliance, and legally covered by the fact that East Prussia lay outside the boundaries of the *Reich*, in which no kingships were permitted beneath the Imperial dignity itself. The Prussian monarchy, however, still remained a small and backward state perched on the edges of North-Eastern Germany. The total population of the Hohenzollern lands had been a mere 1,000,000 in the last years of the Great Elector – some 270,000 in Brandenburg, 400,000 in East Prussia, 150,000 in Cleves-Mark and perhaps another 180,000 in the smaller domains. By the death of Frederick I in 1713, the Prussian realm still contained no more than 1,600,000 inhabitants.

This modest legacy was to be remarkably nurtured by the new monarch, Frederick William I. The 'Sergeant King' devoted his career to building up the Prussian Army, which doubled in size from 40,000 to 80,000 under a ruler who was symbolically the first European prince permanently to wear uniform. Military drill and training were royal obsessions; ordnance works and cloth factories for supplying the field were tirelessly promoted; conscription was introduced; a cadet college for young noblemen was founded, and officer service in foreign armies was rigorously banned; the war commissariat was reorganized under Von Grumbkow's son. The use of the new troops was extremely prudent: Western Pomerania was finally taken from Sweden in 1719, when Prussia joined Russia and Denmark against Charles XII in the closing stages of the Great Northern War. Otherwise, the army was cautiously husbanded behind a pacific diplomacy. The bureaucracy was meanwhile streamlined and rationalized. The State apparatus had

10. Carsten, *The Origins of Prussia*, pp. 266–71.

hitherto been divided into the 'domain' and 'commissariat' columns –
i.e. the private and public financial agencies of the monarchy, responsible
respectively for administration of the royal estates and collection of
civic taxes. These were now merged into one central pillar, memorably
designated the *General-Ober-Finanz-Kriegs-und-Domänen-Direktorium*,
with responsibility for all administrative duties outside foreign affairs,
justice and the church. A corps of secret police or special 'fiscals', was
created to exercise surveillance over the civil service.[11] The economy
was no less carefully tended. Dikes, drainage and settlement projects
were financed in the countryside, using Dutch skills and technicians.
French and German immigrants were recruited for local manufactories
under State control. Royal mercantilism promoted textiles and other
exports. At the same time, court expenses were held to a frugal minimum. The result was that the Sergeant King commanded an annual
income of 7 million thaler by the end of his reign, and left a surplus of
8 million thaler in the exchequer for his successor. Perhaps even more
important, the population of his realm had increased to some 2,250,000
– or nearly 40 per cent within less than three decades.[12] Prussia in 1740
had quietly accumulated the social and material preconditions which
were to make it a major European power under the generalship of
Frederick II, and ultimately to assure its leadership of German
unification.

The question can now be asked: what was the total political configuration of Germany that made the later dominance of Prussia within
it possible and logical? Vice-versa, what specific traits distinguished
Hohenzollern Absolutism from the rival territorial States within the
Holy Roman Empire with an equally plausible claim to German
ascendancy in the early modern epoch? At the outset, a single basic line
of division can be drawn through the *Reich*, separating its Western
from its Eastern regions. Western Germany was by and large thickly
sprinkled with towns. From the High Middle Ages onwards, the

11. For an account of the structure and operation of the *Generaloberdirektorium*,
see R. A. Dorwart, *The Administrative Reforms of Frederick William I of Prussia*,
pp. 170–9. Within the administration, the 'fiscals' were not salaried, but paid
commissions on fines from successful prosecutions initiated by their investiga-
tions.

12. H. Holborn, *A History of Modern Germany 1648–1840*, London 1965, pp.
192–202.

Rhineland was one of the most flourishing commercial zones in Europe, lying across the trade-routes between the two urban civilizations of Flanders and Italy, and profiting from the longest natural waterway used in the continent. In the Centre and North, the Hanseatic League dominated the North Sea and Baltic economies, stretching from Westphalia all the way across to the colonial outposts of Riga and Reval in Livonia and up to Stockholm and Bergen in Scandinavia, while also enjoying privileged positions in Bruges and London. In the South-West, the Swabian cities benefited from transalpine trade, and from the exceptional mining resources of their hinterland. The specific weight of these numerous towns had never been great enough to create city-states of the Italian type, with extensive agrarian territories subject to them; those which did come to possess a modest rural circumference, like Nuremberg, were the exception rather than the rule. For their size was on average considerably smaller than the Italian cities. By 1500, out of some 3,000 German towns, only 15 had populations larger than 10,000, and 2 larger than 30,000:[13] Augsburg, the biggest, numbered some 50,000 at a time when Venice or Milan were over 100,000. On the other hand, their strength and vitality had secured them in the Middle Ages the position of free imperial cities, subject only to the nominal suzerainty of the Emperor (there were 85 of these), and they had shown a political capacity for collective action on a regional scale which alarmed the territorial princes of the Empire. In 1254, the Rhenish towns had formed a defensive military League; in 1358, the Hansa towns completed their economic federation; in 1376, the Swabian towns created an armed association against the Count of Württemberg. The Golden Bull of the mid-14th century officially banned urban leagues, but this did not prevent the Rhenish and Swabian cities from signing a united South German pact in 1381, which was finally crushed by an army of princes seven years later, during the depths of the late feudal depression and concomitant anarchy in the *Reich*. The economic growth of the Teutonic towns, however, picked up rapidly again in the latter half of the 15th century, and reached its apogee in the period 1480–1530, when Germany became something like the diversified centre of the whole European trading

13. H. Holborn, *A History of Modern Germany. The Reformation*, London 1965, p. 38.

system. The Hanseatic League was essentially a mercantile association, without much manufacturing enterprise in the cities themselves: its profits came from entrepôt trade in grain, and control of herring fisheries, combined with international financial transactions. The Rhineland, with the oldest towns in Germany, had traditional linen, woollen and metal industries besides its control of the commercial routes from Flanders to Lombardy. The prosperity of the Swabian cities was newest, and most flourishing of all: textiles, mining and metallurgy gave them an advanced productive base, to which were added the banking fortunes of the Fuggers and Welsers in the epoch of Charles V. At the turn of the 16th century, the South German cities surpassed, if anything, their Italian counterparts in technical invention and industrial progress. It was they who spearheaded the first, popular advance of the Reformation.

The growth of the urban economy in Germany, however, suddenly tailed off at mid-century. Adversity took a number of inter-related forms. To start with, there was a slow reversal of the relationship between agrarian and industrial prices, as demand outpaced supply in foodstuffs, and cereal prices rose rapidly. Lack of structural integration became increasingly apparent in the German commercial network itself. The Northern and Southern ends of the long arc of towns running from the Alps to the North Sea had never been properly linked together in an articulated system.[14] The Hanseatic League and the Rheno-Swabian cities always constituted separate mercantile sectors, with distinct hinterlands and markets. Maritime trade proper, the ace-card of medieval commerce, was confined to the Hansa, which had once dominated the seas from England to Russia. But from the mid-15th century onwards, the competitive shipping of Holland and Zeeland – better designed and equipped – had broken the monopolistic grip of the Hanseatic ports in Northern waters. Dutch herring-fleets captured the fisheries, which had migrated from the Baltic to the Norwegian coasts, while Dutch cargoes cut into the Danzig grain trade. By 1500, Dutch vessels moving through the Sound outnumbered German by 5:4. Hanseatic wealth had thus already passed its peak

14. This has often been emphasized by Marxists: see *inter alia* Lukàcs's representative essay, 'Uber einige Eigentümlichkeiten der geschichtlichen Entwicklung Deutschlands', *Die Zerstörung der Vernunft*, Neuwied/Berlin 1962, p. 38.

during the period of maximum German commercial expansion as a whole. The League still remained rich and powerful: in the 1520's, as we have seen, Lübeck was instrumental in installing Gustavus Vasa in Sweden and bringing down Christian II in Denmark. The very large absolute increase in Baltic traffic during the 16th century to some extent compensated for the precipitate decline of its relative share of it. But the League lost its vantage-points in Flanders, was deprived of its privileges in England (1556), and by the end of the century was reduced to a mere quarter of the volume of Dutch shipping through the Sound.[15] Increasingly divided between its Westphalian and Wendish wings, it was a spent force. Meanwhile, the Rhenish towns were likewise victims, in a different way, of Dutch dynamism. For the Revolt of the Netherlands had led to the closure of the Scheldt in 1585, after the Spanish conquest of Antwerp – the traditional terminus for downstream traffic; and to tight control by the United Provinces over the Rhine estuaries themselves. The great expansion of Netherlands naval and manufacturing power in the later 16th and early 17th centuries thus progressively compressed or thwarted the Rhenish economy upstream from it, since Dutch capital commanded its outlets to the sea. The oldest cities of the Rhineland consequently tended to shrink into a routine conservatism, their archaic guild-systems stifling any adjustment to new circumstances: Cologne, the most illustrious, was one of the few large German cities to remain a bastion of traditional Catholicism throughout the century. New industries in the region tended to settle in smaller and more rural localities, free of corporative restrictions.

The South-Western towns, on the other hand, had a stronger manufacturing foundation and their well-being survived longer. But with the enormous expansion of international overseas trade from the epoch of the Discoveries onwards, their inland position became a critical economic handicap; while compensation along the Danube was blocked by the Turks. The spectacular operations of the Augsburg banking houses in the Habsburg imperial system, financing Charles V and Philip II in successive military adventures, brought their own retribution. The Fuggers and the Welsers were in the end ruined by their loans to the dynasty. Paradoxically, the Italian cities – whose relative

15. Holborn, *A History of Modern Germany. The Reformation*, pp. 81–2.

decline had started earlier – actually ended the 16th century more prosperous than the German towns, whose future had seemed better assured at the time of the Sack of Rome by an army of *Landsknechten*. The Mediterranean economy had resisted the effects of the rise of Atlantic trade longer than that of landlocked Swabia. Naturally, the contraction of urban centres in Germany in this epoch was not uniform. Isolated cities – notably Hamburg, Frankfurt and to a lesser extent Leipzig – made rapid gains and first achieved major economic importance in the period 1500–1600. Western Germany still remained by the standards of the time a generally wealthy and urbanized zone in the early 17th century, although it had ceased to register substantial growth. The comparative density of towns thus marked out a complicated political pattern similar to that of Northern Italy. For here too, just because of the power and plurality of mercantile cities, there was no expanding space for aristocratic absolutism. The social environment of the whole zone was rebarbative to major princely states, and no territorial monarchy of any importance ever emerged there. The predominant nobility necessary for one was lacking. Yet at the same time, the towns of the Rhineland or Swabia themselves, despite their number, were weaker than those of Tuscany or Lombardy. They had as a rule never possessed a rural *contado* of the Italian type in the mediaeval period, and in the early modern epoch they proved incapable of evolving into city-states proper, comparable to the lordships of Milan and Florence or the oligarchies of Venice and Genoa.[16] The political relationship of the seigneurial class to the towns was consequently quite distinct in Western Germany. Instead of a simplification of the map into a few medium-sized urban states ruled by neo-aristocratic adventurers or patricians, there was a multiplicity of small free cities amidst a maze of dwarfish princedoms.

The petty territorial states of Western Germany were distinguished, in particular, by a prominent contingent of ecclesiastical principalities.

16. Brecht's comments on the civic mentality of the free cities of Germany in general, and on his native Augsburg in particular, as reported by Benjamin, were scathing: Walter Benjamin, *Understanding Brecht*, London 1973, p. 119. They form a curious counterpoint to Gramsci's disabused reflections on the Italian cities of the same epoch. For Brecht admired the Renaissance towns of Italy, while Gramsci lauded the urban Reformation in Germany: each sought historical virtue in the national vice of the other.

Of the four Western Electors of the Empire, three were Archbishoprics – Cologne, Mainz and Trier. These curious constitutional fossils dated from the early feudal epoch, when the Saxon and Swabian Emperors had used the Church apparatus in Germany as one of its major instruments of regional rule. Whereas in Italy episcopal rule was early overthrown in the Northern cities, where the main danger to the communes became the political designs of successive Emperors and their main ally against these the Papacy, in Germany the Emperors by contrast had generally sponsored both municipal autonomy and episcopal authority, against the pretensions of secular barons and princes in collusion with Papal intrigues. The result was that both petty ecclesiastical States and free cities survived into the early modern epoch. In the countryside, agrarian property nearly everywhere took the form of the *Grundherrschaft*, in which free peasant tenants paid dues in kind or cash for their holdings to feudal landlords who were frequently absentee owners. In South-Western Germany, large numbers of smaller nobles had successfully resisted absorption into territorial principalities by acquiring the status of 'imperial knights' owing unmediated allegiance to the Emperor himself rather than homage to any ascendant local lord. By the 16th century, there were some 2,500 of these *Reichsritter*, whose total landed possessions amounted to no more than some 250 square miles. Many of them, of course, became embittered or reckless mercenaries; but many other families interpenetrated with the peculiar politico-ecclesiastical complexes that were dotted throughout Western Germany, occupying offices and prebends in them[17] – two anachronistic social forms mutually perpetuating each other. In this littered landscape, there was no room for the growth of a substantial or conventional Absolutist State, even on a regional scale. The two most significant secular principalities in the West were the Rhine Palatinate and the Duchy of Württemberg. Both contained many imperial knights and small cities, neither a serious territorial nobility. Württemberg, with 400–500,000 inhabitants, never played a major role in German politics as a whole, or looked as if it might do so. The Palatinate, which supplied the fourth Western Elector in the Empire, and controlled the tolls of the middle Rhine, was a richer and more considerable State, whose rulers achieved a comparatively early absolutist authority

17. Holborn, *A History of Modern Germany. The Reformation*, pp. 31, 38.

in the 16th century.[18] But its one attempt at major expansion – Frederick V's fatal bid for Bohemia in the early 17th century, which triggered the Thirty Years' War – brought lasting disaster on it: few areas of Germany were so put to the torch by contending armies in the European military conflict which ensued. The later 17th and early 18th centuries brought little respite for recovery. Both the Palatinate and Württemberg were in the front line of Louis XIV's wars, from 1672 to 1714, and were savagely devastated by French and Imperial troops alike. The strategic vulnerability of these two Western principalities compounded their territorial limitations. By the mid-18th century, they were merely the small change of international diplomacy, of no political weight within Germany itself.

The historical terrain presented by Western Germany as a whole thus proved incompatible with the emergence of any major Absolutism. The same sociological necessity which determined this absence in the West ensured that all the important experiences of Absolutist State-construction, which showed a real possibility of establishing an ultimate hegemony within the Empire, came from the East. Excluding for the moment the Habsburg lands in Austria and Bohemia, which will be considered later, the future chances of German unity basically lay with the three Eastern States which formed a tier from the Tyrol to the Baltic – Bavaria, Saxony and Brandenburg. From the 16th century onwards, these were the only real contenders for the leadership of a nationally unified Germany, apart from the House of Austria. For it was in the more recently colonized and more backward East, where cities were much fewer and weaker, that a strong machinery of Absolutism – unfettered by urban proliferation and upheld by a powerful nobility – was alone possible. To see why it was the northernmost of these three States which won final ascendancy in Germany, it is necessary to look at the internal structure of each. Bavaria was much the oldest, a major unit of the Carolingian Empire and one of the great stem duchies of the 10th century. In the late 12th century, the Wittelsbach house became lords of Bavaria. No other line ever supplanted it thereafter: the Wittelsbach dynasty was to achieve the longest unbroken record of rule over its hereditary region of any reigning family

18. For social conditions in Württemberg and the Palatinate, see F. L. Carsten, *Princes and Parliaments in Germany*, Oxford 1959, pp. 2–4, 341–7.

in Europe (1180–1918). Its possessions were frequently subdivided during the Middle Ages, but by 1505 were reunited once again by Albert IV into a single and powerful Duchy, some three times larger than the Mark of Brandenburg. During the religious upheavals of the 16th century, the Bavarian Dukes opted without hesitation for the Catholic cause, and made their realm the most solid bulwark of the Counter-Reformation in Germany. Their brisk suppression of Lutheranism was accompanied by firm subordination of the local Estates, the main focus of Protestant resistance in the Duchy. Dynastic control was achieved over the Archbishopric of Cologne, which remained an important family connection to the Rhineland for nearly two centuries after 1583. The Wittelsbach rulers who were responsible for this religious and political programme, also introduced the first bureaucratic appurtenances of absolutism into Bavaria: a Financial Chamber, a Privy Council and a War Council modelled on Austrian lines, were all established by the 1580's.

Administrative influences from Austria did not, however, mean that Bavaria was in any sense a Habsburg satellite in this epoch. In fact, the Bavarian Counter-Reformation was well ahead of the Austrian, and supplied both example and personnel for the recatholicization of the Habsburg lands: the future Emperor Ferdinand II himself was a product of Jesuit training at Ingolstadt, at a time when Protestantism was still the dominant faith of the landed classes in Bohemia and Austria. In 1597, Maximilian I acceded to the Ducal title and soon proved himself the most resolute and capable ruler in Germany. Summoning a submissive Landtag only twice before the Thirty Years' War, he concentrated all judicial, financial, political and diplomatic powers in his person, doubling taxes and accumulating 2 million guilders' reserves for a war chest. Thus when the Thirty Years' War broke out, Bavaria was the natural leader of the Catholic states of Germany against the threat of a Calvinist take-over in Bohemia. Maximilian I recruited and equipped an army of 24,000 for the Catholic League, which played a vital role in the victory of the White Mountain in 1620, and then attacked and conquered the Palatinate in the following year. Throughout the long vicissitudes of the ensuing military struggle, the Duke taxed his realm ferociously, with complete disregard for the protests of the Estates committee against the price of his war effort: by 1648, Bavaria had paid no less than 70 per cent of the total costs incurred by the armies of the Catholic League during the Thirty Years' War, which had meanwhile devastated the local economy and decimated the population, leading to an acute depression in the Duchy.[19] Maximilian nervertheless emerged from Westphalia the strongest autocrat in Germany, practising an Absolutism more uninhibited and unyielding than that of Frederick William in Brandenburg after him. Bavaria had been enlarged by the annexation of the Upper Palatinate, and had acquired the Electoral dignity. It seemed the most powerful ethnically German State in the Empire.

The future, however, was to belie this appearance. Bavarian Absolutism was early consummated: but it rested on very limited and inelastic foundations. The social structure of the Duchy, in fact, did not permit any further major expansion, checking the Wittelsbach State short of an ascendant all-German role. The Bavarian social formation, unlike that of Württemberg or the Palatinate, contained few free cities or imperial knights. Much less urbanized than these western principalities, its towns were nearly all diminutive in size: Munich, the capital city, had only 12,000 inhabitants in 1500 and less than 14,000 in 1700. The local aristocracy were traditional landowners, who owed direct allegiance to ducal authority. It was this social configuration, of course, which rendered possible the rapid emergence of an Absolutist State in Bavaria, and its subsequent stability and longevity. On the other hand, the nature of Bavarian rural society was not propitious to any dynamic enlargement of the realm. For if the nobility was numerous, its estates were also small and scattered. The peasantry beneath it formed a free tenantry, owing relatively light dues to its landlords: labour services never acquired real importance, amounting to no more than 4–6 days a year in the 16th century. Nor did the nobility enjoy higher justice over their labour force. There was little consolidation of aristocratic demesnes, partly perhaps because of the lack of export outlets for cereals, given Bavaria's geographical position deep in the Central European land-mass, without river routes to the sea. The most notable feature of the *Grundherrschaft* agriculture in South-Eastern Germany was the economic protuberance of the Church, which owned no less than 56 per cent of all peasant farms by the mid-

19. Carsten, *Princes and Parliaments in Germany*, pp. 392–406.

18th century, compared with a mere 24 per cent controlled by the aristocracy and 13 per cent by the dynasty.[20] The relative weakness of the noble class revealed by this property pattern was reflected in its juridical position. It did not achieve full fiscal immunity, although it was naturally taxed much less than any other estate: and its efforts to prevent any non-noble acquisition of its domains, formally embodied in a law banning such purchases in the last Landtag of the 17th century, was effectively sabotaged by covert clerical operations in the land market. Moreover, the acute labour shortage caused by the depopulation of the Thirty Years' War redounded to the disadvantage of the Bavarian aristocracy, given its prior lack of juridical purchase over the villages. It meant that in practice the peasantry was able to bargain successfully for alleviation of dues and amelioration of leases, while many noble properties fell into mortgage. This social background imposed narrow political limits to the potential of Bavarian Absolutism, which soon became evident. The same pattern – 'small noble estates, small towns and small peasants'[21] – which offered very little resistance to the emergence of a ducal Absolutism, also infused it with very little impetus.

The Duchy ended the Thirty Years' War with a population equivalent to that controlled by the Hohenzollern Elector in the north – some 1,000,000 subjects. Maximilian I's successor, Ferdinand Maria, strengthened the civil apparatus of Wittelsbach rule, establishing the supremacy of the Privy Council and using the all-purpose *Rentmeister* as the key official for local administrative intendancy; the last Landtag was dismissed in 1669, although a 'permanent committee' of it survived somewhat ineffectually into the next century. But while the Great Elector was steadily building up a permanent army in Brandenburg, Bavarian troops were disbanded after Westphalia. It was not until 1679 that the new Duke, Max Emmanuel, reconstituted a Wittelsbach military force. But even then, it was never able to attract the Bavarian nobility as a whole into its service: local aristocrats were a small minority of the officer corps in what anyway remained a very modest army (some 14,000 in the mid-18th century). Max Emmanuel, an ambitious and carefree general who had won his spurs against the

20. Carsten, *Princes and Parliaments in Germany*, pp. 350–2.
21. *Ibid.*, p. 352.

Turks in the relief of Vienna, became Regent of the Spanish Netherlands by marriage in 1672 and a candidate for the Hispanic inheritance itself at the turn of the 18th century. Gambling for the highest stakes, he threw in his lot with Louis XIV in 1702, at the outbreak of the War of the Spanish Succession. The Franco-Bavarian alliance briefly dominated the field in Southern Germany, threatening Vienna itself: but Blenheim shattered its chances of victory in Central Europe. Bavaria was occupied by Austrian troops for the rest of the conflict, while Max Emmanuel – stripped of his rank and put under the ban of the Empire – fled to Belgium. The attempt to use French power to establish Wittelsbach ascendancy in Germany had failed disastrously. At the Peace of Utrecht, the Duke had so little confidence in the prospects of his Bavarian patrimony that he proposed to Austria to swap it for the Southern Netherlands – a scheme vetoed by England and France, which was to reappear again at a later date. The dynasty returned to a land enfeebled by a decade of pillage and destruction. Post-war Bavaria gradually sank into a semi-comatose condition of introversion and corruption. The extravagance of the court in Munich absorbed a higher proportion of the budget than in perhaps any other German State of the time. State debts steadily increased as tax-farmers dissipated public revenues, the rural populace remained blighted with religious superstition, the nobles more inclined to ecclesiastical prebends than military duties.[22] The size of the Duchy, and the preservation of a small army, ensured Bavaria's diplomatic importance within the Empire. But by 1740, it was no longer a convincing candidate for the political leadership of Germany.

Saxony, the next realm to the north, represented a somewhat different version of Absolutist development in the Eastern tier of German States. The local ruling house, the Wettin dynasty, originally acquired the Duchy and Electorate of Saxony in 1425, a few years after the Hohenzollern line had obtained the Mark of Brandenburg, and in much the same way – as a grant by the Emperor Sigismund for military services rendered in the wars against the Hussites, in which Frederick of Meissen, the first Wettin Elector, had been one of his chief lieutenants. Partitioned between Ernestine and Albertine branches of the family in 1485, with capitals respectively at Wittenberg and

22. Holborn, *A History of Modern Germany 1648–1840*, pp. 292–3.

Dresden-Leipzig, the Saxon lands nonetheless remained the wealthiest and most advanced region of Eastern Germany. They owed their pre-eminence to the rich silver and tin mines of the mountains, and textile industries which developed in the towns. The commercial cross-roads of Leipzig, as we have seen, was one of the few German cities to grow uninterruptedly throughout the 16th century. The relatively high degree of urbanization in Saxony, by contrast with Bavaria or Branden-burg, and the regalian rights of the local princes in the mining industry, produced a social and political pattern distinct from that of its southern or northern neighbour. There was no manorial reaction in the late mediaeval or early modern epoch comparable to that of Prussia: the power of the Saxon nobility was not great enough to reduce the peasantry to serfdom, given the weight of the towns in the social formation. Seigneurial demesnes were larger than in Bavaria, partly because clerical lands were much less significant. But the basic trend in the countryside was towards free tenant farming, with commutation of labour services for cash rents – in other words, the milder regime of the *Grundherrschaft*. The aristocracy did not achieve complete fiscal immunity (its allodial possessions were subject to tax), and was unable to secure the legal closure of noble property to commoner purchase. It was well represented in the Estates system, however, which became increasingly stable and influential in the course of the 16th century. On the other hand, the towns were also vigorously present in the Landtage, although they had to bear the brunt of the excise on alcohol which pro-vided a staple of princely revenues, to the advantage of the nobility; urban representatives were also excluded from the *Obersteuercollegium* which from the 1570's administered tax-collection in the Electorate.

The Wettin dynasty was able, in this socio-economic context, to amass wealth and force without any direct attack on the Estates or considerable development of bureaucratic government. It had never relinquished higher judicial prerogatives, and controlled a large independent income from its mining rights – which supplied some two-thirds of Albertine cameral revenue in the 1530's, while the pros-perity of the region permitted both profitable and tolerable consump-tion taxes from an early date.[23] It is thus not surprising that Saxony

23. Carsten, *Princes and Parliaments in Germany*, pp. 191–6, 201–4.

became the first princely State to dominate the German arena politically, in the epoch of the Reformation. The Ernestine Electorate was the religious cradle of Lutheranism from 1517 onwards: but it was the Albertine Duchy, which did not go over to the Protestant camp until 1539, that commanded the centre of the political stage in the complex drama that followed the outbreak of the Reformation in Germany. For Maurice of Saxony, who succeeded to the Duchy in 1541, rapidly out-manoeuvred all rival princes and the Emperor himself, in the pursuit of dynastic advantage and territorial aggrandizement. Joining in the Imperial attack on the Schmalkaldic League with Charles V, he participated in the annihilation of the Protestant armies at Mühlberg, and so acquired the bulk of the Ernestine lands and the Electoral title. Orchestrating the Franco-Lutheran attack on Charles V five years later, he destroyed Habsburg chances of reconverting Germany and clinched the unification of Saxony under his rule. At his death, the new Saxon State was the most powerful and prosperous principality in Germany. Fifty years of peaceful growth, during which the Estates were regularly summoned and taxes were steadily increased in the Electorate, ensued.

The onset of the Thirty Years' War, however, caught Saxony militarily and diplomatically unprepared in the early 17th century. While Bavaria played a star role among the German States in the conflict, Saxony was reduced to a hesitant weakness very similar to that of Brandenburg. Both the Wettin and Hohenzollern Electors, although Protestant, sided with the Habsburg imperial camp in the initial stages of the war; both were subsequently occupied and devastated by Sweden, and forced over to the anti-Habsburg bloc; both then defected for a separate peace with the Emperor. Saxony acquired Lusatia by the Treaty of Westphalia, and its princes a regular war-tax which was used to create a modest permanent army. The wealth of the country allowed it to recover comparatively quickly from the effects of the Thirty Years' War. Direct taxation rose some 5 to 6 times between 1660 and 1690. The military apparatus of the Wettin State had increased in size to some 20,000 men by the end of the century, when it performed adequately, together with analogous Bavarian contingents, against the Turks in the relief of Vienna. In 1700, Saxony still had an edge on Brandenburg as an East German power. Its army was somewhat smaller, and its Estates system had not been quashed. But it contained perhaps twice the population, was much more industrially developed, and possessed a proportionately larger treasury. The early 18th century, in fact, now witnessed the major Saxon bid for political primacy within the German State system. For in 1697, the Elector Frederick Augustus I adopted Catholicism in order to win Austrian backing for his candidature to the Polish monarchy. This exercise proved successful. The Elector became the first German ruler to achieve a royal title as Augustus II, and obtained a political lien on nearby Poland, separated from Saxony only by the slender length of Silesia. At the same time, a general sales tax was successfully imposed in Saxony, against the resistance of the Estates: significantly, however, the Saxon excise – unlike the Brandenburger – was extended from the towns into the countryside, at the cost of the nobility.[24] The army was now raised to 30,000, nearer to its counterpart in Brandenburg.

The Saxon-Polish Union, however, was no sooner achieved than the last great drive of Swedish imperialism shattered it. Charles XII marched into Poland, expelled Augustus II from the country, and then invaded Saxony itself in 1706, crushing the Wettin army and imposing a ruthless occupation on the Duchy. The Russian victory over Sweden in the Ukraine eventually repaired the Saxon position internationally, at the end of the Great Northern War. The Polish dignity was restored to Augustus II; the army was built up again in the 1730's; the Estates were increasingly flouted. But the outward show of the Wettin State, displayed in the baroque elegance of its capital in Dresden, no longer corresponded to its inner strength. The Polish connection was a decorative lure, which brought more expense than gain, because of the fictive character of the *szlachta* monarchy: the Saxon investiture had been accepted precisely because Russia and Austria calculated that the Wettin house was too slight to be a dangerous rival. The war which it had occasioned had wrought great damage to the economy of the Duchy. Moreover, unlike the Sergeant King in Berlin, Augustus II was notorious for the extravagance of his court, in addition to his military ambitions. These combined burdens critically weakened Saxony in the years when Prussia was accumulating assets for the contest within Germany ahead. The population of Saxony, 2,000,000 in 1700, had

24. Carsten, *Princes and Parliaments in Germany*, pp. 245–6.

sunk to 1,700,000 or so in the 1720's, while that of Prussia had increased from about 1,000,000 in 1688 to 2,250,000 in 1740: the relative demographic values of each had been reversed.[25] The Saxon nobility had shown little ardour for the adventures of the Elector abroad, and was losing ground at home in the land market to burghers as the century progressed. The Estates survived, partly because of the Polish distractions of the dynasty, and within them the importance of the towns if anything grew. The bureaucratic machinery of the State remained unimpressive, less developed than that of Bavaria. In the absence of any auditing discipline, princely finances became waterlogged with debts. The result was that Saxon Absolutism, despite its promising start and the autocratic propensities of successive Wettin rulers, never achieved real firmness or consistency: the social formation was too fluid and mixed in character.

It is now possible to see why Brandenburg was to be picked out so singularly for dominance in Germany. There was a progressive elimination of alternatives. The Absolutist State was everywhere in Europe fundamentally a political apparatus of aristocratic rule: the social power of the nobility was the central spring of its existence. Within the fragmented arena of the post-mediaeval *Reich*, only those regions which possessed an economically strong and stable landowning class were likely ever to achieve a diplomatic or military leadership of Germany: for they alone could generate an Absolutism capable of equalizing with the greater European monarchies. Western Germany was thus cancelled out from the start, because of the density of its urban civilization. Bavaria possessed no towns of any undue importance, and did develop an early Absolutism under the sign of the Counter-Reformation: but its nobility was too weak, its clergy too endowed, its peasantry too free, to found a dynamic princedom. Saxony contained a more spacious aristocracy, but its cities were also much stronger, and its peasantry no more servile. By 1740, both States had passed their peak. In Prussia, by contrast, the junker class maintained an iron serfdom on its estates, and a vigilant tutelage over the towns: seigneurial power achieved its purest expression in the Hohenzollern lands, the remotest outposts of German settlement in the East. It was thus not the external frontage of Prussia onto Poland that determined its ascent within Germany, as

25. Carsten, *Princes and Parliaments in Germany*, pp. 250–1.

Engels thought.[26] In fact, as we have seen, entanglement with Poland (Engels's word) was actually one of the precipitates of the decline of Saxony; the later Prussian role in the Polish partitions was merely the epilogue to the decisive military victories it had already won within Germany itself, and did little to strengthen it internationally. It was the *internal* nature of the Prussian social formation which explains its sudden overshadowing of all other German States in the epoch of the Enlightenment, and ultimate presidency over the unification of Germany. This rise was overdetermined by the complex historical totality of the *Reich* as a whole, which prevented the emergence of a Western-type Absolutism in the Rhineland, fragmented the territory of the Empire into some 2,000 political units, and extruded the House of Austria towards its non-Germanic borderlands. The key external force affecting the respective fates of Prussia and Austria within Germany was not Poland, but Sweden. For it was Swedish power which destroyed the chance of a Habsburg unification of the Empire in the Thirty Years' War, and Swedish proximity which was the main foreign threat acting as a centripetal pressure on the construction of the Hohenzollern State – whose compulsion Bavaria and Saxony, the other East German principalities, never experienced to the same extent, although Saxony did not escape from becoming the final victim of Nordic militarism. The capacity of Prussia to resist Swedish expansion, and to outfight every rival within Germany, must in turn be related to the peculiar cast of the junker class itself, with the consolidation on a transparently class basis of a dynastic Absolutism by the Great Elector and Sergeant King.

To start with, the scale of the country itself, in the late 17th and early 18th centuries, left its stamp on the Prussian aristocracy. The combined Hohenzollern lands in the East – Brandenburg, East Prussia and later West Pomerania – were still small in size and very thinly settled. Their total population in 1740 was below 2,000,000 if the Western enclaves of the dynasty were excluded; the relative density of

26. See above, p. 236. Weber seems to have shared a similar belief. See his comment that 'enemy attacks on the marches' of mediaeval Germany were responsible for the fact that 'their governors were everywhere endowed with strong powers'. He concluded: 'It is for this reason that in Germany the strongest development towards a unified territorial state occurred in Brandenburg and Austria.' *Economy and Society*, III, p. 1051.

habitation was probably less than half that of Saxony. One of the most constant motifs of State policy from the Great Elector onwards was to be the quest for immigrants to colonize this underpopulated region. The Protestant character of Prussia was to prove a critical asset in this respect. Refugees from Southern Germany after the Thirty Years' War and Huguenots after the Edict of Nantes were eagerly planted in the early years: Dutch, German and more French under Frederick II. But it must always be borne in mind that Prussia remained an extremely modest country, down to the conquest of Silesia, by comparison with the general run of European monarchies at the time. This provincial scale reinforced certain notable traits of the junker class. For above all, the Prussian aristocracy was peculiar among major European nobilities in that it did not have a very wide spectrum of fortunes within it: we shall see that the Polish *szlachta*, similar in many other ways, were in this respect its polar opposite. Thus the average *Rittergüter* – the feudal commercial farms of the Prussian nobility – were of medium size. There was no stratum of great magnates, with huge latifundia far larger than the properties of the smaller gentry, such as was to be found in most other European countries.[27] The old *Herrenstand* of the higher nobility had lost its dominance to the mass of the *Ritterschaft* by the mid-16th century.[28] The one really big landed proprietor was the monarchy itself: the royal demesnes accounted for one-third of the arable land in the 18th century.[29] Two important consequences followed for the character of the junker class. On the one hand, it was socially less divided than many other European aristocracies: it formed, on the whole, a cohesive bloc of like-minded middling landowners,

27. Thus the average value of a sample of 100 estates in the wealthiest region of Brandenburg was no more than 60,000 thalers – perhaps £15,000 – in the 18th century: Walter Dorn, 'The Prussian Bureaucracy in the Eighteenth Century', *Political Science Quarterly*, Vol. 47, 1932, No. 2, p. 263. Partly because of the lack of a primogenitural tradition, many of even the largest holdings were encumbered with debts.

28. It still dominated the committees of the Landtag in this epoch, from which smaller and poorer nobles were excluded; but the tension between the whole aristocracy and the towns was much more acute, economically and politically, than any rift within the landed class itself: Otto Hintze, *Die Hohenzollern und ihr Werk*, Berlin 1915, pp. 146–7.

29. Goodwin, 'Prussia', in Goodwin (ed.), *The European Nobility in the Eighteenth Century*, p. 86.

without undue regional divergences. On the other, it meant that the average junker tended to exercise a direct function in the organization of production, when not engaged in service duties. In other words, he was very often the real, and not merely nominal, manager of his estates. (The residence pattern of the Prussian nobility naturally encouraged this tendency, since towns were few and far between.) The phenomenon of great absentee landowners, with devolution of administrative functions on the demesne to bailiffs and stewards, was uncommon. If relative equality of wealth distinguished the junkers from their Polish opposites, careful husbandry of the demesne separated them from the Russian nobility. The discipline of the export market doubtless contributed to more rational management of the *Gutherrschaft*. The Prussian junkers of the late 17th and early 18th century were thus a compact social class, in a small country, with rough rural business traditions. Thus when the Great Elector and Frederick William I were building their new Absolutist State, the distinctive prior patterns of the nobility produced a *sui generis* administrative structure.

For unlike virtually every other Absolutism, the Prussian model was able to make productive use of the traditional representative institutions of the aristocracy, once their central node had been dissolved. The provincial estates or Landtage did, as we have seen, progressively lapse after the 1650's; the last real session of the Brandenburg Landtag in 1683 was largely devoted to lamenting the omnipotence of the *Generalkriegskommissariat*. But the local 'county' estates or *Kreistage* became the basic bureaucratic unit in the countryside. From 1702 onwards, these junker councils elected candidates from the local nobility to the post of *Landrat*, from whom one was then formally appointed to the office by the monarchy. The institution of the *Landrat*, who was vested with all administrative, fiscal and military powers in the rural districts, to some extent recalls the Justice of the Peace in England, in its savant compromise between the autonomous self-administration of the gentry and the unitary authority of the central State. However, the resemblance is a misleading one, since the partition of spheres in Prussia was founded on a bedrock of servile labour. Serfdom could technically take two forms in Prussia. *Leibeigenschaft* was the hereditary personal subjection of peasants, with no civil or property rights whatever, who could be sold apart from the land. *Erbuntertänigkeit* was the condition of hereditary estate dependence, with some minimal legal rights, but bondage to the demesne and obligatory services to the lord both in house and field. In practice there was little distinction between the two. The State thus exercised no direct jurisdiction at all over the mass of the rural population, who were governed by the junkers in their *Gutsbezirke* under the supervision of the *Landrat*, and whose taxes – two-fifths of peasant income[30] – were collected directly by their lords. The towns, on the other hand, and the royal demesne itself, were ruled by a professional bureaucracy, which was the direct arm of Absolutism. A painstaking toll and traffic control system regulated movements of persons and goods from one sector to another of this dual administration.

The military caste itself, as we have seen, was overwhelmingly co-opted from the nobility: in 1739, all 34 Generals, 56 out of 57 Colonels, 44 out of 46 Lieutenant-Colonels, and 106 out of 108 Majors, were aristocrats.[31] The higher civil bureaucracy was also extensively and increasingly recruited from the junker class. The Sergeant King was careful to balance nobles with burghers in its provincial chambers, but his son deliberately promoted aristocrats at the expense of middle-class functionaries. Rigorously collegial principles governed the organization of this civil service, whose basic cell was the 'board' of co-responsible officials, not the individual functionary – a system well designed to inculcate impersonal collective duty and probity, in a Lutheran nobility.[32] The remarkable discipline and efficacy of these institutions was a reflection of the unity of the class which staffed them. There were no grandee rivalries with clientages inside the State apparatus; there was minimal venality of office because of the nullity of the towns; there was not even tax

30. Holborn, *A History of Modern Germany 1648–1840*, p. 196.

31. Alfred Vagts, *A History of Militarism*, London 1959, p. 64. Up to 1794, the Prussian Army had been commanded by 895 Generals, from 518 noble families. Foreigners outnumbered burghers in the officer corps throughout.

32. Dorn, 'The Prussian Bureaucracy in the Eighteenth Century', *Political Science Quarterly*, Vol. 46, 1931, No. 3, p. 406, who discusses the workings of the *Kriegs-und-Domänen-Kammern*. Collegial organization had by no means led to administrative efficacy or dispatch in Spain: the contrast is doubtless in part to be explained by the distinct ethical bearing of Protestantism in Prussia – a variable to which Engels, among others, attached much importance for its rise as a whole.

farming until Frederick II (who imported a *Régie* from France), because the squires were themselves entrusted with collection of fiscal exactions from their peasants in the countryside, and the urban excise was controlled by professional *Steuerräte*, while the royal demesne provided a large cameral income of its own. The Prussian junkers were so firmly in command of State and society in the 18th century that they felt no need for the vinculism of their Western counterparts: Frederick II tried to promote the primogenitural *maiorat* to consolidate aristocratic estates, but his ideological zeal found little response from the landowners, who even preserved ancient feudal rules of collective agnate consent for family loans.[33] They were not threatened by an ascendant bourgeoisie gradually prising open the land market, and so felt little need to protect their social position by disinheriting their cadet children: junker estates were habitually divided on the death of their owners (which in turn helped to keep down their size). Free from intra-noble tensions, paramount over the towns, lords of their peasants, the Prussian landowning class was more stolidly at one with its State than any other in Europe. Bureaucratic unity and rural autonomy were uniquely reconciled in this cabbage paradise. Junker Absolutism, built on these foundations, contained a formidable potential for expansion.

In 1740, Frederick William I and the Emperor Charles VI both died. The Prussian heir, Frederick II, immediately fell upon Silesia. This rich Habsburg province was rapidly occupied by the Hohenzollern army. France seized the opportunity to secure Prussian support for a Bavarian candidate to the Imperial dignity. In 1741 the Wittelsbach Duke Charles Albert was elected Emperor, and Franco-Bavarian troops marched into Bohemia. Prussian war aims did not include the resurrection of Bavarian primacy in South Germany, or the domination of France in the Empire. Frederick II, having defeated Austria in the field, therefore made a separate peace with Vienna in 1742, leaving Prussia in possession of Silesia. Habsburg military recovery in the struggle against France, and the alignment of Saxony with Austria, precipitated his re-entry into the war two years later, to protect his gains. Saxony was defeated and ransacked: Austrian armies were successfully held off, after very hard fighting. In 1745, the international conflict was concluded, with the restoration of the Imperial title and

33. Goodwin, 'Prussia', pp. 95–7.

the Bohemian kingdom to the Habsburg heiress, Maria Theresa, and the confirmation of the Hohenzollern conquest of Silesia. The victories of Frederick II in the War of the Austrian Succession, long prepared by the work of his predecessors, were the strategic turning-point in the European career of Prussian Absolutism, making it for the first time a triumphant power in Germany. Berlin, in fact, had scored simultaneously against Munich, Dresden and Vienna. The last Bavarian chance of political expansion had been foiled; the Saxon armies had been routed; and the Austrian Empire had been deprived of its most industrialized province in Central Europe, containing the commercial hub of Breslau. Conversely, the acquisition of Silesia increased the population of Prussia by 50 per cent at one blow, bringing it up to some 4 million inhabitants, and endowing it for the first time with a relatively advanced economic region in the East, with a long tradition of urban manufactures (textiles). The feudal order in Prussia as a whole was not seriously modified by this extension, however: the mass of the rural population of Silesia, no less than that of Brandenburg, were *Erbuntertänigen*. The local nobility merely owned larger estates. The annexation of Silesia was, in fact, in relative terms perhaps the most important and lucrative single addition to any European continental State in the epoch.[34]

It was the magnitude of Prussian success in 1740–5, the swift and decisive shift in the balance of power which it portended, which explains the extraordinary scale of the coalition woven against it by the Austrian Chancellor Kaunitz in the succeeding decade. Revenge was to be on a scale fitting the enormity of the upset: by 1757, Kaunitz's 'diplomatic revolution' had united Austria, Russia, France, Sweden, Saxony and Denmark against Prussia. The combined population of these powers was at least twenty times that of the intended victim of their alliance: the aim of the coalition was nothing less than to erase the Prussian State from the map of Europe. Surrounded from all sides, Frederick II in desperation struck first, formally inaugurating the Seven Years' War with the invasion of Saxony. The bitter struggle that ensued was the first truly all-European war, in which every major power from Russia to England and Spain to Sweden was simultaneously involved, since the continental conflict interlocked with the

34. See Dorn's judgement: *Competition for Empire*, pp. 174–5.

maritime and colonial conflict between Britain and France. The Prussian military apparatus commanded by Frederick II, now comprising an army of some 150,000 troops, survived shattering setbacks and defeats, to emerge with a final, thin margin of victories against all its enemies. The diversionary campaigns financed by England in Westphalia, drawing off French forces, and the eventual defection of Russia from the coalition, were critical factors in the 'miracle' of the House of Brandenburg. But the real secret of Prussian resilience was the burnished efficacy of its Absolutism: the State structure that had been scheduled for rapid and complete destruction by Kaunitz proved far more capable of withstanding the enormous economic and logistic strains of the war than the rambling empires arrayed against it in the East. No territory changed hands at the peace in 1763. Silesia remained a Hohenzollern province and Vienna ended the war in more parlous financial condition than Berlin. The repulse of the grand attack by Austria was to prove a conclusive defeat for Habsburg arms in Germany, as subsequent events were to show: its deeper consequences only became apparent later. Saxony, repeatedly and relentlessly plundered by Frederick II, had to bear half the entire Prussian war costs; it now sank into political insignificance past recall, losing its Polish medallion a few months after the peace. Prussia, although it had achieved no geographical gains and won no decisive campaigns, was strategically stronger within the balance of Germany after the Seven Years' War than before it.

The purposes of Frederick II's foreign policy, meanwhile, were complemented by the work of his domestic rule. The top ranks of the bureaucracy and army were consciously aristocratized by the monarchy. The judiciary was reformed by Von Cocceji, and venality largely eliminated from the legal system.[35] The economy was fostered by official programmes for both agriculture and industry. Rural drainage, land settlement and transport improvements were organized. State manufactures were founded, shipping and mining promoted, and textile industries developed. The first systematic 'populationist' policies in Europe were pursued, with immigrant recruitment centres abroad.[36]

35. For Von Cocceji's role, see Rosenberg, *Bureaucracy, Aristocracy and Autocracy*, pp. 122–34.

36. Bluche gives a vivid account, *Le Despotisme Eclairé*, pp. 83–5.

Frederick II was also responsible for one audacious innovation of Prussian Absolutism, destined to have far-reaching consequences in the next century, if largely a paper measure when first decreed: the institution of compulsory primary education for the whole male population, with the *Generallandschulreglement* of 1763. On the other hand, gestures to protect the peasantry from landlord oppression and eviction were largely motivated by fears of depleting the able-bodied manpower for the army, and proved uniformly ineffectual. Mortgage banks to help straitened landowners, although suspiciously received by the junker class at the outset, were destined to have greater importance. Public finances, scrupulously controlled and purged of virtually any court expenses, increased remarkably despite the wars of the reign. Annual royal revenues trebled from 7 million to 23 million thalers (1740–86), while reserves quintupled from 10 to 54 million.[37] The overwhelming bulk of State expenditure went, of course, on the Army, which rose from 80,000 to 200,000 troops under Frederick II – the highest ratio to population of any country in Europe; the proportion of foreign regiments – hired or empressed abroad – was deliberately maximized to spare the limited productive population at home. The partition of Poland in 1772, in agreement with Russia and Austria, added West Prussia and the Ermland to the Hohenzollern domains in the East, consolidating them into a single territorial bloc and increasing the demographic potential of the State. The total population of Prussia had doubled from 2·5 to 5·4 million towards the end of the reign.[38] Internationally, the military reputation of Prussian Absolutism after the Seven Years' War was by now so formidable that Frederick II could effectively dictate the outcome of the two main crises within Germany of the next decades without having to resort to a serious passage of arms. In 1778–9 and again in 1784–5, Austria tried to recoup its position within Germany by achieving an exchange of the Southern Netherlands for Bavaria, twice reaching an understanding with the Wittelsbach Elector to this end. The merger of Bavaria with Austria would have transformed German history, making the Habsburg dynasty unassailably strong in the South and redirecting the whole political orientation of Vienna centrally back into the *Reich*. On both

37. Holborn, *A History of Modern Germany 1648–1840*, p. 268.
38. *Ibid.*, p. 262.

occasions, Prussian interdiction sufficed to kill the project. On the first, some token skirmishes in Bohemia were enough. On the second, the diplomatic alignment by Berlin of Hanover, Saxony, Mainz and other principalities in a common bloc against Austria was an adequate veto: the 'Association of Princes' collected by Frederick II in 1785, a year before his death, advertised and sealed the Hohenzollern preponderance in Northern Germany.

Four years later, the French Revolution broke out and the viability of every *ancien régime* in Europe, no matter how politically new, was thrown into question, as different historical times crossed on the battle-fields of revolutionary war. Prussia, performing poorly in the first counter-revolutionary coalition against France in the West, seized the opportunity to divide the rest of Poland with Russia and Austria in the East, and then promptly pulled out of the struggle with the Republic in 1795. The day of reckoning was only postponed by Hohenzollern neutrality during the next decade of European war. In 1806, Napoleon's attack put the Prussian Absolutist State to its supreme test. Its armies were crushed at Jena, and it had to sign a peace treaty at Tilsit which reduced it to satellite status. All its territory west of the Elbe was confiscated, French garrisons were planted in its fortresses, and huge indemnities were imposed on it. This was the crisis that produced the 'Era of Reforms'. In this, its moment of greatest peril and weakness, the Prussian State was able to draw on a remarkable reserve of political, military and cultural talent to save its existence and renovate its structure. Many of these gifted reformers were in fact from the West and Centre of Germany, socially much more advanced regions than Prussia itself. Stein, the political leader of the come-back against Napoleon, was an imperial knight from the Rhineland. Gneisenau and Scharnhorst, the architects of the new Army, were respectively from Hanover and Saxony. Fichte, the philosophical ideologue of the 'war of liberation' against the French, was a resident of Hamburg. Harden-berg, the noble most responsible for the final shape of the Reforms, was a Hanoverian.[39] The mixed provenance of the reformers was

39. Virtually the only important political figure involved in the reforms who was a native Prussian was the educationalist Von Humboldt, although Clause-witz – the greatest intellectual eminence of this generation – was also by birth a Brandenburger.

premonitory. Prussian Absolutism was henceforward to undergo new leases of life, and deep shifts in character, from the basic fact of its cultural and territorial contiguity with the rest of Germany. From the appearance of Napoleon at the gates of Berlin, there was no longer any possibility of the Hohenzollern State developing *en vase close*. For the moment, however, the reforming impulse did not reach very far. Stein, a Francophobe emigré influenced by Montesquieu and Burke, introduced plans for civic equality, agrarian reform, local self-government and nationalist mobilization against Napoleon. In his year of office (1807–8), he did away with the now cumbersome *Generaldirektorium* and instituted a conventional Ministerial system with functional departments modelled on the lines of the French monarchy, while special officials were dispatched from the capital to supervise provincial affairs. The result was in practice an enhanced centralization of the whole State apparatus, only nominally offset by the grant of limited municipal autonomy to the towns. In the countryside, serfdom was formally abolished and the three-estates juridical system abrogated. These policies encountered vehement opposition among the junker class for their 'radicalism', and when Stein started to move against the patrimonial jurisdictions and fiscal immunity of the nobility, and to plan a general armed *levée* against France, he was promptly ejected.

His successor Hardenberg, a court politician, then applied a skilful dose of legislation exactly measured to modernize Prussian Absolutism, and the class which it represented, to the extent necessary to reinvigorate them, without affecting the essential nature of the feudal State. Agrarian 'reform' was implemented from 1810 to 1816 in such a way as to intensify rural misery still further. In exchange for legal emancipation, the peasants suffered economic despoliation of some 1,000,000 hectares and 260,000,000 marks in 'compensation' to their former masters for their new liberty.[40] The so-called *Bauernlegen* was a cold instrument for the expropriation of the peasantry. Communal lands and the three-field system were swept away. The result was to enlarge

40. W. M. Simon, *The Failure of the Prussian Reform Movement 1807–1819*, New York 1971, pp. 88–104. Peasants had to pay compensation both in land and cash, for the commutation of their labour services to their former masters. These services were still being redeemed by peasants right down to 1865. The estimate for redemption payments given above is drawn from Theodore Hamerow, *The Social Foundations of German Unification*, Princeton 1969, p. 37.

the manorial estates and create a growing mass of landless agricultural labourers, kept at the disposal of the junkers by strict legal ordinances. Hardenberg simultaneously widened access to landownership for the bourgeoisie (who could now purchase estates) and to the professions for the nobility (who no longer dropped rank by taking up law or business). The vitality and versatility of the junker class was thereby increased, without any serious loss of privileges. An attempt to end the role of the *Landrat* was speedily scuttled by the aristocracy, and the traditional county assemblies remained unreformed. In fact, noble control of the countryside was actually augmented by the extension of *Landrat* authority to rural towns. Seigneurial dues persisted long after the abolition of serfdom. The exemption of the *Rittergut* from land taxes lasted until 1861; manorial police jurisdiction until 1871; junker monopoly of county administration until 1891. In the cities, Hardenberg abolished guild monopolies, but was unable to end fiscal dualism; while Humboldt drastically extended and modernized the public educational system, from the elementary *Volksschule* to the foundation of the new University of Berlin. Meanwhile, Scharnhorst and Gneisenau organized a reserve system to evade the post-Tilsit provisions limiting the size of the Prussian army establishment, 'popularizing' recruitment but also thereby increasing the institutional militarization of the whole social order. Field regulations and tactical training were updated. Command functions were rendered formally open to bourgeois recruits, but officers could veto new admissions to their regiments – ensuring that junker control was not endangered.[41] The net effect of the Reform Era was to strengthen rather than moderate the royal state in Prussia. Significantly, however, it was in this period that the junker class – the most loyal nobility in Europe during the difficult growth of Absolutism in the 17th and 18th centuries, the only such class never to resort to civil strife against the monarchy – now for the first time became vocally restive. The Reformers' threat to its privileges, even though soon retracted, stirred up ideological opposition of a consciously neo-feudal character. Von Marwitz, the leader of Brandenburger dissidence against Hardenberg, revealingly denounced both absolutism

41. For the military reforms, see Gordon Craig, *The Politics of the Prussian Army, 1640–1945*, New York 1964, pp. 38–53, 69–70.

and parliamentarism in the name of the long-forgotten Estates constitution prior to the advent of the Great Elector. Henceforward, there always existed a choleric junker conservatism in Prussia, a mood curiously displaced from the 17th to the 19th century, that was often to be at odds with the monarchy.

The sum of the Reforms allowed Prussia to participate competently in the final coalition which defeated Napoleonic France. Yet it was essentially a traditional *ancien régime* which attended the Congress of Vienna, in company with its neighbours Austria and Russia. Although the Prussian Reformers were disliked as near 'Jacobins' by Metternich, the Hohenzollern State was still in certain respects less socially advanced than the Habsburg Empire after the Josephine Reforms of the late 18th century. The real turning-point in the history of Prussian Absolutism is to be dated, not from the work of the Reforms, but from the gains it made at the Peace. To prevent it obtaining Saxony, and to compensate it for Russian absorption of most of Poland, the Allies awarded it Rhine-Westphalia at the other end of Germany – much against the will of the court in Berlin. With this act, they shifted the whole historical axis of the Prussian State. Designed by Austria and Britain to check its territorial consolidation in East-Central Germany, the Rhenish provinces were separated from Brandenburg by Hanover and Hesse, leaving the Hohenzollern domains strategically straggled across Northern Germany, and assigned hazardous defense duties against France in the West. The actual consequences of the settlement were expected by none of the parties to it. The new Hohenzollern possessions contained a population larger than that of all the old provinces put together – 5,500,000 in the West to 5,000,000 in the East. At one stroke, the demographic weight of Prussia doubled to more than 10,000,000: Bavaria, the next largest German state, had only 3,700,000.[42] Moreover, Rhine-Westphalia was one of the most advanced regions of Western Germany. The peasantry still paid customary dues and the landowners enjoyed special hunting and other rights; but small-holder agriculture was deeply entrenched and the noble class were generally absentee landlords, not their own estate managers as in Prussia. Rural *Amt* assemblies included peasant representation, unlike the junker *Kreistage*. Social relations in the

42. J. Droz, *La Formation de l'Unité Allemande 1789–1871*, Paris 1970, p. 126.

countryside were thus much milder in pattern. The new provinces contained in addition a large number of flourishing towns, with long traditions of municipal autonomy, commercial exchange and manu-facturing activities. Much more important even than this, of course, was the fact that because of its mineral resources – as yet unexploited – the region was destined to become the most colossal industrial zone in Europe. The military acquisitions of the feudal Prussian State thus came to incorporate the natural heartland of German capitalism.

The development of the new composite State into a unified Germany in the course of the 19th century forms in essence part of the cycle of bourgeois revolutions, which will be considered elsewhere. It will be enough here to stress three crucial aspects of the socio-economic evolution of Prussia which rendered possible the later success of the Bismarckian programme. Firstly, within the East itself, Harden-berg's agrarian reform of 1816 led to a rapid and imposing advance of the whole corn economy. By freeing the land market, the reform pro-gressively sieved out incapable and endebted junkers from the country-side. Correspondingly, the number of bourgeois investors in land increased, a stratum of prosperous peasant farmers or *Grossbauern* emerged, and there was a marked rationalization of agrarian manage-ment: by 1855, 45 per cent of the *Rittergüter* in the six Eastern pro-vinces had non-aristocratic owners.[43] At the same time, those junkers who were left on the land were now proprietors of larger and more productive estates, aggrandized both by purchase from fellow nobles and by eviction of peasants from commons and small-holdings. In the 1880's, 70 per cent of the largest agrarian properties (over 1,000 hec-tares) were owned by nobles.[44] The whole agricultural sector entered a phase of expansion and prosperity. Crop yields and sown acreage rose together: in fact, both of them doubled in Ostelbian Prussia from 1815 to 1864.[45] The new latifundia were now tilled by wage-labourers,

---

43. John Gillis, 'Aristocracy and Bureaucracy in Nineteenth Century Prussia', *Past and Present*, No. 41, December 1968, p. 113.

44. Hamerow, *The Social Foundations of German Unification*, p. 59.

45. David Landes, 'Japan and Europe: Contrasts in Industrialization' in W. Lockwood (ed.), *The State and Economic Enterprise in Japan*, Princeton 1965, p. 162. Landes's essay is essentially an extended comparison between Prussian and Japanese development, and contains many reflections and insights into 19th century German history.

and becoming increasingly orthodox capitalist enterprises. This wage-labour, however, was itself regulated by a feudal *Gesindeordnung* which survived into the 20th century, and imposed a ruthless manorial discipline on agricultural labourers and domestic servants, with imprisonment for striking and strict limits to mobility. The *Bauernlegen* had not meant an exodus from the countryside: it had produced a large rural proletariat, whose numbers now rose as output increased, helping to keep wages low. The junker aristocracy thus achieved a successful cumulative conversion to capitalist agriculture, while still exploiting every patrimonial privilege it could keep. 'The nobles easily made the transition from manorial to capitalistic agriculture, while large numbers of the peasantry were permitted to drown in the cleansing waters of economic freedom.'[46]

Meanwhile, the Prussian bureaucracy was performing a fundamental service in bridging the Eastern agrarian economy with the industrial revolution simultaneously getting under way in the Western provinces. In the early 19th century, the civil service – which had always provided an occupational refuge for the underdeveloped middle class of the traditional Hohenzollern domains, although it had never dominated its top ranks – was responsible for the gradual establishment of the *Zollverein* uniting most of Germany with Prussia in a single trading zone. Von Motz and Maassen, of the Finance Ministry, were the two architects of this system, built up from 1818 to 1836, which effectively excluded Austria from German economic development and bound the smaller states commercially to Prussia.[47] The surge of railway construction from the 1830's onwards in turn stimulated rapid economic growth within the Customs Union. Bureaucratic initiatives were also of some importance in providing technological and financial aids to nascent Prussian industry (Beuth, Rother). In the 1850's, the *Zollverein* was extended to most of the remaining Northern principalities; Austrian intrusion into it was later deftly blocked by Delbrück, in the Commerce Ministry. The low-tariff policies steadily pursued by the Prussian civil service, culminating in the Treaty of Paris with France

46. Simon, *The Failure of the Prussian Reform Movement*, p. 104.

47. See Pierre Benaerts, *Les Origines de la Grande Industrie Allemande*, Paris 1934, pp. 31–52; Droz has some perceptive general comments on the role of the bureaucracy, *La Formation de l'Unité Allemande*, p. 113.

in 1864, were a critical weapon in the diplomatic and political competition between Berlin and Vienna within Germany: Austria could not afford the economic liberalization which drew the South German States, dependent on international trade, to the side of Prussia.[48]

At the same time, however, the fundamental course of German unification was being set by the tempestuous industrial growth of the Ruhr, within the Western provinces of Prussia itself. The Rhenish bourgeoisie whose fortunes were founded on the new manufacturing and mining economy in the West were a much more politically ambitious and outspoken group than the obedient Ostelbian townsmen. It was their spokesmen – Mevissen, Camphausen, Hansemann and others – who organized and led German liberalism and fought for the granting of a bourgeois constitution with a responsible assembly in Prussia during this period. Their programme meant, in fact, the end of Hohenzollern Absolutism, and naturally aroused the obdurate hostility of the junker ruling class in the East. The popular upheavals of 1848, whose mass combustion was furnished by artisans and peasants, briefly gave this liberal bourgeoisie ministerial office in Berlin, and an ideological platform in Frankfurt, before the royal army crushed the revolution a few months later. The Prussian Constitution which was the aborted product of the crisis of 1848, established a national Landtag for the first time, with one chamber based on a three-class electoral system candidly ensuring the dominance of large property, and another recruited overwhelmingly from the hereditary nobility – both without any powers over the executive: an assembly so pale that only some 30 per cent of eligible voters on average participated in the elections to it.[49] The Rhenish capitalist class thus remained oppositional even when it won majorities to this token institution. The Ostelbian junkers vigilantly eyed the monarchy for any signs of weakness, actually getting its manorial police powers – abolished in a moment of panic by Frederick William IV in 1848 – restored in 1856. The 'constitutional conflict' between the Liberals and the State in the 1860's thus appeared to be a frontal clash for political power between old and new orders.

48. The importance of the trade treaty with France is especially emphasized by Helmut Boehme, *Deutschlands Weg zur Grossmacht*, Cologne/Berlin 1966, pp. 100–20, 165–6 – a pioneering, if unduly economist, work.

49. Hamerow, *The Social Foundations of German Unification*, pp. 301–2.

Nevertheless, the economic bases of a rapprochement between the two classes were being laid by the steady capitalization of Eastern agriculture during the corn boom, and the vertical increase in the weight of heavy industry within the Prussian social formation as a whole. By 1865, Prussia contained nine-tenths of coal and iron production, two-thirds of steam-engines, half of textile output and two-thirds of industrial labour in Germany.[50] The mechanization of German industry had already overtaken that of France. The former extreme reactionary Bismarck, once the truculent champion of ultra-legitimism, was the first political representative of the nobility to see that this burgeoning force could be accommodated in the structure of the State, and that under the aegis of the two possessing classes of the Hohenzollern realm – Prussian junkerdom and Rhenish capital – the unification of Germany was possible. The triumph of the Prussian Army over Austria in 1866 suddenly quieted the discord between the two. Bismarck's bargain with the National Liberals, which produced the North German Constitution of 1867, sealed a momentous social pact, virtually against the political grain of both the parties to it. Three years later, the Franco-Prussian War completed with éclat the work of national unity. The Prussian Kingdom was merged into a German Empire. The fundamental structure of the new State was unmistakably *capitalist*. The Constitution of Imperial Germany in the 1870's included a representative assembly elected by universal male suffrage; a secret ballot; civic equality; a uniform legal code; a single monetary system; secular education; and complete internal free trade. The German State thus created was by no means a 'pure' example of its type (none such existed in the world at the time).[51] It was heavily marked by the feudal nature of the Prussian State which preceded it. Indeed, in a literal and visible way, the *combined* development which defined the conjuncture, was embodied in the architecture of the new State. For the Prussian Constitution was not abrogated; it survived inside the Imperial Constitution, since Prussia was now one of the federal units of the Empire,

50. Pierre Ayçoberry, *L'Unité Allemande (1800–1871)*, Paris 1968, p. 90.
51. Taylor points out that the North German Confederal Constitution of 1867, from which the Imperial Constitution was derived, contained, indeed, the widest suffrage of any major European country, and the only one with a real secret ballot – preceding the Second Reform Act in England and the advent of the Third Republic in France: A. J. P. Taylor, *Bismarck*, London 1955, p. 98.

complete with its disenfranchising 'three-class' electoral system. The officer corps of its army, which naturally composed the overwhelming bulk of the Imperial military apparatus, was not responsible to the Chancellor, but swore fealty directly to the Emperor, who controlled it personally through his military household.[52] The senior ranks of its bureaucracy, purged and reorganized by Von Puttkamer, became if anything more of an aristocratic sanctuary than ever in the decades after 1870. Moreover, the Imperial Chancellor was not responsible to the Reichstag, and could rely on permanent revenues from customs and excise beyond parliamentary control; although budgets had to be approved and laws passed by the Reichstag. Certain lesser fiscal and administrative rights were left in the control of the various federal units of the Empire, formally limiting the unitarianism of the Constitution.

These anomalies lent the German State in the late 19th century a disconcerting cast. Marx's own characterization of the Bismarckian State reveal a mixture of vexation and bafflement. In a celebrated, enraged phrase that Luxemburg was fond of quoting, he described it as *nichts anderes als ein mit parliamentärischen Formen verbrämter, mit feudalem Beisatz vermischter, schon von der Bourgeoisie beeinflusster, bürokratisch gezimmerter, polizeilich gehüteter Militärdespotismus* – 'nothing but a military despotism, embellished with parliamentary forms, alloyed with a feudal admixture, already influenced by the bourgeoisie, furnished by the bureaucracy and protected by the police'.[53] The agglutination of epithets indicates his conceptual difficulty, without providing a solution to it. Engels saw much more clearly than Marx that the German State, despite its peculiarities, had now joined the ranks of its English and French rivals. He wrote of the Austro-Prussian War and its author: 'Bismarck understood the German civil war of 1866 to be what it really was, namely a *revolution* . . . and he was prepared to carry it through by revolutionary means.'[54] The historical result of the conflict with Austria was that 'the very victories of the Prussian army shifted the entire basis of the Prussian

52. For a good account of the Imperial German Constitution, see K. Pinson, *Modern Germany. Its History and Civilization*, New York 1966, pp. 156–63.
53. The formula is from the *Critique of the Gotha Programme*: Marx-Engels, *Werke*, Bd 19, p. 29.
54. F. Engels, *The Role of Force in History*, London 1968, pp. 64–5.

State structure', so that 'the social foundations of the old State underwent a complete transformation'.[55] Comparing Bismarckism with Bonapartism, he stated roundly that the Constitution created by the Prussian Chancellor was 'a modern form of state which presupposes the abolition of feudalism'.[56] In other words, the German State was now a capitalist apparatus, over-determined by its feudal ancestry, but fundamentally homologous with a social formation which by the early 20th century was massively dominated by the capitalist mode of production: Imperial Germany was soon the largest industrial power in Europe. Prussian Absolutism had thus after many vicissitudes been transmuted into *another* type of State. Geographically and socially, socially because geographically, it had slowly been tugged over from East to West. The theoretical *conditions of possibility* of this 'transmutation' remain to be established: they will be considered elsewhere.

55. Marx-Engels, *Selected Works*, pp. 246–7.
56. Ibid., p. 247.

4

Poland

The rise of Prussia from the mid-17th century onwards was counter-pointed by the decline of Poland in the East. The one major country which failed to produce an Absolutist State in the region eventually disappeared, in a graphic *a contrario* demonstration of the historical rationality of Absolutism for a noble class. The reasons why the Polish *szlachta* were never able to generate a centralized feudal State do not seem to have been adequately studied; the debacle of this class poses a problem that has not yet been genuinely resolved by modern his-toriography.[1] At most certain critical elements emerge from the exist-ing materials, which suggest partial or possible answers.

Poland suffered less from the late feudal crisis than any other country in Eastern Europe; the Black Death (if not ancillary plagues) largely passed it by, while its neighbours were ravaged. The Piast monarchy, reconstituted in the 14th century, achieved its political and cultural apogee under Casimir III, after 1333. With the decease of this ruler in 1370, the dynasty died out, and the royal title passed to Louis of Anjou, King of Hungary. An absentee monarch, Louis was obliged to grant the Polish nobility the 'Privilege of Košice' in 1374, in exchange for confirmation of the right of his daughter Jadwiga to succeed him in Poland: the aristocracy was guaranteed economic immunity from new taxation and administrative autonomy in its localities, in a charter inspired by earlier Hungarian models.[2] Twelve

1. This emerges unmistakably from a representative recent survey of the causes adduced for the Partitions by Polish historians, many of which do little more than restate the problem: Boguslaw Lesnodarski, 'Les Partages de la Pologne. Analyse des Causes et Essai d'une Théorie', *Acta Poloniae Historica*, VII, 1963, pp. 7–30.
2. For this episode, see O. Halecki, 'From the Union with Hungary to the

years later, Jadwiga was married to Jagiello, Grand Duke of Lithuania, who became King of Poland, founding a personal union between the two realms. This conjunction was to have deep and permanent effects on the whole subsequent course of Polish history. The Lithuanian Duchy was one of the most recent and remarkable structures of the age. A Baltic tribal society, so remote in its marshes and woods that it was still pagan in the late 14th century, had suddenly thrown up a conquering State that became one of the largest territorial empires in Europe. The western pressure from the German military orders in Prussia and Livonia had set off the precipitate formation of a centralized principality among the tribal confederations of Lithuania; the eastern vacuum created by the Mongol subjugation of post-Kievan Russia permitted its rapid expansion outwards in the direction of the Ukraine. Under its successive rulers Gedymin, Olgerd, Jagiello and Witold, Lithuanian power reached to the Oka and the Black Sea. The population of these vast regions was mostly Slav and Christian – Belorussian or Ruthenian; Lithuanian domination of them was exercised by a military overlordship that reduced local lords to vassal status. This powerful but primitive State was now linked to the smaller, but much older and more advanced realm of Poland. Jagiello accepted Christianity and moved to Poland to secure the Union of 1386, while his cousin Witold was left in the east to govern Lithuania; with the accession of a foreign prince, the Polish *szlachta* succeeded in establishing the principle that the monarchy was elective, although in practice it was to be continuously vested in the Jagellonian dynasty for the next two hundred years.

The accrued strength and dynamism of the new Polish-Lithuanian Union was soon demonstrated. In 1410, Jagiello inflicted the historic defeat of Grünewald on the Teutonic Knights, which proved to be the turning-point in the fortunes of the Order in Prussia. At mid-century, Polish attack on Prussia was renewed, when the local German Estates revolted against the rule of the Order. The Thirteen Years' War ended in 1466 with a decisive Jagellonian victory. By the Second Peace of Torun, Poland annexed West Prussia and Ermland: East Prussia became a Polish fief, held as a vassal by the Grand Master of the

Union with Lithuania', W. F. Reddaway *et al.* (ed.), *The Cambridge History of Poland*, I, Cambridge 1950, pp. 19–193.

Teutonic Order, who henceforward owed homage and service in war to the Polish monarchy. The power of the Order was definitively broken, and Poland acquired territorial access to the Baltic. Danzig, the major port of the whole region, became an autonomous city with special municipal rights under Polish royal sovereignty. Casimir IV, the victor of the war, ruled over the most extensive realm in the continent.

Meanwhile, within Poland itself, the later 15th century saw a steady rise in the political and social position of the gentry at the expense both of the monarchy and the peasantry. To secure the succession of his son, Jagiello granted to the nobility in 1425 the principle of *neminem captivabimus* – legal immunity from arbitrary arrest – in the 'Privilege of Brześć'. Casimir IV, in his turn, was led to make further concessions to the landowning class. The long struggle of the Thirteen Years' War necessitated hire of mercenary troops from all over Europe. To obtain the funds needed to pay them, the king granted the aristocracy the 'Privilege of Nieszawa' in 1454, which provided for regular *conventiones particulares* to be held by the gentry in their localities; neither troops nor taxes could henceforward be raised without their consent.[3] Under his son John Albert, a consolidated national Assembly or Sejm came into being in 1492, relayed by the provincial and local assemblies (*sejmiki*) of the landowning class. The Sejm formed a bi-cameral assembly, composed of a Chamber of Deputies and a Senate; the former was composed of elected representatives of the *sejmiki*, the latter of high clerical and lay dignitaries of the State. Towns were excluded from both: the Polish Estates system which now emerged was exclusively aristocratic.[4] In 1505, the Constitution of Radom formally solemnized the powers of the Sejm: the law of *nihil novi* deprived the monarchy of the right to legislate without the consent of the Estates, while the authority of royal officials was carefully restricted.[5] The convocation of the Sejm was still, however, at the discretion of the monarchy.

Meanwhile, it was in this period too that the legal enserfment of the Polish peasantry was decreed. The Statutes of Piotrkow in 1496 banned

3. See A. Gieysztor, in S. Kieniewicz (ed.), *History of Poland*, Warsaw 1968, pp. 145–6.

4. Burghers from Cracow and (later) Wilno were admitted to the proceedings of the Sejm but had no vote.

5. J. Tazbir, in Kieniewicz (ed.), *History of Poland*, p. 176.

all labour movement from villages, with the exception of a single peasant from each community a year. They were followed by further measures of adscription in 1501, 1503, 1510 and 1511: signs of the difficulties of implementation. Finally in 1520, an ordinance governing feudal dues was passed which imposed labour services of up to 6 days a week on the Polish *wloka* or villein.[6] The serfdom of the peasantry, which became increasingly rigorous in the course of the 16th century, founded the new prosperity of the *szlachta*. For the Polish nobility benefited from the Baltic grain boom of the epoch more than any other social group in the region. Peasant plots were steadily whittled down, while demesne farming expanded to meet the demand of the export market. In the second half of the century, the volume of cereals shipped out of the country doubled. During the zenith of the corn traffic from 1550 to 1620, Western inflation assured the landowning class of vast windfall profits from the terms of trade. Over the longer run, it has been calculated that between 1600 and 1750 the value of the magnates' commercialized production tripled, that of the gentry doubled, while that of the peasantry declined.[7] These gains were not, however, productively reinvested. Poland became the granary of Europe, but techniques of arable farming remained primitive, with low yield ratios. Increased agrarian output was achieved by extensive expansion, especially in the frontier lands of the south-east, rather than by intensive improvements of cultivation. Moreover, the Polish aristocracy used its economic power for a more systematically anti-urban policy than any other ruling class in Europe. In the early 16th century, price-ceilings were statutorily imposed on native manufactures in the towns, whose merchant communities were mostly German, Jewish or Armenian. In 1565, foreign merchants were granted exorbitant privileges, whose objective effect was inevitably to weaken and ruin local traders.[8] The commercial prosperity of the epoch was still accompanied by urban growth, and wealthy lords founded private

6. R. F. Leslie, *The Polish Question*, London 1964, p. 4.

7. Witold Kula, 'Un' Economia Agraria senza Accumulazione: La Polonia dei Seicoli XVI–XVIII', *Studi Storici*, No. 3–4, 1968, pp. 615–16. Income variations were much less, of course, because of the subsistence character of most peasant production (reckoned by Kula at some 90 per cent).

8. Tazbir minimizes the immediate practical results of this measure, but its intention is clear enough: Tazbir, *History of Poland*, p. 178.

towns subject to them, while other nobles were converting iron-works into corn-mills in the countryside. But the municipal autonomy of the urban patriciates was virtually everywhere suppressed, and with it the chances of a developing industry. The Germanic port of Danzig alone escaped the elimination of mediaeval urban privileges by the *szlachta*: the monopolistic export control which it consequently enjoyed further stifled the inland towns. An agrarian monoculture was thus increasingly created, which imported its manufactured goods from the West in an aristocratic prefiguration of the overseas economies of the 19th century.

The noble class which emerged on these economic foundations had no exact parallel anywhere else in Europe The degree of predial pressure it exercised on the peasantry – with labour services legally permitted of up to 6 days a week – was extreme enough; in 1574 it acquired a formal *jus vitae et necis* over its serfs, which technically allowed it to execute them at will.[9] The aristocracy which controlled these powers was notably unlike its neighbours in composition. For the web of clan kinship, sure sign of a pre-feudal social structure, had survived in the relatively backward and amorphous society of early mediaeval Poland much later than anywhere else, to affect the whole contours of the feudal nobility, as it eventually emerged in a period without any articulated vassal hierarchy.[10] For when heraldic insignia were imported from the West in the Middle Ages, they were adopted, not by individual families, but by whole clans, whose kin and client networks still subsisted in the countryside. The result was to create a relatively numerous noble class, comprising perhaps some 700,000 persons or 7–8 per cent of the population in the 16th century. Within

9. Leslie, *The Polish Question*, pp. 4–5.
10. These clans were not direct descendants of tribal units of organization, but more recent formations modelled on them. For the whole problem of clan heraldry in Poland, see K. Gorski, 'Les Structures Sociales de la Noblesse Polonaise au Moyen Age', *Le Moyen Age*, 1967, pp. 73–85. Etymologically, the world *szlachta* probably derives from the Old High German *slahta* (Modern German *Geschlecht*), meaning family or race, although its origin is not absolutely certain. It may be noted that the Hungarian nobility was not dissimilar to the Polish in size and character, again because of the presence of pre-feudal clan principles in its initial formation: but the two cases should not be confused, since the Magyars were, of course, a nomadic people until the late 10th century, and hence had a very different anterior history and social structure from the Western Slavs.

this class, there were no titles of rank distinguishing one grade of lordship from another.[11] But this juridical equality within the nobility – which had no equivalent elsewhere in early modern Europe – was accompanied by an economic inequality which also had no parallel elsewhere at the time. For a great mass of the *szlachta* – perhaps more than half their number – owned tiny holdings of 10 to 20 acres, often no larger than those of an average peasant. This stratum was concentrated in the old provinces of Western and Central Poland: in Mazovia, for example, it made up perhaps a fifth of the total population.[12] Another large section of the gentry were petty squires with small estates, owning no more than a village or two. Yet side by side within nominally the same nobility, existed some of the largest territorial magnates in Europe, with colossal latifundia, mainly situated in the Lithuanian or Ukrainian East of the country. For in these newer lands, the bequest of the Lithuanian expansion of the 14th century, no comparable heraldic diffusion had occurred, and the higher aristocracy always retained much of the character of a small potentate caste superimposed over an ethnically alien peasantry. In the course of the 16th century, the Lithuanian nobility became increasingly assimilated in culture and institutions to its Polish counterpart, as the local gentry gradually gained rights comparable to the *szlachta*.[13] The constitutional result of this convergence was the Union of Lublin in 1569, which finally merged the two realms into a single polity, the *Rzeczpospolita Polska*, with a common currency and parliament. On the other hand, no such fusion occurred among the mass of the population in the Eastern provinces, most of whom remained Orthodox in religion and Belorussian or Ruthenian in language. Less than half of the inhabitants of the combined Polish Commonwealth were thus ethnically and

11. For a sociological sketch, see Andrzej Zajaczkowski, 'Cadres Structurels de la Noblesse', *Annales ESC*, January–February 1968, pp. 88–102. Lithuanian magnates claiming descent from Gedymin or Rurik used the honorific title 'Prince', but this pretension had no legal force.

12. P. Skwarczyński, 'Poland and Lithuania', *The New Cambridge Modern History of Europe*, III, p. 400.

13. For this process, see Vernadsky, *Russia at the Dawn of the Modern Age*, pp. 196–200. Vernadsky's book includes one of the fullest accounts of the Lithuanian State available, under the rubric of 'West Russia'. For the background and provisions of the Union of Lublin, partly determined by military pressure on Lithuania by Muscovy, see pp. 241–8.

linguistically Polish. The 'colonial' character of the landlord class in the east and south-east was reflected in the magnitude of its domains. In the late 16th century, the Chancellor John Zamoyski was master of some 2,000,000 acres, mainly in Little Poland, and exercised jurisdiction over some 80 towns and 800 villages.[14] In the early 17th century, the Wisnowiecki empire in the Eastern Ukraine extended over lands with 230,000 subjects on them.[15] In the 18th century, the Potocki family in the Ukraine owned some 3,000,000 acres; the Radziwill house in Lithuania possessed estates estimated at some 10,000,000 acres.[16] There was thus always an extreme tension between the ideology of legal parity and the reality of tremendous economic disparity within the Polish aristocracy.

During the 16th century, nevertheless, the *szlachta* as a whole probably benefited more than any other group in Eastern Europe from the price revolution. This was the epoch of Brandenburger somnolence and East Prussian decline; Russia was expanding, but amidst fearful convulsions and regressions. Poland was by contrast the largest and wealthiest power in the East. The bulk of the Baltic prosperity fell to it, in the most prosperous epoch of the grain trade. The cultural brilliance of the Polish Renaissance, the background of Copernicus, was one result. Politically, however, it is difficult not to suspect that the early and abundant good fortune of the *szlachta* in a sense paralysed their capacity for constructive centralization in a later age. Poland, *infernus rusticorum* for the peasantry, provided an *aurea libertas* for the nobility: no compelling need was felt for a strong State in this squire's elysium. The comparatively trouble-free passage of Poland through the great economic and demographic crisis of European feudalism in the later Middle Ages, from which it emerged less scathed than any other country of the region, followed by the commercial manna of the early

14. Tazbir, *History of Poland*, p. 196: in addition to his own domains, Zamoyski controlled vast tracts of the royal demesne. The lands belonging to the monarchy in Poland were widely alienated as security on loans to magnate creditors.

15. A. Maczak, 'The Social Distribution of Landed Property in Poland from the 16th to the 18th Century', *Third International Conference of Economic History*, p. 461.

16. B. Boswell, 'Poland', in A. Goodwin (ed.), *The European Nobility in the 18th Century*, pp. 167–8.

modern epoch, thus perhaps prepared the political disintegration that was to come. Strategically, moreover, the Polish Commonwealth of the 16th century confronted no major military threat. Germany was gripped in the internecine strife of the Reformation. Sweden was still a minor power. Russia was expanding more towards the Volga and the Neva than the Dnieper; the development of the Muscovite State, although starting to look formidable, remained crude and its stability precarious. In the South, the weight of Turkish pressure was directed against the Habsburg frontiers in Hungary and Austria, while Poland was buffered by Moldavia – a weak vassal-State of the Ottoman system. Irregular Tartar raids from the Crimea, although destructive, were a localized problem in the south-east. There was thus no urgent necessity for a centralized royal State, to build up a large military machine against external enemies. The huge size of Poland, and the traditional valour of the *szlachta* as a heavy feudal cavalry, seemed to guarantee the geographical safety of the possessing class.

Thus just at a time when Absolutism was advancing elsewhere in Europe, the powers of the Polish monarchy were drastically and definitively reduced by the aristocracy. In 1572, the Jagellonian dynasty was extinguished by the death of Sigismund Augustus, leaving the succession vacant. An international auction for the royal dignity followed. In 1573, 40,000 gentry gathered in a *viritim* assembly on the plains of Warsaw, and elected Henry of Anjou to the monarchy. A foreigner without any links to the country, the French prince was induced to sign the famous Henrician Articles which henceforward became the constitutional charter of the Polish Commonwealth; while a separate device or *Pacta Conventa* between the monarch and the nobility set the precedent for personal contracts, with specific and binding obligations, to be signed by Polish kings at their accession. By the terms of the Henrician Articles, the non-hereditary character of the monarchy was expressly reconfirmed. The monarch himself was deprived of virtually any substantive powers in the government of the realm. He could not dismiss the civil or military officials in his administration, or enlarge the minuscule army – 3,000 men – at his disposal. The consent of the Sejm, henceforth to be convened every two years, was necessary for any political or fiscal decision of importance. Contravention of these restrictions legalized rebellion against the monarch.[17] In other words, Poland became in all but name a nobiliary republic, with a royal figure-head. No native Polish dynasty was ever to preside over the kingdom again: French, Hungarian, Swedish and Saxon rulers were deliberately preferred by the landowning class to ensure the weakness of the central State. The Jagellonian line had enjoyed a large hereditary demesne in its Lithuanian lands: the expatriate kings who now succeeded each other in Poland had no such economic base within the country to sustain them. Both the revenue and troops at the command of the largest magnates were henceforward often to be as large as those of the sovereign himself. Although successful soldier-princes – Bathory, Sobieski — were on occasion to be elected, the monarchy never recovered permanent or substantial powers again. Beneath the dynastic vicissitudes and ethnic heterogeneity of the Polish-Lithuanian Union, there was perhaps also a longer political tradition behind this anomalous outcome. Poland had shared neither in the imperial heritage of the Byzantine nor of the Carolingian realms; its nobility had not experienced an original integration into a royal polity comparable to those of either Kievan Russia or Mediaeval Germany. The clan genealogy of the *szlachta* had been a token of their distance from them. Its Renaissance thus saw not the autocratic cult of a Tudor or Valois or Habsburg monarchy, but the flowering of an aristocratic commonwealth.

The closing phase of the 16th century gave little hint of the crises ahead. The Pacta Conventa of 1573 were succeeded three years later, after the departure of Henry for France, by the election of the Transylvanian prince Stephen Bathory as King of Poland. Bathory, an able and experienced Magyar general, controlled a personal treasury and army from his nearby Principality, whose relatively prosperous and urbanized economy provided him with independent resources and professional troops. His political authority in Poland was thus powerfully buttressed by his territorial base across the Tatras. A Catholic ruler himself, he promoted the Counter-Reformation in Poland with discretion, avoiding religious provocations to those sections of the

17. For the Henrician Articles and the Pacta Conventa, see F. Nowak, 'The Interregna and Stephen Batory', *The Cambridge History of Poland*, I, pp. 372–3. The best general account of the Polish constitutional system as it emerged in this epoch is provided by Skwarczyński, 'The Constitution of Poland Before the Partitions', *The Cambridge History of Poland*, II, pp. 49–67.

nobility which had become Protestant. His reign was illustrated, above all, by military victory in the Baltic Wars against Russia. Taking the field against Ivan IV in 1578, with a mixed army of Polish cavalry, Transylvanian infantry, and Ukrainian Cossacks, Bathory conquered Livonia and swept Russian forces back beyond Polotsk. At his death in 1586, Poland's primacy in Eastern Europe had never seemed greater. The *szlachta*'s next choice for the monarchy was Swedish: Sigismund Vasa. In the course of his reign, Polish expansionism appeared to reach its height. Exploiting the political and social upheavals in Russia during the Time of Troubles, Poland sponsored the brief rule of the False Dimitri in 1605–6, a usurper guarded in his capital by Polish troops. Then in 1610, Polish forces under the Hetman Zolkiewski seized Moscow again and installed Sigismund's son Władysław as Tsar. Russian popular reaction and Swedish counter-manoeuvres compelled the Polish garrison to evacuate Moscow in 1612, and the Tsardom was secured by the Romanov dynasty the following year. But Polish intervention in the Time of Troubles nevertheless ended with major territorial gains at the Truce of Deulino in 1618, by which Poland annexed a large belt of White Russia. The *Rzeczpospolita* attained its widest frontiers in these years.

Nevertheless, two fatal geo-political flaws marred this Polish State even while the prowess of the gentry *husarja* was unmatched in cavalry warfare. They were both symptoms of the monadic individualism of the Polish ruling class. On the one hand, Poland had failed to finish off German rule in East Prussia. The Jagellonian victories over the Teutonic Order in the 15th century had reduced the German knights to vassals of the Polish monarchy. In the early 16th century, the secularization of the Order by its Grand Master was accepted, in exchange for the maintenance of Polish overlordship over what now became Ducal Prussia. In 1563, Sigismund August – the last Jagellonian ruler – had then accepted coinfeudation of the Duchy by the Margravate of Brandenburg, for transient diplomatic advantages. Fifteen years later, Bathory sold the guardianship of the East Prussian Duke to the Brandenburg Elector, for cash to wage the war with Russia. Finally, in 1618, the Polish monarchy permitted the dynastic unification of East Prussia with Brandenburg, under a common Hohenzollern ruler. Thus, in a series of juridical concessions which was eventually to end with a full renunciation of Polish suzerainty, the Duchy was delivered over to the Hohenzollerns. The strategic folly of this course was soon to become clear. By failing to secure and integrate East Prussia, Poland lost the chance of controlling the Baltic littoral and never became a maritime power. Lack of a fleet was thus to render it readily vulnerable to amphibious invasions from the North. The reasons for this inertia are doubtless to be found in the character of the nobility. Mastery of the coast and construction of a navy both demanded a powerful State machine, capable of evicting the Junkers from East Prussia and mobilizing the public investment necessary for forts, shipyards and port establishments. The Petrine State in Russia could do this as soon as it reached the Baltic. The Polish *szlachta* were not interested. They were content to rely on the traditional arrangement of corn transport through Danzig in Dutch or German cargoes. Royal control over the commercial policies of Danzig was relinquished in the 1570's; the few harbours built for a small navy were abandoned in the 1640's.[18] The gentry were indifferent to the fate of the Baltic. Their expansion was to take quite another form – a drive into the south-east frontier regions of the Ukraine. Here private penetration and colonization was possible and profitable; there was no state system to resist this advance; and no economic innovations were needed to create new latifundia from the exceptionally fertile lands on either side of the Dnieper. In the early 17th century, Polish landlordism thus sprawled ever deeper beyond Volhynia and Podolia, into the Eastern Ukraine. The enserfment of the local Ruthenian peasantry, exacerbated by religious conflicts between Catholic and Orthodox Churches, and complicated by the turbulent presence of the Cossack settlements, made this wild zone a constant security problem. Economically the most profitable projection of the Commonwealth, it was socially and politically the most explosive region within the nobiliary State. The reorientation of the *szlachta* away from the Baltic towards the Black Sea was thus to prove doubly disastrous for Poland. Its ultimate consequences were to be the Ukrainian Revolution and the Swedish Deluge.

In the first years of the 17th century, disquieting signs of incipient

18. H. Jablonowski, 'Poland-Lithuania 1609–1648', *The New Cambridge Modern History of Europe*, IV, Cambridge 1970, pp. 600–1.

crisis were already becoming visible within Poland. By the turn of the century, the limits of the traditional agrarian economy in the central zone, which had provided the productive basis of Polish power abroad, were starting to be felt. The growth of manorialism had not been accompanied by any real improvements in productivity: the arable acreage had increased while techniques remained largely stationary. Moreover, the penalties for the inordinate extension of demesne cultivation at the expense of peasant tenures now became evident. There were symptoms of rural exhaustion even before corn prices started to drop with the European depression that set in slowly from the 1620's onwards. Production started to fall off, and more seriously, yields to decline.[19] At the same time, the political cohesion of the State was critically weakened by new derogations from the central authority tenuously maintained by the monarchy. In 1607–9, a serious gentry revolt against Sigismund III – the Zebrzydowski rebellion – forced the king to abandon plans for a reformed royal power. From 1613 onwards, the national Sejm devolved tax-assessments downwards to the local *sejmiki*, making any effective fiscal system still more difficult to achieve. In the 1640's, the *sejmiki* gained further financial and military autonomy in their localities. Meanwhile, the contemporary revolution in military techniques was passing the *szlachta* by: its skill as a cavalry class was increasingly anachronistic in battles decided by trained infantry and mobile artillery. The central army of the Commonwealth was still only some 4,000 at mid-century, and was subtracted from royal control by the independent command of life-long hetmans over it; while border magnates often kept private armies of virtually equivalent size.[20] In the 1620's, the rapid Swedish conquest of Livonia, mastery of the East Prussian littoral and extortion of heavy Baltic tolls, had already revealed the vulnerability of Polish defences in the North; while in the South, repeated Cossack risings in the 1630's had been pacified with difficulty. The stage was now set for the spectacular breakdown of the country in the reign of the last Vasa king, John Casimir.

In 1648, the Ukrainian Cossacks revolted under Khmelnitsky, and a

19. Jerzy Topolski, 'La Régression Economique en Pologne du XVIe au XVIIIe Siècle', *Acta Poloniae Historica*, VII, 1962, pp. 28–49.

20. Tazbir, *History of Poland*, p. 224. In theory, of course, a general levy of the gentry was supposed to provide the main force for foreign wars.

peasant *jacquerie* against the Polish landlord class spread in their wake. In 1654, the Cossack leaders took vast portions of the South-East with them into the enemy Russian State, with the Treaty of Pereyaslavl; Russian armies marched westwards, capturing Minsk and Wilno. In 1655, Sweden launched a devastating pincer attack through Pomerania and Courland; Brandenburg allied with it for a joint invasion. Warsaw and Cracow rapidly fell to Swedish and Prussian troops, while the Lithuanian magnates hastened to defect to Charles X, and John Casimir fled to an Austrian refuge. The Swedish occupation of Poland aroused the *szlachta* to fierce local resistance. International intervention to block the enlargement of the Swedish Empire followed: Dutch fleets covered Danzig, Austrian diplomacy aided the fugitive king, Russian troops assailed Livonia and Ingria, and finally Denmark struck at Sweden in the rear. The result was to clear Poland of Swedish armies by 1660, after immense destruction. War with Russia lasted another seven years. By the time the Commonwealth was at peace again in 1667, after nearly two decades of fighting, it had lost the Eastern Ukraine with Kiev, the long border lands centred on Smolensk, and all residual claims over East Prussia; in the next decade, Turkey seized Podolia. Geographical losses amounted to a fifth of Polish territory. But the economic, social and political effects of these disastrous years were much graver. The Swedish armies which had swept the country had left it ravaged and depopulated from end to end: the rich Vistula valley was worst hit of all. The population of Poland dropped by a third between 1650 and 1675, while grain exports through Danzig fell by over 80 per cent between 1618 and 1691.[21] Cereal output collapsed in many regions because of the devastation and demographic decline; yields never recovered. There was a contraction of cultivated area, and many *szlachta* were ruined. The economic crisis after the war accelerated the concentration of land, in conditions where the great magnates alone had the resources to reorganize production and many smaller estates were up for sale.

21. Henry Willetts, 'Poland and the Evolution of Russia', in Trevor-Roper (ed.), *The Age of Expansion*, p. 265. For a close-up of the ravages of the Deluge in one region, Mazovia, see I. Gieysztorowa, 'Guerre et Régression en Mazovie aux XVIe et XVIIe Siècles', *Annales ESC*, October–November 1958, pp. 651–68, which also shows the economic decline that had set in there before the war, from the early 17th century onwards. The population of Mazovia decreased from 638,000 to 305,000 between 1578 and 1661, or some 52 per cent.

Servile exactions intensified amidst a new stagnation. Debasement of currency and depression of wages withered the towns.

Culturally, the *szlachta* took its revenge on the history which had disappointed it by a morbid mythomania: an astonishing cult of imaginary 'Sarmatian' ancestors in the pre-feudal past was combined with provincial Counter-Reformation bigotry, in a country where urban civilization now largely ebbed away. The pseudo-atavistic ideology of Sarmatianism was not a mere aberration: it reflected the state of the whole class, which found its most vivid expression in the constitutional realm proper. For politically, the combined impact of the Ukrainian Revolution and the Swedish Deluge shattered the brittle unity of the Polish Commonwealth. The great divide in the history and prosperity of the noble class did not rally it to the creation of a central state that could have withstood further external attacks: it plunged, on the contrary, into a suicidal *fuite en avant*. From the mid-17th century onwards, the anarchic logic of the Polish polity achieved a kind of institutional paroxysm with the rule of parliamentary unanimity – the famous *liberum veto*.[22] A single negative vote could henceforward dissolve the Sejm and paralyse the State. The *liberum veto* was first exercised by a deputy to the Sejm in 1652: its use increased rapidly thereafter, and was extended downwards to the provincial *sejmiki*, of which there were now more than seventy. The landowning class, which had long rendered the executive virtually impotent, thus now neutralized the legislature as well. The eclipse of royal authority was henceforward complemented by the disintegration of representative government. In practice, chaos was only avoided by the enhanced dominance within the nobility of the great Eastern magnates, whose vast latifundia tilled by Ruthenian and White Russian serfs gave them preponderance over the smaller squires of Western and Central Poland. A clientage system thus gave some organized framework to the *szlachta* class, although rivalries between the magnate families – Czartoryski, Sapieha, Potocki, Radziwill and so on – constantly rent the unity of the nobility: for at the same time it was they who used the *liberum veto*

22. The classic study of this singular device is L. Konopczynski, *Le Liberum Veto*, Paris 1930. Konopczynski was able to find only one parallel to it elsewhere: the formal right of *dissentimiento* in Aragon. But the Aragonese veto was comparatively innocuous in practice.

most frequently.[23] The constitutional obverse of the 'veto' was the 'confederation': a juridical device which permitted aristocratic factions to proclaim themselves in a state of armed insurrection against the government.[24] Ironically, majority voting and military discipline were legally prescribed for rebel confederations, while the unitary Sejm was constantly immobilized by political intrigue and unanimous voting. The successful noble rising led by the Grand Marshal Lubomirski, which prevented any election *vivente rege* of a successor to John Casimir in 1665–6, and precipitated the abdication of the king, presaged the future pattern of magnate politics. In the age of Louis XIV and Peter I, a radical and total negation of Absolutism was born on the Vistula.

Poland still remained the second largest country in Europe. In the last decades of the 17th century, the soldier-king John Sobieski restored something of its external position. Brought to power by the danger of renewed Turkish attacks in Podolia, Sobieski managed to increase the central army to 12,000, and modernized it by the addition of dragoon and infantry units. Polish forces played the premier role in the relief of Vienna in 1683, and Ottoman advances in the Dniester region were checked. But the major benefits of this last successful mobilization of the *szlachta* were reaped by the Habsburg Emperor; Polish aid against Turkey merely allowed Austrian Absolutism to expand rapidly towards the Balkans. At home, Sobieski's international reputation availed him little. All his projects for a hereditary monarchy were blocked; the *liberum veto* became ever more frequent in the Sejm. In Lithuania, where the Sapieha clan wielded vast powers, the royal writ virtually ceased altogether. In 1696, the gentry rejected his son as a successor: a disputed election ended with the installation of another expatriate prince, Augustus II of Saxony, backed by Russia. The new Wettin ruler tried to use Saxon industrial and military resources to

23. Deputy Sicinski, who inaugurated the use of the veto in 1652, was the catspaw of Boguslaw Radziwill. For a statistical analysis of the exercise of the *liberum veto* over the next hundred years which shows its pronounced regional pattern – 80 per cent of deputies exercising it originated from Lithuania or Little Poland, see Konopczynski, *Le Liberum Veto*, pp. 217–18. The Potocki family held the record for magnate use of the veto.

24. For the device of the 'confederation', see Skwarczyński, 'The Constitution of Poland before the Partitions', p. 60.

establish a more conventional royal State, with a more cogent economic programme. A Saxo-Polish trading company was planned for the Baltic, and port construction renewed, while Wettin troops brought Lithuania to heel.[25] The *szlachta* soon reacted: in 1699 *pacta conventa* were imposed on Augustus II stipulating the withdrawal of his German army from the country. In collusion with Peter I, he then moved it north across the border for an attack on Swedish Livonia. This action precipitated the Great Northern War in 1700. The Sejm strenuously disavowed the private schemes of the king, but Swedish counter-attack against Saxon forces in 1701–2 soon plunged the country into the vortex of the war. Charles XII, after much destructive fighting, overran Poland, declared Augustus II deposed, and installed a native pretender, Stanislas Leszczynski. Confronted with occupation, the nobility split: the great Eastern magnates (as in 1655) opted for Sweden, while the mass of the smaller Western squires reluctantly rallied to the Saxo-Russian alliance. Charles XII's defeat at Poltava restored Augustus II to Poland. But when in 1713–14 the Saxon king tried to reintroduce his army and to augment royal power, an insurgent Confederation was promptly formed, and Russian military intervention imposed the Treaty of Warsaw on Augustus II in 1717. At the dictation of a Russian envoy, the Polish army was fixed at 24,000, Saxon troops were limited to 1,200 personal guards for the king, and German officials in the administration were repatriated.[26]

The Great Northern War had proved to be a second Deluge. The harshness of Swedish occupation and the desolation left by successive campaigns of Scandinavian, German and Russian armies over Polish soil took a massive toll. The population of Poland, damaged by war and plague, dropped to some 6,000,000. The economic exactions of the three powers which disputed strategic control of the country – some 60 million thalers in all – amounted to three times the total public

25. For a recent revaluation of early Saxon plans in Poland, see J. Gierowski and A. Kaminski, 'The Eclipse of Poland', *The New Cambridge Modern History of Europe*, VI, pp. 687–8.

26. Actually, although 24,000 troops were permitted by the Treaty of Warsaw, only some 12,000 were subsequently raised; since the pre-war size of the central army had been 18,000, the result was another reduction of Polish military strength: E. Rostworowski, *History of Poland*, pp. 281–2, 289.

revenues of the Commonwealth during the conflict.[27] More gravely still, Poland was for the first time a prostrate object of the international struggle fought across it. The political passivity of the *szlachta* in the triangular contest between Charles XII, Peter I and Augustus II was broken only by its sullen resistance to any move that might strengthen royal power in Poland, and with it Polish defence capacity. Augustus II, whose base in Saxony was wealthier and more advanced than Transylvania had been, was unable to repeat the experience of Bathory, over a century later. To frustrate any fruition from the Saxo-Polish Union, the gentry were prepared to accept a Russian protectorate. The invitation to St Petersburg to invade in 1717 inaugurated an epoch of increasing submission to Tsarist manoeuvres in Eastern Europe.

In 1733, the election to the monarchy was again disputed. France tried to secure the candidature of Leszczynski, as a native Pole and ally of Paris. Russia, backed by Prussia and Austria, opted for a Saxon succession as the weaker alternative: despite Leszczynski's legitimate election, Augustus III was duly imposed by foreign bayonets. The new ruler, unlike his father an absentee monarch who resided in Dresden, made no attempt to recast the political system in Poland. Warsaw ceased to be a capital, as the country became one vast provincial backwater, occasionally traversed by neighbouring armies. Saxon ministers distributed sinecures in State and Church, while magnate factions lowered vetos on the Sejm at the behest or hire of competing foreign powers – Russia, Austria, Prussia, France.[28] The *szlachta*, which during the height of the Reformation and Counter-Reformation had maintained standards of religious tolerance rare in Europe, was now in the epoch of the Enlightenment gripped with a forgotten Catholic fanaticism: the persecutory fevers of the gentry became the ruined symptom of its 'patriotism'. Economically, there was a gradual recovery in the later 18th century. Population rose once again to pre-Deluge levels, while cereal exports through Danzig doubled in the forty years after the Great Northern War, although still

27. Gierowski and Kaminski, 'The Eclipse of Poland', pp. 704–5. In 1650, the population of Poland had been some 10,000,000.

28. After the initial imposition of Augustus III, every session of the Sejm, of which there were thirteen during the reign, was broken up by use of the *liberum veto*.

remaining far below peak levels of the previous century. Concentration of lands and serfs continued, to the benefit of the magnates.[29]

In 1764, Poniatowski – a Polish paramour of Catherine II, linked to the Czartoryski clique – became the new Russian-picked monarch. Initial permission from St Petersburg to proceed to centralist reforms was soon revoked, on the pretext of the suppression (advocated by the Czartoryskis) of rights for Orthodox and Protestant subjects in Poland. Russian troops intervened in 1767, finally provoking a gentry reaction against foreign dominance, under the flag not of political reform but religious intolerance. The Confederation of Bar in 1768 revolted against both Poniatowski and Russia, in the name of Catholic exclusivism. Ukrainian peasants seized the opportunity to rise against their Polish landlords, while French and Turkish aid was sent to the Confederate levies. After four years of fighting, the Confederation was crushed by Tsarist armies. The diplomatic imbroglio of Russia with Prussia and Austria over this affair resulted in the first Partition of Poland in 1772, a scheme to reconcile the three courts. The Habsburg monarchy took Galicia; the Romanov monarchy seized much of White Russia; the Hohenzollern monarchy acquired West Prussia, and with it the prize of complete control of the South Baltic littoral. Poland lost 30 per cent of its territory and 35 per cent of its population. Physically, it was still larger than Spain. But the advertisement of its impotence was now unmistakable.

The shock of the First Partition created a belated majority within the nobility for a revision of the structure of the State. The growth of an urban bourgeoisie in Warsaw, which quadrupled in size during the reign of Poniatowski, helped to secularize the ideology of the land-owning class. In 1788–91, the unreliable consent of Prussia was won for a new constitutional settlement: the Sejm in its last hours voted the abolition of the *liberum veto* and the suppression of the right of con-federation, the establishment of a hereditary monarchy, the creation of

29. Montesquieu's comments on the country were typical enough of En-lightenment opinion at the time: 'Poland . . . has virtually none of those things which we call the movable goods of the universe, apart from the wheat of its lands. A few lords possess entire provinces; they squeeze the peasants for a greater quantity of wheat to send abroad, with which to procure themselves the objects of their luxury. If Poland did not trade with any other nation, its people would be happier.' *De L'Esprit des Lois*, Paris 1961, II, p. 23.

an army of 100,000, and the introduction of a land tax and somewhat wider franchise.[30] Russian retribution was swift and condign. In 1792, Catherine II's soldiers invaded behind a front of Lithuanian magnates, and the Second Partition was executed. Poland lost three-fifths of its remaining territory in 1793 and was reduced to a population of 4,000,000; this time Russia took the lion's share, annexing the whole of the rest of the Ukraine, while Prussia absorbed Poznania. The finale of the *Rzeczpospolita* came two years later, amidst an apocalyptic confusion and explosion of epochs and classes. In 1794, a national and liberal insurrection erupted under Kosciuszko, a veteran of the American Revolution and a citizen of the French Republic: the mass of the gentry enlisted in a cause which called for the emancipation of the serfs and rallied the plebeian masses of the capital, mingling cross-currents of Sarmatianism and Jacobinism in a desperate, distorted awakening of the nobility under the combined impact of alien Absolutism in the East and bourgeois revolution in the West. The radicalism of the Polish Insurrection of 1794 pronounced the death-sentence on the *szlachta* State. For the legitimist courts which surrounded it, a remote, reflected glare from the fires of the Seine could suddenly be seen along the Vistula. The territorial ambitions of the three neighbouring Empires now acquired the ideological urgency of a counter-revolutionary mission. After Kosciuszko had defeated a Prussian attack on Warsaw, Suvorov was dispatched with a Russian army to stamp out the uprising. The defeat of the revolt was the end of Polish independence. In 1795, the country disappeared altogether under the Third Partition.

The inner reasons why the uniquely wayward and riotous nobility that ruled Poland was unable to achieve a national Absolutism have doubtless yet to be fully explored:[31] only some elements of an

30. For the Constitution of 1791, see R. F. Leslie, *Polish Politics and the Revolution of November 1830*, London 1956, pp. 27–8.

31. Foreign political tutelage was certainly accepted more readily by the *szlachta* because of its relative lack of impingement on the economic interests of the gentry as a class. On the other hand, it is also clear that the gentry tolerated the progressive erosion of national independence for so long, partly just because it had previously failed to produce a centralized State of its own. Had there been a Polish Absolutism of any sort, partition would have deprived a critical sector of the nobility of its positions in the State machine – so important and so lucrative for aristocracies elsewhere in Europe; and there would have been a much earlier

explanation have been proposed here. But the feudal State it produced provided a singular clarification of the reasons why Absolutism was the natural and normal form of noble class power after the late Middle Ages. For in effect, once the integrated chain of mediate sovereignties which constituted the mediaeval political system was dissolved, the nobility had no natural spring of unification. The aristocracy was customarily divided into a vertical hierarchy of ranks, which were in structural contradiction with any horizontal distribution of representation, such as was later to characterize bourgeois political systems. An external principle of unity was therefore imperative to weld it together: the function of Absolutism was precisely to impose a rigorous formal order on it from without. Hence the possibility of the constant conflicts between Absolutist rulers and their aristocracies, which, as we have seen, occurred all over Europe. These tensions were inscribed in the very nature of the solidary relationship between the two, since no immanent mediation of interests was practicable within the noble class. Absolutism could only govern 'for' the aristocracy by remaining 'above' it. In Poland alone, the paradoxical size of the *szlachta* and formal absence of any titles within it, produced a self-destructive caricature of a representative system proper, within the gentry. The incompatibility of the two was bizarrely demonstrated by the *liberum veto*. For within such a system, there was no reason why any individual noble should forego his sovereignty: the provincial *sejmiki* could be dissolved by a single squire, and the Sejm by the delegate of a single *sejmik*. Informal clientage could not provide an adequate substitute principle of unity. Anarchy, impotence and annexation were the inevitable results. The nobiliary republic was finally obliterated by the neighbouring Absolutisms. It was Montesquieu who wrote the epitaph on this experience, some years before the end: 'No monarchy, no nobility; no nobility, no monarchy.'

---

and fiercer reaction to the prospect of annexation. The final change of mood and aims behind the belated attempt to create a reformed monarchy in the 18th century also needs to be better understood, for a satisfactory explanation of the record of the *szlachta*.

5

Austria

The Austrian State in a sense represented the constitutional antipode of the Polish Commonwealth. For it was more exclusively and entirely founded on the organizing principle of dynasticism than any other in Europe. The Habsburg line was to have few equals in the length of its rule: it held sway in Austria from the late 13th uninterruptedly through to the early 20th centuries. More significantly, the only political unity of the varied lands that eventually came to be the Austrian Empire was the identity of the regnant dynasty above them. The Habsburg State always remained, to a unique degree, a familial *Hausmacht* – an assortment of dynastic heritages, without a common ethnic or territorial denomination. Monarchy here achieved its most unadulterated ascendancy. Yet Austrian Absolutism, for this very reason, never succeeded in creating a coherent and integrated state structure comparable to that of its Prussian and Russian rivals. It always to some extent represented a hybrid of 'Western' and 'Eastern' forms, because of the political and territorial divisions of its constituent lands lying across the Baltic-Adriatic line, in the geometrical centre of Europe. The Austrian case thus in certain important respects cross-cuts a regional typology of European Absolutism. It is this peculiar geographical and historical position that lends a special interest to the development of the Habsburg State: 'Central Europe' appropriately produced an Absolutism formally intermediate in character, whose divergence from the strict norms of West or East both confirms and nuances their polarity. The heteroclite structures of Austrian Absolutism reflect the composite nature of the territories over which it presided, and which it was never able in any lasting fashion to compress into a single political framework. Yet at the same time, its blend of motifs did not preclude a dominant key. The Austrian Empire which emerged in the course of the 17th century proved – despite appearances – not to be readily fissile, because it contained one essential social uniformity that rendered its variant parts compatible with each other. Serf agriculture predominated, with different shades and patterns, in the Habsburg lands as a whole. The great majority of the peasant populations ruled by the dynasty – Czech, Slovak, Hungarian, German or Austrian – were tied to the soil, owing labour services to their lords and subject to seigneurial jurisdictions. The respective peasantries of these lands did not constitute an undifferentiated rural mass: the distinctions in their condition were of considerable importance. But there can be no doubt of the overall prevalence of serfdom within the Austrian Empire, in the age of the Counter-Reformation when it first took durable shape. Taxonomically, therefore, the Habsburg State must in its total configuration be classified as an Eastern Absolutism; and in practice, as will be seen, its unusual administrative traits did not conceal its ultimate descent.

The Habsburg family originated in the Upper Rhineland, and first achieved prominence in 1273, when Count Rudolph of Habsburg was elected Emperor by German princes anxious to thwart the rise of the Premyslid king of Bohemia, Ottokar II, who had annexed most of the Austrian lands in the East and was the leading contender for the imperial dignity. The Habsburg domains were clustered along the Rhine, in three separate clumps: in Sundgau to the west of the river, Breisgau to the east of it and Aargau to the south of it, beyond Basle. Rudolph I successfully mobilized an imperial coalition to attack Ottokar II, who was defeated at Marchfeld five years later: the Habsburg line therewith acquired control of the Austrian Duchies – far larger than their Rhenish territories – to which it henceforward transferred its principal seat. The strategic objectives of the dynasty were now two-fold: to keep hold of the imperial succession, with its nebulous but considerable political and ideological leverage within Germany, and to consolidate and enlarge the territorial basis of its power. The newly won Austrian duchies formed a substantial block of hereditary *Erblande*, making the Habsburgs for the first time an important force within German politics. But they remained somewhat excentric to the *Reich*: the obvious route of aggrandizement was to link up the new Austrian bastions with the old Rhenish lands of the dynasty, to form a single geographical block running across South Germany, with direct access to the centres of Imperial wealth and power. To secure his election, Rudolph I had given pledges of non-aggression in the Rhineland,[1] but all the early Habsburg rulers pressed vigorously for the expansion and unification of their domains. This first, historic drive to construct a magnified Germanic State encountered, however, a fatal obstacle in its path. In between the Rhenish and Austrian lands lay the Swiss cantons. Habsburg encroachments in this pivotal region provoked a popular resistance that again and again defeated Austrian armies, and eventually led to the creation of Switzerland as an autonomous confederation outside the Empire altogether.

The peculiarity, and interest, of the Swiss revolt is that it coalesced two social elements within the complex inventory of European feudalism not found anywhere else together in similar union: mountains and towns. This was, also, the secret of its unique success in a century where everywhere else peasant insurrections were defeated. From the very outset of the Middle Ages, as we have seen, the feudal mode of production always had a very uneven topographical spread: it never penetrated the uplands to the extent to which it conquered the plains and the marshes. Mountainous regions all over Western Europe represented remote fastnesses of small peasant property, allodial or communal, whose rocky and exiguous soil offered relatively little attraction for manorialism. The Swiss Alps, the highest range in the continent, were naturally a foremost example of this pattern. They also, however, lay across one of the main overland commercial routes of mediaeval Europe, between the two densely urbanized zones of Southern Germany and Northern Italy. Their valleys were thus also settled with local trading towns, taking advantage of a strategic situation among the high passes. The Swiss cantonalism of the 14th century was the product of the conflux of these forces. Initially influenced by the example of the nearby Lombard communes in their struggle against the Empire, the Swiss revolt against the Habsburgs united rural mountaineers and urban burgesses – a victorious combination. The political lead was taken by the three 'forest cantons', whose peasant infantry routed the Austrian seigneurial cavalry, hobbled in the narrow

1. A. Wandruszka, *The House of Habsburg*, London 1964, pp. 40–1.

valleys, at Morgarten in 1315. Serfdom was consequently abolished in
Uri, Schwyz and Unterwalden within a decade.[2] In 1330 there was a
municipal revolution in Lucerne, in 1336 in Zurich, both against pro-
Habsburg patriciates. By 1351, a formal alliance between these two
cities and three forest cantons existed. Finally, their joint troops
repulsed and defeated the Habsburg armies at Sempach and Näfels, in
1386 and 1388. In 1393 the Swiss Confederation was born: a unique
independent republic in Europe.[3] Swiss peasant pikemen were to go
on to become the crack military force of late mediaeval and early
modern warfare, bringing to an end the long dominance of cavalry
with their victories over the Burgundian knights summoned to
Austrian aid in the next century, and inaugurating the new prowess of
mercenary infantry. By the early 15th century, the Habsburg dynasty
had lost its lands below the bend of the Rhine to the Swiss, and had
failed to unite its possessions in Sundgau and Breisgau.[4] Its Rhenish
provinces were no more than scattered enclaves, symbolically re-
labelled *Vorderösterreich* and administered from Innsbruck. The whole
orientation of the dynasty henceforward shifted to the East.

In Austria itself, meanwhile, Habsburg power had not encountered
the same misadventures. The Tyrol was acquired in 1363; the title of
Archduke assumed at about the same time; the Estates which emerged
after 1400 were, after some sharp struggles, kept in reasonable check.
By 1440, the Imperial office – lost in the early 14th century, after the
first defeats in Switzerland – had been recaptured by the dynasty with
the collapse of Luxemburg power in Bohemia, and was never to pass

2. W. Martin, *A History of Switzerland*, London 1931, p. 44.

3. The singular emergence of the plebeian Swiss Confederation within aristocratic and monarchist Europe underlines an important and general characteristic of
the feudal polity in the later Middle Ages: the same parcellization of sovereignty
which existed at 'national' level could also operate at an 'international' level, so to
speak, permitting anomalous gaps and interstices in the total system of feudal
suzerainty. The Italian communes had already demonstrated this at a municipal
level, by throwing off Imperial authority. The Swiss cantons achieved the auto-
cephaly of a whole region, by their confederation – an anomaly impossible in any
political system other than European feudalism. The Habsburg dynasty did not
forgive them for it: four hundred years later, Switzerland was still 'an asylum of
dissolutes and criminals' for Maria Theresa.

4. H-F. Feine, 'Die Territorialbildung der Habsburger im deutschen Süd-
westen', *Zeitschrift der Savigny-Stiftung für Rechtsgeschichte (Germ. Abt.)*
LXVII, 1950, pp. 272, 277, 306; the lengthiest recent treatment of the subject.

seriously out of its control again thereafter. In 1477, a marital alliance with the House of Burgundy – Austrian ally in the anti-Swiss struggle – secured it the temporary windfall of the Franche-Comté and Netherlands. Before they passed into the Spanish orbit in the epoch of Charles V, however, the Burgundian domains probably furnished the House of Austria with the inspiration for its first steps towards administrative modernity. Maximilian I, surrounded by an entourage of Burgundian-Netherlandish nobles, created a central treasury in Innsbruck, and established the first conciliar agencies of government in Austria. A final attack into Switzerland proved abortive; but Gorizia was absorbed in the Southern marchlands, while Maximilian pursued a forward Italian and Imperial foreign policy. It was his successor Ferdinand I, however, whose reign suddenly marked out the capacious site of future Habsburg power in Central Europe, and laid the foundations of the strange State structure that was to be erected above it. In 1526, the Jagiello King of Bohemia and Hungary, Louis II, was defeated and killed at Mohacs by advancing Ottoman armies; Turkish troops overran most of Hungary, pushing the power of the Sultanate deep into Central Europe. Ferdinand successfully laid claim to the vacant monarchies, his marriage ties to the Jagiello line seconded by the Turkish threat, as far as the Czech and Magyar nobility were concerned. In Moravia and Silesia, the two outlying provinces of the Bohemian Realm, Ferdinand was accepted as a hereditary ruler; but the Bohemian and Hungarian Estates themselves categorically refused him this title, extracting an express acknowledgement from the Archduke that he was merely an elective prince in their lands. Ferdinand, moreover, had to fight a long three-cornered struggle against the Transylvanian pretender Zapolyai and the Turks, which ended in 1547 with the partition of Hungary into three zones: a Habsburg-ruled West, a Turkish-occupied Centre, and a Transylvanian principality in the East that was henceforward an Ottoman vassal state. War dragged on against the Turks in the Danubian plains for another decade, from 1551 to 1562: throughout the 16th century, Hungary cost the Habsburg dynasty more in defence expenditure than it yielded in revenues.[5]

Nevertheless, with all their internal and external limitations, the new

5. V. S. Mamatey, *Rise of the Habsburg Empire 1526–1815*, New York 1971, p. 38.

domains represented a vast potential increase in Habsburg international power. Ferdinand persistently endeavoured to build up royal authority throughout his lands, creating new dynastic institutions and centralizing old ones. The various Austrian Landtage were relatively compliant at this stage, assuring Habsburg rule a reasonably secure political base in the Archduchy itself. The Bohemian and Hungarian Estates were by no means so docile, and foiled Ferdinand's plans for a supreme Assembly covering all his dominions, capable of imposing a single currency and levying uniform taxes. But a cluster of new governmental agencies in Vienna greatly increased the reach of the dynasty, among them the *Hofkanzlei* (Court Chancellery) and the *Hofkammer* (Court Treasury). The most important of these institutions was the Imperial Privy Council, set up in 1527, which soon became the formal apex of the whole Habsburg administrative system in Central Europe.[6] The 'imperial' origins and orientation of this council were an index of the abiding importance of its German ambitions in the *Reich* to the House of Austria. Ferdinand attempted to further these by reviving an Imperial Aulic Council as the highest judicial court of the Empire, under the direct control of the Emperor. But since the Imperial Constitution had been reduced by the German princes to an empty legislative and judicial shell without any executive or coercive authority, the political gains were limited.[7] Much more significant in the long-run was the introduction of a permanent War Council, the *Hofkriegsrat*, created in 1556 and firmly focussed from the start on the 'Eastern' front of Habsburg operations rather than the 'Western'. Designed to organize military resistance to the Turks, the *Hofkriegsrat* was relayed by a local War Council in Graz, which coordinated the special 'Military Borders' created along the South-Eastern frontiers, in which were planted soldier-colonies of free-booting Serb and Bosnian Grenzers.[8]

6. H. F. Schwarz, *The Imperial Privy Council in the Seventeenth Century*, pp. 57–60.

7. See the discussion in G. D. Ramsay, 'The Austrian Habsburgs and the Empire', *The New Cambridge Modern History*, III, pp. 329–30.

8. For an account of the origins of the Grenzers, see Gunther Rothenburg, *The Austrian Military Border in Croatia, 1522–1747*, Urbana 1960, pp. 29–65. The Grenzers, in addition to their defense role against the Turks, were used as a dynastic weapon against the local Croat nobility, who were always extremely hostile to their presence in the frontier zones.

Ottoman strength had by no means relaxed. From 1593 onwards, the Thirteen Years' War raged across Hungary; at the end of it, after successive devastations of the country which left Magyar agriculture in ruins and the Magyar peasantry in serfdom, Habsburg troops had been held in check by the Turks.

By the turn of the 17th century, the House of Austria had registered moderate gains in its State-construction; but the political unity of its possessions was still very tenuous. Dynastic rule was on a different legal footing in each of them, and no common institutions apart from the War Council linked them together. The Austrian lands themselves were only first declared indivisible in 1602. The Imperial aspirations of Habsburg rulers were no substitute for practical integration of the territories owing allegiance to them: Hungary lay outside the *Reich* anyway, so there was not even an inclusive relationship between the realm of the Empire and the lands of the Emperor. Moreover, in the later half of the 16th century, latent opposition in the various aristocratic Estates in the Habsburg domains had been given a new and sharp edge by the advent of the Reformation. For while the dynasty remained a pillar of the Roman Church and Tridentine orthodoxy, the majority of the nobility in every one of its constituent lands went over to Protestantism. First the bulk of the Czech landowning class, long habituated to local heresy, became Lutheran, then the Magyar gentry adopted Calvinism, and finally the Austrian aristocracy itself, in the heartland of Habsburg power, was won to the Reformed religion. By the 1570s the greatest noble families in the *Erblande* were Protestant: Dietrichstein, Starhemberg, Khevenhüller, Zinzendorf.[9] This minatory development was a sure sign of deeper conflicts to come. The impending accession of Ferdinand II to power in Vienna in 1617 thus set off more than a local explosion: Europe was soon engulfed in the Thirty Years' War. For Ferdinand, trained by Bavarian Jesuits, had been a grim and effective champion of the Counter-Reformation as Duke of Styria from 1595 onwards: unrelenting administrative centralization and religious repression were the hallmarks of his provincial regime in Graz. Spanish Absolutism was the international sponsor of his candidature, within the Habsburg family, to the dynastic succession in the Empire and Bohemia; truculent Hispanic diplomats

9. Mamatey, *Rise of the Habsburg Empire*, p. 40.

and generals guided his court from the start. The Bohemian Estates, nervous and erratic, accepted Ferdinand as monarch, and then at the first departure from religious toleration in the Czech lands, raised the banner of rebellion.

The Defenestration of Prague opened the greatest crisis of the Habsburg State system in Central Europe. Dynastic authority collapsed in Bohemia itself; more dangerously still, the Austrian and Hungarian Estates started to veer towards compacts of sympathy with the Bohemian Estates, conjuring up the spectre of a general nobiliary mutiny, fired by smouldering particularism and protestantism. In this emergency, the Habsburg cause was saved by the operation of two decisive factors. The Czech aristocracy, after the historic suppression of the popular Hussite movements in Bohemia, was unable to rally any profound social enthusiasm among the rural or urban masses for its revolt; some two-thirds of the population was Protestant, but at no point did religious zeal serve to cement an inter-class bloc against Austrian counter-attack, of the type which had marked the Dutch struggle against Spain. The Bohemian Estates were socially and politically isolated: the House of Austria was not. The militant solidarity of Madrid with Vienna turned the tide, as Spanish arms, allies and money were mobilized to crush Czech secessionism, effectively organizing Ferdinand II's whole war effort.[10] The result was the Battle of the White Mountain, which destroyed the old Bohemian noble class. The next decade saw Imperial armies led by Wallenstein marching victoriously to the Baltic, extending Habsburg power into North Germany for the first time, and dangling the possibility of a renovated, centralized German Empire ruled by the House of Austria. Swedish intervention in the 1630's destroyed this ambition; the aggressive impetus of Habsburg Imperial policy was lost forever. The Peace of Westphalia which ended the Thirty Years' War consecrated the verdict of the military struggle. The House of Austria was not to dominate the Empire; but it had achieved mastery of Bohemia, the original stake of the conflict. The whole internal pattern of Habsburg

10. Ferdinand II himself declared that the Spanish envoy Oñate was 'the man with whose friendly and frank help all the affairs of the Habsburg family are being managed'. For an account of Oñate's decisive political role in the crisis, see Bohdan Chudoba, *Spain and the Empire 1529–1643*, Chicago 1952, pp. 220–8.

power within the dynastic lands of Danubian Europe was set by the consequences of this settlement.

By its victory in Bohemia, the Hofburg had achieved an enormous domestic advance towards Absolutism. In 1627, Ferdinand II had promulgated a new Constitution for the conquered Bohemian lands. The *Verneuerte Landesordnung* made Habsburg rule into a hereditary monarchy, no longer subject to election; converted all local officials into regal agents; made Catholicism the sole religion and restored the clergy to the Estates; invested the dynasty with supreme judicial rights; and elevated German to the rank of an official language equal to Czech.[11] The Snem was not abolished, and the necessity of its consent to taxation was reaffirmed. But in practice its survival proved no barrier to the implantation of Absolutism in Bohemia. The local assemblies which had once been the pulse of landowner politics faded away in the 1620's, while participation in the Estates declined steeply, as the Snem lost political significance. This process was facilitated by the dramatic war-time upheaval in the social composition and role of the nobility itself. The military reconquest of Bohemia had been accompanied by the political proscription of the bulk of the old seigneurial class, and the economic expropriation of its estates. Over half the manors in Bohemia were confiscated after 1620;[12] this vast agrarian booty was distributed to a new, motley aristocracy of fortune, expatriate captains and emigrant bravos of the Counter-Reformation. No more than a fifth or an eighth of the nobility in the later 17th century was Old German or Old Czech in origin: only some eight or nine major Czech lines, which had remained loyal to the dynasty for religious reasons, survived into the new order.[13] The great majority of the Bohemian aristocracy was now of foreign origin, mixing Italians (Piccolomini), Germans (Schwarzenberg), Austrians (Trautmansdorff), Slovenes (Auersperg), Walloons (Bucquoy), Lorrainers (Desfours) or

11. For the *Verneuerte Landesordnung*, see R. Kerner, *Bohemia in the Eighteenth Century*, New York 1932, pp. 17–22.

12. J. Polišensky, *The Thirty Years' War*, London 1971, pp. 143–4: the confiscated estates were on average much larger than those which escaped expropriation, so that the actual proportion of land which changed hands was considerably greater than the number of manors themselves.

13. H. G. Schenk, 'Austria', in Goodwin (ed.), *The European Nobility in the 18th Century*, p. 106; Kerner, *Bohemia in the Eighteenth Century*, pp. 67–71.

Irish (Taaffe). Landed property by the same stroke underwent a notable concentration: lords and clergy controlled nearly three-quarters of all land, while the share of the former small gentry tumbled from one-third to one-tenth. The lot of the peasantry correspondingly worsened. Already tied to the soil and thinned by the war, it was now loaded with increased labour services; the average *robot* obligations came to be 3 days a week, while more than a quarter of serfs worked every day except Sundays and saints' days for their lords.[14] Moreover, whereas prior to the Thirty Years' War, Bohemian landowners – unlike their Polish or Hungarian counterparts – had paid taxes together with their villeins, after 1648 the new, cosmopolitan nobility in practice achieved fiscal immunity, shifting virtually the whole tax burden downwards onto their serfs. This transfer naturally smoothed the course of deliberations between monarchy and aristocracy in the Estates: henceforward the dynasty merely requested lump sums from the Estates, leaving them to fix and collect the taxes to meet its demands. Fiscal pressures could easily be augmented under this system, where larger budgets usually meant that the Estates 'simply agreed to increase the charges which they themselves laid on their tenants and subjects'.[15] Bohemia had always been much most lucrative domain of the Habsburg lands, and the new financial grip of the monarchy over it significantly strengthened Viennese Absolutism.

Meanwhile, in the *Erblande* themselves, centralized and autocratic administration had made considerable progress. Ferdinand II had created the Austrian Court Chancellery – an enlarged version of his chosen instrument of power in Styria – to top the machinery of government in the Archduchy. This body gradually achieved ascendancy within the counsels of the State, at the expense of the Imperial Privy Council, whose importance inevitably receded after the reluctant withdrawal of Habsburg power from Germany. More vitally still, a permanent army of some 50,000 – 10 infantry and 9 cavalry regiments – was created for the first time in 1650, in the aftermath of Westphalia: the conduct of the Austrian and Bohemian Estates was henceforward inevitably tempered by the presence of this weapon. At the same time,

14. Polišensky, *The Thirty Years' War*, pp. 142, 246; Betts, 'The Habsburg Lands', *The New Camridge Modern History*, V, Cambridge 1969, pp. 480–1.

15. J. Stoye, *The Siege of Vienna*, London 1964, p. 92.

Habsburg Absolutism achieved a unique cultural and ideological feat: Bohemia, Austria and Hungary – the three constitutive zones of its rule – were all progressively folded back into the Church of Rome. Protestantism had been repressed in Styria in the 1590's; the Reformed religions were banned in Lower Austria in 1625, in Bohemia in 1627, and in Upper Austria in 1628. In Hungary, an authoritarian solution was impossible, but the Magyar Primates Pazmány and Lippay successfully reconverted most of the Hungarian magnate class. Austrian lords and peasants, Bohemian towns and Hungarian landowners alike were eventually recatholicized by the skill and drive of the Counter-Reformation, under the auspices of the Habsburg dynasty: a record without equal anywhere else in the continent. The crusading vigour of Danubian Catholicism appeared to find its apotheosis with the triumphant relief of Vienna from the Turks in 1683, and the subsequent victories which cleared Ottoman power out of Hungary and Transylvania, recovering long-lost territories for Christendom and expanding Habsburg rule impressively to the East. The military establishment which achieved these gains, now considerably enlarged, proved equally able to play a major role in the Alliance which held off Bourbon progress on the Rhine. The War of the Spanish Succession demonstrated the new international weight of the House of Austria. The Peace of Utrecht endowed it with Belgium and Lombardy.

Yet the peak of Austrian power, suddenly reached, was soon passed. No other European Absolutism had quite such a brief phase of military confidence and initiative. Begun in 1683, it was over by 1718, with the short capture of Belgrade and the Peace of Passarowitz. Thereafter Austria can virtually be said never to have won a war with a rival state again.[16] An unending series of defeats extended dismally down the next two centuries, relieved only by inglorious participation in the victories of others. This external atony was an index of the internal impasse and incompletion of Austrian Absolutism, even at the height of its powers. The most imposing and distinctive achievements of Habsburg rule in Central Europe were its gathering of disparate lands under a single dynastic roof, and its reconversion of them to Catholicism. Yet the ideological and diplomatic triumphs of the House of Austria – its feline religious and marital flair – were also substitutes for more substantial

16. Its campaigns against Piedmont in 1848 were to be the single exception.

bureaucratic and military gains. The influence of the Jesuits at the Court of Vienna during the epoch of the Counter-Reformation was always far greater than at the sister court of Madrid, where Catholic fervour was typically combined with watchful anti-Papalism. Clerical advisers and agents permeated the whole Habsburg administrative system in Central Europe during the 17th century, performing many of the most crucial political tasks of the day: the construction of the Tridentine bastion in Styria under Ferdinand II – in many ways the pilot experience for Austrian Absolutism – was largely their work. Likewise, the recovery of the Magyar magnate class for the Roman faith – without which the ultimate maintenance of Habsburg suzerainty over Hungary would probably have been impossible – was accomplished by the patient and adroit ideological missions of the priesthood. But such a success also had its limits. Catholic universities and schools won back the Hungarian nobility from Protestantism – but by carefully respecting and upholding the traditional corporate privileges of the Magyar 'nation', assuring the Church spiritual control but leaving the State encumbered with awkward impediments. Habsburg reliance on the clergy in internal political affairs thus had its price: no matter how astute, priests could never be functionally equivalent to *officiers* or *pomeshchiki* as building-blocks of Absolutism. Vienna was not to become a metropolitan centre of sale of offices, or of a service nobility; its hallmarks remained a malleable clericalism and a jumbled administration.

Similarly, the extraordinary fortune of the dynastic marriage policy of the Habsburg dynasty always tended to outrun its martial capacity, without ultimately compensating for it. The nuptial facility with which Hungary or Bohemia were initially acquired led to the coercive difficulty of enforcing Austrian centralism in the one and the eventual impossibility of imposing it in the other: diplomacy could not replace armaments, in the last resort. Yet the military record of Austrian Absolutism was also always somewhat defective and anomalous. The dynasty's three greatest successes were the initial acquisition of Bohemia and Hungary in 1526, the subjugation of Bohemia in 1620 and the defeat of the Turks in 1683, resulting in the reconquest of Hungary and Transylvania. Yet the first was the negative fruit of the Jagiellon defeat at Mohacs, not the product of any Habsburg victory: the Turks won the first and most important battle of Austrian Absolutism for it. The White Mountain, too, was to a large extent a Bavarian victory of the Catholic League; while the troops mustered under the Imperial command itself included Italian, Walloon, Flemish and Spanish contingents.[17] Even the relief of Vienna itself was essentially achieved by Polish and German armies, after the Emperor Leopold I had hastily quitted his capital: Habsburg troops numbered only a sixth of the force that won Sobieski fame in 1683.[18]

This recurrent reliance on allied arms had its curious complement in Austrian generalship itself. For most of the major military commanders who served the House of Austria down to the 19th century were independent entrepreneurs or foreign soldiers of fortune: Wallenstein, Piccolomini, Montecuccoli, Eugene, Laudun, Dorn. Wallenstein's host was in comparative terms perhaps the most formidable ever to fly the Austrian colours; yet it was in fact a private military machine created by its Czech general, which the dynasty hired but did not control – hence Wallenstein's assassination. Eugene, by contrast, was completely loyal to Vienna, but a Savoyard without any roots in the Habsburg lands themselves: the Italian Montecuccoli and the Rhinelander Dorn were lesser versions of the same pattern. The constant use of foreign mercenaries was, of course, a normal and universal feature of Absolutism: but these were rank-and-file troops, not officers in overall command of the armed forces of the State. The latter were naturally recruited from the ruling class of the lands concerned – the local nobility. In the Habsburg domains, however, there was no single seigneurial class, but a number of territorially distinct landowning groups. It was this lack of a unified aristocracy which told on the whole fighting capacity of the Habsburg State. Feudal nobilities, as we have seen, were never primarily 'national' in character; they could be transposed from one country to another, and fulfill their role as a landowning class without necessarily possessing any common ethnic or linguistic links with the subject population beneath them. The cultural separation of a language barrier might often be preserved to heighten the natural distance between rulers and ruled. On the other hand, ethnic or linguistic heterogeneity *within* the landed aristocracy

17. Chudoba, *Spain and the Empire*, pp. 247-8.
18. Stoye, *The Siege of Vienna*, pp. 245, 257.

of a single feudal polity was usually a source of potential weakness and disintegration, for it tended to undermine the political solidarity of the dominant class itself. The disarranged and haphazard aspects of the Habsburg State undoubtedly derived very largely from the composite and unreconciled character of its constituent nobilities. The drawbacks of aristocratic diversity were thus predictably evident in the most sensitive sector of the State machine, the Army. In the absence of a socially unitary nobility, Habsburg armies rarely attained the performance of their Hohenzollern or Romanov counterparts.

Thus Austrian Absolutism, even at its apogee, lacked structural congruence and certainty, because of the conglomerate character of the social formations over which its rule was exercised. The Germanic lands of Austria proper always represented the reliable inner core of the Habsburg Empire – the oldest and most loyal possessions of the dynasty in Central Europe. Nobles and towns retained many traditional privileges in the Landtage of Lower and Upper Austria, Styria and Carinthia; in the Tyrol and Vorarlberg, the peasantry itself was actually represented in the Estates, exceptional sign of the Alpine character of these provinces. The 'intermediate' institutions inherited from the mediaeval epoch were never suppressed, as in Prussia: but by the early 17th century they had been rendered obedient instruments of Habsburg power, whose survival was never seriously to obstruct the will of the dynasty. The Archducal lands thus formed the secure, central base of the ruling House. Unfortunately, they were too modest and circumscribed to impart a unitary royal dynamism to the Habsburg State as a whole. Economically and demographically, they were outweighed by the richer Bohemian lands already in the mid 16th century: in 1541, Austrian tax contributions to the Imperial Treasury were only half those of Bohemia, and this ratio of 1:2 remained in force down to the end of the 18th century.[19] The Swedish defeat of Wallenstein's armies during the Thirty Years' War blocked any expansion of the Germanic base of the dynasty, effectively isolating the Archduchy from the traditional *Reich*. Moreover, rural society in Austria was least representative of the dominant agrarian pattern in the Habsburg lands. For the semi-mountainous character of much of the region rendered it

19. Kerner, *Bohemia in the Eighteenth Century*, pp. 25–6. The Bohemian realm included Bohemia proper, Moravia and Silesia.

ungrateful terrain for large feudal estates. The result was the persistence of small peasant property in the highland zones, and the prevalence of the Western type of *Grundherrschaft* on the plains, stiffened by Eastern norms of exploitation;[20] patrimonial jurisdictions and feudal dues were general, labour services were heavy in many parts, but the opportunities for consolidated demesne farming and vast latifundia were comparatively limited. The solvent action of the capital city on the labour force of the surrounding countryside was later to become a further deterrent to the emergence of a *Gutsherrschaft* economy.[21] The 'critical mass' of the Austrian aristocracy itself was thus too slight to produce an effective magnetic centre for the whole landowning class of the Empire.

The crushing of the Bohemian Estates during the Thirty Years' War, on the other hand, gave Habsburg Absolutism its most basic political success; the substantial and fertile Czech lands now lay unequivocally within its grasp. No rebellious nobility in Europe met such a summary fate as the Bohemian aristocracy: after its downfall, a new landowning class, owing everything to the dynasty, was planted on its estates. The history of European Absolutism reveals no comparable episode. Yet there was still a revealing peculiarity in the Habsburg settlement of Bohemia. The new nobility created there by it was not principally composed of houses from the Austrian bulwark of the dynasty; apart from a few Catholic Czech families, it was imported from abroad. The extraneous origins of this stratum indicated the lack of a home aristocracy to transfer to Bohemia – enhancing Habsburg power in the Czech zone in the short-run, a symptom of weakness in the long-run. The Bohemian lands were the wealthiest and most densely populated in Central Europe: for the next century or so, the largest magnates of the Habsburg Empire nearly always possessed huge serf-tilled estates in Bohemia or Moravia, and the economic centre of gravity of the governing class shifted correspondingly northwards. But the new Bohemian aristocracy revealed little *esprit de corps* or even notable fidelity to the dynasty: the bulk of it deserted at a blow to the Bavarian occupier during the War of the Austrian Succession in the 1740's. This class was

20. V-L. Tapié, *Monarchie et Peuples du Danube*, Paris 1969, p. 144.
21. For conditions in Lower Austria, see Jerome Blum, *Noble Landowners and Agriculture in Austria 1815–1848*, Baltimore 1947, pp. 176–80.

the nearest equivalent to a service nobility in the State system of Austrian Absolutism; but it was the arbitrary product of past services rather than the bearer of organic and ongoing public functions, and although it provided many of the administrative cadres of the Habsburg monarchy, it failed to become a dominant or organizing force within it.

Nevertheless, whatever the limitations of the landowning classes in each sector, the consolidation of imperial power in both the Austrian and Bohemian units of the Habsburg domains by the mid-17th century seemed to create the premises for a more homogeneous, centralized Absolutism. It was to be Hungary which proved the insurmountable obstacle to a unitary royal state. If an analogy were to be made between the two Habsburg Empires, centred in Madrid and Vienna, in which Austria might be compared to Castile and Bohemia to Andalusia, Hungary was a sort of Eastern Aragon. The comparison is very imperfect, however, for Austria never possessed the economic and demographic predominance of Castile, as the hub of the imperial system, while the power and privileges of the Hungarian nobility exceeded even those of the Aragonese aristocracy: and the critical unifying trait of a common language was always missing. The Magyar landowning class was extremely numerous, some 5–7 per cent of the total population of Hungary. While many of these were 'moccasin' squires with tiny plots, the critical sector of the Hungarian gentry was the stratum of so-called *bene possessionati*, who owned medium-sized properties and dominated the political life of the provinces:[22] it was they who characteristically gave to the Magyar nobility as a whole social leadership and unity. The Hungarian Estates system was fully operative, and had never conceded serious regalian rights to the Habsburg dynasty, which reigned merely by virtue of a 'personal union' in Hungary and whose authority was elective and revocable there; the feudal constitution expressly included a *jus resistendi* legitimating noble uprisings against any royal encroachments on the hallowed liberties of the Magyar 'nation'. The gentry had

22. Bela Király, *Hungary in the Late Eighteenth Century*, New York 1969, pp. 33, 108. It looks as if the role of the *bene possessionati* within the Hungarian landowning class was one of the most important factors which distinguished it from the similarly numerous Polish nobility, whom it otherwise so much resembled; the latter were much more polarized between magnates and petty squires, and consequently lacked the cohesion of their Magyar counterparts.

controlled its own unit of county administration – the *comitatus* – ever since the later Middle Ages, assemblies whose permanent committees, vested with judicial, financial and bureaucratic functions, were all-powerful in the countryside and ensured a high degree of political cohesion in the landowning class. The Habsburgs had generally tried to divide the Hungarian aristocracy by splitting away its wealthiest section with honours and privileges: they thus introduced titles – hitherto unknown in Hungary as in Poland – in the 16th century, and secured a juridical separation of the magnates from the gentry in the early 17th century.[23] These tactics had not made appreciable inroads against Hungarian particularism, now further fortified by the spread of Protestantism. Above all, the proximity of Turkish military power – the occupying and suzerain force in two-thirds of the Magyar lands after Mohacs – was a decisive objective hindrance to the extension of a centralized Austrian Absolutism into Hungary. For throughout the 16th and 17th centuries, there were Magyar noblemen living directly under Turkish rule in Central Hungary; while further to the East, Transylvania formed an autonomous princely state under local Hungarian rulers, many of them Calvinist, within the Ottoman Empire. Any attempt by Vienna to attack the venerable prerogatives of the Hungarian aristocracy could thus always be countered by resort to alliance with the Turks; while ambitious Transylvanian rulers repeatedly tried to foment their compatriots in Habsburg terrain against the Hofburg in their own interests, frequently with a well-trained army at their disposal and with the goal of creating a greater Transylvania. The tenacity of Magyar particularism was thus also a function of its potent backstops across the Ottoman frontier, which again and again allowed the gentry of 'Christian' Hungary to summon to their aid military forces superior to their own local strength.

The 17th century – the great epoch of noble unrest and strain in the West, with its cortège of aristocratic conspiracies and rebellions – thus also witnessed one uniquely persistent and successful seigneurial resistance to increased monarchical power in the East, within a developing Absolutism. The first major round of the struggle occurred during the Thirteen Years' Austro-Ottoman War. Habsburg military advances against the Turks were accompanied by religious persecution and

23. Mamatey, *Rise of the Habsburg Empire*, p. 37.

administrative centralization in the conquered zones. In 1604 the Calvinist magnate Bocskay revolted, rallying Magyar gentry and *haiduk* free-booters of the borderlands against the imperial occupation forces, in alliance with the Turks; in 1606 the Porte secured an advantageous peace, the Hungarian aristocracy religious toleration from Vienna, and Bocşkay the princedom of Transylvania. In 1619–20, the new Transylvanian ruler Gábor Bethlen profited by the Bohemian rising to invade and seize large tracts of Habsburg Hungary, joined by local Protestant landowners. In 1670, Leopold I stamped out a magnate conspiracy and moved troops into Hungary in force: the old constitution was liquidated and a new, centralist administration under a German lieutenant-governor, decked with extraordinary tribunals for repression, was imposed. Fighting soon broke out, led by Count Imre Tökölli, from 1678 onwards; and in 1681, Leopold had to retract his constitutional coup and reaffirm traditional Magyar privileges, as Tökölli beckoned Turkish assistance. Ottoman armies duly arrived and the famous siege of Vienna ensued in 1683. Eventually, Turkish forces were expelled from Hungary altogether in 1687, and Tökölli fled to exile. Leopold was not strong enough to restore the former centralist regime of the *Gubernium*, but was now able to secure from the Magyar Estates at Bratislava the acceptance of the Habsburg dynasty as a hereditary – no longer elective – monarchy in Hungary, and the abrogation of the *jus resistendi*. The Austrian conquest of Transylvania in 1690–1, moreover, henceforward surrounded the Magyar gentry with a strategic block of territory to its rear, directly subject to Vienna; the Special Military Border Zones subject to the *Hofkriegsrat* now extended from the Adriatic to the Carpathians; while Turkish power in the Danubian basin was largely spent by the early 18th century. The newly acquired lands were distributed to foreign military adventurers and a select circle of Hungarian lords, whose political loyalty was now cemented by enormous estates in the East.

Nevertheless, the first opportunity for armed sedition afforded by an international conflict was once more avidly seized by the Hungarian gentry. In 1703, war-taxes and confessional persecution drove the north-western peasantry into revolt; capitalizing on this popular unrest, the magnate Ferenc Rakóczi led a final, formidable rebellion in military alliance with France and Bavaria, whose pincer attack on

Vienna was only just stopped by the Battle of Blenheim. Habsburg troops had brought the insurrection to an end by 1711; and four years later, the Magyar landowning class for the first time had to accept imperial taxation of its serfs, and army cantonments in its counties, while the military frontiers beyond them were managed by the *Hofkriegsrat*. A Hungarian Chancellery was now stationed in Vienna. But by the Peace of Szatmár, the traditional social and political privileges of the Hungarian landowners were otherwise confirmed: the administration of the country remained substantially in its control.[24] There were no more rebellions after this settlement, for another 150 years; but the relationship joining the Magyar nobility to the Habsburg dynasty remained unlike that between any other Eastern aristocracy and monarchy in the age of Absolutism. Extreme aristocratic decentralization, entrenched in mediaeval laws and institutions, had proved irreducible on the *puszta*. The Austrian base of the imperial system was too small, the Bohemian extension too brittle, the resistance of the Hungarian polity too strong, for a typically Easternized Absolutism to emerge along the Danube. The result was to block any final rigour or uniformity in the composite state structures presided over by the Hofburg.

Within twenty years of the Peace of Passarowitz, high water-mark of its Balkan expansion and European prestige, Habsburg Absolutism suffered a humiliating defeat at the hands of its far smaller Hohenzollern rival. The Prussian conquest of Silesia in the War of the Austrian Succession deprived it of the most prosperous and industrialized province of its Central European empire: Breslau had become the premier commercial centre of the traditional dynastic lands. Control of the Imperial office was temporarily lost to Bavaria, and the bulk of the Bohemian aristocracy defected to the new Bavarian Emperor. Bohemia was eventually recovered; but in the next decade Austrian Absolutism was profoundly shaken again by the Seven Years' War, in which despite alliance with Russia and France, overwhelming numerical superiority and immense losses, it failed to regain Silesia. Prussia, with a third of the treasury and a sixth of the population of Austria, had

24. In many ways, the best synoptic comments on the successive Hungarian revolts of this epoch are to be found in McNeill, *Europe's Steppe Frontier*, Chicago 1964, pp. 94–7, 147–8, 164–7.

twice triumphed over it. This double shock precipitated two drastic bouts of reforms within the Habsburg State under Maria Theresa, conducted by the Chancellors Haugwitz and Kaunitz, with the aim of modernizing and renovating the whole apparatus of government.[25] The Bohemian and Austrian Chancelleries were fused into a single organ, the corresponding appellate courts were merged, and the separate legal order of the Bohemian nobility abolished altogether. Taxes were for the first time imposed on the aristocracy and clergy of both lands (but not in Hungary), and their Estates coerced into decennial grants of revenue to raise an enlarged permanent army of 100,000. The *Hofkriegsrat* was reorganized and given plenary powers throughout the Empire. A supreme State Council was created to integrate and direct the machinery of Absolutism. Permanent royal officials – the *kreis-hauptmänner* – were posted into every 'circle' of Bohemia and Austria, to enforce centralized justice and administration. Customs barriers between Bohemia and Austria were abolished, and protectionist tariffs erected against foreign imports. Labour services performed by the peasantry were legally limited. Regalian fiscal rights were ruthlessly exploited to increase imperial revenues. Organized emigration was mounted to colonize Transylvania and the Banat. These Theresan measures were soon overtaken, however, by the sweeping programme of further reforms imposed by Joseph II.

The new Emperor broke spectacularly with the Austrian tradition of suffuse official clericalism. Religious toleration was proclaimed, church lands were dissolved, monasteries cut down, church services regulated, and universities taken over by the State. An advanced penal code was introduced, the law courts reformed and censorship abolished. Secular education was vigorously promoted by the State, until by the end of the reign perhaps one out of every three children was in elementary school. Modernized curricula were designed to produce better trained engineers and functionaries. The civil service was professionalized, and its ranks organized on a merit basis, while secret surveillance of it was ensured by a network of police agents modelled on the Prussian system. Taxation ceased to be administered by the Estates, and was henceforward collected directly by the monarchy. Fiscal burdens were steadily increased. Annual sessions of the Estates were suppressed: the

25. Bluche, *Le Despotisme Eclairé*, pp. 106–10 provides a succinct survey.

Landtage now only assembled at the summons of the dynasty. Conscription was inaugurated, and the army expanded to some 300,000 troops.[26] Tariffs were relentlessly raised to assure command of the domestic market, while at the same time urban guilds and corporations were struck down to further free competition within the Empire. The transport system was improved. These steps were radical but not yet outside the range of the conventional moves of Absolutist States in the Age of the Enlightenment. The Josephine programme, however, did not stop at this. In a series of decrees unique in the history of Absolutist Monarchy, serfdom was formally abolished in 1781 – after serious peasant risings in Bohemia during the previous decade – and all subjects were guaranteed the right of free choice in their marriage, migration, work, occupation, and property. Peasants were given security of tenure where they did not possess it, and nobles forbidden to acquire peasant plots. Finally, all labour services were abolished for peasants on 'rustical' land (i.e. villein plots) paying two florins or more a year in taxes, fiscal rates were equalized, and official norms for the distribution of the gross agricultural output of these tenants were decreed – 12·2 per cent for the State in taxes, 17·8 per cent for the lords and clergy in rents and tithes, and 70 per cent to be retained by the peasant himself. Although very partial in its coverage – little more than one-fifth of the Bohemian peasantry was affected by it[27] – this last measure threatened drastic changes in social relations in the countryside, and struck directly at vital economic interests of the landowning nobility throughout the Empire. The proportion of the agrarian product at the disposal of the direct producer was generally about 30 per cent at the time[28] – the new law would double this, by the same stroke all but halving the surplus extracted by the feudal class. Aristocratic outcry was vociferous and universal, backed by widespread obstruction and evasion.

Meanwhile, Joseph II's centralism was causing political uproar at the two extremities of the Empire. The urban corporations and

26. Conscription was introduced in 1771. In 1788, Joseph II mobilized 245,000 infantry, 37,000 cavalry and 900 cannon for his war against Turkey: H. L. Mikoletzky, *Osterreich. Das grosse 18. Jahrhundert*, Vienna 1967, pp. 227, 366.

27. Wright, *Serf, Seigneur and Sovereign*, p. 147.

28. Kerner, *Bohemia in the Eighteenth Century*, pp. 44–5.

mediaeval charters of the distant Belgian provinces had been over-ridden from Vienna; bruised clerical sentiment, patrician hostility and popular patriotism combined to produce an armed revolt concurrent with the French Revolution. More menacing still were the tremors in Hungary. For Joseph II had also been the first Habsburg ruler forcibly to integrate Hungary into a unitary imperial framework. Eugene of Savoy had urged the dynasty to make of their disparate lands an organized whole – *ein Totum*: this ideal was now at last methodically implemented. All the main Josephine reforms – ecclesiastical, social, economic and military – were enforced in Hungary, over the protests of the Magyar gentry. The *Kreis* bureaucracy was extended to Hungary and the ancient county system subordinated to it; the fiscal immunity of the landowning class was abolished; royal justice was imposed. The Hungarian Estates were visibly preparing an insurrection by 1789. At the same time, the foreign policy of the monarchy was foundering. Joseph II had twice made efforts to acquire Bavaria, the second time proposing to swap it for Belgium: this logical and rational objective, whose attainment would have transformed the strategic position and inner structure of the Austrian Empire, shifting it decisively back westwards into Germany, was blocked by Prussia. Significantly, Austria was unable to risk war with Prussia over the issue, even after its great military build-up under Joseph. The result was to divert Austrian expansionism into the Balkans again, where Ottoman armies now inflicted a series of reverses on the Emperor. The ultimate goal of the entire strenuous overhaul of Austrian Absolutism – the recovery of its international military rank – thus escaped it. Joseph's reign ended in disillusionment and failure. War taxes and conscription were unpopular with the peasantry, inflation created great hardships in the towns, censorship was reimposed.[29] Most conclusively, relations between monarchy and aristocracy had reached breaking-point. To avert rebellion in Hungary, centralization had to be jettisoned there. Joseph II's death was the signal for a rapid and general seigneurial reaction. His successor Leopold II was immediately forced to rescind

29. The isolation of the regime in its last years is well conveyed by Ernst Wangermann, *From Joseph II to the Jacobin Trials*, Oxford 1959, pp. 28–9. The peasantry was disappointed with the limits of its land reform and shocked by its anti-clericalism.

the Land Laws of 1789, and restore the political powers of the Magyar nobility. The Hungarian Estates legally annulled Joseph's reforms, and ended taxation of noble land. The onset of the French Revolution and the Napoleonic Wars henceforward drove the dynasty and aristocracy together throughout the Empire, clinching them in a common conservatism. The singular episode of a too 'enlightened' despotism was over.

Paradoxically, it was the very aporia of Austrian Absolutism that had made it possible. The great weakness and limitation of the Habsburg Empire was its lack of any unitary aristocracy, to form a full service nobility of the Eastern type. Yet it was precisely this social absence which permitted the 'irresponsible' latitude of the Josephine autocracy. Just because the landowning class was not built into the Austrian State apparatus in the way that it was in Prussia or Russia, the Absolute Monarchy could sponsor a programme effectively injurious to it. Unrooted in any one territorial nobility, with a strong and single class cohesion, the monarchy could achieve a degree of volatile autonomy unknown to its neighbours. Hence the uniquely 'anti-feudal' character of the Josephine decrees, by contrast with the comparable later reforms of the other Eastern Absolutisms.[30] The instrument of royal renovation in the Habsburg Empire was likewise a bureaucracy more distinct from the aristocracy than any other in the region: recruited primarily from the German upper-middle class of the towns, culturally and socially separate from the landowning class. But the relative detachment of the monarchy from the heterogeneous landowners of its realm was also, of course, the cause of its inner debility. Internationally, the Josephine programme ended in debacle. Internally, the social laws of nature of the Absolutist State rigorously reasserted themselves, in an eloquent demonstration of the impotence of the personal will of the ruler, once it transgressed the collective interests of the class which Absolutism historically functioned to defend.

The Austrian Empire thus emerged from the Napoleonic era as the central pillar of European reaction, Metternich the doyen of monarchist and clerical counter-revolution throughout the continent. Habsburg Absolutism drifted sluggishly through the first half of the nineteenth

---

30. All three reform programmes – the Austrian, Prussian and Russian – were, of course, motivated by military defeats.

century. Meanwhile, incipient industrialization was creating a new urban population, both working-class and middle-class, and commercial agriculture was spreading from the West, with the arrival of new crops – sugar-beet, potatoes, clover – and the growth of wool production. The peasantry had been emancipated from serfdom: but it was still subject to the patrimonial jurisdiction of its landlords throughout the Empire, and nearly everywhere owed heavy labour services to the nobility. In these respects, *Erbuntertänigkeit* of a traditional type still prevailed over some 80 per cent of its territory, including all the main regions of Central Europe – Upper Austria, Lower Austria, Styria, Carinthia, Bohemia, Moravia, Galicia, Hungary and Transylvania – and the *robot* remained the main source of labour in the agrarian economy.[31] The typical German or Slav peasant still kept only some 30 per cent of his produce, after payment of taxes and dues, in the 1840's.[32] At the same time, increasing numbers of landowners were becoming aware that the average productivity of hired labour was much greater than that of *robot* labour, and were seeking to switch to it; a shift of attitude statistically illustrated by their willingness to accept monetary commutation of the *robot* at rates well below the minimum wages for equivalent hired labour.[33] Increasing numbers of landless peasants were simultaneously migrating to the towns, where many of them became urban unemployed. National consciousness was inevitably now aroused, in the post-Napoleonic epoch, first in the cities and later washing back into the countryside. Bourgeois political demands were soon more national than liberal: the Austrian Empire became the 'prison of peoples'.

These accumulated contradictions fused and exploded in the revolutions of 1848. The dynasty eventually quelled urban riots and suppressed national risings throughout its lands. But the peasant revolts that had given the revolutions their mass force could only be pacified by granting the basic demands of the villages. The Assembly of 1848 performed this service for the monarchy, before it was cashiered by the victory of the counter-revolution. Seigneurial jurisdictions were lifted, the rustical-dominical division of land was eliminated, all tenants given

31. Blum, *Noble Landowners and Agriculture in Austria*, pp. 45, 202.
32. *Ibid.*, p. 71.
33. *Ibid.*, pp. 192–202.

equal security of tenure, and feudal dues in labour, kind or cash were formally abolished – with indemnification for lords, of which half was to be paid by the tenant and half by the State. The Austrian and Bohemian landowning class, already instructed in the benefits of free labour, did not oppose this settlement: its interests were generously secured by the compensation clauses, passed against the resistance of peasant spokesmen.[34] The Magyar Estates, led by Kossuth, ended the *robot* in an even more advantageous manner for the gentry: compensation in Hungary was integrally paid by the peasantry. The Agrarian Law of September 1848 assured the predominance of capitalist relations in the countryside. Landed property became even more concentrated, as smaller gentry sold out and poor peasants flocked to the towns, while the great noble magnates increased their latifundia and rationalized their management and production with compensation funds. A stratum of well-off *Grossbauern* was consolidated beneath them, especially in the Austrian lands, but the fundamental distribution of the soil remained perhaps more polarized than ever after the advent of capitalist farming. In the 1860s, 0·16 per cent of landholdings in Bohemia – the huge magnate estates – covered 34 per cent of the land.[35]

An increasingly capitalist agriculture now underlay the Habsburg polity. The Absolutist State, however, emerged unreconstructed from the ordeal of 1848. Liberal demands for civic freedoms and suffrage were silenced, national aspirations suppressed. The feudal dynastic order had survived the popular 'springtime' of Europe. But its capacity for active evolution or adaptation was now past. The Austrian agrarian reforms had been the work of the ephemeral Assembly of the revolution, not the initiative of the royal government – unlike the Prussian Reforms of 1808–11; they had merely been accepted by the Hofburg after the event. Likewise, the military defeat of the most menacing national insurrection in Central Europe – the constitution of a separate State by the Hungarian gentry, to include its own ministry, budget, army and foreign policy, linked to Austria merely by a 'personal union' once again – had been accomplished not by Austrian, but by Russian armies: lowering repetition of the traditions of the dynasty. Henceforward, the Habsburg Monarchy was more and more the passive object of events

34. Blum provides a trenchant analysis of the settlement, pp. 235–8.
35. Tapié, *Monarchie et Peuples du Danube*, p. 325.

and conflicts abroad. The fragile restoration of 1849 allowed it for a brief decade to achieve the long-envisaged goal of complete administrative centralization. The Bach system imposed a uniform bureaucracy, law, taxation and customs zone throughout the Empire; Hungary was filled with hussars to enforce its submission. But no stabilization of this centralist autocracy was possible: it was too weak internationally. Defeat by France at Solferino and the loss of Lombardy in 1859 shook the monarchy so badly that a domestic political retreat was necessary. The Patent of 1861 conceded an Imperial Parliament or *Reichsrat* elected indirectly from the provincial Landtage, with four curias, restricted suffrage and loading to ensure Germanic superiority. The *Reichsrat* had no control over ministers, conscription or collection of existing taxes; it was a powerless and token entity, unaccompanied by any freedom of the press or even immunity for deputies.[36] The Magyar gentry refused to accept it, and all-out military rule was reinstituted in Hungary. Defeat by Prussia at Sadowa, once again damaging and enfeebling the monarchy, undid this provisional regime within six years.

The whole traditional structure of the Absolutist State now underwent a sudden and drastic tilt. For over three centuries, the oldest and most formidable enemy of Habsburg centralism had always been the Hungarian nobility – the most obdurately particularist, culturally cohesive and socially repressive landowning class in the Empire. The final expulsion of the Turks from Hungary and Transylvania in the 18th century had, as we have seen, brought Magyar turbulence to an end, for a time. But the next hundred years, while apparently consecrating Hungarian political integration into the Austrian Empire, was in fact preparing an ultimate and spectacular reversal of roles within it. For the reconquest of Ottoman Hungary and Transylvania, and the agrarian reclamation and colonization of the vast spaces in the East, decisively increased the economic weight of the Hungarian ruling class within the Empire as a whole. Peasant emigration had initially been induced to the Central Hungarian Plain by advantageous tenancies; but once it was repopulated, landlord pressures immediately tightened, demesnes were enlarged and peasant plots expropriated.[37] The agri-

36. A. J. P. Taylor, *The Habsburg Monarchy*, London 1952, pp. 104–27.
37. Kiraly, *Hungary in the Late Eighteenth Century*, pp. 129–35.

cultural boom of the Enlightenment epoch had, despite the discriminating tariff policies of Vienna,[38] greatly benefited most of the gentry and laid the foundations of magnate fortunes which were to be of unparalleled dimensions. Historically, the Bohemian-based nobility had been much the richest in the Habsburg domains: by the 19th century, this was no longer so. The Schwarzenberg family might own 479,000 acres in Bohemia; the Esterhazy family was master of some 7,000,000 in Hungary.[39] The confidence and aggressivity of the Magyar landowning class as a whole, squires and magnates alike, was thus gradually enhanced by the new extent of its possessions and the growth of their importance within the Central European economy.

Yet the Hungarian aristocracy was never admitted to the inner counsels of the Habsburg State in the 18th and early 19th centuries: it was always kept at a distance from the imperial political apparatus itself. Its opposition to Vienna remained the greatest domestic danger to the dynasty: the revolution of 1848 had shown its mettle, when it both imposed a more ruthless agrarian settlement on its peasantry than the Austrian or Bohemian aristocracy were able to do, and resisted royal armies of repression until overwhelmed by the Tsar's expedition against it. Thus as Austrian Absolutism became steadily weaker, after successive foreign disasters, and popular unrest in the Empire steadily stronger, the dynasty was driven, logically and irresistibly, towards its hereditary foe – the most combative and feudal nobility left in Central Europe, and the only landed class now capable of shoring up its power. The Prussian victory over Austria in 1866 assured the Hungarian rise to dominance within the Empire. To save itself from disintegration, the monarchy accepted a formal partnership. The Dualism which created 'Austria-Hungary' in 1867, gave the Magyar landowning class complete domestic power in Hungary, with its own government, budget, assembly and bureaucracy, retaining only a common army and foreign policy, and a renewable customs union. While in Austria, civic equality, freedom of expression and secular education now had to be yielded by the monarchy, in Hungary no such concessions were made

38. Emphasized by traditional Hungarian historians: see, for example, H. Marczali, *Hungary in the Eighteenth Century*, Cambridge 1910, pp. 39, 99.

39. Mamatey, *Rise of the Habsburg Empire*, p. 64; C. A. Macartney, 'Hungary', in Goodwin (ed.), *The European Nobility in the 18th Century*, p. 129.

by the gentry. The Hungarian nobility henceforward represented the militant and masterful wing of aristocratic reaction in the Empire, which increasingly came to dominate the personnel and policy of the Absolutist apparatus in Vienna itself.[40]

For in Austria, political parties, social agitation and national conflicts were gradually undermining the viability of autocratic rule. Within four decades, in 1907, manhood suffrage was forced from the dynasty in Austria, amidst urban strikes and popular echoes of the Russian Revolution of 1905. In Hungary, the landowners firmly kept their class monopoly of the franchise. The Austrian Empire thus failed ever to achieve the transmutation which had made the German Empire into a capitalist state. When the First World War broke out, there was still no parliamentary control of the Imperial government, no Prime Minister, no uniform electoral system. The *Reichsrat* had 'no influence on policy, and its members had no hope of public careers'.[41] Over 40 per cent of the population – the inhabitants of Hungary, Croatia and Transylvania – was excluded from a secret vote or universal male suffrage; the 60 per cent who possessed them in the Austrian lands enjoyed a merely nominal right, since their votes had no purchase on the affairs of the State. Ironically, despite blatant rigging, the nearest to an effective electorate and responsible ministry existed in Hungary – just because both were confined to the landowning class. Above all, of course, the Austrian Empire was the mouldering negation of the bourgeois national state: it represented the antithesis of one of the essential tokens of the capitalist political order in Europe. Its German rival had achieved its structural transformation precisely by presiding over the national construction which the Austrian State refused. The contrary social evolution of each Absolutism thus had its geo-political counterpart. The Prussian State was dragged reluctantly but inexorably

---

40. The major exception was the army, whose supreme command remained a largely Austrian preserve throughout the final period down to the First World War. But the institutional importance of the military establishment in the Austrian State was always, as we have seen, below the average for Absolutism. The General Staff played a fatal role in the crisis of August 1914, but its failures once the fighting had started soon relegated it to a comparative back-seat again (in diametric contrast to the rise of its German counterpart in Berlin), while Magyar political influence in Vienna markedly increased as the War went on.

41. Taylor, *The Habsburg Monarchy*, p. 199.

towards the West as the 19th century wore on, with the industrialization of the Ruhr and the capitalist development of the Rhineland. The Austrian State in the same epoch shifted in the opposite direction, towards the East, with the growing ascendancy of Hungary and its last-ditch landlordism. Appropriately, the final acquisition of the dynasty formed the most backward territory of all in the Empire – the Balkan provinces of Bosnia and Herzegovina, annexed in 1909, where the traditional servitude of the local *kmet* peasants was never seriously modified.[42] The outbreak of the First World War took the trajectory of Austrian Absolutism to its conclusion: German armies fought its battles and Hungarian politicians determined its diplomacy. While the Prussian general Mackensen commanded the field, the Magyar leader Tisza ended as effective Chancellor of the Empire. Defeat razed the prison of nationalities to the ground.

42. O. Jászi, *The Dissolution of the Habsburg Monarchy*, Chicago 1929, pp. 225–6.

6

Russia

We now come to the last, and most durable Absolutism in Europe. Tsarism in Russia outlived all its precursors and contemporaries, to become the only Absolutist State in the continent to survive intact into the 20th century. The phases and pauses in the genesis of this State set it apart early on. For the economic downturn which marked the onset of the late feudal crisis occurred, as we have seen, under the shadow of Tartar tutelage. Wars, civil conflicts, plagues, depopulation and abandoned settlements characterized the 14th and first half of the 15th centuries. From 1450 onwards, a new era of economic revival and expansion set in. In the course of the next hundred years, the population multiplied, agriculture prospered, and internal trade and the use of money picked up rapidly, while the territory of the Muscovite State increased over six times in size. The three-field system – hitherto virtually unknown in Russia – started to supersede traditional and wasteful peasant assartage, in conjunction with the dominance of the wooden plough: somewhat later, mills came into general village use.[1] There was no export farming, and estates were still largely autarkic, but the presence of sizeable towns controlled by the Grand Duchy provided a certain outlet for manorial production; monastic domains were to the forefront in this trend. Urban manufactures and exchange were assisted by the territorial unification of Muscovy and the standardization of currency. Hired labour in town and country grew notably, while international trade across Russia flourished.[2] It was in

1. A. N. Sakharov, 'O Dialektike Istoricheskovo Razvitiya Russkovo Krest'-yantsva', *Voprosy Istorii*, 1970, No. 1, pp. 21–2.

2. It has been claimed that the size of the internal market was larger in the 1560's than in the mid 17th century, and the proportion of free labour in the

this phase of upswing that Ivan III laid the first foundations of Russian Absolutism by his inauguration of the *pomest'e* system.

Hitherto, the Russian landowning class had been essentially composed of autonomous and separatist princes and boyar nobles, many of Tartar or Oriental origin, in possession of large allodial domains and often considerable numbers of slaves. These magnates had gradually gravitated towards the recomposed Muscovite court, where they henceforward formed the entourage of the monarch, while retaining their own military levies and retainers. Ivan III's conquest of Novgorod in 1478 allowed the nascent ducal state to expropriate large tracts of land and settle a new gentry on them, which henceforward formed the military service class of Muscovy. The grant of the *pomest'e* was conditional on seasonal campaigns in the armies of the ruler, whose legal servitor its holder became, subject to a strictly defined statute. The *pomeshchiki* were cavalrymen, equipped for archery and swordthrusts in a disorganized battle mêlée: like the Tartar horsemen whom they were basically designed to confront, they did not use fire-arms. Most of the lands allocated to them were in the centre and south of the country, nearest to the permanent front of war with the Tartars. Whereas the typical boyar *votchina* was a large domain with an abundant supply of dependent peasant and slave labour (the average in the early 17th century was some 520 households in the Moscow region itself), the gentry *pomest'e* was usually a small estate with an average of some 5 to 6 peasant households working on it.[3] The limited size of the *pomeshchik* tenures, and the initial rigour of government control over their exploitation of them, probably meant that their productivity was generally well below that of the allodial boyar and monastic lands. Their economic dependence on the Grand Ducal donor of their lands was thus a tight one, which at first left them little margin for social or political initiatives. But already by 1497, it may have been partly their pressure which resulted in Ivan III's Sudebnik decree restricting

---

work-force greater in the 16th than in the 18th century: D. I. Makovsky, *Razvitie Tovarno-Denezhnykh Otnoshenii v Sel'skom Khozyaistve Russkovo Gosudarstva v XVI Veke*, Smolensk 1960, pp. 203, 206.

3. R. Hellie, *Enserfment and Military Change in Muscovy*, Chicago 1971, p. 24. This important work is the major recent synthesis on the whole question of the formation of Russian serfdom and the role of the service gentry in the early Tsarist state.

peasant mobility through Muscovy to two weeks in every year, before and after St George's Day in November: the first critical step towards the legal enserfment of the Russian peasantry, although the full process had still a considerable distance to go. Vassily III, who succeeded in 1505, followed the same path as his predecessor: Pskov was annexed, and the *pomest'e* system extended, with its political and military advantages for the dynasty. In some cases, the allodial lands of appanage princes or boyars were taken under control and their owners resettled elsewhere on conditional tenures, owing warrior service to the State. Ivan IV, proclaiming himself Tsar, extended and radicalized this process by outright expropriation of hostile landowners and the creation of a terrorist guard corps (*oprichniki*), who were granted confiscated estates for their services.

Ivan IV's work, while a decisive further step towards the construction of a Tsarist autocracy, has often been endowed with undue retrospective coherence. In fact, his rule did mark three critical accomplishments for the future of Russian Absolutism. Tartar power in the East was broken by the liberation of Kazan in 1556, and the annexation of the Khanate of Astrakhan – lifting a secular incubus from the growth of the Muscovite state and society. This signal victory had been preceded by the development of two crucial innovations in the Russian military system – the massive use of heavy artillery and mining charges against fortification (decisive in reducing Kazan), and the formation of the first permanent infantry of *strel'tsy* musketeers: both of major import for the prospects of foreign expansion. Meanwhile, the *pomest'e* system was generalized on a new scale, which lastingly shifted the balance of power between the boyars and tsar. The *oprichnina* confiscations for the first time made conditional tenures the dominant form of landholding in Russia, while *votchina* estates were simultaneously made liable for service themselves, and the growth of monastic domains was checked. This change was reflected in the diminished role of the Boyar Duma during Ivan IV's reign, and the summoning of the first Zemsky Sobor or Assembly of the Land, in which the smaller gentry were prominently represented.[4] Most important of all, Ivan IV now granted the *pomeshchik* class the right to

4. The example of the Polish Sejm can perhaps be detected in the convocation of this institution, which Ivan IV may have designed to attract West Russian

determine the level of rents extracted from the peasantry on their lands, and to collect these themselves – thereby making them for the first time masters over the labour-force on their estates.[5] At the same time, the administrative and tax system was modernized, by the abolition of the *kormlenie* provisioning system (in effect, salaries in kind) for provincial officials, and the creation of a central treasury for fiscal receipts. A local network of *guba* self-administration, manned essentially by the service gentry, further integrated this class into the emergent governmental apparatus of the Russian monarchy. Together, these military, economic and administrative measures tended to strengthen very considerably the political power of the central Tsarist State.

On the other hand, both foreign and domestic advances were subsequently undermined by the disastrous conduct of the interminable Livonian Wars, which exhausted the State and economy, and by the terrorist exactions of the *oprichnina* at home. The *oprichnik* 'state above the state',[6] composed of some 6,000 military police, was entrusted with the administration of Central Russia. Its repressions had no rational objective: they merely answered to Ivan IV's own semi-insane personal vendettas. It did not threaten the boyars as a class, merely selected individuals among them; while its rampages in the towns, disruption of the land system and super-exploitation of the peasantry was a direct cause of the utter centrifugal collapse of Muscovite society in the last years of Ivan's reign.[7] For at the same time, Ivan had committed a fundamental miscalculation after his victories in the East, by pursuing a policy of Western expansion towards the Baltic, rather than turning South to deal with the Crimean Tartar menace, which constituted a

---

nobles from Lithuania into the Muscovite orbit: Billington, *The Icon and the Axe*, pp. 99–100.

5. Hellie, *Enserfment and Military Change in Muscovy*, pp. 37, 45, 115.

6. Phrase coined by R. G. Skrynnikov, and cited by A. L. Shapiro, 'Ob Absoliutizme v Rossii', *Istoriya SSSR*, May 1968, p. 73. Shapiro's article is a reply to the essay by Avrekh alluded to earlier (see p. 19 above), which initiated a homeric debate among Soviet historians on the nature and path of Russian Absolutism, revealing an extremely wide range of positions, with a dozen or so contributions to *Istoriya SSSR* and *Voprosy Istorii* at the time of writing. There is much of interest in this discussion, to which we shall have occasion to refer.

7. See the concordant judgements of Vernadsky, *The Tsardom of Moscow*, Vol. I, pp. 137–9, and Shapiro, 'Ob Absoliutizme v Rossii', pp. 73–4.

permanent drain on Russian security and stability. Capable of defeating comparatively primitive if ferocious Oriental nomads, the new Russian military forces were unable to match the more advanced Polish and Swedish armies, equipped with Western weapons and tactics The twenty-five year long Livonian War ended in a crushing setback , after wracking Muscovite society with its huge expense and dislocation of the rural economy. Defeats on the front in Livonia combined with demoralization at home under the *oprichnik* scourge, to precipitate a disastrous exodus of the peasantry of Central and North-Western Russia to the recently acquired periphery of the country, leaving whole regions in desolation behind them. Calamities now succeeded one another in a familiar cycle of fiscal extortions, crop failures, plague epidemics, domestic pillage and foreign invasions. The Tartars plundered Moscow in 1571, and the *oprichniki* sacked Novgorod. In a desperate attempt to stem this social chaos, Ivan IV banned all peasant movements in 1581, closing the St George's period for the first time; the decree was expressly an exceptional one, covering a specific year, although it was repeated irregularly later in the decade. These bans were unable to check the immediate problem of mass flights, as great expanses of the traditional Muscovite homelands were laid waste of habitation. In the worst-hit areas, the land cultivated per peasant household sank to a third or a fifth of its previous levels; there was a widespread agrarian regression to extensive fallows; in the province of Moscow itself, it has been estimated that from 76 to 96 per cent of all settlements may have been abandoned.[8] Amidst this caving in of the whole rural order laboriously constructed over the past century, there was a sharp recrudesence of slavery, many peasants selling themselves as chattels to escape starvation. The concluding debacle of Ivan IV's reign was to impair the political and economic progress of Russian feudal society for decades thereafter, corroding even its initial successes.[9] The ferocity of Ivan's rule was a symptom of the hysterical and

8. Hellie, *Enserfment and Military Change*, pp. 95–7.

9. It is an error, however, to exaggerate the long-term set-back to the Russian economy which occurred in these years. Makovsky presents it as striking down burgeoning Russian capitalism just when it was on the point of fruition, and inflicting a secular regression of more than two centuries, with the consolidation of the *pomeshchik* class and of serfdom. 'Thus in the 60's and 70's of the 16th century, the necessary economic conditions were ready in the Russian State for

artificial character of much of his drive towards Absolutism, in conditions where any systematic autocracy was still premature.

The next decade saw some mitigation of the profound economic depression into which Russia had been plunged, but the *pomeshchik* gentry were still critically short of adequate peasant labour to till their lands, and were now suffering from acute price inflation as well. Boris Godunov, the magnate who had seized power after Ivan's death, reoriented Russian foreign policy towards peace with Poland in the West, attack on the Crimean Tartars in the South, and above all, annexation of Siberia in the East: for which he needed the loyalty of the military service class. It was against this background that, in order to rally gentry support, Godunov issued a decree in 1592 or 1593 banning all peasant movements until further notice, thereby lifting any temporal restrictions from adscription to the soil. 'This decree was the culminating point of the policies of enserfment of the late 16th and early 17th centuries.'[10] It was promptly followed by a widespread increase in labour services, and legal measures closing entry from lower social groups into the *pomeshchik* class. Godunov's elimination of the last heir of the Rurik dynasty, however, abruptly precipitated his downfall. The Russian State now disintegrated into near chaos with the Time of Troubles (1605–13), a delayed-action political sequel to the economic collapse of the 1580's. Succession intrigues and rival usurpations, magnate conflicts within the boyar class, and foreign invasions from Poland and Sweden, criss-crossed the country. The multiple splits in the ruling order now permitted a Cossack-led peasant rebellion of the type that was to punctuate the next two centuries, Bolotnikov's insurrection in 1606–7. Led by a runaway slave turned freebooter, a motley popular force drawn from the towns and country-

---

large-scale production, but the active intervention of the superstructure (with the mighty instruments of a strong feudal state) within economic relations in the interests of the gentry, not only hindered the development of new relations, but undermined the condition of the whole economy of the country': *Razvitie Tovarno-Denezhnykh Otnoshenii*, pp. 200–1. The *oprichnina*, once presented as a salutary anti-feudal episode, becomes in this version a maleficent instrument of feudal reaction, capable of diverting the whole of Russian history from its previously progressive course. Such a judgement is manifestly unhistorical.

10. V. I. Koretsky, *Zakreposhchenie Krest'yan i Klassovaya Bora v Rossii vo Vtoroi Polovine XVI v*, Moscow 1970, p. 302. Koretsky's research has pin-

side of the South-West marched on Moscow, attempting to raise the urban poor of the capital against the usurper boyar regime in power. This threat rapidly united mutually hostile gentry and magnate armies against the insurgents, who were eventually defeated at Tula.[11] But the first social revolt from below against the growth of seigneurial repression and serfdom was a warning to the landowning classes as a whole of possible storms to come.

By 1613, the aristocracy had closed ranks sufficiently to elect the young boyar Michael Romanov to become Emperor. The advent of the Romanov dynasty, indeed, was now slowly to replant an Absolutism in Russia that was not to be uprooted for 300 years. The central clique of boyar and *d'iak* functionaries who had secured Michael I's elevation preserved for a transitional period the Zemsky Sobor which had formally voted it. Energetic recovery of fugitive peasants, including those who had enrolled in the anti-foreign militias of the Time of Troubles, was implemented by the new government in response to gentry demands, as economic production revived. The Patriarch Filaret, Michael's father, who became the real ruler of the country in 1619, provided further emollients to the *pomeshchik* class by handing over to it black-earth peasant lands in the North. But the basic character and orientation of the new Romanov regime was magnate, determined by the interests of the metropolitan boyars and venal bureaucrats of the capital, rather than the provincial gentry.[12] The 17th century henceforward witnessed a growing divorce and conflict between the mass of the *pomeshchik* service class – numerically the largest group of Russian landowners, some 25,000 strong – and the Absolutist State, of a type which was common to most European countries in the same epoch, but which assumed peculiar features in the

---

pointed more accurately than any previous work the precise phases and circumstances of legal adscription in the late 16th century: for his discussion of Godunov's presumptive decree, whose text has not been recovered, see pp. 123–5, 127–34.

11. For Bolotnikov's revolt, see Paul Avrich, *Russian Rebels*, London 1973, pp. 20–32.

12. J. L. H. Keep, 'The Decline of the Zemsky Sobor', *Slavonic and East European Review*, 36, 1957–8, pp. 105–7; and 'The Regime of Filaret 1619–1633', *Slavonic and East European Review*, 38, 1960, pp. 334–60, which provides a judicious account of the general policies of the Patriarch.

more backward Eastern environment. The small boyar elite of the Russian aristocracy – some 40 to 60 families – was vastly richer than the rank-and-file gentry: it was also highly heterogeneous in character, its original Tartar admixture receiving Polish, Lithuanian, German and Swedish infusions in the course of the 17th century. It enjoyed close links with the top echelons of the central bureaucracy, which were juridically adjacent to it in the complex stratification of ranks in the Muscovite service hierarchy, both groups holding positions well above the gentry itself. It was this magnate-official complex, itself constantly divided by personal or factional feuds, which erratically steered government policies from Moscow in the early Romanov epoch.

Two major contradictions separated it from the service gentry. Firstly, the military superiority of Sweden and Poland – proven in the Livonian Wars and confirmed once again during the Time of Troubles – dictated the renovation and modernization of the Russian Army. The haphazard *pomeshchik* cavalry, innocent of either concerted discipline or regular fire-power, was an anachronism in the age of the Thirty Years' War in Europe, as were the demoralized urban *strel'tsy*: the future lay with trained infantry regiments, used in line formations and equipped with light muskets, combined with picked dragoons. Filaret's regime therefore started to build up permanent troops of this type, employing foreign officers and mercenaries. The service gentry, however, refused to adapt to the contemporary forms of warfare and join these Western-style regiments, which were first used in the unsuccessful Smolensk War with Poland (1632–4).[13] Thereafter, a widening divergence developed between the nominal service role of the *pomeshchik* class and the actual structure and composition of the Russian armed forces, which came more and more to consist of professional regiments of new-style infantry and cavalry, rather than seasonal levies of mounted gentry. The whole military rationale of the latter was increasingly threatened from the 1630's onwards, its traditional performance becoming obsolete and redundant. At the same time, there was constant boyar-gentry friction within the landed class as a whole over the disposal of the rural labour-force. For although the Russian peasantry was now legally bound to the soil, flights were still widespread amidst the immense and primitive expanse of the country, with

13. Hellie, *Enserfment and Military Change*, pp. 164–74.

its lack of any clearly defined frontiers in the North, East and South. In practice, larger magnates could lure serfs from the estates of smaller squires to their own latifundia, where agrarian conditions were usually more secure and prosperous, and feudal exactions correspondingly less onerous. The gentry thus clamoured ravenously for the abrogation of all restrictions on the recovery of fugitive peasants, while the magnates manoeuvred successfully to maintain the legal time-limits after which forcible recuperation was no longer possible – ten years after 1615, five years (under increasing *pomeshchik* pressure) after 1642. The tension between boyars and squires over the anti-fugitive laws was one of the leit-motifs of the epoch, and gentry turbulence in the capital was repeatedly used to extract concessions from the Tsar and higher nobility.[14] On the other hand, neither military nor economic conflicts of interest, however temporarily acute, could override the fundamental social unity of the landowning class as a whole against the exploited rural and urban masses. The great popular upheavals from below in the 17th and 18th centuries invariably acted to re-cement the solidarity of the feudal aristocracy above it.[15]

14. N. I. Pavlenko, 'K Voprosu o Genezisa Absoliutizma v Rossii', *Istoriya SSSR*, April 1970, pp. 78–9. Pavlenko correctly rejects the idea advanced by other participants in current Soviet historiographic discussion, under the influence of Engels's famous formula, that the urban bourgeoisie played any central or independent role in the advent of Russian Absolutism – stressing, by contrast, the importance of inter-feudal frictions between large and small land-owners. The latter are extensively explored by Hellie, *Enserfment and Military Change*, pp. 102–6, 114, 128–38.

15. This is acknowledged, but never adequately integrated into his general analysis, by Hellie. The major weakness of his book is its unduly restrictive notion of the State: Russian 'government' is frequently reduced to the uppermost handful of magnates and counsellers in Moscow, and its 'purposes' to their adventitious private appetites, precluding any concern with adscription of the peasantry (*Enserfment and Military Change*, p. 146). The result is to divorce the social process of enserfment from the political structure of the State, by conjuring away the basic unity of the landed class which determined their linkage. Serfdom becomes a fortuitous and illogical product of the crisis of 1648, an unpredictable concession to the gentry at the very moment when they had lost their military utility to the State, which might otherwise never have occurred (p. 134). In fact, it is obvious that two centuries of Russian serfdom did not depend on the 'chance' events of one year. Hellie's own account subsequently demonstrates that the fundamental relationship between the boyar and gentry sections of the landowning class was not governed by their respective administrative roles or labour facilities, but by their common control of the major means of production, and

It was just such a conjuncture which led to the final codification of Russian serfdom. In 1648, tax and price increases provoked violent artisan riots in Moscow, combined with a flare-up of peasant revolts in the provinces, and a mutiny of the *strel'tsy*. Alarmed by these renewed dangers, the current boyar government accepted a rapid convocation of the decisive Zemsky Sobor which finally lifted all limits on the forcible reclamation of fugitive peasants – thereby conceding the fundamental programme of the provincial gentry, and rallying them to the central State. The Zemsky Sobor now drew up the comprehensive legal code that was to be the social charter of Russian Absolutism. The *Sobornoe Ulozhenie* of 1649 definitively codified and promulgated the serfdom of the peasantry, which was henceforward bound irreversibly to the soil. Both *votchina* and *pomest'e* lands were declared hereditary, and sale or purchase of the latter was banned: all estates were henceforward liable for military service.[16] Towns were subjected to tighter controls by the Tsar than ever before, and sealed meticulously off from the rest of the country: their *posadskie* poor were assimilated to state serfs, only tax-payers could be resident in them, and no inhabitant could leave without royal permission. The top merchant stratum of *gosti* received monopoly privileges in trade and manufacturing, but in fact the future growth of the towns was choked off by the cessation of rural migration to them with the generalization of adscription, which inevitably created scarcity of labour in the small urban sector of the economy. The similarity of the Russian *Ulozhenie* to the Prussian *Recess* of four years later needs no emphasis. Both laid the foundations for Absolutism by a compact between monarchy and nobility, in which the political fealty sought by the one was exchanged for the patrimonial serfdom demanded by the other.

The last half of the century revealed the solidity of this union by the

---

joint interest in the exploitation and repression of the peasantry. The numerous and serious disputes between them always remained within this structural framework: hence their instinctive solidarity in social crises, when State power and agrarian property alike were threatened by peasant insurgency.

16. The main provisions of the *Ulozhenie* are set out in Vernadsky, *The Tsardom of Moscow*, I, pp. 399–411. The remaining municipal autonomy of Novgorod and Pskov was also terminated by the new code: L. A. Fedosov, 'Sotsialnaya Sushchnost' i Evoliutsiya Rossiiskovo Absoliutizma', *Voprosy Istorii*, July 1971, pp. 52–3.

very intensity of the political tests to which it was put. The Zemsky
Sobor, soon rendered redundant, faded away after 1653. In the next
year, the Ukrainian Cossacks formally transferred their allegiance to
Russia with the Treaty of Pereyaslavl; the result was the Thirteen
Years' War with Poland. Tsarist troops pushed forward with initial success, taking Smolensk and advancing into Lithuania, where Wilno was
captured. The Swedish attack on Poland of 1655 soon complicated the
strategic situation, however; Polish recovery led to a decade of costly
fighting, and in the end Russian territorial gains proved limited, if still
substantial. By the Treaty of Andrussovo in 1667, the Tsarist State
acquired the eastern half of the Ukraine beyond the Dnieper, including
Kiev, and recovered the Smolensk region to the north. In the next
decade, massive Turkish thrusts into the South from the Black Sea
were painfully checked, at the price of making a wilderness of much of
the settled Ukraine. These moderate external successes were, meanwhile, accompanied by radical internal changes in the nature of the
military apparatus of emergent Russian Absolutism. For it was during
this period, as the Estates system waned, that the Army steadily waxed,
eventually more than doubling in size from 1630 to 1681, when it
numbered 200,000 – up to the levels of the largest Western military
establishments of the time.[17] The role of the unreconstructed *pomeshchik* levies declined commensurately. Not only did the new fortified
Belgorod line increasingly immunize the Southern frontier from the
Crimean Tartar raids against which they had originally been pitted.
Above all, semi-permanent 'new formation' regiments became the
dominant component of Russia's armies during the Thirteen Years'
War with Poland. By 1674, the gentry provided only two-fifths of the
cavalry, itself henceforward strategically outweighed by the hand-gun
infantry. Meanwhile, the *pomeshchiki* were being equally edged out of
the civilian administration. Predominant in the central chancelleries
during the 16th century, they were increasingly excluded from the
bureaucracy in the 17th century, which came to be the preserve of a

17. For computations of the size of the armed forces during the 17th century,
see Hellie, *Enserfment and Military Change*, pp. 267–9 who incorrectly claims
that by the late 1670's the Russian army was 'much the largest in Europe' (p. 226).
In fact, the French military establishment was at least as great, and probably
greater. But the comparative size – if not yet the skill – of the Muscovite armed
forces was all the same formidable.

quasi-hereditary caste of clerks at lower levels, and corrupt high-ranking officials linked to the magnates in its upper reaches.[18] In 1679, moreover, the Romanov dynasty abolished the local *guba* self-administration which had previously been run by provincial squires, integrating it into the central machinery of *voevoda* governorships, appointed from Moscow.

Nor was the labour situation on the *pomeshchik* estates very satisfactory. Further laws making peasant flights a criminal felony were passed in 1658, but the continued existence of the Southern borderlands and the Siberian wilds left significant territorial loopholes in the legal consolidation of serfdom, although within the Central regions of the country the debasement of the peasantry became ever more marked: while taxes trebled in the course of the 17th century, the average peasant plot declined by a half from 1550 to 1660, to a mere 4 or 5 acres.[19] This relentless constriction of the peasant condition set off the great rural insurrection of cossacks, serfs, suburban poor and slaves in the South-East, led by Razin in 1670 – rallying dispossessed Chuvash, Mari, and Mordva tribesmen, and setting off popular outbreaks in the towns along the Volga valley. The extreme social peril this spreading jacquerie posed to the entire ruling class immediately welded boyars and gentry together: the acute intra-landowner strains of recent decades were forgotten in a common and implacable repression of the poor. The military victory of the Tsarist State over the Razin rebellion, in which the new permanent regiments played an indispensable role, re-bonded the monarchy and nobility once again. In the last two decades of the century, it was the turn of the boyar magnates – hitherto the shifting forces behind successive *fainéant* tsars – to be curbed and remoulded by the exigencies of an ascendant Absolutism. The great potentates who had emerged from the Time of Troubles were often of mixed provenance and recent origin: they had little reason to cling to the antiquated and divisive hierarchy of the *mestnichestvo* or labyrinthine ranking system within the boyar families, which dated from the 14th century, and was deleterious to the command system of the new military apparatus of the State. In 1682, the Tsar Theodore ceremoniously burned the venerable books of ancestral precedence that

18. Hellie, *Enserfment and Military Change*, pp. 70–2.
19. *Ibid.*, pp. 372, 229.

recorded this hierarchy, which was therewith abolished – a precondition of wider aristocratic unity.[20] The stage was now set for a drastic reconstruction of the whole political order of Russian Absolutism.

The State machine erected over these new social foundations was above all, of course, the monumental work of Peter I. His first move on acceding to power was to disband the old and unreliable *strel'tsy* militia in Moscow, whose turbulence had been a frequent source of disquiet to his predecessors, and to create the crack Preobrazhensky and Semenovsky guards regiments which were henceforward the elite corps of the Tsarist repressive apparatus.[21] The traditional duality between boyar and gentry sections of the landowning class was recast by the creation of a new and comprehensive ranking system, and the universalization of the service principle, which yoked both nobles and squires back into a single political framework. New titles were imported from Denmark and Prussia (Count, Baron) to introduce more sophisticated and modern scales within the aristocracy, henceforward socially and etymologically derivative *en bloc* from the court (*dvoriantsvo*). Independent magnate power was ruthlessly suppressed; the Boyar Duma was eliminated, and succeeded by an appointed Senate. The gentry were reincorporated into a modernized army and administration, of which they once again made up the central personnel.[22] The *votchina* and *pomest'e* were united into a single pattern of hereditary landownership, and the nobility soldered to the State by universal service obligations, from the age of 14 onwards, in the army and bureaucracy. To finance the latter institutions, a new census of the population was drawn up, and former slaves were merged with the serf class, while serfs were henceforward bound to the person of their lord rather than to the land which they tilled and could thus be sold like Prussian *Leibeigene*, by their masters. Formerly free black-earth communities in the North and colonists in Siberia became by the same stroke 'state serfs', their conditions somewhat superior to that of private serfs, but increasingly degraded towards it. The Patriarchate was

20. J. L. H. Keep, 'The Muscovite Elite and the Approach to Pluralism', *Slavonic and East European Review*, XLVIII, 1970, pp. 217–18.

21. M. Ya. Volkov, 'O Stanovlenii Absoliutizma v Rossii', *Istoriya SSSR*, January 1970, p. 104. A third regiment of Bodyguards or household cavalry was also formed.

22. Hellie, *Enserfment and Military Change*, p. 260.

abolished, and the Church firmly subordinated to the State by the new office of the Holy Synod, whose highest official was a secular functionary. A new, occidentalized capital was built at St Petersburg. The administrative system was reorganized into gubernias, provinces and districts, and the size of the bureaucracy doubled.[23] Government departments were concentrated into nine central 'Colleges', run by collective boards. A modern iron industry was installed in the Urals, which was to make Russia one of the largest metal producers of the epoch. The budget was quadrupled, largely with resources from a new soul tax on serfs. Average peasant taxes quintupled from 1700 to 1707–8.

The bulk of this greatly enlarged State revenue – two-thirds to four-fifths – was devoted to the construction of a professional army and modern navy:[24] the two over-riding goals of the whole Petrine programme, to which all other measures were subordinated. In the Great Northern War from 1700 to 1721, the Swedish assault on Russia was initially successful: Charles XII routed Tsarist forces at Narva, overran Poland and raised the Cossack hetman Mazeppa against Peter I in the Ukraine. The Russian victory of Poltava in 1709, completed by naval triumph in the Gulf of Finland and invasion of Sweden itself, reversed the whole balance of forces in Eastern Europe. Swedish power was finally repulsed and defeated, and with its fall two decisive geopolitical gains were made by the Tsarist Empire. By the Treaty of Nystadt in 1721, the Russian frontiers at last reached the Baltic: Livonia, Estonia, Ingria and Karelia were annexed, and direct maritime access to the West was assured. In the South, Turkish armies had nearly inflicted catastrophe on over-extended Russian troops in a separate conflict, and the Tsar was fortunate to extricate himself without serious losses. No significant gains were secured along the Black Sea: but the menace of the free-booting *Sech* of the Zaporozhe Cossacks, who had always hindered any permanent settlement of the Ukrainian hinterland, was brought to an end with the suppression of Mazeppa's rebellion. Russian Absolutism emerged from the twenty-year struggle of the Great Northern War a looming force over Eastern

23. I. A. Fedosov, 'Sotsialnaya Sushchnost' i Evoliutsiya Rossiiskovo Absoliutizma', pp. 57–60.

24. Hellie, *Enserfment and Military Change*, p. 256. For tax-increases, see Avrich, *Russian Rebels*, p. 139.

Europe. Domestically, Bulavin's rebellion against official serf-recovery and labour-conscription in the lower Don region was successfully suppressed, and the more protracted Bashkir revolt against Russian colonization in the Ural-Volga region was isolated and defeated. Yet the profile of the Petrine State, with its tireless coercion and territorial advances, must be set against the dismal backwardness of its environment, which deeply affected its real character. For all the reorganization and repression exercised by Peter I, haphazard corruption and peculation were endemic: one guess is that perhaps only a third of tax-revenues actually reached the State.[25] The forcible attempt to draft the whole nobility for life into the services of Tsarism proved supernumerary soon after Peter's death. For once an aristocracy inured to Absolutism was solidly formed and stabilized, Peter's successors could afford to relax and then eliminate the compulsory character of its obligations, which were terminated by his grandson Peter III in 1762; by then the gentry was securely and spontaneously integrated into the apparatus of the State.

Under a succession of weak rulers – Catherine I, Peter II, Anna and Elizabeth – the Guards Regiments which Peter I had created became after his death the cockpit of magnate struggles for power in St Petersburg, whose very putsches were a tribute to the consolidation of the Tsarist institutional complex: nobles henceforward intrigued within the Autocracy, not against it.[26] The arrival of another resolute sovereign in 1762 was thus the signal, not for an outbreak of tension between the monarchy and nobility, but for their most harmonious reconciliation. Catherine II proved to be the most ideologically conscious ruler of Russia and the most amply generous to her class. Aspiring to a European reputation for political Enlightenment, she promulgated a new educational system, secularized church lands, and promoted a mercantilist development of the Russian economy. The currency was stabilized, the iron industry expanded, and the volume of foreign trade increased. The two great landmarks of Catherine II's reign, however, were the extension of organized serf agriculture to the

25. Dorn, *Competition for Empire*, p. 70. Prussian tax revenues were greater than those of Russia in the 1760's, with a population a third the size.

26. The one attempt to impose constitutional limitations on the monarchy was Golitsyn's scheme for rule by an oligarchic Privy Council in 1730, vaguely inspired by Swedish example; it was speedily scotched by a Guards revolt.

whole of the Ukraine, and the promulgation of the Charter of the Nobility. The condition of the first was the destruction of the Tartar Khanate of the Crimea, and the breaking of Ottoman power along the northern coastline of the Black Sea. The Crimean Khanate, as a Turkish vassal state, not only kept Russia out of the Euxine: its perpetual raiding churned and devastated the Pontic plains inland, keeping much of the Ukraine an insecure and depopulated no-man's-land long after its formal incorporation into the Romanov realm. The new Empress directed the full force of the Russian armies against Islamic control of the Black Sea. By 1774, the Khanate had been detached from the Porte, and the Ottoman frontier pushed back to the Bug. In 1783, the Crimea was annexed outright. A decade later, the Russian border had reached the Dniester. Sevastopol and Odessa were founded on the new Tsarist littoral; naval entry into the Mediterranean through the Straits appeared to be within reach.

Much more important in the short-run, however, were the consequences of this Southern advance for Russian agriculture. The final elimination of the Tartar Khanate permitted the organized settlement and reclamation of the vast Ukrainian steppes, large tracts of which were now for the first time converted into arable tillage and planted with a stable, sedentary peasant population on large estates. Managed by Potemkin, the agrarian colonization of the Ukraine represented probably the largest single geographical clearance in the history of European feudal agriculture. No technical progress in the rural economy was registered by this great territorial advance, however: it was a purely extensive gain. Socially, it subjugated the once free or semi-free inhabitants of the border regions to the condition of the central peasantry, increasing the total serf population of Russia steeply. During Catherine II's reign, the volume of money rents paid by serfs increased in some cases up to five times over; any upper limit on the extraction of labour services was rejected by the government; huge numbers of State peasants were handed over to leading nobles for intensified private exploitation. This dramatic, concluding episode of the enserfment of the rural masses was met by the last and greatest of the cossack-inspired rebellions, led by Pugachev – a seismic revolt that shook the whole Volga and Ural regions, mobilizing huge, confused masses of peasants, iron-workers, nomads, mountaineers, heretics and homesteaders in a final, desperate assault on the ruling order.[27] The Tsarist towns and garrisons held firm, however, while the imperial army was deployed to crush the revolt. Its defeat marked the closure of the Eastern frontier. Russian villages sank into stillness thereafter. The Charter of the Nobility granted by the Empress in 1785 completed the long journey of the peasantry into servitude. By it, Catherine II guaranteed the aristocracy all its privileges, released it from compulsory duties, and ensured it total jurisdictional control of its rural labour force: devolution of a measure of provincial administration smoothly transferred local functions to the gentry.[28] The typical parabola of ascendant Absolutism was now complete. The monarchy had risen in concord with the gentry in the 16th century (Ivan IV); they had at times clashed violently in the 17th century, amidst magnate predominance, complex shifts and dislocations within the State, and social turbulence outside it (Michael I); the monarchy had achieved an implacable autocracy by the early 18th century (Peter I); nobility and monarchy thereafter regained a reciprocal serenity and harmony (Catherine II).

The strength of Russian Absolutism was soon revealed in its international successes. Catherine II, the main initiator of the Partitions of Poland, was also their major beneficiary when the operation was completed in 1795. The Tsarist Empire was increased by some 200,000 square miles, and now stretched nearly to the Vistula. Within the next decade, Georgia was annexed in the Caucasus. It was the grandiose trial of strength constituted by the Napoleonic Wars, however, which demonstrated the new European pre-eminence of the Tsarist State.

27. Avrich deems Pugachev's rebellion the most formidable mass upheaval in Europe between the English and French Revolutions: for his analysis of its varied social composition, see *Russian Rebels*, pp. 196–225. The progressive geographical shift in the series of Russian peasant revolts, from Bolotnikov to Pugachev, is evident: they moved in a wide band from the South towards the East, along the least administered and controlled sectors of the frontier. No major upheaval ever occurred in the Central provinces of traditional Muscovy, by contrast – with their older settlement, ethnic homogeneity, and proximity to the capital.

28. Dukes, in a carefully documented volume, concludes that the 'subservience' of the Russian nobility to the Tsarist Autocracy has been much exaggerated: there was rather an easy social unity between the two. Paul Dukes, *Catherine the Great and the Russian Nobility*, Cambridge 1967, pp. 248–50.

Socially and economically the most backward Absolutism in the East, Russia proved politically and militarily the only *ancien régime*, from one end of the continent to the other, to be capable of withstanding French attack. Already in the last decade of the 18th century, Russian armies were for the first time in history dispatched deep into the West – into Italy, Switzerland and Holland – to stamp out the flames of the bourgeois revolution still fanned by the Consulate. The new Tsar Alexander I participated in the unsuccessful Third and Fourth Coalitions against Napoleon. But while Austrian and Prussian Absolutism were undone at Ulm and Wagram, Jena and Auerstadt, Russian Absolutism won a respite at Tilsit. The division of spheres concluded between the two Emperors in 1807 permitted Russia to proceed to the conquest of Finland (1809) and Bessarabia (1812), at the expense of Sweden and Turkey. Finally, when Napoleon launched his full-scale invasion of Russia, the *Grande Armée* proved incapable of smashing the structure of the Tsarist State. Victorious at the outset on the field, the French attack was ostensibly ruined by climate and logistics; but in reality by the impenetrable resistance of a feudal environment too primitive to be vulnerable to the blade of bourgeois expansion and emancipation from the West, now long blunted by Bonapartism.[29] The retreat from Moscow signalled the end of French dominance throughout the continent: within two years, Russian troops were bivouacked in Paris. Tsarism crossed into the 19th century the victorious gendarme of European counter-revolution. The Congress of Vienna sealed its triumph: another great wedge of Poland was annexed, and Warsaw became a Russian city. Three months later the Holy Alliance was solemnized, at the personal insistence of Alexander I, to guarantee royal and clerical restorationism from the Guadarrama to the Urals.

The structures of the Tsarist State which emerged from the Vienna

29. The absence of any radical middle-class in Russia deprived the French invasion of any local political resonance. Napoleon refused to countenance emancipation of the serfs during his advance into Russia, although peasant deputations initially welcomed him, and the Governor-General of Moscow lived in fear of urban and rural rebellions against the Tsarist government. Napoleon, however, planned to come to a deal with Alexander I after defeating him, as he had done with Francis II, and did not intend to compromise this prospect with irreparable social measures in Russia. See the perceptive comments of Seton-Watson, *The Russian Empire*, pp. 129–30, 133.

settlement, untouched by any transformation comparable to the Austrian or Prussian Reforms, had no parallel anywhere in Europe. The State was officially proclaimed an Autocracy: the Tsar ruled for the whole nobility, in his name alone.[30] Under him, a feudal hierarchy was cemented into the very rungs of the State system itself. By a decree of Nicholas I in 1831, a modernized hierarchy of ranks was created within the noble class corresponding to the stepped echelons of the State bureaucracy. Vice-versa, all those occupying determinate positions in the service of the State were given corresponding noble rank, which above certain levels became hereditary. Aristocratic titles and privileges thus continued to be related by the political system to different administrative functions, down to 1917. The landowning class thus welded to the State controlled some 21,000,000 serfs. It was itself highly stratified: four-fifths of these serfs were tied to the lands of one-fifth of proprietors, while the greatest nobles – a mere 1 per cent of the *dvoriantsvo* as a whole – owned estates with nearly one-third of the total population of private serfs. Petty squires with holdings of less than 21 souls were excluded from gentry assemblies from 1831–2 onwards. The Russian aristocracy retained its service orientation down into the 19th century, and its aversion from agrarian management. Few gentry families had local roots going back more than 2 or 3 generations, and absentee ownership was widespread: urban residence – provincial or metropolitan – was the normal ideal of the middle and upper aristocracy alike.[31] Positions in the State apparatus were the by now traditional means of achieving it.

The State itself owned land with 20,000,000 serfs on it – two-fifths of the peasant population of Russia. It was thus directly the most colossal feudal proprietor in the country. The Army was built on random conscription of serfs, with the hereditary nobility dominating its command structure, in accordance with its rank. The Grand Dukes occupied the General Inspectorates of the Army and the War Council: down to and into the First World War, the Commanders-in-Chief were the cousins or uncles of the Tsar. The Church was a subdivision

30. H. Seton-Watson, *The Decline of Imperial Russia*, London 1964, pp. 5–27 provides a clear general survey of Russian society under Nicholas I.

31. T. Emmons, *The Russian Landed Gentry and the Peasant Emancipation of 1861*, Cambridge 1968, pp. 3–11.

of the State, subordinated to a bureaucratic department (the Holy Synod) whose head – the Senior Procurator – was a civil official designated by the Tsar. The Synod had the status of a Ministry, with an Economic Administration dealing with Church Property, and was mainly staffed by lay officials. Priests were treated as functionaries, who owed duties to the government (they had to report confessions which revealed 'evil intent' towards the State). The educational system was contolled by the State, and Rectors and Professors of Universities were by mid-century appointed directly by the Tsar and his Ministers. The vast, proliferating bureaucracy was integrated at the top only by the person of the Autocrat, and the corridor rule of his private chancellery[32] – there were Ministers, but no Cabinet, three competing swarms of police, and generalized peculation. The ideology of clerical and chauvinist reaction which presided over this system was proclaimed by the official trinity: Autocracy, Orthodoxy, Nationality. The military and political power of the Tsarist State in the first half of the 19th century found continued demonstration in foreign expansion and interventionism. Azerbaijan and Armenia were occupied, and mountaineer resistance in Circassia and Daghestan gradually broken; neither Persia nor Turkey was in any position to resist Russian annexations in the Caucasus. In Europe itself, Russian armies struck down the national revolt in Poland in 1830, and wiped out the revolution in Hungary in 1849. Nicholas I, high executioner of monarchist reaction abroad, ruled at home over the only major country in the continent unaffected by the popular upsurges of 1848. The international strength of Tsarism had never seemed greater.

In fact, the industrialization of Western Europe was rendering its confidence anachronistic. The first serious shock to Russian Absolutism came with the humiliating setback inflicted on it by the capitalist States of England and France, in the Crimean War of 1854–6. The fall of Sevastopol can be compared in its domestic consequences with the

32. Soviet historians tend to interpret the Personal Chancellery, which descended from Peter I's *Preobraʒhensky Prikaʒ*, as a 'dualist' decomposition of Absolutist centralization, and a symptom of the administrative decadence of Tsarism by the 19th century. See, for example, A. Avrekh, 'Russkii Absoliutizm i Evo Rol' v Utverzhdenii Kapitalizma v Rossii', *Istoriya SSSR*, February 1968, p. 100; I. A. Fedosov, 'Sotsialnaya Sushchnost' Evoliutsiya Rossiiskovo Absoliutizma', *Voprosy Istorii*, July 1971, p. 63.

rout at Jena. Military defeat by the West led to the abolition of serfdom by Alexander II, as the most elementary social modernization of the bases of the *ancien régime*. But the parallel should not be exaggerated. For the extent of the blow to Tsarism was a much milder and more limited one: the Peace of Paris was by no means the Treaty of Tilsit. The Russian 'Reform Era' of the 1860's was thus only a faint echo of its Prussian predecessor. Juridical procedures were somewhat liberalized; the rural nobility was given *zemstvo* organs of self-administration; municipal councils were conferred on the towns; general conscription was introduced. Alexander's emancipation of the peasantry in 1861 was itself executed in a fashion no less lucrative to the *dvoriantsvo* than Hardenberg's had been to the junkers. Serfs were allocated the land they had previously cultivated from noble estates, in exchange for payment of monetary compensation to their lords. The State advanced this compensation to the aristocracy, and then reclaimed it over a period of years from the peasantry, in the form of 'redemption payments'. In Northern Russia, where land values were low and servile dues were paid in kind (*obrok*), the landowners extorted nearly twice the market price of the land in cash compensation. In Southern Russia, where servile dues took the form mainly of labour services (*barshchina*) and the rich, black soil permitted profitable cereal exports, the gentry defrauded their peasants of up to 25 per cent of the best land owing to them (the so-called *otrezki*).[33] The peasantry, weighed down with redemption debts, thus suffered a net subtraction from the total land they had previously cultivated for their families. Moreover, the abolition of serfdom did not mean the end of feudal relations in the countryside, any more than it had done earlier in Western Europe. In practice, a labyrinth of traditional forms of extra-economic surplus extraction, embodied in customary rights and dues, continued to prevail on Russian estates.

In his pioneering study on *The Development of Capitalism in Russia*, Lenin wrote that after the abolition of serfdom, the 'capitalist economy could not emerge at once, and the *corvée* economy could not disappear at once. The only possible system of economy was, accordingly, a transitional one, a system combining the features of both the *corvée*

33. Geroid T. Robinson, *Rural Russia under the Old Regime*, New York 1932, pp. 87–8.

and the capitalist systems. Indeed, the post-Reform system of farming practised by the landlords bears precisely those features. With all the endless variety of forms characteristic of a transitional epoch, the economic organization of contemporary landlord farming amounts to two main systems – the *labour-service* system and the *capitalist* system. . . . The systems mentioned are actually interwoven in the most varied and fantastic fashion: on a mass of landlord estates there is a combination of the two systems, which are applied to quite different farming operations.'[34] Computing the relative incidence of the two economies, Lenin calculated that by 1899 'although the labour-service system predominates in the purely Russian gubernias, the capitalist system of landlord farming must be considered the predominant one at present in European Russia as a whole'.[35] A decade later, however, the tremendous peasant upsurges against the feudal exactions and oppressions of the Russian countryside during the 1905 Revolution led Lenin to modify the balance of this judgement significantly. In his basic text of 1907, *The Agrarian Programme of Social-Democracy in the First Russian Revolution*, he stressed that: 'In the purely Russian gubernias large-scale capitalist farming definitely drops into the background. Small-scale farming preponderates on large latifundia, comprising various forms of tenant farming based on servitude and bondage.'[36] After a careful statistical assessment of the whole agrarian situation, covering the distribution of land during the first year of the Stolypin reaction, Lenin summed up his survey with the following general conclusion: 'Ten and a half million peasant households in European Russia own 75,000,000 dessiatins of land. Thirty thousand, chiefly noble, but partly also upstart, landlords each own 500 dessiatins – altogether 70,000,000 dessiatins. Such is the main background of the picture. Such are the main reasons for the predominance of feudal landlords in the agricultural system of Russia and, consequently, in the Russian State generally, and in the whoe of Russian life. The owners of the latifundia are feudal landlords in the economic sense of the term: the basis of their landownership was created by the history of serfdom, by the history of land-grabbing by the nobility through the centuries.

34. V. I. Lenin, *Collected Works*, Vol. 3, Moscow 1964, pp. 194–5.
35. *Ibid.*, p. 197.
36. *Ibid.*, Vol. 13, p. 225.

The basis of their present methods of farming is the labour-service system, i.e. a direct survival of the *corvée*, cultivation of the land with the implements of the peasants and by the virtual enslavement of the small tillers in an endless variety of ways: winter hiring, annual leases, half-share *métayage*, leases based on labour rent, bondage for debt, bondage for cut-off lands, for the use of forests, meadows, water, and so on and so forth, *ad infinitum*.'[37] Five years later, Lenin reaffirmed this judgement even more categorically, on the eve of the First World War: 'The difference between "Europe" and Russia stems from Russia's extreme backwardness. In the West, the bourgeois agrarian system is fully established, feudalism was swept away long ago, and its survivals are negligible and play no serious role. The predominant type of social relationship in Western agriculture is that between the *wage-labourer* and the employer, the farmer or landowner. . . . Undoubtedly a system of agriculture just as capitalist has already become firmly established and is steadily developing in Russia. It is in this direction that both landlord and peasant farming is developing. But purely capitalist relations in our country are still overshadowed to a *tremendous* extent by *feudal* relations.'[38]

The capitalist development within Russian agriculture which Lenin and other socialists predicted would occur if Tsarism succeeded in re-establishing its power durably after the counter-revolution of 1907, was the 'Prussian road' of rationalized junker-type estates using wage-labour and integrated into the world market, accompanied by the emergence of a stratum of auxiliary *Grossbauern* in the countryside. Lenin's writings in the period 1906–14 repeatedly warn that such an evolution was possible in Tsarist Russia, and was a serious danger to the revolutionary movement. Stolypin's reforms, in particular, were designed to accelerate just such an evolution by their 'wager on the strong' – the conversion of repartitional into hereditary peasant tenure in the villages, in order to promote the rise of a kulak class. In fact, Stolypin's programme fell considerably short of its objective at the level of the peasantry itself. For while half of all peasant households

37. Lenin, *Collected Works*, Vol. 13, p. 421.
38. Lenin, *Collected Works*, Vol. 18, p. 74. This important article, 'The Essence of "The Agrarian Problem of Russia" ', written in May 1912, is normally overlooked by students of Lenin's writings on the subject.

had juridically hereditary plots by 1915, only one-tenth of them had allotments that were physically consolidated into single units: the survival of the separate-strip and open-field system ensured that the communal constraints of the village *mir* thus remained.[39] Meanwhile, the burden of redemption arrears and taxes increased year by year. The instinctive solidarity of the Russian peasantry against the landowning class was not seriously breached by the reforms. The Bolsheviks were to be surprised by the passionate unity of popular anti-feudal sentiment in the countryside in 1917, as Trotsky later testified.[40] Over-population in the villages became an endemic problem in late Tsarist Russia. The share of peasant farms in total landed property increased by a half – mainly kulak purchases – in the last four decades before 1917, while actual *per capita* holdings of the peasantry dropped by a third.[41] The rural masses remained mired in secular backwardness and poverty.

On the other hand, the last decades of Tsarism did not witness a dynamic conversion of the landowning nobility to capitalist agriculture either. The fears of a 'Prussian Road' did not, in fact, materialize. The *dvoriantsvo* proved organically incapable of following the path of the junkers. Initially, the shake-out in noble estate ownership looked as if the Prussian experience might repeat itself, a re-selection and rationalization of the landowning class. For there was a decline in gentry-owned land of perhaps a third in the three decades before 1905, and the major purchasers – as in Prussia – were initially wealthy merchants and bourgeois. However, after the 1880's, rich peasant acquisitions overtook those of urban investors. By 1905, the average merchant estate was larger than that of the average noble, but kulak gains in total acreage were half as great again as those of townsmen.[42] Thus a stratum of *Grossbauern* was, in fact, clearly emerging in Russia before the First

39. Robinson, *Rural Russia under the Old Regime*, pp. 213–18.

40. *History of the Russian Revolution*, London 1965, Vol. I, pp. 377–9. It should be added that there were widespread attacks in 1917 by villagers on 'secessionist' peasants who had taken advantage of Stolypin's reforms to leave their communes, and lands were now collectively repossessed by them, such was the strength of solidary feelings among the mass of the peasantry. See Launcelot Owen, *The Russian Peasant Movement 1906–1917*, New York 1963, pp. 153–4, 165–72, 182–3, 200–2, 209–11, 234–5.

41. Owen, *The Russian Peasant Movement*, p. 6. Population increased from some 74 million in 1860 to 170 million in 1916.

42. Robinson, *Rural Russia under the Old Regime*, pp. 131–5.

World War. But what was completely missing was any capitalist jump in productivy of the Prussian type. Grain exports to Europe, of course, developed throughout the century, both before and after the Reform of 1861: Russia in the 19th century attained the same position in the international market as Poland or East Germany in the 16th to 18th centuries, although international grain prices drifted downwards from 1870 onwards. However, output and yields remained very low throughout Russian agriculture, which was extremely backward technically. The three-field system still prevailed on a very wide scale, there were virtually no forage crops, and half the peasantry used wooden ploughs. Moreover, as we have seen, innumerable feudal economic relationships continued to characterize the twilight era after the Reform, hampering economic advance on the large estates of Central Russia. The nobility did not achieve the transition to a modern or rational capitalist agriculture. It was symptomatic that while specially created Land Banks had proved a highly successful device for the junkers after the Reform Era in Prussia, providing them with the capital for mortgages and investment, the Land Bank created by the State for the nobility in 1885 was a lugubrious fiasco: its credits were generally squandered, while their recipients sank into debt.[43] Thus, while there is no doubt at all that capitalist relations of production were steadily spreading through the countryside before the First World War, they never acquired the impetus of cumulative economic success, and always remained entangled in the prevalent pre-capitalist undergrowth. The predominant sector of Russian agriculture in 1917 was consequently characterized by feudal relations of production.

Meanwhile, of course, industrialization was rolling rapidly forward in the towns. By the early 20th century, Russia had acquired large coal, iron, oil and textile industries, and an extensive railway network. Many of its metallurgical complexes were among the most technologically advanced in the world. There is no need to stress here the notorious internal contradictions of Tsarist industrialization: capital investment was essentially financed by the State, which was dependent on foreign

43. M. P. Pavlova-Sil'vanskaya, 'K Voprosu Osobennostyakh Absoliutizma v Rossii', *Istoriya SSSR*, April 1968, p. 85. Lenin himself was well aware of the difference between the junkers and the *dvoriane*, whom he characterized as respectively capitalist and feudal landowning classes: *Collected Works*, Vol. 17, p. 390.

loans; to raise these loans, budget solvency was necessary and hence very heavy tax burdens had to be maintained on the peasantry; these then blocked the expansion of the internal market, which was necessary to sustain further investment.[44] For our purposes, the important fact is rather that, despite all these obstacles, the Russian industrial sector – based squarely and fully on capitalist relations of production – trebled in size in the two decades before 1914, recording one of the fastest growth rates in Europe.[45] On the eve of the First World War, Russia was the fourth largest producer of steel (above France) in the world. The absolute size of the industrial sector was the fifth in the world. Agriculture now accounted for about 50 per cent of the national income, while industry provided perhaps 20 per cent, excluding the large railway system.[46] Thus calculating the weight of the rural and urban economies *together*, there can be no doubt that by 1914, the Russian social formation was a composite structure, with a pre-dominantly feudal agrarian sector, but a *combined* agro-industrial capitalist sector that was now overall preponderant. Lenin expressed this laconically on the eve of his departure from Switzerland when he said that by 1917 the bourgeoisie had already ruled the country economically for some years.[47]

Yet, while the Russian *social formation* was dominated by the capitalist mode of production, the Russian *State* remained a feudal Absolutism. For no basic change in its class character or political structure supervened in the epoch of Nicholas II. The feudal nobility continued, as before, to be the ruling class of Imperial Russia: Tsarism was the political apparatus of its domination, from which it was never shifted. The bourgeoisie was far too weak to pose a serious autonomous challenge, and never succeeding in occupying commanding positions

44. There is an elegant analysis of this circle in T. Kemp, *Industrialization in Nineteenth Century Russia*, London 1969, p. 152.

45. T. H. Von Laue, *Sergei Witte and the Industrialization of Russia*, New York 1963, p. 269.

46. Raymond Goldsmith, 'The Economic Growth of Tsarist Russia 1860–1913', *Economic Development and Cultural Change*, IX, No. 3, April 1961, pp. 442, 444, 470–1: one of the most careful analyses of the economy in this period. The share of agriculture in the national income in 1913 was perhaps some 44 per cent in European Russia, and 52 per cent in the Tsarist Empire as a whole. Exact computations are very difficult because of statistical deficiencies.

47. *Collected Works*, Vol. 23, p. 303.

in the administration of the country. The Autocracy was a feudal Absolutism that had survived into the 20th century. Military defeat by Japan, and the massive popular explosion against the regime which followed on its heels in 1905, forced a series of modifications on Tsarism whose direction appeared to Russian liberals to permit an evolution towards a bourgeois monarchy. The formal possibility of such a cumulative change of character existed, as we have seen in the case of Prussia. Historically, however, the hesitant steps of Tsarism never seriously approached this goal. The aftermath of the 1905 Revolution led to the creation by the regime of a powerless Duma and a paper Constitution. The latter was torn up within a year by the dissolution of the former, and by a revision of the electorate that conferred on every landowner voting rights equivalent to those of 500 workers. The Tsar could veto any legislation proposed even by this tame assembly, while Ministers – now grouped in a conventional Cabinet – had no responsibility to it. The Autocracy could decree laws at will merely by proroguing this representative facade. There was thus no comparison with the situation in Imperial Germany, where universal male suffrage, regular elections, parliamentary budgetary control and unrestricted political activity existed. The qualitative political transmutation of the feudal Prussian State when it produced the capitalist German State never occurred in Russia. Both the organizing principles and personnel of Tsarism remained unaltered to the end.

Lenin expressly and repeatedly emphasized this difference in his polemics with the Mensheviks in 1911: 'To maintain that the system of government in Russia has *already* become bourgeois (as Larin says), and that governmental power in our country is no longer of a feudal nature (see Larin again), and at the same time to refer to Austria and Prussia as an example, is to refute oneself! . . . You cannot *transfer* to Russia the German completion of the bourgeois revolution, the German history of a democracy that had spent itself, the German "revolution from above" of the 1860's, and the *actually* existing German legality.'[48] Lenin did not, of course, overlook the necessary *autonomy*

48. *Collected Works*, Vol. 17, pp. 235, 187. This theme recurs again and again in Lenin's writings of this period; see Vol. 17, pp. 114–15, 146, 153, 233–41; Vol. 18, pp. 70–7. We shall have reason to revert to the crucial texts of these years for another purpose, in a later study.

of the Tsarist State apparatus from the feudal landowning class – an autonomy inscribed in the very structures of Absolutism. 'The class character of the tsarist monarchy in no way militates against the vast independence and self-sufficiency of the tsarist authorities and of the "bureaucracy", from Nicholas II down to the last police officer.'[49] He took care to stress the increasing impact of industrial and agrarian capitalism on the policies of Tsarism, and the objective interposition of the bourgeoisie in its workings. But he was always categorical in his characterization of the fundamental social nature of Russian Absolutism in his own time. In April 1917, he stated unequivocally: 'Before the February–March revolution of 1917, state power in Russia was in the hands of one old class, namely, the feudal landed nobility, headed by Nicholas Romanov.'[50] The very first sentence of the *Tasks of the Proletariat in Our Revolution*, written immediately after his arrival in Petrograd, reads: 'The old tsarist power . . . represented only a handful of feudalist landowners who commanded the entire state machinery (the army, police and the bureaucracy).'[51] This limpid formulation was the simple truth. Its consequences, however, have yet to be explored. For, to recapitulate the analysis developed above, there was a *dislocation* between the social formation and State in the last years of Tsarism. The Russian *social formation* was a complex ensemble dominated by the capitalist mode of production, but the Russian *State* remained a feudal Absolutism. The disjunctive articulation between the two remains to be explained, and founded, theoretically.

For the moment, the empirical consequences of this disjuncture for the structures of the Russian State must be considered. Tsarism remained down to its last hour in essence a feudal Absolutism. Even in its final phase, it continued to expand territorially outwards. Siberia was extended beyond the Amur, and Vladivostok was founded in 1861. After two decades of fighting, Central Asia was absorbed by 1884. Administrative and cultural russification was intensified in Poland

49. *Collected Works*, Vol. 17, p. 363. Lenin emphasized that the autonomy of the Tsarist bureaucracy was in no sense due to an influx of bourgeois functionaries into it; its commanding echelons were manned by the landed nobility: p. 390. In fact, it seems probable that after the emancipation of the serfs, the nobility came to rely on employment in the State apparatus more than ever before: see Seton-Watson, *The Russian Empire*, p. 405.

50. *Collected Works*, Vol. 24, p. 44.   51. *Ibid.*, p. 57.

and Finland. Institutionally, moreover, the State was in certain decisive respects far more powerful than any Western Absolutism had ever been, because it survived into the epoch of European industrialization, and therefore was able to import the most advanced technology in the world and appropriate it to itself. For the State had relinquished its grip on agriculture by the sale of its lands, only to entrench itself securely in industry. It had traditionally owned the mines and metal-lurgical works in the Urals. It now financed and built most of the new railway system, which accounted for the second largest budgetary out-lay – after the armed forces. Public contracts dominated Russian indus-try generally – two-thirds of engineering output was taken by the State. Tariffs were extremely high (4 times German or French levels and 2 times US levels), so that local capital depended critically on State supervision and protection. The Ministry of Finance manipulated the State Bank's loaning policy to private entrepreneurs, and established general ascendancy over them with its large gold reserves. The Absolutist State in Russia was thus the major engine of rapid indus-trialization from above. In the laissez-faire capitalist epoch of 1900, its swollen economic role had no comparison in the developed West. Combined and uneven development thus produced in Russia a colossal State apparatus, covering and suffocating the whole society beneath the level of the ruling-class. It was a State that had integrated feudal hierarchy bodily into the bureaucracy, incorporated the Church and education, and supervised industry, while spawning a gargantuan army and police-system.

This late feudal apparatus was, of course, inevitably over-determined by the rise of industrial capitalism in the late 19th century, just as the Absolute Monarchies in the West in their time had been over-determined by the rise of mercantile capitalism. Paradoxically, however, the Russian bourgeoisie remained politically far weaker than its Western pre-decessors, although the economy it represented was far stronger than theirs had been during the epoch of transition in the West. The his-torical reasons for this weakness are well-known, and are discussed again and again in Trotsky and Lenin: absence of petty-bourgeois artisanate, small numbers due to large enterprises, fear of the tumul-tuous working-class, dependence on State tariffs, loans and contracts. 'The farther East one goes, the more cowardly and weak becomes the bourgeoisie', proclaimed the first Manifesto of the RSDLP. The Russian Absolutist State, however, did not fail to reveal the imprint of the class which became its sullen and timorous auxiliary, rather than its antagonist. Just as the sale of offices in an earlier age provided a sensitive register of the subordinate presence of the mercantile class within the Western social formations, so the notorious bureaucratic contradiction between the two main pillars of the Russian State, the Ministry of the Interior and the Ministry of Finance, was a signal of the 'effects' of industrial capital in Russia. By the 1890's, there was constant conflict between these central institutions.[52] The Ministry of Finance pursued policies that were consonant with orthodox bourgeois aims. Its factory inspectorate supported employers in refusing to make wage concessions to workers; it was hostile to the village communes which represented an obstacle to the free market in land. Locked in struggle with it, the Ministry of the Interior was obsessed with the maintenance of the political security of the feudal State. It was above all concerned to prevent any public disorders or social strife. In pursuit of these aims, its repressive network of police spies and provocateurs was immense. Simultaneously, however, it had little sympathy for the corporate interests of industrial capital. Thus it pressured employers to make economic concessions to workers, so as to avoid the danger of their making political demands. It suppressed all strikes, which were illegal anyway, but wanted to get permanent police officials into the factories to study conditions there and ensure they did not provoke explosions. The employers and the Finance Ministry naturally resisted this, and a struggle ensued for control of the Factory Inspectorates, which were retained by the Finance Ministry only after an engagement to collaborate with the police. In the countryside, the Ministry of the Interior looked with bureaucratic paternalism on the village communes, from which it – not the Finance Ministry – collected taxes, since it regarded them as bulwarks of submissive tradition and barriers against revolutionary agitation. This comedy of reactionary contrasts culminated in the invention of police trade-unions by the Ministry of the Interior, and the instituting of labour laws by the executioner Plehve. The boomerang results of this experiment – the *Zubatovshchina* – which

52. There is an instructive discussion of their contradictions in Seton-Watson, *The Decline of Imperial Russia*, pp. 114, 126–9, 137–8, 143.

eventually produced Gapon, are well-known. What is symptomatically more important here is this final, delirious bid by the Absolutist State, after having at one time or another incorporated nobility, bourgeoisie, peasantry, education, army and industry, to produce even its own trades-unions under the aegis of the autocracy. Gramsci's abrupt dictum that: 'In Russia the State was everything, civil society was primordial and gelatinous',[53] thus contained a real historical truth.

Gramsci, however, failed to see *why* this was so: a scientific definition of the historical character of the Absolutist State in Russia escaped him. We may now be in a position to remedy this gap in his text. Once Russian Absolutism is set into an epochal European perspective, everything falls into place. Its lineaments become immediately evident. The Autocracy was a *feudal* State, although Russia was by the 20th century a composite social formation *dominated* by the capitalist mode of production: a dominance whose remote effects are legible in the structures of Tsarism. Its time was not that of the Wilhelmine Empire or the Third Republic, its rivals or partners: its true contemporaries were the Absolute Monarchies of the transition from feudalism to capitalism in the West. The crisis of feudalism in the West produced an Absolutism which succeeded serfdom; the crisis of feudalism in the East produced an Absolutism that institutionalized serfdom. The Russian *ancien régime* survived its counterparts in the West so long, despite their common class nature and functions, because it was born from a different matrix. In the end, it drew its top-heavy strength from the very advent of industrial capitalism, by bureaucratically implanting it from above, as its Western predecessors had once promoted mercantile capitalism. The ancestors of Witte were Colbert or Olivares. The international development of capitalist imperialism, radiating into the Russian Empire from the West, was what made possible this combination of the most advanced technology in the industrial world with the most archaic monarchy in Europe. Eventually, of course, imperialism,

53. Gramsci's purpose was to contrast Russia here with Western Europe: 'in the West, there was a proper relation between State and civil society, and when the State trembled a robust structure of civil society was at once revealed.' *Note sul Machiavelli*, p. 68. We shall return at length elsewhere to the implications of this crucial passage, in which Gramsci tried to analyse the different strategic problems confronting the working-class movement in Eastern and Western Europe during the 20th century.

which had initially armoured Russian Absolutism, engulfed and destroyed it: the ordeal of the First World War was too much for it.[54] It might be said that it was literally 'out of its element' in a direct confrontation between industrial imperialist states. In February 1917, it was overturned by the masses in a week.

If all this is so, it is necessary to have the courage to draw the consequences. *The Russian Revolution was not made against a capitalist State at all.* The Tsarism which fell in 1917 was a feudal apparatus: the Provisional Government never had time to replace it with a new or stable bourgeois apparatus. The Bolsheviks made a *socialist revolution*, but from beginning to end they never confronted the *central enemy* of the workers' movement in the West. Gramsci's deepest intuition was in this sense correct: the modern capitalist State of Western Europe remained – after the October Revolution – a *new* political object for Marxist theory, and revolutionary practice. The profound crisis which shook the whole battle-ravaged continent in 1917–20 left its own significant, and selective heritage. The First World War brought to an end the long history of European Absolutism. The Russian imperial State was overthrown by a proletarian revolution. The Austrian imperial State was erased from the map by bourgeois national revolutions. The destruction and disappearance of both was permanent. The cause of socialism triumphed in Russia in 1917; and flickered briefly in Hungary in 1919. In Germany, however, the strategic key to Europe, the capitalist transmutation of the Prussian monarchy assured the integral survival of the old State apparatus into the Versailles epoch. The two last great feudal States of Eastern Europe fell to revolutions from below, of contrasted character. The capitalist State that had once been their legitimist consort resisted every revolutionary upsurge, amidst the despair and debris of its own defeat by the Entente. The failure of the November Revolution in Germany, as momentous for the history of Europe as the success of the October Revolution in Russia, was grounded in the differential nature of the State machine

54. Tsarist imperialism itself was, of course, a mixture of feudal and capitalist expansion, with an inevitable and critical preponderance of the feudal component. Lenin took care in 1915 to make this necessary distinction: 'In Russia, capitalist imperialism of the latest type has fully revealed itself in the policy of Tsarism towards Persia, Manchuria and Mongolia, but in general, military and feudal imperialism is predominant in Russia.' *Collected Works*, Vol. 21, p. 306.

with which each was confronted. The mechanisms of socialist victory and defeat in these years go to the bottom of the deepest problems of bourgeois and proletarian democracy, which have still to be theoretically and practically solved in the second half of the 20th century. The political lessons and implications of the fall of Tsarism, for a comparative study of contemporary social formations, remain to this day largely unexplored. The historical obituary of the Absolutism that expired in 1917 has in that sense yet to be completed.

7

The House of Islam

The First World War, which flung the major capitalist States of the West against each other, and destroyed the last feudal States of the East, originated in the one corner of Europe where Absolutism never took root. The Balkans constituted a distinct geo-political sub-region, whose whole anterior evolution separated it from the rest of the continent: it was, in fact, precisely its lack of any traditional or stable integration into the international State-system of the late 19th and early 20th century which made it the 'powder-keg' of Europe, that eventually detonated the conflagration of 1914. The overall pattern of development in this sector of the continent thus provides a suitable control and epilogue to any survey of Absolutism. The Ottoman Empire remained through its existence on the continent a social formation apart. The Balkans under the rule of the Porte appeared to be curtained off from the general prospect of Europe, by Islamic subjection. But the regulative structure and dynamic of the Turkish State remains of great comparative significance, for the contrast it presents with either variant of European Absolutism. The character of the Ottoman system, moreover, provides the basic explanation of why the Balkan peninsula continued after the late mediaeval crisis to evolve in a pattern altogether divergent from that of the rest of Eastern Europe, with consequences lasting well into this century.

The Turkish warriors who overran Eastern Anatolia in the 11th century were still desert nomads. They had owed their success in Asia Minor, where the Arabs had failed, partly to the similarity of its climatic and geographical environment with that of the cold, dry Central Asian plateaux from which they came: the Bactrian camel, their essential means of transport, was ideally suited to the Anatolian highlands, which had proved impassable to the tropical Arab drome-dary.[1] Yet they did not arrive merely as primitive steppe-dwellers. Turkish slave soldiers from Central Asia had served both Abbasid and Fatimid dynasties in the Middle East from the 9th century onwards, both as rank-and-file troops and as officers, often with the highest rank. The analogy with the role of the Germanic border tribes in the Later Roman Empire has often been pointed out. Fifty years before the battle of Manzikert, the Seljuks had descended from their oases in Turkestan into Persia and Mesopotamia, overthrowing the languishing Buyid State and creating a Greater Seljuk Empire with its capital in Baghdad. The bulk of these Turkish conquerors rapidly became sedentarized as the professional army and administration of the new Sultanate, which itself now inherited and assimilated the long and settled urban traditions of 'Old Islam' – with its pervasive Persian influences mediated through the legacy of the Abbasid Caliphate. At the same time, however, a constant fringe of unpacified Turcoman nomads pushed forward in disorderly surges on the edges of the new Empire. It was with the aim of rounding up and disciplining these irregulars that Alp Arslan had journeyed to the Caucasus and on his way stumbled into the fateful destruction of the Byzantine army at Manzikert.[2] As we have seen earlier, no organized invasion of Anatolia by the Seljuk Sultanate followed this victory: its military preoccupations lay elsewhere, in the direction of the Nile, not the Bosphorus. It was the Turcoman pastoralists who inherited the fruits of Manzikert, and henceforward could ride virtually unopposed into the Anatolian interior. These frontier warriors and adventurers not only sought lands for their flocks: they were also, by a process of self-selection, typically stamped with the so-called *ghaʐi* outlook – a militant, crusading Muslim faith that rejected any accommodation with the infidel, such as had come to characterize the established states of Old Islam.[3] Yet once Anatolia had effectively been occupied, in successive waves of migra-

1. Xavier de Planhol, *Les Fondements Géographiques de l'Histoire de l'Islam*, Paris 1968, pp. 39–44, 208–9.
2. C. Cahen, 'La Campagne de Manzikert d'Après les Sources Musulmanes', *Byʐantion*, IX, 1934, pp. 621–42.
3. Paul Wittek, *The Rise of the Ottoman Empire*, London 1963, pp. 17–20. This short and brilliant monograph is the basic work on the nature of early Ottoman expansion.

tion from the 11th to the 13th century, the same conflict was reproduced in Asia Minor. The offshoot Seljuk Sultanate of Rum, centred in Konya, had soon recreated a prosperous, Persian-inspired State that was at constant loggerheads with the much more anarchic *ghazi* Emirates neighbouring it, especially the Danishmend, over which it eventually won the upper hand. However, all the contending Turkish States of Anatolia, of whatever type, were soon laid low by the Mongol invasions of the 13th century. The region reverted to a mosaic of petty emirates and wandering pastoralists. It was from out of this confusion that the Osmanli Sultanate emerged, from 1302 onwards, to become the dominant power, not merely in Turkey but throughout the whole Islamic world.

The peculiar dynamic animating the Ottoman State, which lifted it so far beyond the ranks of its rivals in Anatolia, lay in its unique combination of *ghazi* and Old Islamic principles.[4] Fortuitously situated at the outset on the Nicaean plains immediately next to the residual Byzantine Empire, its frontier proximity in the Christian world kept its military and religious fervour at full pitch, when other emirates in the hinterland lapsed into relative laxity. The Osmanli rulers from the start conceived themselves as *ghazi* missionaries in a holy war against the infidel. At the same time, their territory lay on the main inland trade route across Asia Minor, and hence attracted the merchants and artisans, as well as religious ulemas, who were the indispensable social elements for an Old Islamic State with a non-nomadic, non-crusading institutional solidity. The Osmanli Sultanate that was steeled in constant mounted warfare from 1300 to 1350 thus came to yoke the legal and administrative sophistication of the Old Islamic cities to the

4. Wittek, *The Rise of the Ottoman Empire*, pp. 37–46. Wittek's analysis of the dual principles of the Ottoman State is, in fact, an indirect echo of Ibn Khaldun's famous division of Islamic history into alternating phases of nomadic *asabiyya* (characterized by religious fervour, social solidarity and military prowess) and urban *farâgh* or *dia* (characterized by economic prosperity, administrative sophistication and cultural leisure), which he believed mutually incompatible – urban civilization being unable to resist nomadic conquest, nomadic fraternity then being unable to survive urban corruption, producing a cyclical history of state formation and disintegration. Wittek's account of the Ottoman Empire can be read as a subtle reversal of this formula: in the Turkish State, the two contradictory principles of Islamic political development for the first time came into structural harmony.

fierce military and proselytizing zeal of the *ghaẓi* frontiersmen. At the same time, some of its basic social impetus still lay in the nomadic quest for land which had been the driving force of the original Turkish occupation of Anatolia.[5] Territorial expansion was also a process of economic and demographic colonization.

The explosive potential of this political formula was soon felt in Christian Europe. The triumphant advance of the Turkish armies into the Balkans, driving deep into the Peninsula and so enveloping the beleagured Byzantine capital from behind, is well-known. In 1354, they were established in Gallipoli. In 1361, they had seized Adrianople. In 1389, Serbian, Bosnian and Bulgarian forces were annihilated at Kossovo, destroying further organized Slav resistance throughout most of the region. Thessaly, Morea and the Dobrudja were taken soon afterwards. In 1396, the Crusader expedition sent to stave off their advance was routed at Nicopolis. A brief pause followed, when Bayazid's army, engaged in forcible annexations of fellow-Muslim emirates in Anatolia, encountered Tamerlane's host sweeping through the region, and was shattered at Ankara, largely because its *ghaẓi* contingents deserted what they deemed an unholy and fratricidal cause. Rudely recalled to its religious vocation, the Osmanli State slowly reconstituted itself over the next fifty years on the other side of the Bosphorus, transferring its capital to Adrianople, in the front line of the war with Christendom.[6] In 1453, Constantinople was taken by Mehmet II. In the 1460's, Bosnia to the North and the Karamanid Emirate in Cilicia were seized. In the 1470's, the Tartar Khanate in the Crimea was reduced to client status, and a Turkish garrison planted in Caffa. In the first twenty years of the 16th century, Syria, Egypt and the Hejaz were conquered by Selim I. In the next decade, Belgrade was captured, most of Hungary subjugated and Vienna itself besieged. By now, nearly the whole Balkan peninsula had been overrun. Greece, Serbia, Bulgaria, Bosnia and Eastern Hungary were Ottoman provinces.

5. Ernst Werner, *Die Geburt einer Grossmacht – Die Osmanen*, pp. 19, 95. Werner's work is the major Marxist study of the growth of Ottoman power; his criticism of Wittek's neglect of the tribal drive for land behind early Osmanli expansionism, however, is supported by the research of the Turkish historian Omer Barkan.

6. P. Wittek, 'De la Défaite d'Ankara à la Prise de Constantinople (un demi-siècle d'histoire ottomane)', *Revue des Etudes Islamiques*, 1948, I, pp. 1–34.

Moldavia, Wallachia and Transylvania were tributary principalities under satellite Christian rulers, surrounded by directly ruled Turkish territories on the Danube and the Dniester. The Black Sea was an Ottoman lake. In the Middle East, meanwhile, Iraq was annexed; the Caucasus was subsequently absorbed. In the Maghreb, Algiers, Tripoli and Tunis were successively subjected to Turkish sovereignty. The Sultan was henceforward Caliph over all the Sunni lands of Islam. At its apogee under Suleiman I in the mid-16th century, the Osmanli realm was the most powerful Empire in the world. Overshadowing his nearest European rival, Suleiman I enjoyed a revenue twice that of Charles V.

What was the nature of this Asian colossus? Its contours provide a strange contrast with those of the European Absolutism that was contemporary with it. The economic bedrock of the Osmanli despotism was the virtually complete absence of private property in land.[7] The whole arable and pastoral territory of the Empire was deemed the personal patrimony of the Sultan, with the exception of *waqf* religious endowments.[8] For Ottoman political theory, the cardinal attribute of sovereignty was the Sultan's unlimited right to exploit all sources of wealth within his realm as his own Imperial Possessions.[9] It followed that there could be no stable, hereditary

7. This was for Marx the fundamental characteristic of all forms of what he called, following a long tradition, 'Asiatic despotism'. Commenting on Bernier's famous description of Moghul India, he wrote to Engels: 'Bernier rightly considered the basis of all phenomena in the East – he refers to Turkey, Persia, Hindustan – to be the *absence of private property in land*. This is the real key, even to the Oriental heaven.' (*Selected Correspondence*, p. 81). Marx's comments on the 'Asiatic mode of production' raise many problems, which will be considered later. If we retain for the moment the use of the term 'despotism' for the Ottoman State, this should be understood in a strictly provisional and merely descriptive sense. Scientific concepts for the analysis of Oriental states in this epoch are still largely lacking.

8. H. A. R. Gibb and H. Bowen, *Islamic Society and the West*, Vol. I, Part I, London 1950, pp. 236–7. House-sites, vineyards and orchards within village precincts were private property (*mulk*), as was most urban land (the significance of these exceptions – horticulture and towns – will be discussed in their general Islamic context). In 1528, some 87 per cent of Ottoman land was *miri* or State property: Halil Inalcik, *The Ottoman Empire*, London 1973, p. 110.

9. Stanford Shaw, 'The Ottoman View of the Balkans', in C. and B. Jelavich (ed.), *The Balkans in Transition*, Berkeley-Los Angeles 1963, pp. 56–60, graphically conveys this conception.

nobility within the Empire, because there was no security of property which could found it. Wealth and honour were effectively coterminous with the State, and rank was simply a function of positions held within it. The State itself was loosely divided into parallel columns, subsequently designated by European historians (significantly, not by Ottoman thinkers themselves) as the 'Ruling Institution' and the 'Muslim (or Religious) Institution', although there was never any absolute separation between the two.[10] The Ruling Institution comprised the total military and bureaucratic apparatus of the Empire. Its top stratum was overwhelmingly recruited from ex-Christian slaves, the core of whom were inducted into it by the invention of the *devshirme*. This institution, created probably in the 1380's, was the most remarkable expression of the interpenetration of *ghazi* and Old Islamic principles that defined the ascendant Ottoman system as a whole.[11] Every year, a levy was made of male children from Christian families of the subject population in the Balkans: taken from their parents, they were sent to Constantinople or Anatolia to be reared as Muslims and trained for posts of command in the army or administration, as the immediate servitors of the Sultan. In this way, both the *ghazi* tradition of religious conversion and military expansion, and the Old Islamic tradition of tolerance and tribute-collection from unbelievers, were conciliated.

The *devshirme* levy provided between 1,000 and 3,000 slave recruits for the Ruling Institution a year: they were supplemented by another 4–5,000 from war prisoners or foreign purchase, who underwent the same training process for elevation to prepotence and servitude.[12] The Sultan's slave corps so constituted provided the top ranks of the

10. The terms 'Ruling Institution' and 'Muslim Institution' were first coined by A. H. Lybyer, *The Government of the Ottoman Empire in the Time of Suleiman the Magnificent*, Cambridge USA, 1913, pp. 36–8. Their general acceptance by subsequent scholars has been criticized by N. Itzkowitz, 'Eighteenth Century Ottoman Realities', *Studia Islamica*, XVI, 1962, pp. 81–5, but without substantiating a probant case against their use for the 16th century.

11. S. Vryonis, 'Isidore Glabas and the Turkish Devshirme', *Speculum*, XXXI, July 1956, No. 3, pp. 433–43, has established the modern dating of the institution.

12. Inalcik, *The Ottoman Empire*, p. 78; L. S. Stavrianos, *The Balkans Since 1453*, New York 1958, p. 84. Exceptionally, in Bosnia the *devshirme* was extended to local Muslim families.

imperial bureaucracy, from the supreme office of Grand Vizir down-wards through the ranks of provincial beylerbeys and sanjakbeys; and the totality of the permanent army of the Porte, which was composed both of the special cavalry of the capital, and the famous janissary regi-ments that formed the elite infantry and artillery arms of Ottoman power. (One of the key early functions of the *devshirme* was precisely to provide disciplined and reliable foot-soldiers in an age when the international dominance of cavalry was just coming to an end, and mounted Turcomans were proving very unsuitable material for con-version into professional infantry.) The astonishing paradox of a slave synarchy – unthinkable within European feudalism – has its intelligible explanation within the whole social system of Osmanli despotism.[13] For there was a structural link between the absence of private property in land, and the eminence of State property in men. In effect, once any strict juridical concept of ownership was suspended in the funda-mental domain of the basic wealth of the society, the conventional connotations of possession in the domain of manpower were by the same stroke diluted and transformed. Once all landed property was a prerogative of the Porte, it ceased to be degrading to be the human property of the Sultan: 'slavery' was no longer defined by opposition to 'liberty', but by proximity of access to the Imperial command, a necessarily ambiguous vicinity that involved complete heteronomy and

13. The Ottoman system, of course, had deep roots in prior Muslim traditions, There were significant precedents in Islamic history for elite slave guards and commanders, as we shall see. The historical condition of the political rule of these palatine troops was the absence of *economic* use of slave labour in the dominant branch of production, agriculture. The Muslim world traditionally imported slaves mainly for domestic and sumptuary purposes, and these were always sharply distinguished from the privileged 'military' slaves. Only in the excep-tional case of Southern Iraq under the Abbasids was slavery ever predominant in the agrarian economy, and there it was a relatively brief episode, which pro-voked the Zanj insurrections in the late 9th century. In the Turkish Empire, some estates outside the regular land system seem to have been tilled by slave share-croppers, acquired abroad by war or purchase; but this marginal labour-force generally became assimilated to ordinary peasant status in the course of the 16th century. At the same time, the legal monopoly of land enjoyed by the Ottoman Sultans was also based on earlier Islamic traditions, going back to the first Arab conquests in the Middle East. The two features of the Turkish system discussed above were thus not arbitrary or isolated phenomena, but the culmination of a long and coherent historical development, which will be touched on later.

immense privilege and power. The paradox of the *devshirme* was thus perfectly logical and functional within Ottoman society at its prime.

At the same time, the Sultan's slave corps did not exhaust the Ruling Institution. For it coexisted with the native Islamic military stratum of *sipahi* warriors, who occupied a very different but complementary position within the system. These Muslim mounted soldiers formed a 'territorial' cavalry in the provinces. They were allocated by the Sultanate landed estates or *timars* (in some cases, these could be larger units or *ziamets*), from which they were entitled to draw carefully fixed revenues in exchange for providing military service. The income from the *timar* determined the scope of the obligation of its holder: for every 3,000 aspers, the *timariot* had to provide an additional horseman. First instituted by Murad I in the 1360's, it has been estimated that by 1475 there were some 22,000 *sipahis* in Rumelia and 17,000 in Anatolia (where *timars* were usually smaller).[14] The total cavalry reserve that could be mobilized through this system was, of course, much larger. There was constant competition for *timars* in the European borderlands of the Empire; among others, successful janissaries were often awarded them for their services. The system was never fully extended by the Porte to the remoter Arab lands conquered in its rear in the early 16th century, where it could afford to dispense with the cavalry-service that was necessary on its Christian frontiers and in the Turkish hinterland close behind them. Thus the provinces of Egypt, Baghdad, Basra and the Persian Gulf had no *timar* lands, but were garrisoned by janissary troops and paid an annual fixed sum in taxes to the central Treasury. These regions typically played a much more important economic than military role in the Empire. The original axis of the Ottoman order lay across the Straits, and it was the institutions that prevailed in the 'home countries' of Rumelia and Anatolia – above all, Rumelia – that defined its basic form.

The *timariots* and *zaims* represented the nearest analogy to a knight class within the Ottoman Empire. But the *timar* estates were in no sense genuine fiefs. Although the *sipahis* performed certain administrative

14. Inalcik, *The Ottoman Empire*, pp. 108, 113. Ottoman history is still little researched: statistical estimates within it are regularly discrepant in alternative authorities. Inalcik's own study contains two apparently contradictory figures for the number of *sipahis* in the reign of Suleiman I: pp. 48 and 108.

and policing functions for the Sultanate in their localities, they exercised no feudal lordship or seigneurial jurisdiction over the peasants who worked on their *timars*. The *timariots* played virtually no role in rural production at all: they were essentially external to the agrarian economy itself. The peasants, indeed, actually had hereditary security of tenure on the plots they tilled, while the *timariots* did not: *timars* were not inheritable, and at the access of every new Sultan their holders were systematically reshuffled in order to prevent them becoming entrenched in them. Closer to the *pronoia* system which juridically and etymologic- ally preceded it, the *timars* were much more limited in scope and firmly controlled from the centre than the Greek system had been.[15] In the Ottoman Empire, they comprised less than half the cultivated land in Rumelia and Anatolia, the rest of which (apart from the *waqfs*) was reserved for the direct use of the Sultan, the imperial family or high functionaries of the palace.[16] The *timariot* stratum was thus in this epoch both economically and politically a subordinate, if prominent component of the ruling order.

Set somewhat apart from the military-bureaucratic complex of the 'Ruling Institution' was the 'Muslim Institution'. This comprised the religious, legal and educational apparatus of the State, and was naturally manned with few exceptions by orthodox Islamic natives. *Kadi* judges, *ulema* theologians, *medresa* teachers and a mass of other clerical stipendiaries performed the essential ideological and jural tasks of the system of Ottoman domination. The apex of the 'Muslim Institution' was the Mufti of Istanbul, or *Sheikh-ul-Islam*, a supreme religious dignitary who interpreted the sacred law of the *Shar'ia* for the faithful. Islamic doctrine had never admitted any separation or distinction between Church and State; the notion had scarcely any meaning for it. The Osmanli Empire was now the first Muslim political system to create a specially organized religious hierarchy with a clergy comparable to that of a full-scale church. Moreover, it was this hierarchy which pro- vided the key judicial and civil personnel of the State apparatus on the ground; for the *kadis* recruited from the ulemate were the mainstay of

15. S. Vryonis, 'The Byzantine Legacy and Ottoman Forms', *Dumbarton Oaks Papers*, 1969–70, pp. 273–5.

16. Gibb and Bowen, *Islamic Society and the West*, I/I, pp. 46–56; L. Stavri- anos, *The Balkans Since 1453*, pp. 86–7, 99–100.

Ottoman provincial administration. Thus here too, a novel compound of *ghazi* and Old Islamic pressures was at work. The religious zeal of the former found an outlet in the fanatical obscurantism of the Turkish ulemate, while the social *gravitas* of the latter was respected by its firm integration into the machinery of the Sultanate. One consequence was that the *Sheikh-ul-Islam* could, on occasion, block initiatives of the Porte by invoking tenets of the *Shar'ia* of which it was the official guardian.[17] This formal limitation of the Sultan's authority was in a sense the counterpart of the enhanced power accruing to the Ottoman State from its creation of a professional ecclesiastical apparatus. It in no way cancelled the political despotism exercised by the Sultan over his Imperial Possessions, which fully corresponded to Weber's definition of a patrimonial bureaucracy in which problems of law everywhere tend to become simple questions of administration, bound by customary tradition.[18]

Given that the whole arable territory of the Empire was deemed the property of the Sultanate, the central domestic purpose of the Ottoman State, which determined its administrative organization and division, was naturally fiscal exploitation of the Imperial Possessions. To this end, the population was divided into the *Osmanlilar* ruling class, incorporating both the Ruling and Religious Institutions, and the *rayah* subject class, whether muslim or infidel. The vast bulk of the latter, of course, were the peasantry, who were Christian in the Balkans. No attempt was ever made to enforce mass conversion of the Balkan Christian populations under Ottoman rule. For to do so would have been to negate the economic advantages of an infidel *rayah* class,

17. Gibb and Bowen, *Islamic Society and the West*, I/I, pp. 85–6.

18. See Weber's remarks, *Economy and Society*, II, pp. 844–5. In fact, Weber regarded the Near East as the 'classic locale' of what he precisely called 'sultanism': *Economy and Society*, III, p. 1020. At the same time, he was careful to stress that even the most arbitrary personal despotism always operated within a custom-bound ideological framework: 'Where domination is primarily traditional, even though it is exercised by virtue of the ruler's personal autonomy, it will be called *patrimonial authority*; where it operates primarily on the basis of discretion, it will be called *sultanism*. . . . Sometimes it appears that sultanism is completely unrestrained by tradition, but this is never in fact the case. The non-traditional element is not, however, rationalized in impersonal terms, but consists only in an extreme development of the ruler's discretion. It is this which distinguishes it from every form of rational authority.' *Economy and Society*, I, p. 232.

which by long traditions of Old Islam and the *Shar'ia* could be burdened with special taxes that were not extendable to Muslim subjects: there was thus a direct conflict between tribute-oriented toleration and missionary-oriented conversion. The *devshirme*, as we have seen, resolved this for the Osmanlis by siphoning off an islamized child levy, while leaving the rest of the Christian population in their traditional faith, and paying the traditional price for it. All Christian *rayahs* owed a special capitation tax to the Sultan, and tithes for the maintenance of the ulemate. In addition, those peasants who tilled the land of *timars* or *ziamets* owed money dues to the holders of these benefices. The rate of these dues was carefully fixed by the Porte, and could not be arbitrarily altered by the *timariot* or *zaim*. Tenants were granted security of tenure, to assure stability of fiscal yield, and protected against landlord exactions, to prevent local drainage of the surplus away from the imperial centre. The labour services that had existed under Christian princes were reduced or abolished.[19] The right of peasants to shift residence was controlled, although not altogether eliminated; while in practice competition for labour among *timariots* encouraged informal mobility on the land. Thus during the 15th and 16th centuries, the Balkan peasantry suddenly found itself delivered from increasing servile degradation and seigneurial exploitation under its Christian rulers, and transferred to a social condition that was paradoxically in most respects milder and freer than anywhere else in Eastern Europe at the time.

The fate of the Balkan peasantry contrasted with that of their traditional lords. In the initial phases of Turkish conquest, sections of the local Christian aristocracies in the Balkans had gone over to the Ottomans, often fighting with them in the field as tributary allies and auxiliaries. This collaboration had occurred in Serbia, Bulgaria, Wallachia and elsewhere. With the consolidation of Ottoman imperial power in Rumelia, however, the residual autonomy of these lords came to an end. A few were converted to Islam and assimilated to the

19. Dushan's Code had obliged the Serbian peasant to work on his lord's land two days a week. According to Inalcik, under Ottoman rule, the *rayah* owed the *sipahi* only three days of labour a year: *The Ottoman Empire*, p. 13. His own subsequent account of the services due to *timar*-holders does not altogether tally with this very low claim (pp. 111–12). But there is no reason to doubt the relative improvement in the position of the Balkan peasantry.

Ottoman ruling class, mainly in Bosnia. Some were granted *timars* in the new agrarian system, without conversion. But Christian *timariots* were not numerous, and their estates were usually modest, with small incomes. Within a few generations, they had died out completely.[20] Thus throughout most of the Balkans, the local ethnic nobility was soon eliminated – a fact of great consequence for the future social development of the region. Beyond the Danube, in Wallachia, Moldavia and Transylvania alone, the Sultanate never proceeded to direct occupation and administration. In Wallachia and Moldavia, the recently formed Rumanian boyar class, which had itself only just emerged into the phase of political unification and economic subjection of the native peasantry, was permitted to preserve its lands and provincial power, merely paying a heavy annual tribute in kind to Istanbul. In Transylvania, Magyar landowners were left in dominion over an ethnic population mostly alien to them – Rumanian, Saxon or Szekler. Otherwise, Ottoman rule in South-Eastern Europe swept the Balkans clear of a local nobility. The ultimate results of this profound modification of the indigenous social systems were complex and contradictory.

On the one hand, as we have seen, it led to a definite amelioration of the material condition of the peasantry, after Turkish conquest was consolidated. Not only were rural dues and taxes lowered; but the long Ottoman peace in the subjugated South-East behind the front in Central Europe also lifted the bane of constant noble warfare from the countryside. On the other hand, however, the social and cultural results of the complete destruction of the native ruling classes were undoubtedly retrogressive. The Balkan aristocracies had exploited the peasantry much more oppressively than did Ottoman administration in its prime. But the very constitution of a landed nobility, in the late mediaeval and early modern epoch, represented an indubitable historical advance in these laggard social formations. For it signalled a rupture with clan principles of organization, tribal fragmentation, and the rudimentary cultural and political forms attendant on these. The price paid for this advance was, precisely, class stratification and increased economic exploitation. The late mediaeval Balkan States were notoriously weak and vulnerable, as we have seen. But their collapse

20. H. Inalcik, 'Ottoman Methods of Conquest', *Studi a slamica*, II, 195, pp. 104–16.

prior to the Turkish invasions did not mean that they had no further potential for development: in fact, a pattern of apparent 'false starts' and subsequent recoveries was typical of early feudal Europe, both Western and Eastern, as we have seen, and usually took the initial form of 'prematurely' centralized administrative structures such as went under in the late mediaeval Balkans. The elimination of the local land-owning class by the Turks henceforward precluded any such endogenous dynamic. On the contrary, its main cultural and political result was an actual regression to clannic institutions and particularist traditions among the Balkan rural population. Thus in the Serb lands – where this phenomenon has been particularly studied – the tribal *plemena*, the chiefly *knez* and the kin-webbed *zadruga*, which were fast disappearing before Ottoman conquest, now revived as pervasive units of social organization, in the countryside.[21] The general relapse into a patriarchal localism was accompanied by a notable decline in literacy. Cultural articulation of the life of the subject population became largely a monopoly of the Orthodox clergy, whose servility to the Turkish rulers was matched only by its ignorance and superstition. Towns lost their commercial or intellectual importance, becoming military and administrative centres of Ottoman rule, planted with

21. The Bosnian historian Branislav Djurdjev has been mainly responsible for bringing to light this process of social regression. For an account of his work, and the discussions it has provoked, see W. S. Vucinich, 'The Yugoslav Lands in the Ottoman Period: Post-War Marxist Interpretations of Indigenous and Ottoman Institutions', *The Journal of Modern History*, XXVII, No. 3, September 1955, pp. 287–305. Djurdjev's emphasis on the contradictory character of the initial Ottoman impact on Balkan society contrasts with the predominant Russian and Turkish views, which tend to emphasize unilaterally either destruction and repression, or pacification and prosperity, as the outcome of Ottoman conquest. For an example of Soviet interpretations, see Z. V. Udal'tsova, 'O Vnutrennykh Prichinakh Padeniya Vizantii v XV Veke', *Voprosy Istorii*, July 1953, No. 7, p. 120 – an article commemorating, or deploring, the 500th anniversary of the fall of Constantinople, which claims that Turkish rule led straightaway to intensified exploitation of the rural masses. For a Turkish position, see H. Inalcik, 'L'Empire Ottomane', *Actes du Premier Congrès International des Etudes Balkaniques et Sud-Est Européennes*, Sofia 1969, pp. 81–5. The tension between the two tendencies is marked in the contributions to this Congress, which also includes a crisp statement by Djurdjev recapitulating his judgements: B. Djurdjev, 'Les Changements Historiques et Ethniques chez les Peuples Slaves du Sud Après la Conquête Turque', pp. 575–8.

Turkish craftsmen and shopkeepers.[22] Thus, although the great mass of the rural population benefited materially from the initial impact of the Turkish conquest, because it led to a decline in the volume of surplus extracted from the immediate producers in the countryside, the other side of the same historical process was an interruption of any indigenous social development towards a more advanced feudal order, a regression to pre-feudal patriarchal forms, and a long stagnation in the whole historical evolution of the Balkan peninsula.

The Asian provinces of the Turkish Empire, meanwhile, experienced a notable revival and advance during the apogee of Ottoman power in the 16th century While Rumelia remained the main theatre of war for the Sultan's armies, Anatolia, Syria and Egypt enjoyed the benefits of peace and unity brought to the Middle East by Osmanli conquest. The insecurity created by the decadence of the Mamluk States in the Levant gave way to firm and centralized administration, which suppressed brigandage and stimulated inter-regional trade. The late mediaeval depression of the Syrian and Egyptian economies, hard hit by invasion and plague, was reversed, as agriculture recovered and population rose. These two provinces came to provide a third of the receipts of the imperial treasury.[23] In Anatolia, demographic growth may have been especially marked – a clear sign of agrarian expansion: the rural population perhaps increased by as much as two-fifths in the course of the century. Commerce flourished, both within the Eastern provinces themselves, and more especially along the international trade routes linking Western Europe to Western Asia, whether via the Mediterranean or the Black Sea. Roads were well-maintained, and official staging-posts constructed along them; waters were patrolled by Ottoman fleets against piracy. Spices, silks, cotton, slaves, velvets, alum and other commodities were shipped or caravaned across the Empire in large quantities. The transit trade of the Middle East throve under the protection of the Porte, to the benefit of the Ottoman State.

This commercial prosperity, in turn, led to an upswing of urban growth. The population of the towns may have nearly doubled in the

22. See W. S. Vucinich, 'The Nature of Balkan Society under Ottoman Rule', *Slavic Review*, December 1962, pp. 603, 604–5, 614.

23. Inalcik, *The Ottoman Empire*, p. 128.

16th century.[24] Osmanli society at its prime possessed a limited but flourishing number of manufacturing centres in Bursa, Edirne and other cities, producing or processing silks, velvets and other exports.[25] When he conquered Byzantium, Mehmet II pursued a more enlightened economic policy than the Comneni or Paleologue Emperors, by abolishing Venetian and Genoese trading privileges and instituting a very mild protectionist tariff to promote local commerce. Within a century of Turkish rule, the size of Istanbul itself had increased from perhaps 40,000 to 400,000. In the 16th century, it was far the largest city in Europe.

However, the economic growth of the Empire in its ascendancy had definite limits from the start. The agricultural revival of the Asian provinces during the 16th century does not seem to have been accompanied by any major improvements in rural technology. The most significant innovation in the Middle Eastern countryside in the early modern epoch, the introduction of American maize, occurred in a later phase, when overall imperial decline had already set in. The demographic upsurge in Anatolia can be largely attributed to the restoration of peace and the sedentarization of nomadic tribes, as the stabilization of Ottoman rule permitted agricultural settlement to expand again after the late Byzantine depopulation. It was soon to reach negative limits, as the availability of land ran out at existing technical levels. At the same time, the revival of trade across the Empire did not necessarily find an equivalent reflection in the activity of domestic manufactures, or even the importance of local merchants. For the particular character of the urban economy and government in the Ottoman lands was always governed by the constraints of the Sultanate. Neither provincial workshops, nor a vast capital, nor periodic concern by individual rulers, could alter the basically inimical relationship of the Ottoman State to cities and industries. Islamic political traditions possessed no

24. Omer Lutfi Barkan, 'Essai sur les Données Statistiques des Registres de Recensement dans l'Empire Ottomane aux XVe et XVIe Siècles', *Journal of the Economic and Social History of the Orient*, Vol. I/I, August 1957, pp. 27–8: apart from the macrocephaly of Istanbul itself (accompanied by a decline of Aleppo and Damascus), the population of twelve representative provincial towns grew by some 90 per cent in the 16th century.

25. Halil Inalcik, 'Capital Formation in the Ottoman Empire', *The Journal of Economic History*, XXIX, No. 1, March 1969, pp. 108–19.

conception of urban liberties. Towns had no corporate or municipal autonomy: indeed, they had no legal existence at all. 'Just as there was no state, but only a ruler and his agents, no courts but only a judge and his helpers, so there was no city but only a conglomeration of families, quarters and guilds, each with their own chiefs or leaders.'[26] The towns, in other words, were without defense against the will of the Commander of the Faithful, and his servants. Official regulation of commodity prices and enforced purchase of raw materials controlled urban markets. Craft guilds were carefully supervised by the State, and their technical conservatism typically reinforced by it. Moreover, the Sultanate nearly always intervened against the interests of the indigenous merchant communities in the cities, which were regarded with consistent suspicion by the ulemate, and were detested by the artisan populace. State economic policy tended to discriminate against large-scale commercial capital, and to patronize petty production, with its guild archaism and religious bigotry.[27] The characteristic Turkish town eventually came to be dominated by a stagnant and backward menu peuple that prevented any entrepreneurial innovation or accumulation. Given the nature of the Ottoman State, there was no protective space in which a Turkish mercantile bourgeoisie could develop, and from the 17th century onwards commercial functions devolved increasingly onto infidel minority communities, Greek, Jewish or Armenian, which had always anyway dominated the export trade with the West. Muslim traders or producers were thereafter generally confined to small shopkeeping and artisanal occupations.

Thus even at its height, the level of the Ottoman economy never achieved a degree of advance commensurate with the Ottoman polity. The basic motor-force of imperial expansion remained relentlessly military in character. Ideologically, the structure of Turkish dominion knew no natural geographical bounds. In Osmanli cosmogony the planet was divided into two great zones – the House of Islam and the House of War. The House of Islam comprised those lands inhabited by true believers, to be progressively assembled beneath the banners of the Sultan. The House of War covered the rest of the world, peopled by

26. Bernard Lewis, *The Emergence of Modern Turkey*, London 1969, p. 393. Lewis plainly exaggerates in claiming that there was 'no state', of course.
27. Inalcik, 'Capital Formation in the Ottoman Empire', pp. 103–6.

unbelievers whose destiny was to be conquered by the Soldiers of the Prophet.[28] For practical purposes, this meant Christian Europe, at whose gates the Turks had established their capital. Throughout the history of the Empire, in fact, the real centre of gravity of the *Osman-lilar* ruling class was Rumelia – the Balkan Peninsula itself – not Anatolia, the Turkish homeland. It was from here that army after army would set forth, marching northwards to the House of War, to enlarge the abode of Islam. The fervour, mass and skill of the Sultan's troops rendered them invincible in Europe for two hundred years after they first crossed into Gallipoli. The *sipahi* cavalry that rode out for seasonal campaigns and surprise forays, and the picked janissary infantry, proved deadly weapons of Ottoman expansion in South-Eastern Europe. The Sultans, moreover, did not hesitate to utilize Christian manpower and lore in ways other than the *devshirme* which provided its foot-regiments. Turkish artillery was among the most advanced in Europe, on occasion specially cast for the Porte by renegade Western engineers. The Turkish navy soon rivalled that of Venice, because of the experience of its Greek captains and crews.[29] Voraciously appropriating military technicians and craftsmen from Europe, the Ottoman war machine at its peak combined the qualitative modernity of the best Christian armies with a quantitative mobilization far beyond that of any single Christian State ranged against it. Coalitions alone could withstand it along the Danubian frontiers. It was not until the siege of Vienna in 1529 that Spanish and Austrian pikes were able to lower the sabres of the janissaries.

The decay of Turkish despotism, however, gradually set in from the epoch in which its expansion was halted. The closure of the Osmanli frontiers in Rumelia was to have a chain series of repercussions backwards into the Empire. Compared with the Absolutist States of late 16th and early 17th century Europe, it was commercially, culturally and technologically backward. It had thrust its way into Europe through the continent's weakest angle of defence – the crumbling socia revetments of the late mediaeval Balkans. Confronted with the far

28. Gibb and Bowen, *Islamic Society and the West*, I/I, pp. 20–1.

29. For particular emphasis on the use of European technicians and artisans by the Porte, see R. Mousnier, *Les XVIe et XVIIe Siècles*, Paris 1954, pp. 463–4, 474.

robuster and more representative Habsburg monarchies, it was ultimately incapable of prevailing, whether by land (Vienna) or by sea (Lepanto). Since the Renaissance, European feudalism had been giving birth to a mercantile capitalism that no Asian despotism could reproduce: least of all that of the Porte, with its complete innocence of inventions and contempt for manufactures. The cessation of Turkish expansion was determined by the ever-increasing economic, social and political superiority of the House of War. The results of this reversal of forces were manifold for the House of Islam. The structure of the *Osmanlilar* ruling class had rested on perpetual military conquest. It was this which permitted the anomalous dominance of the State apparatus by a slave-elite of non-Muslim origin; so long as the frontier unwound before the march of the Ottoman armies, the necessity and rationality of the janissary corps and the *devshirme* were justified in practice for the whole ruling order: the victories of Varna, Rhodes, Belgrade, Mohacs, were at this price. It was also this which rendered possible the initially moderate level of rural exploitation in the Balkans, and the tight central supervision exercised over it. For the *Osmanlilar* class as a whole could expect to make its fortunes by extensive seizure of more and more lands from the House of War, as *timars* and *ʒiamets* multiplied with the advance northwards. The social mechanisms of booty were thus basic to the rigid unity and discipline of the Turkish State at its meridian.

Once territorial expansion ceased, however, a slow involution of its whole enormous structure was inevitable. The privileges of an extraneous slave corps, deprived of its military functions, gradually became intolerable to the bulk of the dominant class of the Empire, which eventually exerted its inert weight to normalize and recover command of the political apparatus of the Ruling Institution. The surplus rural population that had been enlisted as auxiliaries or freebooters in the armies of the Porte, turned to social revolt or brigandage once the military machine could no longer absorb it. Moreover, the stoppage of extensive acquisition of lands and treasure was inevitably to lead to much more intensive forms of exploitation within the bounds of Turkish power, at the expense of the subject *rayah* class. The history of the Ottoman Empire from the late 16th to the early 19th century is thus essentially that of the disintegration of the central imperial State, the consolidation of a provincial landowning class, and the degradation of the peasantry. This long drawn-out process, which was not without transient political and military recoveries, did not occur in Balkan isolation from the rest of the European continent. It was, on the contrary, deepened and aggravated by the international impact of West European economic supremacy, under whose sway the Ottoman Empire – stagnating in technological parasitism and theological obscurantism – increasingly fell. From the Price Revolution of the 16th to the Industrial Revolution of the 19th century, Balkan society was to be more and more affected by the development of capitalism in the West.

The long-term decline of the Ottoman Empire was determined by the military and economic superiority of Absolutist Europe. In the short-term, its worst reverses were suffered in Asia. The Thirteen Years' War with Austria, from 1593 to 1606, proved a costly stalemate. But the longer and more destructive wars with Persia, which lasted with brief interruptions from 1578 to 1639, ended in frustration and defeat. It was the victorious consolidation of the Safavid State in Persia which was the immediate turning-point in the fortunes of the Osmanli State. The Persian wars, which resulted in the eventual loss of the Caucasus, inflicted immense damage on the army and bureaucracy of the Porte. Anatolia, the homeland of the ethnic Turkish population of the Empire, had never been its political centre, as we have seen. It was in Rumelia that the new Ottoman social system had been systematically implanted in the 14th and 15th centuries, land tenure and military administration shaped to the international needs of the imperial State. Anatolia, by contrast, remained much more traditional in its social and religious structure, with strong remnants of older nomadic and clan organization in the *beyliks* of the interior and latent hostility to the cosmopolitan laxism of Istanbul. The Anatolian *timars* were typically smaller and poorer than those of Rumelia. The local *sipahi* class, suffering from the rising costs of participation in seasonal campaigns because of the steep inflation of the late 16th century, showed less and less enthusiasm for the inter-muslim struggle with Persia. At the same time, the agrarian expansion in rural Anatolia had by now ceased; the major increase in population had ended by creating a growing class of landless peasants or *levandat* in the highlands. Widely recruited into the armed levies raised by provincial governors for the Persian front, the *levandat* acquired military training, but not discipline. The strain of the wars, and enemy victories on the eastern frontier, thus gradually precipitated a collapse of civic order in Anatolia. *Timariot* disaffection fused with peasant distress in a series of tumultuous upheavals – the so-called *jelali* risings which broke out from 1594–1610 and again in 1622–8, mingling provincial mutiny, social banditry and religious revivalism.[30] It was in these years, too, that Cossack raids across the Black Sea struck with humiliating success at Varna, Sinope, Trebizond, and even pillaged the suburbs of Istanbul itself. Eventually, the *sipahi* leaders of the *jelali* rebellions of Anatolia were bought off, while their *levandat* following were repressed. But the damage to the internal morale of the Ottoman system caused by the spread of brigandage and anarchy in Anatolia was very great. The later 17th century was to see further *jelali* outbreaks, in a countryside where pacification was never complete.

In the Porte itself, meanwhile, the costs of the long Persian contest were acutely aggravated by mounting inflation caught from the West. The influx of American bullion into Renaissance Europe had worked its way through to the Turkish Empire by the last decades of the century. The gold-silver ratio within the Ottoman domains was lower than in the West, making the export of silver currency into them highly profitable for European traders, recouping in gold. The result of this massive injection of silver was naturally a steep rise in prices, which the Sultanate vainly tried to offset by debasing the asper. The value of Treasury revenues fell by half between 1534 and 1591.[31] Thereafter, the annual budgets were regularly and deeply in deficit, as the wars dragged on against Austria and Persia. The consequence was inevitably a great increase in fiscal pressures on the whole subject population within the Empire. The *rayah* poll tax paid by the Christian peasantry multiplied six times over between 1574 and 1630.[32] These measures, however, could only palliate a situation in which the State apparatus itself was now showing signs of deepening malaise and crisis.

---

30. For the phenomenon of the Anatolian *levandat*, and the *jelali* revolts generally, see V. J. Parry, 'The Ottoman Empire 1566–161 7', *The New Camridge Modern History*, III, pp. 372–4, and 'The Ottoman Empire 1617–1648', *The New Cambridge Modern History*, IV, pp. 627–30.

31. Inalcik, *The Ottoman Empire*, p. 49.

32. Inalcik, 'L'Empire Ottomane', pp. 96–7.

The janissary corps and *devshirme* stratum which had formed the cupola of the Ottoman imperial apparatus in the age of Mehmet II were among the first to reveal the general symptoms of decomposition. Early in the 16th century, during the rule of Suleiman I, the janissaries won the right to marry and raise children, encumbrances that had originally been forbidden them. This naturally increased the cost of their maintenance, which had anyway risen enormously because of the inflation transmitted from the influx of silver from Western Europe via the Mediterranean trade of the Empire, which produced virtually no manufactures of its own. Thus janissary pay quadrupled between 1350 and 1600, while the Turkish silver asper was repeatedly devalued and the general price-level decupled.[33] To support themselves, the janissaries were consequently now allowed to supplement their incomes by engaging in crafts or commerce, when not on a war-footing. Then in 1574, at the accession of Selim II, they extorted the right to enroll their sons in the janissary regiments. A professional, skill-selected military elite was thus progressively converted into a hereditary, semi-artisanal militia. Its discipline disintegrated pro-portionately. In 1589, the first successful janissary mutiny for higher pay ousted the current Grand Vizir, and set a pattern that was to become endemic in Istanbul political life; in 1622, the first Sultan was deposed by a janissary rising. Meanwhile, the weakening of the once hermetic insulation of the *devshirme* stratum from the rest of the *Osmanlilar* ruling class predictably led to the dissolution of its separate *devshirme* identity altogether. In the reign of Murad III, at the end of the 16th century, native Muslims acquired the right to enter the ranks of the janissaries. Finally, by the time of Murad IV, in the 1630's, the *devshirme* levies had died out altogether. The janissary regiments, however, still possessed tax exemption and other traditional privileges. There was thus a permanent demand for enlistment in them on the part of the Muslim population; while the social unrest of the *jelali* period led to the spread of janissary garrisons throughout the provincial towns of the Empire for the purposes of internal security. Thus from the mid-17th century onwards, the janissaries increasingly became vast bodies of semi- or untrained urban militia, many of whom no longer resided in

33. Stavrianos, *The Balkans Since 1453*, p. 121; Lewis, *The Emergence of Modern Turkey*, pp. 28-9.

barracks but in their booths and workshops as petty traders and artisans (where their presence in the guilds often undermined craft standards), while the more prosperous acquired rights over local land. The military value of the janissaries soon became minimal; their main political function in the capital was to form a fanaticized *masse de manoeuvre* for ulemate bigotry or palace intrigues.

Meanwhile, the *timar* system had undergone a no less drastic degeneration. The light cavalry provided by the *sipahis* fell into military obsolescence with the improvement of European weaponry, and the consolidation of standing armies by the Christian powers: reluctant summer sorties by *timariot* horsemen, their fortitude in the field weakened by the depreciation of their incomes, were quite inadequate against the heavy fire-power of German fusiliers. Thus amidst growing corruption in Istanbul, the State tended to assign more and more *timars* for non-military purposes to high officials, or to absorb them back into the Treasury. The result was a steep drop in *sipahi* effectives by the early 17th century. The Ottoman armies henceforward came to rely largely on companies of paid musketeers or *sekban* units – originally irregular provincial auxiliaries, which now became the central military formations of the Empire.[34] The upkeep of *sekban* troops as a permanent force both intensified and monetized the tax-burden in the Ottoman lands, in a conjuncture of probable economic recession in much of the Eastern Mediterranean. New cultivable land had run out in Anatolia. The spice and silk trades were captured and diverted by English and Dutch shipping, whose operations in the Indian Ocean now encircled the Ottoman Empire from behind. Egypt, on the other hand, where traditional agriculture held up well,[35] slipped increasingly back into local Mamluk control. The financial and political difficulties of the State were compounded by the degeneration of the dynasty. For in the 17th century, the calibre of the imperial rulers – whose despotic authority had hitherto generally been exercised with considerable ability – collapsed because of a new succession system. From 1617 onwards, the Sultanate passed to the eldest surviving male of the Osmanli line, who had typically been sequestered from birth within the

34. Inalcik, *The Ottoman Empire*, p. 48.

35. See Stanford Shaw, *The Financial and Administrative Organization and Development of Ottoman Egypt, 1517–1798*, Princeton 1962, p. 21.

'Cage of Princes', damascened dungeons virtually designed to produce pathological imbalance or imbecility. Such Sultans were in no position to control or check the steady deterioration of the State system beneath them. It was in this epoch that clericalist manoeuvres by the *Sheikh-ul-Islam* started to encroach on the system of political decision,[36] which became steadily more venal and unstable.

Nevertheless, the Ottoman Empire proved capable of one last, great military heave into Europe in the second half of the 17th century. The setbacks of the Persian wars, the disorders of Anatolian brigandage, the humiliations of Cossack raids, and the demoralization of the janissary corps, were succeeded by an effective, if temporary reaction within the Porte. The Köprülü Vizirates, from 1656 to 1676, restored once again a vigorous and martial administration in Istanbul. Ottoman finances were redressed by forced loans and tributary extortions; expenditure was cut by pruning of sinecures; infantry training and equipment were improved in the permanent regiments; good use was made of the still punishing Tartar cavalry in the Pontic theatre. The decline of the Safavid regime in Persia concomitantly eased pressure in the East, and permitted a final Turkish push in the West. The Danubian principalities, whose rulers had become increasingly restless, were brought to heel. A twenty-year war with Venice was successfully concluded with the capture of Crete in 1669. Then in 1672, mobilizing the mounted contingents of the Crimean Khanate, Ottoman forces conquered Podolia from Poland. For the next decade, a long and savage struggle was waged against Russia for mastery of the Ukraine. Eventually blocked in this conflict, which ended with a truce confirming the *status quo ante* in 1682 after great devastation of the Ukraine, Turkish power was next turned against Austria in 1683. The new and even more aggressive Vizir Kara Mustapha, who had succeeded Mehmet Köprülü, assembled a large army for a frontal attack on Vienna. A hundred and fifty years after Suleiman II's siege of the Habsburg capital, a second Osmanli assault was now launched. The failure of the first had merely stabilized the front-line of Turkish advance into Christendom. The defeat of the second, with the victorious relief of Vienna by a mixed force of Polish, Imperial, Saxon and Bavarian troops in 1683, led to a collapse of the whole Ottoman position in Central Europe. The

36. Inalcik, 'L'Empire Ottomane', p. 95.

Köprülü recovery thus proved artificial and short-lived: its initial successes led the Porte to over-reach itself, with disastrous and irreversible results. The Viennese fiasco was followed by a protracted retreat, which ended in 1699 with the complete loss of Hungary and Transylvania to the Habsburgs, while Poland regained Podolia and Venice occupied the Morea. Henceforward, the House of Islam was to be perpetually on the defensive in the Balkans, capable at best of temporarily holding up infidel advances, at worst repeatedly and definitively yielding before them.

The brunt of the roll-back of the Turkish Empire over the next hundred years fell to Russian, rather than Austrian, Absolutism. Habsburg military impetus petered out relatively soon, after the conquest of the Banat in 1716–18. Ottoman forces checked Austrian armies in 1736–9, regaining Belgrade. But in the North, Romanov expansion in the Euxine zone could not be halted. Defeat by Russia in 1768–74 resulted in the loss of lands between the Bug and the Dniester, and the establishment of Tsarist rights of intervention in Moldavia and Wallachia. In 1783, the Crimea was absorbed into Russia; in 1791, Yedisan was annexed. Meanwhile, the whole administrative fibre of the Ottoman State was steadily deteriorating. The Divan became the pawn of rapacious cliques in the capital, bent on maximizing the profits of venality and malversation. Turkish civilian bureaucrats and Greek Phanariot merchants from Istanbul gained growing power and influence in the Porte after 1700, as the military capacity of the Ottoman State further weakened – the former increasingly rising to become pashas and provincial governors,[37] while the latter won control of lucrative treasury positions and the Rumanian hospodarships. Offices which had once been the reserve of the *devshirme*, with promotion according to merit, were now sold wholesale to the highest bidders: but since, unlike the European systems, there was no security of tenure after purchase, office-holders had to squeeze the gains from their investment at top speed before they were evicted in their turn, thereby greatly increasing the pressure of extortion downwards on the masses beneath, that had to bear the burden of such an administration. A spreading racket in janissary pay-tickets developed, which came to be bought and sold to fictional members amidst universal administrative corruption. By the

37. N. Itzkowitz, 'Eighteenth Century Ottoman Realities', pp. 86–7.

end of the century, there were about 100,000 registered janissaries, of whom a mere fraction had real military training: but a great many had access to weapons, and could use them for local extortion and intimidation.[38] The janissaries now lay everywhere like a gangrenous mass across the towns of the Empire. Their most powerful members were often to furnish many of the local *ayan* notables that henceforward became a prominent feature of Ottoman provincial society.

Meanwhile, the whole land system was undergoing a transformation. The *timar* had long declined as an institution, together with the *sipahi* cavalry it had supported. The Porte pursued a deliberate policy of recovering the estates of former *timariots*, either by annexing them to the domains of the imperial house and then re-leasing them to speculators to gain greater cash revenues, or simply allocating them to dummy holders manipulated by palace officials. There was thus a general shift in the form of Ottoman exploitation from the *timar* to the *iltizam*: military benefices were converted into tax-farms, which yielded increased monetary flows to the Treasury. The *iltizam* system had been first developed by the Porte in the further Asian provinces, such as Egypt, where it had no need of mounted warriors of the type massed in Rumelia.[39] The generalization of these tax-farms throughout the Empire, however, corresponded not merely to the financial needs of the Osmanli State, but also to the Muslim homogenization of the whole ruling class with the decline and disappearance of the *devshirme* .One of the major structural reasons for the latter process, indeed, was the alteration in the total composition of the Empire with the conquest of the Arab provinces. The spread of the *iltizam* fiscal unit from its Islamic homelands at the expense of the *timar* thus accomplished the dissolution of the institution that had been the functional complement of the *devshirme* in the original system of Ottoman expansionism. A concomitant phenomenon was the increase in *waqf* lands, nominally corporate religious estates endowed by the pious, which were the only important form of agrarian tenure that was not the ultimate property

38. For accounts of the decadence of the janissary system, see Gibb and Bowen, *Islamic Society and the West*, I/I, pp. 180–4; Stavrianos, *The Balkans since 1453*, pp. 120–2, 219–20.

39. For the emergence and character of the *iltizam* system in Egypt, see Shaw, *The Financial and Administrative Organization and Development of Ottoman Egypt*, pp. 29–39.

of the Sultanate.[40] These were traditionally much used as a camouflaging device to render land hereditary in a single family, vested with the 'administration' of the *waqf*. The early Osmanli rulers had kept a vigilant control of this devout institution; Mehmet II, in fact, had effected a general reappropriation of *waqf* lands by the State. In the epoch of Ottoman decline, however, *waqf* holdings multiplied once again, above all in Anatolia and the Arab provinces.

The advent and influence of the *iltizam* system transformed the situation of the peasantry. The *timariot* had not been able to evict or to exact dues above the statutory limits prescribed by the Sultan. The landlords of the new epoch brooked no such restrictions: the very brevity of their initial tenures incited them to super-exploitation of the peasants on their estates. In the course of the 18th century, increasing numbers of 'life-farms' or *malikane* were granted by the Porte, which moderated the short-term demands of these rural notables, but stabilized their long-term power over the villages.[41] Thus in the Balkans, the *timar* eventually generally gave way to what became known as the *chiflik* system. The *chiflik*-holder had practically unfettered control of the labour-force at his disposal: he could drive his peasants off the land, or prevent them leaving it by entangling them in debt obligations. He could enlarge his own manorial reserve or *hassa-chiflik* at the expense of his tenants' plots; and this became the general pattern. He would typically exact one half of the harvest of the direct

40. Bulgarian historians have laid great – too great – emphasis on the importance of *waqf* lands in the Ottoman social formation, in developing their claim that it was essentially feudal in character – a classification rejected, correctly in my view, by most Turkish historians. Since *waqf* lands were the nearest juridical category to private agrarian property, their extent can be used to argue that a feudal content lay concealed behind legal fictions of imperial-religious control. In fact, there is no reason to believe that *waqf* lands ever predominated in the Balkan and Anatolian countryside, or determined basic relations of production in the Ottoman social formation. But their increase in the epoch of Ottoman decline is well attested. For an able survey of the *waqf* phenomenon, see V. Mutafcieva and S. Dimitrov, 'Die Agrarverhältnisse im Osmanischen Reiches im XV – XVI Jh.', *Actes du Premier Congrès des Etudes Balkaniques*, pp. 689–702, which estimates them at perhaps one third of the total land area of the home countries, concentrated in the Balkans mainly in Thrace, the Aegean and Macedonia: they were virtually or completely unknown in Serbia or the Morea.

41. Gibb and Bowen, *Islamic Society and the West*, I/I, pp. 255–6. The most oppressive landlords were always tax-farmers, closely followed by religious authorities; op. cit., p. 247.

producers, who were left with a mere third of their output after payment of the land-tax and the fees for its collection.[42] In other words,
the condition of the Balkan peasantry sank together with that of the
rest of Eastern Europe, towards a common misery. In practice, it was
now bound to the soil and villagers could be legally recovered by landowners if they abandoned their lands. Just as the corn traffic with
Western Europe had led to an intensification of the rate of servile
exploitation in Poland or Eastern Germany, without occasioning it, so
the commercial production of cotton or maize for export along the
coasts and up the valleys of Greece, Bulgaria and Serbia increased
landlord pressures on the *chifliks*, and contributed to their spread. The
most distinctive feature of rural relations in the South-East was the
break-down of any firm civic order imposed from above: banditry
became rampant, encouraged by the mountainous relief of the region,
which made it the Mediterranean equivalent of flight on the Baltic
plains, for the peasantry. Landlords, conversely, maintained bands of
armed thugs or *kirjali* irregulars on their estates, to protect themselves
from revolt and repress their tenantry.[43] For the final term of the long
involution of the Ottoman State was the virtually complete paralysis
of the Porte and the usurpation of provincial power, first by military
pashas in Syria or Egypt, next by *derebeys* or valley lords in Anatolia,
and then by *ayans* or dynasties of local notables in Rumelia. By the end
of the 18th century, the Sultanate controlled only a fraction of the
26 *eyalets* into which the imperial administration was formally divided.

The protracted decomposition of the Osmanli despotism, however,
did not generate any ultimate feudalism. The imperial title to all secular
land within the Empire was not abandoned, however many *malikane*
grants were made for usufruct of it. The *chiflik* system never received
formal legal sanction; nor were peasants ever juridically bound to the
soil. Right down to 1826, the fortunes of the bureaucrats and tax-
farmers who battened on the subject population could be arbitrarily
confiscated by the Sultan at their death.[44] There was no positive

42. Stavrianos, *The Balkans since 1453*, pp. 138–42.

43. T. Stoianovich, 'Land Tenure and Related Sectors of the Balkan Economy
1600–1800', *The Journal of Economic History*, XII, Summer 1953, No. 3, pp. 401,
409–11.

44. Şerif Mardin, 'Power, Civil Society and Culture in the Ottoman Empire',
Comparative Studies in Society and History, Vol. 11, 1969, p. 277.

security of property; still less any titular nobility. The liquefaction of the old social and political order did not lead to the emergence of any cogent new one. The Osmanli State in the 19th century remained a sodden morass, artificially sustained by the rivalry of the European powers for its inheritance. Poland could be divided between Austria, Prussia and Russia, because all three were land powers with congruent access and interests in it. The Balkans could not, because there was no compatibility between the three main contenders for dominance of the region – Britain, Austria and Russia. Britain possessed maritime supremacy in the Mediterranean and commercial primacy in Turkey; the Ottoman market, indeed, imported more English goods by 1850 than France, Italy, Austria or Russia, making it a vital region for Victorian economic imperialism. British naval and industrial power precluded any harmonious arrangement for the disposition of the Ottoman Empire, baulking Russian efforts to partition it. At the same time, the progressive national awakening of the Balkan peoples after the Napoleonic epoch prevented any stabilization of the political situation in South-Eastern Europe. Serbian rebellion had broken out already in 1804; Greek insurrection followed it in 1821. Tsarist invasion in 1828–9 routed Turkish armies, and imposed the formal autonomy of Serbia, Moldavia and Wallachia from the Porte; while Anglo-French and Russian intervention both secured and confined Greek independence in 1830. These losses, derived from local movements that London or Vienna could not control, still left Turkey with a Balkan empire stretching from Bosnia to Thessaly, and Albania to Bulgaria.

International protection was to delay the ultimate demise of the Ottoman State for nearly a century, inspiring in the interim successive attempts at 'liberal' renovation to conform with Western capitalist norms. These were inaugurated by Mahmud II in the 1820's, in an attempt to modernize the administrative and economic apparatus of the Sultanate. The janissaries were disbanded, and *timars* wound up; *waqf* lands were nominally recalled to the imperial Treasury; foreign officers were imported to train a new army. Central control was reasserted over the provinces, and the reign of the *derebeys* brought to an end. These measures rapidly proved ineffective to staunch the decay of the imperial system. Mahmud's armies were routed by the Egyptian troops of Mehmet Ali, while his governors and functionaries often proved even more corrupt and oppressive than the local notables before them. Renewed Anglo-French pressure to liberalize and reorganize Ottoman rule followed this debacle. The result was the Tanzimat reforms of the mid-century, more closely geared to Western legal and commercial preoccupations. The Rescript of the Rose Chamber in 1839 finally assured juridical security of private property within the Empire, and religious equality before the law.[45] Both had been insistently demanded by the diplomatic corps in Istanbul. State property in land, however, still remained dominant in the home countries of the Empire. It was not until 1858 that an agrarian law was passed, giving limited rights of inheritance to those in control or usufruct of them. Unsatisfied with this measure, the Western powers pressed for an extension of these rights, which was conceded in 1867, when local landowners finally acquired juridical ownership of their estates.[46] But the artificial character of the new political course soon became evident. When Turkish nationalists attempted to impose a representative constitution, Sultan Abdul Hamid II had little difficulty in reimposing a brutal if rickety personal despotism in 1878. By the end of the century, a stabilization of the office-holding and landowning class had occurred, with the guarantees of security of property afforded by the Tanzimat measures. But otherwise no new social and political order arose within the Ottoman Empire, as it gradually contracted before the successive struggles for liberation fought by the subject Balkan peoples, and the manoeuvres of the major European powers to thwart or exploit them. In 1875, a popular revolt in Bulgaria was suppressed. Russia intervened and Turkey was again defeated in the field, while England once more mobilized to save it from the consequences of debacle. The result was a settlement between the European powers which granted full independence to Serbia, Rumania and Montenegro; created an autonomous Bulgaria under residual Ottoman suzerainty; and turned Bosnia over to Austrian control. In the next decade, Greece purchased Thessaly and Bulgaria gained independence.

It was the combined frustrations of accelerating imperial decline, and

45. Lewis, *The Emergence of Modern Turkey*, pp. 106–8.
46. H. Inalcik, 'Land Problems in Turkish History', *The Moslem World*, XLV, 1955, pp. 226–7. Inalcik comments that Western legal concepts were only fully applied to landownership, without conditions or stipulations, for the first time in 1926.

unwonted bureaucratic fixity during Abdul Hamid's rule, that inspired the military officers who came to be known as the Young Turks to seize power by a putsch in 1908. Career ambitions satisfied and Comtean slogans forgotten, the political programme of the Young Turks was reduced to further dictatorial centralism and repression of the subject nationalities of the Empire.[47] Defeat in the First Balkan War and disintegration in the First World War were its ignominious end. The Ottoman State thus underwent subtractions and modifications in the last century of its existence, but never acquired a new social spring. The old one simply became ever more tortured and broken. The negative reform of 'abuses' was inherently incapable of issuing into a positive reconstruction of the Empire, whether in the form of a new political system or a restoration of the old. Feudalism had not presided over the formation of the Ottoman Empire; Absolutism was distant from its decline. Attempts by the European powers to 'align' the Porte with the different institutional norms of Vienna, St Petersburg or London were equally futile: it belonged to another universe. The abortive reforms of Mahmud II and the Tanzimat epoch, followed by the Hamidian reaction and the Young Turk fiasco, produced neither a Turkish neo-despotism, nor an Eastern Absolutism, nor – naturally – a Western parliamentarism. The birth of a new form of State had to wait until the diplomatic conservation of the relics of the old ended with the international conflict of the First World War, which finally released the Osmanli realm from its misery.

The Balkans, however, were delivered from Ottoman domination before the *dénouement* in Turkey itself. The expulsion of the whole system of Ottoman occupation from country after country, from the early 19th century onwards, led to an unexpected agrarian pattern in the peninsula, distinct from that of the rest of both Eastern and Western Europe. Rumania, historically a late no man's land between the Balkan and Transalbingian types of regional development, experienced the strangest twist of all the new countries that emerged after 1815. For it became the one country in Europe where a true 'second serfdom',

47. Even the most indulgent recent study of the Young Turk regime concludes that it was unable to create any new institutions, but merely exploited traditional mechanisms of rule for its own purposes: Feroz Ahmed, *The Young Turks*, Oxford 1969, pp. 164–5.

unquestionably determined by the grain trade, occurred after a 'first' serfdom had previously come to an end. The Rumanian lands had, as we have seen, been uniquely left under their own boyar class by the Ottoman State, when it overran them in the 16th century. The formation of a stratified rural society with seigneurial lords and a subject peasantry had been very recent, because of the long retardation imposed on this area by predator nomadic rule, which only came to an end with the gradual expulsion of the Cumans and Tartars in the 13th century.[48] Communal village property was widespread down to the 14th century, and it was only with the emergence of the Moldavian and Wallachian principalities in the 15th century that a landed aristocracy took shape, at first exploiting the rural producers fiscally rather than feudally – much in the fashion of the Turkic nomads that had schooled it.[49] The brief unification of the two states by Michael I in the late 16th century marked the generalized adscription of the Rumanian peasantry. Serfdom was thereafter consolidated under Ottoman overlordship. In the 18th century, the Porte entrusted administration of these provinces to Greek Phanariot families from Istanbul, who came to form an intermediate ruling dynasty of so-called Hospodars in the Principalities, where tax-collection and trade were already controlled by expatriate Greeks.

Boyar manorialism was now increasingly harassed by peasant resistance, in the characteristic Eastern form of mass flights to escape dues and taxes. Austrian officials, anxious to settle the newly won Habsburg borderlands in South-Eastern Europe, calculatedly offered Rumanian refugees haven across the frontiers.[50] Seriously concerned with the deteriorating labour situation in the Principalities, the Sultan in 1744 ordered one of the Hospodars, Constantine Mavrokordatos, to pacify and repopulate the Principalities. Influenced by the European

48. The historical origins of the Rumanian social formation in the late mediaeval epoch are charted in H. H. Stahl, *Les Anciennes Communautés Villageoises Roumaines. Asservissement et Pénétration Capitaliste*, Bucharest 1969, pp. 25–45: a very distinguished work, which casts light on many aspects of the social development of Eastern Europe.

49. There is a meticulous periodization of this whole process in Stahl, *Les Anciennes Communautés Villageoises*, pp. 163–89.

50. W. H. MacNeill, *Europe's Steppe Frontier 1500–1800*, Chicago 1964, p. 204.

Enlightenment, Mavrokordatos decreed the gradual abolition of servile bonds in both Wallachia (1746) and Moldavia (1749), by granting every peasant the right to purchase emancipation;[51] a measure facilitated by the absence of any equivalent juridical category of serfdom within the Turkish-administered provinces of the Empire. There was in this century no export trade in cereals because the Porte controlled a state commercial monopoly, and merely shipped tribute in kind down to Istanbul. However, the Treaty of Adrianople in 1829, which gave Russia virtually co-suzerainty over the Rumanian lands with Turkey, abrogated Ottoman export controls. The result was a sudden and spectacular grain boom along the Danube. For by the mid 19th century, the advent of the industrial revolution in Western Europe had created a capitalist world market of a type that had never existed in the 16th and 17th centuries, with a pulling power that could transform backward agrarian regions within a few decades. Corn output in the Rumanian Principalities doubled from 1829–32, and export values from 1831–3. The acreage of cereal cultivation actually increased ten times within a decade, from 1830 to 1840.[52] The rural labour for this phenomenal growth was found by reimposing servile obligations on the Rumanian peasantry and stepping up labour services to levels greater than those before Mavrokordatos's decrees in the previous century. The one genuine case of a second serfdom in Europe was thus the work of *industrial*, not mercantile capitalism; and it could only have been so. Here, direct and massive inter-economic causality, operating across the length of the continent, was possible, where it had never been two or three centuries earlier. The Rumanian peasantry remained depressed and land-hungry thereafter, in conditions very similar to those of the Russian peasantry. Servile restrictions were once again legally abolished by a Reform in 1864, directly modelled on the Tsarist proclamation of 1861; as in Russia, the countryside remained dominated by feudal landlords down to the First World War.

Rumania, however, was the exception in the Balkans. Virtually

51. For a discussion of the emancipation decrees and boyar reaction to them, see A. Oțetea, 'Le Second Asservissement des Paysans Roumains (1746–1821)', *Nouvelles Etudes d'Histoire*, I, Bucharest 1955, pp. 299–312.

52. A. Oțetea, 'Le Second Servage dans les Principautés Danubiennes', *Nouvelles Etudes d'Histoire*, II, Bucharest 1960, p. 333.

everywhere else, something like the opposite process occurred. For in Croatia, Serbia, Bulgaria and Greece, the local aristocracies had been wiped out by Ottoman conquest, the land directly annexed to the Sultanate, and Turkish occupiers planted on it – by the 19th century, mostly the powerful and parasitic class of local *ayan* notables. Successive national revolts and wars of liberation now drove Turkish armies out of Serbia (1804–1913), Greece (1821–1913) and Bulgaria (1875–1913). The conquest of political independence in these countries was thus automatically accompanied by an economic upheaval in the countryside. For Turkish landlords normally and comprehensibly decamped with the troops that had guarded them, abandoning their estates to the peasants that had tilled them. This pattern varied considerably, according to the duration of the independence struggle. Wherever it was slow and protracted, as in Serbia and Greece, there was much more time for a native landowning stratum to emerge and expand in the course of it, appropriating *chifliks* outright in the later phases: wealthy Greek families, for example, bought many Turkish estates intact in Thessaly, when it was acquired from the Porte in 1881.[53] In Bulgaria, on the other hand, the briefer and fiercer tempo of the independence struggle gave much less opportunity for such transfers to happen. But in all three countries, the ultimate rural economy that emerged was very similar.[54] Independent Bulgaria, Greece and Serbia became essentially countries of small peasant proprietors, at a time when Prussia, Poland, Hungary and Russia were still lands of noble latifundia. Rural exploitation, naturally, did not come to an end: usurers, merchants and functionaries now relayed it in new forms in the independent states. But the fundamental agrarian pattern of the Balkan countries remained based on petty production, amidst increasing overpopulation, divided holdings and village debts. The recession

53. Stavrianos, *The Balkans since 1453*, pp. 478–9.
54. Albania formed a distinct case, because of the Islamization of the majority of the population under Ottoman rule, and the preservation of tribal social patterns in the mountains. Turkish recruitment of Albanians into the Osmanli State apparatus was traditional; the Hamidian reaction had especially relied on their loyalty. Thus the local Muslim notables opted for independence only at the last moment in 1912, when it was obvious that Turkish power was finished in the Balkans. Landlordism was consequently unimpaired by the end of Ottoman rule; the alpine tribalism of much of the country, on the other hand, inevitably limited large-estate agriculture.

of Turkish rule signified the end of traditional landlordism. Eastern Europe suffered a common social and economic backwardness at the turn of the 20th century, which separated it from Western Europe: but the South-East remained a peninsula apart, within it.

III. Conclusions

Conclusions

The Ottoman State, occupant of South-Eastern Europe for five hundred years, camped in the continent without ever becoming naturalized into its social or political system. It always remained largely a stranger to European culture, as an Islamic intrusion into Christendom, and has posed intractable problems of presentation to unitary histories of the continent to this day. In fact, the long and intimate presence on European soil of a social formation and State structure in such contrast with the prevalent pattern of the continent, provides an apposite measure against which to assess the historical specificity of European society before the advent of industrial capitalism. From the Renaissance onwards, indeed, European political thinkers in the age of Absolutism repeatedly sought to define the character of their own world by opposition with that of the Turkish order, so close and yet so remote from it; none of them reduced the distance simply or mainly to one of religion.

Machiavelli, in the Italy of the early 16th century, was the first theorist to use the Ottoman State as the antithesis of a European monarchy. In two central passages of *The Prince*, he singled out the autocratic bureaucracy of the Porte as an institutional order which separated it from all the States of Europe: 'The entire Turkish empire is ruled by one master, and all other men are his servants; he divides his kingdom into *sandjaks* and dispatches various administrators to govern them, whom he transfers and changes at his pleasure . . . they are all slaves, bounden to him.'[1] He added that the type of standing army at the disposal of the Osmanli rulers was something unknown anywhere else in the continent at the time: 'No prince today possesses professional

1. *Il Principe e Discorsi*, pp. 26–7.

troops entrenched in the government and administration of the provinces. . . The Turk is an exception, for he controls a permanent army of 12,000 infantry and 15,000 cavalry, on which the security and strength of his realm rests; the supreme principle of his power is to safe-guard its loyalty.'[2] These reflections, it has rightly been pointed out by Chabod, constitute one of the first implicit approaches to a self-definition of 'Europe'.[3] Sixty years later, in the throes of the Religious Wars in France, Bodin developed a political contrast between mon-archies bound by respect for the persons and goods of their subjects, and empires unrestricted in their dominion over them: the first repre-sented the 'royal' sovereignty of European States, the second the 'lordly' power of despotisms such as the Ottoman State, which were essentially foreign to Europe. 'The King of the Turks is called the Grand Seignior, not because of the size of his realm, for that of the King of Spain is ten times larger, but because he is complete master of its persons and property. Only the servitors brought up and trained in his household are called slaves. But the *timariots*, of whom his subjects are tenants, are merely vested with their *timars* at his sufferance; their grants must be renewed every decade, and when they die their heirs can inherit only their movable goods. There are no such lordly monarchies elsewhere in Europe. . . . The peoples of Europe, prouder and more warlike than those of Asia or Africa, have never tolerated or known a lordly monarchy since the time of the Hungarian invasions.'[4] In the England of the early 17th century, Bacon emphasized that the funda-mental distinction between European and Turkish systems was the social absence of a hereditary aristocracy in the Ottoman realm. 'A monarchy where there is no nobility at all, is ever a pure and absolute tyranny; as that of the Turks. For nobility attempers sovereignty, and draws the eyes of the people somewhat aside from the line royal.'[5] Two decades later, after the overthrow of the Stuart monarchy, the repub-

2. *Il Principe e Discorsi*, pp. 83–4.

3. F. Chabod, *Storia dell'Idea d'Europa*, Bari 1964, pp. 48–52.

4. *Les Six Livres de la République*, pp. 201–2. European thinkers had noticeable difficulty in finding a terminology to discuss the peculiarities of the Ottoman State in this epoch. Hence the curiously inapposite title of 'Grand Seignior' bestowed on the Sultan. The notion of 'despotism', later customarily applied to Turkey, was a neologism of the 18th century.

5. *The Essays or Counsels Civil and Moral*, London 1632, p. 72.

lican Harrington shifted the stress of the contrast to the economic foundations of the Ottoman Empire as the basic line of division between Turkish and European States: the Sultan's juridical monopoly of landed property was the real hallmark of the Porte: 'If one man be sole landlord of a territory, or overbalance the people, for example, three parts in four, he is Grand Seignior: for so the Turk is called from his property; and his Empire is absolute Monarchy . . . it being unlawful in Turkey that any should possess land but the Grand Seignior.'[6]

By the late 17th century, the power of the Ottoman State had passed its peak; the tone of comment on it now perceptibly altered. For the first time, the theme of the historical superiority of Europe started to become central to discussion of the Turkish system, while the defects of the latter were generalized to all the great Empires of Asia. This new step was taken, decisively, in the writings of the French physician Bernier, who travelled through the Turkish, Persian and Mughal realms, and became the personal doctor of the Emperor Aurangzeb in India. On his return to France, he projected Mughal India as a yet more extreme version of Ottoman Turkey: the basis of the desolate tyranny of both, he reported, was the absence of private property in land, whose effects he graphically compared to the smiling countryside ruled by Louis XIV. 'How insignificant is the wealth and strength of Turkey in comparison with its natural advantages! Let us only suppose that country as populous and cultivated as it would become if the right of private property were acknowledged, and we cannot doubt that it could maintain armies as prodigious as formerly. I have travelled through nearly every part of the empire, and witnessed how lamentably it is ruined and depopulated. . . . Take away the right of private property in land, and you introduce, as an infallible consequence, tyranny, slavery, injustice, beggary and barbarism; the ground will cease to be cultivated and become a wilderness; the road will be opened to the destruction of nations, the ruin of kings and states. It is the hope by which a man is animated that he shall retain the fruits of his industry, and transmit them to his descendants, that forms the main foundation of everything excellent and beneficial in this world; and if we take a review of the different kingdoms of the globe, we shall find that they prosper or decline according as it is acknowledged or condemned: in

6. *The Commonwealth of Oceana*, London 1658, pp. 4, 5.

a word, it is the prevalence or neglect of this principle which changes and diversifies the face of the earth.'[7] Bernier's acrid account of the Orient exercised a deep influence on subsequent generations of thinkers, during the Enlightenment. In the early 18th century, Montesquieu echoed his depiction of the Turkish State closely: 'The Grand Seignior grants most of the land to his soldiers and disposes of it at his whim; he can seize the entire inheritance of the officers of his empire; when a subject dies without male descent, his daughters are left with the mere usufruct of his goods, for the Turkish ruler acquires the ownership of them; the result is that possession of most assets in society is precarious. . . . There is no despotism so injurious as that whose prince declares himself proprietor of all landed estates and heir of all subjects: the consequence is always the abandonment of cultivation, and if the ruler interferes in trade, the ruin of every industry.'[8]

By now, of course, European colonial expansion had explored and traversed virtually the whole globe, and the scope of political notions originally derived from the specific encounter with the Ottoman State in the Balkans had expanded accordingly, to the confines of China and beyond. Montesquieu's work thus embodied for the first time a full-scale comparative theory of what he categorically termed 'despotism' as a general extra-European form of government, whose whole structure was opposed to the principles born of European 'feudalism', in *De l'Esprit des Lois*. The generality of the concept nevertheless retained a traditional geographical denotation, explained by the influence of climate and terrain: 'Asia is that region of the world where despotism is so to speak naturally domiciled.'[9] Bequeathed by the Enlightenment, the fortunes of the notion of Oriental Despotism in the 19th century are famous and need not concern us here:[10] it will suffice to say that from Hegel onwards most of the same basic conceptions of Asian society were retained, whose intellectual function was

7. *Travels in the Mogul Empire* (translated by Archibald Constable), re-edited Oxford 1934, pp. 234, 238. The Victorian luxuriance of Constable's translation has been slightly trimmed above, to bring it closer to the text of Bernier's original: for which see François Bernier, *Voyages*, I, Amsterdam 1710, pp. 313, 319–20.

8. *De l'Esprit des Lois*, I, pp. 67–66.

9. *Ibid.*, p. 68.

10. They are discussed in the note on the 'Asiatic Mode of Production', pp. 462–95 below.

always to draw a radical *contrast* between European history, whose original specificity Montesquieu had located in feudalism and whose modern descendant he had discerned in absolutism, and the destiny of other continents.

In this century, Marxist scholars, persuaded of the universality of the successive phases of socio-economic development registered in Europe, have by contrast generally asserted that feudalism was a world-wide phenomenon, embracing Asian or African states as much as European. Ottoman, Egyptian, Moroccan, Persian, Indian, Mongolian or Chinese feudalism have been discerned and studied. Political reaction against the imperial ideologies of European superiority has led to intellectual extension of historiographic concepts derived from the past of one continent to explain the evolution of others, or all. No term has undergone such an indiscriminate and pervasive diffusion as that of feudalism, which has often in practice been applied to any social formation between tribal and capitalist poles of identity, unstamped by slavery. The feudal mode of production is minimally defined in this usage as the combination of large landownership with small peasant production, where the exploiting class extracts the surplus from the immediate producer by customary forms of extra-economic coercion – labour services, deliveries in kind, or rents in cash – and where commodity exchange and labour mobility are correspondingly restricted.[11] This complex is presented as the economic nucleus of feudalism, which can subsist within a wide number of alternative political shells. In other words, juridical and constitutional systems become facultative and external elaborations on an invariant productive centre. Political and legal superstructures are divorced from the economic infrastructure that alone constitutes the actual feudal mode of production as such. In this view, now widespread among contemporary Marxist scholars,

11. A single example, defining the Ottoman social formation with which we have been specifically concerned, must suffice here: 'Relations of production of a purely feudal type developed under the Ottomans. The preponderance of a small peasant economy, domination of agriculture over handicrafts and country over town, monopoly of landownership by a minority, appropriation of the surplus product of the peasantry by a ruling class – all these hallmarks of the feudal mode of production are to be found in Ottoman society.' Ernst Werner, *Die Geburt einer Grossmacht, die Osmanen*, p. 305. This passage is rightly singled out for criticism by Ernest Mandel, *The Formation of the Economic Thought of Karl Marx*, London 1971, p. 127.

the type of agrarian property, the nature of the possessing class, and the matrix of the State may vary enormously, above a common rural order at the base of the whole social formation. In particular, the parcellized sovereignty, vassal hierarchy and fief system of mediaeval Europe cease to be in any respect original or essential characteristics of feudalism. Their complete absence is compatible with the presence of a feudal social formation, so long as a combination of large-scale agrarian exploitation and peasant production, founded on extra-economic relations of coercion and dependence, obtains. Thus Ming China, Seljuk Turkey, Genghisid Mongolia, Safavid Persia, Mughal India, Tulunid Egypt, Ummayad Syria, Almoravid Morocco, Wahabite Arabia – all become equally amenable to classification as feudal, on a par with Capetian France, Norman England or Hohenstaufen Germany. In the course of this enquiry, three representative examples of such categorization have been encountered: as we have seen, the nomadic Tartar confederations, the Byzantine Empire, and the Ottoman Sultanate have each of them been designated feudal States by serious scholars of their respective histories,[12] who have argued that their overt superstructural divergences from Western norms concealed an underlying convergence of infrastructural relations of production. All privilege to Western development is thereby held to disappear, in the multiform process of a world history secretly single from the start. Feudalism, in this version of materialist historiography, becomes an absolving ocean in which virtually any society may receive its baptism.

The scientific invalidity of this theoretical ecumenicism can be demonstrated from the logical paradox in which it results. For if, in effect, the feudal mode of production can be defined independently of the variant juridical and political superstructures which accompany it, such that its presence can be registered throughout the globe wherever primitive and tribal social formations were superseded, the problem then arises: how is the unique dynamism of the European theatre of international feudalism to be explained? No historian has yet claimed that industrial capitalism developed spontaneously anywhere else except in Europe and its American extension, which then, precisely, conquered the rest of the world by virtue of this economic primacy,

12. See above, pp. 386–7; *Passages from Antiquity to Feudalism*, pp. 219–22, 282–3.

arresting or implanting the capitalist mode of production abroad according to the needs and drives of its own imperial system. If there was a common economic foundation of feudalism right across the whole land mass from the Atlantic to the Pacific, divided merely by juridical and constitutional forms, and yet only one zone produced the industrial revolution that was eventually to lead to the transformation of all societies everywhere, the determinant of its transcendant success must be sought in the political and legal superstructures that alone distinguished it. Laws and States, dismissed as secondary and insubstantial, reemerge with a vengeance, as the apparent authors of the most momentous break in modern history. In other words, once the whole structure of sovereignty and legality is *dissociated* from the economy of a universal feudalism, its shadow paradoxically governs the world: for it becomes the only principle capable of explaining the differential development of the whole mode of production. The very omnipresence of feudalism in this conception reduces the fate of the continents to the surface play of mere local usages. A colour-blind materialism, incapable of appreciating the real and rich spectrum of diverse social totalities within the same temporal band of history, thus inevitably ends in a perverse idealism.

The solution to the paradox lies, obvious yet unremarked, in the very definition given by Marx of pre-capitalist social formations. *All* modes of production in class societies prior to capitalism extract surplus labour from the immediate producers by means of extra-economic coercion. Capitalism is the first mode of production in history in which the means whereby the surplus is pumped out of the direct producer is 'purely' economic in form – the wage contract: the equal exchange between free agents which reproduces, hourly and daily, inequality and oppression. All other previous modes of exploitation operate through *extra-economic* sanctions – kin, customary, religious, legal or political. It is therefore on principle always impossible to read them off from economic relations as such. The 'superstructures' of kinship, religion, law or the state necessarily enter into the constitutive structure of the mode of production in pre-capitalist social formations. They intervene *directly* in the 'internal' nexus of surplus-extraction, where in capitalist social formations, the first in history to separate the economy as a formally self-contained order, they provide by contrast its 'external' preconditions. In consequence, pre-capitalist modes of production cannot be defined *except* via their political, legal and ideological superstructures, since these are what determine the type of extra-economic coercion that specifies them. The precise forms of juridical dependence, property and sovereignty that characterize a pre-capitalist social formation, far from being merely accessory or contingent epiphenomena, compose on the contrary the central indices of the determinate mode of production dominant within it. A scrupulous and exact taxonomy of these legal and political configurations is thus a precondition of establishing any comprehensive typology of pre-capitalist modes of production.[13] It is evident, in fact, that the complex *imbrication* of economic exploitation with extra-economic institutions and ideologies creates a much wider gamut of possible modes of production prior to capitalism than could be deduced from the relatively simple and massive generality of the capitalist mode of production itself, which came to be their common and involuntary *terminus ad quem* in the epoch of industrial imperialism.

Any *a priori* temptation to pre-align the former with the uniformity of the latter should thus be resisted. The possibility of a plurality of post-tribal and non-slave, pre-capitalist modes of production is inherent in their mechanisms of surplus extraction. The immediate producers and the means of production – comprising both the tools of labour and the objects of labour, e.g. land – are always dominated by the exploiting class through the prevalent property system, the nodal intersection between law and economy: but because property relations are themselves directly articulated on the political and ideological order, which indeed often expressly governs their distribution (confining landownership to aristocrats, for example, or excluding nobles from trade), the total apparatus of exploitation always extends upwards into the sphere of the superstructures themselves. 'Social relations in

13. This fundamental need has been clearly perceived by the Soviet historian Zel'in, in his remarkable essay, 'Printsipy Morfologicheskoi Klassifikatsii Form Zavisimosti', in K. K. Zel'in and M. V. Trofimova, *Formy Zavisimosti v Vostochnom Sredizemnomor'e Ellenisticheskovo Perioda*, Moscow 1969, pp. 11–51, especially 29–33. Zel'in's text contains a criticism of the antinomies of conventional discussions of feudalism by Marxists; his own concerns are essentially with more rigorous definition of the forms of dependence – neither feudal nor slave in character – characteristic of the Hellenistic world.

their totality form what is now designated property', wrote Marx to Annenkov.[14] This does not mean that juridical ownership itself is therefore a mere fiction or illusion, that can be waived or dispelled by a direct analysis of the economic substructure beneath it, a procedure which leads straight to the logical collapse already indicated. It means that for historical materialism, on the contrary, juridical property can never be separated either from economic production or politico-ideological power: its absolutely central position within any mode of production derives from its linkage of the two, which in pre-capitalist social formations becomes an outright and official fusion. It is thus no accident that Marx devoted virtually the whole of his pivotal manuscript on pre-capitalist societies in the *Grundrisse* – his only work of systematic theoretical comparison of different modes of production – to a profound analysis of the *forms of agrarian property* in successive or contemporary modes of production in Europe, Asia and America: the guiding thread of the whole text is the changing character and position of landownership, and its interlocking relationship with political systems, from primitive tribalism to the eve of capitalism.

We have already seen that Marx specifically distinguishes nomadic pastoralism from all forms of sedentary agriculture as a distinct mode of production, based on collective property of immobile wealth (land) and individual property of mobile wealth (herds), contrary to later Marxist writers.[15] It is thus no surprise either that Marx emphasized that one of the fundamental traits defining feudalism was *private, noble property in land*. His comments on Kovalevsky's study of the dissolution of communal village property are in this respect especially revealing. Kovalevsky, a young Russian historian who admired and corresponded with Marx, dedicated a substantial portion of his work to what he claimed was the slow emergence of feudalism in India, after the Muslim conquests. He did not dismiss the political and legal differences between the Mughal and European agrarian systems as altogether unimportant, and conceded that the juridical persistence of exclusive imperial ownership of land led to a 'lower intensity' of feudalization in India than in Europe. But he nevertheless argued that

14. Marx-Engels, *Selected Correspondence*, p. 38 (retranslated).
15. See *Passages from Antiquity to Feudalism*, p. 220.

in reality an extended fief system, with a full hierarchy of subinfeudation, had developed into an Indian feudalism before British conquest
broke off its consolidation.[16] Although Kovalevsky's study was to a
considerable extent influenced by his own work, and the tone of his
unpublished notes on the copy sent to him by the Russian scholar was
generally benevolent, it is striking that Marx repeatedly criticized those
passages where Kovalevsky assimilated Indian or Islamic socio-
economic institutions to those of European feudalism. The most
trenchant and illuminating of these interventions rejecting the attribution of a feudal mode of production to Mughal India reads: 'On the
grounds that the "benefice system", "sale of offices" (the latter, however, is by no means purely feudal, as is proved by Rome) and "commendation" are to be found in India – Kovalevsky regards this as
feudalism in the Western European sense. Kovalevsky forgets, among
other things, that serfdom – which represents an important element in
feudalism – does not exist in India. Moreover, as for the *individual role*
of feudal lords (exercising the function of counts) as *protectors* not
merely of unfree but also of free peasants (cf. Palgrave), this plays an
insignificant role in India, apart from the *waqfs*. Nor do we encounter
that *poetry of the soil* (*Bodenpoesie*) so characteristic of Romano-
Germanic feudalism (cf. Maurer) in India, any more than in Rome. In
India, land is nowhere *noble* in the sense of being, for example, inalien-
able to commoners! On the other hand, Kovalevsky himself sees one
fundamental difference: the absence of *patrimonial justice in the field of
civil law in the Empire of the Great Mughal.*'[17] Elsewhere Marx again
pointedly contradicted Kovalevsky's claim that the Muslim conquest of
India, by imposing the Islamic land tax or *kharaj* on the peasantry,
thereby converted hitherto allodial into feudal property: 'The payment
of the *kharaj* did not transform their lands into feudal property, any
more than the *impôt foncier* rendered French landed property feudal.

---

16. M. Kovalevsky, *Obshchinnoe Zemlevladenie, Prichiny, Khod i Posled-
stviya evo Razlozheniya*, Moscow 1879, pp. 130–55.

17. 'Materialy Instituta Marksizma-Leninizma pri Tsk KPSS. Iz Neopubliko-
vannykh Rukopisei Karla Marksa', *Sovetskoe Vostokovedenie*, No. 5, 1968, p. 12.
Marx's notes on Kovalevsky have been published only in Russian, in *Sovetskoe
Vostokovedenie*, 1958, No. 3, pp. 4–13, No. 4, pp. 3–22, No. 5, pp. 3–28; *Problemy
Vostokovedenie*, 1959, No. 1, pp. 3–17. There is an introduction to the manu-
scripts by L. S. Gamayunov, in *Sovetskoe Vostokovedenie*, 1958, No. 2, pp. 35–45.

All Kovalevsky's descriptions here are in the highest degree useless.'[18]
Nor was the nature of the State similar to that of the feudal principalities of Europe: 'By Indian law political power was not subject to
division between sons: thereby an important source of *European
feudalism* was blocked up.'[19]

These critical passages show very clearly that Marx himself was well
aware of the dangers of a promiscuous extension of the rubric of
feudalism beyond Europe, and refused to accept the India of the Delhi
Sultanate or the Mughal Empire as a feudal social formation. His
marginalia reveal, moreover, an extreme penetration and sensitivity
towards precisely those 'superstructural' forms whose irreducible
importance for the classification of pre-capitalist modes of production
has just been emphasized. Thus his objections to Kovalevsky's designation of Indian agrarian society after the Islamic conquest as feudal cover
virtually the whole range of legal, political, social, military, judicial,
fiscal and ideological fields. They could perhaps be summarized, without undue stretching, thus: feudalism typically involves the juridical
serfdom and military protection of the peasantry by a social class of
nobles, enjoying individual authority and property, and exercising an
exclusive monopoly of law and private rights of justice, within a
political framework of fragmented sovereignty and subordinate
fiscality, and an aristocratic ideology exalting rural life. It will be seen
at once how remote this comprehensive heuristic schedule is from the
few, simple tabs since often used to label a social formation as feudal.
To revert to our initial point of departure, there can be no question
that Marx's own view of feudalism, in this condensed definition,
excluded the Turkish Sultanate from its scope – a State that was, in
fact, in many ways the inspiration and model of Mughal India.

The contrast so intensely felt by contemporaries between European
and Ottoman historical forms was thus well-founded. The Turkish
socio-political order was radically distinct from that which characterized Europe as a whole, whether in the Western or Eastern regions

18. *Sovetskoe Vostokovedenie*, 1958, No. 4, p. 18.
19. *Sovetskoe Vostokovedenie*, 1958, No. 5, p. 6. Note elsewhere Marx's criti-
cisms of Kovalevsky for describing Turkish military colonies in Algeria as feudal,
by analogy with Indian examples: 'Kovalevsky baptizes these "feudal" on the
weak grounds that under certain conditions something like the Indian *jagir*
could develop out of them.' *Problemy Vostokovedenie*, 1959, No. 1, p. 7.

of the continent. European feudalism had, in fact, no likeness anywhere in the geographical zones abutting onto it; it was, at the far occidental extremity of the Eurasian land-mass, alone. The original feudal mode of production which triumphed during the early Middle Ages was never simply composed of an elementary set of economic indices. Serfdom provided, of course, the primary ground-work of the total system of surplus-extraction. But the combination of large-scale agrarian property controlled by an exploiting class, with small-scale production by a tied peasantry, in which surplus labour was pressed out of the latter by *corvées* or dues in kind, was in its generality a very widespread pattern throughout the pre-industrial world. Virtually any post-tribal social formation that did not rest on slavery or nomadism, revealed in this sense forms of landlordism. The singularity of feudalism was never exhausted merely by the existence of seigneurial and serf classes as such.[20] It was their specific organization in a vertically articulated system of parcellized sovereignty and scalar property that distinguished the feudal mode of production in Europe. It was this concrete nexus which spelt out the precise type of extra-economic coercion exercised over the direct producer. The fusion of vassalage-benefice-immunity to produce the fief system proper created an entirely *sui generis* pattern of 'sovereignty and dependence', in Marx's words. The peculiarity of this system lay in the double character of the relationship it established, both between the immediate producers and the stratum of non-producers appropriating their surplus labour, and within the exploiting class of non-producers themselves. For the fief was in essence an economic grant of land, conditional on performance of military service, and vested with judicial rights over the peasantry tilling it. It was consequently always an amalgam of property and sovereignty, in which the partial nature of the one was matched by the private character of the other: conditional tenure was structurally linked to individual jurisdiction. The original dilution of absolute ownership in land was thus complemented by the fragmentation of public authority in a stepped hierarchy. At the level of the village itself, the result was the

20. For a particularly clear and trenchant critique of promiscuous uses of the term 'feudalism', in this and other ways, see Claude Cahen, 'Réflexions sur l'Usage du Mot "Féodalité" ', *The Journal of the Economic and Social History of the Orient*, III, 1960, I, pp. 7–20.

emergence of a class of nobles enjoying *personal* rights of exploitation and jurisdiction over dependent peasants, consecrated in law.

Inherent in this configuration was rural residence by the possessing class, as opposed to the urban location of the aristocracies of classical Antiquity: the exercise of seigneurial protection and justice presupposed the direct presence of the feudal nobility in the countryside itself, symbolized by the castles of the mediaeval period and later idealized in the 'poetry of the soil' of the subsequent epoch. The individual property and power which was the mark of the feudal class in the agrarian landscape could consequently be accompanied by an organizing role in production itself, whose typical form in Europe was the manor. The division of the manorial estate into the lord's demesne and tenants' virgates reproduced below, as we have seen, the scalar economic articulation characteristic of the feudal system as a whole. Above, the prevalence of the fief established unique internal bonds within the nobility. For the combination of vassalage, benefice and immunity into a single complex created the ambivalent mixture of contractual 'reciprocity' and dependent 'subordination' which always set a true feudal aristocracy off from any other form of exploitative warrior class, in alternative modes of production. Enfiefment was a synallagmatic contract:[21] the oath of homage and the act of investment bound both parties to the respect of specific obligations and the performance of specific duties. Felony was a rupture of this contract which could be committed by vassal *or* lord, and freed either side if injured from its terms. At the same time, this synallagmatic pact was also the hierarchical dominion of a superior over his inferior: the vassal was the liege-man of his lord, and owed him personal, bodily fealty. The composite ethos of the feudal nobility thus held 'honour' and 'loyalty' together in a dynamic tension foreign to either the free citizenry of classical Antiquity, which in Greece or Rome had known only the first, or the servitors of a despotic authority like the Sultanism of Turkey, who knew only the second. Contractual mutuality and positional inequality were merged in the full device of the fief. The result was to generate an aristocratic ideology which rendered compatible pride of rank and humility of homage, legal fixity of obligations and personal

21. This is Boutruche's apposite term: *Seigneurie et Féodalité*, II, pp. 204–7.

fidelity of allegiance.[22] The moral dualism of this feudal code was rooted in the fusion and diffusion of economic and political powers within the mode of production as a whole. Conditional property instituted the subordination of the vassal within a social hierarchy of lordship: parcellized sovereignty, on the other hand, vested the feoffee with autonomous jurisdiction over those below him. Both were solemnized by transactions between particularized individuals within the noble estate as a whole. Aristocratic power and property were quintessentially *personal*, at all levels of the chain of protection and dependence.

This politico-legal structure, in turn, had further critical consequences. The overall parcellization of sovereignty permitted the growth of autonomous towns in the interstitial spaces between disparate lordships. A separate and universal Church could cross-cut all secular principalities, concentrating cultural skills and religious sanctions in its own independent clerical organization. Moreover, within each particular realm of mediaeval Europe, an estates system could develop which characteristically represented in a tripartite assembly the nobility, clergy and burghers as distinct orders within the feudal polity. The basic precondition of such an estates system was, once again, the de-totalization of sovereignty which conferred on the members of the aristocratic ruling class of the society private prerogatives of justice and administration, such that their collective consent was necessary for any extra-suzerain actions by the monarchy at the top of the feudal hierarchy, outside the mediatized chain of personal obligations and rights. Mediaeval parliaments were thus a necessary and logical exten-

22. Weber was the first to emphasize the originality of this combination: see his excellent discussion, *Economy and Society*, III, pp. 1075–8. In general, Weber's analytic contrasts between 'feudalism' and 'patrimonialism' are of great force and acuity. His overall use of them, however, is vitiated by the notorious weaknesses of the notion of 'ideal-types' characteristic of his later work. Thus both feudalism and patrimonialism are in practice treated as detachable and atomic 'traits' rather than as unified structures; consequently they can be distributed and mixed at random by Weber, who lacked any *historical* theory proper after his pioneering early work on Antiquity. One result is Weber's inability to provide any stable or accurate definition of Absolutism in Europe: sometimes it is 'patrimonialism' which is 'dominant in Continental Europe up to the French Revolution', while at other times Absolute monarchies are deemed 'already bureaucratic-rational'. These confusions were inherent in the increasing formalism of his later work. In this respect Hintze, who learnt much from Weber, was always his superior.

sion of the traditional presentation of *auxilium et consilium* – aid and advice – by the vassal to his overlord. Their ambiguity of function – instruments of royal will or devices of baronial resistance to it – was inherent in the contradictory unity of the feudal compact itself, at once reciprocal and unequal itself.

Geographically, as we have seen, the 'full' feudal complex was born in continental Western Europe, in the former Carolingian lands. It thereafter expanded slowly and unevenly outwards, first to England, Spain and Scandinavia; later, and less perfectly, it spread into Eastern Europe, where its constituent elements and phases underwent numerous local dislocations and torsions, without the region ever losing an unmistakable general affinity with Western Europe, as its comparatively undeveloped periphery. The boundaries of European feudalism, so formed, were fundamentally set neither by religion nor by topography; although both manifestly overdetermined them. Christendom was never coextensive with this mode of production: there was no feudalism in mediaeval Ethiopia or Lebanon. Nomadic pastoralism, adapted to the arid terrain of much of Central Asia, the Middle East and North Africa, for long periods bordered Europe on every side, except for the Atlantic across which the latter would eventually escape to dominate the world. But the frontiers between nomadism and feudalism were not drawn in any linear fashion merely by topography: the Pannonian plain and the Ukrainian steppe, classical habitats of predatory pastoralism, were both ultimately integrated into the sedentary agriculture of Europe. Feudalism, born in the Western sector of Europe, propagated itself in the Eastern sector by force of settlement and example. Conquest played an additional, but subordinate role: its most spectacular achievement also proved to be its most ephemeral, in the Levant. Unlike either the slave mode of production before it or the capitalist mode of production after it, the feudal mode of production as such did not lend itself to imperialist expansionism on a wide scale.[23] Although each baronial class strove ceaselessly to widen its area of power by military aggression, the construction of vast territorial empires was precluded by the systematic fission of authority that defined the feudalism of mediaeval Europe. There was conse-

23. This point is effectively made by Porshnev, *Feodalizm i Narodnye Massy*, pp. 517–18.

quently no superordinate political unification of the different ethnic communites of the continent. A common religion and learned language linked together states otherwise culturally and constitutionally separate from each other. The dispersal of sovereignty in European feudalism permitted the great diversity of populations and tongues within the continent after the Germanic and Slavic migrations to subsist. No mediaeval state was founded on nationality, and aristocracies were often mobile in trajectory, undergoing transplantation from one territory to another; but the very divisions of the dynastic map of Europe allowed the consolidation of ethnic and linguistic plurality beneath it. The feudal mode of production, itself wholly 'pre-national' in character, objectively prepared the possibility of a multi-national state system in the epoch of its subsequent transition to capitalism. A final trait of European feudalism, born of conflict and synthesis between two anterior modes of production, was thus the extreme differentiation and internal ramification of its cultural and political universe. In any comparative perspective, this was not the least important of the peculiarities of the continent.

Feudalism as a historical category was a coinage of the Enlightenment. Ever since it first entered circulation, the question has been debated as to whether the phenomenon existed outside Europe, where it obtained its name. Montesquieu, as is well-known, declared it to be wholly singular: it was 'an event which happened once in the world and will perhaps never happen again'.[24] Voltaire's disagreement is equally notorious: 'Feudalism is not an event, it is a very old form which, with different administrations, subsists in three-quarters of our hemisphere.'[25] Clearly, feudalism was indeed an institutional 'form' rather than an instantaneous 'event': but the latitude of the 'differences of administration' attributed to it, as we have seen, has often tended to evacuate it of any determinate identity altogether.[26] On balance, there is no doubt today that Montesquieu, with a much deeper historical sense, was nearer to the truth. Modern research has only discovered *one*

24. *De l'Esprit des Lois*, II, p. 296.

25. *Oeuvres Complètes*, Paris 1878, XXIX, p. 91.

26. Generic inflation of the term 'feudalism' has not, it should be emphasized, been confined to Marxists: the same tendency is evident in a collection of a very different persuasion, R. Coulborn (ed.), *Feudalism in History*, most of whose essays discover feudalism where they seek for it.

major region of the world where a feudal mode of production comparable to that of Europe indisputably prevailed. At the other extreme end of the Eurasian land-mass, beyond the oriental empires familiar to the Enlightenment, the islands of Japan were to reveal a social panorama that vividly recalled the mediaeval past to European travellers and observers of the later 19th century, after Commodore Perry's arrival in the Bay of Yokohama in 1853 had brought to an end its long seclusion from the outside world. Within little more than a decade, Marx himself commented in *Capital*, published in the year before the Meiji Restoration: 'Japan with its purely feudal organization of landed property and its developed *petite culture*, gives a much truer picture of the European middle ages than all our history books.'[27] In this century, scholarly opinion has overwhelmingly concurred in considering Japan to have been the historical site of an authentic feudalism.[28] For our purposes here, the essential interest of this Far Eastern feudalism lies in its distinctive combination of structural similarities and dynamic divergences from European evolution.

The Japanese feudalism which emerged as a developed mode of production from the 14th–15th centuries onwards, after a long period of prior incubation, was characterized by essentially the same essential nexus as European feudalism: the fusion of vassalage, benefice and immunity into a fief system which constituted the basic politico-legal framework in which surplus labour was extracted from the direct producer. The links between military service, conditional landownership and seigneurial jurisdiction were faithfully reproduced in Japan. The graded hierarchy between lord, vassal, and rear-vassal, to form a chain of suzerainty and dependence, was equally present. An aristocracy of mounted knights formed a hereditary ruling class: the peasantry was juridically bound to the soil in a close replica of glebe serfdom. Japanese feudalism also, of course, possessed local traits of its own, which contrasted with European feudalism. The technical conditions

27. *Capital*, I, p. 718.

28. See the famous passages in Bloch, *Feudal Society*, pp. 446–7; Boutruche, *Seigneurie et Féodalité*, I, pp. 281–91. The major comparative study of European and Japanese feudalism is F. Joüon des Longrais, *L'Est et L'Ouest*, Paris 1958, *passim*. Documentation for the comments on Japanese development made below will be found in the references in a separate note on Japanese feudalism as such, pp. 435–61.

of riziculture dictated different village structures, which lacked a three-field system. The Japanese manor, for its part, rarely contained a demesne or home-farm. More importantly, within the intra-feudal relationship between lord and overlord, above the village level, vassalage tended to predominate over benefice: the 'personal' bond of homage was traditionally stronger than the 'material' bond of investiture. The feudal compact was less contractual and specific than in Europe: the duties of a vassal were more diffuse and the rights of his liege more imperative. Within the peculiar balance of honour and subordination, reciprocity and inequality, which marked the feudal tie, the Japanese variant was consistently tilted towards the second term. Although clan organization was – as in all true feudal social formations – superseded, the expressive 'code' of the lord-vassal relationship was provided by the language of kinship, rather than the elements of law: the authority of the lord over his follower was more patriarchal and unquestionable than in Europe. Seigneurial felony was foreign as a concept; vassal courts did not exist; legalism generally was very limited. The most critical general consequence of the more authoritarian and asymmetrical cast of the intra-seigneurial hierarchy in Japan was the absence of any Estates system, either at regional or national level. This was undoubtedly the most important political line of division between Japanese and European feudalism, considered as self-enclosed structures.

But having registered these significant second-order differences, the fundamental resemblance between the two historical configurations as a whole are unmistakeable. Above all, Japanese feudalism too was defined by a rigorous parcellization of sovereignty and scalar private property in land. Parcellization of sovereignty, indeed, achieved a more organized, systematic and stable form in Tokugawa Japan than it ever did in any European country; while scalar private property in land was actually more universal in feudal Japan than in mediaeval Europe, since there were no allodial tenures in the countryside. The basic parallelism of the two great experiences of feudalism, at the opposite ends of Eurasia, was ultimately to receive its most arresting confirmation of all, in the posterior destiny of each zone. European feudalism, as we have seen, proved the gateway to capitalism. It was the economic dynamic of the feudal mode of production in Europe which released the elements for primitive accumulation of capital on a continental scale, and it was the social order of the Middle Ages which preceded and prepared the ascent of the bourgeois class that accomplished it. The full capitalist mode of production, launched by the industrial revolution, was the gift and malediction of Europe to the globe. Today, in the second half of the twentieth century, only one major region outside Europe, or its overseas settlements, has achieved an advanced industrial capitalism: Japan. The socio-economic preconditions of Japanese capitalism, as modern historical research has amply demonstrated, lie deep in the Nipponic feudalism which so struck Marx and Europeans in the later 19th century. For no other area of the world already contained such propitious internal constituents for a rapid industrialization. Just as in Western Europe, feudal agriculture had generated remarkable levels of productivity: perhaps greater than most of monsoon Asia today. There too, there had emerged a pervasive market-centred landlordism, in a countryside whose overall index of commercialization was astonishingly high: possibly a half or more of total output. Moreover, and even more tellingly, late feudal Japan had witnessed a type of urbanization probably without equivalent anywhere else except in contemporary Europe: in the early 18th century, its capital Edo was larger than London or Paris, and perhaps one out of every ten inhabitants lived in towns over 10,000 in size. Last, but not least, the educational stock of the country bore comparison with the most developed nations of Western Europe: on the eve of the Western 'opening up' of Japan, some 40–50 per cent of the adult male population were literate. The formidable speed and success with which industrial capitalism was implanted in Japan by the Meiji Restoration had their determinate historical presuppositions in the uniquely advanced character of the society which was the bequest of Tokugawa feudalism.

Yet at the same time there was a decisive divergence between European and Japanese development. For although Japan was ultimately to achieve a tempo of industrialization more rapid than that of any capitalist country in Europe or North America, the fundamental impetus for its tempestuous transition to the capitalist mode of production in the late 19th and 20th century was *exogenous*. It was the impact of Western imperialism on Japanese feudalism that suddenly galvanized internal forces into a total transformation of the traditional order. The depth of these changes was in no way already within reach of the Tokugawa realm. When Perry's squadron anchored off Yokohama in 1853, the historical gap between Japan and the Euro-American powers menacing it was, despite everything, enormous. Japanese agriculture was remarkably commercialized at the level of distribution, but it was far less so at the level of production itself. For feudal dues, predominantly collected in kind, still accounted for the bulk of the surplus product, even if they were finally converted into cash: direct farming for the market remained subsidiary within the rural economy as a whole. Japanese cities were huge urban agglomerations, with very sophisticated financial and exchange institutions. But manufactures were still rudimentary in character, dominated by artisanal crafts organized in traditional guilds; factories proper were virtually unknown; wage-labour was not yet organized on any major scale; technology was simple and archaic. Japanese education was a mass phenomenon, which had made perhaps every other man literate. But culturally, the country was still overwhelmingly backward compared with its Western antagonists; there was no growth of science, little development of law, scarcely any philosophy, even less political or economic theory, and a virtually complete absence of critical history. In other words, nothing remotely comparable to the Renaissance had touched its shores. It was thus logical that the structure of the State itself was fragmented and frozen in form. Japan knew a long and rich experience of feudalism: but it never produced an Absolutism. The Tokugawa Shogunate which presided over the islands for the last two and a half centuries of its existence before the intrusion of the industrialized West, assured a long peace and maintained a rigorous order: but its regime was the negation of an Absolutist State. The Shogunate commanded no monopoly of coercion in Japan: regional lords kept their own armies, whose total was greater than the troops of the Tokugawa house itself. It enforced no uniform law: the writ of its own regulations basically ran only over a fifth to a quarter of the country. It possessed no bureaucracy with competence throughout the area of its suzerainty: every major fief had its own separate and autonomous administration. It collected no national taxation: three-quarters of the land lay outside its fiscal reach. It conducted no diplomacy: offici l seclusion forbade regular relations to be established with the external world. Army, fiscality, bureaucracy, legality and diplomacy – all the key institutional complexes of Absolutism in Europe were defective or missing. The *political* distance in this respect between Japan and Europe, the two homelands of feudalism, manifests and symbolizes the profound disjuncture in their historical development. A comparison, not of the 'nature', but of the 'position' of feudalism within the trajectory of each, is necessary and instructive here.

The feudal mode of production in Europe, as we have seen, was the result of a fusion of elements released from the shock and dissolution of two antagonistic modes of production anterior to it: the slave mode of production of classical antiquity, and the primitive-communal modes of production of the tribal populations on its periphery. The slow Romano-Germanic synthesis during the Dark Ages eventually produced the new civilization of European feudalism. The specific history of every social formation in mediaeval and early modern Europe was marked by the differential incidence of this original synthesis that gave birth to feudalism. A consideration of the entirely separate experience of Japanese feudalism underlines an important general truth, which we owe to Marx: that the *genesis* of a mode of production must always be distinguished from its *structure*.[29] For the same articulated structure may come into existence by a number of different 'paths'. The constitutive elements which compose it can be released in variant ways and sequences, from previous modes of production, before interlocking to form a coherent and self-reproducing system as such. Thus Japanese feudalism had neither a 'slave' nor a 'tribal' past behind it. It was the product of the slow disintegration of a Sinified imperial system, based on state monopoly of land. The Taihō State, created in the 7th–8th centuries A.D. under Chinese influence, was a type of Empire absolutely unlike that of Rome. Slavery was minimal in it; there was no municipal liberty; private landownership was abolished. The gradual dislocation

29. Marx's analyses of primitive accumulation in *Capital*, I, Part VIII, pp. 713–74, furnish, of course, the classical example of this distinction. See also many statements in the *Grundrisse*, for example: 'Thus although money becomes capital as a result of *presuppositions* which are determined and external to capital, as soon as capital as such comes into existence, it creates its own presuppositions ... through its own process of production.' *Grundrisse*, London 1973, p. 364.

of the centralized bureaucratic polity constituted by the Taihō Codes was a spontaneous and endogenous process, which extended from the 9th to the 16th centuries. There were no foreign invasions comparable to the barbarian migrations in Europe: the only serious external threat, the maritime attack by the Mongols in the 13th century, was decisively repulsed. The mechanisms of the transition to feudalism in Japan were thus totally different from those in Europe. There was no cataclysmic collapse and dissolution of two conflicting modes of production, accompanied by a profound economic, political and cultural regression, that nevertheless cleared the way for the dynamic subsequent advance of the new mode of production born of their dissolution. Rather, there was an extremely long drawn-out decline of a central imperial state, within the framework of which local warrior nobles imperceptibly usurped provincial lands and privatized military power, until eventually – after a continuous development of seven centuries – a virtually complete feudal fragmentation of the country had occurred. This involutionary process of feudalization 'from within' was finally completed by the recomposition of independent territorial lordships into an organized pyramid of feudal suzerainty. The Tokugawa Shogunate represented the arrested end-product of this secular history.

The whole *genealogy* of feudalism in Japan, in other words, presents an unequivocal contrast with the descent of feudalism in Europe. Hintze, whose work contains analyses that still remain among the profoundest reflections on the nature and incidence of feudalism, was nevertheless wrong to believe that a close analogy existed between Japanese and European experience in this respect. For him, feudalism everywhere resulted from what he called the 'deflection' (*Ablenkung*) of an advancing tribal society through the shell of a former empire, which deviated its path towards State-formation into a unique configuration. Rejecting any linear evolutionism, he insisted on the necessity of a conjunctural 'interweaving' (*Verflechtung*) of imperial and tribal effects to release a true feudalism. The emergence of Western European feudalism after the Roman Empire could thus be compared with the emergence of Japanese feudalism after the Taihō Empire: in both cases it was an 'external' combination (Germany/Rome and Japan/China) of elements that determined the formation of the order. 'Feudalism is not the creation of an immanent national development, but of a world-historical constellation'.[30] The fault in this comparison is the assumption of any resemblance between the Sinic and Roman imperial states, beyond their abstract nomenclature as Empire. Antonine Rome and T'ang China, or its counterpart Taihō Japan, were in fact utterly dissimilar civilizations, founded on distinct modes of production. It is the *diversity* of the roads of feudalism, not their identity, that is a basic lesson of the separate appearance of the same historical form at the two corners of Eurasia. Against the background of this radical diversity of origins, the *structural* similarity of European and Japanese feudalism is only the more striking: the most eloquent demonstration of all that a mode of production, once constituted, reproduces its own rigorous unity as an integrated system, 'clear' of the disparate presuppositions which initially gave birth to it. The feudal mode of production had its own order and necessity, which imposed itself with the same serried logic in two extremely contrasted environments, when the processes of transition had been accomplished. Not only were the main governing structures of the feudalism that first developed in Europe reproduced in Japan: perhaps more significantly still, these structures had visibly similar historical effects. The development of landlordism, the growth of mercantile capital, the spread of literacy in Japan were such, as we have seen, that the country proved to be the only major region in the world of non-European derivation that was able to rejoin Europe, North America and Australasia on the march towards industrial capitalism.

Yet, having stressed the fundamental parallelism between European and Japanese feudalism, as internally articulated modes of production, there remains the simple, enormous fact of their divergent outcome. Europe, from the Renaissance onwards, accomplished the transition to capitalism under its own impulsion, in a process of constant global expansion. The industrial revolution which was ultimately set off by the primitive accumulation of capital on an international scale during the

30. Hintze, 'Wesen und Verbreitung des Feudalismus', *Gesammelte Abhandlungen*, I, p. 90. Hintze believed that there there was a Russian feudalism after the Byzantine Empire, and an Islamic feudalism after the Sassanid Empire, which presented two other cases of the same process. In fact, Russian development formed part of European feudalism as a whole, while there was never any true Islamic feudalism. But Hintze's whole discussion, pp. 89–109, is nevertheless full of interest.

early modern epoch, was a spontaneous, gigantic combustion of the forces of production, unexampled in its power and universal in its reach. Nothing comparable occurred in Japan, and despite all the advances of the Tokugawa epoch, there was no sign that anything like it was imminent. It was the impact of Euro-American imperialism which destroyed the old political order in Japan, and it was the import of Western technology which rendered an indigenous industrialization possible from the materials of its socio-economic heritage. Feudalism permitted Japan – alone among Asian, African or Amerindian societies – to enlist in the ranks of advanced capitalism, once imperialism had become a world-conquering system: it did not generate a native capitalism of its own momentum, in Pacific isolation. There was thus no inherent drive within the feudal mode of production which inevitably compelled it to develop into the capitalist mode of production. The concrete record of comparative history suggests no easy evolutionism.

What, then, was the specificity of European history, which separated it so deeply from Japanese history, despite the common cycle of feudalism which otherwise so closely united the two? The answer surely lies in the perdurable inheritance of classical antiquity. The Roman Empire, its final historical form, was not only itself naturally incapable of a transition to capitalism. The very advance of the classical universe doomed it to a catastrophic regression, of an order for which there is no real other example in the annals of civilization. The far more primitive social world of early feudalism was the result of its collapse, internally prepared and externally completed. Mediaeval Europe then, after a long gestation, released the elements of a slow ulterior transition to the capitalist mode of production, in the early modern epoch. But what rendered the unique passage to capitalism possible in Europe was *the concatenation of antiquity and feudalism*. In other words, to grasp the secret of the emergence of the capitalist mode of production in Europe, it is necessary to discard in the most radical way possible any conception of it as simply an evolutionary subsumption of a lower mode of production by a higher mode of production, the one generated automatically and entirely from within the other by an organic internal succession, and therewith effacing it. Marx rightly insisted on the distinction between the genesis and the structure of modes of production. But he was also wrongly tempted to add that the reproduction of the latter, once assured, absorbed or abolished the traces of the former altogether. Thus he wrote that the anterior 'presuppositions' of a mode of production, 'precisely as such *historic* presuppositions, are past and gone, and hence belong to the *history of its formation*, but in no way to its *contemporary* history, i.e. not to the real system of the mode of production . . . as the historical prelude of its becoming, they lie behind it, just as the processes by means of which the earth made the transition from a liquid sea of fire and vapour to its present form now lie beyond its life as finished earth.'[31]

In fact, even triumphant capitalism itself – the first mode of production to become truly global in reach – by no means merely resumed and internalized all previous modes of production it encountered and dominated in its path. Still less did feudalism do so before it, in Europe. No such unitary teleology governs the winding and divided tracks of history in this fashion. For concrete *social formations*, as we have seen, typically embody a number of coexistent and conflicting modes of production, of varying date. In effect, the advent of the capitalist mode of production in Europe can only be understood by breaking with any purely linear notion of historical time as a whole. For rather than presenting the form of a cumulative chronology, in which one phase succeeds and supersedes the next, to produce the successor that will surpass it in turn, the course towards capitalism reveals a *remanence* of the legacy of one mode of production within an epoch *dominated* by another, and a *reactivation* of its spell in the passage to a third. The 'advantage' of Europe over Japan lay in its classical antecedence, which even after the Dark Ages did not disappear 'behind' it, but survived in certain basic respects 'in front' of it. In this sense, the concrete historical genesis of feudalism in Europe, far from vanishing like fire and vapour into the terrestrial solidity of its accomplished structure, had tangible effects on its final dissolution. The real historical temporality governing the three great historical modes of production that have dominated Europe up to the present century was thus radically distinct from the continuum of an evolutionary chronology. Contrary to all historicist assumptions, time was as if at certain levels inverted between the first two, to release the critical shift to the last. Contrary to all structuralist

31. *Grundrisse*, pp. 363–4.

assumptions, there was no self-moving mechanism of displacement from the feudal mode of production to the capitalist mode of production, as contiguous and closed systems. The *concatenation* of the ancient and feudal modes of production was necessary to yield the capitalist mode of production in Europe – a relationship that was not merely one of diachronic sequence, but also at a certain stage of synchronic articulation.[32] The classical past awoke again within the feudal present to assist the arrival of the capitalist future, both unimaginably more distant and strangely nearer to it. For the birth of capital also saw, as we know, the rebirth of antiquity. The Renaissance remains – despite every criticism and revision – the crux of European history as a whole: the double moment of an equally unexampled expansion of space, and recovery of time. It is at this point, with the rediscovery of the Ancient World, and the discovery of the New World, that the European state-system acquired its full singularity. A ubiquitous global power was eventually to be the outcome of this singularity, and the end of it.

The concatenation of ancient and feudal modes of production which distinguished European development can be seen in a number of original traits in the mediaeval and early modern epochs, which set it off from Japanese (let alone, say, Islamic or Chinese) experience. To start with, the whole position and evolution of the cities was quite different. Feudalism as a mode of production, as we have seen, was the first in history to render possible a dynamic *opposition* between town and country; the parcellization of sovereignty inherent in its structure permitted autonomous urban enclaves to grow as centres of production within an overwhelmingly rural economy, rather than as privileged or parasitic centres of consumption or administration – the pattern Marx believed to be typically Asiatic. The feudal order thus promoted a type of urban vitality unlike that of any other civilization, whose common products can be seen in both Japan and Europe. There was, however, at the same time a critical difference between the towns of mediaeval Europe and those of Japan. The former possessed a degree of even density and autonomy unknown to the latter: their specific weight

32. The re-emergence of slavery on a mass scale in the New World was in itself to be one of the most graphic developments of the early modern epoch, of course – an indispensable condition of the primitive accumulation necessary for the victory of industrial capitalism in Europe. Its role, which lies outside our scope here, will be discussed in a subsequent study.

within the feudal order as a whole was much greater. The major wave of urbanization in Japan was comparatively late, developing from the 16th century onwards, and was dominated by a few huge concentrations. Moreover, no Japanese cities acquired lasting municipal self-government: their apogee coincided with maximum control by baronial or shogunal lords over them. In Europe, on the other hand, the general structure of feudalism allowed the growth of producer towns based on craft-manufactures too, but the *specific social formations* which emerged from the peculiar local form of transition to feudalism ensured a much greater urban and municipal 'input' from the start. For, as we have seen, the actual movement of history is never a simple change-over from one pure mode of production to another: it is *always* composed of a complex series of social formations in which a number of modes of production are enmeshed together, under the dominance of one of them. This is, of course, why the determinate 'effects' of the ancient and primitive-communal modes of production prior to the feudal mode of production, could survive *within* mediaeval social formations in Europe, long after the disappearance of the Roman and Germanic worlds themselves. Thus European feudalism enjoyed from the outset a municipal legacy which 'filled' the space left by the new mode of production for urban development far more positively and dynamically than was the case anywhere else. The most telling testimony to the direct importance of Antiquity in the emergence of the characteristic urban forms of the Middle Ages in Europe has been noted: the primacy of Italy in this development, and the adoption of Roman insignia in its first municipal regimes, from the 'consulates' of the 11th century onwards. The whole social and juridical conception of an urban *citizenry* as such was classical in memory and derivation, and had no parallel outside Europe. Naturally, within the feudal mode of production once constituted, the whole socio-economic *basis* of the city-republics which gradually developed in Italy and the North was radically different from that of the slave mode of production from which they inherited so many superstructural traditions: liberated craft labour rendered them forever distinct from their predecessors, at once cruder and capable of wider creativity. Like Antaeus, in Weber's comparison, the city culture of the classical world, which sank back to the cavernous depths of the rural earth in the Dark Ages, re-emerged stronger and freer once again in the urban communities of the early modern epoch.[33] Nothing like this historical process occurred in Japan and *a fortiori* in the great Asian Empires that never knew feudalism – Arab, Turkic, Indian or Chinese. The *cities* of Europe – communes, republics, tyrannies – were the unique product of the combined development that marked the continent.

At the same time, the countryside of European feudalism also underwent an evolution that had no parallel elsewhere. The extreme rarity of the fief system as a type of rural property has already been emphasized. It was never known in the great Islamic states, or under successive Chinese dynasties, both of which had their own characteristic forms of agrarian land tenure. Japanese feudalism, however, did reveal the same nexus of vassalage, benefice and immunity which defined the mediaeval order in Europe. But it did not, on the other hand, ever demonstrate the critical *transformation* of rural property that distinguished early modern Europe. The pure feudal mode of production was characterized by conditional private property in land, vested in a class of hereditary nobles. The *private* or *individual* nature of this landownership demarcated it, as Marx saw, from a whole range of alternative agrarian systems outside Europe and Japan, where formal State monopoly of land, either original or durable, corresponded to much less strictly 'aristocratic' possessing classes than knights or samurai. But, once again, European development branched beyond that of Japan with the transition from *conditional* to *absolute* private property in land, in the epoch of the Renaissance. Here too, it was essentially the classical heritage of Roman law which facilitated and codified this decisive advance. Quiritary ownership, the highest legal expression of the commodity economy of Antiquity, remained waiting to be refound and set to work, once the spread of commodity relations within feudal Europe had reached levels at which its precision and clarity were demanded once more.[34] Seeking to define the specificity of the European path to

33. See Weber's concluding passage, in all its splendour, of 'Die Sozialen Gründe des Untergangs der antiken Kultur', *Gesammelte Aufsätze zur Sozial- und Wirtschaftsgeschichte*, pp. 310–11.

34. Engels could write: 'Roman law is so much the classical expression of the living conditions and collisions of a society dominated by pure private property, that all subsequent legislation was unable to improve on it in any essential way.

capitalism, by contrast with development in the rest of the world, Marx wrote to Zasulich that: 'In this Western movement the point in question is the *transformation of one form of private property into another form of private property*.'[35] By this he meant the expropriation of small peasant holdings by capitalist agriculture, which he (mistakenly) believed could be avoided in Russia by a direct transition from communal peasant property to socialism. The formula, however, contains a profound truth if applied in a somewhat different sense: the transformation of one form of private property – conditional – into another form of private property – absolute – within the landowning nobility was the indispensable preparation for the advent of capitalism, and signified the moment at which Europe left behind all other agrarian systems. In the long transitional epoch in which land remained quantitatively the predominant source of wealth across the continent, the consolidation of an unrestricted and hereditary private property in it was a fundamental step towards the release of the necessary factors of production for the accumulation of capital proper. The very 'vinculism' which the European aristocracy displayed in the early modern age was already evidence of the objective pressures towards a free market in land that was ultimately to generate a capitalist agriculture. Indeed, the legal order born of the revival of Roman law created the *general* juridical conditions for a successful passage to the capitalist mode of production as such, in both town and country. The security of onwership and fixity of contract, the protection and predictability of economic transactions between individual parties assured by a written civil law, was never repeated elsewhere. Islamic law was at best vague and uncertain in matters of real estate; it was inextricably religious and therefore confused and contentious in interpretation. Chinese law was single-mindedly punitive and repressive; it was scarcely concerned with civil relations at all, and provided no stable grid for economic activity. Japanese law was rudimentary and fragmented, with only the timid beginnings of a justiciable, commercial law emerging at the crossing-

---

The burgher property of the Middle Ages was by contrast much alloyed by feudal limitations, and consisted in large measure of privileges; Roman law was consequently in this respect far in advance (*weit voraus*) of the bourgeois relationships of the time.' *Werke*, Bd 21, p. 397.

35. Marx-Engels, *Selected Correspondence*, p. 340.

points between a diversity of domanial fiats.[36] Roman law, by contrast with all of these, provided a coherent and systematic framework for the purchase, sale, lease, hire, loan and testation of goods: remoulded in the new conditions of Europe and generalized by a body of professional lawyers unknown to Antiquity itself, its influence was one of the fundamental institutional preconditions for the quickening of capitalist relations of production on a continental scale.

The revival of Roman law, moreover, was accompanied or succeeded by the reappropriation of virtually the whole cultural inheritance of the classical world. The philosophical, historical, political and scientific thought of Antiquity – not to speak of its literature or architecture – suddenly acquired a new potency and immediacy in the early modern epoch. The critical and rational components of classical culture, compared with that of any other ancient civilization, gave a further and sharper edge to the return to it. Not only were these intrinsically more advanced than any equivalent in the past of other continents, but they were divided from the present by the great gulf of the religious divide between the two epochs. Classical thought could thus never be embalmed as a venerable and innocuous tradition, even in its selective assimilation in the Middle Ages: it always retained an antagonistic and corrosive content as a non-Christian universe. The radical potential of its greatest works was fully seen once new social conditions themselves permitted European minds to look steadily back across the abyss separating them from Antiquity, without vertigo. The result, as we have seen, was an intellectual and artistic revolution of a kind that could only occur because of specific historical precession of the classical over the mediaeval worlds. The astronomy of Copernicus, the philosophy of Montaigne, the politics of Machiavelli, the historio-graphy of Clarendon, the jurisprudence of Grotius – all were indebted in different ways to the messages of Antiquity. The very birth of modern physics itself in part took the form of a rejection of one classical legacy – Aristotelianism – under the sign of another – the Neo-Platonism which inspired its 'dynamized' conception of nature.[37] The

36. These contrasts are explored below, pp. 453, 497–9, 543.

37. For the role of Neo-Platonism in the growth of modern science, see Frances Yates, *Giordano Bruno and the Hermetic Tradition*, London 1964, pp. 447–55. More directly, of course, the heritage of Euclidean geometry and Ptole-

increasingly analytic and secular culture that gradually unfolded, still with many theological blockages and reversions, was the historical phenomenon which perhaps most unerringly singled Europe out from all other major zones of civilization in the pre-industrial epoch. The becalmed traditionalism of Japanese feudal society, virtually innocent of contrary ideological gusts in the Tokugawa era, furnishes an especially striking contrast. The intellectual stagnation of Japan, amidst its economic effervescence, of course was to a considerable extent due to the deliberate isolation of the country. But in this respect too, European feudalism had the advantage of its Japanese counterpart from the very outset of their respective origins.

Whereas the feudal mode of production in Japan resulted from the slow involution of an imperial order whose structures were borrowed from abroad, and was ultimately stabilized in conditions of complete seclusion from the external world, the feudal mode of production in Europe emerged from the frontal clash of two conflicting anterior orders over a great land-mass, whose after-effects extended over an ever wider geographical expanse. Insular feudalism in Japan moved inwards, away from the whole Far Eastern matrix of the initial Taihō State. Continental feudalism in Europe moved outwards, as the ethnic diversity which was inherent in the original synthesis that gave birth to it actually increased with the spread of the mode of production beyond its Carolingian homelands, and eventually produced a dynastic and proto-national mosaic of great complexity. In the Middle Ages, this great diversity ensured the autonomy of the Church, which was never subjected to a single imperial sovereignty such as it had known in Antiquity, and encouraged the emergence of Estates, characteristically summoned to rally a local nobility to one monarchy or principality against the attack of another, in the military conflicts of the time.[38] Both ecclesiastical independence and estates-representation, in turn, were features of mediaeval society in Europe that were never duplicated in the Japanese variant of feudalism. They were in this sense functions

---

maic astronomy was the indispensable precondition for the emergence of Galilean physics.

38. The inter-state determinants of estates representation were stressed by Hintze: 'Weltgeschichtliche Bedingungen der Repräsentativverfassung', *Gesammelte Abhandlungen*, I, pp. 168–70.

of the *international* character of European feudalism, which was by no means the least profound of the reasons why its fate was to be so different from that of Japan. The haphazard multiplicity of political units in late mediaeval Europe became in the early modern epoch an organized and interconnected state-system: the birth of diplomacy formalized the novelty of a plural *set* of partners – for war, alliance, trade, marriage or propaganda – within a single political arena, whose bounds and rules became ever clearer and more definite. The cross-cultural fecundity that resulted from the formation of this highly integrated yet extremely diversified system was one of the peculiar hallmarks of pre-industrial Europe: the intellectual achievements of the early modern epoch were probably inseparable from it. No comparable political set existed anywhere else in the world: the institutionalization of diplomatic exchange was an invention of the Renaissance, and remained a European particularity long afterwards.

The Renaissance, then, was at once the moment in which the collocation of antiquity and feudalism suddenly produced its most original and astonishing fruits, and the historical turning-point at which Europe outdistanced all other continents in dynamism and expansion. The new and singular type of *State* that arose in this epoch was Absolutism. The Absolute Monarchies of the early modern period were a strictly European phenomenon. Indeed they represent the precise *political* form of the headway of the whole region. For, as we have seen, it was just at this point that Japanese evolution stopped: Far Eastern feudalism never passed over into Absolutism. The emergence of Absolutism from European feudalism was, in other words, the tally of its political lead. A creation of the Renaissance, the development of Absolutism was made possible by the long prior history that stretched back behind feudalism, and was conjured up again at the dawn of the early modern age. The dominant state structure in Europe down to the end of the Enlightenment, its ascendancy coincided with the exploration of the globe by the European powers, and the beginnings of their supremacy over it. In nature and structure, the Absolute monarchies of Europe were still feudal states: the machinery of rule of the same aristocratic class that had dominated the Middle Ages. But in Western Europe where they were born, the *social formations* which they governed were a complex combination of *feudal and capitalist modes of production*, with a gradually rising urban bourgeoisie and a growing primitive accumulation of capital, on an international scale. It was the intertwining of these two antagonistic modes of production within single societies that gave rise to the transitional forms of Absolutism. The royal States of the new epoch brought to an end the parcellization of sovereignty that was inscribed in the pure feudal mode of production as such, although without themselves ever achieving a fully unitary polity. This change was in the final instance determined by the increase in commodity production and exchange attendant on the spread of mercantile and manufacturing capitalism, which tended to dissolve primary feudal relations in the countryside. But at the same time, the disappearance of serfdom did not mean the abolition of private extra-economic coercion to extract surplus labour from the immediate producer. The landed nobility continued to own the bulk of the fundamental means of production in the economy, and to occupy the great majority of positions within the total apparatus of political power. Feudal coercion was displaced upwards, to a centralized monarchy; and the aristocracy typically had to exchange its estates representation for bureaucratic office, within the renovated structures of the State. The acute strains of this process produced many seigneurial revolts; royal authority was often exercised implacably against members of the noble class. The term 'Absolutism' itself – in fact always technically a misnomer – is a testimony of the weight of the new monarchical complex on the aristocratic order itself.

But there was nevertheless one basic characteristic which divided the Absolute monarchies of Europe from all the myriad other types of despotic, arbitrary or tyrannical rule, incarnated or controlled by a personal sovereign, which prevailed elsewhere in the world. *The increase in the political sway of the royal state was accompanied, not by a decrease in the economic security of noble landownership, but by a corresponding increase in the general rights of private property.* The age in which 'Absolutist' public authority was imposed was also simultaneously the age in which 'absolute' private property was progressively consolidated. It was this momentous social difference which separated the Bourbon, Habsburg, Tudor or Vasa monarchies from any Sultanate, Empire or Shogunate outside Europe. Contemporaries confronted with the Ottoman State on European soil itself were constantly and acutely aware of this great crevasse. Absolutism did not mean the end of aristocratic rule: on the contrary, it protected and stabilized the social dominion of the hereditary noble class in Europe. The kings who presided over the new monarchies could never transgress the unseen limits to their power: those of the material conditions of reproduction of the class to which they themselves belonged. Commonly, these sovereigns were aware of their membership of the aristocracy which surrounded them; their individual pride of station was founded on a collective solidarity of sentiment. Thus while capital was slowly accumulated beneath the glittering superstructures of Absolutism, exerting an ever greater gravitational pull on them, the noble landowners of early modern Europe retained their historical predominance, in and through the monarchies which now commanded them. Economically guarded, socially privileged and culturally matured, the aristocracy still ruled: the Absolutist State adjusted its paramountcy to the steady burgeoning of capital within the composite social formations of Western Europe.

Subsequently, as we have seen, Absolutism also emerged within Eastern Europe – the much more backward half of the continent, which had never experienced the original Romano-Germanic synthesis that gave birth to mediaeval feudalism. The contrasting traits and temporality of the two variants of Absolutism within Europe, Western and Eastern, which have formed a central theme of this study, in their own way serve to underline the common final character and context of both. For in Eastern Europe, the social power of the nobility was unqualified by any ascendant urban bourgeoisie such as marked Western Europe: seigneurial domination was unfettered. Eastern Absolutism thus more patently and unequivocally displayed its class composition and function than its Western counterpart. Built on serfdom, the feudal cast of its State structure was blunt and manifest; the enserfed peasantry below were a permanent reminder of the forms of oppression and exploitation its apparatus of coercion perpetuated. But at the same time, the genesis of Absolutism in Eastern Europe was fundamentally distinct from that of Absolutism in Western Europe. For, precisely, it was not directly the growth of commodity production and exchange which brought it into being: capitalism was still far off beyond the Elbe. It was the two intersecting forces of an uncompleted process of feudalization – which had started chronologically later, without benefit of the heritage of Antiquity, and in more difficult topographic and demographic conditions – and an accelerating military pressure from the more advanced West, which led to the paradoxical pre-formation of Absolutism in the East. With the establishment of the Absolutist regimes of Eastern Europe, in turn, the international state-system that defined and demarcated the continent as a whole was completed. The birth of a multilateral political order, as a single field of competition and conflict between rival States, was thus itself both cause and effect of the generalization of Absolutism in Europe. The construction of this international system, from Westphalia onwards, naturally did not render the two halves of the continent homogeneous. On the contrary, representing distinct historical lineages from the start, the Absolutist States of Western and Eastern Europe followed divergent trajectories down to their respective conclusions. The gamut of fates that resulted is well-known. In the West, the Spanish, English, and French monarchies were defeated or overthrown by bourgeois revolutions from below; while the Italian and German principalities were eliminated by bourgeois revolutions from above, belatedly. In the East, on the other hand, the Russian empire was finally destroyed by a proletarian revolution. The consequences of the division of the continent, symbolized by these successive and opposite upheavals, are still with us.

Two Notes

A. Japanese Feudalism

In the 7th century A.D., a centralized imperial polity was formed in Japan under strong Sinic influence: the Taika reform of 646 abolished the previous loose congeries of noble lineage-groups and dependent cultivators, and installed a unitary state system for the first time. Administratively modelled on the T'ang Empire in contemporary China, the new Japanese State, which came to be regulated by the Taihō Codes issued in the early 8th century (702), was based on an imperial monopoly of landownership. Soil was allocated in small allotments, which were periodically redistributed, to tenant cultivators who owed taxes in kind or corvée duties to the State: initially applied to the house domains of the imperial line itself, the allotment system was gradually extended throughout the country over the next century or so. An extensive central bureaucracy composed of a civilian aristocratic class, recruited to office by heredity rather than examination, maintained unified political control of the country. The realm was systematically divided into circuits, provinces, districts and villages, all under tight governmental supervision. A permanent conscript army was also created, if somewhat insecurely. Symmetrically planned imperial cities were built, along Chinese lines. Buddhism, syncretically mixed with indigenous Shinto cults, became an official religion, formally integrated into the apparatus of the State itself.[1] From 800 or so onwards, however, this Sinicized Empire started to dissolve under centrifugal pressures.

The lack of anything like a mandarinate proper within the bureaucracy rendered it prone to noble privatization from the start. The Buddhist religious orders preserved special privileges on the lands

1. For a lucid account of the Taihō State, see J. W. Hall, *Japan from Prehistory to Modern Times*, London 1970, pp. 43–60.

donated to them. Conscription was effectively abandoned in 792; redistribution of allotments in 844 or so. Semi-private estates or *shōen* increasingly sprang up in the provinces, the proprietary domains of nobles or monasteries: initially subtracted from State ownership of land, they eventually gained fiscal immunity and finally exemption from cadastral inspection by the central government altogether. The larger such estates – often originating from newly reclaimed land – covered several hundred acres. The peasants tilling the *shōen* now paid dues directly to their lords, while within this emergent manorial system superimposed rights of access to the produce (mainly, of course, rice) were acquired by intermediate layers of managers or bailiffs. The internal organization of Japanese manors was greatly influenced by the nature of riziculture, the basic branch of agriculture. There was no three-field system of the European type, and commons were comparatively unimportant, given the lack of livestock. Peasant strips were much smaller than in Europe, and village-clusters fewer, amidst a considerably density of rural population and shortage of land. Above all, there was no real demesne system within the farm: the *shiki*, or divisible rights of appropriation of the product, were collected uniformly from the whole output of the *shōen*.[2] Meanwhile, within the political system, the court aristocracy or *kuge* developed a refined civilian culture in the capital, where the house of Fujiwara gained a prolonged ascendancy over the imperial dynasty itself. But outside Kyōtō, the imperial administration was increasingly allowed to lapse. At the same time, once conscription disappeared, armed force in the provinces gradually came to be the appurtenance of a new military nobility of samurai warriors or *bushi* who first became prominent in the course of the 11th century.[3] Both public officials in the central government and local *shōen* proprietors gathered personal bands of such warriors about them, for purposes of defense and aggression. Civil strife escalated together with the privatization of coercive power, as provincial *bushi* troops intervened in the struggles of court cliques for control of the imperial capital and administrative framework.

2. For a comparative analysis of the *shōen*, see Joüon des Longrais, *L'Est et l'Ouest, Institutions du Japon et de l'Occident Comparées*, Paris 1958, pp. 92–103.
3. The origins of the *bushi* are sketched in J. W. Hall, *Government and Local Power in Japan 500–1700*, Princeton 1966, pp. 131–3.

The breakdown of the old Taihō system culminated with the victorious foundation of the Kamakura Shogunate by Minamoto-no-Yoritomo in the late 12th century. The Imperial dynasty and court in Kyōtō, and the traditional civil administration, were preserved by the new ruler, who was Kyōtō-bred and showed great respect for their legacy.[4] But side by side with them a new military apparatus of rule was created under the command of the Shogun or 'generalissimo', manned by the *bushi* class and centred in a separate capital at Kamakura. Real power in Japan was henceforward exercised by this para-imperial authority. The Shogunate, which came to be referred to as the *Bakufu* ('tent' or military headquarters), at the outset controlled the loyalty of some 2,000 *gokenin* 'housemen' or personal vassals of Yoritomo, and appropriated or confiscated many *shōen* for its use. In the provinces, it appointed military governors or *shugo*, and land stewards or *jitō*, drawn from its retainers. The former in practice became the dominant local power in their regions, while beneath them the latter were charged with tax-collection from the *shōen* manors, over which they gradually came to acquire increasing *shiki* rights themselves, at the expense of their former proprietors.[5] The new *shugo-jitō* network, created by and responsible to the Shogunate, represented a preliminary form of benefice system: repressive and fiscal functions were delegated to *bushi* followers by it, in exchange for titles to income from land. Formal 'letters of confirmation' granted local vassal rights to both land-revenues and men-at-arms.[6] Imperial legality and bureaucracy, however, still subsisted: the Shogun was technically appointed by the Emperor, the *shōen* remained subject to public law, and the bulk of the land and population stayed under the old civil administration.

Financially and militarily weakened by the Mongol attacks in the late 13th century, Kamakura rule eventually collapsed in civil strife. It was during the Ashikaga Shogunate which succeeded it, that the next decisive step towards a full feudalization of Japanese society and polity occurred, in the course of the 14th century. The Shogunate was now transferred to Kyōtō itself, and the lingering autonomy of the imperial

4. M. Shinoda, *The Founding of the Kamakura Shogunate 1180–1185*, New York 1960, pp. 112–13, 141–4.

5. See the extensive discussion of the *jitō* in Hall, *Government and Local Power in Japan*, pp. 157–8, 182–90.

6. Shinoda, *The Founding of the Kamakura Shogunate*, p. 140.

court abolished: the sacred dynasty and *kuge* aristocracy were deprived of most of their lands and wealth, and relegated to purely ceremonial roles. Civilian administration in the provinces was completely eclipsed by the military *shugo* governorships. But at the same time, the Ashikaga Shogunate itself was much weaker than its Kamakura predecessor: consequently the *shugo* themselves became increasingly unbridled regional lords, absorbing the *jitō*, levying their own corvées, and annexing half the proceeds of the local *shōen* on a province-wide scale; sometimes even 'receiving' the whole *shōen* outright from their absentee owners.[7] By now a true fief or *chigyō* system had developed, which for the first time represented a direct fusion of vassalage and benefice, military service and conditional landholding: the *shugo* themselves both possessed such fiefs and distributed them to their followers. The adoption of primogeniture within the aristocratic class consolidated the new feudal hierarchy within the countryside.[8] The peasantry below underwent a corresponding degradation, as their mobility was restricted, and their prestations were increased: the petty rural warriors of the *bushi* stratum were in a better position to squeeze the surplus from the direct producers than the absentee *kuge* nobles had been. There was a spread of commodity production in the countryside, especially in the central regions round Kyōtō where *sake* brewing was concentrated, and the volume of monetary circulation increased. Rural productivity improved with better farm tools and increased use of animal traction, and agrarian output rose steeply in many areas.[9] Foreign trade expanded, while artisan and merchant guilds of a type similar to those of mediaeval Europe developed in the towns. But the archaic imperial framework still persisted, although now honeycombed by new feudal hierarchies, under a comparatively weak central Shogunate. The gubernatorial jurisdictions of the *shugo* continued to be much wider than their enfeoffed land, and by no means all the *bushi* within them were their personal vassals.

It was the eventual collapse of the Ashikaga Shogunate after the outbreak of the Ōnin Wars (1467–77), which finally dissolved the last vestiges of the Taihō administrative legacy, and completed the process

7. H. P. Varley, *The Ōnin War*, New York 1967, pp. 38–43.
8. *Ibid.*, pp. 76–7.
9. Hall, *Japan from Prehistory to Modern Times*, p. 121.

of country-wide feudalization. Amidst a wave of anarchy in which 'lower ruled higher', the regional *shugo* were overthrown from below by usurper vassals – often their ex-deputies, and the *shōen* clusters and provincial jurisdictions over which they had presided disappeared altogether. The war-born adventurers of the new Sengoku epoch carved out their own principalities, which they henceforward organized and ruled as purely feudal territories, while any real central power disintegrated in Japan. The *daimyō* or magnates of the late 15th or early 16th centuries controlled compact domains, in which all warriors were their vassals or rear-vassals, and all land was their suzerain property. Divisible *shiki* rights were concentrated into single *chigyō* units. Feudalization was territorially more complete than in mediaeval Europe, for allodial plots were unknown in the countryside. Samurai retainers swore oaths of military loyalty to their lords, and received full fiefs – grants of land together with rights of jurisdiction – from them.[10] Enfeoffment was calculated in terms of 'villages' (*mura* – administrative units more than actual hamlets), and the tenantry submitted to direct *bushi* supervision. Castle-towns and subinfeudation developed in the *daimyō* domains, which were regulated by new feudal 'house laws' codifying the prerogatives of their overlord and the hierarchy of personal dependences beneath him. The bond between lord and vassal in Japanese feudalism remained marked by two peculiarities. The personal link between seigneur and retainer was stronger than the economic link of the retainer to the land: vassalage tended to predominate over benefice within the fief nexus itself.[11] At the same time, the relationship between lord and vassal was more asymmetrical than that in Europe. The contractual component of homage was much weaker; vassalage had a semi-familial and sacred character, rather than a legal one. The notion of seigneurial 'felony' or breakage of the bond by the lord was unknown: nor did multiple lordship exist. The intra-feudal relationship proper was thus more unilaterally hierarchical; its terminology was borrowed from that o paternal authority and the kinship system. European feudalism was

10. For the textual wording of a vassal oath and land grant of this epoch, see Hall, *Government and Local Power in Japan*, pp. 253–4: Sengoku feudal organization generally is depicted, pp. 246–56.

11. This characteristic is much stressed by Joüon: *L'Est et l'Ouest*, pp. 119–20, 164.

always rife with inter-familial quarrels, and was characterized by an extreme litigiousness; Japanese feudalism however, not only lacked any legalistic bent, but its quasi-patriarchal cast was rendered the more authoritarian by extensive paternal rights of adoption and disinheritance, which effectively deterred filial insubordination of the type common in Europe.[12] On the other hand, the coefficient of feudal warfare, with its premium on the valour and skill of armoured knights, was fully as great as in late mediaeval Europe during this epoch. Fierce fighting was constant between contending *daimyō* principalities. Moreover, in the gaps left by the political fragmentation of Japan, autonomous merchant towns reminiscent of those of mediaeval Europe – Sakai, Hakata, Ōtsu, Ujiyamada and others – were able to flourish: the port of Sakai was to be termed an oriental 'Venice' by Jesuit travellers.[13] Religious sects created their own armed enclaves in Kaga and Noto on the Japan Sea. Even insurrectionary rural communes, led by disaffected gentry and based on a rebellious peasantry, briefly appeared: the most notable being established in the central Yamashiro region itself, where commercialization had created acute indebtedness among the rural population.[14] The turmoil of the times was further increased by the impact of European fire-arms, techniques and ideas after the arrival of the Portuguese in Japan in 1543.

In the second half of the 16th century, a series of massive civil wars between the major *daimyō* potentates led to the victorious reunification of the country by successive military commanders – Nobunaga, Hideyoshi and Ieyasu. Odo Nobunaga forged the first regional coalition to establish control of central Japan. He liquidated Buddhist militarism, broke the independence of the merchant towns, and gained mastery of a third of the country. The formidable work of conquest was completed by Toyotomi Hideyoshi, leading huge armies equipped

12. See the acute comments by Joüon, *L'Est et l'Ouest*, pp. 145–7, 395–6. It should be noted, however, that despite the terminological bias of Japanese feudalism towards pseudo-kin relationships, in practice vassalage was considered a more secure bond of loyalty than consanguinity by baronial lords of the epoch: significantly, branch families of a magnate line were typically assimilated to vassal status. See Hall, *Government and Local Power in Japan*, p. 251.

13. For an account of Sakai, see G. Sansom, *A History of Japan 1334–1615*, London 1961, pp. 189, 272–3, 304–5.

14. The circumstances which produced the Yamashiro commune are sketched in Varley, *The Ōnin War*, pp. 192–204.

with muskets and cannons, and composed of a block of allied *daimyō* forces grouped under him.[15] The result of Hideyoshi's subjection of all other magnates to his own authority was not, however, a restoration of the vanished centralized state of the Taihō tradition. It was rather a reintegration of the mosaic of regional lordships into a unitary feudal system for the first time. The *daimyō* were not dispossessed of their domains, but were vassalized in their turn to the new ruler, from whom they henceforward held their territories as fiefs and to whom they granted kin as hostages for their fealty. The imperial dynasty was retained as a religious symbol of legitimacy, above and apart from the operational system of feudal suzerainty. A new cadastral survey stabilized the landowning system, consolidating the reorganized pyramid of lordships over it. The population was divided into four closed orders – nobles, peasants, artisans and merchants. *Bushi* were separated from the villages and congregated in the castle-towns of their *daimyō*, as disciplined men-at-arms ready for immediate military deployment. Their numbers were officially registered, and the size of the samurai class was henceforward fixed at some 5–7 per cent of the population, a comparatively large sword-bearing stratum. Peasants were by the same token deprived of all arms, bound to the soil and juridically forced to deliver two-thirds of their product to their masters.[16] The autonomous cities of the Ashikaga and Sengoku epochs were suppressed, and the merchant class forbidden to purchase land (just as the samurai were excluded from commerce). On the other hand, the castle-towns of the feudal magnates themselves grew prodigiously in this period. Trade developed rapidly, under the protection of the *daimyō* whose castellar headquarters provided the central nodes of a greatly enlarged network of cities in Japan. At Hideyoshi's death, supreme power was won by Tokugawa Ieyasu, a *daimyō* from the original Toyotomi bloc, who mobilized a new coalition of lords to defeat his rivals at the battle of Sekigahara in 1600 and become Shogun in 1603. Ieyasu founded the Tokugawa state which was to last two hundred and fifty years, down to the epoch of the industrial revolution

15. 'Hideyoshi's victory represented not a true unification but the conquest of Japan by one *daimyō* league over the entire country': Hall, *Government and Local Power in Japan*, p. 284.

16. Sansom comments that the actual proportion collected was nearer two-fifths, because of widespread evasion: *A History of Japan 1334–1615*, p. 319.

in Europe. The stability and longevity of the new regime was greatly reinforced by the formal closure of Japan to virtually all contact with the outside world: a device initially inspired by Ieyasu's well-founded fear that the Catholic missions which had become established in Japan were an ideological spear-head for European political and military infiltration. The effect of the rigorous seclusion of the country was, of course, to insulate it from any external shocks or disturbances for the next two centuries, and petrify the structures established by Ieyasu after Sekigahara.

The Tokugawa Shogunate imposed unity on Japan, without centralism. It in effect stabilized a kind of condominium between the suzerain shogunal regime, based on the Tokugawa capital of Edo, and the autonomous *daimyō* governments in their provincial fiefs. Japanese historians have consequently designated the epoch of its dominance as the *Baku-han* period, or combination of rule by the *Bakufu* – the Tokugawa governing complex – and the *han* or baronial houses in their own domains. This hybrid system was integrated by the dual foundations of Shogunal power itself. On the one hand, the Shogunate possessed its own Tokugawa domains, the so-called *tenryō* lands which amounted to some 20–25 per cent of the country – a far larger block than that possessed by any other feudal lineage – and strategically commanding the central plains and coasts of Eastern Japan. Just over half of these were administered directly by the *Bakufu* apparatus itself; the rest were granted as minor fiefs to the *hatamoto* or 'banner-men' of the Tokugawa house, of which there were some 5,000 in all.[17] In addition, the Shogunate could rely, firstly on the 20 or so large Tokugawa collateral lines or *shimpan* lords, who were entitled to provide successors to the Shogunate, and secondly on the numerous smaller lords who had been loyal regional vassals of Ieyasu, prior to his rise to supreme power. These latter composed the so-called *fudai* or 'house' *daimyō*: there were about 145 of them by the 18th century, and their lands covered another 25 per cent of the surface of Japan. The *fudai* provided the bulk of the higher officialdom of the *Bakufu* administration, whose lower echelons were recruited from the *hatamoto*, whereas the major

17. A Craig, *Chōshū in the Meiji Restoration*, Cambridge USA, 1961, p. 15. Land in Japan was officially assessed from Hideyoshi onwards by its rice-yield in *koku* (about 5 bushels).

collateral houses were excluded from the Shogunal government itself, as potentially overmighty in their own right, although they could act as advisors to it. The Shogunate itself gradually underwent a process of 'symbolization' comparable to that of the Imperial line itself. Tokugawa Ieyasu had not displaced the Imperial dynasty any more than had his predecessors Nobunaga and Hideyoshi: if anything, he had carefully restored much of the religious aura surrounding it, while segregating both the Emperor and the *kuge* court nobility more completely than ever from any secular power. The monarch was a divine authority, relegated to spiritual functions in Kyōtō which were wholly divorced from the conduct of political affairs. The residual duality of Imperial and Shogunal systems in one respect provided a kind of attenuated correlate of the separation of Church and State within European feudalism, because of the religious aura of the former; there were always potentially two sources of legitimacy within Japan in the Tokugawa epoch. In other ways, however, since the Emperor was also a political symbol, this duality reproduced the fissured sovereignty characteristic of any secular feudalism as a whole. The Shogun ruled in the name of the Emperor, as his delegate, by an official fiction which institutionalized 'government from behind the screen'. The Tokugawa dynasty which provided the successive Shoguns who formally controlled the *Bakufu* state apparatus, however, eventually ceased to exercise personal authority within it themselves: after several generations, substantive political power receded to the Shogunal Council of *rōjū*, composed of nobles recruited from the medium *fudai* lineages – in a second degree of 'government from behind the screen'.[18] The Shogunal bureaucracy was extensive and amorphous, with widespread confusion of functions and plurality of tenures within it. Tenebrous vertical cliques manoeuvred for office and patronage within its shrouded machinery. About half of the bureaucracy was civilian and half military in duties.

The *Bakufu* government could theoretically call on a feudal levy of 80,000 mounted warriors, composed of 20,000 or so banner-men and house-men, plus their rear-vassals: in practice, its real armed potential

18. The successive phases of this process within the Shogunate are carefully traced in C. Totman, *Politics in the Tokugawa Bakufu 1600–1843*, Cambridge USA, 1967, pp. 204–33.

was much smaller, and relied on the strength of loyal *fudai* and *shimpan* contingents. The peace-time strength of its permanent guard-units was some 12,200.[19] The revenues of the Shogunate were basically derived from the rice-yields of its own domains (initially some two-thirds of its total income),[20] supplemented by its monopoly of gold and silver mines, from which it minted coinage (a declining asset from the 18th century onwards); later, when it ran into increasing financial difficulties, it resorted to frequent debasements of currency and forced loans or confiscations of merchant wealth. The extent of both its army and treasury was thus set by the limits of the domanial territory of the Tokugawa house itself. At the same time, however, the Shogunate exercised formally tight external controls over the *daimyō* outside the boundaries of its own direct jurisdiction. All the lords of the *han* domains were, in fact, its tenants-in-chief: they were invested in their fiefs by the Shogun, as his vassals. Their territories could in principle be revoked or transferred, although this practice died out in the later phases of the Tokugawa epoch, when *han* domains were effectively hereditary.[21] Shogunal marriage policy at the same time sought to tie the major baronial lines to the Tokugawa dynasty. The *daimyō* were, moreover, obliged to maintain an alternate residence in the *Bakufu* capital of Edo, where they had to displace themselves every other year or six months, and leave family hostages behind when they returned to their fiefs. This so-called *sankin-kōtai* system was designed to ensure a permanent watch over the conduct of regional magnates, and to hamper independent actions by them in their strongholds. It was backed by an extensive system of informers and inspectors, who provided an intelligence service for the Shogunate. Movements along the main highways were tightly policed by use of internal passports and road-blocks; while marine transport was subject to government regulations which forbade the construction of craft above a certain size. The *daimyō* were permitted to keep one castle-complex only, and ceilings on their armed retinues were fixed in the official rolls of the Shogunate. There was no economic taxation of the *han* domains, but

19. Totman, *Politics in the Tokugawa Bakufu*, pp. 45, 50.
20. P. Akamatsu, *Meiji 1868: Révolution et Contre-Révolution au Japon*, Paris 1968, p. 30.
21. Hall, *Japan from Prehistory to Modern Times*, p. 169.

irregular contributions could be requested from them by the *Bakufu*, for extraordinary expenditure.

This imposing and inquisitorial set of controls appeared to give the Tokugawa Shogunate complete political paramountcy in Japan. In fact, its real power was always less than its nominal sovereignty, and the actual gap between the two increased over time. The founder of the dynasty, Ieyasu, had defeated the rival lords of the South-West at Sekigahara: he had not destroyed them. The *daimyō* numbered some 250–300 under the Tokugawa Shogunate. Of these, about 90 represented *tozama* or 'outside' houses, whom had not been early vassals of the Tokugawa, and many of which had fought against Ieyasu. The *tozama* houses were regarded as potentially or traditionally hostile to the Shogunate, and were rigorously excluded from participation in the machinery of the *Bakufu*. They included the great majority of the largest and richest domains: of the 16 biggest *han*, no less than 11 were *tozama*.[22] These were located in the peripheral regions of the country, the South-West or North-East. The *tozama* houses together accounted for some 40 per cent of the land in Japan. However, in practice, their wealth and power became more formidable than their official listings on the *Bakufu* registers revealed. Towards the end of the Tokugawa epoch, the Satsuma *han* controlled 28,000 armed samurai, or twice the official rating permitted it; the Chōshū *han* mustered 11,000, again more than it was supposed to possess; while the loyal *fudai* houses were generally under their nominal strength, and the Shogunate itself could in practice field only some 30,000 or so warriors by the early 18th century – less than half its theoretical levy.[23] At the same time, the newer lands in the outlying *tozama* domains contained more unreclaimed surface for conversion to riziculture than the older *tenryō* house-lands of the Shogunate itself in the centre of the country. The rich Kantō plain, the most developed zone in Japan, was controlled by the *Bakufu*;

22. Craig, *Chōshū in the Meiji Restoration*, p. 11.
23. Craig, *Chōshū in the Meiji Restoration*, pp. 15–16; Totman, *Politics in the Tokugawa Bakufu*, pp. 49–50. The origin of the exceptionally high samurai ratios in the South-Western *tozama* fiefs lay in the post-Sekigahara settlement, when Ieyasu drastically reduced the domains of his enemies. The result was to concentrate their retainers into much smaller areas. The *tozama* lords, for their part, concealed the real output of their lands in order to minimize the scale of the reductions ordered by the *Bakufu*.

but precisely the newer commercialized crops which characterized it tended to elude traditional Tokugawa fiscal collection, based on rice units. Certain of the *toȥama* tax-yields thus eventually came to be higher than those of the Shogunal domains.[24] Although aware of the discrepancy between the nominal rice-assessment for the *toȥama*-fiefs and their real output, which in some cases existed from the outset of the *Baku-han* period, the cessation of Shogunal authority at *han* borders prevented Edo from redressing the situation. Moreover, when commercialized agriculture reached the outlying regions of Japan, the more compact and vigorous *han* governments were able to establish lucrative local monopolies in cash crops (such as sugar or paper), increasing *toȥama* revenues while *Bakufu* income from mining was falling. The economic and military strength of any daimiate were closely linked, since samurai warriors had to be supported from rice-revenues. The material position of the great *toȥama* houses was thus much more powerful than it readily appeared, and grew more so with the passage of time.

Within their domains, moreover, all the *daimyō* – whether *toȥama*, *shimpan* or *fudai* – commanded an untempered authority: the direct writ of the Shogunate stopped at the frontiers of their fiefs. They issued laws, administered justice, raised taxes, and maintained troops. The political centralism of the *daimyō* was actually greater within their *han* than that of the Shogunate in its *tenryō* lands, because it was no longer mediatized by subinfeudation. Initially, the *han* territories were divided into *daimyō* house-lands and vassal fiefs granted to their armed retainers. However, in the course of the Tokugawa epoch, there was a steady increase in the number of samurai within every *han* who were simply paid stipends in rice, rather than enfeoffed with land as such. By the end of the 18th century, virtually all *bushi* retainers outside the Shogunal territory itself received rice salaries from the domain granaries, and most resided in the castle-towns of their lords. This shift was facilitated by the traditional tilt within the intra-feudal relationship towards the pole of vassalage rather than benefice. The divorce of the samurai class from agrarian production was accompanied, in both the

24. See the tentative calculations in W. G. Beasley, 'Feudal Revenues in Japan at the Time of the Meiji Restoration', *Journal of Asian Studies*, XIX, No. 3, May 1960, pp. 255–72.

Bakufu and *han* sectors of Japan, by its entry into bureaucratic administration. For the Shogunal State apparatus, with its proliferating posts and uncertain departments, was reproduced in the territories of the provincial lords. Each *daimyō* house came to acquire its own bureaucracy, staffed by vassal samurai, and directed by a council of higher retainers or *kashindan*, which like the *rōjū* board within the Shogunate often exercised effective power in the name of the *han* lord himself, who frequently became a figure-head.[25] The class of *bushi* was now itself stratified into a complex hereditary ranking system, only the top grades of which provided the senior officials of the *han* governments. A further result of the bureaucratization of the samurai was to make it an educated class, with an increasingly impersonal loyalty to the *han* as a whole, rather than to the person of the *daimyō* – although revolts against the latter were virtually unknown.

At the base of the whole feudal system, the peasantry were juridically tied to the soil and forbidden to migrate or exchange their holdings. Statistically, the average peasant plot was extremely small – some 2 to 3 acres – and dues on it owed to the lord amounted to some 40–60 per cent of the product in the early Tokugawa epoch; this declined to 30–40 per cent towards the end of the Shogunate.[26] Villages were collectively responsible for their dues, which were generally paid in kind (although cash conversions were to increase) and collected by the *daimyō*'s fiscal officials. Since the samurai no longer performed any manorial functions, all direct relationship between knights and peasants on the land was eliminated, apart from rural administration by the *han* magistrates. The long peace of the Tokugawa epoch, and the fixed assessment methods of surplus extraction established under it, permitted an impressive advance of agrarian output and productivity in the first century after the installation of the Shogunate. Major reclamations of land were undertaken, with the official encouragement of the *Bakufu*, and there was an increased diffusion of iron field-implements. Irrigation was intensified and the area of paddy-fields extended; fertilizers were more widely used; and crop variants multiplied. The

25. The role of the *daimyō* varied greatly, however: in the *Bakumatsu* period, for example, while the Chōshū lord was a cipher, the Satsuma or Tosa lords were politically active.

26. Kohachiro Takahashi, 'La Place de la Révolution de Meiji dans L'Histoire Agraire du Japon', *Revue Historique*, October–December 1953, pp. 235–6.

official estimates for rice acreage increased by some 40 per cent in the 17th century: in fact, these assessments always undercalculated the real situation because of concealments, and total cereal production probably nearly doubled in this epoch.[27] Population increased by 50 per cent to some 30 million in 1721. Thereafter, however, it levelled off as bad harvests and famines henceforward struck down excess labour, and villages started to practise malthusian controls to fend off these dangers. Thus in the 18th century, demographic increase was minimal. At the same time, the growth in gross output seems to have slowed down considerably: land under cultivation increased by less than 30 per cent according to official reckoning.[28] On the other hand, the later Tokugawa period was characterized by much more intensive commercialization of agriculture. Riziculture continued to make up two-thirds of rural production down to the end of the Shogunate, benefiting from the introduction of improved threshing-machines.[29] The rice surplus siphoned off by seigneurial dues was ultimately monetized by the feudal class in the towns. At the same time, regional specialization developed rapidly in the course of the 18th century: cash crops such as sugar, cotton, tea, indigo and tobacco were produced directly for the market, their cultivation often promoted by *han* monopoly ventures in specific commodities. By the end of the Shogunate, it is clear that a remarkably high proportion of total agricultural output was commercialized,[30] either directly by peasant production for the market, or

27. Hall, *Japan from Prehistory to Modern Times*, p. 201.

28. Hall, *Japan from Prehistory to Modern Times*, pp. 201–2. Reclamations of new land had in some cases, as in feudal Europe or mediaeval China, led to deterioration of older lands, and over-extended riparian works had resulted in disastrous floods. See J. W. Hall, *Tanuma Okitsugu, 1719–1788*, Cambridge USA, 1955, pp. 63–5.

29. The new threshing-machines of the 18th century seem to have been the only major technical invention in Japanese agriculture during this period: T. C. Smith, *The Agrarian Origins of Modern Japan*, Stanford 1959, p. 102.

30. The exact extent of this commercialization is a matter of considerable dispute. Crawcour asserts that 'it is safe to say' that over one half and perhaps nearer two-thirds of gross production was marketed in one form or another by the mid 19th century: E. S. Crawcour, 'The Tokugawa Heritage', in W. Lockwood (ed.), *The State and Economic Enterprise in Japan*, Princeton 1965, pp. 39–41. Ohkawa and Rozovsky, on the other hand, discount any such high estimate, stressing that even in the early 1960's, only some 60 per cent of Japanese agrarian output reached the market: they reckon that, excluding tax-rice, the index of real

indirectly via the sale of feudal rice revenues from the tax-system.

The invasion of a money economy into the villages and the sharp conjunctural fluctuations of rice prices inevitably accelerated social differentiation among the peasantry. From the very outset of the Tokugawa epoch, land tenure within the Japanese villages had always been very unequal. Rich peasant families typically possessed larger than average holdings, which they worked with the aid of dependent labour masked in various forms of pseudo-kin or customary relationships with poorer peasants, while they dominated village councils as a traditional commoner elite.[31] The spread of commercial agriculture greatly enhanced the power and wealth of this social group. Although sale or purchase of land by them was technically illegal, in practice poor peasants were widely driven in desperation to mortgage their plots to village usurers when harvests were poor and prices were high, during the 18th century. There thus emerged within the rural economy a second exploiting stratum, intermediary between the seigneurial officialdom and the immediate producer: the *jinushi* or usurer-landlords, who were usually by origin the richest peasants or headmen (*shōya*) within the village, and who often increased their wealth by financing new cultivation, undertaken by dependent sub-tenants or wage-labour. The pattern of land-holding within the *mura* thus became steadily more concentrated, and kin fictions were abandoned for cash relationships between villagers. Thus while *per capita* income probably increased during the later Tokugawa period with the halt in demographic growth,[32] and the *jinushi* stratum expanded and prospered, the net

(peasant) commercialization was probably not more than 20 per cent in the 1860's: 'A Century of Japanese Economic Growth', in Lockwood, *The State and Economic Enterprise in Japan*, p. 57. It should be emphasized that the structural distinction between noble and peasant forms of commercialization is crucial to an understanding of both the dynamic and limits of Tokugawa agriculture.

31. Smith, *The Agrarian Origins of Modern Japan*, pp. 5–64, presents a comprehensive account of this traditional pattern.

32. The overall performance of the later Tokugawa agrarian economy is still a focus of controversy. In his important study, revising official rice-estimates at the start of the Meiji epoch upwards, Nakamura develops a set of hypotheses which indicate an increase in *per capita* product of some 23 per cent over the period 1680–1870: see J. Nakamura, *Agricultural Production and the Economic Development of Japan 1873–1922*, Princeton 1966, pp. 75–8, 90, 137. Vigorous objections to his assumptions, however, have been made by Rozovsky, who argues that the yield-ratios imputed to Tokugawa riziculture by Nakamura must

result of the same process was also to undermine the pitiful livelihood of the poorer peasantry. Punctuated by ruinous dearths, the 18th and 19th centuries saw increasing numbers of popular rebellions in the countryside. Initially local in character, these tended as time went on to acquire a regional and finally quasi-national incidence, to the alarm of both *han* and *Bakufu* authorities.[33] The peasant revolts of the Tokugawa epoch were still too random and unorganized to be a serious political threat to the *Baku-han* system: they were, however, symptoms of a gathering economic crisis within the old feudal order.

Meanwhile, within this agrarian economy, as in feudal Europe, there had developed important urban centres, engaged in mercantile operations and manufactures. The municipal autonomy of the trading towns of the Ashikaga and Sengoku epochs had been durably suppressed at the end of the 16th century. The Tokugawa Shogunate permitted no urban self-government: at most, honorific merchant councils were allowed in Ōsaka and Edo, under the firm control of the *Bakufu* magistrates charged with the administration of the cities.[34] The *han* castle-towns naturally afforded no space for municipal institutions either. On the other hand, the pacification of the country and the establishment of the *sankin-kōtai* system gave an unprecedented commercial impetus to the urban sector of the Japanese economy. The consumption of luxury goods by the higher aristocracy developed

---

be too high, since they exceed those of all other countries of monsoon Asia in the 20th century: H. Rozovsky, 'Rumbles in the Rice-Fields: Professor Nakamura versus the Official Statistics', *Journal of Asian Studies*, XXVII, No. 2, February 1968, p. 355. Two recent articles give euphoric but impressionistic accounts of *Baku-han* agriculture, without any attempt at quantification: S. B. Hanley and K. Yamamura, 'A Quiet Transformation in Tokugawa Economic History', *Journal of Asian Studies*, XXX, No. 2, February 1971, pp. 373–84, and Kee Il Choi, 'Technological Diffusion in Agriculture under the *Baku-han* System', *Journal of Asian Studies*, XXX, No. 4, August 1971, pp. 749–59.

33. Between 1590 and 1867, modern research has so far identified some 2,800 peasant riots; another 1,000 popular outbreaks occurred in the towns: Kohachiro Takahashi, 'La Restauration de Meiji au Japon et la Révolution Française', *Recherches Internationales*, No. 62, 1970, p. 78. In the 19th century, the number of inter-peasant (as opposed to anti-seigneurial) riots increased: Akamatsu, *Meiji 1868*, pp. 44–5.

34. C. D. Sheldon, *The Rise of the Merchant Class in Tokugawa Japan 1600–1868*, Locust Valley 1958, pp. 33–6, who comments that peasant headmen exercised more real power in the villages than merchants in the towns.

rapidly, while the conversion of the knight class into salaried officials augmented the demand for comforts beneath it (both Shogunal and *han* bureaucracies were congenitally overmanned because of the size of the samurai class). There was an overwhelming drainage of *daimyō* wealth to Edo and Ōsaka, caused by the costly construction and ostentatious itineraries attendant on the serial residence of the major feudal lords in the Tokugawa capital. It is estimated that up to 60–80 per cent of *han* cash outlays were accounted for by *sankin-kōtai* expenditure.[35] There were over 600 official residences or *yashiki* maintained by the *daimyō* in Edo (most major lords had more than three each). These residences were in fact sprawling estate-compounds, the largest of which could be up to 400 acres in extent, including mansions, offices, barracks, schools, stables, gymnasia, gardens and even prisons. Perhaps a sixth of the *han* retinues were permanently stationed in them. The great urban agglomeration of Edo was dominated by a concentric system of such *daimyō* residences, carefully distributed about the vast Chiyoda fortress-palace of the Shogunate itself in the centre of city. In all, half of the population of Edo lived in samurai households, and no less than two-thirds of the entire area of the city was the property of the military class.[36] To sustain the enormous costs of this system of compulsory feudal consumption, the *han* governments were obliged to convert their tax-revenues, extracted for the most part from the peasantry in kind, into cash incomes. Their rice surplus was thus marketed in Osaka, which came to be a distribution centre that was the commercial pendant to the consumption centre of Edo: it was there that specialized merchants managed *han* warehouses, advanced credit against taxes or stipends to lords or their vassals, and speculated in commodity futures. The enforced monetization of feudal revenues thus

35. T. G. Tsukahira, *Feudal Control in Tokugawa Japan: The Sankin-Kōtai System*, Cambridge USA 1966, pp. 96–102. For a graphic account of the new urban life-styles affected by nobles and merchants in Edo, see Hall, *Tanuma Okitsugu*, pp. 107–17.

36. After the Restoration, the Meiji government released the following figures for urban property in Edo: 68·6 per cent was 'military land', 15·6 per cent belonged to 'temples and shrines', and only 15·8 per cent was the property of townspeople or *chōnin* themselves: Tsukahira, *Feudal Control in Tokugawa Japan*, pp. 91, 196. Totman reckons the size of the whole Chiyoda castle at one square mile, and the administrative complex of the Main Enceinte alone at 9 acres: *Politics in the Tokugawa Bakufu*, pp. 92, 95.

prepared the conditions for a rapid expansion of mercantile capital in the cities. At the same time, the *chōnin* class of town-dwellers was legally forbidden to acquire agricultural land: the Japanese merchants of the Tokugawa epoch were consequently prevented from diverting their capital into rural property, after the manner of their Chinese counterparts.[37] The very rigidity of the class-system created by Hideyoshi thus paradoxically encouraged the steady growth of purely urban fortunes.

There thus developed in the course of the 17th and 18th centuries an extremely prosperous stratum of merchants in the larger towns, who engaged in a wide range of commercial activities. *Chōnin* companies in the cities accumulated capital through marketing of the agricultural surplus (dealing in both rice and newer crops like cotton, silk or indigo), transport services (coastal shipping developed intensively), exchange transactions (there were over thirty major currencies in circulation in this period, since the *han* issued paper notes in addition to the *Bakufu* metallic coinages), manufacture of textiles, porcelain or other commodities (either concentrated in urban workshops or dispersed in the villages via a putting-out system), lumber and construction enterprises (frequent fires necessitated constant rebuilding in the towns), and loans to the *daimyō* or the Shogunate. The largest merchant houses came to control incomes equivalent to those of the most prominent territorial lords, for whom they acted as financial agents and sources of credit. The spreading commercialization of agriculture, accompanied by massive illegal migration to the towns, permitted an enormous expansion of the urban market. By the 18th century, Edo may have had a population of 1,000,000 – larger than contemporary London or Paris; Ōsaka and Kyōtō had perhaps 400,000 inhabitants each; and perhaps a tenth of the total population of Japan lived in towns of over 10,000.[38] This rapid wave of urbanization led to a scissors effect in the prices of manufactured and agricultural goods, given relative supply rigidity in the rural sector from which the nobility derived its income. The result was to create chronic budgetary difficulties for both the *Bakufu* and *han* governments, which became increas-

---

37. The *chōnin* class technically included both merchants (*shōnin*) and artisans (*kōnin*). Subsequent discussion of them here refers essentially to merchants.

38. Hall, *Japan from Prehistory to Modern Times*, p. 210.

ingly indebted to the merchants who advanced them loans against their fiscal revenues.

The deepening aristocratic deficits of the later Tokugawa epoch, however, did not betoken any corresponding ascent of the *chōnin* community within the social order as a whole. The Shogunate and the *daimyō* reacted to the crisis in their incomes by cancelling their debts, coercively extracting large 'gifts' from the merchant class, and cutting the rice stipends of their samurai retainers. For the *chōnin* were juridically at the mercy of the nobility whom they supplied with credit, and their gains could arbitrarily be erased by obligatory benevolences and special levies on them. Tokugawa law was 'socially shallow and territorially limited': it covered only the *tenryō* domains themselves, lacked any real judiciary and was mainly concerned with repression of crime. Civil law was rudimentary, grudgingly administered as 'a matter of grace' in litigation between private parties by the *Bakufu* authorities.[39] Legal security for capital transactions was thus always precarious, although the large Shogunal cities afforded merchants protection against *daimyō*, if not *Bakufu*, pressures. On the other hand, the preservation of the *Baku-han* system blocked the emergence of a unified domestic market and hampered the growth of mercantile capital on a national scale, once the limits of *sankin-kōtai* expenditures had been reached. *Han* checkpoints and border guards impeded free passage of goods and persons, while many of the major *daimyō* houses followed protectionist policies of import restriction. Most decisive of all for the fate of the *chōnin* class in Japan, however, was Tokugawa isolationism. From the 1630's onwards, Japan was closed to foreigners, except for a Dutch-Chinese enclave off Nagasaki, and no Japanese was permitted to leave the country. These sealed frontiers were henceforward a permanent noose on the development of merchant capital in Japan. One of the fundamental preconditions of primitive accumulation in early modern Europe was the dramatic internationalization of commodity exchange and exploitation from the epoch of the Discoveries onwards. Lenin repeatedly and rightly emphasized that: 'It is impossible to conceive a capitalist nation without foreign trade, nor is there any

39. D. F. Henderson, 'The Evolution of Tokugawa Law', in J. Hall and M. Jansen, *Studies in the Institutional History of Early Modern Japan*, Princeton 1968, pp. 207, 214, 225–8.

such nation,'[40] The Shogunal policy of seclusion, in effect, precluded any possibility of a transition to the capitalist mode of production proper within the Tokugawa framework. Deprived of foreign trade, commercial capital in Japan was constantly reined in and re-routed towards parasitic dependence on the feudal nobility and its political systems. Its remarkable growth, despite this insurmountable limit to its expansion, was only possible because of the density and scale of the domestic markets, despite their division – with 30 million inhabitants, Japan in the mid-18th century was more populous than France. But there could be no 'capitalism in one country'. Tokugawa isolationism condemned the *chōnin* to a fundamentally subaltern existence.

The great metropolitan boom caused by the *sankin-kōtai* system came to an end in the early 18th century, together with the tapering off of population growth as a whole. Restrictive official monopolies were licensed by the Shogunate in 1721. From about 1735, construction and expansion ceased in the large *Bakufu* cities.[41] Commercial vitality had, in fact, by then already shifted from the Ōsaka bankers and merchants to smaller inter-regional wholesalers. These in turn acquired monopolistic privileges towards the end of the 18th century, and entrepreneurial initiative moved further outwards into the provinces. In the early 19th century, it was the rural landlord-trader stratum of *jinushi* who proved the most dynamic business group, profiting from the lack of guild restrictions in the countryside to implant village industries such as *sake* brewing or silk manufacture (which migrated from the towns in this epoch).[42] There was thus a progressive diffusion of commerce outwards, which was transforming the countryside at the close of the Tokugawa epoch, rather than revolutionizing the towns. For manufacturing activity itself remained extremely primitive: there was little division of labour in either urban or rural enterprises, no major technical inventions, and relatively few concentrations of wage-labour. Japanese industry, in fact, was overwhelmingly artisanal in character, and exiguous in equipment. The extensive development of

40. Lenin, *Collected Works*, Vol. 3, p. 65; see also 1, pp. 102–3, 2, pp. 164–5.
41. Sheldon, *The Rise of the Merchant Class in Tokugawa Japan*, p. 100.
42. For these successive shifts in the centre of commercial gravity under the Shogunate, see E. S. Crawcour, 'Changes in Japanese Commerce in the Tokugawa Period', in Hall and Jansen, *Studies in the Institutional History of Early Modern Japan*, pp. 193–201.

organized commerce was never matched by an intensive advance in methods of production. Industrial technology was archaic, its improvement foreign to *chōnin* traditions. The prosperity and vitality of the Japanese merchant class had produced a distinctive urban culture of great artistic sophistication, above all in painting and literature. But it had not generated any growth in scientific knowledge or innovation in political thought. *Chōnin* creativity within the *Baku-han* order was confined to the domains of imagination and diversion; it never extended to enquiry or criticism. The merchant community as a class lacked intellectual autonomy or corporate dignity: it was circumscribed to the end by the historical conditions of existence imposed on it by the feudal autarky of the Shogunate.

The immobility of the *Bakufu* itself in turn perpetuated the structural paradox of the State and society to which the Shogunate had given birth. For unlike any variant of feudalism in Europe, Tokugawa Japan combined a notably rigid and static parcellization of sovereignty with an extremely high velocity and volume of commodity circulation. The social and political framework of the country remained comparable to that of 14th century France, in the judgement of one of its major modern historians,[43] yet the economic magnitude of Edo was greater than that of 18th century London. Culturally, too, overall educational levels in Japan were remarkable: perhaps 30 per cent of the adult population, and 40–50 per cent of men, were literate by the mid 19th century.[44] No other region in the world, outside Europe and North America, contained such integrated financial mechanisms, such advanced commerce or such high literacy. The ultimate compatibility between the Japanese polity and economy in the Tokugawa epoch fundamentally rested on the disproportion between commodity *exchange* and *production* within the country: for, as we have seen, the monetization of the seigneurial surplus which was the basic motor of urban growth did not correspond to the real scale of commercial agriculture by the peasantry as such. It was an 'artificial' conversion of feudal deliveries in kind, superimposed on a primary production that was still predominantly subsistence, despite an increasing market orientation of its own in the later phases of the Shogunate. It was this

43. Craig, *Chōshū in the Meiji Restoration*, p. 33.
44. R. P. Dore, *Education in Tokugawa Japan*, Berkeley 1965, pp. 254, 321.

objective disjuncture at the base of the economic system which *internally* permitted the conservation of the original juridical and territorial fragmentation of Japan, dating from the settlement after Sekigahara. The *external* precondition of Tokugawa stability – fully as vital – was the sedulous insulation of Japan from the outside world, which sealed it off from ideological infections, economic disruptions, diplomatic disputes or military contests of any kind. Nevertheless, even within the airless world of the Chiyoda keep, the strains of maintaining an antiquated 'mediaeval' machinery of government in a dynamic 'early modern' economy were becoming increasingly evident by the early 19th century.

For the *Bakufu* was gradually gripped, just as much as the provincial daimiates, by a creeping revenue crisis: at the material intersection of sovereignty and productivity, its fiscal system was logically the most vulnerable link of the Shogunate. The Tokugawa government itself did not, of course, have to bear the expenses of the *sankin-kōtai* system which it imposed on the *han*. But since the whole social rationale of the ostentatory consumption involved in it was to demonstrate grades of rank and prestige within the aristocratic class, the Shogunate's own voluntary costs of display were necessarily even greater than those of the *daimyō*: the palatine household alone, composed of the women of the court, absorbed a larger share of the budget in the 18th century than the combined defense establishment of Ōsaka and Kyōtō.[45] Moreover, the *Bakufu* had to perform certain quasi-national functions as the unitary apex of the pyramid of feudal sovereignty in Japan, while itself disposing of only about one-fifth of the land-resources of the country: there was thus always a potential imbalance between its responsibilities and its tax-capacity. Its extensive bureaucracy of *bushi* retainers was naturally far larger than that of any *han*, and was extremely expensive to maintain. The total cost of the rank and office stipends of its liege vassals covered about half its annual budget; while official corruption within the *Bakufu* eventually became widespread.[46] At the same time,

45. Totman, *Politics in the Tokugawa Bakufu*, p. 287.
46. For salary costs, see Totman, *Politics in the Tokugawa Bakufu*, p. 82. For corruption and purchase of office, see the engaging candour of Tanuma Okitsugu, Grand Chamberlain in the Bakufu in the late 18th century: 'Gold and silver are treasures more precious than life itself. If a person brings this treasure with an expression of his desire to serve in some public capacity, I can be assured that he

the fiscal yield of its house-lands tended to decline in real terms, because it could not prevent increasing cash commutation of rice taxes, which depleted its treasury because the conversion rate was usually below market prices and coinage values were themselves steadily depreciating.[47] In the early phase of the Tokugawa epoch, the bullion monopoly of the Shogunate had been a hugely profitable asset: Japanese silver output at the turn of the 17th century, for example, was about half the volume of total American exports to Europe, at the height of the Spanish convoys.[48] But by the 18th century, the mines were suffering from flooding and production declined greatly. The *Bakufu* responded by resorting to systematic debasements of the existing coinage: between 1700 and 1854, the volume of nominal currency in circulation issued by the Shogunate increased by 400 per cent.[49] These devaluations eventually came to supply something between a quarter and a half of its annual income: since no competing specie was entering the country and demand was expanding within the economy as a whole, there was relatively little long-term price inflation. No regular taxation of commerce existed, but periodic and major confiscations were made from the merchant class from the early 18th century onwards, when the Shogunate so decided. Repeated budgetary shortfalls and financial emergencies nevertheless continued to harass the *Bakufu*, whose annual deficits were well over half a million gold ryō by 1837–41;[50] while short-term price oscillations during bad harvests could precipitate crises in countryside and capital alike. After nearly a decade of crop failures, much of Japan was haunted by famine in the 1830's, while the incumbent *rōjū* clique vainly strove to beat down prices and consolidate house income. In 1837, Ōsaka was the scene of a desperate attempt at plebeian insurrection, which revealed how charged the political climate of the country was becoming. At the same time, the armed apparatus of the Shogunate had – after over two centuries of domestic peace – been drastically corroded: the outmoded and incompetent

---

is serious in his desire. A man's strength of desire will be apparent in the size of his gift.' Hall, *Tanuma Okitsugu*, p. 55.

47. Totman, *Politics in the Tokugawa Bakufu*, pp. 78–80. The legal limit for cash conversion was $\frac{1}{3}$ of the tax, but the average actually came to be over $\frac{2}{3}$.

48. Vilar, *Oro y Moneda en la Historia*, p. 103.

49. P. Frost, *The Bakumatsu Currency Crisis*, Cambridge USA 1970, p. 9.

50. W. G. Beasley, *The Meiji Restoration*, London 1973, p. 51.

guard units of the *tenryō* were to prove incapable of assuring security within Edo itself in a civil crisis;[51] while the *Bakufu* no longer had any operative superiority over the forces that could be mustered in the *tozama han* of the South-West. The military evolution of Tokugawa feudalism was the antithesis of that of European Absolutism: a progressive diminution and dilapidation of its troop-strength occurred.

The Japanese feudal order was thus already in the throes of a slow internal crisis by the early 19th century: but if the commodity economy had eroded the stability of the old social and institutional instructure, it had not yet generated the elements for a political solution to supersede it. The Tokugawa peace was still intact at mid-century. It was the exogenous impact of Western imperialism, with the arrival of Commodore Perry's squadron in 1853, which suddenly condensed the multiple latent contradictions of the Shogunal state, and set off a revolutionary explosion against it. For the aggressive intrusion of American, Russian, British, French and other warships into Japanese waters, demanding the establishment of diplomatic and trade relations at gun-point, posed an ominous dilemma for the *Bakufu*. For two centuries, it had systematically instilled xenophobia into all classes in Japan, as one of the most sacred themes of official ideology: the total exclusion of foreigners had, indeed, been one of the sociological lynch-pins of its rule. Yet it now confronted a military menace whose technological power – embodied in the iron-clad steam-ships hovering in the Bay of Yokohama – it immediately became aware was easily capable of crushing its own armies. It therefore had to temporize and concede the Western demand for the 'opening up' of Japan, to preserve its own survival. By doing so, however, it immediately rendered itself vulnerable to xenophobic attacks from within. Important collateral lineages of the Tokugawa house itself were rabidly hostile to the presence of foreign missions in Japan: the first assassinations of Westerners in their enclave at Yokohama were often the work of samurai from the fief of Mito, one of the three main cadet branches of the Tokugawa dynasty. The Emperor in Kyōtō, guardian and symbol

51. A striking sign of the military archaism of the Shogunate was the continued official precedence given to swords over muskets, despite all the experience of the Sengoku epoch in the superiority of fire-arms: Totman, *Politics in the Tokugawa Bakufu*, pp. 47–8.

of traditional cultural values, was also ferociously opposed to dealing with the intruders. With the onset of what all sections of the Japanese feudal class felt to be a national emergency, the imperial court was suddenly reactivated as an effective secondary pole of power, and the *kuge* aristocracy in Kyōtō soon became a constant focus of intrigue against the Shogunal bureaucracy in Edo. The Tokugawa regime was, in effect, now in an impossible situation. Politically, it could only justify its progressive retreats and concessions before Western demands by explaining to the *daimyō* the military inferiority which necessitated them. But to do so was to admit its own weakness and thereby invite armed subversion and revolt against itself. Pinned down by the external danger, it became increasingly unable to cope with the internal unrest that its delaying tactics provoked.

Economically, moreover, the abrupt end of Japanese seclusion upset the whole viability of the Shogunal monetary system: for since the Tokugawa coinages were essentially fiat issues, with far less bullion content than their denominational value, foreign merchants refused to accept them at parity with Western currencies based on real silver weightages. The advent of foreign trade on a large scale thus forced the *Bakufu* to devalue steeply to the actual bullion content of its coinage, and to issue paper money, while external demand for key local products – silk, tea and cotton – soared. The result was a catastrophic domestic inflation: the price of rice quintupled between 1853 and 1869,[52] causing acute popular unrest in towns and countryside. The Shogunal bureaucracy, convoluted and divided, was unable to react with any clear or decisive policy to the dangers now pressing in upon it. The lamentable state of its security apparatus was revealed when the one resolute leader produced by the *Bakufu* in its last phase, Ii Naosuke, was assassinated by xenophobic samurai in Edo in 1860;[53] two years later, another *attentat* forced his successor to resign. The *tozama* fiefs of the South-West – Satsuma, Chōshū, Tosa and Saga – by their structural position always antagonists of the *Bakufu*, were now emboldened to pass over to the offensive and conspire for its overthrow. Their own military and economic resources, husbanded by regimes more compact and efficacious than the Edo government, were put on a war footing.

52. Frost, *The Bakumatsu Currency Crisis*, p. 41.
53. For this critical episode, see Akamatsu, *Meiji 1868*, pp. 165–7.

Han troops were modernized, enlarged and reequipped with Western armaments; while Satsuma already possessed the largest samurai cadre in Japan, Chōshū commanders recruited and drilled rich peasants, to create a commoner force capable of use against the Shogunate. Popular expectations of great changes were now spreading in superstitious forms among the crowds of Nagoya, Ōsaka and Edo, while the tacit support of certain *chōnin* bankers was won to provide the necessary financial reserves for a civil war. Constant liaison with the *kuge* malcontents in Kyōtō ensured the *tozama* leaders of crucial ideological coverage for the projected operation: it was to be nothing less than a revolution whose formal aim was to restore the Imperial authority that had been usurped by the Shogunate. The Emperor thus supplied a transcendental symbol to which all classes could in theory be rallied. A swift coup delivered Kyōtō to Satsuma troops in 1867. With the city under military control, the Emperor Meiji read a proclamation drafted by his court formally ending the Shogunate. The *Bakufu*, subverted and demoralized, proved incapable of any determined resistance: within a few weeks, the whole of Japan had been seized by the insurgent *tozama* armies, and the unitary Meiji State had been founded. The fall of the Shogunate spelt the end of Japanese feudalism.

Economically and diplomatically undermined from abroad, once the safety of its seclusion had gone, the Tokugawa State was politically and militarily undone from within by the very parcellization of sovereignty that it had always preserved: its lack of any monopoly of armed force, and its failure to suppress imperial legitimacy, eventually rendered it impotent before a well-organized insurrection in the name of the Emperor. The Meiji State that succeeded it promptly proceeded to a sweeping arc of measures to abolish feudalism from above – the most radical such programme ever to be enacted. The fief system was liquidated, the four-estate order destroyed, the equality of every citizen before the law proclaimed, calendar and dress reformed, a unified market and single currency created, and industrialization and military expansion systematically promoted. A capitalist economy and polity emerged directly from the elimination of the Shogunate. The complex historical mechanisms of the revolutionary transformation accomplished by the Meiji Restoration remain to be examined. Here it is only necessary to stress that, contrary to the supposition of some

Japanese historians,[54] the Meiji State was not in any categorical sense an Absolutism. Initially an emergency dictatorship of the new ruling bloc, it soon proved itself a peremptory capitalist state, whose mettle was within a few decades to be fittingly tested in action against a genuine Absolutism. In 1905, the Russian debacles at Tsushima and Mukden revealed to the world the difference between the two. The passage from feudalism to capitalism was effected, to a unique extent, without political interlude in Japan.

54. See, for example, the classic Marxist study of the Restoration, available outside Japan only in Russian: Shigeki Toyama, *Meidzi Isin, Krushenie Feodalizma v Yaponii*, Moscow 1959, pp. 183, 217–18, 241, 295. There is no space here to do more than make the bald assertion above: a full discussion of the historical character of the Meiji Restoration must be reserved for a later study. Lenin's view of the nature of the victor in the Russo-Japanese War may, however, be noted. He believed that 'the Japanese bourgeoisie' had inflicted 'a crushing defeat' on the 'feudal autocracy' of Tsarism: 'autocratic Russia has been defeated by constitutional Japan'. Lenin, *Collected Works*, Vol. 8, pp. 52, 53, 28.

B. The 'Asiatic Mode of Production'

I

It has been seen that Marx expressly rejected the qualification of Mughal India as a feudal social formation: and by necessary implication, of Ottoman Turkey. This *negative* delimitation, however, which reserved the concept of feudalism for Europe and Japan, poses the question of what *positive* classification Marx ascribed to the socio-economic systems of which they furnished prominent examples. The answer, it has increasingly been conceded since the sixties, is that Marx believed them to represent a specific pattern which he called the 'Asiatic mode of production'. This notion has come to be the focus of a wide international discussion among Marxists in recent years, and in the light of the conclusions to this study, it may be useful to recall the intellectual background from which he wrote. Theoretical juxtaposition and contrast of European and Asian state structures formed, as we have seen, a long tradition from Machiavelli and Bodin onwards: prompted by the proximity of Turkish power, it was indeed coeval with the new birth of political theory as such in the Renaissance, and thereafter accompanied its development step by step down to the Enlightenment.

We have noted above the successive and significant reflections of Machiavelli, Bodin, Bacon, Harrington, Bernier and Montesquieu on the Ottoman Empire itself, intimate and enemy of Europe from the 15th century onwards.[1] By the 18th century, however, the geographical application of ideas initially conceived in contact with Turkey had spread steadily further east, in the wake of colonial exploration and expansion: to Persia, then India and finally to China. With this geographical extension came a conceptual generalization of the complex of traits initially discerned or confined to the Porte. The notion of political

1. See above, pp. 397–401.

'despotism' was born – a term hitherto lacking in the vocabulary of European commentary on Turkey, even if its substance was already long present to it. The traditional designation of the Osmanli Sultan, in Machiavelli, Bodin or Harrington, was the 'Grand Seignior' – an awkward projection of the terminology of European feudalism onto a Turkish State explicitly declared to be distinct from any political system in Europe. Hobbes was the first major writer to speak of despotic power in the 17th century – commending it, paradoxically, as the normal and proper form of sovereignty. This connotation was naturally to be an isolated one. On the contrary, as the century proceeded, despotic power was everywhere increasingly equated with tyranny; while in France, 'Turkish tyranny' was frequently attributed to the Bourbon dynasty in the polemical literature of its opponents, from the Fronde onwards. Bayle seems to have been the first philosopher to use the generic concept of *despotism* as such, in 1704;[2] while himself questioning it, he implicitly accepted that the idea was now a widely current one.

The definite emergence of the notion of 'despotism', moreover, coincided with its extrojection onto the 'Orient' from the start. For the central canonical passage in classical Antiquity where the original Greek word itself (an unusual term) could be found was a famous statement by Aristotle: 'Barbarians are more servile by nature than Greeks, and Asians are more servile than Europeans; hence they endure despotic rule without protest. Such monarchies are like tyrannies, but they are secure because they are hereditary and legal.'[3] Despotism was thus expressly attributed to Asia in the *fons et origo* of all political philosophy in Europe. The Enlightenment, which could now mentally encompass the whole globe after the great voyages of colonial discovery and conquest, was for the first time in a position to provide a general and systematic formulation of this connection. This task was undertaken by Montesquieu, with his mature theoretical categorization of 'Oriental Despotism'. Montesquieu, deeply influenced by Bodin and an assiduous reader of Bernier, inherited from his predecessors the basic axioms that

2. R. Koebner, 'Despot and Despotism: Vicissitudes of a Political Term', *The Journal of the Warburg and Courtauld Institutes*, XIV, 1951, p. 300. This essay also traces the pre-history of the word in the Middle Ages, before it was banished during the Renaissance for the impurity of its philological pedigree.

3. Aristotle, *Politics*, III, ix, 3.

Asiatic States lacked stable private property or a hereditary nobility, and were therefore arbitrary and tyrannical in character – views which he repeated with all the lapidary force peculiar to him. Oriental despotism, moreover, not merely rested on an abject fear, but also on an erasive *equality* among its subjects – for all were alike in their common subjection to the lethal caprices of the despot. 'The principle of despotic government is fear . . . it is uniform throughout.'[4] This uniformity was the sinister antithesis of the municipal unity of classical Antiquity: 'Men are all equal in a republican state; they are also equal in a despotic state; in the first, because they are everything; in the second, because they are nothing.'[5] The lack of a hereditary nobility, long ago perceived in Turkey, here became something much stronger: a condition of denuded, egalitarian servitude throughout Asia. Montesquieu also added two further notions to the tradition he had inherited, both of them specifically reflecting Enlightenment doctrines of secularism and progress. Thus he argued that Asian societies were devoid of legal codes, religion operating as a functional substitute for law in them: 'There are states where laws are nothing, or no more than the capricious and arbitrary will of the sovereign. If the laws of religion in these states were similar to the laws of men, they would be null too; but since a society must have some principle of fixity, it is religion which provides it.'[6] At the same time, he believed that these societies were essentially unchanging: 'The laws, customs and manners of the Orient – even the most trivial, such as mode of dress – remain the same today as they were a thousand years ago.'[7]

4. *De l'Esprit des Lois*, I, pp. 64, 69. Montesquieu's discourse on despotism, of course, was not just an overt theorization of Asia. It also contained a coded warning of the dangers of absolutism in France, which if unchecked by the 'intermediary powers' of nobility and clergy might ultimately – Montesquieu hinted – approximate to Oriental norms. For these polemical undertones of the *Esprit des Lois*, see the generally excellent discussion in L. Althusser, *Montesquieu – La Politique et l'Histoire*, pp. 92–7. Althusser, however, overstates the propagandist dimension of Montesquieu's theory of despotism, by minimizing altogether its geographical demarcation. To superpoliticize the significance of the *Esprit des Lois* is to parochialize it. In fact, it is abundantly clear that Montesquieu took his analyses of the Orient extremely seriously: they were not merely or primarily allegorical devices, but an integral component of his attempt at a global science of political systems, in both senses.

5. *De l'Esprit des Lois*, I, p. 81.

6. *De l'Esprit des Lois*, II, p. 168.   7. *De l'Esprit des Lois*, I, p. 244.

Montesquieu's declared principle of explanation for the differential character of European and Asian States was, of course, geographical: climate and topography determined their separate destinies. Thus he synthesized his views on the nature of each in an artistically dramatic comparison: 'Asia has always been the home of great empires; they have never subsisted in Europe. For the Asia of which we know has vaster plains than Europe; it is broken up into greater masses by the surrounding seas; and as it is further south, its springs run more easily dry, its mountains are not so covered with snow, and its rivers are lower and form lesser barriers. Power therefore must always be despotic in Asia, for if servitude were not extreme, the continent would suffer a division which the geography of the region forbids. In Europe, the natural dimensions of geography form several states of a modest size, in which the rule of laws is not incompatible with the survival of the state; on the contrary, it is so propitious to it that without laws a state would fall into decay, and become inferior to every other. It is this which has created that spirit of liberty which renders each part of the continent so resistant to subjugation or submission by a foreign power, except law or the advantage of commerce. In Asia, by contrast, there reigns a spirit of servitude which has never quitted it; and in the entire history of the continent, it is impossible to find a single trait that marks a free soul: only the heroism of slavery is to be seen.'[8]

Montesquieu's canvas, although contested by a few critics in his own time,[9] was generally accepted by the age, and became a central legacy

8. *De l'Esprit des Lois*, I, pp. 291–2.

9. The most notable of these was Voltaire, who – preoccupied with cultural rather than political problems – vigorously disputed Montesquieu's account of the Chinese Empire, which he admired for what he believed to be the rational benevolence of its government and manners: 'enlightened despotism' was, as we have seen earlier, a positive ideal for many of the bourgeois *philosophes*, for whom it represented the suppression of feudal particularism – precisely the reason why Montesquieu, a nostalgic aristocrat, feared and denounced it. Another very different critic of *De l'Esprit des Lois*, who has won the commendation of recent writers, was Anquetil-Duperron, a scholar of Zoroastrian and Vedic sacred texts who spent some years in India and wrote a volume entitled *Législation Orientale* (1778), devoted entirely to denying the existence of despotism in Turkey, Persia and India, and asserting the presence of rational legal systems and private property in these countries. Montesquieu and Bernier were singled out specifically for attack (pp. 2–9, 12–13, 140–2), for having maintained otherwise. Anquetil-Duperron dedicated his book to the 'Unhappy peoples of India', pleading for

for political economy and philosophy thereafter. Adam Smith took what was perhaps the next important step in developing the received opposition between Asia and Europe, when for the first time he redefined it as a contrast between two types of *economy*, dominated respectively by different branches of production: 'As the political economy of the nations of modern Europe has been more favourable to manufactures and foreign trade, the industry of the towns, than to agriculture, the industry of the country; so that of other nations has followed a different plan, and has been more favourable to agriculture than to manufactures and foreign trade. The policy of China favours agriculture more than all other employments. In China, the condition of a labourer is said to be as much superior to that of an artificer, as in

---

their 'wounded rights', and accused European theories of Oriental despotism of merely providing ideological cover for colonial aggression and rapine in the East: 'Despotism is the government in these countries, where the sovereign declares himself the proprietor of all the goods of his subjects: let us become that sovereign, and we will be the master of all the lands of Hindustan. Such is the reasoning of avid greed, concealed behind a facade of pretexts which must be demolished.' (p. 178). On the strength of these sentiments, Anquetil-Duperron has subsequently been hailed as an early and noble champion of anti-colonialism. Althusser has, with some naiveté, pronounced his *Législation Orientale* an 'admirable' panorama of the 'real East', as opposed to Montesquieu's image of it. Two recent articles have repeated his commendation: F. Venturi, 'Despotismo Orientale', *Rivista Storica Italiana*, LXXII, I, 1960, pp. 117–26, and S. Stelling-Michaud, 'Le Mythe du Despotisme Oriental', *Schweizer Beiträge zur Allgemeinen Geschichte*, Bd 18/19, 1960/1961, pp. 344–5 (which in general follows Althusser closely). In fact, Anquetil-Duperron was an altogether more equivocal and trivial figure than these encomia suggest, as a little further enquiry would have revealed to their authors. Rather than a principled foe of colonialism in general, he was a disappointed French patriot, chagrined by the success of British colonialism in ousting its Gallic rival from the Carnatic, and the sub-continent. In 1782, he wrote another volume, *L'Inde en Rapport avec l'Europe*, now dedicated to the 'Shades of Dupleix and Labourdonnais', a violent requisitory against 'audacious Albion, which has usurped the trident of the oceans and the sceptre of India', that called for the 'French flag to float with majesty once again in the seas and lands of India'. Published in 1798 during the Directory, Anquetil-Duperron argued in this book that 'the tiger must be attacked in its lair', and proposed a French naval expedition to 'seize Bombay' and so 'overthrow English power beyond the Cape of Good Hope' (pp. i–ii, xxv–xxvi). None of this could be guessed from the immaculate piety of the entry in the *Dictionnaire Historique* from which much of his later reputation appears to have derived.

most parts of Europe, that of an artificer is to that of a labourer.'[10]
Smith went on to postulate a novel correlation between the agrarian
character of Asian or African societies and the role of hydraulic works –
irrigation and transport – in them; for since, he argued, the State was
proprietor of all land in these countries, it was directly interested in the
public improvement of agriculture. 'The works constructed by the
ancient sovereigns of Egypt for the proper distribution of the waters of
the Nile were famous in antiquity; and the ruined remains of some of
them are still the admiration of travellers. Those of the same kind
which were constructed by the ancient sovereigns of Indostan, for the
proper distribution of the waters of the Ganges as well as of many
other rivers, though they have been less celebrated, seem to have been
equally great. . . . In China, and in several other governments of Asia,
the executive power charges itself both with the reparation of the high
roads, and with the maintenance of the navigable canals. . . . This
branch of public police accordingly is said to be very much attended to
in all those countries, but particularly in China, where the high roads,
and still more the navigable canals, it is pretended, exceed very much
everything of the same kind which is known in Europe.'[11]

In the 19th century, the successors of Montesquieu and Smith prolonged much the same lines of thought. Within German classical
philosophy, Hegel studied both men deeply, and in *The Philosophy of
History* restated most of Montesquieu's notions of Asian despotism,
without intermediary ranks or powers, in his own characteristic idiom.
'Despotism, developed in magnificent proportions' was in the Orient
the 'form of government strictly appropriate to the Dawn-Land of
History.'[12] Hegel enumerated the major regions of the continent to

10. *An Inquiry into the Nature and Causes of the Wealth of Nations*, London
1778, II, p. 281.

11. *An Inquiry into the Nature and Causes of the Wealth of Nations*, II, pp.
283, 340. Smith characteristically added: 'The accounts of those works, however,
which have been transmitted to Europe, have generally been drawn up by weak
and wondering travellers; frequently by lying and stupid missionaries. If they
had been examined by more intelligent eyes, and if the accounts of them had been
reported by more faithful witnesses, they would not, perhaps, appear to be so
wonderful. The account which Bernier gives of some works of this kind in
Indostan, falls very much short of what had been reported of them by other
travellers, more disposed to the marvellous than he was.'

12. *The Philosophy of History*, London 1878, p. 260.

which this rule applied: 'In India, therefore, the most arbitrary, wicked, degrading despotism has its full swing. China, Persia, Turkey – in fact Asia generally is the scene of despotism, and in a bad sense, of tyranny.'[13] The Heavenly Kingdom, which had aroused such mixed sentiments among Enlightenment thinkers, was the special object of his interest, as the model of what he saw as an egalitarian autocracy. 'In China, we have the reality of absolute equality, and all the differences that exist are possible only in connection with that administration, and in virtue of worth which a person may acquire, enabling him to fill a high post in the government. Since equality prevails in China, but without any freedom, despotism is necessarily the mode of government. Among us, men are equal only before the law, and in the respect paid to the property of each; but they have also many interests and peculiar privileges, which must be guaranteed, if we are to have what we call freedom. But in the Chinese Empire these special interests enjoy no consideration on their own account, and the government proceeds from the Emperor alone, who sets it in motion as a hierarchy of officials or mandarins.'[14] Hegel, like many of his predecessors, expressed a certain qualified admiration for Chinese civilization. His account of Indian civilization, although also nuanced, was much more sombre. He believed that the Indian caste system was quite unlike anything in China, and represented a progress of hierarchy over equality, but one which nevertheless immobilized and debased the whole social structure. 'In China there prevailed an equality among all the individuals composing the empire; consequently all government was absorbed in its centre, the Emperor, so that individual members could not attain to independence and subjective freedom. . . . In this respect, the essential advance is made in India, viz: that independent members ramify from the unity of despotic power. Yet the distinctions which these imply are referred to Nature. Instead of stimulating the activity of a soul as their centre of union, and spontaneously realizing that soul – as is the case in organic life – they petrify and become rigid, and by their stereotyped character condemn the Indian people to the most degrading spiritual serfdom. The distinctions in questions are the *Castes*.'[15] The result was

· 13. *The Philosophy of History*, p. 168.
  14. *Ibid.*, pp. 130–1.
  15. *Ibid.*, pp. 150–1.

that 'while we found a moral despotism in China, whatever may be called a relic of political life in India is a despotism without a principle, without any rule of morality or religion.'[16] Hegel went on to characterize the nuclear basis of Indian despotism as a system of inert village communities, governed by hereditary custom and distribution of crops after taxation, unaffected by political alterations in the State above them. 'The whole income belonging to every village is, as already stated, divided into two parts, of which one belongs to the Rajah, the other to the cultivators; but proportionate shares are also received by the Provost of the place, the Judge, the Water-Surveyor, the Brahmin who superintends religious worship, the Astrologer (who is also a Brahmin, and announces the days of good and ill omen), the Smith, the Carpenter, the Potter, the Washerman, the Barber, the Physician, the Dancing Girls, the Musician, the Poet. This arrangement is fixed and immutable, and subject to no one's will. *All political* revolutions, therefore, are matters of indifference to the common Hindu, for his lot is unchanged.'[17] These formulations, as will be seen, were to have a notable after-life. Hegel ended by repeating the by now traditional theme of historical stagnation, which he attributed to both countries: 'China and India remain stationary, and perpetuate a natural vegetative existence even to the present time.'[18]

While in German classical philosophy, Hegel had followed Montesquieu very closely, if we turn to English political economy, we find that Smith's themes were not immediately adopted by his heirs. The elder Mill added little to traditional notions of Asian despotism in his study of British India.[19] The next English economist to develop a more original analysis of Oriental conditions was Richard Jones, the successor of Malthus at the East India College, whose *Essay on the Distribution of Wealth and the Sources of Taxation* was published in London in 1831, the same year in which Hegel was delivering his lectures on China and India in Berlin. Jones's work, whose aim was a critique of Ricardo, included probably the most careful attempt at a concrete survey of agrarian tenures in Asia hitherto produced. Jones

16. *The Philosophy of History*, p. 168.
17. *Ibid.*, p. 161.   18. *Ibid.*, p. 180.
19. James Mill, *The History of British India*, London 1858 (re-edition), I, pp. 141, 211.

stated at the outset that: 'Throughout Asia, the sovereigns have ever been in the possession of an exclusive title to the soil of their dominions and they have preserved that title in a state of singular and inauspicious integrity, undivided, as well as unimpaired. The people are there universally the tenants of the sovereign, who is the sole proprietor; usurpations of his officers alone occasionally break the links of the chain of dependence for a time. It is this universal dependence on the throne for the means of supporting life, which is the real foundation of the unbroken despotism of the Eastern world, as it is of the revenue of the sovereigns, and of the form which society assumes beneath their feet.'[20] Jones, however, was not content with the generic assertions of his predecessors. He tried to demarcate with some precision the four great zones in which what he called 'ryot rents' – i.e. taxes paid by peasants directly to the State as proprietor of the soil which they tilled – prevailed: India, Persia, Turkey and China. The uniform nature of the economic system and political government in these diverse lands could be traced, he thought, to their common conquest by the Tartar tribes of Central Asia. 'China, India, Persia and Asiatic Turkey, all placed at the outward edge of the great basin of central Asia, have been subdued in their turn by irruptions of its tribes, some of them more than once. China seems even at this moment hardly escaping from the danger of another subjugation. Wherever these Scythian invaders have settled, they have established a despotic form of government, to which they have readily submitted themselves, while they were obliging the inhabitants of the conquered countries to submit to it. . . . The Tartars have everywhere either adopted or established a political system, which unites so readily with their national habits of submission in the people, and absolute power in the chiefs: and their conquests have either introduced or re-established it, from the Black Sea to the Pacific, from Pekin to the Nerbudda. Throughout agricultural Asia (with the exception of Russia) the same system prevails.'[21]

Jones's general hypothesis of nomadic conquest as the origin of state

20. Richard Jones, *An Essay on the Distribution of Wealth and the Sources of Taxation*, London 1831, pp. 7–8.

21. *An Essay on the Distribution of Wealth*, pp. 110, 112. Jones's allusion to the Tartar dangers threatening China is probably a reference to the Khoja rebellions in Kashgaria of 1830. Note his express exclusion of Russia from the Asian system under discussion.

ownership in land was combined with a new set of discriminations in his assessment of the degree and effects of this property in the respective countries with which he was concerned. Thus he wrote that later Mughal India witnessed 'an end to all system, moderation, or protection; ruined rents, arbitrarily imposed, were collected in frequent military circuits, at the spear's point; and the resistance often attempted in despair, was unsparingly punished by fire and slaughter.'[22] The Turkish State, on the other hand, formally maintained milder levels of exploitation, but the corruption of its agents often in practice rendered any restraints nugatory. 'There are evidently some advantages in the Turkish system compared with those of India or Persia. The permanence and moderation of the *miri* or land rent, is a very great one. . . . But its comparative moderation and strength have remained useless to its unhappy subjects, from a degree of supineness and indifference as to the malversations of its distant officers.'[23] In Persia, royal rapacity was without bounds, but the local irrigation system tempered its range – in contrast to its role in Smith's schema – by introducing forms of private property: 'Of all the despotic governments of the east, that of Persia is perhaps the most greedy, and the most wantonly unprincipled; yet the peculiar soil of that country has introduced some valuable modifications of the general Asiatic system of ryot rents . . . (for) he who brings water to the surface, where it never was before, is guaranteed by the sovereign in the hereditary possession of the land fertilized by him.'[24] Finally, Jones saw very clearly that Chinese agriculture formed a special case that could not be simply assimilated to that of the other countries he had described; its immense productivity set it apart. 'The whole conduct indeed of the Empire presents a striking contrast to that of the neighbouring Asiatic monarchies. . . . While not one half of India has ever been reclaimed, and still less of Persia, China is as fully cultivated, and more fully peopled than most European monarchies.'[25] Jones's work thus undoubtedly represented the most advanced point reached by political economy in its discussion of Asia, in the first half of the 19th century. The younger Mill, writing nearly two decades later, revived Smith's surmise that Oriental states typically patronized public hydraulic works – 'the tanks, wells, and canals for irrigation, without

22. *An Essay on the Distribution of Wealth*, p. 117.
23. *Ibid.*, pp. 129–30.   24. *Ibid.*, pp. 119, 122–3.   25. *Ibid.*, p. 133.

which in most tropical climates cultivation could hardly be carried on'[26] – but otherwise merely repeated the generic characterization of 'the extensive monarchies which from a time beyond historical record have occupied the plains of Asia'[27] that had long since become a consensual formula in Western Europe.

It is thus essential to grasp that the two main intellectual traditions which decisively contributed to the formation of the work of Marx and Engels, contained a common pre-existent conception of Asian political and social systems – a shared complex of ideas that ultimately went back to the Enlightenment before them. This complex can be summarized in something like the following form:[28]

State property of land	H_1 B_3 M_2 J
Lack of juridical restraints	B_1 B_3 M_2
Religious substitution for law	M_2
Absence of hereditary nobility	M_1 B_2 M_2
Servile social equality	M_2 H_2
Isolated village communities	H_2
Agrarian predominance over industry	S B_3
Public hydraulic works	S M_3
Torrid climatic environment	M_2 M_3
Historical immutability	M_2 H_2 J M_3

=

Oriental Despotism

No one author combined all of these notions in a single conception, as can be seen. Bernier alone had studied Asian countries at first hand. Montesquieu alone had formulated a coherent general theory of Oriental despotism as such. The geographical referents of successive writers had widened from Turkey to India and eventually to China: Hegel and Jones alone had sought to distinguish regional variations within a common Asiatic pattern.

26. John Stuart Mill, *Principles of Political Economy*, London 1848, I, p. 15.
27. *Principles of Political Economy*, p. 14.
28. H_1 = Harrington; H_2 = Hegel; B_1 = Bodin; B_2 = Bacon; B_3 = Bernier; M_1 = Machiavelli; M_2 = Montesquieu; M_3 = Mill; S = Smith; J = Jones.

II

We can now turn to the famous passages of Marx's correspondence with Engels, in which the two first discussed the problems of the Orient. On 2 June 1853, Marx wrote to Engels, who had been studying Asian history and learning some Persian, to recommend Bernier's account of Oriental cities, as 'brilliant, graphic and striking'. He went on to endorse the major thesis of Bernier's book in a celebrated and unequivocal fashion: 'Bernier rightly considered the basis of all phenomena in the East – he refers to Turkey, Persia, Hindustan – to be the *absence of private property in land*. This is the real key, even to the Oriental heaven.'[1] In his reply a few days later, Engels conjectured that the basic historical explanation for this lack of private landed property

1. Marx-Engels, *Selected Correspondence*, pp. 80–1. The central passage from Bernier to which Marx was referring is well worth reproducing here, for its content and tone: 'These three countries, Turkey, Persia and Hindustan, have no idea of the principles of *meum* and *tuum*, relatively to land or other real possessions; and having lost that respect for the right of property, which is the basis of all that is good and useful in the world, necessarily resemble each other in essential points: they fall into the same pernicious errors, and must, sooner or later, experience the natural consequences of them – tyranny, ruin and desolation. How happy and thankful should we feel that the monarchs of Europe are not the sole proprietors of the soil! Were they so, we should seek in vain for countries well cultivated and populous, for well-built and prosperous cities, for a polite and flourishing people. If this principle prevailed, far different would be the real riches and power of the sovereigns of Europe, and the loyalty and fidelity with which they are served: they would soon reign over solitudes and deserts, mendicants and barbarians. Actuated by a blind passion, ambitious to be more absolute than is warranted by the laws of God and of nature, the Kings of Asia grasp at everything, until at length they lose everything; coveting too many riches, they find themselves without wealth, or far less than the goals of their cupidity. If the same system of government existed with us, where should we find Princes, Prelates or Nobles, opulent Burghers and thriving Merchants, or ingenious Artisans? Where should be look for such cities as Paris, Lyon, Toulouse, Rouen, or if you will, London, and so many others? Where should we see that infinite number of small towns and villages; all those beautiful country houses, those fine fields and hills, cultivated with so much care, art and labour? What would become of the ample revenues they yield to both subjects and sovereign? Our large towns would become uninhabitable in consequence of their unwholesome air, and fall into ruins without exciting in any person a thought of repairing their decay; our hills would be abandoned and our plains would be overrun with thorns and weeds, or covered with pestilential morasses.' *Travels in the Mogul Empire*, pp. 232–3.

must lie in the aridity of North African and Asian soil, which necessitated intensive irrigation and hence hydraulic works by the central
State and other public authorities. 'The absence of property in land is
indeed the key to the whole of the East. Herein lies its political and
religious history. But how does it come about that the Orientals did not
arrive at landed property, even in its feudal form? I think it is mainly
due to the climate, taken in connection with the nature of the soil,
especially with the great stretches of desert which extend from the
Sahara straight across Arabia, Persia, India and Tartary up to the
highest Asiatic plateau. Artificial irrigation is here the first condition
of agriculture and this is a matter either for the communes, the provinces or the central government. An Oriental government never had
more than three departments: finance (plunder at home) war (plunder
at home and abroad) and public works (provision for reproduction). . . . This artificial fertilization of the land, which immediately
ceased when the irrigation system fell into decay, explains the otherwise
curious fact that whole stretches which were once brilliantly cultivated
are now waste and bare (Palmyra, Petra, the ruins in the Yemen,
districts in Egypt, Persia and Hindustan); it explains the fact that one
devastating war could depopulate a country for centuries and strip it of
its whole civilization.'[2]

A week later, Marx wrote back, agreeing on the importance of public
works for Asian society and stressing the coexistence of self-sufficient
villages with them: 'The stationary character of this part of Asia –
despite all the aimless movement on the political surface – is fully
explained by two circumstances which supplement each other: (1) the
public works which were the business of the central government;
(2) besides this the whole empire, not counting the few larger towns,
was divided into *villages*, each of which possessed a completely separate
organization and formed a little world in itself. . . . In some of these
communities the lands of the village are cultivated in common, in most
cases each occupant tills his own field. Within them there is slavery and
the caste system. The waste lands are for common pasture. Domestic
weaving and spinning is done by wives and daughters. These idyllic
republics, which only jealously guard the boundaries of their village

2. Marx-Engels, *Selected Correspondence*, p. 82. Note that Engels speaks
specifically of 'civilization' here.

against the neighbouring village, still exist in a fairly perfect form in the North-Western parts of India, which were recent English accessions. I do not think anyone could imagine a more solid foundation for stagnant Asiatic despotism.' Marx added, significantly: 'In any case it seems to have been the Mohammedans who first established the principle of "no property in land" throughout the whole of Asia.'³

During this same period, Marx presented their common reflections to the public in a series of articles for the *New York Daily Tribune*: 'Climate and territorial conditions, especially the vast tracts of desert, extending from the Sahara, through Arabia, Persia, India and Tartary, to the most elevated Asiatic highlands, constituted artificial irrigation by canals and waterworks the basis of Oriental agriculture. As in Egypt and India, inundations are used for fertilizing the soil of Mesopotamia, Persia and so on; advantage is taken of a high level for feeding irrigative canals. This prime necessity of an economical and common use of water, which in the Occident drove private enterprise to voluntary association, as in Flanders and Italy, necessitated in the Orient, where civilization was too low and the territorial extent too vast to call into life voluntary association, the interference of the centralizing power of Government. Hence an economical function devolved upon all Asiatic Governments, the function of providing public works.'⁴ Marx went on to emphasize that the social basis of this type of government in India was the 'domestic union of agricultural and manufacturing pursuits' in the 'so-called *village system*, which gave to each of these small unions their independent organization and distinct life.'⁵ British rule had smashed the political superstructure of the Mughal imperial state, and was now attacking the socio-economic infrastructure on which it rested, by the forcible introduction of private property in land: 'The *zamindari* and *ryotwari* themselves, abominable as they are, involve two distinct forms of private property in land – the great desideratum of Asiatic society.'⁶ In a sweeping strophe, of the

---

3. *Selected Correspondence*, pp. 85–6.
4. Marx-Engels, *On Colonialism*, Moscow 1960, p. 33: 'The British Rule in India', article of June 10, 1853.
5. *On Colonialism*, p. 35.
6. *On Colonialism*, p. 77: 'The Future Results of British Rule in India', article of July 22, 1853.

greatest passion and eloquence, Marx surveyed the historical consequences of European conquest of Asian soil that were now unfolding:
'Sickening as it must be to human feeling to witness those myriads of
industrious patriarchal and inoffensive social organizations disorganized and dissolved into their units, thrown into a sea of woes, and
their individual members losing at the same time their ancient form of
civilization and their hereditary means of subsistence, we must not
forget that these idyllic village communities, inoffensive though they
may appear, had always been the solid foundations of Oriental despotism, that they restrained the human mind within the smallest
possible compass, making it the unresisting tool of superstition,
enslaving it beneath traditional rules, depriving it of all grandeur and
historical energies. We must not forget the barbarian egotism which,
concentrating on some miserable patch of land, had quietly witnessed
the ruin of empires, the perpetration of unspeakable cruelties, the
massacre of the population of large towns, with no other consideration
bestowed upon them than on natural events, itself the helpless prey of
any aggressor who deigned to notice it at all.'[7] He added: 'We must
not forget that these little communities were contaminated by distinctions of caste and by slavery, that they subjugated man to external
circumstances instead of elevating man to be the sovereign of circumstances, that they transformed a self-developing social state into never-
changing natural destiny.'[8]

Marx's private correspondence and publicistic intervention of 1853
were thus very close to the main themes of traditional European commentary on Asian history and society, in both direction and tone. The
continuity, avowed at the outset by the appeal to Bernier, is especially
striking in Marx's repeated assertion of the stagnation and immutability of the Oriental world. 'Indian society has no history at all, at
least no known history',[9] he wrote; a few years later, he characteristically referred to China as 'vegetating in the teeth of time'.[10] Two
main emphases, however, can be distilled from the course of his
exchange with Engels. Both had been partially adumbrated in the
preceding tradition. The first was the notion that public irrigation
works, necessitated by climatic aridity, were a basic determinant of

7. *On Colonialism*, p. 36.   8. *Ibid.*, p. 37.
9. *Ibid.*, p. 76.   10. *Ibid.*, p. 188.

centralized despotic states, with a monopoly of land, in Asia. This was, in effect, a fusion of three themes that had hitherto been relatively distinct – hydraulic agriculture (Smith), geographical destiny (Montesquieu), and state agrarian property (Bernier). A second thematic element was added by the claim that the basic social cells on which oriental despotism was superimposed were self-sufficient village communities, embodying a union of domestic crafts and cultivation. This conception had also, as we have seen, been advanced in the earlier tradition (Hegel). Marx, taking his evidence from reports of the British colonial administration in India, now gave it a new and more prominent position within the general schema he had inherited. The hydraulic State 'above' and the autarchic village 'below' were linked into a single formula, in which there was a conceptual equipoise between the two.

Four or five years later, however, when Marx was drafting the *Grundrisse*, it was the latter notion of the 'self-sustaining village community' which acquired an unmistakably *predominant* function in his account of what he was to call the 'Asiatic mode of production'. For Marx now came to believe that State property of the soil in the Orient concealed a tribal-communal ownership of it, by self-sustaining villages which were the socio-economic reality behind the 'imaginary unity' of the title of the despotic sovereign to the land. 'The *all-embracing unity* which stands above all these small common bodies may appear as the higher or *sole proprietor*, the real communities only as *hereditary* possessors. . . . The despot here appears as the father of all the numerous lesser communities, thus realizing the common unity of all. It therefore follows that the surplus product belongs to this highest unity. Oriental despotism therefore appears to lead to a legal absence of property. In fact, however, its foundation is tribal or common property, in most cases created through a combination of manufacture and agriculture within the small community which thus becomes entirely self-sustaining and contains within itself all conditions of production and surplus production.'[11] This thematic innovation was accompanied by a considerable extension of the field of application of Marx's conception of this mode of production, which was no longer tied so directly to Asia. Thus, he went on: 'In so far as this type of

11. *Pre-Capitalist Economic Formations*, pp. 69–70. [*Grundrisse*, pp. 472–3.]

common property is actually realized in labour, it can appear in two ways. The small communities may vegetate independently side by side, and within each the individual labours independently with his family on the land allotted to him. Secondly, the unity can involve a common organization of labour itself, which in turn can constitute a veritable system, as in Mexico, and especially Peru, among the ancient Celts, and some tribes of India. Furthermore, the communality within the tribal body may tend to appear either as a representation of its unity through the head of the tribal kinship group, or as a relationship between the heads of families. Hence either a more despotic or a more democratic form of the community. The communal conditions for real appropriation through labour, such as irrigation systems (very important among the Asian peoples), means of communication, and so on, will then appear as the work of the higher unity – the despotic government which is poised above the lesser communities.'[12] Such despotic governments, Marx seems to have believed, levied irregular and unskilled labour drafts from their populations, which he called the 'generalized slavery of the Orient'[13] (not to be confused, he stressed, with the slavery proper of classical Antiquity in the Mediterranean). Towns in these conditions were generally contingent or supererogatory in Asia: 'Cities in the proper sense arise by the side of these villages only where the location is particularly propitious to external trade, or where the head of the state and his satraps exchange their revenue (the surplus product) against labour, which they expend as labour-funds. . . . Asian history is a kind of undifferentiated unity of town and country (the large city, properly speaking, must be regarded merely as a princely camp superimposed on the real economic structure).'[14] Here the echo of Bernier, the original prompter of Marx's reflections on the Orient in 1853, is once again manifestly audible.

The decisively new element in Marx's writings of 1857–8 on what he a year later, for the first and only time, formally dubbed the 'Asiatic mode of production',[15] was the idea that there existed in Asia and

12. *Pre-Capitalist Economic Formations*, pp. 70–1. [*Grundrisse*, pp. 437–74.]
13. *Ibid.*, p. 95.   14. *Ibid.*, pp. 71, 77–8. [*Grundrisse*, pp. 495, 474, 479.]
15. 'In broad outlines, the Asiatic, ancient, feudal and modern bourgeois modes of production may be designated as epochs marking progress in the economic development of society.' *Preface* to *A Contribution to the Critique of Political Economy*, London 1971, p. 21.

elsewhere tribal or communal ownership of the soil by self-sufficient villages, behind the official veil of State property of land. In his completed and published writings, however, Marx never explicitly endorsed this novel conception again. In *Capital*, on the contrary, he substantially reverted to the earlier positions of his correspondence with Engels. For on the one hand, he re-emphasized again, at greater length than ever before, the importance of the peculiar structure of Indian village communities, which he asserted were prototypical of Asia as a whole. These he described as follows: 'These small and extremely ancient Indian communities, some of which have continued down to this day, are based on possession in common of the land, on the blending of agriculture and handicrafts, and on an unalterable division of labour. . . . The constitution of these communities varies in different parts of India. In those of the simplest form, the land is tilled in common, and the produce divided among the members. At the same time, spinning and weaving are carried on in each family as subsidiary industries. Side by side with the masses thus occupied with one and the same work, we find the "chief inhabitant", who is judge, police and tax-gatherer in one; the book-keeper, who keeps the accounts of the tillage and registers everything relating thereto; another official who prosecutes criminals, protects strangers travelling through and escorts them to the next village; the boundary man, who guards the boundaries against neighbouring communities; the water-overseer, who distributes the water from the common tanks for irrigation; the Brahmin, who conducts the religious services; the schoolmaster who on the sand teaches the children reading and writing; the calendar-Brahmin, or astrologer, who makes known the lucky or unlucky days for seed-time and harvest, and for every other kind of agricultural work; a smith and a carpenter, who make and repair all the agricultural implements; the potter, who makes all the pottery of the village; the barber, the washerman, who washes clothes, the silversmith, here and there the poet, who in some communities replaces the silversmith, in others the school-master. This dozen of individuals is maintained at the expense of the whole community. If the population increases, a new community is founded, on the pattern of the old one, on unoccupied land.'[16] It will

16. *Capital*, I, pp. 357–8.

be noticed that this account, down to the very order of the roll-call of rustic occupations in the village (judge-water-surveyor-brahmin-astrologer-smith-carpenter-potter-barber-washerman-poet) is virtually word for word that of Hegel's *Philosophy of History* cited above. The only changes in the *dramatis personae* are a lengthening of the list, and a substitution of Hegel's 'physician, dancing girls and musician' by Marx's more prosaic 'boundary-man, silversmith and school-master'.[17]

The political conclusions Marx drew from his miniature social diorama were no less exactly reminiscent of those Hegel had proposed thirty-five years earlier: the formless plethora of self-sufficient villages, with a union of crafts and agriculture, and collective tillage, was the social basis of Asiatic immutability. For the unchanging rural communities were insulated from the fortunes of the State above them. 'The simplicity of the organization for production in these self-sufficing communities that constantly reproduce themselves in the same form, and when accidentally destroyed, spring up again on the same spot and with the same name – this simplicity supplies the key to the secret of the unchangeableness of Asiatic societies, an unchangeableness in such striking contrast with the constant dissolution and refounding of Asiatic societies, and the never-ceasing changes of dynasty. The structure of the economic elements of society remains untouched by the storm-clouds of the political sky.'[18] On the other hand, while he maintained that these villages were characterized by common possession of land, and often common cultivation of it, Marx no longer claimed that they embodied communal or tribal *property* of the soil. On the contrary, he now reverted to a straightforward and unambiguous restatement of his original position that Asian societies were typically defined by State property of land. 'Should the direct producers not be confronted by a private landowner, but rather, as in Asia, under direct subordination to a state which stands over them as their landlord and simultaneously as sovereign, then rent and taxes coincide, or rather,

17. Hegel and Marx were obviously both using some common source. Louis Dumont has pointed out that the original paradigm for these stereotypical descriptions was a report by Munro in 1806: see 'The "Village Community" from Munro to Maine', *Contributions to Indian Sociology*, IX, December 1966, pp. 70–3. Munro's account was then constantly reiterated and enlarged upon in subsequent decades.

18. *Capital*, I, p. 358.

there exists no tax which differs from this form of ground rent. Under such circumstances, there need exist no stronger political or economic pressure than that common to all subjection to that state. The state is then the supreme lord. Sovereignty here consists in the ownership of land concentrated on a national scale. But, on the other hand, no private ownership of land exists, although there is both private and common possession of land.'[19] The mature Marx of *Capital* itself thus remained substantially faithful to the classical European image of Asia which he had inherited from a long file of predecessors.

It remains to consider the later, informal interventions of Marx and Engels with a bearing on the whole question of 'oriental despotism'. It can be said at the outset that virtually all of these dicta after *Capital* – most of them in correspondence – take up once again the characteristic leitmotif of the *Grundrisse*: they repeatedly link communal property of land, by self-sustaining villages, with centralized Asiatic despotism, and pronounce the former to be the socio-economic basis for the latter. Thus Marx, in his draft letters to Zasulich in 1881, defining the Russian *mir* community under Tsarism as a type in which 'property in land is communal, but each peasant cultivates and manages his own plot on his own account', stated: 'The isolation of the village communities, the lack of links between their lives, this locally bounded microcosm, is not everywhere an immanent characteristic of the last of the primitive types. However, wherever it does occur, it permits the emergence of a central despotism above the communities.'[20] Engels, for his part, twice reproduced the same theme. In 1875, well before Marx's exchange with Zasulich, he had written in an article on Russia: 'The complete isolation of these communities, which creates identical but in no way common interests in the country, is the natural basis of *oriental despotism*: from India to Russia, wherever this social form has predominated, it has engendered such a State as its complement.'[21] In 1882, in an unpublished manuscript on the Frankish epoch in Western European history, he again remarked: 'There where the State arises in an epoch when the village community cultivates its land in common, or at least merely

19. *Capital*, III, pp. 771–2.
20. These remarks are from the second draft letter to Zasulich; they are reproduced in the supplementary texts to *Pre-Capitalist Economic Formations*, p. 143.
21. Marx-Engels, *Werke*, Bd 18, p. 563.

allocates it temporarily to different families, and where consequently no private property of the soil has yet emerged, as with the Aryan peoples of Asia and the Russians, State power assumes the form of a despotism.'[22] Finally, in his major published work of this epoch, Engels reaffirmed both of the two ideas which had from the start been the most distinctive emphases of his common reflections with Marx. On the one hand, he reiterated – after a lapse of two decades – the importance of hydraulic works for the formation of despotic states in Asia. 'However great the number of despotisms which rose and fell in Persia and India, each was fully aware that above all it was the entrepreneur responsible for the collective maintenance of irrigation throughout the river valleys, without which no agriculture was possible there.'[23] At the same time, he once again asserted the typical subsistence of village communities with collective property of land beneath Asiatic despotisms. For while commenting that 'in the whole of the Orient . . . the village community or the state owns the land',[24] he went on to declare that the oldest form of such communities – i.e. precisely those to which he attributed communal landownership – were the foundation of despotism. 'Where the ancient communes have continued to exist, they have for thousands of years formed the basis of the cruellest form of state, Oriental despotism, from India to Russia.'[25]

This categorical statement may conclude our survey of the views of the founders of historical materialism on Asian history and society. How should they be summarized? It is clear that Marx's negative refusal to generalize the feudal mode of production beyond Europe had its counterpart in his positive conviction, shared by Engels, that there was a specific 'Asiatic mode of production' characteristic of the Orient, which separated it historically and sociologically from the Occident. The hallmark of this mode of production, which set it off immediately from feudalism, was the absence of private property in land: for Marx, this was the first 'key' to the whole structure of the Asiatic mode of production. Engels attributed this lack of individual agrarian property to climatic aridity, necessitating large-scale irrigation works and hence state supervision of the forces of production. Marx toyed for a moment with the hypothesis that it was first introduced

22. *Werke*, Bd 19, p. 475.   23. *Anti-Dühring*, Moscow 1947, p. 215.
24. *Anti-Dühring*, p. 211.   25. *Ibid.*, p. 217.

into the Orient by Islamic conquest; but then he too adopted Engels's thesis that hydraulic agriculture was probably the geographical basis of the absence of private property in land that distinguished the Asiatic mode of production. Later, however, Marx came to believe in the *Grundrisse* that State property of the soil in the Orient concealed a tribal-communal ownership of it by self-sustaining villages. In *Capital* he abandoned this notion, reaffirming the traditional European axiom of a State monopoly of land in Asia, while retaining his conviction of the importance of self-enclosed rural communities at the base of Oriental society. In the two decades after the publication of *Capital*, however, both Marx and Engels reverted to the idea that the social basis of Oriental despotism was the self-sufficient village community, with communal agrarian property. No wholly consistent or systematic account of the "Asiatic mode of production' can be derived from their writings, because of these oscillations indicated above. But allowing for this, Marx's sketch of what he believed to be the archetypal Asian social formation included the following fundamental elements: the absence of private property in land, the presence of large-scale irrigation systems in agriculture, the existence of autarchic village communities combining crafts with tillage and communal ownership of the soil, the stagnation of passively rentier or bureaucratic cities, and the domination of a despotic state machine cornering the bulk of the surplus and functioning not merely as the central apparatus of repression of the ruling class, but as its principal instrument of economic exploitation. Between the self-reproducing villages 'below' and the hypertrophied state 'above', dwelt no intermediate forces. The impact of the State on the mosaic of villages beneath it was purely external and tributary; its consolidation or destruction alike left rural society untouched. The political history of the Orient was thus essentially cyclical: it contained no dynamic or cumulative development. The result was the secular inertia and immutability of Asia, once it had attained its own peculiar level of civilization.

III

Marx's notion of the 'Asiatic mode of production' has in recent years been revived on a considerable scale: many writers, aware of the impasse of a quasi-universal feudalism, have welcomed it as a theoretical emancipation from a too rigid and linear scheme of historical development. After having fallen into oblivion for a long period, the 'Asiatic mode of production' has today achieved a new fortune.[1] For the purposes of this note, it is evident that the Ottoman occupation of the Balkans confronts any Marxist study of even European history with the question of whether it is a valid guide for the Turkish State that existed in the same continent, on the other side of feudalism. The original function of Marx's notion is clear enough: it was designed essentially to account for the failure of the major non-European civilizations of his own day, despite their very high level of cultural achievements, to evolve towards capitalism, as Europe had done. The Oriental despotisms which Marx initially had in mind were the recent or contemporary Asian Empires of Turkey, Persia, India and China – those which had formed the focus of Jones's study. Most of his evidence, in fact, was drawn from the single case of Mughal India, destroyed a century earlier by the British. However, in the somewhat later passages of the *Grundrisse*, Marx proceeded to extend his application of 'Asiatism' to a very different range of societies, actually outside Asia altogether: notably, to the American social formations of Mexico and Peru before the Spanish conquest, and even to Celtic and other tribal societies. The reason for this conceptual slippage is evident from the draft texts of the *Grundrisse* themselves. Marx came to believe that the fundamental reality of the 'Asiatic' mode of production was not state property in land, centralized hydraulic works or a political despotism, but the 'tribal or communal property' of land in self-sustaining villages, combining crafts and agriculture. Within the terms of his original scheme, the whole emphasis of his interest shifted from the bureau-

1. Two volumes provide sufficient illustration: the ample symposium of essays, *Sur Le 'Mode de Production Asiatique'*, Paris 1969, which contains a bibliography of further contributions to the topic; and the general conspectus in G. Sofri, *Il Modo di Produzione Asiatico*, Turin 1969.

cratic State above to the autarkic villages below, and once the latter were designated 'tribal' and ascribed a communal, more or less egalitarian system of production and property, the way was open for an indefinite extension of the notion of the Asiatic mode of production to societies of a totally distinct type from those which initially seem to have been envisaged by Marx and Engels in their correspondence – neither 'Oriental' in location nor comparably 'civilized' in development. In *Capital*, Marx hesitated over the logic of this evolution, and returned in part more closely to his original conceptions. Thereafter, however, both Engels and Marx developed the themes of communal or tribal property of land by self-sufficient villages, as the foundation of despotic states, without major qualifications.

Today, it is noticeable that contemporary discussion and utilization of the notion of the Asiatic mode of production has largely focussed on the draft sketches of 1857-8, and their scattered sequels of 1875-82, and in doing so has tended to radicalize the centrifugal tendencies of the concept that first start to appear in the *Grundrisse*. The notion has, in effect, typically been extended in two different directions. On the one hand, it has been cast far backwards to include Ancient societies of the Middle East and Mediterranean prior to the classical epoch: Sumerian Mesopotamia, Pharaonic Egypt, Hittite Anatolia, Mycenaean Greece or Etruscan Italy. This use of the notion retains its original emphasis on a powerful centralized state, and often hydraulic agriculture, and focusses on 'generalized slavery' in the presence of arbitrary and unskilled labour drafts levied from primitive rural populations by a superior bureaucratic power above them.[2] At the same time, a second extension has occurred in another direction. For the 'Asiatic mode of production' has also been enlarged to embrace the first state organizations of tribal or semi-tribal social formations, with a level of civilization far below those of pre-classical Antiquity: Polynesian islands, African chieftainries, Amerindian settlements. This usage normally discards any emphasis on large-scale irrigation works

2. The best example of this tendency is the study by Charles Parrain, 'Proto-Histoire Mediterranéenne et Mode de Production Asiatique', in *Sur Le 'Mode de Production Asiatique'*, pp. 169–94, which discusses Megalithic, Creto-Mycenaean and Etruscan social formations; an essay in itself full of interest, even where it is impossible to assent to its basic classifications.

or a particularly despotic state: it focusses essentially on the survival of kin relationships, communal rural property and cohesively self-sufficient villages. It deems this whole mode of production 'transitional' between a classless and a class society, preserving many pre-class features.[3] The result of these two tendencies has been an enormous inflation of the scope of the Asiatic mode of production – chronologically backwards to the earliest dawn of civilization, and geographically outwards to the farther edge of tribal organization. The consequent supra-historical melange defies all scientific principles of classification. A ubiquitous 'Asiatism' represents no improvement on a universal 'feudalism': in fact it is even less rigorous as a term. What serious historical unity exists between Ming China and Megalithic Ireland, Pharaonic Egypt and Hawaii? It is perfectly clear that such social formations are unimaginably distant from one another. Melanesian or African tribal societies, with their rudimentary techniques of production, minimal population and surplus, and lack of literacy, are poles apart from the massive and sophisticated *Hochkulturen* of the Ancient Middle East. These in turn represented manifestly distinct levels of historical development from the civilizations of the Early Modern Orient, separated by huge revolutions in technology, demography, warfare, religion and culture across the intervening millennia. To mix

3. Much the most distinguished work along these lines are the two studies by Maurice Godelier, 'La Notion de "Mode de Production Asiatique" et Les Schémas Marxistes d'Evolution des Sociétés', in *Sur Le 'Mode de Production Asiatique'*, pp. 47–100, and the long 'Preface' to *Sur Les Sociétés Pré-Capitalistes: Textes Choisis de Marx Engels Lénine*, Paris 1970, especially pp. 105–42. The latter text also contains by far the most scrupulous and accurate analysis of the evolution of the thought of Marx and Engels on the problem of 'Oriental' societies (pp. 13–104). The taxonomic conclusions of Godelier's works are, however, untenable. By realigning the Asiatic mode of production' along the axis of tribal societies in passage from acephalous to State forms of organization, thereby shifting the whole notion enormously backwards in evolutionary 'time', he is paradoxically obliged to end by denoting the massive civilizations of early modern China or India once again as 'feudal', even if with some dubitation, to distinguish between the two. The logic of his procedure dictates this solution, whose aporia has already been shown above, despite his own evident unease with it: see *Sur Le 'Mode de Production Asiatique'*, pp. 90–1; *Sur Les Sociétés Pré-Capitalistes*, pp. 136–7. Disembarrassed of the whole inappropriate framework of 'Asiatism', on the other hand, Godelier's anthropological account of the different phases and forms of transition of tribal social formations towards centralized State structures is extremely illuminating.

such immensely disparate historical forms and epochs under a single rubric[4] is to end with the same *reductio ad absurdum* produced by an indefinite extension of feudalism: if so many different socio-economic formations, of such contrasting levels of civilization, are all contracted to one mode of production, the fundamental divisions and changes of history must derive from another source altogether, that has nothing to do with the Marxist conception of modes of production. The inflation of ideas, like coins, merely leads to their devaluation.

The license for later minting of Asiatisms, however, is to be found in Marx himself. For it was his gradual shift of emphasis from the despotic oriental state to the self-sufficient village community, which was to make possible the discovery of the same mode of production outside the Asia with which he had initially been concerned. Once all the weight of his analysis was transferred away from the 'ideal' unity of the State to the 'real' foundations of communal-tribal property in the egalitarian villages below, it imperceptibly became natural to assimilate tribal social formations or ancient states with a still comparatively primitive rural economy to the same category as the modern civilizations with which Marx and Engels had started: Marx himself, as we have seen, was the first to do so. The subsequent theoretical and historiographic confusions point unmistakeably to the whole notion of the 'self-sustaining village' and its 'communal property' as the basic empirical fault in Marx's construction. The central elements of the 'self-sustaining village' in this conception were: union of domestic crafts and agriculture, absence of commodity exchange with the external world, hence isolation and detachment from the affairs of the State, common property of land, and in some cases also common cultivation of the soil. Marx founded his belief in the palingenesis of these rural communities and their egalitarian property systems virtually entirely on his study of India, where English administrators had reported their existence after the conquest of the subcontinent by

4. The most extreme form of this confusionism is, of course, not the work of a Marxist, but of a more or less Spencerian survival: K. Wittfogel, *Oriental Despotism*, New Haven 1957. This vulgar charivari, devoid of any historical sense, jumbles together pell-mell Imperial Rome, Tsarist Russia, Hopi Arizona, Sung China, Chaggan East Africa, Mamluk Egypt, Inca Peru, Ottoman Turkey, and Sumerian Mesopotamia – not to speak of Byzantium or Babylonia, Persia or Hawaii.

Britain. In actual fact, however, there is no historical evidence that communal property ever existed in either Mughal or post-Mughal India.[5] The English accounts on which Marx relied were the product of colonial mistakes and misinterpretations. Likewise, cultivation in common by villagers was a legend: tillage was always individual in the early modern epoch.[6] Far from the Indian villages being egalitarian, moreover, they were always sharply divided into castes, and what co-possession of landed property did exist was confined to superior castes who exploited lower castes as tenant cultivators on it.[7] Marx, in his first comments on Indian village systems in 1853, had mentioned in passing that 'within them there is slavery and the caste system', and that they were 'contaminated by distinctions of caste and by slavery'; but he never seems to have attached much importance to these 'contaminations' of what he in the same paragraphs described as these 'inoffensive social organisms'.[8] Thereafter he virtually ignored the whole massive structure of the Hindu caste system – the central social mechanism of class stratification in traditional India – altogether. His subsequent accounts of these 'self-sufficient village communities' are effectively innocent of any reference to it.

Although Marx believed that there was a hereditary political leadership of such villages, whether in India or Russia, of a 'patriarchal' type, the whole drift of his analysis – expressly set out in his correspondence with Zasulich in the 1880's, in which he approved the idea of a direct transition from the Russian village commune to socialism – was that the fundamental character of the self-sufficient rural communities was a primitive economic *egalitarianism*. This illusion was all the more strange in that Hegel, whom Marx otherwise so closely followed in his accounts of India, was far more conscious of the brutal omnipresence of caste inequality and exploitation than Marx himself: *The Philosophy of History* devotes a graphic section to a subject on which the *Grundrisse*

5. See Daniel Thorner, 'Marx on India and the Asiatic Mode of Production', *Contributions to Indian Sociology*, IX, December 1966, p. 57: an astringent and salutary article.

6. Thorner, op. cit., p. 57.

7. Louis Dumont, 'The "Village Community" from Munro to Maine', pp. 76–80; Irfan Habib, *The Agrarian System of Mughal India (1556–1707)*, London 1963, pp. 119–24.

8. See above, pp. 474, 476.

and *Capital* are silent.[9] The caste system, in fact, rendered Indian villages – both before and during Marx's day – one of the most extreme negations of 'inoffensive' bucolic community or social equality anywhere in the world. Furthermore, the rural villages of India were never in any real sense 'detached' from the State above them, or 'isolated' from its control. Imperial monopoly of land in Mughal India was enforced by a fiscal system which extracted heavy taxes from the peasantry to the State, mostly payable in cash or in commercial crops subsequently re-sold by the State, hence limiting even the 'economic' autarky of the humblest rural communities. Administratively, moreover, Indian villages were always subordinated to the central State through its appointment of their headmen.[10] Thus far from being 'indifferent' to Mughal rule above them, the Indian peasantry eventually rose in great jacqueries against its oppression, and directly hastened its downfall.

The self-sufficiency, equality and isolation of the Indian village communities was thus always a myth; both the caste system within them and the State above them precluded either.[11] The empirical falsity of Marx's image of the Indian village communities, indeed,

9. *The Philosophy of History*, pp. 150–61. Hegel, tranquilly affirming that 'Equality in civil life is something absolutely impossible' and that 'this principle leads us to put up with variety of occupations, and distinctions of the classes to which they are entrusted', nevertheless could not contain his revulsion against the Indian caste-system, in which 'the individual belongs to such a class by *birth*, and is bound to it for life. All the concrete vitality that makes its appearance sinks back into death. A chain binds down the life that was just upon the point of breaking forth.' (p. 152).

10. 'All over the country, the top group in the village were allies of the state, co-beneficiaries in the system of exploitation. In every village the bottom layer were untouchables squeezed tight against the margin of subsistence. The extra-village exploitation was sanctioned by military force, intra-village exploitation by the caste system and its religious sanctions.' Angus Maddison, *Economic Growth and Class Structure. India and Pakistan since the Moghuls*, London 1971, p. 27. See the accounts in Dumont, 'The "Village Community" from Munro to Maine', pp. 74–5, 88; Habib, *The Agrarian System of Mughal India*, pp. 328–38.

11. In fact, it could be said that the only accurate element in Marx's image of Indian villages was their union of crafts and cultivation: but this trait was common to virtually any pre-industrial rural community in the world, whatever its mode of production. It revealed nothing specific about the Asian countryside. In India, moreover, it did not exclude considerable commodity exchange beyond the village, in addition to the domestic pattern of labour.

could have been guessed from the theoretical contradiction which they introduced into the whole notion of the Asiatic mode of production. For the presence of a powerful, centralized State presupposes a developed class stratification, according to the most elementary tenets of historical materialism, while the prevalence of communal village property implies a virtually pre-class or classless social structure. How could the two in fact be combined? Likewise, the original insistence by Marx and Engels on the importance of public irrigation works by the despotic state was quite incompatible with their later emphasis on the autonomy and self-sufficiency of the village communities: for the former precisely involves the direct intervention of the central state in the local productive cycle of the villages – the most extreme antithesis of their economic isolation and independence.[12] The combination of a strong, despotic state and egalitarian village communes is thus intrinsically improbable; politically, socially and economically they virtually exclude one another. Wherever a powerful central state occurs, advanced social differentiation exists, and there is always a complex skein of exploitation and inequality reaching into the lowest units of production themselves. The tenets of 'communal' or 'tribal property' and 'self-sufficient villages', which prepared the way for the later inflation of the Asiatic mode of production, cannot survive a critical examination. Their elimination frees consideration of the subject from the false problematic of tribal or ancient social formations. We are thereby returned to the original focus of Marx's concern: the great empires of early modern Asia. These were the Oriental despotisms, characterized by the absence of private property in land, which formed the starting-point for the correspondence between Marx and Engels on the problems of Asian history. If the 'village communities' disappear under the scrutiny of modern historiography, what verdict does it permit on the 'hydraulic state'?

For it will be remembered that the two central traits of the Oriental State initially noted by Engels and Marx were the absence of private

---

12. Thorner points out a still further contradiction: Marx believed Indian communal ownership to be the most ancient form of rural property in the world, which provided the starting-point and key to all later types of village development, and yet also maintained that the Indian villages were quintessentially stagnant and non-evolutionary, thereby squaring the circle: 'Marx on India and the Asiatic Mode of Production', p. 66.

property in land and the presence of public hydraulic works on a large scale. The one presupposed the other: for it was the state's construction of large-scale irrigation systems which rendered possible the sovereign's monopoly of agrarian land. The interconnection of these two was the foundation of the comparatively stationary character of Asian history, as the common ground of all the Oriental Empires which dominated it. It must now be asked whether the empirical evidence available today confirms this hypothesis. The answer is that it does not do so. On the contrary, it might be said that the two phenomena singled out by Marx and Engels as the key-notes of Asian history paradoxically represented not so much *conjoint* as *alternative* principles of development. Very crudely, the historical evidence shows that of the great Oriental Empires of the early modern epoch with which they were originally concerned, those which were marked by the absence of private property in land – Turkey, Persia and India – never possessed any public irrigation works of importance, while that which possessed major irrigation systems – China – was vice-versa marked by private property in land.[13] The two terms of the combination posited by Marx and Engels diverged rather than coincided. Russia, moreover, which they repeatedly assimilated to the Orient as a whole, as an example of 'Asiatic despotism', never knew either major irrigation systems or absence of private property in land.[14] The similarity which

13. The evidence will be discussed later in this note.
14. The history of the successive 'locations' of Russia in Western political thought since the Renaissance is a significant and revealing subject in itself, for which there is no space to do more than allude to here. Machiavelli still regarded Russia as the classical 'Scythia' of Antiquity, 'a land that is cold and poor, where there are too many men for the soil to support, so that they are forced to migrate from it, many pressures driving them to leave and none to remain': it was thus beyond the bounds of Europe, which for him stopped at Germany, Hungary and Poland, the bulwarks against further barbarian invasions of the continent: *Il Principe e Discorsi*, p. 300. Bodin, on the other hand, did include 'Muscovy' in Europe, but isolated it as the single example of a 'despotic monarchy' in the continent, at variance with the whole constitutional pattern of the rest of Europe, which otherwise contrasted with that of Asia and Africa: 'Even in Europe the Princes of Tartary and Muscovy rule over subjects called *kholopi*, that is to say, slaves': *Les Six Livres de La République*, p. 201. Montesquieu, by contrast, was two centuries later commending the Russian government for having broken with the habits of despotism: 'See with what industry the government of Muscovy seeks to leave behind a despotism that is a greater burden for it than even for its peoples.' He had no doubt that Russia was now part of the comity of Europe:

Marx and Engels perceived between all the States they deemed Asian was a deceptive one, to a large extent the product of their own inevitable lack of information, at a time when historical study of the Orient was only just starting in Europe. Indeed, nothing is more striking than the extent to which they inherited virtually *en bloc* a traditional European discourse on Asia, and reproduced it with few variations. The two main innovations – each already anticipated *in nuce* by previous authors, as we have seen – that they introduced were the self-sustaining village community and the hydraulic state: both of which in different ways proved scientifically unsound. In certain respects, it can even be said that Marx and Engels regressed behind their ancestors in the tradition of European reflections on Asia. Jones was more aware of the political variations within the States of the Orient; Hegel perceived the role of caste in India more clearly; Montesquieu revealed a more acute interest in the religious and legal systems of Asia. None of these authors identified Russia so nonchalantly with the Orient as Marx, and all of them showed more serious knowledge of China.

Marx's comments on China furnish, indeed, a final illustration of the limits of his comprehension of Asian history. Omitted from the main discussions between Marx and Engels on the Asiatic mode of production, which revolved largely on India and the Islamic world, China was not thereby exempted from the notions which they yielded.[15] Both

---

'Peter I gave the customs and manners of Europe to a nation of Europe, and in doing so, found facilities which he himself did not expect.' *De L'Esprit des Lois*, I, pp. 66, 325–6. Naturally, these debates were not without repercussions within Russia itself. In 1767, Catherine II officially declared in her famous *Nakaz*: 'Russia is a European power.' Thereafter, few serious thinkers questioned the claim. Marx and Engels, however, both deeply scarred by Tsarist counter-revolutionary intervention in 1848, repeatedly and anachronistically referred to Tsarism as an 'Asiatic despotism' and amalgamated India with Russia in a common obloquy. The general tenor of Marx's opinions on Russian history and society, in particular, often lacks balance or control.

15. It has sometimes been suggested that Marx's omission of China from the original discussions of 1853 on Asian despotism may have been due to his knowledge of the fact that private landed property existed in the 19th century Chinese Empire. In an article of 1859, Marx cited an English account which, among other things, mentioned the existence of peasant ownership in China: 'Trade with China', *Marx on China*, London 1968, p. 91; there is also a passage in *Capital* which implies that the property system of Chinese villages was more advanced – i.e. less communal – than those of Indian villages: *Capital*, III, p. 328.

Marx and Engels repeatedly referred to China in terms indistinguishable from their general characterization of the Orient. In fact, their allusions were if anything especially unqualified. The 'imperturbable Celestial Empire' was a strong-hold of 'arch-reaction and arch-conservatism' that was 'the very opposite of Europe', enclosed in a 'barbarous and hermetic isolation from the civilized world'. The 'rotting semi-civilization' of the 'oldest empire in the world' inculcated 'hereditary stupidity' in its population; 'vegetating in the teeth of time', it was a 'representative of the antiquated world' contriving 'to dupe itself with delusions of celestial perfection'.[16] In a significant article of 1862, Marx once again applied his standard formulation for Oriental Despotism and the Asiatic Mode of Production to the Chinese Empire. Commenting on the Taiping Rebellion, he remarked that China, 'this living fossil', was now convulsed with a revolution, and added: 'There is nothing extraordinary in this phenomenon, since Oriental Empires exhibit a permanent immobility in their social foundations, and restless change in the persons and tribes who seize control of the political superstructure.'[17] The intellectual consequences of this conception are strikingly evident in Marx's judgments of the Taiping Rebellion itself – the largest single upheaval of exploited and oppressed masses anywhere in the world in the whole course of the 19th century. For Marx, paradoxically, displayed the greatest hostility and acrimony towards the Taiping rebels, whom he actually described thus: 'They are a still greater abomination for the popular masses than for the old rulers. Their destiny appears to be no more than to oppose conservative stagnation with a reign of destruction grotesque and loathsome in form, a destruction without any new or constructive kernel whatever.'[18] Recruited from 'lumpen elements, vagabonds and bad characters', who were given 'carte-blanche to commit every conceivable outrage on women and girls', the Taiping 'after ten years of noisy pseudo-activity have destroyed everything and

---

In fact, however, as the passages discussed above show, Marx clearly did not make any general distinction between China and the Orient.

16. Marx-Engels, *On Colonialism*, pp. 13–16, 111, 188.

17. 'Chinesisches', *Werke*, Bd 15, p. 514. This article is not included in the English-language collection *Marx on China*, and is subsequent to the items in it.

18. *Werke*, Bd 15, p. 514. In fact, the Taiping 'Kingdom of Heaven' contained a broad utopian programme, of an egalitarian character.

produced nothing.'[19] Such vocabulary, taken over uncritically from English consular reports, shows more clearly than anything else the gulf of incomprehension that separated Marx from the realities of Chinese society. In practice, neither Marx nor Engels seem to have been able to give Chinese history much study or thought: their essential preoccupations lay elsewhere.

Modern attempts to build a developed theory of the 'Asiatic mode of production' from the scattered legacies left by Marx and Engels – whether in the 'communal-tribal' or 'hydraulic-despotic' avenues of direction – are thus essentially misguided. They underestimate both the weight of the prior problematic which Marx and Engels accepted, and the vulnerability of the limited modifications which they brought to it. The 'Asiatic mode of production', even shorn of its village myths, still suffered the inherent weakness of functioning essentially as a generic residual category for non-European development,[20] and so blending features found in distinct social formations into a single, blurred archetype. The most obvious and pronounced distortion resulting from such a procedure was the persistent attribution of a 'stationary' character to Asian societies. In fact, the absence of a feudal

19. *Werke*, Bd 15, p. 515. Puritan abstinence and discipline, of course, were formally enjoined on the Taiping rank-and-file.

20. Ernest Mandel rightly emphasizes that its real and original function for Marx and Engels was to attempt an explanation of 'the *special* development of the East in comparison with Western and Mediterranean Europe': *The Formation of the Economic Thought of Karl Marx*, London 1971, p. 128. This book contains the most perceptive Marxist criticism of the 'tribal-communal' versions of the Asiatic mode of production, pp. 124–32. It suffers, however, from undue confidence in the 'hydraulic' versions. Mandel reproaches Godelier and others, with justice, of 'gradually reducing the characteristics of the Asiatic mode of production to those that mark *every* first manifestation of the state and of ruling classes in a society still essentially based on the village community', and correctly emphasizes that 'in the writings of Marx and Engels, the idea of an Asiatic mode of production is related not just to some 'primitive' Indian or Chinese society, lost in the mists of the past, but to Indian and Chinese society as they were when European industrial capital encountered them in the eighteenth century, on the eve of the conquest (India) or the massive penetration (China) of these countries by this capital' – a society which was 'not at all a "primitive" one, in the sense that there are no clearly defined or constituted social classes': pp. 125, 127, 129. But he overlooks the extent to which Marx himself was the source of this confusion. Reasserting, on the other hand, the centrality of the motif of the hydraulic functions exercised by a highly developed – indeed hypertrophied – State for the Asiatic mode of production, Mandel is insufficiently aware of its factual fragility.

dynamic of the Western type in the great Oriental Empires did not mean that their development was therefore merely stagnant or cyclical. Very great changes and advances marked much of early modern Asian history, even if these did not debouch onto capitalism. This comparative ignorance produced the illusion of the 'stationary' and 'identical' character of Oriental Empires, where in fact it is their *diversity* and *development* that today naturally commands the attention of the historian. Without attempting anything more than the briefest suggestions, the contrast between the Islamic and Chinese sociopolitical systems, in the Asia with which Marx and Engels were originally concerned, is eloquent enough. The epochal expansion of both had, in fact, been enormous and ceased at a comparatively recent date. The maximum sway of Islamic civilization was geographically reached at the turn of the 17th century; South-East Asia had been attained, most of Indonesia and Malaya converted, and above all the three powerful Islamic Empires of Ottoman Turkey, Safavid Persia and Mughal India coexisted in the same epoch, each of great economic wealth and military power. The greatest spread and highest prosperity of Chinese civilization was achieved during the 18th century, when the vast inner spaces of Mongolia, Sinkiang and Tibet were conquered by the Ch'ing dynasty, and the population doubled in a century, to levels some five times those of three hundred years before. Yet the characteristic socioeconomic structures and State systems of each were strikingly distinct, in their very different geographical contexts. In the following remarks, no attempt will be made to pose the central question of defining the fundamental *modes of production* and their complex combinations which constituted the successive social formations of Islamic or Chinese history: the generic term 'civilization' can be taken here as simply a conventional verbal scaffolding concealing these concrete, unresolved problems. But even without broaching them directly, certain preliminary contrasts can be made, subject to necessary and inevitable ulterior correction.

IV

The Muslim Empires of the early modern epoch, of which the Ottoman Empire was the most visible to Europe, had a long institutional and political ancestry behind them. For the original Arabian model of conquest and conversion had set the course of Islamic history along certain lines to which it always thereafter seems to have remained comparatively faithful. Desert nomads and urban merchants were the two social groups which, although both had initially rejected him, assured the success of Muhammad in the Hejaz: his teaching, indeed, precisely provided an ideological and psychic unification for a society whose clan and kin cohesion was increasingly rent by class divisions in the streets and tribal feuds in the sands, as commodity exchange dissolved traditional customs and ties along the Northern trade routes of the peninsula.[1] The beduin tribes of Arabia, like virtually all nomadic pastoralists, had combined individual ownership of herds with collective use of land:[2] private agrarian property was foreign to the deserts of Northern Arabia as much as to Central Asia. The wealthy merchants and bankers of Mecca and Medina, on the other hand, owned land both in the urban precincts themselves and in their immediate rural circumference.[3] When the first Islamic victories occurred, in which both groups participated, the disposal of conquered soil on the whole reflected the conceptions of the townsmen: Muhammad sanctioned the division of booty – including land – among the faithful. But when the Arab armies swept across the Middle East in the great Islamic *jihads* of the 7th century after Muhammad's death, beduin traditions gradually reasserted themselves in a new form. To begin with, royal or enemy estates in the Byzantine and Persian Empires, whose proprietors had been subdued by force of arms, were confiscated and appropriated to the Islamic community or *Umma*, commanded by the Caliph who had succeeded to the authority of the

1. For the social background to the emergence of Islam, see Montgomery Watt, *Muhammad at Mecca*, Oxford 1953, pp. 16–20, 72–9, 141–4, 152–3.

2. B. Lewis, *The Arabs in History*, London 1950, p. 29.

3. F. Løkkegaard, *Islamic Taxation in the Classical Period*, Copenhagen 1950 pp. 20, 32.

Prophet; lands belonging to infidels who had accepted a negotiated surrender were left in their possession, subject to payment of tribute; while Arab soldiers were granted leases or *qat'ia* on confiscated domains, or could buy their own land outside Arabia, subject to a religious tithe.[4]

By the mid-8th century, however, a more or less uniform land-tax or *kharaj* had emerged, which all cultivators had to pay to the Caliphate whatever their faith, while unbelievers owed in addition a discriminatory poll-tax or *jizya*. At the same time, the category of 'subdued' land underwent a notable extension at the expense of 'negotiated' land.[5] These changes were clinched by the formal establishment under Umar II (717–20) of the doctrine that all land was by right of conquest the property of the sovereign, on which subjects paid rents to the Caliph. 'In its fully developed form this conception of *fay'* (booty) means that the State in all the subdued countries reserves for itself the absolute title to all land.'[6] The vast, newly acquired territories of the Muslim world were thus technically henceforward the property of the Caliphate; and despite many variant interpretations and local derogations, State monopoly of land became a traditional legal canon of Islamic political systems thereafter – from the Umayyad and Abbasid States down to Ottoman Turkey or Safavid Persia.[7] Marx's original suspicion that the diffusion of the principle in Asia was largely due to Islamic conquest was thus not wholly unfounded. Of course, its practical operation was nearly always loose and defective, especially in the earlier epochs of Islamic history – the 'Arab' centuries proper, after the Hegira. For no political machinery of the time was capable of enforcing a full and effective State control of all agrarian property. Moreover, the very juridical existence of such a monopoly inevitably blocked the emergence of precise and univocal categories of *property* altogether on the land, since the notion of 'property' always involves plurality and negativity: the plenitude of a single possessor excludes the

4. R. Mantran, *L'Expansion Musulmane (VIIe–XIe Siècles)*, Paris 1969, pp. 105–6, 108–10; Lewis, *The Arabs in History*, p. 57.

5. Løkkegaard, *Islamic Taxation in the Classical Period*, p. 77.

6. *Ibid*, p. 49.

7. R. Levy, *The Social Structure of Islam*, p. 401; X. De Planhol, *Les Fondements Géographiques de l'Histoire de l'Islam*, p. 54.

necessary divisions that give ownership its hard boundaries and edges.

The characteristic state of Islamic law with respect to landed property was thus one of endemic 'vacillation' and 'chaos', as has often been remarked.[8] This confusion was compounded by the religious character of Muslim jurisprudence. The sacred law or *shari'a*, which developed during the second century after the Hegira, and achieved formal acceptance by the Abbasid Caliphate, comprised 'an all-embracing body of religious duties, the totality of Allah's commands that regulate the life of every Muslim in all its aspects.'[9] Precisely for this reason, its interpretation was riven by theological disputes between rival schools. Moreover, although its claims were in principle universal, in practice secular government existed as a separate realm apart: the sovereign enjoyed virtually unlimited discretionary power to 'complete' the sacred law in matters directly affecting the State – above all, war, politics, taxation and crime.[10] There was thus a permanent gulf between juridical theory and legal practice in classical Islam, the inevitable expression of the contradiction between a secular polity and a religious community in a civilization that lacked any distinction between Church and State. There were always 'two justices' at work within the *Umma*. Moreover, the diversity of religious schools of jurisprudence rendered impossible any systematic codification of even the sacred law. The result was to prevent the emergence of any lucid or precise legal order whatever. Thus, in the agrarian sphere, the *shari'a* developed virtually no clear and specific concepts of property, while administrative practice anyway frequently dictated norms without relation to it.[11] Hence, beyond the ultimate claim of the ruler to the totality of the soil, there typically prevailed an extreme juridical *indetermination* on the land. After the initial Arab conquests in the Middle East, the local peasantry in the subject lands were typically left

8. See the characteristic asides of Løkkegaard, *Islamic Taxation in the Classical Period*, pp. 44, 50.

9. J. Schacht, *An Introduction to Islamic Law*, Oxford 1964, pp. 1–2, 200–1.

10. *Ibid.*, pp. 54–5, 84–5.

11. Schacht, *An Introduction to Islamic Law*: 'The theory of Islamic law has thus developed only a few rudiments of a special law of real estate; conditions of land tenure in practice were often different from theory, varying according to place and time' (p. 142).

in undisturbed possession of their plots; as *kharaj* lands, the latter were regarded as part of the collective *fay'* of the conquerors, and so formally were state property. In practice there was in most regions little restriction – or conversely, guarantee – of their disposition by the villagers who cultivated them; while in other areas, such as Egypt, the proprietary rights of the State were very strictly enforced.[12] Likewise, the *qat'ia* distributed to the Islamic soldiery in the Umayyad epoch were in theory emphyteutic leases of public domains, but in practice could become personal liens of quasi-ownership. On the other hand, partible inheritance governed such *qatia*, and other forms of individual holding, and customarily prevented the consolidation of large hereditary estates within the framework of the sacred law. A pervasive ambiguity and improvisation characteristically haunted landownership within the Muslim world.

The corollary of the legal absence of stable private property in land was the economic spoliation of agriculture in the great Islamic Empires. At its most extreme, this typical phenomenon took the form of the 'beduinization' of wide areas of settled peasant cultivation, which reverted to arid scrub or wasteland under the impact of pastoral invasion or military pillage. The original Arab conquests in the Middle East and North Africa in general seem initially to have preserved or repaired pre-existent agricultural patterns, if without adding notably to them. But the subsequent waves of nomadic invasion which punctuated the development of Islam often proved to be durably destructive in their impact on settled cultivation. The two most extreme cases were to be the Hillali devastation of Tunisia and the Turcoman beduinization of Anatolia.[13] The long-run historical curve in this sense was to point steadily downwards. But from the outset, a permanent division was established virtually everywhere between agrarian production and

12. Claude Cahen, *L'Islam des Origines au Début de l'Empire Ottomane*, Paris 1970, p. 109: for agrarian conditions generally in this epoch, see pp. 107–13. Cahen's book is the most solid recent synthesis on the Arab epoch of Islam.

13. Cahen, *L'Islam*, p. 103, insists on the distinction between the initial 7th century conquests and later nomadic devastations, tending to attribute the worst of the latter to the non-Islamic Mongol invasions of the 13th century, p. 247. De Planhol is much more sweeping: for his graphic account of the process of beduinization within Islamic agriculture generally, see *Les Fondements Geographiques de l'Histoire de l'Islam*, pp. 35–7.

urban surplus appropriation, mediated by the tributary structure of the State. No direct relationship between lord and peasant typically arose in the countryside: rather the State leased certain rights of rural exploitation to military or civilian functionaries, resident in towns – essentially the collection of the *kharaj* land tax. The result was the Arab *'iqta*, the precursor of the later Ottoman *timar* or Mughal *jagir*. The Abbasid *iqtas* were in effect land grants to warriors, which took the form of fiscal licenses distributed to absentee urban rentiers to squeeze small peasant cultivators.[14] The Buyid, Seljuk and early Osmanli States exacted military services from the holders of these rents or their successor versions, but the natural tendency of the system was always to degenerate into parasitic tax-farming – the *iltizam* of the later Ottoman epoch. Even under rigorous central control, state monopoly of land filtered through commercialized rights of absentee exploitation constantly reproduced a general ambience of legal indetermination and precluded any positive bond between the profiteer and tiller of the soil.[15] Large-scale hydraulic works were consequently at best maintained or redressed from previous regimes; at worst damaged or neglected. The first centuries of Umayyad and Abbasid rule saw a general upkeep of inherited canals in Syria and Egypt, and some extension of the sub-terranean *qanat* system in Persia. But already by the 10th century, the Mesopotamian canal network was in decay, as ground levels rose and waterways were abandoned.[16] No new irrigation systems were ever

14. For the changing form and function of the *'iqta*, see C. Cahen, 'L'Evolution de l'Iqta du XIe au XIIe Siècle', *Annales ESC*, January–March 1953, No. 1, pp. 25–52.

15. See the memorable pages in Planhol, *Les Fondements Géographiques*, pp. 54–7. Ibn Khaldun with typical contempt lumped peasants together with pastoralists in a common opprobrium as primitive inhabitants of the rural backlands: as Goitein remarks, 'Fellah and Beduin alike are beyond the pale of civilization' for him: *A Mediterranean Society*, I, p. 75.

16. D. and J. Sourdel, *La Civilisation de l'Islam Classique*, Paris 1968, pp. 272–87, surveys the role and fate of hydraulic works in the Umayyad and Abbasid epochs; see especially pp. 279, 289. They emphasize that the Iraqi irrigation system was in complete decline long before the Mongol invasions, to which its collapse was often later attributed. The underground *qanats* of Persia, of course, antedated Islamic conquest by well over a millennium, having been a major feature of the Achaemenid State: see H. Goblot, 'Dans l'Ancien Iran, Les Techniques de l'Eau et la Grande Histoire', *Annales ESC*, May–June 1963, pp. 510–11.

constructed comparable in scale to the Yemeni dams of Antiquity, whose ruin was the fitting prologue to the birth of Islam in Arabia.[17] The single important invention on the land after the Arab conquest of the Middle East, the advent of the windmill, was a Persian device born in the region of Sistan, and eventually seems to have benefited European agriculture more than Islamic. Indifference or contempt for agriculture precluded even a stabilized serfdom: labour was never regarded as so precious by the exploiting class that peasant adscription became a main desideratum. In these conditions, agrarian productivity again and again stagnated or regressed in Islamic countries, leaving a rural panorama of often 'desolate mediocrity'.[18]

Two notable exceptions confirm in their own way these general rules of the countryside. On the one hand, Lower Iraq under Abbasid rule in the 8th century was the scene of sugar, cotton and indigo plantations, organized as advanced commercial enterprises on reclaimed marsh land by Basra merchants. The rationalized exploitation of this plantation economy, a prefiguration of the later sugar complexes of European colonialism in the New World, was remote from the usual pattern of indolent fiscalism: but it precisely rested on massive use of African slaves imported from Zanzibar. Rural slavery, however, was always foreign to Islamic agriculture as a whole: the Iraqi plantations remained an isolated episode which only underlined the absence of a comparable capitalization of production elsewhere.[19] On the other hand, it is noticeable that horticulture always occupied a special position within the Islamic agrarian systems, achieving high technical levels and inspiring specialist treatises on plants and shrubs, from

17. The mysterious fall of the great Marib barrages in the Yemen coincided with the shift of economic and social vitality from Southern to Northern Arabia in the 6th century A.D.; Engels was aware of the background importance of the regression of the Yemen for the ascent of Islam in the Hejaz, although he antedated it unduly and attributed it too exclusively to Ethiopian invasion: Marx-Engels, *Selected Correspondence*, pp. 82–3.

18. The phrase is Planhol's: *Les Fondements Géographiques*, p. 57. A more optimistic account can be found in C. Cahen, 'Economy, Society, Institutions', *The Cambridge History of Islam*, II, Cambridge 1970, pp. 511–12ff. Planhol uncritically assimilates Islamic agricultural patterns to those of Classical Antiquity, and generalizes unduly, but his concrete geographical analyses of the ultimate results of Muslim disdain for cultivation are often of the greatest force.

19. For the Zanj plantations, see Lewis, *The Arabs in History*, pp. 103–4.

Andalusia to Persia.[20] The reason was revealing: gardens and orchards were normally concentrated in towns or suburbs, and as such were specifically exempt from the State ownership of soil prescribed by tradition, which had always permitted private property of urban land. Horticulture thus formed the equivalent of a 'luxury' sector in industry, patronized by the rich and powerful, that partook of the prestige of cities themselves, in the shadow of whose minarets and palaces its carefully tended gardens grew.

For the Islamic world was always, from the first Arab conquests onwards, a vast, catenary system of cities separated by a neglected or despised countryside. Born in the transit town of Mecca and heir to the metropolitan legacy of late Mediterranean and Mesopotamian Antiquity, Muslim civilization was indefectibly urban, promoting commodity production, mercantile enterprise and monetary circulation in the cities which linked it together, from the first. Initially, the Arab nomads who conquered the Middle East formed their own military encampments in the desert, on the edge of the pre-existent capitals, which later often became major cities in their own right – Kufa, Basra, Fostat, Kairuan. Then, with the stabilization of Islamic rule from the Atlantic to the Persian Gulf, urban expansion of a perhaps unequalled speed and scale occurred in the most privileged regions of the Caliphate. According to one recent (doubtless exaggerated) calculation, the city of Baghdad grew to a population of two million within less than half a century, from 762 to 800.[21] This concentrated urbanization in selected sites in part reflected the 'gold boom' of the Umayyad and Abbasid epochs, when Egyptian and Persian treasures were released into circulation, Sudanese output was canalized into the Muslim world, and mining techniques notably improved with the use of the mercury

20. Planhol, *Les Fondements Géographiques*, p. 57; Andre Miquel, *L'Islam et Sa Civilisation, VIIe–XXe Siècles*, Paris 1968, pp. 130, 203; Irfan Habib, 'Potentialities of Capitalist Development in the Economy of Mughal India', *The Journal of Economic History*, XXIX, March 1969, pp. 46–7, 49.

21. M. Lombard, *L'Islam dans sa Première Grandeur (VIIe–XIe Siècles)*, Paris 1972, p. 121. G. Von Grunebaum, *Classical Islam*, London 1970, p. 100, estimates the population of Baghdad, by contrast, at 300,000. Cahen deems it impossible to assess the size of any such cities as Baghdad accurately in this epoch: 'Economy, Society, Institutions', p. 521. Mantran cautions against Lombard's estimates of the scale of early Islamic urbanization: *L'Expansion Musulmane*, pp. 270–1.

amalgam; and in part was the result of the creation of a unified trading zone of intercontinental dimensions. The Arab merchant class which rode the crest of this wave of commercial prosperity was respected and honoured by religious law and social opinion: the vocation of the trader and manufacturer was sanctioned by the Koran, which never dissociated profit from piety.[22] The financial and entrepreneurial devices of Islamic commerce soon became very advanced; it was in the Middle East, indeed, that the institution of the *commenda* – which was later to play such an important role in mediaeval Europe – was perhaps first invented.[23] The fortunes made by Arab traders, moreover, were no longer confined to overland caravan routes. Few aspects of early Islamic expansion were more striking than the speed and facility with which the sea was mastered by the Arabs of the desert. The Mediterranean and Indian Ocean were reunited into a linked maritime system for the first time since the Hellenistic epoch: while Muslim shipping in the Abbasid Caliphate ventured all the way from the Atlantic to the China Sea. The Islamic world, poised between Europe and China, was master of East-West trade. The wealth gathered in commerce correspondingly stimulated manufactures, above all textiles, paper and porcelain. While prices steadily rose and the countryside became depressed, urban handicrafts and voluptuary consumption flourished in the towns. This configuration was not peculiar to the Abbasid Caliphate. The later Islamic Empires were always characterized by dramatic increases in the size of the largest towns: Constantinople, Isfahan and Delhi are celebrated examples.

But the economic magnitude or opulence of these Islamic cities was not accompanied by any municipal autonomy or civic order. Towns had no corporate political identity; their merchants little collective social power. Urban charters were unknown, and town life was everywhere subject to the more or less arbitrary will of princes or emirs. Individual merchants could rise to the highest political positions in the

22. The commanding discussion of this question is Maxime Rodinson, *Islam and Capitalism*, London 1974, pp. 28–55. Rodinson also effectively criticizes Weber's contention that Islamic ideology was generally inimical to rationalized commercial activity: pp. 103–17.

23. See the discussion in A. L. Udovitch, 'Commercial Techniques in Early Mediaeval Islamic Trade', in D. S. Richards (ed.), *Islam and the Trade of Asia*, Oxford 1970, pp. 37–62.

counsels of dynasties;[24] but their personal success was invariably exposed to intrigue or hazard, while the wealth of their houses could always be confiscated by military rulers. The municipal symmetry and order of the late classical cities that had originally fallen to Arab armies exercised a certain initial influence on the successor towns of the new imperial system: but this soon waned, remembered only in a few private or palatine ensembles laid out for later rulers.[25] Islamic cities thus typically came to lack any coherent internal structure, whether administrative or architectonic. They were confused, amorphous mazes of streets and buildings, without public centres or spaces: focused only on mosques and bazaars, and the local trades huddled about them.[26] Just as no mercantile or professional associations organized the body of the propertied, no artisan guilds protected or regulated the activity of the small craftsmen in the great Arab cities.[27] At most, neighbourhood clusters or religious fraternities provided a humble collective hearth for popular life, within an urban milieu that straggled away indistinctly into the suburbs or rural villages beyond. Beneath the devout artisanate, there typically floated an underworld of criminal and mendicant gangs among the unemployed and lumpenproletariat.[28] The one institutional group which functioned to confer a certain quasi-unity on the towns was the ulemate, whose clinging combination of clerical and secular roles and voluble religious zeal to some extent mediated and bound together the population below the prince and his

24. For examples, see S. D. Goitein, *Studies in Islamic History and Institutions*, Leiden 1966, pp. 236–9.

25. D. and J. Sourdel, *La Civilisation de l'Islam Classique*, pp. 424–7.

26. Planhol, *Les Fondements Géographiques*, pp. 48–52, etches a sharp portrait, if perhaps antedating the typical disorder of Islamic cities somewhat: compare Sourdel, *La Civilisation de l'Islam Classique*, pp. 397–9, 430–1.

27. For the most recent restatement of the complete absence of Islamic guilds before the late 15th century, see G. Baer, 'Guilds in Middle Eastern History', in M. A. Cook (ed.), *Studies in the Economic History of the Middle East*, London 1970, pp. 11–17.

28. These characteristics are depicted in I. M. Lapidus, *Muslim Cities in the Later Middle Ages*, Cambridge USA 1967, pp. 170–83 (criminal and mendicant gangs), and 'Muslim Cities and Islamic Societies', in Lapidus (ed.), *Middle Eastern Cities*, Berkeley-Los Angeles 1969, pp. 60–74 (lack of delimited urban communities or self-contained cities). Lapidus protests against traditional contrasts between West European and Islamic cities in the Middle Ages, but his own accounts graphically reinforce, if refine, them.

guards.[29] It was the latter, however, who ultimately dominated the destiny of the towns. Grown in disorder, lacking plan or charter, the fate of the Islamic cities was normally determined by that of the State whose fortune had conferred their prosperity on them.

Islamic States, in their turn, were usually of nomadic descent: the Umayyad, Hamdanid, Seljuk, Almoravid, Almohad, Osmanli, Safavid and Mughal political systems were all derived from nomadic desert confederations. Even the Abbasid Caliphate, perhaps the most urban and settled in background, drew most of its initial armed strength from the recent tribal colonists of the Khorasan. All these Islamic States, like the Ottoman Empire itself, were essentially warrior and plunderer in cast: founded on conquest, their whole rationale and structure was military. Civilian administration proper, as a functional sphere in its own right, never became dominant within the ruling class: a scribal bureaucracy did not develop much beyond the needs of tax-collection. The State machine was largely a consortium of professional soldiers, organized either in tightly centralized corps or a more diffuse form, in either case customarily supported by revenue-assignments from public lands. The political wisdom of the typical Islamic State was condensed in the expressive apothegm of its manuals of rule: 'The world is before all else a verdant garden whose enclosure is the State, the State is a government whose head is the prince, the prince is a shepherd who is assisted by the army, the army is a body of guards which is maintained by money, and money is the indispensable resource which is provided by subjects.'[30] The linear logic of these syllogisms had curious structural consequences. For it was the combination of military predation and contempt for agrarian production that seems to have given rise to the distinctive phenomenon of elite slave guards who again and again came to cap the State apparatus itself. The Ottoman *devshirme* was only the most developed and sophisticated example of this specifically Islamic system of military recruitment, which was to be found all over the Muslim world.[31] Turkish slave officers from

29. Lapidus, *Muslim Cities in the Later Middle Ages*, pp. 107–13.
30. Sourdel, *La Civilisation de l'Islam Classique*, p. 327.
31. For some incomplete remarks, see Levy, *The Social Structure of Islam*, pp. 74–5, 417, 445–50. There is no adequately systematic survey of this phenomenon. Cahen observes that slave-guards were somewhat less prominent in the Islamic West (Spain and North Africa), politically a less developed zone: *L'Islam*, p. 149.

Central Asia founded the Ghaznavid State in Khorasan, and dominated the Abbasid Caliphate in its decadence in Iraq; Nubian slave regiments ringed the Fatimid Caliphate, and Circassian and Turkish slaves brought from the Black Sea manned the Mamluk State in Egypt; Slav and Italian slaves commanded the last armies of the Umayyad Caliphate in Spain, and created their own *taifa* kingdoms in Andalusia when it fell; Georgian or Armenian slaves supplied the crack *ghulam* regiments of the Safavid State in Persia under Shah Abbas.[32] The alien and servile character of these palatine corps corresponded to the strange structural logic of successive Islamic polities. For nomadic tribal warriors, who typically founded them, could not maintain their beduinism long after conquest: clans and transhumance together disappeared after sedentarization. On the other hand, they were not readily convertible into a rural nobility, living on hereditary estates, or a scribal bureaucracy, organized in a civil administration: traditional scorn for agriculture and letters impeded either, while their turbulent independence made them resistant to a strict military hierarchy. Victorious dynasties were thus repeatedly led to create special guard units of slaves as the core of their regular armies, once they became established in power. Since predial slavery scarcely existed in agriculture, praetorian slavery could become an honour. The various Islamic guard corps, in effect, represented the nearest thing to a purely military elite conceivable at the time, divorced from any agrarian or pastoral role and broken from any clan organization – hence capable in theory of unconditional loyalty to the ruler, their slavery a pledge of soldierly obedience; in practice, of course, capable thereby of seizing supreme power for themselves. Their prevalence was a sign of the constant absence of a territorial nobility in the Islamic world.

The social traits outlined above were, of course, always unevenly distributed in the various epochs and regions of Muslim history; but a family resemblance between most of the Islamic States seems *prima*

32. The final case cited above provides a particularly clear and documented example of the political purposes which these guard-corps in general served, perhaps because it was chronologically the latest. The Georgian *ghulam* cavalry units were specifically created by the dynasty to free it from the turbulence of the Qizilbash Turcoman tribesmen that had originally brought the Safavid house to power. See R. M. Savory, 'Safavid Persia', *The Cambridge History of Islam*, I, Cambridge 1970, pp. 407, 419–30.

facie – at least by contrast with the other major imperial civilization of the Orient – to be discernible. This does not mean, however, that Islamic history was therefore merely one of cyclical repetition. On the contrary, a marked periodization of development appears evident within it. The Umayyad State which was planted on the subject territories of the Middle East in the 7th century essentially represented the Arab tribal confederations that had achieved the initial conquests, in which the merchant oligarchy of Mecca had regained an advantageous position. The Caliphate in Damascus coordinated more or less autonomous beduin sheikhs commanding their own warriors in the military camp-towns outside the great cities of Syria, Egypt and Iraq. Arab desert troops monopolized pensions from the central treasury, fiscal exemptions and military privileges. The civilian bureaucracy was for a long time left in the hands of former Byzantine or Persian officials, who managed technical administration for their new overlords.[33] Non-Arab converts to Islam (and poorer, marginalized Arabs) were confined to inferior *mawali* status, paying heavier taxes and serving the tribal encampments as petty artisans, menials and footsoldiers. The Umayyad Caliphate thus established an 'Arab political sovereignty'[34] over the Middle East rather than an Islamic religious ecumene. With the stabilization of the conquests, however, the ruling Arab warrior class became increasingly anachronistic; its ethnic exclusiveness and economic exploitation of the mass of Muslims among the former subject population of the Empire provoked the ever greater discontent of its *mawali* co-religionists, who soon came to outnumber it.[35] Intertribal frictions between Northern and Southern groups simultaneously weakened its unity. Meanwhile frontier colonists in farther Persia resented traditional administrative methods to which they were submitted. It was this settler community which seems to have set off the final upheaval against the Syrian-based State centred in Damascus, whose popular success was assured by the widespread *mawali* disaffection in Persia and Iraq. Organized and secret agitation against Umayyad rule, utilizing heterodox Shi'ite religious fervour, but above all

33. Lewis, *The Arabs in History*, pp. 65–6.

34. The phrase is that of F. Gabrieli, *Muhammed and the Conquests of Islam*, London 1968, p. 111.

35. Lewis, *The Arabs in History*, pp. 70–1.

mobilizing *mawali* hostility to the narrow Arabism of the dynasty in Damascus, unleashed the political revolution which brought the Abbasid house to power, sweeping westwards from its base in Khorasan across Persia and Iraq.[36]

The Abbasid Caliphate signalled the end of the Arab tribal aristocracy; the new State apparatus created in Baghdad was sustained by Persian administrators and shielded by Khorasani guards. The formation of a permanent bureaucracy and army, with a cosmopolitan discipline, rendered the new Caliphate a political autocracy with much more centralized power than its predecessor.[37] Shedding its heretical background, it preached religious orthodoxy and claimed divine authority. The Abbasid State presided over the maximum floresence of Islamic trade, industry and science: at its apogee in the early 9th century, it was the wealthiest and most advanced civilization in the world.[38] Merchants, bankers, manufacturers, speculators and tax-farmers accumulated huge sums in the great cities: urban crafts diversified and multiplied; a commercial sector emerged in agriculture; long-distance shipping girded the oceans; astronomy, physics and mathematics were transposed from Greek into Arabic culture. Yet the limits

36. The exact social composition and significance of the Abbasid upheaval have been the subject of much dispute. Traditional accounts have interpreted it essentially as a popular and ethnic revolt of the non-Arab *mawali* population, although the presence of Arab tribal factions (Yemeni in filiation) within it has always been acknowledged. The degree of importance ascribed to religious heterodoxy in the movement has been doubted by Cahen, 'Points de Vue sur la Révolution Abbaside', *Revue Historique*, CCXXX, 1963, pp. 336–7. The most recent and complete account of the origins of the revolt is M. A. Shaban, *The Abbasid Revolution*, Cambridge 1970, which gives central emphasis to the grievances of the Arab settlers in Khorasan, subjected to the traditional rule of local Persian *diqhān* by the conservative administrative policies of the Umayyad State: pp. 158–60. It is clear, in any case, that the insurgent army which launched the overthrow of the Caliphate in Damascus by seizing Merv was in practice composed of both Arab and Iranian elements.

37. Lewis, *The Arabs in History*, pp. 83–5.

38. Goitein has termed the period ushered in by the consolidation of Abbasid power the 'intermediate' civilization of Islam: a world between Hellenic and Renaissance epochs in time, Europe/Africa and India/China in space, and secular 4nd religious cultures in character: *Studies in Islamic History and Institutions*, p. a6ff.

to Abbasid development were reached relatively soon. Despite the soaring commercial prosperity of the 8th and 9th centuries, few productive innovations in manufactures were registered, and little technological progress was yielded by the introduction of scientific studies. The most important native invention was probably the lateen sail – a transport improvement that merely facilitated trade; cotton, the most significant new cash crop of the time, derived from pre-muslim Turkestan; the formula for paper, the major new industry of the epoch, was externally acquired from Chinese prisoners of war.[39] The very volume and fever of mercantile activity, outstripping any impetus from production proper, appears to have led to a series of explosive social and political tensions in the Caliphate. Corruption and mercenarization of the administration went hand in hand with increased fiscal exploitation of the peasantry; generalized inflation struck at petty craftsmen and shopkeepers; plantation enclaves concentrated slave-labourers in desperate, massed gangs. While the internal security of the regime deteriorated, professional Turkic guards increasingly usurped power at the centre, as the military rampart against the rising tide of diverse social revolts from below. In the late 9th and 10th centuries, successive insurrections and conspiracies shook the whole structure of the Empire. The Zanj slaves rebelled in Lower Iraq and waged war successfully against regular armies for fifteen years, before being suppressed; the Qarmatian movement, a breakaway Shi'ite sect, created an egalitarian slave-owning republic in Bahrein; while the Ismaili faith, another Shi'ite movement, plotted and organized for the overthrow of the established order throughout the Middle East, until it eventually seized power in Tunisia and then established a rival empire in Egypt, the Fatimid Caliphate.[40] By now Abbasid-held Iraq had lapsed into

39. After the battle of Talas in Central Asia, in 751, where Arab troops defeated a force of Uighur and Chinese contingents. For general surveys of Islamic commercial and manufacturing activity in the Abbasid epoch, see P. K. Hitti, *History of the Arabs*, London 1956, pp. 345–9; Sourdel, *La Civilisation de l'Islam Classique*, pp. 289–311, 317–24; Lombard, *L'Islam dans sa Première Grandeur*, pp. 161–203 (particularly informative on the slave-trade – one of the great staples of Abbasid commerce, drawing on the Slav, Turkish and African hinterlands). For the spread of cotton, see Miquel, *L'Islam et Sa Civilisation*, p. 130.

40. For these diverse revolts, see the acute discussion in Lewis, *The Arabs in History*, pp. 103–12. From his account, the Qarmatian regime in the Gulf appears to have been the nearest Islamic equivalent that ever existed to a city-state of

irremediable economic and political decline, and the whole centre of gravity of the Islamic world shifted to the new Fatimid State in Egypt, the victor of the social upheavals of the epoch, and the founder of Cairo.

Unlike its predecessor, the Fatimid Caliphate did not disavow its heterodoxy after the conquest of power, but aggressively propagated it. Slave plantations were never re-created; on the other hand, the mobility of the peasantry was more closely controlled in Fatimid Egypt. International trade was now revived on a grand scale, to both India and Europe: Egyptian commercial prosperity of the 11th and 12th centuries once again demonstrated the international enterprise of the Arab merchant class, and the traditional skills of Arab craftsmen. But the transfer of economic and political ascendancy within the Muslim world from the Tigris to the Nile also signified the pull of a new force which was to affect the whole future course of Islamic development. For the pre-eminence of Fatimid Egypt was geographically a function of its relative proximity to the Central Mediterranean, and to mediaeval Europe. 'The impact of European trade on the local market was overwhelming.'[41] The dynasty had already established close contacts with Italian traders at the outset of its career, in 10th century Tunisia, whose commercial prosperity had provided the basis for its subsequent conquest of Egypt. The ascent of Western feudalism was henceforward a constant historical presence on the flank of the Islamic world. Initially, maritime traffic with the Italian cities quickened the economic growth of Cairo; eventually, the military intrusion of Frankish knights into the Levant was to upset the whole strategic balance of Arabic civilization in the Middle East. The benefits of trade were soon to be followed by the blows of the Crusades. A great watershed in Islamic history was now at hand.

Already in the mid-11th century, Turcoman nomads had overrun Persia and Iraq, seizing Baghdad, while Arab beduin from the Hejaz had devastated North Africa, sacking Kairuan: these Seljuk and Hillali invasions revealed the weakness and vulnerability of large regions of

---

classical Antiquity – a Spartan community of equal citizenry based on agricultural slavery. It was eventually swept away in Bahrein in the later 11th century.

41. S. D. Goitein, *A Mediterranean Society*, Vol. I, *Economic Foundations*, Berkeley-Los Angeles 1967, pp. 44-5.

the settled Muslim world. Neither created a stable new order, either in the Maghreb or the Middle East. Seljuk armies took Jerusalem and Damascus, but were unable to consolidate their rule in Syria or Palestine. The sudden Christian offensive in the Levant during the 12th century thus precipitated a general strategic crisis in the Middle East. For the first time, the frontiers of Islam receded, as punishing defeats were inflicted on the fragmented principalities of the Syro-Palestinian coastlands. Egypt itself, the hub of Arab wealth and power in the region, was now exposed to direct attack. The Fatimid dynasty had meanwhile reached the last stages of corruption and decay; by 1153 Crusader power was at the gates of Sinai. But amidst the turmoil and disorientation of the time, a new type of Muslim political order started to emerge, and with it a fresh phase in the development of Islamic society. For confronted with the expansionism of the West, everything henceforward happened as if Islamic reaction took the form of an extreme militarization of the dominant state structures of the Middle East, and a corresponding de-commercialization of the economies of the region, under the aegis of new ethnic rulers. In 1154, Nur al-Din Zangi, grandson of a Turkish slave soldier and lord of Aleppo and Mosul, seized Damascus. From now on, the Christian-Muslim contest for the control of Cairo was to decide the fate of the whole Levant. The race for the Nile Delta was won by Saladin, a Kurdish officer sent south by Nur al-Din, who conquered Egypt, destroyed the Fatimid Caliphate and founded the Turkish-style Ayyubid regime in its stead. Soon gaining control of Syria and Mesopotamia as well, Saladin decisively beat back the Crusaders, retaking Jerusalem and most of the Palestinian coast. European counter-attacks by sea re-established Crusader enclaves; and in the early 13th century, maritime expeditions twice invaded Egypt itself, capturing Damietta in 1219 and 1249. But these thrusts proved of no avail. Christian presence on the mainland of Levant was finished off by Baybars, a commander who created the fully Turkish Mamluk Sultanate,[42] whose power extended from Egypt up to Syria. Meanwhile, to the North the Seljuks had conquered most of Anatolia; the rise of the Ottomans was to complete their work in Asia Minor. In Iraq and Persia, the Mongol and Timurid invasions installed Tartar and

42. Goitein, *A Mediterranean Society*, I, pp. 35–8.

Turcoman States. Aided by the general crisis of European feudalism in the later Middle Ages, a new wave of Islamic expansion was now set in motion, which was not to come to a halt for another four centuries. Its most spectacular manifestation was, of course, the conquest of Constantinople and the Ottoman drive into Europe. But it was the general structural characteristics of the new Turkic States of the early modern epoch which were of most significance for the development of Islamic social formations as a whole. The Greater Seljuk Sultanate of Iraq and, above all, the Mamluk Sultanate in Egypt were the late mediaeval prototypes of these regimes; the three great Empires of Ottoman Turkey, Safavid Persia and Mughal India exemplified their accomplished form.

In every case, it was as if the Turkification of the Islamic political order decisively accentuated the military cast of the original Arab systems, at the expense of their mercantile component. The Turcoman nomads of Central Asia who invaded the Muslim world from the 11th century onwards in tide after tide were in social and economic background apparently very similar to the Arab beduin from South-West Asia who had originally overrun the Middle East. The historical congruence of the two great pastoralist zones above and below the Fertile Crescent, indeed, was what assured the fundamental continuity of Islamic civilization after the Turkic conquests: the newcomers were attuned by their own past to much of its cultural tenor. There were, nevertheless, certain critical differences between the pastoral nomadism of Central Asia and Arabia, which were to leave their stamp on the whole subsequent pattern of Muslim society. Whereas the Islamic homeland of Arabia had combined desert and towns, merchants and nomads, and was a major residuary legatee of the urban institutions of Antiquity, the steppes of Central Asia which supplied the pastoral conquerors of Turkey, Persia and India, had known few cities and little commerce by comparison. The fertile region of Transoxiana, between the Caspian and the Pamirs, had always been densely populated and relatively urbanized: Bokhara and Samarkand, lying across the great overland trade routes to China, were more than worthy counterparts to Mecca or Medina. But this wealthy territorial belt, which the Arabs were to call Mawarannahr, was historically Iranian in character. Beyond it, lay the immense, empty vortex of steppe, desert, mountain and forest stretching all the way to Mongolia and Siberia, which knew virtually no urban settlements at all, and from which issued tribe after tribe of Altaic nomads – Seljuks, Danishmends, Ghuzz, Mongols, Oirots, Uzbeks, Kazakhs, Kirghiz – whose successive eruptions precluded any lasting sedentarization of the Turkic world of Central Asia. The Arabian peninsula was relatively small, and encircled by sea: surrounded by maritime trade from the first, it also had a strictly limited demographic potential. In fact, after the original conquests of the 7th and 8th centuries, Arabia proper sank back into complete political insignificance throughout the rest of Islamic history, to the present century. Central Asia, by contrast, represented an enormous land-mass isolated from the sea, with constantly replenished reserves of war-like and migratory peoples.[43] The terms of the balance between nomad and urban traditions within classical Islamic civilization were thus inevitably shifted by the new Turkish predominance within it, from the late Middle Ages onwards. Martial organization hardened, as commercial enterprise receded. This change was never absolute or uniform, but its general direction was unmistakable. Moreover, the slow alteration in the metabolism of the Islamic world after the Crusades was not, of course, due merely to internal forces: its external setting was no less determinant – both in war and trade.

The Turcoman nomads of Central Asia had initially established their supremacy in the Middle East by their mastery of mounted archery, an art foreign to the spear-wielding Arab beduin. But the military strength of the new Imperial states of the early modern epoch rested on regular

43. For two anthropological comparisons, see R. Patai, 'Nomadism: Middle Eastern and Central Asian', *Southwestern Journal of Anthropology*, Vol. 7, No. 4, 1951, pp. 401–14, and E. Bacon, 'Types of Pastoral Nomadism in Central and South-West Asia', *Southwestern Journal of Anthropology*, Vol. 10, No. 1, 1954, pp. 44–65. Patai proposed an organized series of contrasts between Turkic and Arabian nomadism (horse vs camel, yurt vs tent, bow vs sword, exogamy vs endogamy, and so on). Bacon justly criticized these for lack of an adequate historical perspective, pointing out that Patai had unwarrantably projected backwards in time the agrarian cultivation practised by 18th and 19th century Kazakhs, and wrongly assumed greater class stratification in Central than in South-West Asian pastoralism. But both articles in their own way confirm the essential divergences outlined above: Turkic nomadism both lacked any stable symbiosis with sedentary agriculture (Bacon, pp. 46, 52), and was the predominant 'culture' in Central Asia, where Arab nomadism was a more subordinate 'culture' in South-West Asia (Patai, pp. 413–14).

field troops, equipped with fire-arms and backed by artillery: gunpowder was essential to their might. Heavy cannons for siege purposes were first adopted by the Mamluk State in Egypt, in the late 14th century. But the conservative mounted traditions of the Mamluk army blocked the use of field artillery or musketry. The Ottoman conquest of Egypt was precisely due to the superiority of Turkish arquebusiers over Mamluk cavalry. By the mid-16th century, Ottoman use of muskets and cannon had been perfected from European example. Safavid armies soon learnt the importance of fire-arms, after their initial defeat by Ottoman gunnery at Caldiran, and endowed themselves with modern ordnance. Mughal troops in India were armed from the outset of Babur's conquest with artillery and musketry.[44] The generalization of gunpowder in the Middle East, in fact, was certainly one of the most visible reasons for the notably greater stability and staying-power of the new Turkic states over the Arab regimes of the earlier Islamic epoch. The Ottoman military apparatus could hold European attacks at bay, even long after it had itself lost the strategic initiative in the Balkan or Pontic regions. Safavid and Mughal armies finally halted further Turcoman invasions of Persia and India, with the defeat of the Uzbek nomads who occupied the Mawarannahr in the 16th century: henceforward a strategic breakwater protected the three great imperial States of Islam from the tribal turbulence of Central Asia.[45] The superiority of these early modern empires was not, however, merely one of military technology: it was administrative and political, too. Mongol state-craft, in the epoch of Genghis-Khan and his successors, had already been organizationally more advanced than that of the Arab world, and its conquest of much of the Middle East perhaps left certain lasting lessons of rule behind it. At all events, the Ottoman, Safavid and Mughal armies at their peak embodied a discipline

44. For a survey of the role of musketry and cannonry in the Ottoman, Safavid and Mughal armies, see the article 'Bārūd' (gunpowder), in the *Encyclopaedia of Islam* (New Edition), Leiden 1967, Vol. I, pp. 1061-9. The Mamluk failure to master field artillery or hand-guns is analyzed in D. Ayalon, *Gunpowder and Fire-Arms in the Mamluk Kingdom*, London 1956, pp. 46-7, 61-83.

45. The Uzbek conquest of Transoxiana both Turkified it ethnically for the first time, and precipitated its economic stagnation and decline. Mughal campaigns to reconquer the Mawarannahr in the 17th century had no success: overextended lines of communication nearly led to disaster for Aurangzeb in 1645-7, averted only by his superior fire-power.

and training unknown to their predecessors. Their administrative substructures were also tighter and more integrated. The traditional Arab *'iqta* had been a largely parasitic fiscal device, which dissolved rather than reinforced the martial vocation of the urban assignee who enjoyed its revenue. The new-style Ottoman *timar* or Mughal *jagir* grant, on the other hand, was tied to much stricter obligations of warrior service and consolidated the pyramid of military command, which was now organized in a more formal hierarchy. In these Turkic political systems, moreover, State monopoly of land was enforced with a recharged verve: for less alloyed nomadic traditions now prevailed more than ever before in the regulation and disposal of agrarian property. Nizam-ul-Mulk, the famous Grand Vizir of the first Seljuk ruler in Baghdad, declared the Sultan the sole ruler of all land; the extent and rigour of Ottoman rights over the soil was notorious; the Safavid Shahs reinvigorated juridical claims to a monopoly of landownership; the Mughal Emperors imposed a ruthlessly exploitative fiscal system based on royal claims over all rural cultivation.[46] Suleiman, Abbas or Akbar commanded an imperial power in their realms greater than that of any Caliph.

On the other hand, the commercial vitality of the Arab epoch, which had coursed through the 'intermediate' civilization of classical Islam, now progressively ebbed away. This shift was, of course, correlated with the rise of European trade. The military expulsion of the Crusaders from the Levant had not been accompanied by the recovery of commercial mastery in the Eastern Mediterranean. On the contrary, already in the 12th century, Christian shipping had won a dominant position in Egyptian waters.[47] The Kurdo-Turkish counter-offensive on land, symbolized by Saladin and Baybars, was achieved at the cost of deliberate renunciation of naval power: to block renewed European landings, the Ayyubid and Mamluk rulers were reduced to dismantling ports and devastating the coast-line of Palestine.[48] The Ottoman State, by contrast, did build up a large and formidable naval force in

46. See A. Lambton, *Landlord and Tenant in Persia*, Oxford 1953, pp. 61, 66, 105–6 (Seljuks and Safavids); Gibb and Bowen, *Islamic Society and the West*, I/I, pp. 236–7 (Ottomans); W. H. Moreland, *India at the Death of Akbar*, London 1920, p. 256 (Mughals).

47. Goitein, *A Mediterranean Society*, I, p. 149.

48. See 'Bāhriyya', *Encyclopaedia of Islam* (New Edition), Vol. I, pp. 945–7.

the 16th century, with liberal use of Greek seamen, which regained control of the Eastern Mediterranean, and marauded into the Western Mediterranean from the corsair lairs in North Africa. But Osmanli sea-power was comparatively short-lived and artificial: it was always restricted functionally to warfare and piracy, never developing a merchant marine proper, and relied too heavily on the skills and man-power of subject groups to last. Moreover, just at the moment when Mamluk Egypt was absorbed into the Ottoman Empire, giving it direct access to the Red Sea for the first time, the Portuguese voyages of Discovery outflanked the entire Islamic world by establishing strategic ascendancy round the whole rim of the Indian Ocean in the early 16th century, with bases in East Africa, the Persian Gulf, the Indian subcontinent, and the Malay and Indonesian islands. Thereafter, international shipping lanes were permanently dominated by Western powers, depriving the Islamic Empires of the maritime commerce which had provided so much of the fortune of their predecessors. This development was all the more serious in that mediaeval Arab economies themselves had always prospered more in the sphere of exchange than of production, trade than manufactures; the discrepancy between the two was one of the basic reasons for their crisis in the later Middle Ages, and the success of European economic advance at their expense.[49] At the same time, the traditional Arab esteem for the merchant was now no longer shared by their Turkic successors: contempt for trade was a general hallmark of the ruling class of the new States, whose commercial policy was at best one of tolerance, and at worst one of discrimination against the mercantile classes in the towns.[50] The business climate of Constantinople, Isfahan and Delhi in the early modern

49. Claude Cahen has suggested, in an important note, that the balance of payments surpluses achieved by mediaeval Islam on its external account, partly because of its superior stock of precious metals, were themselves a disincentive to increase output of manufactures, since there was rarely a trade deficit of the type which stimulated West European economies of the same period to produce more exports: 'Quelques Mots sur le Déclin Commercial du Monde Musulman à la Fin du Moyen Age', in Cook (ed.), *Studies in the Economic History of the Middle East*, pp. 31–6.

50. For example, Mamluk Emirs in Syria deliberately unloaded their grain surpluses in the cities at the expense of urban traders, or forced them to purchase stocks at inflated prices, and frequently confiscated their capital: Lapidus, *Muslim Cities in the Later Middle Ages*, pp. 51–7.

epoch was never reminiscent of that of mediaeval Baghdad or Cairo. Alien minorities – Greek, Jewish, Armenian or Hindu – characteristically cornered trading and banking functions. Conversely, artisan guilds now made their appearance for the first time, in the Ottoman realm, as deliberate instruments of government control over the urban population,[51] which normally became repositories of theological and technical obscurantism. The legal systems of the late Empires, too, were typically re-clericalized, religious doctrines gaining enhanced administrative force over previously casual secular customs, with the passage of time.[52] Official Safavid bigotry was particularly intense.

Military rigidity, ideological zealotry and commercial lethargy thus became the usual norms of government in Turkey, Persia and India. The last generation of major Islamic States before European colonial expansion overwhelmed the Muslim world already bore witness to the twin pressures of the West. Economically surpassed from the Discoveries onwards, they still excelled for another century in war or conversion, from the Balkans to Bengal. Territorially, the bounds of Islam continued to widen in the Orient. But the new conversions in South and East Asia hid a demographic stagnation or recession within the combined lands of classical Muslim civilization. After 1600, the most optimistic calculations indicate a slight but actual decline in a total population of about 46 million in the great zone stretching from Morocco to Afghanistan, and the Sahara to Turkestan, over the next two centuries.[53] Proselytism in India or Indonesia, an extension in width of the Muslim world, could not compensate for its absence of demographic vitality in depth. The contrast with either Europe or China in the same epoch is unmistakable. The Islamic Empires of the 17th century, even in their hours of martial fervour or success, were at a concealed disadvantage within the pattern of populations in the Old World as a whole.

The Mughal Empire, with which Marx was specifically concerned,

51. Baer, 'Guilds in Middle Eastern History', pp. 27–9.
52. Schacht, *An Introduction to Islamic Law*, pp. 4, 89–90, 94; 'Law and Justice', *The Cambridge History of Islam*, II, p. 567.
53. Miquel, *L'Islam et Sa Civilisation*, pp. 280–3, who estimates that by 1800 there may have been a drop to some 43 million. These figures are subject to considerable caution, as Miquel emphasizes, because of the lack of reliable evidence. But the general balance-sheet is unlikely to be far wrong.

illustrates most of the motifs of the late Muslim State, although since it was furthest removed from Europe and ruled the least islamized population, it also presented in some ways a more varied and vital panorama than its Turkish or Persian homologues. Its administrative similarity to the Ottoman Empire had already struck Bernier in the 17th century. Agrarian land was subject to the sole economic and political power of the Emperor. The indigenous peasantry was guaranteed permanent and hereditary occupation of its plots (as in the Turkish system), but had no rights of disposal or alienation over them; tillers who failed to cultivate their holdings were liable to expulsion by the State.[54] There was no communal tenure in the villages, which were divided by social castes and great economic inequality.[55] The State always appropriated up to half of total peasant output, as its 'land-revenues'.[56] These were often paid in cash taxes, or deliveries in kind subsequently re-sold by the State, leading to widespread cultivation of commercial crops (wheat, cotton, sugar, indigo or tobacco). Land was relatively abundant and agrarian productivity not lower than in 20th century India; canal irrigation was insignificant, rain-water and local wells or ponds providing soil moisture.[57] The massive fiscal pressure of the Mughal State on the rural population, however, led to

54. Habib, *The Agrarian System of Mughal India*, pp. 113–18. The absence of any real conception of ownership in land was classically emphasized by W. More-land, *The Agrarian System of Moslem India*, Cambridge 1929, pp. 3–4, 63, who believed that it dated back to the prior Hindu epoch of Indian history.

55. Habib, *The Agrarian System of Mughal India*, pp. 119–24.

56. Habib, *The Agrarian System of Mughal India*, pp. 195–6, thinks that the level of surplus extraction by the central State was comparatively stable, as against Moreland, who had reckoned that the norm fluctuated from $\frac{1}{3}$ to $\frac{2}{3}$, according to the policy of respective rulers.

57. Perhaps 5 per cent of the cultivated land was irrigated under the Mughals: Maddison, *Class Structure and Economic Growth. India and Pakistan since the Moghuls*, London 1971, pp. 23–4. Marx believed that Indian agriculture was defined by an intensive irrigation, and that British colonialism would destroy traditional Indian society by industrializing it. Ironically, after the ephemeral railway-boom of the mid 19th century, the effects of British rule were the sym-metrical opposite. There was minimal implantation of industry in India by the British; on the other hand, much agriculture was for the first time converted to irrigation. By the end of the Raj, irrigated land had increased 8 times over, and covered a quarter of total acreage, including some spectacular canalization in the Punjab and Sind. See Maddison, p. 50.

spiralling usury and indebtedness in the villages, and increasing peasant flights.

The apex of the State apparatus itself was the elite *mansabdar* stratum, some 8,000 military officers graded in a complex ranking system, who were allocated the vast bulk of the land-revenues in the form of *jagirs* or temporary assignments, by the Emperor. In 1647, 445 of these received over 60 per cent of the total income of the State; 73 took some 37·6 per cent alone.[58] Ethnically, the *mansabdar* corps was predominantly, and predictably, alien in origin – mostly Persian, Turanian or Afghan. Some 70 per cent of Akhbar's *mansabdars* were foreign-born or sons of foreigners; the remainder were local 'Indian' Muslims or Hindu Rajputs. By 1700, the proportion of Indian-born Muslims had risen to perhaps 30 per cent of the total.[59] The degree of hereditary continuity was very limited: appointment to *mansabdar* rank was at the personal discretion of the Emperor. The corps possessed no horizontal social unity as an aristocratic order, although its top members were granted the title of 'nobles': its disparate components always remained conscious of their various ethnic origins, which characteristically gave rise to factions within it. They were held together only by vertical obedience to the imperial command. The *mansabdars* resided in cities and were obliged to maintain the cavalry army of 200,000 on which the military power of the Mughal State depended: the cost of the upkeep of these troops absorbed about two-thirds of their income from *jagir* assignments or salaries from the central treasury. The average tenure of a *jagir* was less than three years, and all were resumable at will by the Emperor, who constantly shuffled their holders to prevent them sinking regional roots. Interspersed with this system across the countryside were native *zamindars* or local rural potentates, commanding infantry retainers and castles, and licensed to collect a much smaller slice of the surplus from the peasantry, some 10 per cent of the land-revenues accruing to the State in Northern India.[60]

58. Habib, 'Potentialities of Capitalistic Development', pp. 54–5.
59. P. Spear, 'The Mughal "Mansabdari" System', in E. Leach and S. N. Mukherjee (ed.), *Elites in South Asia*, Cambridge 1970, pp. 8–11.
60. Habib, *The Agrarian System of Mughal India*, pp. 160–7ff.; 'Potentialities of Capitalistic Development', p. 38. Allowing for their divergent origins, there is a certain similarity between the respective structural position of the *mansabdar* and *zamindar* classes within the Mughal system and the *devshirme* and *timariot*

Agrarian rents were overwhelmingly consumed in the towns, where royal and *mansabdar* outlays on palaces, gardens, orchards, servants and luxuries were sumptuous. Urbanization was consequently relatively high, accounting for perhaps a tenth of the population. The major Indian cities at the start of the 17th century were sometimes reckoned by travellers larger than those of Europe. The urban work-force was largely Muslim, and artisanal crafts were numerous and skilled. These crafts gave rise in some areas to a putting-out system under the control of mercantile capital. But the only large manufactories, employing hired labour, were royal or 'noble' *karkhana*, which produced exclusively for household consumption.[61] Merchant fortunes were always liable to arbitrary confiscation by the sovereign and no proto-industrial capital ever developed. The Mughal State, principal instrument of economic exploitation of the ruling class, lasted for 150 years until it succumbed to peasant revolts, Hindu separatism, and British invasion.

V

Much compressed, such seem to be some of the central elements of Islamic social history. The character and course of Chinese civilization, on the other hand, appears to present a whole series of traits contrapuntal to Islamic development. There is no space here to discuss the long and complex evolution of Ancient China proper, from the bronze-age Shang epoch of 1400 B.C. onwards, down to the end of the Chou era in the 5th century B.C. and the formation of the unitary Ch'in State in the 3rd century B.C. It will be enough to summarize briefly the material legacies of a continuous record of literate civilization stretching back some two millennia before the final emergence of the Imperial

---

sectors of the Ottoman State apparatus: in both cases, a central military elite was superimposed on a local warrior stratum. On the other hand, their composition was contrasted: the Turkish *devshirme* formed an ex-Christian slave corps and the *timariots* were Muslim cavalrymen, while the Mughal *mansabdars* conversely formed a Muslim 'aristocracy' and the *ʒamindars* were Hindu regional exploiters. The relative honorific roles of each within the total political system were thus quite distinct.

61. Habib, 'Potentialities of Capitalistic Development', pp. 61–77.

State system which was to become the distinctive mark of Chinese political history as a whole.

The cradle of Sinic civilization was North-West China, whose economy was based on a dry cereal agriculture; the dominant crops of Ancient China were always millet, wheat and barley. Within its intensive settled agriculture, however, Chinese civilization early developed significant hydraulic systems for grain cultivation in the loess highlands and valleys of North-Western China; the first major contour canals for leading water off river-courses to irrigate fields were built during the Ch'in State in the 3rd century B.C.[1] In the lower-lying basin of the Yellow River further towards the North-East, the successor Han State subsequently erected an important series of dikes, dams and reservoirs for the complementary purpose of flood control and regulated release of water for agriculture;[2] square-pallet chain pumps were designed;[3] while terraced paddy-fields of rice seem to have emerged for the first time in the 1st century B.C., further south.[4] At this stage, however, dry cereal cultivation of millet and wheat was still overwhelmingly predominent in the rural economy. Both Ch'in and Han States also constructed imposing transport canals for the swift shipment of grain-taxes to their treasuries – probably the first to be built anywhere in the world: throughout Chinese history, in fact, the State was always to give priority to transport waterways, with their fiscal and military (logistic) functions, over irrigation systems proper, for agricultural purposes.[5] Quite apart from hydraulic engineering, however, key technical advances were registered in the countryside at an early date, in general well before their comparable appearance in Europe. The rotary-mill was invented about the same time as in the Roman West, in the 2nd century B.C. The wheel-barrow, on the other

1. For the three main types of hydraulic system in China, and their regional location, see the original analysis by Chi Ch'ao Ting, *Key Economic Areas in Chinese History*, New York 1963 (re-edition), pp. 12–21; and now the magisterial survey in J. Needham, *Science and Civilization in China*, Vol. IV/3 (*Civil Engineering and Nautics*), Cambridge 1971, pp. 217–27, 373–5.

2. Chi Ch'ao Ting, *Key Economic Areas in Chinese History*, pp. 89–92.

3. Needham, *Science and Civilization in China*, IV/2 (*Mechanical Engineering*), Cambridge 1965, pp. 344, 362.

4. Yi-Fu Tuan, *China*, London 1970, p. 83.

5. Needham, *Science and Civilization in China*, IV/3, p. 225.

hand, was discovered a millennium earlier than in Europe, in the 3rd century A.D.; the stirrup came into use at much the same time; equine traction was decisively improved with the emergence of modern collar-harness in the 5th century A.D.; segmental arch bridges were built by the 7th century A.D.[6] More strikingly still, techniques for casting iron were pioneered as early as the 6th–5th centuries B.C., while in Europe they came into use only in the later Middle Ages; and steels were actually produced from the 2nd century B.C. onwards.[7] Chinese metallurgy was thus far in advance of that of any other region of the world from an extremely early date. At the same time, three major manufactures were pioneered in Ancient China: silk was produced from the remotest origins of its history; paper was invented in the 1st–2nd century A.D.; and porcelain was perfected by the 5th century A.D.[8] This remarkable fund of technological acquisitions provided the material foundations for the first great dynastic Empire to reunify China durably after the regional strife and division of 300–600 A.D. – the T'ang State, which is generally taken as the coherent and decisive inception of Chinese imperial civilization proper.

The land system of the T'ang Empire was in many respects curiously close to the Asiatic archetype imagined by later European thinkers, including Marx. The State was juridically sole proprietor of the soil, according to the rule: 'Under the whole heaven every spot is the Emperor's ground.'[9] Agrarian cultivation was based on the so-called *chün-t'ien* or 'equal allotment' system, originally inherited from the Northern Wei, which was administratively enforced to a degree that has surprised subsequent historians. Fixed plots of land, in principle some 13·3 acres in extent, were granted by the State to peasant couples for the duration of their working life, with the obligation of paying taxes in kind – mainly grain and cloth – and providing prestations of

6. Needham, *Science and Civilization in China*, IV 2, pp. 190, 258–65ff., 312–27; IV 3, p. 184.

7. J. Needham, *The Development of Iron and Steel Technology in China*, London 1958, p. 9; steel was made by a combination of wrought iron and cast iron as early as the 6th century A.D.: pp. 26, 47.

8. Needham, *Science and Civilization in China*, I (*Introductory Orientations*), Cambridge 1954, pp. 111, 129.

9. D. Twitchett, *Financial Administration under the T'ang Dynasty*, Cambridge 1963, pp. 1, 194.

labour; a fifth of these plots, reserved for silk or hemp production, could be inherited, while the rest was resumed by the State at their retirement.[10] The central purposes of the system were to extend agrarian cultivation and to check the formation of large private estates by aristocratic landowners. State officials themselves were allocated substantial public domains for their own upkeep. Careful registration of all land-holdings and labour was integral to the system. The meticulous administrative control laid down across the countryside was duplicated, or rather intensified, inside the towns – starting with the imperial capital of Chang'an itself, which probably numbered more than 1,000,000 inhabitants. Chinese cities of the early T'ang period were rigorously planned and policed by the imperial State. They were usually geometrical creations, surrounded by moats and ramparts, and divided into rectangular wards which were sealed off from each other by walls with guarded gates for traffic by day, and a curfew between them at night: officialdom resided in a special precinct enclosed by a double wall from the rest of the city.[11] Transgression of these fortified compartments by townsfolk without permission was condignly punished.

The State machine which exercised this vigilance over town and country was originally controlled by a military aristocracy, which had won its position in the constant internecine wars of the preceding epoch, and was still in tradition and outlook a hereditary mounted nobility. The first century of the T'ang epoch, in fact, witnessed a spectacular wave of Chinese military conquests to the North and West. Manchuria and Korea were subjugated; Mongolia was pacified; and Chinese power was extended deep into Central Asia, as far as the region of Transoxiana and the Pamirs. This great expansion was largely the work of the T'ang cavalry, assiduously built up by a programme of elite horse-breeding at home, and commanded by a pugnacious aristocracy.[12] The security system of the new Empire, once gained, was

10. Twitchett, *Financial Administration under the T'ang Dynasty*, pp. 1–6. In densely populated regions, the size of allotments could fall to as little as 2 or 3 acres: pp. 4, 201. The system was never firmly enforced in the rice-growing districts of the South, where it was technically unsuitable for the larger labour demands of irrigated riziculture.

11. E. Balazs, *Chinese Civilization and Bureaucracy*, New Haven 1967, pp. 68–70.

12. J. Gernet, *Le Monde Chinois*, Paris 1972, pp. 217–19: this volume is

then entrusted to infantry colonies of divisional militia, endowed with lands for cultivation and charged with duties of defence; but from the later 7th century onwards, large permanent units became necessary to man the frontiers of the Empire. Strategic expansionism was accompanied by cultural cosmopolitanism; for the first time in Chinese history, major foreign influences shaped official ideology, with the ascent of Buddhism as a State religion. At the same time, however, a much deeper and more lasting change was gradually starting to alter the whole complexion of the State apparatus itself. For it was during the T'ang epoch that the characteristic civilian bureaucracy of imperial China was born. From the mid-7th century onwards, an elite of higher personnel within the governmental system started for the first time to be recruited by a public examination system, although the great majority of posts were still filled by hereditary privilege or recommendation from traditional noble families. The 'censorate' comprised a separate column of civil officials entrusted with criticizing and checking the work of the main body of the imperial bureaucracy, to ensure correct standards of performance and policy.[13] By the mid T'ang period, the political rise of the civilian officialdom through the examination system, whose prestige had come to attract even magnate candidates, was unmistakable. The military branch of the State apparatus, while it was later to provide a long succession of usurper generals, was never again to become functionally predominant in the Chinese Empire. Nomadic conquerors – Turkic, Mongol or Manchu – were in subsequent epochs to over-run China and base their political power on their own garrison troops: but these interloping armies remained outside the normal administrative government of the country, which always survived them. A lettered bureaucracy, by contrast, came to be the permanent hall-mark of the Chinese imperial State.

The T'ang agrarian system in practice disintegrated fairly soon: peasant vagrancy to unoccupied and unregistered land combined with the reclamation schemes of the rich and the sabotage of officials bent on accumulating land themselves, to break down the *chün-t'ien* regulations. Then in 756, there occurred the fateful rebellion of the barbarian

perhaps the best recent overview of Chinese history as a whole, in a European language.

13. R. Dawson, *Imperial China*, London 1972, pp. 56–8.

general An Lu-Shan, just at a point when Chinese external power had been weakened by Arab and Uighur victories in Turkestan. Dynastic stability temporarily collapsed; frontiers contracted with the revolt of subject peoples; there was a general break-down of domestic order. The acute crisis of the mid-8th century completely disrupted the registration schedules of the land allotment system, and in practice effectively ended the *chün-t'ien* order in the countryside. Within five years of An Lu-Shan's rebellion, the number of registered households fell by 80 per cent.[14] Large private estates or *chang-yuan* now emerged, owned by squires, bureaucrats or officers. These were not consolidated latifundia, but collections of lots tilled by peasant tenants, hired labour or occasionally slaves, under the supervision of farm bailiffs. Rents typically amounted to half the produce for tenants on these estates, a considerably higher rate of exploitation than that extracted by the State from the *chün-t'ien* plots.[15] The fiscal system simultaneously shifted from fixed poll taxes in kind and *corvées* to graduated levies on property and land area, paid in cash and grain; indirect taxes on commodities became increasingly lucrative, as commercial transactions and a monetarized economy spread.[16] China prior to the T'ang epoch had been largely a barter economy, and the T'ang economy itself was chronically short of copper for coinage, relying partly on silk as a medium of exchange. The suppression of Buddhist monasteries in the mid-9th century, however, dethesaurized large quantities of copper and relieved monetary circulation. This move in turn was inspired partly by the xenophobic reaction which marked later T'ang rule. Dynastic recovery after the crisis of the mid-8th century was accompanied by a new hostility to alien religious institutions, which terminated the dominance of Buddhism within the ideological complex of the Chinese State. The secular conservatism of Confucian thought, moralizing and anti-enthusiast, replaced it as the main official doctrine of the imperial order. Henceforward, the Chinese Empire was always to be distin-guished by the basically lay character of its system of legitimation. The drive behind this cultural change came, in its turn, largely from the Southern gentry who supplied the most important contingents to the civilian bureaucracy: the imperial retreat from Central Asia and

14. Twitchett, *Financial Administration under the T'ang Dynasty*, pp. 12–17.
15. *Ibid.*, pp. 18–20.   16. *Ibid.*, pp. 24–65.

Manchuria-Korea led to a general weakening of the old military aristocracy of the North-West, with its greater receptivity to foreign influences, and to a strengthening of the position of the official literati within the State.[17] At the same time, population and wealth moved steadily southwards towards the Lower Yangtze valley. Intensive riziculture now started for the first time to acquire major importance, with the development of transplantation beds which eliminated the need for fallows and hence greatly increased output.

In the succeeding Sung epoch, from the 10th to the 13th centuries, the whole rural order thus took on a new shape. The final phase of T'ang rule, marked by disintegration of central dynastic power, spreading regional rebellions, and recurrent barbarian invasions from the North, saw the disappearance of the traditional military aristocracy of the North-West altogether. The Chinese ruling class in the Sung State, which was largely new in immediate social composition, derived its ancestry from the civilian officialdom of the preceding dynasty: it now became a broadened and stabilized scholar gentry. The State apparatus was divided into three functional sectors – civilian, financial and military – with specialist careers in each; provincial administration was likewise reorganized and strengthened. The imperial bureaucracy that resulted was much larger than that of the T'ang epoch, doubling in size during the first century of Sung rule. A regular bureaucratic cursus was established in the 10th century, with entry controlled by examination and promotion determined by merit ratings and sponsorship recommendations. Training for the degree system became much more rigorous, and the average age of graduates rose from the mid-twenties to the mid-thirties. Examinate candidates soon came to dominate every sector of the State except for the army; military careers formally possessed equal rating with civilian, but in practice were far less honoured.[18] By the 11th century, the majority of responsible officials were graduates, who typically resided in towns and controlled rural properties managed by stewards and worked by dependent tenants. The largest such estates came to be concentrated in the new regions of Kiangsu, Anhwei and Chekiang, the homes of the bulk of doctoral

17. Gernet, *Le Monde Chinois*, pp. 255–7.
18. Twitchett, 'Chinese Politics and Society from the Bronze Age to the Manchus', in A. Toynbee (ed.), *Half the World*, London 1973, p. 69.

candidates and higher functionaries of the State.[19] The peasants who cultivated the holdings of these landlords owed dues in labour and kind, while their mobility was restricted by their tenancy contracts. There is no doubt of the critical importance of this estate-system, with its tied labour, in Sung agriculture. On the other hand, it is possible that up to 60 per cent or more of the total rural population were now small-holders in their own right, outside the perimeter of the estates.[20] It was they who paid the bulk of rural taxes. State ownership of all land was nominally retained in Sung legal theory, but was in practice from now on a dead letter.[21] Henceforward private agrarian property, although subject to certain important restrictions, was to characterize Chinese imperial society down to the end.

Its social ascendancy coincided with great advances in the Chinese countryside. The shift in overall settlement and cultivation towards the rice-producing Lower Yangtze valley was accompanied by the rapid development of a third type of hydraulic system – the drainage of alluvial marsh lands, and recovery of lake-bottoms. There was a spectacular rise in the total level of irrigative projects, whose annual average incidence during the Sung epoch more than trebled over that of any previous dynasty.[22] The Sung landlords invested in large-scale reclamations over and above public projects. Indeed, the advent of

19. Twitchett, *Land Tenure and the Social Order in T'ang and Sung China*, London 1962, pp. 26–7.

20. Twitchett, *Land Tenure and the Social Order*, pp. 28–30. The problem of the real balance between the *chang-yuan* estate sector and small-holder agriculture within the Sung economy is one of the most controversial in current historiographic writing on the epoch. In his important recent work, Elvin argues that Chinese 'manorialism', based on 'serf' labour, was dominant in most of the countryside, although he concedes that the number of peasants outside estates was 'not inconsiderable': *The Pattern of the Chinese Past*, London 1973, pp. 78–83. However, he dismisses the quantitative estimates based on the population registers of the time, without offering alternative calculations, and relies for much of his interpretation on two Japanese scholars, Kusano and Sudō, whose views do not appear to be uncontested in their own country. Twitchett, by contrast, is critical of the use of such terms as 'manorialism' to describe the *chang-yuan*, and lays greater stress on the relative importance of Sung small-holders. The present state of evidence does not seem to permit firm conclusions.

21. Twitchett, *Land Tenure and the Social Order*, p. 25.

22. See the computations in Needham, *Science and Civilization in China*, IV/3, pp. 282–4, refined on the basis of calculations initially made by Chi Ch'ao Ting, *Key Economic Areas in Chinese History*, p. 36.

private property in land was concomitant with the dominance of irrigated riziculture within the Chinese agrarian economy as a whole: both were new phenomena of the Sung epoch. The great majority of irrigation works were henceforward always local in character, needing little or no central intervention by the State:[23] landowner or villager initiatives were responsible for the bulk of them, once the much more productive cycles of wet agriculture were established in the Yangtze region. It was in this epoch that more complex water-driven machinery for pumping, milling and threshing became generalized. Field implements – ploughs, hoes, spades and sickles – spread and improved. Champa early-ripening rice was imported from Vietnam; wheat yields multiplied.[24] Commercial crops such as hemp, tea, and sugar were planted. In all, agrarian productivity increased very rapidly, and with it demographic density. The population of China, which had been virtually stationary at about 50 million since the 2nd century B.C., perhaps doubled between the mid-8th and the 10–13th centuries, to some 100 million.[25]

Meanwhile, dramatic industrial progress had been made in mining and metallurgy. The 11th century saw mounting production of coal, involving much larger investments of capital and labour than traditional fuels, and reaching formidable levels of output. Demand was fanned by decisive advances in the iron industry, whose technology was now extremely sophisticated (the piston-bellows was standard equipment), and whose foundries were perhaps the largest anywhere in the world down to the 19th century. In 1078, Northern Sung iron production has been reckoned at somewhere between 75–150,000 tons, a twelve-fold increase in two hundred years: it is possible that Chinese iron output in the 11th century was approximately equivalent to total European production at the start of the 18th century.[26] It was this swift growth of the iron industry which rendered possible the multiplication

23. Dwight Perkins, *Agricultural Development in China 1368–1968*, Edinburgh 1969, pp. 171–2. Perkins's study is concerned with post-Yuan China, but there is every reason to believe that his judgement holds for the whole post-T'ang epoch.

24. Twitchett, *Land Tenure and the Social Order*, pp. 30–1.

25. Gernet, *Le Monde Chinois*, p. 281.

26. R. Hartwell, 'A Revolution in the Chinese Iron and Coal Industries during the Northern Sung, 920–1126 A.D.', *The Journal of Asian Studies*, XXI, No. 2, February 1962, pp. 155, 160.

of the agrarian tools spreading through the countryside, and the enlarged manufacture of weaponry. The same period witnessed an astonishing cluster of new inventions. Fire-arms were pioneered for war; movable type was designed for printing; the magnetic compass was used as a navigation instrument; and mechanical clocks were constructed.[27] The three or four most celebrated technical innovations of Renaissance Europe were thus anticipated long in advance in China. Pound-locks for canalization, stern-post rudders and paddle-wheels for shipping, further improved transport.[28] The ceramic industry developed very rapidly, porcelain ware for the first time possibly overtaking silk as the main export commodity of the Empire. The circulation of copper coinage was vastly increased, and paper notes started to be issued by both private bankers and the State. This combined rural and industrial progress unleashed a tremendous wave of urbanization. By 1100, China possessed perhaps as many as five cities with a population of over 1,000,000.[29] These great agglomerations were much more the product of a spontaneous economic growth rather than deliberate bureaucratic fiat, and were characterized by a much freer urban layout.[30] Curfew was abolished in the Sung capital of Kaifeng in the 11th century, and the old ward compartments within the imperial cities gave way to a more fluid street-system. The new mercantile communities in the towns profited from the advent of a cash-crop agriculture, the boom in mining, the rise of metallurgical industries, the discovery of new devices in banking and credit. The output of copper currency rose up to 20 times over the levels of the T'ang epoch. There was a growing mastery of long-distance trade by sea, assisted by the numerous advances in marine engineering and the creation for the first time of an imperial navy.

The dramatic shift in the total configuration of the Chinese economy

27. Needham, *Science and Civilization in China*, I, pp. 134, 231; IV/2, pp. 446–65; IV/3, p. 562. In practice, block type always predominated in Imperial China, because ideographic script minimized the advantages of movable type relative to it: Gernet, *Le Monde Chinois*, pp. 292–6.

28. Needham, *Science and Civilization in China*, IV/2, pp. 417–27; IV/3, pp. 350, 357–60, 641–2.

29. E. Kracke, 'Sung Society: Change within Tradition', *The Far Eastern Quarterly*, XIV, August 1955, No. 4, pp. 481–2.

30. See Tuan, *China*, pp. 132–5.

in the Sung epoch was accentuated with the conquest of Northern China by the Jürchen nomads in the mid-12th century. Sealed off from the traditional Central Asian and Mongolian hinterland of Sinic civilization, the Sung Empire in South China was turned from an inland to a maritime orientation, that was quite new in Chinese experience: while within it, the specific weight of urban trade grew commensurately. The result was that for the first time in history, agriculture ceased to provide the bulk of State revenues in China. Imperial income from commercial taxes and monopolies was already equal in volume to that from land taxes in the 11th century; in the Southern Sung State of the later 12th and 13th centuries, commercial revenues greatly exceeded agrarian revenues.³¹ This new fiscal balance reflected not merely the growth of domestic and foreign trade, but also the enlargement of the manufacturing base of the whole economy, the expansion of mining, and the spread of cash cropping in agriculture. The Islamic Empire of the Abbasid Caliphate had for a time been the richest and most powerful civilization in the world, in the 8th and 9th centuries; the Chinese Empire of the Sung epoch was unquestionably the wealthiest and most advanced economy on the globe in the 11th and 12th centuries, and its florescence was based far more securely on the diversified production of its agriculture and industry, rather than mainly on the exchange transactions of international trade. The economic dynamism of the Sung State was accompanied by an intellectual ferment, which combined veneration for the Ancient Chinese past with new explorations in mathematics, astronomy, medicine, cartography, archaeology and other disciplines.³² The scholar-gentry which now governed China was characterized by Mandarin contempt for physical sports and martial exercises, and a deliberate cult of aesthetic and intellectual pastimes. Cosmic speculations were com-

31. Gernet, *Le Monde Chinois*, p. 285.

32. Gernet, among others, speaks of a Sung 'Renaissance' comparable to that of Europe in this epoch: *Le Monde Chinois*, pp. 290–1, 296–302. But the analogy is an untenable one, for Chinese scholars never ceased to be preoccupied with the Ancient past: there was no sharp process of cultural *rupture* such as defined the Renaissance rediscovery of classical Antiquity in Europe. Elsewhere Gernet himself warns eloquently against the abusive importation of periods and notions proper to Europe into Chinese history, and insists on the need to forge new concepts specific and appropriate to Sinic experience: *Le Monde Chinois*, pp. 571–2.

bined with a systematized neo-confucianism in the culture of the Sung epoch.

The Mongol conquest of China in the 13th century was to test the resilience of the whole socio-economic system that had matured in this halcyon age. Considerable areas of Northern China were initially 'pastoralized' by the new nomadic rulers, under whom agriculture generally declined; later efforts by Yuan Emperors to redress the agrarian situation met with little success.[33] Industrial innovation largely halted; the most notable technical advance of the Mongol epoch seems, perhaps suggestively, to have been the casting of metal-barrel cannon.[34] The tax-burden on the rural and urban masses increased, while hereditary registration of their occupations was introduced, to immobilize the class structure of the country. Rents and interest rates remained high, and peasant indebtedness steadily rose. Although the Southern landlords had rallied to the invading Mongol armies, the Yuan dynasty showed little trust in the Chinese mandarinate. The examination system was abolished, central imperial authority was strengthened, provincial administration reorganized, and fiscal collection farmed to foreign corporations of Uighurs, on whom the Mongol rulers relied heavily for administrative and business skills.[35] On the other hand, Yuan policies promoted mercantile enterprise and stimulated commerce. The integration of China into the far-flung Mongol imperial system led to an influx of Islamic traders from Central Asia and an expansion of international shipping. A national paper currency was introduced. Large-scale coastal transport for the supply of grain to the North, where a new capital had been founded at Peking, was instituted; while the monumental Grand Canal, linking the economic and political centres of the country by a continuous inland waterway, was completed. But the ethnic discrimination of the dynasty soon antagonized much of the gentry class, while the intensity of its financial exactions, the depreciation of its fiduciary issue, and the spread of oppressive landlordism drove the peasantry into armed revolt. The result was the

33. H. F. Schurmann, *Economic Structure of the Yuan Dynasty*, Cambridge USA 1956, pp. 8–9, 29–30, 43–8.

34. Needham, *Science and Civilization in China*, I, p. 142.

35. Schurmann, *Economic Structure of the Yuan Dynasty*, pp. 8, 27–8; Dawson, *Imperial China*, pp. 186, 197.

social and national upheaval which ended Mongol rule in the 14th century, and installed the Ming dynasty.

The new State represented, with some significant modifications, a reinvigoration of the traditional political structure of scholar-gentry rule. The examination system was promptly restored; but a regional quota system to ensure against Southern monopoly of offices now had to be built into it, reserving some 40 per cent of doctorates to Northern candidates. Large Yangtze landowners were brought to the new Ming capital at Nanking, where their enforced residence facilitated government control; while the Imperial Secretariat, traditionally a check on the arbitrary will of the Emperor, was abolished. The whole authoritarian cast of the State was increased under Ming rule, whose secret police and surveillance systems were much more ruthless and extensive than those of the Sung dynasty.[36] Court politics were increasingly dominated by a swollen corps of eunuchs (definitionally outside Confucian norms of paternal authority and responsibility), and fierce factional struggles. The solidarity of the scholar-bureaucracy was weakened by insecurity of tenure and division of duties, while the age of graduation through the degree system grew steadily later. A very large army of 3,000,000 was initially created, much of which was subsequently diluted into a network of military colonists. The main fiscal innovation of the Ming State was the systematic imposition of public labour services on the rural and urban population, which was organized into carefully supervised 'community' units to execute them.

In the countryside, the restrictive tenancy contracts of the Sung epoch tended to lapse,[37] while the hereditary occupational registers of the Yuan regime were maintained, if in a loosened form. With the re-establishment of civil peace and the relaxation of tenancies, rural forces of production now recorded prodigious advances once again. A huge programme of agrarian rehabilitation was officially launched by the founder of the Ming dynasty, the Hongwu Emperor, to make good the devastations of Mongol rule and the destructions caused by the up-

36. Dawson, *Imperial China*, pp. 214–15, 218–19; Twitchett, 'Chinese Politics and Society', pp. 72–3.

37. This at least is the usual view. Elvin dates the end of the 'servile' tenancy system much later – to the early Ch'ing epoch, which he regards as the first period in which small-ownership became generalized in the countryside: *The Pattern of the Chinese Past*, pp. 247–50.

heavals which ended it. Reclamation of land was organized, hydraulic works were restored and extended, and an unprecedented reforestation was accomplished at the instructions of the imperial State.[38] The results were swift and spectacular. Within six years of the overthrow of the Yuan, the volume of grain taxes received by the central treasury had nearly trebled. The initial impetus given to the rural economy by this reconstruction from above set off extremely rapid agricultural growth from below. Irrigated riziculture steadily expanded and improved in the valleys and plains, with the spread of early-ripening strains and double-cropping outwards from the Lower Yangtze to Hopei, Hunan and Fukien; in the South-West, Yunnan was colonized. Marginal lands in the South were ploughed with wheat, barley and millet adapted from the North. Commercial crops such as indigo, sugar and tobacco were grown on a much broader scale. The population of China, which had probably fallen back to some 65–80 million under Mongol rule, now grew rapidly once again, to somewhere between 120 and 200 million by 1600, as a consequence of this progress.[39] In the towns, silk-weaving, ceramics and sugar-refining underwent notable development; while cotton textiles for the first time came into popular use, replacing traditional hemp garments. The adoption of the new draperies by the peasantry made possible the creation of major manu- facturing centres for cloth production: by the end of the Ming era, the Sungkiang region grouped perhaps some 200,000 craftsmen in its textile industry. Inter-regional trade increasingly knitted the country together, while there was a pronounced shift towards a new monetary system. Paper currency was abandoned because of successive devalua- tions soon after the mid-15th century; eventually, an increasing volume of silver was imported from America (via the Philippines) and Japan, which came to form the dominant medium of exchange within China, until in the end the fiscal system was largely converted to it.

The great initial surge of the Ming economy, however, was not sustained in the second century of the dynasty's rule. The first checks to its growth became evident in agriculture: from about 1520 onwards,

38. Gernet, *Le Monde Chinois*, pp. 341–2.
39. Ping-Ti Ho, *Studies on the Population of China 1368–1953*, Cambridge USA 1969, pp. 101, 277; Perkins, *Agricultural Development in China*, pp. 16, 194–201, 208–9.

land prices started to fall, as the profitability of rural investment declined for the gentry class.[40] Population growth now seems to have slowed down too. The towns, on the other hand, still outwardly exhibited great commercial prosperity, with improved methods of production in some older manufactures and increased supplies of bullion. But at the same time, industrial technology on a more fundamental plane generally ceased to display any fresh dynamism. No new urban inventions of major importance seem to have been recorded under Ming rule; while some earlier advances (clocks and pound-locks) were relinquished or forgotten.[41] The textile industry progressed from hemp to cotton as a raw material; but in doing so, it abandoned the mechanical spinning wheels in use for hemp cloths in the 14th century – a critical technical regression. Organizationally too, whereas Sung rural hemp-cloth production had developed a putting-out system under merchant control, rural cotton manufactures typically reverted to a simple cottage industry in the countryside.[42] Naval expansion reached its apogee in the early 15th century, when Chinese junks of tonnages far beyond any European vessels of the age traversed the oceans to Arabia and Africa; but these maritime expeditions were abandoned by mid-century, and the imperial navy dismantled wholesale, in a gentry-bureaucratic back-lash which presaged a wider official involution and obscurantism.[43] The nativist and restorationist climate of Ming culture, originally formed in xenophobic reaction against Mongol rule, seems to have led to a philological and literary 'displacement' of intellectual activity, which was accompanied by declining interest in science and technique. Politically, the Ming imperial State soon reproduced a more or less familiar parabola: palace extravagance, administrative corruption and landlord tax-evasion depleted its treasury, leading to increased pressure on the peasantry, whose labour *corvées* were commuted to cash taxes that steadily escalated as the regime came under external assault. Japanese piracy infested the seas, effectively closing the interlude of Chinese maritime power; Mongol raids were renewed in the North, with great destruction; and Japanese expeditionary attacks into Korea

40. Gernet, *Le Monde Chinois*, pp. 370–1.

41. Needham, *Science and Civilization in China*, IV/2, p. 508; IV/3, p. 360.

42. Elvin, *The Pattern of the Chinese Past*, pp. 195–9, 162, 274–6.

43. Needham, *Science and Civilization in China*, IV/3, pp. 524–7, summarizes current hypotheses about the reasons for this precipitous change.

were resisted only by massive outlays on the imperial armies.[44] The economic and demographic growth of the country thus gradually came to a halt during the 16th century, with the political decline of the government and the military bill for its incompetence. By the early 17th century, as the first Manchu incursions struck into North-Eastern China, domestic security was already crumbling within the Ming realm, as famines ravaged the countryside and desertions undermined the army. Usurper revolts and peasant insurrections were soon billowing across the landscape, from Shensi and Szechuan to Kiangsu.

The Manchu conquest was thus already prepared by the internal condition of China under the last Ming Emperors: long drawn-out attacks over two generations took the Tungusic Banners from Mukden to Canton. By 1681, the whole of the Chinese mainland had been over-run. The new Ch'ing dynasty, once installed, was to repeat much the same economic cycle as its predecessor, on a wider scale. Politically, its rule was a mixture of Yuan and Ming traditions. Ethnic separatism was maintained by the Manchu ruling class, which garrisoned the country with its own Banner regiments and monopolized top military commands in the State.[45] Manchu governor-generals, commanding two provinces at a time, typically overlaid Chinese governors in charge of the administration of single provinces. But the Chinese gentry class was basically left in possession of the civil bureaucracy, and the examination system was further refined to equalize provincial representation. Traditional cultural censorship by the Imperial State was tightened. For nearly a century, from 1683 to 1753, Manchu rule lowered taxes, checked corruption, maintained internal peace and furthered colonization. The spread of American root crops via the Philippines – maize, potatoes, peanuts, sweet potatoes – permitted the agrarian conquest of the thin-soiled hills for the first time. Peasant migration into forested uplands, hitherto inhabited by tribal peoples, proceeded rapidly, reclaiming large tracts of land for cultivation. Rice strains were still further improved, to yield crops in less than half the

44. For the vicissitudes of the later Ming regime, see Dawson, *Imperial China*, pp. 247–9, 256–7.

45. Chinese 'Green Banner' troops formed a subordinate arm of the Ch'ing State. The dualism between Manchu and Chinese regiments was maintained down to the last years of the dynasty, at the turn of the 20th century: V. Purcell, *The Boxer Uprising*, Cambridge 1963, pp. 20–4.

time taken by the first early-ripening varieties of the Sung epoch. Agrarian acreage and productivity thus once again rose steeply, permitting an explosive demographic increase, which this time surpassed all previous records. The population of China doubled or trebled between 1700 and 1850, when it reached 430 million.[46] While the total population of Europe increased from some 144 million in 1750 to 193 million in 1800, the population of China rose by one calculation from 143 million in 1741 to 360 million in 1812: the more intensive yields of riziculture, always higher than those of dry cereal farming, rendered possible a demographic density without parallel in the Occident.[47] At the same time, Manchu military conquests – which for the first time in history brought Mongolia, Sinkiang and Tibet under effective Chinese control – significantly increased the potential territory available for agrarian cultivation and settlement. China's inland frontiers were extended deep into Central Asia by Ch'ing troops and officials.

By the 19th century, however, relative economic stagnation on the land had set in. Soil erosion was washing away much hill farming and inundating irrigation systems; super-exploitative landlordism and usury were rampant in the most fertile regions; and peasant over-population was starting to be evident in the villages.[48] Manchu military expansion and court extravagance, in the reign of the Ch'ien Lung Emperor in the latter half of the 18th century, had by now restored fiscal pressures to intolerable levels. In 1795, the first great peasant insurrection broke out in the North-West, and was suppressed with difficulty after eight years of fighting. Soon, too, urban manufactures entered a period of growing crisis. The 18th century had witnessed a renewed commercial prosperity in the towns. Textiles, porcelain, silk, paper, tea and sugar had all boomed during the Ch'ing peace. Foreign trade increased considerably, pulled by new European demand for Chinese wares, although at the end of the century it still only yielded about one-sixth of the tax-receipts from internal trade. But there was no qualitative change in

46. Ping-Ti Ho, *Studies on the Population of China*, pp. 208–15.

47. Gernet, *Le Monde Chinois*, p. 424. Even today, average international rice yields are some 75 per cent higher per acre than corn yields; in the 18th century, the advantages of Chinese rice over European wheat were much greater.

48. Dawson, *Imperial China*, pp. 301–2; Ho, *Studies on the Population of China*, pp. 217–21.

the pattern of Chinese industry. The great siderurgical advances of the Sung epoch had not been followed by any comparable progress in early modern China: there was no development of a producer-goods industry as such. The consumer industries, which from the Ming era onwards were always the most buoyant, did not generate any technological breakthrough either in the Ch'ing epoch; nor had the use of wage-labour significantly expanded within them by the early 19th century. The overall balance between urban and rural sectors of the economy under Manchu rule was indicated by the massive predominance of land and poll taxes in the fiscal system; down to the end of the 18th century they accounted for 70–80 per cent of total revenues of the Ch'ing State.[49] Moreover, from the mid-19th century onwards, European imperialist expansion for the first time started to attack traditional Chinese trade and manufactures, and to dislocate the whole defense apparatus of the Ch'ing State. The initial form of Occidental pressure was essentially commercial: the illicit opium traffic conducted by English companies from the second decade of the 19th century onwards in Southern China created an external trade deficit for the Manchu government, as narcotic imports soared. A growing balance of payments crisis was compounded by the fall in silver values on the world market, which led to a depreciation of Chinese currency and mounting domestic inflation. The Ch'ing bid to halt the opium trade was broken by armed force, in the Anglo-Chinese War of 1841–2.

These economic and military setbacks, accompanied by disquieting ideological penetration from abroad, were then followed by the great social earthquake of the Taiping Rebellion. For fifteen years, from 1850 to 1864, this vast peasant and plebeian insurrection – far the largest popular revolt anywhere in the world throughout the 19th century – shook the whole Empire to its foundations. Most of Central China was conquered by the soldiers of the 'Kingdom of Heaven', inspired by the egalitarian and puritan ideals of Taiping doctrine. North China, meanwhile, was convulsed by the separate rural risings of the Nien rebels; while oppressed ethnic and religious minorities – above all Muslim communities – exploded into revolt in Kweichow, Yunnan, Shensi, Kansu and Sinkiang. The ferocious wars of repression unleashed by the Ch'ing State against these successive uprisings of the poor lasted for

49. Gernet, *Le Monde Chinois*, p. 424.

nearly three decades. It was not until 1878 that Manchu operations were completed, with the final 'pacification' of Central Asia; the total casualties of these gigantic struggles were perhaps some 20–30 million, and agrarian destruction was commensurate. The Taiping Rebellion and its concomitants marked the irreversible decline of the Manchu political system. The Imperial State attempted to redress its finances by new commercial taxes, whose combined value rose some seven times between 1850 and 1910: a burden which further weakened domestic industries just as they were hit by full-scale foreign competition.[50] English and North American cotton textiles swamped native production; Indian and Ceylonese tea ruined local plantations; Japanese and Italian silks captured traditional export markets. Imperialist military pressure steadily tightened, culminating in the Sino-Japanese war of 1894–5. Foreign humiliations provoked domestic turbulence (Boxer Rebellion), which led to further foreign intervention. The Ch'ing State, tottering under these multiple blows, was finally demolished with the republican revolution of 1911, in which social and national elements once again mingled.

The concluding agony and demise of Imperial rule in China impressed on European observers of the 19th century the idea of an essentially stagnant society, collapsing before the inrush of the dynamic West. The spectacle of the late Ch'ing debacle was nevertheless in a longer view deceptive. For the course of Chinese imperial history as a whole, from the T'ang to the Ch'ing epochs, reveals in certain basic respects an emphatically cumulative development: the enormous increase in the population of the country, which jumped from some 65,000,000 or so in 1400 to some 430,000,000 in 1850 – a demographic record greatly surpassing that of Europe in the same epoch – testifies by itself to the scale of the expansion of the forces of production in Imperial China after the Yuan epoch. The agricultural advances achieved in early modern China were, in any secular perspective, remarkable. The enormous demographic growth, which multiplied the population six-fold in the course of five centuries, seems to have been constantly matched by increased grain production down to the very end of the imperial order itself: per capita output, in fact, was probably

50. Gernet, *Le Monde Chinois*, pp. 485–6.

relatively steady from 1400 down to 1900.[51] The great absolute increase in grain production registered over this half millennium has been attributed in approximately equal measure to quantitative expansion of cultivated acreage, and qualitative improvement of yield ratios, each of which seems to have been responsible for about half the total growth in output.[52] Within the yield share of this progress, in turn, probably half the improvement registered was due to better seed strains, double-cropping and new plant varieties; while the other half was traceable to increased water-control and fertilizer use.[53] At the end of this long evolution, despite the disastrous final years of Ch'ing rule, the levels of productivity in Chinese riziculture were far higher than those of other Asian countries such as India or Thailand. Yet the whole pattern of agrarian development was virtually devoid of significant *technological* improvements, after the Sung epoch.[54] Grain production was raised, again and again, by more extensive cultivation of land, more intensive application of labour, more variegated planting of seeds, and more widespread use of irrigation and fertilization. Otherwise, the stock of rural technology remained stationary.

Property relations, too, may have altered comparatively little after the Sung epoch, although research into them is still fragmentary and uncertain. One recent estimate is that the overall rate of tenancy by landless peasants may actually have been virtually constant, at some 30 per cent, from the 11th to the 19th centuries.[55] The Ch'ing State left behind it a configuration in the countryside that was, in fact, an expressive summation of the secular trends of Chinese agrarian history. In the 1920's and 1930's, perhaps 50 per cent of the Chinese peasantry were owners of the land they occupied, 30 per cent were tenants and another 20 per cent were both proprietors and tenants.[56] Usury was so widespread that a nominal owner was 'often little more than the tenant of a money-lender'.[57] Three-quarters of the land worked by tenant cultivators under Ch'ing rule was leased at fixed rents in kind

51. Perkins, *Agricultural Development in China*, pp. 14–15, 32.
52. *Ibid.*, pp. 33, 37. 53. *Ibid.*, pp. 38–51, 60–73.
54. *Ibid.*, pp. 56–8, 77. A rare exception seems to have been the introduction of the windmill, first recorded in the early 17th century.
55. Perkins, *Agricultural Development in China*, pp. 98–102.
56. R. H. Tawney, *Land and Labour in China*, London 1937, p. 34.
57. *Ibid.*, p. 36.

or cash, formally permitting improvements in productivity to accrue to the direct producer; one-quarter was governed by harvest-sharing arrangements, mostly in the poorer regions of the North where tenancy was least important.[58] At the outside, some 30–40 per cent of the rural product was marketed by the end of the Ch'ing epoch.[59] Landlord estates, concentrated in the Yangtze region, the South and Manchuria, covered the bulk of the most productive land: 10 per cent of the rural population owned 53 per cent of the cultivated soil, and the size of the average gentry property was 128 times that of the average peasant plot.[60] Three-quarters of landlords were absentee owners. The cities typically formed centres for distinct, concentric circles of agrarian property and production: suburban land monopolized by merchants, officials and gentry and devoted to industrial or horticultural crops, succeeded by commercialized rice or wheat fields dominated by the gentry, and finally by subsistence peasant plots in the highest or most inaccessible regions beyond. Provincial towns had multiplied during Ch'ing rule, but Chinese society was proportionately more urbanized in the Sung epoch, over half a millenium earlier.[61]

For the growth in the forces of production in Imperial China appears, in effect, to have taken a curiously spiral form after the great socio-economic revolutions of the Sung age in the 10–13th centuries. It repeated its motions on ascending levels, without ever twisting away into a new figure altogether, until finally this dynamic recurrence was broken and overwhelmed by forces external to the traditional social formation. The paradox of this peculiar movement of Chinese history in the early modern epoch is that most of the purely technical pre-conditions for a capitalist industrialization were achieved far earlier in China than they were in Europe. China possessed a comprehensive and decisive technological lead over the Occident by the later Middle Ages, anticipating by centuries virtually every one of the key inventions in material production whose conjugation was to release the economic

58. Perkins, *Agricultural Development in China*, pp. 104–6.

59. *Ibid.*, pp. 114–15, 136.

60. Ho, *Studies on the Population of China*, p. 222.

61. Elvin, *The Pattern of the Chinese Past*, pp. 176–8: the percentage of the population living in cities of over 100,000 inhabitants was perhaps some 6 to 7·5 in the 12th century, as against 4 in 1900.

dynamism of Renaissance Europe. The whole development of Sinic imperial civilization, indeed, can in a sense be seen as the most grandiose demonstration and profound experience of the power, and impotence, of technique in history.[62] For the great, unprecedented breakthroughs of the Sung economy – above all in metallurgy – spent themselves in the subsequent epochs: the radical transformation of industry and society they promised never occurred. In this respect, everything points to the Ming epoch as the crux of the Chinese conundrum, which has still to be solved by future historians: for it was at this point that, despite impressive initial advances on land and sea, the mechanisms of scientific and technological growth in the towns ultimately appear to have stopped or gone into reverse.[63] From the early 16th century onwards, just as the Renaissance of the Italian cities was spreading outwards to encompass Western Europe as a whole, the towns in China ceased to provide fundamental innovations or impetus within the Empire. Suggestively perhaps, the last major urban foundation was the construction of the new capital of Peking by the Yuan. The Ming dynasty attempted to relocate the political centre of the country in the old-established town of Nanking, abortively: it added no new creations of its own. Economically, thereafter, everything seems to have happened as if successive phases of formidable agrarian expansion

62. This is, in effect, the unforgettable lesson of Needham's great and passionate work, whose scope is without any precedent in modern historiography. It should be said that Needham's own cursory classification of Chinese imperial society as a 'feudal bureaucratism' falls manifestly short of the scientific standards set by his book as a whole. The yoking of these two terms together does not render 'feudalism' more applicable, or 'bureaucracy' less truistic, for the purposes of defining the Chinese social formation from 200 B.C. onwards. Needham is in practice too lucid to be unaware of this, and is never categorical in his usage. See, for example, the revealing statement: 'Chinese society was a bureaucratism (or perhaps a bureaucratic feudalism), i.e. a type of society unknown in Europe.' *Science and Civilization in China*, II, p. 337. The last clause is of course, the operative one: the 'i.e.' implicitly reduces the antecedent predicates to their true role. Elsewhere, Needham expressly warns against identifying Chinese 'feudalism' or 'feudal bureaucratism' with anything denoted by these words in European experience (IV/3, p. 263) – thereby (involuntarily?) calling into radical question the utility of a common concept to cover the two.

63. Advances in such fields as medicine and botany appear to have been exceptions. See Needham, *Science and Civilization in China*, III (*Mathematics and the Sciences of the Heavens and the Earth*), Cambridge 1959, pp. 437, 442, 457; IV/2, p. 508; IV/3, p. 526.

occurred, without these finding any commensurate industrial counter-part, or receiving any technological momentum from the urban economy, until finally agricultural growth itself came up against insuperable limits of over-population and land-shortage. It seems clear, in fact, that in its own terms traditional Chinese agriculture reached a peak of performance in the early Ch'ing epoch, when its levels of productivity were far higher than those of contemporary European agriculture, and could thereafter only be improved by the supply of industrial inputs proper (chemical fertilizers, mechanical traction).[64] It was the failure of the urban sector to generate these that was decisive for the blockage of the Chinese economy as a whole. The presence of a vast internal market, which reached deep into the countryside, and of very large accumulations of merchant capital, appeared to afford propitious conditions for the emergence of a true factory system, combining mechanized equipment with wage-labour. In fact, neither the jump to mass production of consumption goods by machinery, nor the transformation of urban crafts into an industrial proletariat, ever occurred. Agricultural growth reached satiation, while industrial potential was left slack.

This deep disproportion can doubtless be traced to the whole structure of Chinese state and society itself, for as we have seen the modes of production of any pre-capitalist social formation are

64. Elvin has analysed this impasse most fully: *The Pattern of the Chinese Past*, pp. 306–9ff. The great merit of Elvin's book is to have posed more clearly than any other study the central paradoxes of the early modern Chinese economy, after the Sung florescence. His own solution to the problem of the imperial im-passe, however, is too narrow and cursory to be persuasive. The term 'high equilibrium trap' which he uses to describe the blockage of the post-Sung economy, does not in fact explain it: it simply restates the problem with a de-ceptively technical air. For a high equilibrium obtained only in agriculture, which is all that Elvin's concluding analysis – despite appearances – actually discusses. The 'equilibrum' in industry, by contrast, was rather a low one. Elvin's account, in other words, begs the question as to why there was no industrial revolution in the towns, to provide 'scientific' inputs for agriculture. His remarks dismissing sociological explanations of the inhibitions on Chinese industry (pp. 286–98) are too cavalier to be convincing; they are also visibly at variance with his own account of conditions in the textile industry (pp. 279–82). In general, *The Pattern of the Chinese Past* suffers from a lack of real integration or articulation of its economic and social analyses, which proceed at discrete levels. The final attempt at a 'purely' economic explanation of the Chinese impasse is mani-festly inadequate.

always specified by the politico-juridical apparatus of class rule which enforces the extra-economic coercion peculiar to it. Private property of land, the basic means of production, developed much further in Chinese than in Islamic civilization, and their distinctive trajectories were certainly marked by this fundamental difference. But Chinese notions of ownership nevertheless still fell short of European property concepts. Joint-family ownership was widespread among the gentry, while rights of pre-emption or re-purchase limited land sales.[65] Urban merchant capital suffered from the lack of any norms of primogeniture and from state monopolization of key sectors of domestic output and foreign exports.[66] The archaism of clan bonds – notably absent from the great Islamic States – reflected the lack of any civil legal system as such. Custom or kinship survived as powerful preservatives of tradition in the absence of a codified law: the legal prescriptions of the State were essentially punitive in character, concerned with the simple suppression of crime, and afforded no positive juridical framework for the conduct of economic life.[67] Similarly, Chinese culture failed to develop theoretical concepts of natural laws, beyond the practical ingenuity of its technical inventions and the refinements of its officially sponsored astronomy. Its sciences tended to be classificatory rather than causal, tolerating the irregularities they observed – often more accurately than contemporary Western science – within an elastic cosmology, rather than seeking to attack and explain these: hence their characteristic lack of determinate paradigms whose disproof could have led to theoretical upheavals within them.[68] Moreover, the rigid social

65. H. F. Schurmann, 'Traditional Property Concepts in China', *The Far Eastern Quarterly*, XV, No. 4, August 1956, pp. 507–16, forcefully insists on these limitations of Chinese notions of private agrarian property.

66. Balazs, *Chinese Civilization and Bureaucracy*, particularly stresses the inhibiting role of State monopolies and imperial ownership of much urban real estate, pp. 44–51.

67. This has been emphasized by most scholars. See, for example, D. Bodde and C. Morris, *Law in Imperial China*, Cambridge USA 1967, pp. 4–6. 'The official law always operated in a vertical direction from the state upon the individual, rather than on a horizontal plane between two individuals.' Bodde argues that Chinese culture never at any epoch entertained the idea that written law could be of divine origin – in exact opposition to Islamic jurisprudence, for example (p. 10).

68. See the excellent discussion by S. Nakayama, 'Science and Technology in China', *Half the World*, pp. 143–4; astronomical irregularities that upset

division between scholars and craftsmen prevented the fateful rendez-vous between mathematization and experimentation which in Europe produced the birth of modern physics. Chinese science consequently always remained Vincean rather than Galilean, in Needham's phrase;[69] it never crossed the divide into the 'universe of precision'.

The interleaved absence of juridical laws and natural laws in the superstructural traditions of the imperial system in the long-run could not but subtly inhibit urban manufactures, within towns which them-selves never achieved any civic autonomy. Yangtze merchants often accumulated huge fortunes in commerce, while Shansi bankers were to spread branches across the whole country in the Ch'ing epoch. But the process of production itself was characteristically left untouched by mercantile or financial capital in China. With few exceptions, the inter-mediate stage of a putting-out system did not even develop in the city economy. Merchant wholesalers dealt with contractors who bought direct from artisan producers, and marketed goods without any managerial intervention in their actual manufacture. The barrier between production and distribution was often institutionalized by official allocation of role monopolies.[70] There was thus minimal investment of commercial capital in improvements of manufacturing technology itself: the two were functionally separated. Merchants and bankers, who at no period enjoyed the esteem of traders in the Arab world, typically sought to realize their fortunes by purchase of land and, later, degrees in the examination system. They were denied corporate political identity, but not personal social mobility.[71] Con-versely, gentry were later to appropriate opportunities for profit in

---

traditional calculations were blandly accepted, with the wisdom that 'even the heavens occasionally go astray'.

69. Needham has provided several eloquent analyses: *Science and Civilization in China*, II (*History of Scientific Thought*), Cambridge 1956, pp. 542–3, 582–3; III, pp. 150–68; *The Grand Titration*, London 1969, pp. 36–7, 39–40, 184–6, 299–330. Needham suggests that there was a close connection between the sec-toral backwardness of physics, in particular, and the social heteronomy of the merchant class in Imperial China.

70. Elvin, *The Pattern of the Chinese Past*, pp. 278–84.

71. Ping-Ti Ho, *The Ladder of Success in Imperial China: Aspects of Social Mobility, 1368–1911*, New York 1962, pp. 46–52; for social mobility generally in Ming-Ch'ing China, pp. 54–72. See also Balazs, *Chinese Civilization and Bureaucracy*, pp. 51–2.

mercantile activities. The result was to prevent any crystallization or collective solidarity or organization among the urban commercial class, even when the private sector of the economy increased quantitatively in the final stages of the Ch'ing epoch; merchant associations were characteristically of the regionalist *Landsmannschaft* type,[72] politically more divisive than unitary in function. Predictably, the role of the Chinese merchant class in the republican revolution which finally over-threw the Empire in the early 20th century was prudent and ambivalent.[73]

The Imperial State machine which thus constricted the cities also, by the same token, laid its impress on the gentry. The landlord class of China always possessed a dual economic base: in its estates and its offices. The total size of the imperial bureaucracy itself was always very small by comparison with the population of the country: some 10–15,000 functionaries in the Ming era and less than 25,000 in the Ch'ing epoch.[74] Its efficacy depended on the informal links between the officials dispatched to the provinces, and the local landowners who collaborated with them in the performance of public functions (transport, irrigation, education, religion and so on) and the maintenance of civic order (defence units and so on), from which they received lucrative 'service' incomes.[75] The extensive families of the gentry traditionally included some members who had passed the examinations giving *chin-shih* rank and formal access to the bureaucratic apparatus of the State, and others in small provincial towns or rural districts without such credentials: degree-holders typically occupied central or local administrative positions, while their relations looked after the lands. But the wealthiest and most powerful stratum within the landowning class was always composed of those with offices or links to the State, whose public emoluments (from salaries, corruption, and service

72. Ping-Ti Ho, 'Salient Aspects of China's Heritage', in Ping-Ti Ho and Tang Tsou (eds.), *China in Crisis*, I, Chicago 1968, pp. 34–5.

73. See the long and illuminating essay by M-C. Bergères, 'The Role of the Bourgeoisie', in M. Wright (ed.), *China in Revolution: The First Phase, 1900–1913*, New Haven 1968, pp. 229–95.

74. Gernet, *Le Monde Chinois*, pp. 343–4; Chang-Li Chang, *The Income of the Chinese Gentry*, Seattle 1962, pp. 38, 42. The Ch'ing bureaucracy had an additional oup of some 4,000 Manchu officials.

75. Chang, *The Income of the Chinese Gentry*, pp. 43–7ff.

charges) regularly surpassed their private agrarian incomes in the Ch'ing epoch, perhaps by some 50 per cent again.[76] Thus while the Chinese gentry as a whole owed its social and political power to its control of the basic means of production, realized in qualified private property of land, its mutable elite – perhaps just over 1 per cent of the population in the 19th century – was determined by the degree-system which gave official access to the greatest wealth and highest authority within the administrative system itself.[77] Agrarian investment was thus also diverted by the absorbent role of the Imperial State within the ruling class. The sudden, great advances in agricultural productivity in China typically occurred from below, in phases of lessened fiscal and political pressure by the State on the peasantry, at the beginning of a dynastic cycle. The consequent demographic increases then usually stirred new social unrest on the land, each time progressively more dangerous for the gentry as the population grew, until the final episode of the Taiping 'Kingdom of Heaven'. At the same time, the political authoritarianism of the Imperial State tended, if anything, to intensify after the Sung epoch.[78] Confucianism became steadily more repressive, and the power of the Emperor more extensive, down to the eve of the fall of the Ch'ing dynasty.

Chinese and Islamic civilizations, which in their dissimilar natural settings[79] together lay across the great bulk of the Asian land mass by

76. Chang, *The Income of the Chinese Gentry*, Seattle 1962, p. 197: degree-holders also typically enjoyed large incomes from mercantile activities, which Chang reckons may in aggregate have been about half those yielded by their landed property.

77. Chang, *The Chinese Gentry*, p. 139, calculates degree-holders with their families at 1·3 per cent of the population before the Taiping Rebellion. Chang's studies arbitrarily confine the definition of 'gentry' to this stratum only: but his findings are separable from acceptance of this restriction.

78. Ho, 'Salient Aspects of China's Heritage', pp. 22–4.

79. Strictly geographical determinations of social structure were typically exaggerated by Montesquieu and his age, in their attempts to understand the non-European world. Marxists in this century have often compensated unduly for this legacy of the Enlightenment, by ignoring the relative significance of natural milieux in history altogether. It has been left to modern historians like Braudel to lend a juster weight to them again. In fact, no truly materialist history can put geographical conditions into silent parentheses, as simply external to modes of production. Marx himself emphasized the natural environment as an ¡rreducible prior constituent of any economy: '*The original conditions of production*

the early modern epoch, thus comprised two patently divergent morphologies of State and society. The contrast between them could be made virtually term by term. The military slave-guards who so frequently formed the capstone of Islamic political systems were the antithesis of the civilian scholar-gentry that dominated the Chinese imperial State: power wore a praetorian or mandarin guise, respectively. Religion saturated the whole ideological universe of the Muslim social systems, while kinship was eclipsed or relegated; secular morality and philosophy governed official culture in China, while clan organization remained encrusted in civic life. The social prestige of merchants in the Arab Empires was never matched by the honour accorded to traders in the Celestial Kingdom; the range of their maritime commerce at its height far surpassed anything ever achieved by their Sinic counter-parts. The cities from which they operated were no less dissimilar. Classical towns in China formed bureaucratic, segmented grids while Islamic towns were tangled, aleatory labyrinths. The apogee of inten-sive agriculture, utilizing the most developed hydraulic works in the world, was combined with private ownership of land in China, where the Islamic world typically exhibited juridical monopoly of land by the sovereign and desultory or extensive cultivation of it, without the introduction of irrigation systems of moment. Neither great zone revealed egalitarian village communities; but otherwise the generally stagnant rural productivy of the Middle East and North Africa was thrown into sharp relief by the very great agrarian progress registered in China. Contrasts of climate and soil, of course, were not foreign to these respective performances. The population of the two regions naturally corresponded to the forces of production in the main branch of any pre-capitalist economy: Islamic stability, Chinese multiplication. Technology and science, too, followed opposite directions: Chinese imperial civilization generated many more technical inventions than mediaeval Europe, while Islamic history was vice-versa seemingly infertile by comparison with it.[80] Last but not least, perhaps, the

---

cannot themselves originally *be produced* – they are not the results of production' *Pre-Capitalist Formations*, p. 86. [*Grundrisse*, p. 389.]

80. The relative technical proficiency of Chinese, Islamic and European civili-zations was indicated in the traditional adage reported from Samarkand by the Castilian ambassador to Timur in the 14th century: 'The craftsmen of Cathay are

Islamic world was contiguous with the West, early subjected to its expansion and eventually to its encirclement, whereas the Chinese realm lay in seclusion beyond it, out of the reach of Europe – for long perhaps transmitting more to the Occident than it received from it, while the 'intermediate' civilization of Islam confronted the ascent of Western feudalism and its invincible heir, at the other end of Eurasia.

These elementary contrasts, of course, in no way constitute even the beginnings of a comparison of the real *modes of production* whose complex combination and succession defined the actual social formations of these huge regions outside Europe. They merely resume some of the grossest indices of divergence between Islamic and Chinese civilizations (make-shift terminological objects which themselves need differentiation and retranslation for any scientific analysis), which preclude any attempt to assimilate them as simple examples of a common 'Asiatic' mode of production. Let this last notion be given the decent burial that it deserves. It is perfectly clear that a very great deal of further historical research is necessary before any true scientific conclusions can be drawn from the variant paths of non-European development, in the centuries contemporary with the Western mediaeval and early modern epochs. Only the surface of vast areas and periods has so far been scratched in most cases, by comparison with the closeness and intensity of scholarly study to which European history has been submitted.[81] But one procedural lesson is absolutely plain: Asian development cannot in any way be reduced to a uniform

---

reputed to be the most skilful by far beyond those of any other nation; and the saying is that they alone have two eyes, that the Franks may indeed have one, while the Muslims are but a blind folk.' Needham, *Science and Civilization in China*, IV/2, p. 602. Needham himself supposes a higher degree of direct transmission of inventions from China to Europe than can generally be proved from historical evidence. The virtually complete *social* ignorance in which the two civilizations remained of each other during Antiquity and the Middle Ages – the mutual lack of any accurate information in written records prior to a very late date – is difficult to reconcile with the assumption of frequent *technical* intercommunication between the two, however informal and untraceable in documents. Chinese instruction of Europe in technology is not a necessary corollary of Chinese superiority over Europe: it is the latter that is crucial and unquestionable.

81. Twitchett compares the current state of work on T'ang and Sung China with the stage which English mediaeval historiography had reached by the time of Seebohm and the early Vinogradoff: *Land Tenure and the Social Order*, p. 32.

residual category, left over after the canons of European evolution have been established. Any serious theoretical exploration of the historical field outside feudal Europe will have to supersede traditional and generic contrasts with it, and proceed to a concrete and accurate typology of social formations and State systems in their own right, which respects their very great differences of structure and development. It is merely in the night of our ignorance that all alien shapes take on the same hue.

Index of Names

Index of Authorities